THE
LAST FULL
MEASURE

★ ★ ★

THE
LAST FULL
MEASURE

★ ★ ★

How Soldiers Die in Battle

Michael Stephenson

CROWN PUBLISHERS

NEW YORK

Copyright © 2012 by Michael Stephenson

All rights reserved.
Published in the United States by Crown Publishers, an imprint of the Crown
Publishing Group, a division of Random House, Inc., New York.
www.crownpublishing.com

CROWN and the Crown colophon are registered trademarks of Random House, Inc.

Library of Congress Cataloging-in-Publication Data
Stephenson, Michael, 1946–
The last full measure : how soldiers die in battle / Michael Stephenson.—1st ed.
1. Battle casualties—History.   2. Military history.   I. Title.
D25.5.S74 2011
305.9'06950973—dc22   2011005874

ISBN 978-0-307-39584-9
eISBN 978-0-307-95277-6

Printed in the United States of America

Book design by Ellen Cipriano
Jacket design by Christopher Brand
Jacket photography by Getty Images

1   3   5   7   9   10   8   6   4   2

First Edition

*For Kathryn, who makes everything possible
and for Gabriel Gray Henshaw, who runs so bravely*

Dreading what I might see, yet needing to see it.

ALEX BOWLBY,
The Recollections of Rifleman Bowlby

We moved on, each of us inching along the
brink of his own extinction.

WILLIAM MANCHESTER,
Goodbye, Darkness

Contents

★ ★ ★

PREFACE

★

But in a larger sense, we cannot dedicate—we cannot consecrate—we cannot hallow—this ground. The brave men, living and dead, who struggled here, have consecrated it, far above our poor power to add or detract. The world will little note, nor long remember, what we say here, but it can never forget what they did here. . . . From these honored dead we take increased devotion to that cause for which they gave the last full measure of devotion.

—Abraham Lincoln, Gettysburg, November 19, 1863

THE IDEA THAT remembrance can conjure rescue from oblivion may be only a historian's sleight of hand. But the act of remembering, of memorializing, also invokes a magic as old as humanity. There is an atavistic sense of propitiation: remembrance as a gift to the restless dead. It is an idea powerfully invoked by the First World War doctor and poet John McCrae (who was to die in Flanders in 1918). His line "If ye break faith with us who die / We shall not sleep" was intended to rally the boys to the flag, but to me it makes a different, equally powerful appeal.

The Last Full Measure is about how soldiers have died in combat. This exploration of the central truth of battle involves a recognition of a debt and an attempt to honor an obligation. But it is important to be clear about this. To pay respect to these dead is not at all the same thing as promoting militarism. (The braying of the war lovers and the shrill call of the chicken hawks, will always ensure that their voices are heard loud and clear.) Nor is it to pretend that every slain soldier is a hero—a word hugely devalued by our huckster politicians and their media flacks (what the World War II poet-soldier Alun Lewis, killed in 1944, described as "the loud celebrities / Exhorting us to slaughter"). In fact, by trying to represent death in battle as honestly as possible and with as much regard to the complexities as my "poor power" would allow—in other words, to deal with the whole bloody business as humanely as I can—I hope to honor the slain by helping to rescue them from appropriation by the cynic and the jingoist.

Old wars were once real before they were preserved in the formaldehyde of history. They were chaotically bloody and shockingly immediate in a way that words have always struggled to convey. Reading about combat and death is radically different from experiencing combat and death. In time the blood dries, the agony fades, and battle takes on a pleasing shape, in the way a jagged rock is worn smooth by insistent surf. Looked at from afar, it becomes romantic, and the killed—rescued from the smashed and torn violence of their deaths by the magic powers of our nostalgia—are bathed in the golden aura of some version of the "greatest generation." The stench and screams give way to rousing images. The death agonies settle into the encouraging heroic gestures of the war memorial and the movies. We are wrapped in the warmth and certitudes of History with a capital *H*.

Wehrmacht infantryman Guy Sajer, writing of the experience of combat on the eastern front in Russia in World War II, put it this way in his memoir, *Forgotten Soldier* (1967):

> Too many people learn about war with no inconvenience to themselves. They read about Verdun or Stalingrad without comprehension, sitting in a comfortable armchair, with their feet beside the fire, preparing to go about their business the next day, as usual. One should really read such accounts under compulsion, in discomfort, considering oneself fortunate not to be describing the event in a letter home, writing from a hole in the mud. One should read about war in the worst circumstances, when everything is going badly, remembering that the torments of peace are trivial, and not worth any white hairs. Nothing is really serious in the tranquility of peace. . . . One should read about war standing up, late at night, when one is tired, as I am writing about it now, at dawn . . .

Sajer draws his line in the sand, and only those who have experienced combat may cross it. All others are at best honest observers and at worst voyeurs—those who, as the poet-soldier Siegfried Sassoon accused, "Listen with delight / By tales of dirt and danger fondly thrilled." As I was keenly aware while writing this book, the fates had dealt me a pretty cushy hand as far as military hazard has been concerned. The date and place of my birth has, due to some benevolent turn of the roulette wheel, preserved my sorry ass. It is a fact of which I can be neither proud nor apologetic. Those, like Sajer, who have lived on one side of the line may be observed, but they may not be joined.

Many soldiers act heroically, but death in action is not itself an automatic anointment. The horrible truth is that most have had their lives wrenched from them, far from the embalming salve of the heroic. The last sound from the lips of the stricken is not so much the rousing rallying call "for the motherland" as the heart-breaking cry for mother. In the end, though, there is a kind of democracy among the killed: Heroic Themistocles is as dead as an anonymous soldier who has his life ripped from him in abject terror. And this book is interested equally in both—and seeks to honor both.

The roads that lead a soldier to the grave may be brutally short and straight, or they may be winding and complicated by many smaller byways and detours. But there is always a place where they come to their fatal intersection. What brings a warrior to his death is a convergence of many factors: the weapon that kills him; the tactics that brought him to the place and manner of his death; the strategy that marks the boundaries of the killing field; the decisions he makes or the decisions that others make on his behalf; the ability of medical services to save a life (or, throughout much of history, hasten the extinction). And last, what might be called the cultural context that shapes each and every warrior: a complex amalgam of attitudes and ideas about such things as the heroic, the need for sacrifice, the justness of the cause, the embrace of the aggressive spirit, compassion toward the defeated (to name only a few ingredients in this rich soup), or, indeed, the rejection of all the foregoing. Much of this is quite specific to the historical period, and that is why I chose to organize this book chronologically—soldiers die in the style of their times. But also, much of it is a shared human experience, and that is why I have attempted to trace the great arcs of connection that leap across the centuries.

War is about many things, but at its core it is about killing or getting killed. It is not chess, or a computer game, or a movie, or a book *about* death. It is, implacably and nonnegotiably, the thing itself. Henri Barbusse, in *Le feu* (*Under Fire*, 1916), his great memoir of combat in World War I, puts it this way: "We leave by the trench at right angles . . . towards the moving, living and awful frontier of now." In our "virtual" or ersatz culture we all too often confuse the pretend and the real. In a way unprecedented in history, most of us today are able to get by with acting out rather than acting. Warmed by the glow of the screen, we can choose to inhabit a simulacrum, while a few—comparatively very few—live and die in the searing light of a reality we would much rather read about or game-play than experience.

"Military history must never stray from the tragic story of killing," says Victor Davis Hanson with characteristic forthrightness. "Wars are the sum of battles, battles the tally of individual human beings killing and dying. . . . To write of conflict is not to describe merely the superior rifles of imperial troops or the matchless edge of the Roman *gladius,* but ultimately the collision of a machine-gun bullet with the brow of an adolescent, or the carving and ripping of artery and organ in the belly of an anonymous Gaul. To speak of war in any other fashion brings with it a sort of immorality. Euphemism in battle narrative or the omission of graphic killing altogether is a near criminal offense of the military historian."

In this regard I was acutely aware of the tightrope I had to walk in making this book. There is no way one can write about violent death without describing horrific scenes. Men do not always die with a decorous sigh and fall with composed grace. They often quit this world in a shit-storm of screams and blood, often literally blown to kingdom come. How does one do justice to that without pandering to Rambo-style porno-violence? Tightropes are demanding. I edged along mine as best I could.

The amazingly obvious but generally overlooked point is that we who write or comment, or indeed read, of this melancholy subject are—by the ministrations of the kindly Fates—alive! We have the good luck to be lolling on the sunny bank of the Styx, and although our journey is definitely booked and confirmed, we are still only looking, if humbly and sadly, at the legion upon legion of shades already gathered on the dark side.

★   ★   ★

THE LAST FULL MEASURE, through considerations of length and the stamina, not to say the sanity, of the author, limits itself to ground warfare. In no way are valiant sailors and airmen—among whom was an uncle, USAAF sergeant George Taylor, a left-waist gunner killed in his B-17G over Posen on April 11, 1944—denigrated by omission. What might be called the technological context of their deaths compared with that of soldiers makes the separation possible and, perhaps, logical. In addition, although recognizing that disease, cold, heat, and starvation have killed more soldiers than any weapon, and that death delivered by these Four Horsemen is a direct consequence of warfare, I decided to focus on the sharp end of battle—death caused directly by fighting rather than as a consequence of being in an army during wartime.

ONE

FIRST BLOOD

Death and the Heroic in Ancient Combat

★

The Greeks, as I have learned, are accustomed to wage wars in the most stupid fashion due to their silliness and folly. For once they have declared war against each other, they search out the finest and most level plain and there fight it out. The result is that even the victorious come away with great losses; and of the defeated, I say only that they are utterly annihilated.

—Herodotus, *The Histories*[1]

ERODOTUS: HISTORIAN OR LIAR? Researcher or fabricator? Famously denounced by Cicero as a fraudster, depicted by some modern historians as a fictionalizer, he can be seen as the precursor of some rather distinguished modern historians who have had, to put it delicately, a little difficulty with the all too often indistinct boundary between history and "imagined history." But in looking back to the earliest evidence of warfare and the fates that befell warriors on those prehistoric and ancient killing grounds, the Herodotian dilemma—that confused swirl of myth and fact, of dispassionate observation and passionate "interpretation"—may serve us well, for the reality is that we walk on uncertain ground, and we would be well advised to tread it gingerly.

As the quote that heads this chapter suggests, Herodotus looked at the warfare of his age (fifth century BCE) and saw anything but a heroic clash of arms. Greek warriors could be almost lemminglike in their tunnel-visioned stampede to oblivion. His view echoes the modern debate—a hawks-versus-doves standoff—about our ancient and prehistoric ancestors.

Was it a clash between those who saw their interests best served by ruthless violence and those who saw their interests served by avoiding bloody conflict and reaching some kind of peaceful accommodation? The hawks see primitive man as truly primitive. This hawks-and-doves dichotomy is reflected in modern studies of early battlefield lethality. There are those who contend that early combat was merely ritualistic, full of sound and fury signifying nothing—a great deal of prancing and empty threats that were designed to minimize the body count. The argument is that in societies of low birthrate and high natural mortality, bloodletting, which could only harm both antagonists, would be avoided. Instead of real warfare they organized a mutually agreed-upon charade in which theatrical gesture replaced killing—an argument anthropologist Lawrence H. Keeley dismisses as "the increasingly irrational meandering in a neo-Rousseauian, post-modernist 'woo-woo land.' "[2] However, the "flower-war" school gained traction in the 1960s and 1970s, perhaps as a reaction to what was seen as the military brutalism of much of the twentieth century, which, despite its self-congratulatory "modernity" and humanism, set a new benchmark for savagery.

John Keegan in *A History of Warfare* (1993) promotes the idea of self-restraining warfare being a characteristic of "primitives" who "have recourse to all sorts of devices which spare both themselves and their enemies from the worst of what might be inflicted. . . . Most important of such devices is that of ritual, which defines the nature of combat itself and requires that, once defined rituals have been performed, the contestants shall recognise the fact of their satisfaction and have recourse to conciliation, arbitration and peacemaking."[3] But before we can rest in the comfortable assumption that primitive warriors were simply thwarted peacemakers, Keegan puts us right: "It is important . . . not to idealise primitive warfare. It may take a very violent turn." Indeed, Keegan adds, a little euphemistically, it may "have material effects undesired by those who suffer them"—undesired as in being tortured before being eaten. Our primitive forebears could be unfussy diners.

Robert L. O'Connell in his influential 1989 survey of war and aggression also promotes a view of primitive battle as essentially one of low lethality:

> Most probably fighting was, as it is now among contemporary hunting-and-gathering people, a sporadic, highly personalized affair, homicidal in intent and, occasionally, in effect, but lacking a sustained economic and political motivation beyond that of revenge and, sometimes, women. Under such conditions, ambush and raiding are the preferred modes of operation, and the target often is a single "enemy." Pitched battles, when they occur, represent tactical failure. The object of the foray is rout, not prolonged combat. In such an environment the attacking party will close only if surprise is reasonably certain; otherwise the aim is to stay at long range and exchange missiles.[4]

The distinction O'Connell and Keegan make between "formal" battle and ambush or surprise attack is critical in understanding the risk primitive warriors ran. It has been posited that in formal battle the total casualty rate (wounded and killed) could be quite high—perhaps in the 30 to 40 percent range—compared with, say, an "average" American Civil War battle casualty rate of 12 to 15 percent (although casualties in certain battles, like Gettysburg, ran to almost 25 percent). But because these primitive battles were often standoffs employing relatively unsophisticated missile weaponry, the *death* rate was low compared with that of modern battle: one killed for about thirty wounded; whereas by comparison, one man was killed for about every five wounded at Gettysburg, and at the battle of the Somme in 1916 some British battalions took one killed for every two men wounded.[5] However, some primitive pitched battles could be quite deadly if the protagonists closed with shock weapons such as clubs, axes, and lances (a pattern that would become characteristic of Greek and Roman warfare). For example, combat among the woodland tribes of eastern North America (before Europeans introduced firearms), in which up-close shock weapons such as clubs and axes predominated, could be highly lethal. However, if we look only at pitched battle the true picture of primitive-warrior fatality would be severely distorted because the favored mode of battle was what we might term "irregular": ambushes and raids. The loss rate of each incident may have been quite low relative to modern warfare, but their frequency and ferocity elevated the cumulative kill to "catastrophic mortalities" so that "a member of a typical tribal society, especially a male, had a far higher probability of dying in combat than the citizen of an average modern state."[6]

The picture, then, of our warrior ancestors does not fit notions of heroic warfare in which one warrior meets and defeats another as an equal. Much more likely, the style of doing battle was opportunistic and motivated largely by an intuitive risk/benefit analysis. When life is squeezed into the tight margin of survivability, grandiose gestures will give way to careful calculation. A sure kill by a mob swarming, in a brief moment of advantage, over a numerically inferior enemy may not be pretty, but it cuts the odds of harm to the attackers significantly. Early humans were no different from most hunting packs. This was the way they had learned to overcome animal prey, and it was a tactic equally effective against human enemies. In some ways it is not so different from insurgent warfare of our era, which is also based on isolating and overrunning small groups of the enemy in ambushes and traps—in fact on any opportunistic tactic that increases the odds of success, no matter how "underhanded" it might be. Whether it be Europeans fighting natives in North America (settlers referred to the natives' style of combat as "the skulking way of war"); the French fighting Spanish guerrillas during the Peninsular War of the Napoleonic era; the French and Americans fighting communists in Vietnam in the twentieth century; or the Soviets fighting the mujahideen and Americans the Taliban in modern Afghanistan, insurgent tactics reject a definition of the heroic; based that is, on open and transparent confrontation.

When did we start killing each other in combat? Some scholars date the earliest warfare to 2 million years ago.[7] *Homo habilis* lived 2.3–1.4 million years ago, while we, the relative newcomer *Homo sapiens,* did not make an appearance until about 250,000 years ago. It was among the fraternal interest groups of our hominid hunter ancestors some 400,000 years ago that the territorial instinct turned lethal.[8] They killed one another not only to protect what they already had but also to extend their spheres of influence in order to maximize their chances of surviving and thriving.[9] The self-interest of the band was, and remains, the great motivator of warfare. We may have dressed that self-interest in a flashy rhetorical uniform, and the bands may now be nation-states, but it is nevertheless still connected to our most basic and ancient instincts. We cannot quite rid ourselves of the ripe stink of the pelt.

About 1.7 million years ago *Homo erectus* began to spread out of Africa carrying clubs, and about 400,000 years ago wooden spears with fire-hardened tips were added to the armory.[10] However, it was the introduction of missile weapons that gave a tactical shape to prehistoric warfare that would be characteristic of battle ever since: the proximity of shock versus the long range of missiles. *Homo neanderthalensis,* a competitor of *Homo sapiens,* was physically stronger and long experienced in the use of stone-tipped spears for both throwing and stabbing. But it was the nimbler and more inventive *H. sapiens* who would succeed in driving Neanderthals from the richer hunting grounds, thereby squeezing them into an evolutionary cul-de-sac that reduced their chances of thriving and, ultimately, of surviving.

About 40,000 years ago *H. sapiens* developed a weapons technology that would profoundly shift the balance of combat power: the atlatl.[11] Faced with adversaries who in close combat could make best use of direct muscular power, *H. sapiens* needed a counterpunch. The atlatl was a wooden missile launcher, sharing some of the physics of the sling, for hurling short, spearlike darts. It was one of the first force multipliers, increasing the range of the hand-thrown spear by about four times (from 25 yards to 100, with fairly predictable accuracy up to 30 yards),[12] and it afforded the critical advantage of being able to fend off a physically powerful opponent who could make good use of shock weapons, and grievously hurt him from a distance. It meant that the atlatl-wielding group could start an assault earlier than an enemy armed only with clubs and hand-thrown spears. In some prehistoric actuarial calculation, the increased risk to the attacked and the concomitant reduction of risk to the attacker translated directly into the margin of success. And by the time the bow and arrow made an appearance around 20,000 years ago, *Homo neanderthalensis* was extinct.[13]

The bow brought some very distinct advantages over the atlatl. It had greater range; ammunition was lighter and therefore more of it could be carried; it was an easier weapon to learn to operate. Above all, it offered the great tactical advantage of being much more versatile—it could be used in open combat, but more important, it was better adapted to ambush warfare, where it could be fired from cover (difficult for the atlatl-fiver who needs unencumbered space). But change in history does not work with the crisp exactness of a page being turned. The atlatl, for example, was still used by Aztec and Inca warriors well over 40,000 years after its introduction (as were Stone Age swords, the edges embedded with slivers of razor-sharp obsidian, capable of lopping off a conquistador's horse's head in one terrible strike).[14]

Whether atlatl or bow, the long-range missile weapon radically changed battlefield prospects. Now a David could kill a Goliath; a nincompoop a genius; the lowest the highest. It was the start of the great social leveling of combat killing. The ever-increasing sophistication of missile weaponry (the atlatl of the Aztecs defeated by the arquebuses of the conquistadors, the arquebus by the musket, the musket by the breech-loading rifle, and so on), and the concomitant reduction of high-risk, close-action shock combat is one of the core themes of warfare. Killing from a distance is invariably preferable to the riskiness of close combat. And so, over millennia the evolution of missile weaponry has all but rendered shock weapons redundant. Clubbing and stabbing, although occasionally resorted to, are no longer the tactical lingua franca of modern battle, despite exhortations—even in quite recent history—for soldiers to go in with cold steel. As a consequence, the battlefield has become "empty": In most cases the warrior does not see whom he kills or is killed by. In fact, there is a prospect that we will so increase the distance between combatants that killing may well be done by drones and other smart weapons that will make the heroic traditions of close-combat shock warfare as antiquated as the duel between Achilles and Hector, and "modern" small-arms fighting as quaint as medieval swordplay.

The bullet or heat-seeking bomb does not give a jot for courage or trial-by-arms; they fly to the heart of the matter with unblinking dispassion. But perhaps this was ever so. The arrow is nothing but the uncritical servant of the archer, no better or worse than the unmanned drone or the man with his finger on a computer key, whereas the swordsman and the spearman, the soldier wielding a bayonet, must look into the eye of his fellow warrior, see his fear, hear his cry, smell his blood. And in that contact there is a whole moral world; a world that might be hateful, angry, terrified, disgusted, full of regret, or crazed with exultation—but never dispassionate, never coldly unhuman.

Despite the fact that killing by long-distance missiles is on some level a more efficient handling of risk, earliest warfare endowed close-quarters combat with a much higher heroic status. There were quite pragmatic reasons for the distinction. The most effective warriors had the bravery to close for the kill. The risks were great but the prize greater. The primary benefit was quite straightforward: The decisive killer was the most productive, and the one likely to ensure the well-being of his immediate family and the larger group. In him lay their future; to him was accorded power, influence, status, something the hero can translate into very tangible benefits: power and influence. The prehistoric hunter's claim on the kill would be mirrored, later in the history of combat, in the ancient warrior's claim to the panoply of his defeated enemy (with its echo in modern warfare in the taking of souvenirs from the defeated).

Close-combat killing defined the heroic for millennia. There is a tension, constant for most of military history, between shock and missile tactics that arises from the constraints imposed by the physical properties of the weapons. Put simply, shock weapons—clubs, swords, stabbing spears, maces, et cetera—were more effective killers than missiles, but the warrior had to get close to his enemy, which is dangerous: "These very short ranges create severe psychological and social difficulties that render shock weapons the weapons of choice among only the more severely disciplined armies of high chiefdoms and states. . . . And more important, to reach this closure the warrior must pass through the killing zone of the enemy's fire weapons."[15]

Archers and slingers, although a tactical staple of the armies of the ancient Middle East—especially Egyptian, Assyrian, and Sumerian—were often viewed, especially in ancient Greece, as craven compared with infantrymen. As though to underscore the "unheroic" nature of the missile warrior, there was a long tradition among many primitive societies of employing "dirty" techniques to increase missile lethality. Spear and arrow shafts were sometimes weakened so that the point would break off in the wound when extraction was attempted; animal claws were attached in such a way as to remain in the wound and promote infection; arrowheads were barbed to make extraction difficult; and, of course, many societies tipped heads with various poisons or excrement and otherwise went to great lengths to maximize lethality, including draining the blood from the heart of a sheep, putting it in a section of intestine, burying it until it was nicely rotted, and then smearing the pestilent concoction on their arrowheads. As one anthropologist notes: "The widespread use of such nasty weapons directly contradicts the commonly held idea that primitives took pains to ameliorate the deadliness of their combat."[16]

Nor were our primitive forebears too scrupulous about the treatment of the defeated. The eradication of potential competitors is, perhaps, hardwired into our evolutionary makeup, and warriors on the losing side (and very often their families) were usually terminated without compunction. Fleeing, it might be thought, would elicit some sort of compassion on the part of the victor; but quite the opposite is true. Throughout history retreat has often triggered a deep-rooted *joie de mort*—killing as celebration. Just as the animals of the prehistoric hunt were eaten, so too were the defeated human enemy. Such "communions of triumph,"[17] although disturbing to modern sensibilities, are profoundly embedded in religious rites: the symbolic cannibalism of the Christian Eucharist being one of the more obvious.

There is evidence of cannibalism from early Neolithic southern France (five to six thousand years ago) and prehistoric southwestern North America.[18] In precolonial Mesoamerica, North America, and parts of Oceania and western Africa, captive warriors were often killed publicly and wholly or partially consumed. Aztec cannibalism, for example, has been attributed to religious motives—propitiation of the sun god through blood sacrifice— but also to the more mundane need for protein. Another powerful motivation was simply to subdue potential enemies through astounding acts of very public cruelty: an effective way of bolstering the power of the ruling elite—a technique not lost on even modern despots like the East African dictator Idi Amin, who was reported to enjoy choice cuts of his opponents.[19]

In studies of forty-two primitive societies it has been found that the vast majority (thirty-nine) routinely killed *all* captured enemy warriors.[20] Zapotecs removed hearts and genitals; the ancient Chinese bound and buried their defeated enemies and, like the Aztecs, much preferred to capture an enemy for later ritual sacrifice than kill him outright on the battlefield. Sometimes these acts of torture were carried out by noncombatant women and children (particularly young boys, for whom it was an initiation rite), as was the case among some of the American woodland Indian tribes such as the Iroquois:

> Captured warriors were often subject to preliminary torture during the return journey of a war party. When the party arrived at the home village, the prisoners were beaten by running the gauntlet into the village. At a council, the warrior prisoners who survived these initial torments were

distributed to families who had recently lost men in warfare. After these prisoners were ritually adopted and given the name of the family's dead member, they were usually tortured to death over several days. The victim was expected to display great fortitude during these torments—taunting his torturers and expressing contempt for their efforts. When the prisoner was dead, some parts of his body were eaten (usually including his heart).[21]

It was extremely rare that a captive warrior would be spared and incorporated into his captor's tribe, although it did happen occasionally among, for example, the Fox and Shawnee of midwestern North America, if the captive had endured his torture with outstanding bravery and if there also happened to be a need for replacement manpower due to unusually high combat losses.

If cannibalism in the primitive world was one way of consuming the enemy, the dead warrior's body could also become an object of totemic importance. Sometimes the killed enemy was never quite dead enough, and he had to be rekilled with many postmortem blows. Occasionally they were motivated by hatred but often were a frenzied release of tension, even celebration. A grave pit in Heilbronn, Germany, dating from 5000 BCE contains thirty-four victims, most struck on the back of the head with stone axes while fleeing, then on the back of the neck, the dome and sides of the skull, and, probably after death, the arms, legs, and pelvis.[22] At the prehistoric (9000 BCE) Jebel Sahaba cemetery in Egypt, skeletons have been found with between fifteen and twenty-five arrowheads in each. In more recent times, US soldiers killed by American Indians in the nineteenth century were often struck by many arrows and their bodies mutilated. British redcoats killed by Zulus were disemboweled and often beheaded after death. In some primitive cultures the killed foe was transfigured from corpse into couture: "In Tahiti, a victorious warrior, given the opportunity, would pound his vanquished foe's corpse flat with his heavy war club, cut a slit through the well-crushed victim, and don him as a trophy poncho."[23] Aztec priests would also wear the flayed skin of sacrificed warriors, and one Colombian group flayed their victims, stuffed them, made wax faces for their skulls, and set them up "in places of honor" within their households.[24]

The body itself was also literally and symbolically appropriated by the taking of trophies. Scalping was a custom firmly rooted in North American aboriginal culture and was very widespread from the eastern seaboard across to California, from the subarctic to northern Mexico. But there is also a grave site in Chienkon, China, that dates to 2200 BCE and contains victims who were scalped after having been killed.[25]

Scalping was eschewed by early Europeans, the trophy of choice being the whole head. The ancient Celts were particularly fond of beheading (Trajan's Column in Rome features a striking bas-relief of a Germanic warrior with the hair of the severed head of his conquered foe gripped firmly in his teeth), and not content with decapitating enemy warriors, Celts would often behead their horses as well. The head is probably the most culturally widespread trophy because it is irrefutable in a way that a scalp, or lopped hands, or sliced-off ears, are not; the man is dead. (The samurai were particular fetishizers of severed heads, collecting them assiduously and building them into elaborate after-battle ritual cairns.)

The face is also the token of personality and even after death remains a vital reminder of the living. It can be spoken to, as a Maori warrior did to the severed head of his enemy: "You wanted to run away, did you? But my *meri* [war club] overtook you: and after you were cooked, you made food for my mouth. And where is your father? He is cooked—and where is your brother? He is eaten—and where is your wife? There she sits, a wife for me—and where are your children? There they are, with loads on their backs, carrying food, as my slaves."[26] And if heads could have conversations, albeit one-way, the slain could also be made to play a merry tune; in South America and New Zealand the long bones of the leg and arm were made into flutes.

It is hard to deny that in many cultures throughout history, including our own, killing in combat may be seen as, if not precisely a joyful act, then one that comes close, and is celebrated. But in many primitive cultures the warrior who had just slain a foe was considered by his noncombatant kin to be stained. A crime of a sort (though considered necessary) had been committed, and an expiation was necessary. In some cultures the warrior was forced into isolation for a period, or made to eat only certain foods, or abstain from sex: "Because he was a spiritual danger to himself and anyone he touched, a Huli killer of New Guinea could not use his shooting hand for several days; had to stay awake the first night after the killing, chanting spells; drink "bespelled" water; and exchange his bow for another. South American Carib warriors had to cover their heads for a month after dispatching an enemy. An African Meru warrior, after killing, had to pay a curse remover . . . returning raiders had to cleanse themselves by drinking water and vomiting."[27]

Samurai warriors, although dedicated collectors of their slain enemies' heads, were considered defiled if, by chance, they directly touched the head or any part of the corpse. In ancient Japan there were elaborate ceremonies of purification following battle, and a horror of the pollution associated with decay and death.[28] And in an echo of these ancient rites modern warriors also often need to be "cleansed" through the ministration of a range of care facilities.

★   ★   ★

OF THE VISUAL depictions of prehistoric and ancient war only fragments remain, but they are fragments of extraordinary beauty.

The whole schema has long gone, and we are left to decipher as best we can the enigmatic shards. The Stele of the Vultures (so called because the ruler is seen allowing vultures to devour the enemy dead, a kind of shameful "double death") dates to about 2500 BCE (about thirteen hundred years before the Trojan War). Apart from prehistoric cave paintings delineating intertribal violence, it is the earliest depiction of organized warfare. The stele is a Bronze Age limestone slab that celebrates, in bas-relief images, the victory of Eannatum, ruler of Lagash in Sumeria, over the bordering kingdom of Umma, although victor and vanquished alike are now all fallen into some Ozymandian obscurity. A column of infantry (looking remarkably like a Greek phalanx about twelve hundred years before it appeared in Greece) walks, implacably, over the bodies of its fallen enemy (elsewhere the enemy dead—naked but unmutilated—lie in heaps). The victorious infantrymen's eyes are resolutely fixed forward; every detail is immaculately ordered. They are in a column six files deep, with a nine-man frontage. They are spearmen, and the spears are long and need to be held in both hands; the spear tips extend well beyond the front rank. The warriors are protected to some extent by shields, which, because they cannot be supported by an arm, must have been suspended from a shoulder strap. The commander (perhaps the king) leads them from his chariot. It is an image of organization, of order and fixed intent. It conforms to a seductive notion of warfare: that it is planned and efficiently executed. There are those who have been empowered to give orders, and there are those who obediently execute them. But it is also unsettling, as though we are reviewing SS troops circa 2500 BCE.

Much as the ruling junta might have wished the war to be tightly controlled, the truth is that Bronze Age battle was in all probability an extension of the tactical messiness of earlier warfare. There was a good deal of long-range missile fire, a fair amount of ritualized "posturing," and some dueling between champions or principals (who may or may not have been kings or their equivalents). It has been claimed that the tight formation depicted on the stele reflects a willingness of the troops to "confront adversaries at close quarters and face danger in a cooperative fashion. This is a commitment virtually impossible to draw from any but highly motivated troops, those who view themselves as having a true stake in not just the fighting, but changing the course of their politics."[29] But there seems little reason to imagine that the levies who served a Bronze Age autocrat would have fought in the hope of influencing their fate through political change. Nor is it exclusively true that only those with a stake in the political outcome of battle fight with self-sacrificing resolve. Throughout history there have been dedicated groups of mercenary professionals who have great pride in their skills, a fierce commitment to their fellow mercenaries, and a willingness to fight to the death, irrespective of the political cause.

★   ★   ★

EVER SINCE THE introduction of relatively long-range missile weaponry, the tactical shape of battle has conformed to a fairly predictable pattern. First comes the "softening-up" barrage. It was arrows in the Bronze Age; high-explosive shells, delivered either by artillery or by aircraft, in ours. Following that there has to be a closure, a physical confrontation that claims territory. In the Bronze Age it would have been a combination of chariot-borne warriors and infantry; in ours it is soldiery borne in a variety of armored vehicles, delivered by aircraft (and parachute), or, occasionally, by helicopter.

The earliest chariots may have been used by Sumerians from Uruk in Mesopotamia around 3500–3000 BCE. They were, in their earliest incarnation, lumbering, solid-wheeled battle wagons, drawn by onagers, draft animals somewhere between horses and asses, and intended more as transport than shock weapon. Their primary function was to deliver into the heart of combat the highborn warrior-duelist who, protected from arrows and sling-shots by an accompanying shield bearer, sought out his enemy peer. It was extremely important that there was an appropriate social match: a characteristic found not only in ancient warfare but vestigially into the modern era, where an officer would sur-render only to a fellow officer.

Another role of the early chariot was to carry archers and spear throwers closer to the enemy, where they could loose off some shots and then make their retreat (a tactic that was resurrected with the mounted gunmen of the seventeenth century who performed an intricate maneuver known as the *caracole,* in which pistoleers would ride up to the enemy and fire, then turn back to make way for the next wave). Lighter chariots were developed around 1700 BCE, perhaps in China, and these faster versions not only became a characteristic of Chinese combat but also spread down through Anatolia, Crete, and mainland Greece (they were an important element in Homeric battle) to Mesopotamia and New Kingdom Egypt. The action was swift—a mêlée in which chariot might square off against chariot but also be unlucky enough to find itself the target of several enemy chariots. It was combat not unlike the swirling confusion of aerial dogfighting. If a chariot capsized, the occupants might be rescued if friendly troops were close enough; if not, they would be quickly overwhelmed and dispatched. In *The Iliad,* chariot-borne warriors usually dismount to fight as infantry, "using their chariots for transport to and from the field, as taxis and as ambulances."[30] Chariot warfare was a rough and problem-atic business: The passenger, whether archer or spearman, was banged and rocked about as the unsprung vehicle lurched, raced, and swung along. In consequence, the killing they meted out must have been somewhat random.

Horses are brilliant on the approach and in pursuit of a fleeing enemy (and decidedly useful in retreat, as Richard III discovered to his profound regret) and may on occasion be persuaded to crash through a line of infantry, but they can also be easily spooked by any kind of resolute defense, particularly if it involves something sharp, like spearpoints or bayonets, or by having arrows fired into them. Understandably, no matter how well trained, they fear greatly for their safety and will remove themselves with alarming alacrity, despite the wishes of the mounted warrior or charioteer. This may account for the success of the horse archers of the Asiatic steppes, who used their mounts not as shock weapons but as swift archery platforms. Their skills at firing while guiding the horse only with their knees were astonishing. They could deliver a prodigious rate of accurate fire and had the ability to contort themselves in such a way as to deliver fire behind themselves (the legendary "Parthian shot") while riding forward at full tilt, which made them almost as dangerous in retreat as attack. This style of warfare had a profound effect on much of the area that formed a great crescent of the Russian steppes, Mongolia, through what is now Iraq and Iran, and including the eastern Mediterranean (and was echoed in the cavalry combat style of the North American Plains Indians).

A horse-based style of war-making presented an enormous tactical challenge to the infantry-based military model that characterized settled, agricultural societies in the ancient world. Cavalry archery would stamp itself on the military ethos of the lands bordering the eastern Mediterranean (particularly Persia and, later, the Ottoman Empire) in a way that was not seen in Greece or western Europe, where traditional cavalry tended to be more like mounted infantry, armed with lance, sword, ax, or mace, rather than the bow.

Nevertheless, it is something of a mystery why horses, domesticated in Central Asia by about 5000 BCE, were not pressed into service as cavalry mounts until about 1000 BCE.[31] And, although chariot warfare was a characteristic of Homeric warfare, cavalry as a separate arm was absent, as it was in the hoplite warfare of the Hellenic city-states. The Greek phalanx placed so much emphasis on the virtue of face-to-face combat, for all ranks irrespective of social status, that fighting on horseback was considered, if not cowardly, then not quite appropriate.[32] The Athenian aristocrats Cimon, Alcibiades, and Pericles fought in the phalanx, as did Spartan kings.[33]

Horses are expensive to maintain and, in a society that saw frugality as the handmaiden of democracy, may have been viewed as a symbol of aristocratic indulgence by the burghers of Hellenic Greece. This connection with feudal aristocracy and the horse would be central to western European history, and it is notable that the cavalry that eventually emerged from Greece came from Macedonia and Thessaly ("the truculent baronage of Thessaly," as one historian refers to them),[34] which were not only feudal-type autocracies but, due to their geography, probably much more influenced by the horse cultures of the Asiatic steppes.

What is taking shape, however, during the first millennium BCE is a split in the tactical attitude of two worlds, echoes heard still in modern warfare. One world, its epicenter Greece, attached itself to a battle ethic that was tactically centralized, focused, highly corporate, coherent, disciplined, and, above all, rational. The hoplite order is compact; it drives on with fixed and unwavering intent. It is bureaucratic, even machinelike. These characteristics became the imprimatur of warfare in western Europe and, later, Europeanized North America. The battle ethic of its enemies, however, represented an entirely different tradition based on mobility, on loose and overflowing formations rather than tight critical mass. Asiatic in essence, it is opportunistic and keen to exploit the odds of least risk and highest return. Greek-type warfare, however, seeks to *change* the odds, even at some risk. In one world the clever marauder and ambusher is a model of effectiveness; in the other world those tactics are considered despicable—and only direct confrontation is ultimately effective and has moral virtue. It is heroic.

Some military historians, such as J. F. C. Fuller, have claimed that the Western tradition illustrates a racial superiority (Fuller was a member of the British Fascist Party): "When we look back upon Western warfare as it was before the introduction of firearms, of the differences we see, the one which most boldly stands out is the precedence of valor over cunning. It is out of valor that European history rises: the spear and the sword, and not, as in Asia, the bow and arrow, are its symbols. The bravest and not the most crafty are the leaders of men, and it is their example rather than their skill which dominates the battle."[35] It is easy to mock Fuller's vision of Teutonic warriors as brave as lions but as thick as planks, versus those skulking but "damned clever" Orientals.

In ancient Greek war-making there is also a contradiction seeking reconciliation. On the one hand is a heroic tradition of individual combat; and on the other, the need to subsume individuality in a corporate endeavor: the duelist and the hoplite—those who fight and die with names, and those who sacrifice themselves dutifully and anonymously. This tension is a constant in the history of warfare, seen in the knight or the samurai or the Plains Indian war chief, who must proclaim himself both through heraldic symbolism and lengthy declamations before battle in order to announce his lineage, his separateness from the mass. He proclaims his name and demands recognition. If he is killed, he at least will have died with the dignity due his station. The rest end up in a communal grave, their names lost forever, and their unreplicable *selfness* dissolved by the quicklime of the centuries.

In *The Iliad*, the Athenian general Nestor dresses down his troops: "Let no man in the pride of his horsemanship and his manhood dare to fight alone with the Trojans in front of the rest of us, neither let him give ground, since that way you will be weaker. When the man from his own car [chariot] encounters the enemy chariots let him stab with his spear, since this is the stronger fighting. So the men before your time sacked tower and city."[36] Nestor is trying to impose a rational, controlled war making on a much older tradition that valued heroic dueling. He wanted solid results rather than beautiful gestures; the team over the individual. Nevertheless, *The Iliad* is a great paean to the heroic warrior, the man with the name—he who steps out from the multitude. The Homeric hero is eager not only to engage his peer mano a mano but also to confront and defy a potentially overwhelming mass of the enemy: two scenarios that have always been the benchmarks of the heroic in combat. For example, one of the highest acts of valor among the Kiowa and other North American Plains Indian tribes was to charge the enemy single-handedly while the rest of one's war band was retreating. It was on a par with engaging the leading enemy warrior before general action had started, the hero isolated and unsupported, making an emphatic statement of individuality. As both of these actions carried the highest risk of being killed, they also attracted the highest kudos.[37]

But why? Getting yourself killed, as Nestor points out, is not necessarily best for the general cause. The explanation may well be that self-sacrificial actions are so highly valued precisely because they *can* forward the general cause. First, they may hit a spectacular tactical bull's-eye, such as killing the enemy leader or allowing your comrades to get away. Second, the heroic mythology of the group is reinforced. With repetitions of individual acts of heroism over time, a legendary narrative is created that strengthens general military morale and makes the group a more motivated fighting force. Thus, heroism and self-sacrifice serve a quite utilitarian function and the behavior is reinforced through rewards—sometimes money, sometimes trophies and, later in history, medals—but, most important, through remembrance; and through remembrance the hero is liberated from the engulfing darkness of anonymity. Hector, in full realization of his impending and inevitable death at the hand of Achilles, calls for just such a rescue from oblivion:

And now death, grim death is looming up beside me,
no longer far away. No way to escape it now. This,
this was their pleasure after all, sealed long ago—
Zeus and the son of Zeus, the distant deadly Archer—
though often before now they rushed to my defense.
So now I meet my doom. Well let me die—
but not without struggle, not without glory, no,
in some great clash of arms that even men to come
will hear of down the years![38]

In *The Iliad,* the warrior of the Trojan War is driven by the expectations of the wider group to conform to a heroic model of individual combat, and it cannot be a one-off performance; he must display *aretai*—a combination of strength, speed, courage, and quick-wittedness—repeatedly. In the duel he reinforces his claim to *timē,* or worthiness, but as Homer reminds us, it was "ruthless work":

Peneleos closed with Lycon—
they'd missed each other with spears, two wasted casts,
so now both clashed with swords. Lycon, flailing,
chopped the horn of Peneleos' horsehair-crested helmet
but round the socket the sword-blade smashed to bits—
just as Peneleos hacked his neck below the ear
and the blade sank clean through, nothing held
but a flap of skin, the head swung loose to the side
as Lycon slumped down to the ground . . . There—

at a dead run Meriones ran down Acamas, Acamas
mounting behind his team, and gouged his right shoulder—
he pitched from the car and the mist whirled down his eyes.
Idomeneus skewered Erymas straight through the mouth,
the merciless brazen spearpoint raking through,
up under the brain to split his glistening skull—
teeth shattered out, both eyes brimmed to the lids
with a gush of blood and both nostrils spurting,
mouth gaping, blowing convulsive sprays of blood
and death's dark cloud closed down around his corpse.[39]

There is even a rejoicing in the sheer viciousness of the duel, as when Patroclus dispatches the hapless Thestor:

And next he went for Thestor the son of Enops
cowering, crouched in his fine polished chariot,
crazed with fear, and the reins flew from his grip—
Patroclus rising beside him stabbed his right jawbone,
ramming the spearhead square between his teeth so hard
he hooked him by that spearhead over the chariot-rail,
hoisted, dragged the Trojan out as an angler perched
on a jutting rock ledge drags some fish from the sea,
some noble catch, with line and glittering bronze hook.
So with the spear Patroclus gaffed him off his car,
his mouth gaping around the glittering point
and flipped him down facefirst,
dead as he fell, his life breath blown away.[40]

The manner of Thestor's death, or rather the manner in which it is depicted, is ignominious. He is reduced to a fish, as befits a coward. But even the bravest and most noble, like Hector, may be debased in death. Achilles, his killer, "bent on outrage, on shaming noble Hector" for having killed Achilles' soul-brother, Patroclus:

Piercing the tendons, ankle to heel behind both feet,
he knotted straps of rawhide through them both,
lashed them to his chariot, left the head to drag
and mounting the car, hoisting the famous arms aboard,
he whipped his team to a run and breakneck on they flew,
holding nothing back. And a thick cloud of dust rose up
from the man they dragged, his dark hair swirling round
that head so handsome once.[41]

The combat of *The Iliad,* focused on heroic champions, would certainly have been very different in reality. Death would have come in what Homer describes as "the buck-and-rush" of battle, or as the historian J. E. Lendon depicts it:

Amidst the showers of spears and arrows and stones, amidst the running to and fro and confusion and stabbing by surprise, men of high standing would go down, killed anonymously by stray missiles and the spears of low wretches; trampled by horses, or crushed ingloriously by stray chariots. In the confusion the high deeds of the brave would go unnoticed, along with the cringing of the cowardly. The would-be heroes would emerge from battle with the same demoralizing certainty as survivors of a trench bombardment that this kind of combat was chiefly a matter of luck, not a test of excellence; that the strong and weak, the brave and craven can live or die quite at random; that bravery is not necessarily rewarded with glory or cowardice punished with shame. In the real world, Homeric combat would turn the bright colors of epic to gray.[42]

Euripides, looking back on the Homeric tradition, was also a little skeptical about the apparent clarity of heroic dueling. How did the gladiators find one another? "One thing I will not ask or I'd be laughed at: whom each of these men stood facing in the battle . . . When a man stands face to face with the enemy, he is barely able to see what he needs to see."[43]

The Iliad is part of an essential process to burnish combat killing and present it in a heroic form. We have had to be taught how to love war because seen unadorned it is too despicable to bear. Death in the Homeric era would have come not so much from heroic single-combat confrontations, as promoted in *The Iliad,* but more probably from a type of warfare rooted in prehistoric tribal combat. Peltasts—the hurlers of javelins and stones—would rush from the throng to deliver their missiles, and perhaps get in the occasional javelin thrust on an exposed and isolated enemy, before withdrawing into the safety of the pack. These low-risk opportunists were much more typical of archaic Greek warfare, though certainly not as heroic as duelist or phalangite and therefore not worthy of Homeric attention. *The Iliad* wants us to see the lions rather than the jackals.

In 1879 a German surgeon, H. Frölich, analyzed the wounds suffered by warriors in *The Iliad* and sorted them by weapon type, anatomical location, and relative lethality.[44] Of course, Frölich was analyzing an epic poem in which artistic license plays a role, but nevertheless the general picture of Bronze Age warfare that emerges is revealing. The main weapons are spears, swords, arrows, and rocks (used as missiles). Frölich identifies 147 incidences of wounding, but subsequent computer analysis has identified 139, of which 105 (76 percent) were fatal.[45] The spear was the main killer, with 99 deaths (71 percent) attributed to it. They were mainly hits to the torso (43), with head (16) and neck (10) the next most lethal areas. Although Frölich makes no distinction between thrown spears—javelins—or thrusting spears, it now seems that more Homeric heroes died from javelin hits (54) than from spear thrusts (45), with most of them to the trunk.

The physics of the javelin and spear are very different. The javelin, which is lighter, relies on a weight/momentum relationship: Too light and it bounces off armor; too heavy and it requires more strength than most warriors could muster to be launched with any speed or accuracy. The spear, on the other hand, transfers the force of the spearman directly to the victim; all it requires is a rigid shaft and an effective spearhead for direct transmission of energy.

All bladed weapons—be they thrusting types like spears and certain swords and daggers, hacking types like axes and some swords, or missile types like arrows and javelins—employ a similar physics. The sharp point concentrates the delivered energy into a very small area for greatest possible penetration; the broader blade opens the wound for greatest possible tissue damage and blood loss. And if we look at the much broader tactical picture, we can see the same dynamic: The "physics" of attack tactics follows a similar transmission of force. The smaller, initial assault group punches the hole, and the larger follow-up force exploits the entry.

All sword wounds, arcording to Frölich's analysis of *The Iliad,* were lethal. There are eighteen—13 percent of all fatalities. The neck was the most vulnerable area, followed by the head (decapitation is not unusual). The body blows, although fewer, are horrific and often involve disemboweling, all of which would be expected from a heavy bronze-bladed slashing sword. The Naue II sword (as archeologists designate it), with a bronze blade (broad at its base and tapering to a point, like a lanceolate leaf shape) was introduced into the eastern Mediterranean as well as western Europe and Scandinavia from northern Italy and Carpathia (the modern Czech, Slovakia, Poland area) around 1200 BCE. Perhaps brought in by northern "barbarian" mercenaries, it played an important part in the military revolution that led to the destruction of the chariot-based empires.[46]

The tensile strength of bronze (an alloy of copper and tin) is greater than that of the metals used earlier, and this translated into a longer blade than its daggerlike forerunners, which in turn conferred a significant advantage on the swordsman, who became safer (because his longer blade allowed him greater distance from his foe), while being more lethal. It was a weapon design of extraordinary effectiveness, longevity, and adaptability. Although later it was made of iron, which is easier to keep sharp (although more susceptible to corrosion) than bronze, it retained its basic shape for about seven hundred years. Effectively, the sword carried into Homeric battle would not have appeared strange to the Roman legionary armed with his legendary short sword, the *gladius*.

Missile deaths other than those caused by javelins are fewest in *The Iliad:* four by arrow, four by hurled stone. The stone, of course, takes us back to the very earliest forms of hunting and combat killing and reminds us that Bronze Age warfare is perched between the prehistoric and the "modern." Homer describes Patroclus killing Erylaus:

> *And next he caught Erylaus closing, lunging in—*
> *he flung a rock and it struck between his eyes*
> *and the man's whole skull split in his heavy helmet,*
> *down the Trojan slammed on the ground, head-down*
> *and courage-shattering Death engulfed his corpse.*[47]

A modern baseball player can deliver a fastball at about 95 miles per hour, and one can imagine that a somewhat heavier rock, although delivered at a slower speed, could indeed be lethal as a head shot. But nevertheless it seems anomalous that Homeric heroes, so wedded to the notion of up-close dueling, resorted to as basic and as earthily crude a form of death dealing as pitching rocks.

The most vulnerable areas for the Homeric warrior in terms of fatalities were first the trunk (stomach and chest), which although partly protected by a brass breastplate offered the largest target and contains most of the major organs. Death would probably have been swift, but even those who survived the initial damage to vital organs would have succumbed to lethal infections. Second was the head because brain injuries would have been certainly fatal (although trepanning had been widely practiced for many centuries). This would have included blows to the face that penetrated the cranium, as when Ajax, for example, speared the Trojan Acamas "tall and staunch":

> *The first to hurl, Great Ajax hit the ridge*
> *of the helmet's horsehair crest—the bronze point*
> *stuck in Acamas' forehead pounding through the skull*
> *and the dark came swirling down to shroud his eyes.*[48]

The horsehair crest on the helmet served not only as an intimidating height magnifier (an important function of military headgear throughout history; one thinks, for example, of the plumed headdresses of the Aztecs, of the Plains Indian bonnets, of the wondrous horned helmets of medieval samurai, or of the towering bearskins of Napoleon's Imperial Guard) but also as a blow deflector (Alexander the Great would be saved at the battle of the Granicus in this way). A strike to the helmet that stove it in and penetrated the cranium would cause massive and fatal bleeding. The helmet did not have to be ruptured for the blow to prove deadly. Archeological finds from the classical and Hellenic Greek eras confirm the sometimes limited protection a helmet offered:

> Extant examples of Corinthian helmets show numerous extensive dents, cracks, and caved-in sides, suggesting that such blows, while not actually breaking the metal surface

might have caused considerable brain damage. . . . Nearly all such trauma were likely to be fatal. . . . And even when the Corinthian helmet protected the hoplite against serious brain injury, the sheer force of the running spear thrust could snap the head radically backward or downward, fracturing the cervical vertebrae altogether. This either severed the spinal cord, causing paralysis or perhaps sudden death, or induced hemorrhaging within the spinal canal, and that could lead to intolerable pressure and eventual death or a wasting quadriplegia—a condition that was probably fatal in the ancient world.[49]

The third most vulnerable area was the neck, which was only partially protected at the nape and, to some extent, at the side by the long cheek protectors:

There—quick Oilean Ajax rushed Cleobulus,
took him alive, stumbling blind in the rout
but took his life at once, snapped his strength
with a sword that hewed his neckbone.[50]

The fourth most vulnerable was the arm:

But Maris charged Antilochus,
sweeping in with his lance, enraged for his brother,
planted himself before his corpse but Thrasmyedes,
quick as a god, beat him to it—he stabbed
before Maris stabbed—no miss! right in the shoulder,
the Argive's spearpoint cracked through the bony socket,
shearing away the tendons, wrenched the whole arm out
and down he thundered, darkness blanked his eyes.[51]

And last, the leg:

And Amphiclus went for Meges
but Meges saw him coming and got in first by far
spearing him in the thigh where it joins the body
the spot where a man's muscle bunches thickest:
the tough sinews shredded around the weapons point
as the dark swirled down his eyes—[52]

The rise of the Greek city-states during the seventh century BCE (some five hundred years after the fighting for Troy and perhaps two hundred years or so after Homer wrote his epic account of it) introduced a type of military organization and method of fighting that reflected the civic, political, economic, and social expectations of the states of southern Greece. It was a style of predominantly infantry combat—phalanx warfare—that was adopted around 700 BCE.

The Greek infantry, called hoplites (from *hopla*, "shield"), who made up the phalanx (derived from reeds bound into a tight bundle) were property-owning citizens, many of them small farmers. Their obligation was to defend their territory should it be threatened by an invading force. It was a sacred duty—and one in which every citizen had a say—but it had to be reconciled with their primary obligation to make a living, and so it was in their interest to limit the amount of time spent fighting. The style of warfare they developed reflected their civic obligation as well as their self-interest and was designed to produce short, sharp battles that had, to some extent, been arranged and would be fought by certain rules.[53] Although there was a ritual element in these combats, they could be very bloody: "Hoplite conflict was by deliberate design somewhat artificial, intended to focus a concentrated brutality upon the few in order to spare the many."[54] The opposing closely ordered block formations (phalanxes) were drawn up, usually on preselected and mutually agreed-upon flat terrain, and faced off. At some point the tension was broken and one of the phalanxes started to move toward the other, at first quite slowly, then gathering speed in order to maximize impact.

Each hoplite warrior supplied his own weaponry and armor, and therefore its quality was a reflection of the man's financial means (as, for example, with the militia of the American War of Independence). He wore a thick cuirass (breast- and backplates) weighing about 11 pounds (some modern authorities cite weights as much as 50 pounds)[55] and a helmet of iron or bronze, which if worn by rank-and-file hoplites was heavier because it was cast and weighed 12–15 pounds,[56] while the wealthier wore forged helmets that weighed only 5–8 pounds. The lower leg was protected by brass greaves (shin guards) so molded to the calf that they could be snapped into place without the need for straps (bronze, although heavier than steel, is much more elastic); a pair weighed about 3 pounds. His 3-foot-diameter shield weighed about 16 pounds.

The total weight of the armor, without weapons, was somewhere in the region of 45 pounds. (By comparison, a medieval knight's armor weighed between 60 and 70 pounds, and it is interesting to note that the modern infantryman, far from having his burden lightened by modern materials, is often expected to hump gear weighing more than that of a knight in armor.)[57] But because each man tailored his armor to his individual needs and means, there would have been considerable variation. In addition, a hoplite would often have been accompanied by a servant, who carried his shield and spear and acted as a forager, a dispatcher of enemy wounded, and even as a light infantryman. Nevertheless, there are many references to the excessive weight of the hoplite's armor, and under a burning Greek sun it was no wonder that many incidents of heatstroke are recorded.[58] Hanson speculates that it was the discomfort of fighting in the sun that prompted the Spartan Dienekes at Thermopylae in 480 BCE to coolly remark that the expected avalanche of Persian arrows, massive enough to blot out the sun, would merely provide some much needed shade.[59]

The military historian Jack Coggins tested the protective properties of a breastplate made to the approximate specification of a hoplite piece: "A modern hunting arrow (with a head probably far superior to anything the ancients had) shot at very close range from a 50-pound bow dented the plate and penetrated about 5/8 of an inch. With existing equipment [a bow of the period], at battle ranges, a cuirass made of similar material should have been impenetrable." Coggins concludes that "the hoplite, with Corinthian helm, shoulder-to-knee-length shield and greaves, presented little target vulnerability to the average archer."[60]

The armor of the hoplite and the tactics of phalangite combat were a compromise between mobility and weight. The warrior certainly carried a heavy load, but the design of his armor afforded more physical flexibility than might at first be thought. His limbs were unencumbered (except for light greaves) so that running, bending, and turning, as well as a dexterous manipulation of shield, spear, and sword, would have been possible. (Similarly, the popular perception of, for example, the medieval knight is essentially that of a steel-bound Michelin Man, about as agile as a turtle, but we know that well-crafted suits of armor allowed considerable freedom of movement.)[61] Although the panoply (the technical term for a suit of ancient armor) allowed the hoplite flexibility, the phalanx was a place for corporate rather than individualistic combat; tactically there was little fancy footwork—the mighty shove of pikemen against pikemen would determine the outcome.

Phalangites had an obligation to the group; many would have been blood relatives; all would have had a civic bond. The phalanx, like all crowdlike masses, had its own dynamic, often reflected in the tendency of the whole group to drift to the right as each man sought the protection of his neighbor's shield for his unprotected right side.[62] For amateur soldiers the mass of the phalanx maximized the advantages of corporate heft and helped compensate for an individual's lack of training and experience.

If Homeric mythology provided the duelist with a compelling narrative as the center of heroic combat, the honest burghers and spear carriers, the necessary but unnamed, also needed their sustaining legend, their inspiring vocabulary. And that heroic vocabulary usually revolved around the ideals of steadfastness, tenacity, obligation, loyalty to the greater cause, and the welfare of one's comrades. Standing fast even unto death is a heroic ideal fashioned specifically for the group. It is the heroicizing of a necessary but not necessarily romantic reality, and one specifically fashioned for citizen-warriors. The Spartan poet Tyrtaeus describes this stoic ethos:

> Let each man plant himself firmly, rooted to the ground with
> both feet,
> bite his lip with his teeth, and hold.[63]

As the phalanx drew up against the enemy (perhaps 200 yards away) there may well have been a good deal of barracking, swearing, and general ribald encouragement. When men are tense they tend to mouth off; it lifts the spirits. At some point the psychological trigger would be pulled and one side would move into a steady trot, then into a full-blooded running charge. The point at this stage is to gather momentum, and as the momentum increases so does the level of adrenaline; glucose is released by the liver for extra muscular exertion, all of which incites the charging warrior to greater effort:

> Experience taught the hoplites that the best way to push
> their iron through the bronze and wood of enemy shields

and breastplates was to achieve momentum before both sides became entangled and the chance to drive home a running spear-thrust with real power was lost. This desire on the part of the spearmen to have one clear shot, to crash into the opposing side in one fell swoop, was an enticing narcotic; even the rational argument that the very momentum he gathered on the run might just as easily impale him on the propped spears of a kneeling enemy, or distort his advancing line of protective shields, would have fallen on deaf ears.[64]

The charge also had a protective function. The quicker the warrior covered the last 200 yards or so, the less exposed he was to missile fire by javelin-throwing peltasts (the name derives from their crescent-shaped shield, the *pelte*), archers, or slingers. Missile fire, although disdained by hoplites, could be devastating, as the Athenian general Demosthenes discovered in 426 BCE when his force was routed by Aetolian peltasts who, refusing to close with the Athenian phalanx, destroyed it from a distance, and more than thirty years later it would be the turn of peltasts under the Athenian general Iphicrates to destroy a Spartan *mora* (battalion) at Lechaeum.[65]

The side receiving the charge may also have moved forward—aggression tends to invite aggression—or it may doggedly and determinedly have shaped up to receive the impact. Given that modern warfare is so removed from the collision of massed bodies, one can only imagine the stupendous chaos at impact. Xenophon says that there was no yelling, "but there was not silence either; instead that particular sound was present which both anger and battle tend to produce."[66] Individual noises amalgamated into a great roar. Livy's description of a Roman battle scene would have been applicable to all ancient warfare: "But due to the very din and tumult neither any encouragement nor orders were able to be heard, so much so that the infantry could not recognize their maniples, centuries, or even their own assigned places . . . there was such a cloud of fog that men relied on their ears rather than their eyes. They turned their faces toward the groans of the wounded, the blows of flesh and arms, and the mingled cries of both the frightened and the panicked."[67]

At the moment of impact, the attackers' spears (6–8 feet long, weighing about 4 pounds) would have been held underhand in order to thrust upward into the unprotected groin, the thigh, or the gut under the breastplate:

> *This indeed is a foul thing, that the older man falls*
> *among the forefront and lies before the younger*
> *His white head and his grey beard breathing out his*
> *strong soul in the dust,*
> *Holding in his dear hands his groin all bloody.*[68]

This sounds entirely plausible. Vase paintings show hoplites unprotected on their thighs and, as far as one can judge, on their genitals. But something, nevertheless, seems contrary to common sense. If, over time, warriors find that they have a particular vulnerability—that is, they get killed on a regular basis because of a lack of armor in a vital place, or their tactics expose them to often repeated fatalities, or their gear is defective—they tend to do something about it. On the whole, fighting men have a particular aversion to getting killed. In addition, being gored in the genitals is a very special risk men would passionately seek to avoid (one thinks of the steel codpieces of medieval knights). But this does not seem to have been the case in hoplite warfare (or Roman legion warfare either).

Two ideas present themselves (though neither entirely convincingly). One, that they did have effective protection, or felt they did, in the shield; or, two, that another advantage—a tactical one—outweighed the disadvantage: Was it more important to be mobile, to be relatively unencumbered? (There is, of course, a third possibility—that they did not rate self-preservation very highly. But this would seem unlikely in the context of citizen-soldiers who sought limited warfare.)

Once engaged, hoplites would change to an overhead grip in order to thrust down over the shield into the neck, face, arms, and shoulders. Spears had butt spikes that could be used for stabbing a fallen enemy, but they also posed their own problem to comrades behind. Plutarch relates that in the great press of bodies in Pyrrhus's phalanx during the battle of Árgos in 272 BCE many were killed by "friendly fire"—accidental blows from comrades.[69] Some spears would have shattered on impact with the enemy front line, but the great press of bodies would have made sword fighting difficult (hoplites were usually armed with the double-edged short sword—although there is pictorial evidence of a sicklelike design not dissimilar to a Ghurka kukri—as well as a dagger called the *parazonium,* or "belt companion").[70] In the great shove a disarmed hoplite himself became a weapon, as companions behind pushed him into the enemy ranks.

The heaviest mortality would understandably be in the front rank, and again one can see the function of providing a special heroic status to those who fought there. Men have to be, in the most literal meaning of the word, encouraged to risk their lives. For example, in the age of musketry, it would often be junior officers, young men seeking advancement (but also the most expendable), who were given the honor of carrying the regimental colors. It was a highly dangerous job because the color bearer was an obvious target and, due to the nature of his role, often exposed. But the function had been, over centuries, *invested* with glory, and if he survived he not only progressed in his career but also enhanced his social standing among his peers as well as the wider society. Through his risk taking he had become empowered. The same could be said of the Roman *velites,* lightly armored forward skirmishers of the legion who, young and eager to prove themselves, were rewarded for acts of conspicuous individual bravery.[71] As the Spartan Tyrtaeus expressed it: "Glorious indeed is death in the front rank of the combat, when the brave man falls fighting for his country."[72]

Once the two phalanxes were locked together, the battle came down to *othismos*—the push of shields—by which the rearward ranks sought to shove their comrades deeper into the enemy formation in order to form bridgeheads that could be reinforced and exploited—assuming the pioneers survived long enough to hold the pocket. Hand-to-hand battle would have been frenzied and ugly, rather like the trench-raiding combat of World War I—desperate, fear-choked, grabbing, slashing, brutal killing about as far removed from some heroic model of warfare as one could imagine. Death by trampling and suffocation (a high risk in any close-in combat by massed infantry, as Agincourt eighteen hundred or so years later would demonstrate) was the fate of many who lost their footing. But the need to maintain a heroic aura around battle is compelling (if civilians knew how truly gruesome combat is, societies would be hard-pressed to sustain it), and mass warfare is very rarely depicted on ancient Greek vases; the image that had to be promoted was one of heroic individual combat. The engine of war runs on the intoxicating vapor of mythology.

At some point came the critical moment of resolution when on one side there was a rapid evaporation of morale and the defeated began to peel off from the rear and sides, quickly triggering a general flight (the whiff of defeat is pungent). Retreat often unleashes some primitive bloodlust in the victor, and if there was a complete collapse, undoubtedly men were run down and killed in number, but if some order was maintained by the defeated, a fighting withdrawal would have been a sufficient disincentive to the attackers to take further casualties. Battle, after all, was about driving the enemy off and doing so while minimizing risk. There was a life to return to. Casualties generally remained on the low side compared with modern warfare—5 percent for the victors and about 14 percent for the defeated."[73]

But hoplite battle was far from a bloodless ritual. Victor Davis Hanson describes the aftermath:

> Besides the sheer concentration of bodies, the most common sight to these onlookers would have been the quantity of spilled blood and gore. In some of the larger battles—Delion, Leuktra, or Plataia—thousands of corpses lay with huge, gaping wounds from the spear and the sword. Since the flesh was never incinerated as it came to be in modern battles by the explosion of bomb and shell, and because the entry and exit wounds created by double-edged iron spearheads tend to be larger than those caused by small-arms fire, the bodies would have drained much of their body fluids upon the ground. Walking among the pile of corpses entailed treading everywhere over stained earth and pools of blood. . . . Plutarch recorded a similar picture after the death of some 25,000 Macedonian pikemen at Pydna.[74]

(Pydna, 168 BCE, was the battle in which Macedonian phalanxes were massacred by Roman legions. The Macedonian death toll has been estimated as exceeding 60 percent.)

Victory was usually signaled by the erection of a panoply of armor mounted on a tree or pole, and custom dictated that it should not be permanent (too showy an edifice was considered in bad taste). Under the strict code of hoplite combat the dead were invariably reclaimed by their respective sides and an accounting by tribal affiliation was relayed back to the city. Where the bodies lay would have told its own story reflecting the tribal composition of the phalanx. As with any unit based on geographical proximity, whole communities could be devastated (the British Pals battalions of World War I, and the men from Bedford, Virginia, who died at D-Day, are classic modern examples). At Plataea, for example, (479 BCE) the Athenian dead came from one tribe, the Aiantis. At Leuctra (371 BCE) almost all of the Spartan high command, many of whom were related, were killed.[75] The Roman writer Onasander, describing hoplite warfare, remarked that men fought best when "brother is in rank beside brother, friend beside friend, lover beside lover."[76] The last category is certainly at odds with "Don't ask, don't tell." The Theban "Sacred Band" of 150 homosexual couples died to a man resisting the Macedonian invasion at the battle of Chaeronea in 338 BCE. Plutarch describes the Macedonian king, Philip, reviewing their corpses: "He stopped at the spot where the three hundred lay: all slain where they had met the long spears of the Macedonians. The corpses were still in their armor and mixed up with one another, and so he became amazed when he learned that these were the regiments of lovers and beloved. 'May all perish,' he said, 'who suspect that these men did or suffered anything disgraceful.' "[77]

In Sparta also homosexuality was an institutionalized part of the society and an entirely accepted part of the military.[78]

In Greek warfare, victory went to the side that controlled the battlefield and not necessarily to the side with fewer casualties. At the battle of Paraetacene (c. 316 BCE), for example, Antigonus's army lost more than 3,700 killed, while his opponent, Eumenes, had only about 540 dead. But Eumenes could not persuade or force his army to camp among the corpses, and it insisted on moving off for the night. Antigonus, on the other hand, did cajole his men to sleep among the slain and claimed the victory.[79]

★   ★   ★

SHIFTS IN WEAPONS technology and the tactics that flow from them can spell doom for those warriors on the wrong side of change—the battlefields of history are littered with the corpses of military mastodons. But military change should never be pinned on one factor in isolation. Technical and tactical innovations have a dynamic exchange with social and political ideas. The response to economic pressures such as overpopulation or the dwindling of some natural resource may be expressed in a desire for colonial expansion, or to redress a perceived wrong, and is then packaged in the ideology necessary to the day and to the cause. Ideas, as much as weapons, get warriors killed, and this symbiotic relationship radically alters the lethality of the battlefield. These sea changes happen periodically, and Macedonia in the latter half of the first millennium BCE was the seat of just such a military revolution.

It is sometimes difficult for us to appreciate small changes. We live in an era in which military science, over a period of only a few decades, learned how to potentially evaporate the world. That the Macedonians in about 400 BCE extended the length of a spear by about 8 feet does not seem that much of a big deal. But the extended reach of the 16-to-18-foot *sarissa* multiplied both the potential lethality and the defensive capability of the Macedonian phalanx by an order of magnitude. The longer spear meant that the front five rows (rather than the three of the conventional hoplite phalanx) could present spear points to the enemy—an increase in "firepower" of 40 percent.[80]

It was a densely packed and determined body that offered what must have been a stomach-churning prospect to its opponents. There was also a radical change in personal armor. The relatively heavy hoplite panoply was discarded in favor of much lighter leather and composite elements; and because the warrior needed both hands to hold his much weightier and longer spear, the great hoplite shield was reduced to a vestigial disk hung at the neck or shoulder (a similar diminution of armor is seen in the purely symbolic gorget of an eighteenth-century infantry officer).

This was not the armor of self-preservation that had characterized the southern Greeks but something much more aggressive.
Killing rather than concession drove the Macedonian war ethic,
and unlike the southern Greeks, with their emphasis on limited
war, the Macedonians brought a totalitarian blitzkrieg mental-
ity to the battlefield that was reflected in their general tactical
scheme.

Ancient Macedonia was a frontier of Greece, and there was
perhaps more contact there with the horse-raider societies of the
steppes. It would not be surprising, therefore, that it adopted
from them a horse culture that was lacking in southern Greece.
Macedonian society was rough-hewn and tough. Compared with
southern Greeks, Macedonians had more in common with other
outliers of ancient history—Celts, Picts, Gauls, or Germans:
ruled by clan kings, fierce warriors, and stupendous boozers, and
not much concerned with the etiquette of their more sophisticated neighbors. Cavalry, and particularly an elite-based cavalry
(the Companions), played a critical role in Macedonian tactics.
(The word *aristocratic* is often used to describe the social structure
and the men who made up the Macedonian cavalry, but with its
genteel associations it is perhaps not the best descriptor; we need
something much closer to the raw power of a Mafia consigliere
or Scottish tribal laird than, say, Louis XIV—more clenched fist
than crooked pinkie.)

The general shape of Macedonian battle tactics was in some
ways reminiscent of modern armored warfare. The Companions—
essentially a royal houschold unit (*hetaroi*) armed with sword,
shield, and short cavalry spear (*xyston*) used for throwing and
thrusting—was anchored on the right of the battle line (the
right, throughout history, has been the position of honor and
status). Alexander, in a shift from the tradition of Greek commanders fighting as infantry, fought with the Companions. The
auxiliary cavalry was on the left wing, while the center was filled

by the phalangites with their massed spears. A lighter infantry component—*hypaspists* (from *aspis,* shield)—operated between phalanx and cavalry as mobile attack infantry. The Companions' role was to smash, panzer-style, deep into the enemy cavalry and with the utmost determination fight its way to its command center. While the phalanx held the opposing infantry, the *hypaspists* exploited the confusion caused by their cavalry's incursions. It was a tactical model based on the combination of great speed and concentration of force from the cavalry, and a rock-solid infantry center that could either hold or move forward at a steady and irresistible pace.

This combined-force approach has been described as "an entirely new development in the history of Western warfare," and it took a man of extraordinary ambition (perhaps even to a psychotic degree) to harness its lethality.[81] Alexander of Macedon had inherited the military machine from his father, Philip II, and he drove it with a ferocious intensity through the ranks of his enemies. He was not just the commander of killers but a frontline killer himself. He was an inheritor of a heroic tradition of combat leadership. Greek generals and kings fought in the phalanx, and "there is not a single major Greek battle—Thermopylae, Delium, Mantinea, Leuctra—in which Hellenic generals survived the rout of their troops."[82] The Spartan king Cleombrotus was killed in the phalanx at Leuctra, for example, the usual fate of a defeated Spartan king. This exposure of commanders to the risks of the battlefield lasted until the nineteenth century (one thinks, for example, of the high mortality rate among general officers of the American Civil War), when it was replaced by the bureaucratization of leadership: the commander-as-manager. Plutarch has Alexander recite the cost of his hands-on involvement: "First, among the Illyrians my head was wounded by a stone and my neck by a cudgel. Then at Granicus my head was cut open by an enemy's dagger, at Issus my thigh was pierced by the sword. Next, at Gaza my ankle was wounded by an arrow, my shoulder was dislocated. . . . Then at Macaranda the bone of my leg was split open by an arrow. . . . Among the Mallians the shaft of an arrow sank deep into my breast and buried its steel."[83]

It was a risk shared by his subordinate officers; some 120 were killed in the phalanx at Issus in 333 BCE—and this in a battle he won. At the battle of the Granicus River in 334 BCE, Alexander was the center of attention for the Persian high command. If he could be killed quickly, despondency might break the will of his army. Alexander personally killed Mithridates, the son-in-law of the Persian king, Darius (who was not present), with a spear thrust through the face and, having survived a blow to the head from Rhoesaces,[84] a Lydian nobleman, killed Rhoesaces with a spear thrust to the chest.[85] The death toll among the Persian high command at the Granicus was staggering—perhaps ten of the thirteen major commanders were killed or, as in the case of Arsites, later committed suicide. As for the Macedonian high command, one of the greatest risks of being killed came from Alexander himself. Two of his greatest and most valiant generals, Parmenio and his son, the cavalry commander Philotas, were killed on Alexander's order, as was Cleitus, who had saved Alexander's life at the Granicus; Cleander and Sitacles, Agathon and Heracon were also executed on flimsy pretexts.[86]

Alexander brought a ruthlessness to battle that was reflected in hitherto unprecedented mortality rates. At the Granicus, having destroyed and driven off the main Persian army, he reserved his particular ire for the Greek mercenaries fighting on the Persian side, who had stood their ground and were surrounded. All were put to the sword except 2,000 who were sent back to Macedonia as slaves. About 5,000 Persians were killed plus 2,000–3,000 Greek mercenaries, while some historians have put the figure for the killed Greek mercenaries alone at 15,000–18,000.[87] At the battle of Issus the following year Alexander's army inflicted something in the region of 20,000 deaths on the Greek mercenaries fighting for Darius III, plus "anywhere from 50,000 to 100,000 Persian recruits . . . a formidable challenge of time and space to butcher more than 300 men every minute for eight hours. This was extermination taken to new heights. . . . The Macedonian phalanx did not push men off the battlefield as much as slaughter them from the rear for hours on end after the battle was already decided."[88] (It should also be noted that all the Macedonian wounded whom Alexander left behind in the town of Issus were slaughtered by the returning Persians.) This uninhibited killing of the wounded and defeated set a pattern seen in other Alexandrian battles such as Gaugamela (331 BCE) and the Hydaspes (326 BCE), and served to emphasize that possibly the greatest risk of death for a warrior comes when cohesion breaks and retreat begins, reflected by the disparity between the death count of the victorious and the slaughter of the defeated. (At the Granicus, Macedonian losses were perhaps as few as 150, and at Issus, 450.)

★   ★   ★

AT THE BATTLES of Cynoscephalae in 197 BCE and at Pydna almost thirty years later, the mighty Macedonian phalanxes met their own nemesis in the form of the Roman legions. In defeat, the Macedonian pikemen stood quite still with their *sarissae* upright. It was a signal that they wished to surrender, but the problem was that their opponents could not or would not recognize this convention of the battlefield. The Macedonians, so stalwart in action and so stoical in defeat, were unceremoniously and savagely cut down where they stood. The phalanx died because it had become too good at what they had been good at. Fixed in place, they would be destroyed for it. The legions, for their part, did what they had been rigorously trained to do: They attacked with formidable energy and killed with ferocious single-mindedness. For them, a dead enemy was a peaceful enemy.

Where the old phalanx was deep and solid and unwieldy, the legion was made up of units—maniples and cohorts—that afforded it more tactical flexibility. They were deployed in a quincunx formation: a chessboard pattern where all the black squares are troops and the white squares the spaces between, with the black squares covering the white squares in front of them and able to move up as reinforcement when necessary. And what was writ large was also writ small: The legionaries' armor reflected this highly mobile segmented pattern. The upper-body cuirass, the *lorica segmentata,* was made up of metal bands stitched onto a linen or leather undergarment, thus combining protection with flexibility. The legionary was primarily a swordsman rather than a spear pusher, and he required more maneuverability than the heavy bell cuirass of the old phalanx could have afforded. His weaponry, too, was light and wieldy, quick to the thrust and fast in the slash. Even his shield could be used as an offensive weapon. The heavy central boss gave it the added heft to bang down an opponent, exposing his torso for a *gladius* or *pilum* (a type of javelin) thrust, while the rim of the shield was handy for hooking and smashing. A strong legionary could inflict considerable damage on his opposite number with shield alone.

The first tactical objective (as true whether fighting a Macedonian phalanx or a Gaulish or Germanic host) was to get into the enemy ranks where the wicked short sword, the 2-foot-long double-edged *gladius hispaniensis* ("Spanish sword"), could do its business. First, the carapace of enemy shields had to be cracked in order to expose the flesh. At about twenty paces the first two rows of legionaries would hurl the *pilum*—more harpoon than spear—where its solid weight might penetrate an opponent's shield and wound him. Fighting in Gaul, Caesar writes of *pila* driving through "several of their overlapping shields . . . the iron head would bend and they could neither get it out nor fight properly with their left arms. Many of them, after a number of vain efforts at disentangling themselves, preferred to drop their shields and fight with no protection for their bodies."[89]

Once they were through the outer shell of enemy shields, the legionaries went to work with the *gladius*. To those who had never seen Roman swordsmen in close combat, the results were shocking. Livy writes, "When they had seen bodies chopped to pieces by the Spanish sword, arms torn away, shoulders and all, or heads separated from bodies . . . or vitals laid open . . . they realized in a general panic with what weapons, and what men they had to fight."[90]

Caesar described close combat against the Germans: "When the signal was given, our men rushed forward so fiercely and the enemy came on so swiftly and furiously that there was no time for hurling our javelins. They were thrown aside, and the fighting was with swords at close quarters. The Germans quickly adopted their usual close formation to defend themselves from the sword thrusts, but many of our men were brave enough to leap right on top of the wall of shields, tear the shields from the hands that held them, and stab down at the enemy from above."[91]

Caesar, for obvious reasons, wants us to see his soldiers as dashing heroes, and there's no doubt that this sort of fighting occurred on a regular basis. *Virtus*, the combination of courage, daring, and determination to close with the enemy, was highly prized in the Roman military, but the general truth of close-quarter combat is that it tends to be much more tentative, messy, and confusing at the contact face: "Hand-to-hand fighting was physically very fatiguing and emotionally stressful. Actual hand-to-hand fighting can only have lasted for very short periods and the relatively light casualties suffered at this stage seem to support this."[92]

If no immediate and viable bridgehead was established within the enemy ranks, the opponents tended to stand off. The reluctant had to deal with pressure from officers, the press of men behind making it difficult for the front-rank fighters to escape (*optiones,* the centurions' NCOs, literally pushed men forward from the rear ranks), and the knowledge of severe punishment if they tried it. The practice of decimation, the execution of one man in ten in a unit that had performed particularly poorly, was not a Roman invention. Alexander had used it, and had himself borrowed the practice from earlier Near Eastern armies. All of this, as well as the men's soaring adrenaline, bore down to create the pressure that might lead to reengagement. But:

> The longer the unit was close to the enemy the more its formation and cohesion dissolved. Men increasingly followed their instincts, the bravest pushing to the front, the most timid trying to slip away to the rear, while the majority remained somewhere in the middle. At any time they might follow the example of the timid and the unit would dissolve into rout, a possibility that became greater the longer a unit did not advance or make progress. Significant casualties on an ancient battlefield occurred when a unit fled from combat. The ones who died first were those who were the slowest in turning to flee, so the men in the center of a formation, able to see little of what was going on, were always on the verge of nervous panic.[93]

And what got the legionary killed? As with the Macedonian phalangites the legionary was wedded to specific tactical forms and attitudes and was superb in their execution. But this dedication to a specialized tactical model brought its own potentially fatal weaknesses, which two catastrophic defeats illustrate.

The legion, like the phalanx, was a war machine designed to go forward. And like the phalanx, it was vulnerable to attack on its flanks. Also like the phalanx it needed to strike a balance between compaction (which gave it solidity and heft) and yet allowing enough space between warriors for the effective manipulation of their weapons. At Cannae in 216 BCE, Hannibal lured the legions into a frontal assault that was then compressed by attacks on its flanks and, eventually, its rear, so that legionaries, whose armor was designed primarily to protect the front, were exposed to blows coming in on their sides and backs. Committed to their traditional attack pattern, they would have found it extremely difficult to defend against flank incursions, and as the legionary mass became increasingly compacted, the rear ranks relentlessly and blindly pressed their more forward comrades into an ever more deadly cul-de-sac.

It was only the leading edge of the force that could fight effectively, while those behind were rendered either redundant or, worse, disabling. The result was that in one of the smallest killing fields in the history of warfare the Roman legions were surrounded and annihilated. This, the largest army Rome had ever sent into the field, died where it stood. Sources differ, but somewhere in the region of 60,000 legionaries were cut down.[94] The Romans, themselves traditionally so merciless to their wounded enemies, were shown little compassion: "Many wounded had been hamstrung by marauding small bands, their writhing bodies left to be finished off by looters, the August sun, and the Carthaginian cleanup crews the next day. Two centuries later Livy wrote that thousands of Romans were still alive on the morning of August 3, awakened from their sleep and agony by the morning cold, only to be 'quickly finished off' by Hannibal's plunderers."[95] In the two years or so of his invasion of Italy, Hannibal would kill, wound, or capture more than a third of the Roman military manpower pool.[96] Rome absorbed these huge body blows and took its revenge. At Zama in 202 BCE the Roman general Scipio killed 20,000–25,000 of Hannibal's army for the relatively modest investment of 1,500 of his own dead, and Carthage itself was so comprehensively destroyed that the city existed only in memory, like a golden ghost.

The Roman army was designed to engage, and its tactical ideal was to close, kill, and conquer. But on occasion the discipline, cohesion, and determination of the legion were neutralized by an enemy who simply would not agree to fight according to the Roman rule book. By standing off and bleeding their enemy with long-distance archery, they denied him any tactical traction and robbed him of his most valued assets.

The Roman consul Marcus Crassus was eager to strengthen his political position in Rome by a successful military adventure and to that end invaded Parthia (modern northeastern Iran) with an army of about 40,000. At the battle of Carrhae (53 BCE) his force, deployed in a defensive square, was surrounded by a much smaller Parthian host consisting primarily of horse archers and *cataphracts* (heavy cavalry). The well-supplied horse archers kept up a galling enfilade, and Crassus, desperate to bring on a close-up engagement in which his tactical strengths could be deployed, sent out his son Publius with eight cohorts (about 4,800 men), 500 archers, and 1300 cavalry.[97] It was an instinctive response to tactical frustration, as is seen on many occasions throughout history. It is a particular characteristic of colonial warfare; one thinks, for example, of the US Army in the Indian wars (Fetterman massacre), the British in nineteenth-century Afghanistan (the Kabul expedition), and the French Foreign Legion fighting the Morrocan Rif uprising. The heads tend to come back on pikes, which was precisely the fate of Publius's and, not long after, Crassus's. The Romans were stalked and decimated by the archers and then hit hard with Parthian *cataphract*. None of the abandoned Roman wounded were spared, and the eventual death toll for the legions was 20,000–30,000. Ironically, however, one survivor, the officer Gaius Cassius, would later come to be bitterly regretted—by Julius Caesar.

TWO

TE DEUM AND NON NOBIS

Death on the Medieval Battlefield

It is not we who have made this slaughter but Almighty God.

—Henry V, after the battle of Agincourt, 1415

*V*ISBY. THE ISLAND of Gotland, Sweden. 1361. The peasant army (*army* is perhaps too grand a word for this motley crew) stood outside the walls of the town. Inside, the worthy burghers, merchants, and assorted tradesfolk were disinclined to take up arms and later, when the bloody work was finished, would pay off the army that threatened them. In the meantime they bolted the gates and left the ragtag defenders to do battle with the invading Danes. The combat was swift, predictable, and merciless. After the slaughter, the peasant-soldiers—about eleven hundred of them—were stripped of their pitiably inadequate weaponry (mainly glaives and bills, the spearlike adaptations of farming implements) and armor (a few had some chain mail) and tossed unceremoniously into grave pits.

The naked bodies fell like puppets with their strings cut, limbs akimbo, jumbled and tumbled together in a gruesome confraternity, appalling in its mimicry of intimacy. They would lie together, lost, unnamed, and unremembered, until the pits were uncovered in 1905 and each skeleton was examined to determine the likely cause of its death. Those without marks on their bones—the majority—were killed by lethal flesh wounds, mainly spear and sword thrusts to the abdomen. Four hundred fifty-six wounds spoke of being struck by cutting weapons such as swords and axes. Piercing weapons such as arrows, spears, and the mace-like "morning star," a ball studded with metal spikes and attached to a handle, accounted for 126 wounds. One skull shows evidence of multiple hits. In its base it has three bodkin-tipped arrowheads lodged in a neat cluster. Was the man trying to flee? Or had he turned his back in an instinctive response to a hail of arrows? In addition, though, as a testament to the ferocity of a medieval battlefield, he was also struck twice toward the back of his head with devastating blows from a war hammer that left its telltale square imprint in his shattered skull. The destructive power of medieval weaponry is seen everywhere at Visby, but particularly in the cuts to the legs, where in more than one case a single sword or ax blow had severed both legs in one tremendous scything swipe.

The fate of the anonymous dead of Visby was the lot of most of the slain common soldiers of the time. In many battles the foot soldiers, the archers, the crossbowmen who, through some unlucky turn of battle's fortune, were left exposed and unprotected, were invariably slaughtered. They had little value, could not be ransomed, and were more profitable dead and stripped of their gear, however meager. In a sense, though, they were condemned to death for the same tactical reasons their social betters, the knights, also perished. If they became isolated, unsupported, separated, they would be shot to death by bowmen, ridden down by cavalrymen, or hacked and stabbed by the exultant infantry.

The battle of Falkirk in Scotland (1298) is a good example. The English knights drove off the Scottish cavalry and archers who provided some protection for the pikemen of the infantry massed in dense, circular formations—the *schiltrons*—that were a characteristic of Scottish battle formations of the period. Faced with the bristling hedge of pikes, the English cavalry milled about, unable to break in, but nor could the Scots advance or retreat for fear of being broken. So they stood and died under the devastating hail of Edward I's longbowmen (a significant proportion of whom were Welsh). Their defensive cohesion shot to pieces, the survivors were hacked down by the English horse followed by the infantry. Of the original ten thousand Scots pikemen, more than half were dispatched.[1]

On occasion the infantry were tricked into breaking their defensive unity and suffered the consequences. At Hastings in 1066, the Norman cavalry, riding up and down the Saxon line, had fruitlessly tried to break down the *shieldburgh*—the formidable shield wall behind which the Saxon *frydmen*, the foot militia, stood fast. It was only by feigning retreat that the Normans induced a large block of the Saxons to break ranks and chase downhill, abandoning their strong defensive position on a ridge, in what seemed like victorious pursuit, only to have the pursuer turn around and cut down to a man the exposed Saxon foot soldiers. By nightfall the flower of the English army lay dead around the fallen dragon standards and its slain king.

If the fate of the medieval infantry soldier was in many instances brutal and bloody, what of the warrior from the opposite end of the social and economic scale? How did the knight fight and die?

One of the most significant differences—in both combat and death—between the noble warrior and the common soldier was identity. The medieval knight's surname was a specific identifier, whereas the common soldier had a generic surname very often drawn from his trade—Tanner, Cooper, Fletcher, et cetera. Similarly, the medieval samurai had surnames, whereas the common soldier, the *ashigaru* (literally, "light feet," meaning unarmored), had none. In the time before 1587, when it was possible for an *ashigaru* to fight his way into samurai status, his first acquisition was a surname.[2]

By the mid-twelfth century, the heraldic symbols painted onto the knight's shield proclaimed him uniquely, unlike the signifiers of generic tribal membership with which common soldiers' shields were decorated. The knight's symbol also told the story of his ancestral history and proclaimed his position in the world. Of course, the heraldic advertising had one decided disadvantage in that it attracted the attention of the enemy—either those intent on capture and ransom or those somewhat more homicidally inclined who wished to decapitate (often literally) their opponent's command structure and thereby demoralize his army. The *horo*, a ballooning capelike cloak worn by elite samurai, advertised not only his identity but also his role as a key battlefield messenger (roughly equivalent to an aide-de-camp). As a particularly conspicuous target (similar to the standard-bearer in the Western tradition) it also increased his risk and would serve as the receptacle of his severed head should he be killed in battle. It not only invited attack but, ironically, served to guarantee that its wearer's body would be treated with respect.

In an echo of the Homeric proclamation, knights would on occasion ride out to pronounce their lineage and seek an opponent of similar caste. Like their European counterparts, the samurai were fixated by lineage and determined to establish their status before battle. In the first clash between the Taira and Minamoto clans on July 29, 1156, two samurai approached an opponent and declared: "We are Ōba Kageyoshi and Saburō Kagechika, descendants of Kamakura Gongorō Kagemasa, who when he was sixteen years old . . . went out in the van of battle and was hit in the left eye by an arrow. . . . The arrow tore his eye out and left it hanging on the plate of his helmet, but he sent an arrow in reply and killed his enemy." Quite a declaration before even one blow has been exchanged.[3]

One of the paradoxes of both knight and samurai is that the passion to establish identity through heraldry and proclamation is countered by the anonymity of armor. For example, the close resemblance between the Viking helmet and face mask of the Sutton Hoo burial trove and a samurai mask, complete with its false mustaches, is striking. Other examples of "hiding" identity behind decoration are seen, for example, in the painted faces of North American Indian warriors and the "Huron" haircuts and painted faces of American airborne warriors going into Normandy on D-Day. All chose an adopted identity, terrifying to the beholder and reassuring to the wearer. It is as though the battleground is a theater, and to step into a role, to become a character, makes the warrior's task easier.

The knight was a warrior designed to fight warriors of a similar caste. The mode of fighting—the technology (the most advanced of his day) and the method (drummed in by training since a tender age)—was intended to be not only practically effective but symbolically charged. The way he fought was meant both to overcome his enemy and to proclaim his status. The high stylization of combat (the way the knight was trained in specific techniques; the weaponry and armor that distinguished him; the protocols of combat he was honor-bound to observe; and, almost above all, the identity proclaimed by his heraldic logo) was a reflection and a projection of his social and economic standing. And it was war that sustained him and gave him identity. The noble troubadour Bertran de Born (who ends up in Dante's hell, carrying his severed head before him) revels in it: "I tell you I have no such joy in eating, drinking or sleeping as when I hear the cry from both sides, 'up and at 'em!' or when I hear the riderless horses whinny under the trees, and groans of 'Help me! Help me!' and when I see both great and small fall in the ditches and on the grass, and see the dead transfixed by spear shafts! Barons, mortgage your castles, domains, cities, but never give up war."[4]

Dueling—the mano a mano contest of equally paired opponents—was the gold standard of knightly combat, and considered a direct contact with the perceived nobility of the ancient Greek and Roman tradition. It was the honor paid to an opponent in recognition of a shared culture and social status. Even if the honor ended in death, the combatants were brothers under the skin. The image of the knight riding directly against another knight, the couched lances splintering against or piercing the plate armor of the enemy, is the image most evocatively associated with medieval warfare—but inevitably, it is not the whole story. There was a jarring collision between the rhetoric and the reality. That is not to say that dueling was not a cherished ideal among the knightly class, but only to recognize that sometimes the ideal ended up in the mire of the battlefield.

Our focus on the chivalric as the defining characteristic of medieval warfare reflects a desire, as true now as it was for the balladeers, saga poets, and chroniclers of the Middle Ages, to romanticize the awful truth that the battlefield had more to do with the bloody chaos of a mêlée than with the noble symmetry of the duel. The knight stood as much chance of dying in the bloody scrum of battle (for very often he fought on foot), where he could be stabbed by a peasant-soldier sticking a dagger into an armpit or crotch, or up the unprotected rear end, or ramming it through the slit of a helmet visor, as he did of facing off with his peer. Once unhorsed, by design or accident, he might literally be hammered to death, as was the fate of many French knights at Crécy and Agincourt who fell to the mauls (mallets used to drive in the sharpened stakes that protected the English archers against frontal cavalry assault) of "base villeins."

Agile and skilled infantrymen developed techniques for dealing with mounted knights. Almogavars, for example, were rugged warriors from the mountainous regions of Aragon and Catalonia who wore no armor and fought with javelin and short stabbing sword. They were used extensively as mercenaries in Italy and Greece. One, who was captured by a Crusader army in thirteenth-century Greece, was pitted against a fully armed and armored mounted Angevin knight as an entertainment for his captors,[5] the assumption being that the knight would easily overwhelm so lightly equipped an opponent: "The almogavar awaited the knight's charge, then at the last moment hurled his javelin—the azcona—into his opponent's horse, dodged the latter's lance then jumped on the unfortunate knight as he fell from his wounded horse and held a knife to his throat. At this point the duel was stopped."[6] Armed with a *colltell*, a cross between a knife and a butcher's cleaver, an Almogavar foot soldier could do very serious damage to a knight, armored as he might be. A contemporary source records that at the battle of Kephissos in 1311 the Spanish light infantrymen ran in among the heavily armored Frankish knights of the Duke of Athens and massacred them. One "gave such a cut that the greave with the leg came off in one piece and besides it entered half a palm into the horse's flank."[7]

Our fascination with the mounted knight has somewhat distorted his importance in medieval battle. Not only did infantry play an important part, but an argument can be made that they were, in fact, the predominant element. During the main span of the medieval period (from around AD 500 to about 1400, when guns first made themselves felt on the battlefield), infantry outnumbered cavalry "by at least five to one."[8] Infantry was a cost-effective option compared with cavalry, and tactics, essentially through the mixed use of pikemen and missile firers (at first crossbowmen and archers, who were eventually superseded by arquebusiers and musketeers), developed to maximize the use of foot soldiers. For example, at the battle of Courtrai (in modern Belgium) in 1302, Flemish pikemen warded off French knights by firmly planting the butts of their pikes in the ground in order to present a porcupine hedge of points. They were supported by crossbowmen, and any knights who might have penetrated the hedge were dealt with unceremoniously by soldiers armed with *goedendags*—the Flemish version of the "morningstar"—the crude but effective spiked mace. And at Courtrai the Flemish knights, led by Guy de Namur and Wilhelm van Jülich and their entourages, fought on foot in support of the lowly infantry and crossbowmen. In fact, fighting on foot was almost the preferred style for knights in many battles of the era. The result was a devastating defeat for the French knights who were dragged down from their mounts when the horses were hit by crossbow quarrels or disemboweled on the Flemings' pikes, to be unceremoniously put to death.[9]

If the knights and men-at-arms killed lowly enemies with impunity, it is not surprising that, given half a chance, the base villeins would take their revenge. In 1332 at Dupplin Moor in Scotland an English army, under the capable military leadership of Sir Henry Beaumont, employed tactics that would later be put to effective use in France during some of the great battles of the Hundred Years' War. The English absorbed the spirited mounted frontal attack of the Scots chivalry led by Donald, Earl of Mar, and Lord Robert Bruce (the illegitimate son of the late king, the great Robert Bruce). While battling with the English foot, the Scottish knights were compressed into a suffocatingly (often literally) small killing ground by the combined pressure of their own disorganized infantry barging into their rear and the enveloping folds of the English archery wings determinedly pressing in on their flanks. According to the *Lanercost Chronicle*, "Each crushed his neighbour, and for every one fallen there fell a second, and then a third," until the pile of bodies reached the height of a spear.[10] The English infantry and archers surrounded the heap of wounded, dying, and dead Scots, many of them suffocated, to kill the survivors. Mar and Bruce died this way, along with perhaps as many as 58 other knights, 1,200 men-at-arms, and hundreds, perhaps thousands, of foot soldiers. The English lost only 2 knights and 33 soldiers.[11]

At Crécy in 1346, the historian Jean Froissart records a similar tale of mounted knights and men-at-arms hurling themselves in disorderly passion against the English archers who, having created havoc in the small killing zone of the French knightly vanguard, enabled the lowly English foot soldiers to move in for the kill. "In the English army there were some Cornish and Welsh men on foot, who had armed themselves with large knives, these advancing through the ranks of the [English] men-at-arms and archers, who made way for them, came upon the French when they were in this danger, and falling upon earls, barons, knights, and squires, slew many, at which the king of England was exasperated."[12] Edward III's exasperation was probably due to the abrogation of the chivalric code. Knights were meant to kill knights; underlings were not. It was not only a breach of battlefield decorum but also a threatening rupture of the social order.

Tactically, the story that unfolded at Agincourt in 1415 would be much the same. A French knight, Jehan de Wavrin, described the bloody debacle:

Their horses stumbled among the stakes [of the English longbowmen], and they were speedily slain by the archers, which was a great pity. And most of the rest, through fear, gave way and fell back into their vanguard, to whom they were a great hindrance; and they opened their ranks in several places, and made them fall back and lose their footing in some land newly sown, for their horses had been so wounded by the arrows that the men could no longer manage them. Thus . . . the vanguard of the French was thrown into disorder, and men-at-arms without number began to fall. . . . Soon afterwards the English archers, seeing the vanguard thus shaken, issued from behind their stockade, threw away their bows and quivers, then took their swords, hatchets, mallets, axes, falcon-beaks [macelike weapons] and other weapons, and, pushing into the places where they saw these breaches, struck down and killed these Frenchmen without mercy, and never ceased to kill till the said vanguard which had fought little or not at all was completely overwhelmed.[13]

Many suffocated or were crushed to death, including the rotund Duke of York, whose body, along with that of the Earl of Oxford, Wavrin records, was "boiled, in order to separate the bones and carry them to England" and a decent Christian funeral. Many of the French knights and men-at-arms who escaped the crushing mêlée only to be captured were ordered put to death by Henry V, fearful of a reported French cavalry column that could have linked up with the prisoners. At first the English captors refused Henry's order, no doubt as much deeply angered at the loss of potential ransom as they were offended by a similar breach of the chivalric code that had appalled Edward III at Crécy. But Henry overrode their objections and sent in two hundred of his archers, who "fell on the French, paunching them [as in gutting game] and stabbing them in the face." The cavalry column never materialized, and as a chaplain reported, "We returned victorious through the heaps and piles of the slain." Henry ordered the great hymns of thanksgiving, the Te Deum and Non Nobis, to be sung: "O Lord, let thy mercy lighten upon us, as our trust is in thee."

★   ★   ★

THE WEAPONS OF medieval warfare reflect the great social schism between noble and nonnoble warriors. Unlike the codes of their counterparts in the Islamic world or in the samurai class of medieval Japan, Western chivalry abhorred any kind of missile weaponry for knightly use. Of course, in a broader tactical sense archers and crossbowmen (and, later hand gunners) were an essential element of the battle array, no matter how despised by the noble commanders as an insult to the ideal of close combat. There may also have been another explanation: that combat with edged weapons and lances offered some control to the victorious knight over the outcome of the contest: "It allowed the warrior the opportunity to display magnanimity and it allowed him to supplement his income handsomely by holding his erstwhile opponents captive until they could be suitably ransomed."[14] Missile weapons, once launched, were blind to social class, and they could kill some valuable asset better kept alive. This may help explain the recurring theme of aristocratic outrage at crossbowmen and arquebusiers, who, if captured, were either killed on the spot or had a hand severed so that they would never ply their trade again. The death these underlings meted out was all too democratic. It was not good death. The medieval church would regularly pass down injunctions against missile weapons because they were "unfair" to the nobility.

Magnanimity toward a defeated foe of the same class was an expression of solidarity that went beyond temporary enmity. This was a world that was not yet locked into national identity (that would come with the centralization of power in the monarchy and then the state), and the brotherhood of chivalry transcended geographic boundaries. Profit was intimately bound up with chivalry. The knightly class had risen, through war, to social, economic, and political power. And it was an expensive operation to maintain. Plunder was a major incentive for all classes of warrior, with quite precise calculations on how much each participant would receive; only the style of plunder distinguished social classes, and then quite often not by much. For example, the Hundred Years' War in France was an important profit center for nobleman and ordinary soldier alike. English knights objected "vociferously to any temporary outbreak of peace [and] the English troops' lust for loot was such that special regulations had been introduced to stop men brawling over their prisoners. Not surprisingly, the king kept the most important captured castles, land and enemy personnel. Contracts and sub-contracts determined most of the rest. Usually the senior party took one-third, an ordinary soldier paying a third of his own 'winnings' to his officer, and so on up the chain of command."[15]

Although the lowly foot soldier had little say in his fate, the knight to some extent chose his destiny, one that might well embrace death in battle. The code of honor that enveloped him and signified his superiority also, ironically, could propel him to his doom. The knight's history is filled, as is his samurai counterpart's, with acts of extraordinary bravery and of suicidal hubris. At Dupplin Moor the Earl of Mar, outraged by accusations of his treachery, claimed the right to redeem his reputation by being the first to charge into the English host, only to be upstaged by his companion in arms and honor, Lord Robert Bruce. Both were killed.

At Bannockburn (1314), a great Scots victory over the old enemy, the English Earl of Gloucester, a young man of twenty-two, stung by accusations that he had shown cowardice and incompetence, rode almost unarmored into a Scots *schiltron* to be speared to death. At Crécy, Charles, the blind king of Bohemia and an ally of the French, hearing that the battle was all but lost and that his son, in a funk, had quit the field, ordered his horse's bridle to be linked with those of two attendants and to be led into the killing ground. The chronicler Froissart says that "they rode in among the enemy, and he and his companions were all slain, and on the morrow they were found on the ground with all their horses tied together."

In all cultures where social and economic leadership is intimately tied to personal prowess on the battlefield, such sacrifices are mandated. During the Gempei War (1180–85) between the two great samurai clans the Taira and Minamoto, one of the Minamoto nobles, Yorimasa, with his two sons and a small group of warriors, elected to hold out against a powerful Taira force in order to gain time for the main Minamoto army to make its escape. Both the sons were killed defending their aged father, who, however, managed to commit hara-kiri in such impressive style that it became the enduring model of the way a defeated samurai should quit the world. First he wrote his death poem and then opened his stomach with one great horizontal dagger cut to release his samurai spirit, while a retainer decapitated him and threw his weighted head into the river so as to keep it from enemy trophy hunters.[16]

Honor might also demand that a noble warrior sacrifice himself if his leader was slain. In 1183 the Minamoto leader, Yoshinaka, was attempting to escape from battle when he was hit in the face by a Taira arrow and then decapitated. His retainer, Imai Kanehira, saw this and cried out: "Alas, for whom now have I to fight? See, you men of the East Country. I will show you how the mightiest champion in Japan can end his life!" Putting the point of his sword in his mouth, he flung himself headlong from his horse to be impaled. The codes of honor that governed both samurai and knight are similarly death-centered. Life is impermanent, its outcome determined by God or fate. To die in combat was to reaffirm that connection and to underwrite the currency of their class.

Weaponry was also a social signifier, loaded with meaning beyond its purely military function and imbued with magical, fetishistic attributes. The Vikings "ennobled" their weapons with poetical epithets: Spears were referred to as "flying dragons of the wounds," axes as "witches of the helmet," arrows as "ice of the bow."[17] Swords were particularly magical, and in the Viking sagas their names alone could spell death. Thorstein Vikingsson's sword was the legendary Angrvadil, which his father had taken from the slain Björn Blue-tooth. Its reputation went before it: "When Vikingsson drew it, it was as if lightning flashed from it. Harek, seeing this said 'I should never have fought against thee, I had known thou hadst Angrvadil . . . it was the greatest misfortune when Angrvadil went out of our family'; and at that moment Vikingsson struck down on the head of Harek, and cleft him in two from head to feet, so that the sword entered the ground up to the hilt."[18] The church established a liturgy around AD 950 to bless swords and, at a slightly later date, created a ceremony to bless those who would use them: "Almighty father, who has permitted the use of the sword to repress the malice of the wicked and defend justice . . . cause Thy servant here before Thee never to use this sword . . . to injure anyone unjustly, but always to defend the just and the right."[19]

Weapons and armor of the nobler class were often decorated in ways that we might think irrational and not germane to their purpose. They could be astonishingly beautiful, and we may find it bizarre or disturbing that things of such decorative intricacy were dedicated to killing and maiming. Other weapons, however, those of the rank-and-file infantry, were emphatically not beautiful at all. The bills, axes, and maces had a lethal functionality not too far removed from the implements of farm and abattoir from which they originated. The pole weapons burgeoned into a whole family of specialized implements with exotic-sounding names—*guisarme, voulge,* halberd, *fauchard,* glaive, *partizan* (known in Bohemia as the "ear-spoon"), *ravensbill, Rossschinder* ("horse killer"). There were hundreds of variations for each type, reflecting local taste, but the essence was an ax head mounted on a staff (the "pole"), often with numerous hooks and spikes for pulling mounted enemies from their horses (the Mongols of the fourteenth century were particularly adept at unhorsing Christian knights with hooked spears).[20] The point provided a thrusting element; the ax head, a formidable slashing and cleaving element. They were the Swiss Army knife of the medieval infantryman and in the hands of trained soldiers could inflict terrible wounds.

At Morgarten in 1315, one of the bloodiest battles of the medieval period, the Swiss infantry, "slashing and striking with their terrible halberds, shearing through helms," killed half of the knights of Duke Leopold of Austria's invading force. Excavated skeletons of knights killed by a halberd show that their skulls were cleft down to the teeth.[21] The *Ahlspiess,* a pike with a long square-sectioned blade, was specifically designed to penetrate the joints of a knight's armor. The point of the halberd could do quite terrible damage to a knight who had been thrown off balance. If he was "struck on the back of his head, or between his shoulders, he would fall forward, exposing the unarmored back of his thighs and backside to the halberdier."[22]

The upthrust from an infantryman armed with pike or bill or halberd was a serious threat to the mounted knight in two other ways: The belly of his horse was susceptible to a ripping thrust, and the knight's throat and under-jaw were targets for a piercing upjab. The horse could not be completely encased in armor and be expected to carry a man who, in armor, might easily weigh in excess of 250 pounds. The beast would always be vulnerable to a gutting thrust up through the unprotected belly. In fact the horse, it could be argued, although the defining piece of knightly gear (the word *chivalry* comes from the French for horse, *cheval*), was one of the most vulnerable parts of the knight's equipage.

During the 1500s the knight developed, in response to the vulnerability to his throat, an haute-piece—an armored collar that extended from his shoulder. His counterpart in Japan, the mounted samurai, faced exactly the same threat and added a throat protector (*nodowa*). Nevertheless, it was not foolproof protection, as the fourteenth-century historical epic the *Taiheiki* illustrates when an infantryman (in this case a *sōhei* or monk-warrior) wielding the halberdlike *naginata* (about 12 feet long) attacks a mounted samurai:

> Just then a monk kicked over the shield in front of him and sprang forward, whirling his naginata like a water wheel. It was Kajitsu of Harima. Kaitō [a mounted samurai] received him with his right arm, meaning to cut down into his helmet bowl, but the glancing sword struck down lightly from Kajitsu's shoulder-plate. . . . Again Kaitō struck forcefully, but his left foot broke through its stirrup, and he was likely to fall from his horse. As he straightened his body, Kajitsu thrust up his naginata, and two or three times drove its point quickly into his helmet. Kaitō fell off his horse, pierced cleanly through the throat. Swiftly Kajitsu put down his foot on Kaitō's armor, seized his side hair, and cut off his head, that he might fix it to his naginata.[23]

Every threat had to be countered with a defense until, by the end of the medieval era, the knight, once lightly armored in mail hauberk, helmet, and shield, was transformed into a machine of beautiful and all-encasing steel; and although a basic suit of field armor might weigh in the region of 50 pounds, superb craftsmanship gave the knight a surprisingly high degree of maneuverability (it is said that he could vault onto his horse, for example).[24]

However, as late as the 1640s, Edmund Ludlow, a royalist cuirassier in the English Civil War, noted that when unhorsed, he "could not without great difficulty recover on horse back again, being loaded with cuirassier arms," and Sir Edmund Verney flatly refused to go into battle heavily armored, "for it will kill a man to serve in a whole cuirass. I am resolved to use nothing but back, breast, and gauntlet; if I had a Pott [helmet] for the Head that were Pistoll-proofe it maye bee I would use it if it were light."[25] And he was to pay dearly for his determination, being cut down at the battle of Edgehill in 1642, disdaining even a leather buff coat for protection. On the other hand, the royalist Earl of Northampton was so completely armored that his enemies had to take off his helmet in order to kill him.[26]

A knight fighting dismounted, which was common, would have tired easily (the buildup of heat within the suit alone must have been a serious problem), and if struggling on muddy or uneven terrain, he would have put himself at great risk. In comparison, his counterpart in feudal Japan took a very different tack. Where Europeans emphasized size and weight, the samurai opted for lightness and mobility. It is as though the European knight himself became a weapon, dedicated to shock impact. The samurai, on the other hand, considered excessive protection counterproductive.[27] He carried no shield because his *katana* (main sword) was invariably used two-handed, which precluded using a shield in the European style. The weapon dictated a straight-on style of fighting: He stood squarely before his opponent in, for him, a heroically direct confrontation. The type of weapon, the way it was to be used, and the chivalric code that dictated that use all came together. The samurai, however, unlike the knight, saw no disgrace in using standoff weaponry such as the bow. A principal weapon, though, was the *naginata*, used both mounted and on foot. Some evidence suggests that when engaged against a similarly armed mounted samurai it was wielded rather like the knight's lance during the tourney, that is, couched under the right arm and angled across the horse's neck, but more often it would be employed as a slashing weapon with the mounted warrior standing in the stirrups.[28]

Although the poleax and the war hammer were often favored by knights, the sword was the trademark weapon of the noble warrior. The swords of the early medieval period were ancestors of the Roman *spatha,* a parallel-edged slashing sword that, with the spread of plate armor in the mid-thirteenth century, developed into a more pointed weapon, adapted as much to thrusting (for penetrating chain mail or piercing the joints of plate armor) as cutting. Even if armor were not pierced (and some modern tests suggest that piercing mail armor with a sword thrust is problematic), a blow from a heavy blade could cause bone fractures and internal injuries.[29] A mounted knight might have a large "war" sword weighing about 5 pounds hung from the front of the saddle, while in his sword belt he would carry a smaller, "arming" sword, weighing about 3 pounds.[30]

The transition to plate armor during the thirteenth century was not only a defensive response to pikes but also an attempt to counter the lethality of the very class of weapon the knight held in contempt: the bow and crossbow. Crossbows are known to have been used by Chinese infantry in the fourth century BCE and were used as hunting weapons by the Romans. Their reemergence in Europe during the tenth century seems to have been linked to an upsurge in siege warfare (the Roman siege ballista were essentially huge crossbows), but the Normans took to the crossbow with enthusiasm as an infantry weapon. The advantages to the user were enormous. A knight in whom years of training and a huge amount of money had been invested could be killed by a dolt with a bolt at about 200 yards or less.

The crossbow is a forerunner of machinelike weapons such as

the rifle in that although it was relatively easy to use it was of fairly complex construction, and like all machines, it had its own specialized vocabulary. The bowlike crosspiece ("span" or "lathe"), made of a hardwood such as yew, oak, or maple (though in the Islamic world it might have been made of an amalgam of horn, sinew, and wood), was lashed with whipcord to a stock ("tiller"). The bowstring ("bridle") was made of whipcord or sinew. To "span" the bow (prepare it for firing), the operator put his foot into the stirrup at the bow end of the tiller and drew back the bridle with muscle power—a hook attached to the crossbowman's belt and snagged under the bridle pulled it back when the crossbowman straightened up. It might also be pulled back with the aid of a mechanical crank. Once pulled back, the bridle was secured by a catch made of horn. Dartlike bolts ("quarrels"), made most commonly of yew, ash, witch hazel, or poplar and tipped with wicked little heads of a variety of designs depending on the grief they were meant to inflict, were placed in a groove running down the top face of the tiller, engaging with the bridle by a notch ("knock") at the rear of the bolt. A triggerlike mechanism released the catch, and off flew the bolt—not fired, but "cast," as though its victim was an unsuspecting fish.

The power of the crossbow, in one way, was considerably more than the longbow's. It could "draw" about 750 pounds, compared with the longbow's 70–150 pounds, but its released energy was comparatively inefficient because the span was short and its tips, whose whiplash movement turned stored energy into bolt speed and range, moved through a much shorter trajectory than the long and powerful expanse of the longbow's. Also, the longbow's arrow was heavier than a quarrel, which gave it greater penetrative power over a greater distance. To match the longbow's lethality, the crossbow would have had to be considerably larger, which would have made it impossibly unwieldy. Even in its comparatively light form it already suffered from a lengthy loading procedure that left the crossbowman vulnerable.

These characteristics molded the tactical use of both types of bow. The crossbow tended to be deployed in relatively close action where the flat trajectory would have a potentially devastating effect (the problem was, of course, that the closer the crossbowman was to the action, the greater his chances of being ridden down or shot down during the relatively lengthy periods of reloading). The longbow, on the other hand, tended to be used at longer distance in arcing trajectories where its high speed of reloading (about twelve shafts per minute, compared with perhaps three per minute for the crossbow—about the same rate as a black-powder musket) could inflict a storm of harm on the enemy.

The famous confrontation between the Genoese mercenary crossbowmen fighting for France and the English and Welsh longbowmen at the battle of Crécy in 1346 is a good illustration. The Genoese were the first to advance within range but without the large shields (*pavise*) behind which they could shelter while reloading. In addition the French approach had been chaotic, and the chronicler Jean Froissart writes that "there fell a great rain," which almost certainly slackened the crossbow bridles. In contrast, the longbowmen unstrung their bows during the drenching downpour and coiled the linen strings under their helmets for protection. The Genoese got off the first volley and would almost certainly have had to retighten the strings of their crossbows, which increased their risk of being counterattacked. At this point the three thousand or so longbowmen

knocked [fitted the arrows to the string] and drew, closing their backs, opening their chests, pushing into their bows, anchoring for a second, holding their drawn arrows firm, thumbs of their drawing hands touching right ears or the points of jaws as they aimed for a heartbeat when the drawn shafts slid past their bow hands until the cold steel of the arrowheads touched the first knuckles; letting fly, right hands following the strings almost as swiftly as the shafts' flight past the brown bows, grabbing the next arrow from ground, or belt, or quiver, to knock and draw and anchor and loose, in deadly unrelenting repetition.[31]

The hail of arrows—"so thick that it seemed like snow"—took a terrible toll, and the Genoese broke, many only to fall beneath the hooves of the advancing French knights who contemptuously rode down their own crossbowmen in a mad rush to get at the English.

The essential difference between the crossbow and the longbow had as much to do with relative cost as with relative lethality. A longbow, although mechanically simpler than the crossbow, was not necessarily cheaper. It was made from specialized wood, the supply of which presupposed land use dedicated to growing trees rather than more immediately profitable crops. The crossbow, even if made of wood, did not demand the exacting material of the longbow; in fact it could be, and was, made of a composite of materials. But perhaps more important, the crossbow also had a striking economic advantage that would be a preview of the age of the handgun: It did not take the great deal of training, practice, and physical strength to turn out a competent crossbowman that it took to turn out an archer. The long training of an archer was by far the most significant "below-the-line" cost of the bow. It would be the crossbow, unlovely and unloved, rather than the longbow, romantic and revered, that pointed the way to the future and the victory of technology over muscle.

★   ★   ★

THE CRUSADES WERE a clash not only of religious ideologies (a writhing bag of snakes would have been easier to deal with) but also of tactical ideologies. Christian and Muslim warriors had been shaped by different traditions. The mounted knight sought to bring the matter to the point of decision by a trial of personal arms at close quarters, and his supporting troops—infantry and crossbowmen—were just that: a support that set up the possibility of the decisive charge. Islamic warriors, whose tactical antecedents were from Asiatic raiders, were rarely committed to an all-out charge unless, due to prior softening up by missile weapons, the enemy appeared to be terminally vulnerable. The horse bowmen, like those Parthians who had destroyed the Roman legions at Carrhae in 53 BCE, were still one of the most important elements of Saracen combat. The horse was, of course, one important element that Christian and Muslim shared, but it was used in strikingly different ways. To put it schematically, the Muslim warrior used his horse as a weapons platform, whereas the knight used it as a weapon; the one stood off and fired his arrows, the other sought to make physical contact. An effective cavalry charge relied on a collective and concentrated weight to destroy the enemy. It demanded cohesion and discipline. The problem, however, was that as it got under way, the vagaries of terrain and the individual horse and rider caused it to destabilize and disintegrate, and many knights were killed in the ensuing counterattack, unable to get back to the shelter of the infantry (a similar problem faced by tanks many centuries later).

In the early phases of the Crusades, the Christians' reliance on heavy cavalry cost them dearly. Using tactics not unlike those of the nineteenth-century Plains Indians, Saracen horse bowmen swept around the invading armies, shooting down men and mounts, only to melt away when the Christian cavalry sallied out to engage. If, however, the Saracens, in their initial missile phase, managed to uncover a weak spot, in went the heavier lance-armed cavalry, to be followed by infantry support.

The *Itinerarium*, a chronicle of Richard Lionheart's Third Crusade, describes the frustration of the Crusaders before the battle of Arsuf in 1191 as the Muslim horsemen, "keeping alongside our army as it advanced, struggled to inflict what it could upon us, firing darts and arrows which flew very thickly, like rain. Alas! Many horses fell dead transfixed with missiles, many were gravely wounded and died much later! You would have seen such a great downpour of darts and arrows that where the army passed through you could not have found a space of four foot of ground without shafts stuck in it."[32] However, it says something about the relative lethality of the Asiatic bow compared with the longbow that many a Christian foot soldier managed to weather the storm. The Islamic chronicler Bahā-al-Din, Saladin's secretary, describes the Christian foot, protected by their thick quilted jackets (*gambesons*) and mail shirts (*hauberks*): "I noted among them men who had from one to ten shafts sticking in their backs, yet trudged on at their ordinary pace and did not fall out of their ranks. . . . The Muslims sent in volleys of arrows from all sides, endeavoring to irritate the knights and to worry them into leaving their ramparts of infantry. But it was all in vain."[33]

On the other side, Crusader crossbowmen were effective and feared. Protected by pikemen from the predations of Muslim light cavalry, they inflicted significant casualties. Although it was contrary to Muslim law, captured crossbowmen stood a good chance of being massacred.[34] (Ironically, Richard himself would die from gangrene caused by a crossbow bolt wound in the shoulder at the siege of Châlus, a relatively insignificant little castle near Limoges, France, in 1199—and thus, "the Lion by the Ant was slain.")

If the Muslims favored fluidity and opportunistic attack, the Europeans valued cohesion, organization, and discipline (not always so easily achieved when restraint was challenged by the hair trigger of chivalric hubris). The Christians had to prevent their opponents from breaking down their *solidus inter se conglobati*—meaning, in tactical terms, sticking together (literally, "coagulating"). Maintaining cohesion on the march was paramount, for when they allowed themselves to be "cut out" into smaller units—as they were, for example, at the battle of Hattin in 1187—the Christians were usually, and emphatically, done to death.[35] To prevent this unhappy outcome, Crusader columns had to fashion themselves into forts-on-the-hoof; the cavalry sheltered within the protective walls of pikemen and crossbowmen, who worked in tandem to keep the Muslim horse at bay. Richard Lionheart, on the Third Crusade (1189–92), had his front rank of pikemen, each protected by his shield and shoulder-to-shoulder with his comrades, kneel, presenting his grounded pike toward the Saracen cavalry. Behind them were pairs of crossbowmen, one loading and the other firing.

Richard was also masterful at shepherding his flock as it slowly progressed along the coast of Palestine, the knights on the seaward side, protected by infantry and archers on the exposed landward flank. At Arsuf the Christian chivalry had a rare chance to break out and run down their attackers. Ironically, Richard I's victory was to some extent due to a breakdown in the very discipline he had tried so hard to maintain. He was forced to support an unauthorized attack by the Knights Hospitallers and in the series of ensuing charges scattered and eventually destroyed Saladin's army. For the Muslims, their deaths were also a result of either failing or being prevented from exercising their crucial tactical advantage: mobility. And once caught, they were enthusiastically dispatched. Contemporaries record that the field was bloodily strewn with seven thousand bodies.

★　★　★

GUNPOWDER WAS FIRST used in China, where the earliest written formula for it dates from 1044. It was then adopted by the Muslim world, where it was known, poetically, as "Chinese snow."[36] The English-speaking world had an altogether more blunt-nosed word for it. *Gun* is first used in an English text in 1339, and a new era of battlefield lethality was born.[37]

THREE

A Terrible Thunder

Battlefield Lethality in the Black-Powder Era

Firearms are the most destructive category of weapons, and now more than ever. If you need convincing, just go to the hospital and you will see how few men have been wounded by cold steel as opposed to firearms. My argument is not advanced lightly. It is founded on knowledge.

—Maréchal de Puységur, *Art de guerre par principes et par règles, 1749*

IT IS IRONIC that the warfare of rationality—that is, a way of destroying warriors not with the crude slash and shove of muscle and steel but with the application of science and invention, of formulae and calculation—should have one foot in a pile of ordure. Warfare in the "Modern Age" is based on piss and shit.

One of the primary ingredients of gunpowder—saltpeter (potassium nitrate)—is a by-product of the bacterial decay of organic matter, particularly dung and urine. In the fourteenth century, gunpowder manufacturers in Europe were attempting to set themselves up as a self-sustaining industry independent of importation, not unlike our nervous dependence on foreign oil.[1] Saltpeter "farms" were established in Europe, and by the 1420s it was half the price it had been only fifty years earlier. England was an important center because the English were renowned as redoubtable boozers (a reputation they seem to have enthusiastically sustained over the centuries) and therefore famously productive in the elimination of highly ammoniac urine. Bert S. Hall puts it in scientific language: "Urine from wine and beers is based on the fact that ammonia levels in the urine increase dramatically as the body metabolizes alcohol. . . . A heavy drinker's urine contributes more vitally needed NH4 to the heap than does an abstemious person."[2] Saltpeter forms naturally in warm climates with a regular dry season that dries out the urine-soaked earth, leaving nitrous salts. Until sources were found in Chile, most saltpeter came from India, collected from "the bottoms of the tanks or shallow ponds of water, which, in this country, are often of great extent, where the water being evaporated by the heat of the sun, large quantities of filth are left to corrupt, which furnishes a mud of strongest nitrous quality."

In 1561 Gerard Honrick, a German who had established a saltpeter business in England, recommended "black earth" (composted human fecal matter and dung from horses fed on oats), urine ("namely of those persons whiche drink either wyne or strong bears [sic]"), and two kinds of lime. The mixture was to be kept in a dry environment and turned, like a compost heap, at least once a year. It took about a year for the bacteriological process to make the snowlike deposit that was saltpeter.[3]

Robert Norton writes in 1628 that gunpowder "is compounded of three Principles, or Elements, Saltpetre, Sulpher and Cole, whereof Saltpetre is it that gives the chiefest violence."[4] The approximate relative quantities of these ingredients are 75 percent saltpeter, 10 percent sulphur, and 15 percent carbon (usually charcoal powder), a mixture that will burn at 2,100–2,700°C. The expanding gases (274–360 cubic centimeters per gram of gunpowder), if confined in a tube, will explode a closed tube to create a bomb or, if the tube is open at one end, propel a ball, or, in the very earliest manifestations of the gun, a dart.[5] The problem for the makers and users of early firearms (Edward III had three small cannons at the battle of Crécy in 1346) was that large-grained gunpowder burned at a slower rate than a finer-milled grain and produced less force (it seems counterintuitive, but in fact small grains have a larger surface area, in proportion to their mass, than large ones and therefore burn faster). But if gunners used too fine a grain, the expanding gases could well burst their weapons faster than the projectile could respond by exiting the gun and thus relieving the pressure. This was not too much of a problem in hand arms that used relatively small amounts of powder but was certainly a risk for artillery pieces. James II of Scotland, for example, was killed by an exploding cannon during his siege of Roxburgh Castle in 1460. A piece of the weapon smashed his thigh and he "died hastily."

Apart from being prone to damp, the constituent elements of gunpowder tend to separate out after mixing. Early gunpowder manufacturers overcame this by "corning" (from the Old English for "seed"—*corn*—as in *peppercorn*), wetting the powder (vinegar, wine, and urine were often used) to make a paste, from which pellets were formed and dried. The aggregate had less surface area and therefore did not absorb as much atmospheric moisture. It was easier to store, lasted longer, and became ballistically more potent. Before use, the pellets could be crushed into particles. If they were ground too finely, there would not be enough space between the grains to provide sufficient oxygen for maximal burn; too coarse, and the powder burned too slowly.

By the late fifteenth century there had been a coming together of powder and ordnance technologies. From about the 1430s, gun barrels grew longer (to maximize the effect of the gas expansion behind the ball); improvements in cast-iron technology meant that run-of-the-mill guns could be made more cheaply and that brass was now reserved for premium ordnance. Barrels became more resilient, which, in turn, meant that guns could take a more potent charge, and iron cannonballs replaced stone. Later, the corning of powder would become more refined. Peter White-horne, in 1562, describes the sieving process, an essential part of corning: "The manner of cornyng all sorts of powder is with a Seeve made, with a thicke skinne of Parchement, full of little rounde holes, into whiche seve the powder must be put, while it is danke [moist], and also a little bowle, that when you sifte, maie rolle up and doune, upon the clottes of powder, to breake them, that it may corne, and runne through the holes of the Seeve."[6] And this, in principle but scaled up to an industrial level, is how gunpowder has been corned ever since.

With a now relatively inexpensive source of gunpowder, the fifteenth century saw a proliferation of gun types—culverins and *veuglaires, serpentines, crapaudeaux, basilisks, fauçons, passé-volantes, courtaux,* bombards, and, on a smaller scale, handguns such as *hacquebuses* and arquebuses. At first the small arms were less lethal than the bow and crossbow, but they were noisy—and noise has always been a potent factor on the battlefield, both rais-ing or reducing morale depending on whose side was creating the din. Guns were also a product of the fledgling Industrial Revolu-tion and would become a relatively inexpensive way to kill war-riors by warriors who were, in their turn, relatively inexpensive to train. By the 1520s a handgun cost about 40 percent less than a crossbow.

History, in that inconvenient way it has, does not develop in reassuringly straight lines. There are serpentine loops and oxbow bends that can leave pools of the past, forlornly trapped, as the river meanders on. It takes a while for things to show themselves.

The knight was not one day in full and glorious gallop and the next shot out of his saddle by newfangled weaponry. With the advent of firearms the mounted warrior responded in two ways. He could embrace the new technology, or he could stubbornly stick with the old notion of cold steel.

In any event, he had to find a way to counteract the mutually supporting threats of massed pikes interspersed with shooters—arquebusiers—armed with matchlocks, which, although cumbersome and unreliable (a fairly undependable smoldering piece of cord had to be touched to the powder pan, itself susceptible to damp, to fire a gun so heavy that it had to be supported on a rest), represented a tactical bridge between the ancient and medieval world of muscle weaponry and the "modern" world of technological killing. As firearms became lighter and more plentiful, they in their turn would destroy the massed pikes at such sixteenth-century battles as Marignano, La Bicocca, and Pavia.[7]

In Japan there was a parallel to the European experience. The gun had been introduced there by the Chinese and Portuguese during the late fifteenth and early sixteenth centuries. It made its debut at the battle of Uedahara in 1548, but the first significant victory that can be attributed to the arquebus was the siege of Kajiki the following year. And at the battle of Nagashino in 1575 the great general Oda Nobunaga deployed three thousand lowly *ashigaru* firing their matchlocks in rotating volleys to destroy the mounted samurai of Takeda Katsuyori. As the bullets took their toll, *ashigaru* pikemen moved in to thrust up at those samurai who remained mounted. Takeda left ten thousand dead on the field, a staggering 67 percent fatality rate. Fifty-four of ninety-seven named Takeda-clan samurai were killed.[8]

In Italy, at the river Sesia in 1524, the old French chivalry, finely armored and gloriously confident, were shot out of their saddles. One of them was Pierre Terrail, Seigneur de Bayard, the legendary *chevalier sans peur et sans reproche*. Born in 1473, he was a holdover from another era and was killed by an arquebusier—*sans peur et sans cérémonie.* The valiant Bayard, wedded to a compelling mythology of aristocracy and obligation, had done what was expected; almost every head of his family, going back centuries, had been killed in combat. It was an obligation to death in battle and a defining characteristic of the knightly class.

At Pavia in 1525 the French knights, led by their king, Francis I, were killed in great numbers by Spanish musketeers. The heavy shot "penetrated not only one man-at-arms, but often two, and two horses as well. Thus the field was covered with the pitiful carnage of dying noble knights as well as with heaps of dying horses." They lay, according to a contemporary commentator, "like dung upon the face of the earth, and like the corn after the reaper, which none gathereth."[9] Francis survived but was captured and ransomed.

In Europe the old chivalric order at first tried to adapt to firearm technology by arming itself with the matchlock and then the slightly more advanced wheel-lock pistols, but wellborn warriors could never quite escape the idea that guns were unheroic and therefore unfit for noble combat. François de La Noue, a Huguenot cavalier of the sixteenth century, writes disparagingly in his *Discours politiques et militaires* that pistols were "devilish, invented in some mischevious workshop to turne whole realmes . . . into desolation and replenish the graves with dead carcases. Howbeit man's malice hath made them so necessarie that they cannot be spared."[10]

As though in compensation and defiance of the sheer ugliness of gun-based combat, the horsemen of the sixteenth and seventeenth centuries developed an elaborate set of maneuvers that seem to have more in common with the intricacies of the aristocratic dances of the period than with the exigencies of gun battles. Named after a courtly dance, the caracole, lines of horsemen rode up to the enemy, discharged their pistols usually at too great a distance to be effective, and then peeled away to permit the next line to repeat the slightly farcical exercise.

Even as late as the eighteenth century, cavalrymen were all too aware of the inadequacy of firearms for mounted troops: "At a range of more than fifty paces a pistol shot and a well-thrown stone have just about the same effect. In a mêlée a discharged pistol is useless for parrying, and the only thing you can do is cast it away, for if you replace it in its holster and draw your sword you will receive a cut over your ear for your pains."[11] Against enemy cavalry the problem was accentuated by the fact that both mounted shooters were delivering their fire from highly unstable platforms: "Troopers usually fire at long range when the horses are galloping and the men are shaken about, and the target itself is moving so fast that it is quite impossible to take proper aim." A British artillery officer at Waterloo, Cavalié Mercer, records in his journal:

> Two double lines of skirmishers extended all along the bottom—the foremost of each line were within a few yards of each other constantly in motion, riding backwards and forwards, firing their carbines or pistols, and then reloading, still on the move. This fire seemed to me more dangerous for those on the hills above than for us below; for all, both French and English, generally stuck out their carbines or pistols as they continued to move backwards and forwards, and discharged them without taking any particular aim, and mostly in the air. I did not see a man fall on either side.[12]

As the sixteenth and seventeenth centuries progressed, and the experience with pistol and carbine (a shorter and lighter version of the musket) proved less than stellar, European cavalry tended to respond to the challenge of infantry by reverting to an old tactical role: using the horse as a shock weapon and, armed with sword or saber, attempting to break up blocks of infantry. As it was invariably true that disciplined and compact bodies of infantry, whether they were pike and arquebus configurations of the earlier part of the black-powder era or the bayonet-fitted musketeers of the later part, could hold off most cavalry, frontal charges were to be avoided.

For infantry, cohesion was everything. If it was broken down, perhaps because a flank was vulnerable or enemy artillery had disordered the formation, or—and this was particularly lethal—if the infantry were fleeing, then the cavalry could penetrate, and infantrymen could be killed in large numbers and with terrible speed. During the Seven Years' War, at the first battle of Lutterberg in 1758, the French cavalry fell on the broken and demoralized Anglo-German infantry and "carried everything before it, and killed almost all the enemy among scenes of terrible carnage."[13] At Quatre Bras (the battle ten days before Waterloo) the British Sixty-Ninth Regiment was caught before it could form itself into a defensive square and was terribly mauled by French cavalry.[14] By lying down and allowing the cavalry to ride over him, an infantryman might just possibly escape, but Captain John Kincaid was disgusted to see "the [French] cuirassiers in their retreat stooping and stabbing at our wounded men as they lay on the ground."[15]

Nothing quite ignited the nascent savagery of the *arme blanche* as the prospect of riding down disorganized infantrymen. The Prussian hussars at Hohenfriedeberg in 1745 were itching to get at the Saxon infantry. One of the Prussian officers records: "I heard some commotion and loud chatter among the hussars standing behind me. This was an infraction of our strict standards of discipline, and I asked an NCO what was happening. 'The lads are beside themselves with joy,' he answered. 'They have been ordered to give no quarter to the Saxons.' . . . I cannot recall having seen another battle in which we displayed more enthusiasm or burning anger."[16] One hundred thirty-four years later, at the battle of

Ulundi, fleeing Zulu warriors were subjected to British cavalry on a rampant spree:

> The 94th and the 2nd/21st edged aside, and the blue-jacketed lancers . . . moved out in column of fours. . . . Then, as the lines straightened, "Form line—Gallop—Cha-a-arge!"
>
> A roaring cheer burst from the square as the lances lowered. . . .
>
> It was a riding-school exercise. Hardly breaking formation, the lancers rode down the slope through the retreating Zulus, picking their men from the ruck. The momentum from the horses spitted the warriors on the points, and as they passed, a strong outward flick of the wrist cleared the weapon, which swung back, up and forward again to point. [The movement was] almost too fast for the eye to follow, as lance after lance flipped through its deadly arc. One or two of the lances fouled in a shield, which would not drop off, and the lancers slowed and tried to slough them off against their horses.
>
> . . . The men jammed the lance butts into the leather sockets on their right stirrups, thrust their arms past the elbow through the haft loops and drew their sabers to continue the slaughter.[17]

The charge of cavalry against cavalry tended to be not the grand head-on, crash-dummy collision of popular imagination but something altogether messier. The charging horses, unlike some of their riders, were not inclined to suicidal daftness and sought to avoid slamming into their counterparts. The Comte de Guibert describes the usual model of a cavalry-on-cavalry clash: "When, however, the two squadrons are made up of men and mounts which are equally experienced in war and are equally well-trained, the charge proceeds as follows—the ranks run at each other, the horses seek the intervals [the spaces between] of their own accord . . . the forces are so completely intermingled that the two squadrons cross and emerge in the other's rear."[18] Mercer at Waterloo observed something similar:

> Amongst the multitudes of French cavalry continually pouring over the front ridge, one corps came sweeping down the slope entire . . . when suddenly a regiment of light dragoons (I believe of the German Legion) came up from the ravine at a brisk trot on their [the French] flank. The French had barely time to wheel up to the left and push their horses into a gallop when the two bodies came into collision. They were at very short distance from us, so that we saw the charge perfectly. There was no check, no hesitation on either side; both parties seemed to dash on in a most reckless manner and we fully expected to have seen a horrid crash—no such thing! Each, as if by mutual consent, opened their files on coming near, and passed rapidly through each other, cutting and pointing, much in the same manner one might pass the fingers of the right hand through those of the left. We saw but few fall. The two corps reformed afterwards, and in a twinkling both disappeared, I know not how or where.[19]

Captain L. E. Nolan, a British cavalryman, pointed out that in most cases the heroic fury of the cavalry charge was undermined by the instinct for self-preservation:

> Cavalry seldom meet each other in a charge executed at speed; the one party generally turns before joining issue with the enemy, and this often happens when their line is still unbroken and no obstacles of any sort intervene.
>
> The fact is, every cavalry soldier approaching another at speed must feel that if they come in contact at that pace

they both go down, and probably break every limb in their bodies.

To strike down his adversary, the dragoon must close, and the chances are he receives a blow in return for the one he deals out.

There is a natural repugnance to close in deadly strife . . . the cavalry soldiers, unless they feel confident in their riding, can trust to their horse, and know that their weapons are formidable, will not readily plunge into the midst of the enemy's ranks.[20]

In the hurly-burly it was comparatively easy to allow the horse to take the rider out of the danger zone—not to be wondered at when one considers the anything-but-heroic hacking match of a cavalry mêlée. Francis Hall, an officer of the British Fourteenth Light Dragoons, describes just such an action at Fuentes de Oñoro in Spain in 1811:

I had been carrying a message when the first charge took place, and returned in the midst of the mêlée. It was literally *"auferre, trudidare, rapere"* [essentially, a shoving, pushing scrum]. Horses whose riders had been killed or overthrown ran wildly across the field or lay panting in their blood. The general rencontre was sub-divided into partial combats. Two heavy Dragoons were in the act of felling a Chasseur with their broad swords; his chaco [shako headdress] resisted several blows, but he at length dropped. Another was hanging in the stirrup, while his horse was hurried off by a German Hussar, eager to plunder his valise. Some were driving two or three slashed prisoners to the rear: one wretch was dragged on foot between two Dragoons, but as he was unable to keep pace with their horses, and the enemy were now forming for a second charge, he was cut down.

... Our men had *evidently* the advantage as individuals. Their broad sword, ably wielded, flashed over the Frenchmen's heads.... The alarm was, indeed, greater than the hurt, for their cloaks were so well rolled across their left shoulders, that it was no easy matter to give a mortal stroke with the broad edge of a sabre, whereas their swords, which were straight and pointed, though their effect on the eyes was less formidable, were capable of inflicting a much severer wound.[21]

There were two schools of thought about the most effective weapon for cavalry. One favored the straight sword held pointed forward with the arm fully extended in almost a reconstruction of the medieval knight's lance. The lethality came at the point, as Grandmaison, a French cavalry specialist writing in the mid-eighteenth century, emphasizes: "A single thrust into the body with the point will kill a man, which frequently cannot be achieved with twenty cuts with the edge." There were those, however, who advocated the heavy curved saber. Writing at the same time as Grandmaison, a Hungarian cavalry officer countered the theory of the superiority of the thrust:

I know that straight swords deal a more deadly blow, but they are not nearly as effective in combat. If you need convincing, I will explain the mechanism of the two kinds of weapon. When he is at a full gallop and a cavalryman attacks his enemy with the point, he will inevitably pierce him. But he must stop and break off his part in the action, so as to pull the sword out. During an equivalent amount of time a dragoon with a curved saber will have wounded three or four enemy, without having to stop his horse or stop fighting. The enemy will not be mortally wounded, but at least they will be disabled, which is what we ought to look for in battle.[22]

And there is no doubt that the saber could inflict grotesque injury. At the battle of the Waxhaws in South Carolina during the American War of Independence, in May 1780, the infamous British cavalry commander, the swaggering Banastre Tarleton, surprised and routed an American force. Dr. Robert Brownsfield recorded the results:

A furious attack was made on the rear guard, commanded by Lieut. Pearson. Not a man escaped. Poor Pearson was inhumanely mangled on the face as he lay on his back. His nose and upper lip were bisected obliquely; several of his teeth were broken out in the upper jaw, and the under completely divided on each side. . . .

Capt. John Stokes . . . was attacked by a dragoon, who aimed many deadly blows at his head, all of which by the dextrous use of the small sword he easily parried; when another on the right, by one stroke, cut off his right hand through the metacarpal bones. He was then assailed by both, and instinctively attempted to defend his head with his left arm until the forefinger was cut off, and the arm hacked in eight or ten places from the wrist to the shoulder. His head was then laid open almost the whole length of the crown to the eye brows. After he fell he received several cuts on the face and shoulders.[23]

Despite being also bayoneted and having his wounds dressed by a less-than-sympathetic British surgeon who filled his head wounds with "rough tow, the particles of which could not be separated from the brain for several days," John Stokes, miraculously, survived.

If a breakdown of cohesion spelled doom for infantry at the hands of cavalry, a tight formation and stalwart resistance could turn the tables. Mercer at Waterloo described how French cavalry swarmed around British infantry squares like "an enormous surf bursting over the prostrate hull of a stranded vessel, and then running, hissing and foaming up the beach," filling the spaces between the squares. Horses are sensitive creatures and could be easily spooked by a resolute display of bayonet points. Gunfire would bring down many horses and riders of the first ranks, leaving those behind to negotiate a writhing barricade of screaming beasts and men. In addition, many mounted frontal charges were delivered at nothing more than a trot or even a walk. At Waterloo, an officer of the Ninety-Fifth Foot, whose regiment was drawn up in a defensive square, describes being attacked by French cuirassiers. First, the infantrymen withheld their fire until the French were within thirty yards or so. "I fired a volley from my Company which had the effect, added to the fire of the 71st, of bringing so many horses to the ground, that it became quite impossible for the Enemy to continue their charge. I certainly believe that half of the Enemy were at that instant on the ground; some few men and horses were killed, more wounded, but by far the greater part were thrown down over the dying and the wounded. These last after a short time began to get up and run back to their supporters, some on horseback, but most of them dismounted."[24]

★　　★　　★

THE SOLDIER OF the premodern age (prior to about 1850 and what might be called the era of "high technology") had an intimate relationship with death and killing on the battlefield that the modern warrior rarely experiences. It was an intimacy dictated, to a large extent, by the inadequacies of the weapons with which he fought. The French cavalry knocked over by the Ninety-Fifth Foot at Waterloo came within thirty yards of their enemy. They had to get close because they were fighting mainly with swords; the infantry had to let them get close because the smoothbore muskets with which they defended themselves were grossly inaccurate at distances much beyond 50 yards. The protagonists were drawn closely together and the agency of death was never far away.

Before the age of industrial replication (as far as guns are concerned circa 1825), warfare was a handmade business. There were of course templates that laid out the design of firearms, but there was scant means by which the idea of standardization could be transferred into the actuality of exact uniformity. So, although most soldiers died anonymously, chewed up and spat out by the great maw of war, every combat death was individually crafted. Each gun, cannon, sword, and bayonet was unique. In the seventeenth and eighteenth centuries a tension between the particular and the general became increasingly acute. It was an era that saw a dramatic movement away from the particularization of the feudal, where each nobleman armed his own contingent, toward the increasing standardization of the nation-state.

Designs of gunpowder firearms all face the same basic challenge: A way has to be found to ignite the powder in order to project the missile, and the powder posed problems. The earliest firearms of the fourteenth and fifteenth centuries required a lighted wick ("match") to make direct contact with the powder in the pan, which would flash and ignite the main powder charge in the barrel. (Sometimes the powder would flash without igniting the main charge—hence the phrase "a flash in the pan" for something showy but ultimately useless.) Carrying a lighted wick in the vicinity of gunpowder was not only potentially dangerous but also highly inconvenient. Rain was obviously a problem, and the lighted match advertised any movement at night. The wheel-lock mechanism of the seventeenth century applied a more sophisticated solution (overdesigned, as it turned out) to the ignition problem. A hammer that gripped a piece of iron pyrite was cranked back against a spring ("spanning," the same word used for arming a crossbow) using a tool (from which we get the word *spanner*).

When the trigger was pulled, the pan cover moved to expose the powder and the pyrite sparked against a serrated wheel to ignite the priming charge. The gun was expensive to make and the wheel lock particularly prone to jamming or breaking if cocked for too long; it was, according to a seventeenth-century soldier, "too curious and too soone distempered with an ignorant hand."[25]

In contrast, the flintlock, which became the standard infantry gun for about 150 years (roughly 1700–1850), was a model of simplicity. As the name suggests, the firing mechanism was based on the relatively simple mechanics of a lock. The mechanism was derived from the German-Dutch hunting piece known as a *snaphance* (the name means "pecking cock," describing the action of the hammer, or "cock"). The cock was pulled back against a spring that in turn engaged with a restraining cog, the "sear." When the sear was released by a trigger, the cock "pecked" down and automatically opened the pan cover to expose the priming powder. The flint in the cock struck against a steel plate ("frizzen") to send a spark into the priming-powder pan and thence through a firing hole into the base of the barrel, which held the main powder charge. A sliding cover, manually closed after loading but automatically opened on firing, protected the priming charge from spilling or becoming wet. Another advantage was the introduction of a "half-cock," which to some extent mitigated the danger of carrying a loaded weapon at full cock.[26] Even so, accidents happened and men were killed. The sear that held the cock could become dangerously worn. Richard Holmes in *Redcoat* relates: "At Waterloo Lieutenant Strachan of the 73rd, who had just joined the regiment and was anxious to see action, was marching in front of a line of men with their muskets at the trail carried horizontally, muzzle forwards. A corn-stalk got entangled with the trigger of a half-cock musket, which went off, hitting Strachan in the back and killing him instantly."[27]

The flintlock musket, although a huge improvement on the

wheel-lock, was in some respects hardly more lethal than the bow (in fact, during the American War of Independence, Benjamin Franklin strongly advocated reintroducing the longbow), but unlike the bow, it could be mastered by almost any soldier. The drill stages ("evolutions," as they were called) seem to us quite extraordinarily complicated (even though the forty-four stages for the matchlock were reduced by about half for the flintlock). Nevertheless, the soldier had an imposing number of things to do before his musket was ready to fire. Priming powder had to be poured into the pan, and then a coarser powder, along with the ball, poured into the barrel, followed by a wad of paper or cloth to hold the charge in place; then all had to be tamped down with a ramrod. As the eighteenth century progressed, ball and powder were amalgamated into paper cartridges that the soldier broke open (usually by biting off one end) to enable him to pour powder and ball into the barrel to be followed by the empty paper cartridge, which acted as the wad.

In combat, understandably, much of the fancy rigamarole was dropped in favor of shortcuts. Very often, instead of going through the official loading procedure, soldiers under pressure would pour in the powder, roll in the ball, and give the butt a good whack on the ground to settle the powder and seat the ball on top.

All of these actions took a good deal of dexterity, and it is no wonder that in the heat of battle soldiers fumbled and panicked. Guns were loaded multiple times but not fired (usually because the ball had been put into the barrel before the powder); they became fouled from gunpowder residue; the ramrods bent or broke. To save time between loadings, soldiers stuck their ramrods into the earth, which caused their guns to become fouled with dirt. Some soldiers inadvertently fired off their ramrods because they had forgotten to remove them from the barrel, sometimes with fatal consequences for a man in a row in front.

In order to facilitate speedy loading, the ball was significantly smaller than the bore of the barrel. The resultant space between the ball and the barrel was termed "windage" (in flintlocks of the later eighteenth century, the windage was about .05 inches). Windage may have made loading easier, but there was a price to pay in the loss of gas (from the exploding gunpowder) that escaped around the ball rather than propelling it. The buffeting deformation of the flight of the ball as it traveled up the barrel affected accuracy also. Like a rifle bullet, the smoothbore ball left the barrel with a spin, but neither its axis nor its speed of rotation was controlled, and as it traveled, air resistance further deflected its flight in the same way that a sliced golf shot reacts.[28] Yet if windage was reduced, it caused extensive fouling with the resinous after-burn residue of the powder. It also increased what was already a fairly hefty recoil that could leave a badly bruised shoulder after a period of firing. (The recoil could be powerful enough to kill. A Lieutenant I. Bangs of the American Continental Army in the Revolutionary War records that as a man lowered his gun to cock it, it went off prematurely and the recoiling butt "kicked" him in the chest, "producing instant death.")[29]

The anticipation of the recoil and pan flash of the priming powder caused involuntary flinching, which also affected accuracy.[30] In addition, there was a tendency to let the musket rise during aiming, so that many shots went high. The experienced officer or NCO would have his men aim low, around the knee, so that any rising might result in a torso or head hit. Colonel Charles Scott instructed his Virginia musketeers at the second battle of Trenton in December 1776: "Now I want to tell you one thing. You are all in the habit of shooting too high. You waste your powder and lead, and I have cursed you about it a hundred times. Now I tell you what it is, nothing must be wasted, every crack must count. For that reason boys, whenever you see them fellows first begin to put their feet upon this bridge do you shin 'em. Take care now and fire low. Bring down your pieces, fire at their legs."[31]

Flintlocks were notoriously inaccurate at anything over about 50 yards. An eighteenth-century officer writes: "A soldier's musket, if not exceedingly ill-bored as many are, will strike the figure of a man at 80 yards . . . but a soldier must be very unfortunate indeed who shall be wounded by a common musket at 150 yards, provided his antagonist aims at him, and as for firing at 200 yards you might as well fire at the moon."[32] Modern tests under laboratory conditions (that is, the guns were not fired by humans but clamped and electrically ignited) on actual eighteenth-century muskets have shown 60 percent hits on target at 75 yards; at 100 yards it was pretty much a fifty-fifty proposition. With some guns the deviance was so great that the test had to be halted for safety reasons.[33] Misfiring was also a significant problem. The hydroscopic nature of gunpowder was obviously a major contributory factor, and flint wear also played a part, with each flint being good for about sixty firings.[34] As many as one in four discharge attempts were unsuccessful.[35] These were just some of the technical shortcomings of the weapon itself, and they were, of course, greatly compounded by the complexities of human stress under battle conditions.

The inaccuracy of individual muskets could be compensated for to some degree by reducing the range to target. Men had to get close to maximize the lethality of their weapon. If weapons were discharged at more than 80–100 yards, the chances of a hit were so greatly reduced that the expenditure of lead per casualty inflicted was massively inefficient. The Prussians at Chotusice (1742), for example, loosed off about 650,000 rounds to make 2,500 kills and about the same number of wounded. Some of those fatalities (perhaps as many as half) would have been caused by artillery and some (probably only a very small number, for reasons that will be discussed later), by bayonet. Assuming, therefore, that about

1,200 men were killed by musketry, it took approximately 540 balls or roughly 33 pounds of lead to extinguish one Austrian soldier's life.[36] At the battle of Vitoria (1813) during the Peninsular War, contemporaries estimated that the British fired 60 rounds per man (usually the total allocation) for an expenditure of 3.5 million rounds or 450 per French casualty.[37] (In modern warfare we have far exceeded the shots-to-kill ratio of the early modern period.) The great French general Maurice de Saxe, in his *Reveries on the Art of War* (1757), passes the judgment that "powder is not as terrible as believed. Few men in these affairs are killed from the front while fighting. I have seen whole salvoes fail to kill four men."[38] Some historians of the Napoleonic period put the hit rate as low as .3 percent,[39] others as high as 5–30 percent.[40]

But mortality rates in combat become misleading when they are expressed as a percentage of total combatants or casualties vis-à-vis total rounds expended. Battle is not fought in the statistical median but at the hot spots of localized violence. In these hot spots, casualties could be far higher. At Fontenoy in 1745 the Welsh Regiment of Fusiliers (it became the Royal Welch Fusiliers in 1920) had 200 killed out of a total casualty list of 322 (a massive 62 percent). At the battle of Brooklyn in 1776, 256 Marylanders were killed and 100 wounded out of a total complement of 400.[41] At Salamanca in 1812, Leith's division (about 3,000 strong) took 367 wounded and 51 killed in the front line of the attack (14 percent casualties, of which 1.7 percent were killed), but it was localized. Some battalions, such as the British 1/4th Foot ("1/4" means 1st Battalion of the 4th Regiment), lost only 3.9 percent, while others, such as the 3/1st Foot, lost 21 percent.[42] "It was by no means unusual," writes Major General B. P. Hughes, for a unit to suffer 30 percent casualties in the close combat of the eighteenth century."[43] And the majority of those casualties would usually be taken among the first two ranks at distances of less than 50 yards, and probably within a few seconds of the opening volley, when muskets had been preloaded in the calm before what one combatant called "the smoky, tormented, thunder-shaken vortex of the great fight."[44] Rain could be lethal. A downpour quenched the muskets of Colborne's brigade at the battle of Albuera, allowing the French cavalry to sweep in. The British took 76 percent casualties with a massive killed-to-wounded ratio: 319 killed, 460 wounded.[45]

To compensate for the inaccuracy of individual muskets, men were packed together into a firing formation that theoretically would be able to put out a formidable wall of fire in a concentrated blast. The problem was that they also offered a nicely compacted target that was not only convenient for opposing infantry but particularly tasty to field artillery. For the infantry this would be a devilish contract that lasted well into the modern period. It is sometimes tempting to be smug about the past, and the idiocy of two opposing armies in the eighteenth century blasting away at 30 yards (as they did, for example, at Fontenoy in 1745, where both sides lost about 20 percent of their combatants within the first few minutes of engagement) appears to us to be crazy; but this kind of bloody necessity to try and overwhelm the enemy with massed small-arms firepower brought to bear at close range and at great risk to the attacker would mark infantry warfare throughout the later modern period, of which the American Civil War is a prime example.

Timing was a crucial factor in black-powder combat. The first volley was important, but it could also be hazardous to the firer if it was not effective; for in the time it took to reload, the enemy could deliver a devastating countervolley. Frederick the Great declared: "Battles will be won through superior firepower . . . the infantry that can load the fastest will always defeat those that are slower to reload."[46] In parade-ground conditions a musket could be loaded and fired five times a minute, but in the "thunder-shaken vortex" of battle nothing approaching that rate could be hoped for. Men were sometimes killed by those in the ranks behind them. An Austrian officer at the battle of Kolin in 1757 observed that it "was the first and only action I have ever seen where our troops kept up an orderly and aimed fire in tightly closed ranks, and yet many a brave lad fell dead of wounds inflicted from the back, without having turned tail to the enemy. . . . The surgeons were later ordered to inspect the battlefield, and it transpired that these mortal wounds had been delivered by men of the rearward ranks, who carelessly mishandled their muskets in the heat of fire."[47]

A musket ball weighed about 1 ounce, and a hit at anything up to, say, 100 yards could inflict an appalling wound. Modern conoidal-shaped bullets make a clean entry but tend to tumble when they enter the body, leaving a trail of horrific damage, and create a large exit wound. A heavy round ball does not tumble but creates what in wound ballistics is known as "crushing" on initial impact. "Elastic" tissue such as muscle and skin is good at absorbing the kinetic energy of the projectile. A high-velocity bullet is not necessarily more lethal than a slower, heavier ball because kinetic energy is a function of mass. (In fact, the muzzle velocity of the black-powder period—1,200–1,500 feet per second—compares quite favorably with some modern firearms. For example, a Colt .357 Magnum fires a bullet at 1,200 feet per second, and even modern assault rifles, "beneficiaries of more than three centuries of technical development, were only double those of early muskets.")[48]

An infantryman was most likely to be hit on his left side, as this was most often presented to the enemy (a right-handed shooter turns slightly to the right, exposing his left side).[49] A full-velocity shot to the head or stomach invariably proved fatal. Stomach wounds were particularly feared (due in part to the almost inevitable death from peritonitis if the soldier was not killed outright). Rifleman Harris, in the Peninsular War, describes a comrade who had been gut-shot:

A man near me uttered a scream of agony, and looking from the 29th, who were on my right, to the left, whence the screech had come, I saw one of our sergeants, named Fraser, sitting in a doubled-up position, and swaying backwards and forwards as though he had got a terrible pain in his bowels. He continued to make such complaint that I arose and went to him, for he was rather a crony of mine.

"Oh, Harris," said he, as I took him in my arms, "I shall die! I shall die! The agony is so great that I cannot bear it."

It was, indeed dreadful to look upon him; the froth came from his mouth, and the perspiration poured from his face. Thank Heaven! he was soon out of pain, and, laying him down, I returned to my place. Poor fellow! He suffered more for the short time that he was dying than any man I think I ever saw in the same circumstances.[50]

Men hit by a musket ball did not always drop neatly. A soldier of the Napoleonic era describes the macabre death dance: "I have observed a Soldier, mortally wounded, by a shot through the head or heart, instead of falling down, elevate his Firelock with both hands above his head, & run round & round, describing circles before he fell, as one frequently sees a bird shot in the air. . . . Men, when badly wounded, seek the shelter of a stone or a bush, to which they betake themselves, before they lie down, for support & security, just as birds, or hares do, when in a similar state of suffering."[51]

Prolonged firefights at relatively close ranges could produce high casualties for little gain. A French witness at the slugfest of Kloster Kamp (1760) recalls: "The battlefield was strewn with dead, but we did not notice a single enemy uniform on our ground, or a single French uniform on that of the enemy."[52] Commanders, understandably, tried to prevent this. The model they aspired to was the volley followed by a bayonet charge. Major Macready of the Thirtieth Foot at Waterloo remarks: "All firing beyond one volley in a case where you must charge, seems only to cause a useless interchange of casualties, besides endangering the steadiness of a charge to be undertaken in the midst of sustained file fire, when a word of command is hard to hear."[53]

Sometimes there was to be no firing at all and an entire reliance on the bayonet. Marshal Ney at Montmirail in 1814 had the Guard empty their muskets of priming powder. Before the British bayonet attack on Anthony Wayne's sleeping troops at Paoli in 1777, "no soldier . . . was suffered to load; those who could not draw their pieces [extract the charge] took out the flints." Failure to do so could have its own fatal consequences. When Wayne, in revenge for Paoli, attacked the British garrison at Stony Point in 1779 he ordered it be done at the point of the bayonet, guns unloaded, but one unfortunate "insisted on loading his piece—all was now a profound silence—the officer commanding the platoon ordered him to keep on; the soldier observed that he did not understand attacking with his piece unloaded; he was ordered not to stop [in order to load], at his peril; he still persisted, and the officer instantly dispatched him."[54] In terms of percentages of men killed by the bayonet, the British at Paoli seemed to have had a slight margin. Of 1,500 Americans at Paoli, 200 (13.3 percent) were killed; at Stony Point, of 600 British, the Americans killed 63 (10.5 percent).[55]

The bayonet became something of an idée fixe of the black-powder era and, indeed, way beyond. Its supposed powers were invoked well into the twentieth century. But hard evidence suggests its effectiveness was more in the anticipation than the use, for no other weapon was held in such horror.

The "plug" bayonet had been introduced around the middle of the seventeenth century but by the end of the century was supplanted by the socket version (which, unlike the plug, permitted firing because it was attached to the outer rim of the musket by a ring). Its introduction is one of those innovations that seems, on the face of it, relatively minor, but in fact it condemned a whole class of warrior—the pikemen—to oblivion. No longer did musketeers need the pike for protection, for the bayonet now gave them the means to defend themselves.

There are many eyewitnesses to the warfare of the period who state that the bayonet was rarely employed. Dominique-Jean Larrey, Napoleon's surgeon-in-chief, encountered only five cases of bayonet wounds throughout his career. Although commanders were constantly urging men to withhold fire and charge with the bayonet, actual bayonet fighting seems to have been rare. At the battle of Maida (Italy, 1806), according to the British commander Sir John Stuart, his troops, having exchanged a volley, moved in "awful silence towards [the French] . . . until their bayonets began to cross." However, a British combatant saw it somewhat differently: "I have heard . . . it is stated that the bayonets of the contending forces actually crossed during the charge. They may have done so, in some parts of the line—but *so far as I could see* they did not do so, and I have never heard any one who was in the action say that the bayonets actually crossed."[56]

Lieutenant Colonel Dave Grossman believes that "bayonet combat is extremely rare . . . wound statistics from nearly two centuries of battle indicate that what is revealed here is a basic, profound, and universal insight into human nature. First, the closer the soldier draws to his enemy the harder it is to kill him, until at bayonet range it can be extremely difficult."[57]

One American Civil War veteran, interviewed by Sidney George Fisher, certainly would have agreed: "I said it seemed to me that the most terrible thing in battle must be a charge of bayonets, that a confused melee of furious men armed with such weapons, stabbing each other & fighting hand to hand in a mass of hundreds, was something shocking even to think of. He said it was so shocking that it very rarely happened that bayonets are crossed, one side always giving way before meeting."[58]

Killing with the bayonet may have been rare but it has always appealed to a certain strain of martial bloodlust. Again, the defeated soldier throughout history seems to trigger a psychopathological itch the bayonet scratches. At the battle of Brooklyn in 1776, Scots and Hessians caught units of the American patriot forces in a deadly pincer. A British officer reveled in the use of the bayonet: "The Hessians and our brave Highlanders gave no quarter, and it was a fine sight to see with what alacrity they dispatched the Rebels with their bayonets after we had surrounded them so they could not resist. . . . It was a glorious achievement."[59] As an American officer noted after Brooklyn: "Capt: Jewett had Rc'd: two Wounds with a Bayonet after he was taken, & Strip'd of his Arms & part of his Clothes, one in the Brest & the other in the Belly, of which he Languished with great pain until the Thursday following when he Died; Sargt: Graves was also Stab'd in the Thigh with a Bayonet, after he was taken."[60]

★   ★   ★

EVERY MILITARY SPECIALTY has its own dedicated and evocative vocabulary. Take, for example, the artillerists' term *grazing*. Technically it describes the bounces a cannonball makes during its flight. However, the word also evokes an animal feeding, which describes quite accurately the relationship between smoothbore artillery and the infantry and cavalry on which it preyed. The inadequacies of the individual musket resulted in a dependence on massed infantry arrayed in tight ranks to achieve anything approaching adequate firepower, and those same inadequacies placed a great emphasis on getting close to the enemy. Infantry tactics, therefore, provided large targets ideally suited to cannon that, although not particularly accurate, could cause much havoc on densely packed soldiers. The cannon was a beast of omnivorous and indiscriminate appetite, guzzling greedily on the herds of men conveniently marching toward its muzzle. It is fitting that the open end of a cannon is referred to as its mouth.

There were three main categories of shot used in the blackpowder era. The first and most important (accounting for about 70 percent of the ammunition carried) was solid iron ball. The second was canister, sometimes called "case," or "grape" (although grape, strictly speaking, was a naval munition), which has been described as the machine gun of the era. Tinned galvanized-iron cans filled with small iron balls (usually about sixty per can) burst when they left the cannon's mouth, spraying their payload in a shotgun pattern, which at close range (anything less than 200 yards) could create terrible slaughter. At Fontenoy in 1745 the French gunners allowed the English foot to come close and then ripped it apart with canister: "There was not a single shot from those cannon which failed to produce a dreadful carnage, and the first two discharges threw the enemy into such disorder that they rapidly betook themselves to the rear."[61] The Prussian colonel Eckhart witnessed the destruction of the Kalckstein Regiment at Kolin in 1757: "It was the enemy canister fire in particular which hit the second battalion, leaving not a single survivor among the lieutenants who commanded the platoons."[62] The artillerist Captain Mercer at Waterloo was attacked by French cavalry: "I saw through the smoke the leading squadrons of the advancing column coming on at a brisk trot, and already not more than one hundred yards distant. . . . I immediately ordered the line to be formed for action—case shot! . . . making terrible slaughter . . . in an instant covering the ground with men and horses." They were piled up on one another, remembered another, "like cards, the men not even having been displaced from the saddle." A Frenchman who viewed the same action observed: "Now, I thought, those gunners would be cut to pieces; but no, the devils kept firing with grape, which mowed them down like grass."[63]

In the third category were the exploding shells often fired from short-barreled howitzers and mortars. The gunner's art lay in setting the trajectory and trimming the fuse (which was ignited by the cannon flash) to achieve an airburst that showered troops with balls and bits of the shell case or bounced the spherical shell in among the enemy. And although gunnery as a whole was not particularly accurate, some artillerists showed considerable skill, as witnessed by Dr. James Thacher at Yorktown (1781), who described some American and French gunners: "It is astonishing with what accuracy an experienced gunner will make his calculations, that a shell shall fall within a few feet of a given point, and burst at the precise time, though at a great distance. When a shell falls, it whirls round, burrows, and excavates the earth to a considerable extent, and, bursting, makes dreadful havoc around. I have more than once witnessed fragments of the mangled bodies and limbs of the British soldiers thrown into the air by the bursting of our shells."[64]

Black-powder artillery engaged its target by "direct" fire: The target had to be visible ("indirect" fire at out-of-sight targets relying on mathematical calculation would come later in the nineteenth century). A six-pounder (a cannon firing a 6-pound ball), a workhorse of eighteenth-century artillery, had a range of approximately 1,200 yards. William Müller, of the King's German Legion (a British regiment), did extensive gunnery testing, which he published in *The Elements of the Science of War* in 1811. Firing at a cloth target 6 feet high and 30 feet wide (roughly the frontage of a battalion in line), he found that a six-pounder would make 100 percent hits at up to 520 yards, dropping precipitously to 31 percent at 950 yards, and to only 17 percent at its maximum range of 1,200 yards. The ball, however, had several phases of lethality over its trajectory. At zero degrees elevation (parallel to the ground), its first bounce (graze) would be about 400 yards out; the second graze grounded about 800 yards out; the third, 900 yards from the muzzle. To maximize its destructive potential the gunner attempted to pitch the ball just in front of the first rank of the enemy and have it ricochet and rise, hitting men in several ranks as it ascended, creating what one historian calls "tunnels of carnage."[65] Different infantry dispositions offered different tunnels. Against soldiers arrayed in line, the most lethal artillery placement was to fire round shot in enfilade: from the side, so that the ball would travel down a row. Against column, a head-on shot would have much the same effect, potentially making multiple kills during its brief but bloody career (and on stony ground secondary splinters would add to the shot's destructiveness).

A 6- or 9-pound cannonball traveling at up to 900 feet per second could, obviously, inflict horrendous damage on a soldier. At Bunker Hill in 1776, British warships caught American militia as they crossed the Neck onto Charlestown Peninsula. Peter Brown, a patriot, recalls that "one cannon [ball] cut off three men in two [cut them in half]." Sir John Moore, the British commander in the early stages of the Peninsular War, was mortally wounded by a ball: "The shock threw him from his horse with violence. . . . The dreadful nature of the injury he had received was then noticed; the shoulder was shattered in pieces, and the muscles of the breast were torn into long strips, which were interlaced by their recoil from the strain and dragging of the shot."[66]

Bizarrely, even near misses could be fatal. "I was sitting on the side of the trench," writes the American soldier Joseph Plumb Martin at Yorktown, "when some of the New-York troops coming in, one of the sergeants stepped up to the breastwork to look about him . . . at that instant a shot from the enemy (which doubtless was aimed for him in particular, as none others were in sight of them) passed just by his face without touching him at all; he fell dead into the trench; I put my hand on his forehead and found his skull was shattered all in pieces, and the blood flowing from his nose and mouth, but not a particle of skin was broken."[67] There are several such accounts of men being killed by a nimbus of pressurized air created by the flying ball.

Even a seemingly spent ball could be lethal. Many soldiers were maimed or killed by trying to stop what seemed to be a benignly rolling cannonball. In fact the heavier the shot, the more kinetic energy it retained. John Trumbull was with the American army besieging Boston in 1776 when rewards were offered for the retrieval of British cannonballs. The results, however, could be unfortunate, "for when the soldiers saw a ball, after having struck and rebounded from the ground several times (*en ricochet*), roll sluggishly along, they would run and place a foot before it, not aware that a heavy ball long retains sufficient impetus to overcome such an obstacle. The consequence was that several brave lads lost their feet, which were crushed by the weight of the rolling shot."[68]

Messing about with spent ordnance could literally blow up in your face, as Captain Kincaid reported from Spain in 1812: "Among other things carried from Ciudad Rodrigo, one of our men had the misfortune to carry his death in his own hands, under the mistaken shape of amusement. He thought that it was a cannon ball, and took it for the purpose of playing at the game of nine-holes, but it happened to be a live shell. In rolling it along it went over a bed of burning ashes, and ignited without his observing it. Just as he had got it between his legs, and was in the act of discharging it a second time, it exploded, and . . . blew him to pieces."[69]

Loading smoothbore cannon was a fairly complicated maneuver usually involving a minimum of five men. After each shot the barrel had to be swabbed with a soaked sheepskin "mop" to extinguish any embers before a new cartridge (a linen bag filled ·

with powder and ball) was rammed home. Lieutenant John Peebles of the Royal Highland Regiment fighting in America in 1780 describes the perils: "An artillery man lost an arm and an assistant killed by one of our own guns hanging fire and going off when they put in the spunge [*sic*]."[70] Given the volatility of the materials and the pressure of loading in battle conditions, disasters were waiting to happen. At Waterloo, Captain Mercer recalled:

> One of, if not the first man who fell on our side was wounded by his own gun. Gunner Butterworth was one of the greatest pickles in the troop, but at the same time a most daring, active soldier; he was No. 7 (the man who sponged etc) at his gun. He had just finished ramming down the shot, and was stepping back outside the wheel when his foot stuck in the miry soil, pulling him forward at the moment the gun was fired. As a man naturally does when falling, he threw out both his arms before him, and they were blown off at the elbows. He raised himself a little on his two stumps, and looked up most piteously in my face. To assist him was impossible—the safety of all, everything, depended on our not slackening our fire, and I was obliged to turn from him. The state of anxious activity in which we were kept all day, and the numbers who fell almost immediately afterwards, caused me to lose sight of poor Butterworth; and I afterwards learned that he had succeeded in rising, and was gone to the rear; but on inquiring for him next day, some of my people . . . told me that they saw his body lying by the roadside . . . bled to death.[71]

The killing power of artillery in this period was debated then, just as it has been by modern historians. In the sixteenth century, field artillery was clumsy, difficult to move, and slow to fire—only about eight shots an hour. As a French commentator of the first half of the sixteenth century puts it, "*Il fait plus de peur, que du mal*" (it frightens more than it hurts).[72] It was a sentiment repeated 150 years or so later by a witness of the battle of Vitoria in 1813: "Several of our officers remarked, & I think it just, that cannon make more noise and alarm than they do mischief. Many shots were fired at us but we suffered little from them. A young soldier is much more alarmed at a nine pounder shot passing within 4 y[ar]ds of his head than he is of a bullet at a distance of as many inches, although one would settle him as effectively as the other."[73]

Some modern historians have looked to the records of types of wounds of those soldiers admitted to the French national military hospital, Les Invalides, in Paris. The records of 1762, for example, show that the great majority of men (68 percent) were hit by small arms; sword wounds accounted for 14.7 percent; 13.4 percent were wounded by artillery; and only 2.4 percent by the bayonet.[74] As these statistics represent survivable wounds, the effects of artillery, which often inflicted mortal wounds, are greatly underrepresented (a similar skewing is seen in American Civil War casualty statistics). But Rory Muir, in *Tactics and the Experience of Battle in the Age of Napoleon*, makes the following comment:

> But even if, to correct this, we allow that half of all men killed in action (who seldom amounted to more than one-fifth of all casualties) fell to artillery fire, this still means that only just over 20 per cent of all casualties were the result of artillery.
>
> ... It can however be argued that the figures would be higher for the Napoleonic period. Infantry firefights were less common and intense than during the Seven Years War; while compared to the American Civil War troops

manoeuvred in close formations taking little cover, which made them very vulnerable to artillery fire. Although these arguments smack of special pleading, we might give them sufficient credence to consider a figure of between 20 and 25 per cent as being the maximum normal proportions of casualties caused by the fire of artillery. . . . The most we can say is that where we have evidence of the ammunition consumed and the losses suffered by the opposing army, it took, on average, a number of rounds of artillery fire to inflict one enemy casualty.[75]

Other modern historians credit the artillery of the period with a much more effective lethality: "On average, well-sighted and well-handled artillery [firing case] could expect to inflict between one and 1½ casualties per shot."[76] But as with musketry, the generalization of statistics can mask the horror of localized actions in which artillery could play a devastating part. Captain Kincaid at Waterloo records that "the 27th Regiment were lying literally dead, in square," mainly killed by artillery. In addition, the question has to be asked about the basis of statistical evidence in this period. There was no bureaucratic or forensic capability within any army to record the causes of death in action. The dead were usually dumped unceremoniously into mass graves pretty quickly after the fighting had ended. No one was about to catalog their individual fates. It seems true, however, that artillery became increasingly decisive in the great Napoleonic battles against continental enemies (unlike the fighting in the Peninsular War, which was more infantry-based). Concentrations of cannon could be very large indeed, with batteries of up to a hundred guns, and the French memoirist Sergeant Burgoyne claims that Borodino "like all our great battles was won by the artillery."[77]

★   ★   ★

THE COMBAT OFFICER throughout history has a double-edged intimacy with death in battle. Officers in the field, particularly junior grades, are expected to lead in combat, which, inevitably, increases their risk of being killed. They also send men to their deaths. A bad officer can get his men killed; a good officer will try to minimize the risk to his men if it can be done without compromising the mission. But sometimes it cannot, and so "good" and dedicated officers also get their men killed.

The officer was bound by a code of honor designed to ensure that he would willingly, often passionately, accept his obligation and the death it might bring. Social class still determined almost without exception who would lead and how they were expected to fight and die. The common soldier, it was thought, may well have had an animal vitality, but he lacked the higher qualities that were the inheritance of the officer. The French aristocrat Turpin de Crissé outlined the distinction: "Bravery is in the blood, but courage is in the soul. Bravery is instinctive, almost a mechanical reaction. Courage is a virtue, and a lofty and noble sentiment."[78]

A token of that noble inheritance was a casual disregard for personal safety, the more flamboyantly expressed the better. Death was to be sneered at as though it were a vulgarity. Sangfroid was an expression of the languid disdain a gentleman offered impending oblivion. Alessandro Farnese, the Duke of Parma, was taking his luncheon while besieging the city of Oudenaarde in 1582:

> Hardly had the repast commenced, when a ball came flying over the table, taking off the head of a young Walloon officer who was sitting near Parma. . . . A portion of his skull struck out the eye of another gentleman present. A second ball . . . destroyed two more of the guests as they sat at the banquet. . . . The blood and the brains of these unfortunate

individuals were strewn over the festive board, and the others all started to their feet, having little appetite left for their dinner. Alexander alone remained in his seat. . . . Quietly ordering the attendants to remove the dead bodies, and to bring a clean tablecloth, he insisted that his guests should resume their places.[79]

Parma's reaction may strike us as deranged, but it was meant to demonstrate a degree of self-control thought to be the exclusive preserve of the aristocrat-officer. George Napier recalled, with astonishing detachment, having his arm amputated during the Napoleonic Wars: "I must confess that I did not bear the amputation of my arm as well as I ought to have done, for I made noise enough when the knife cut through my skin and flesh. It is no joke I assure you, but still it was a shame to say a word. . . . Staff Surgeon Guthrie cut it off. However, from want of light, and from the number of amputations he had already performed . . . his instruments were blunted, so it was a long time before the thing was finished, at least twenty minutes, and the pain was great. I then thanked him for his kindness."[80]

George Washington at Yorktown exhibited more of the "right stuff":

During the assault, the British kept up an incessant firing of cannon and musketry from their whole line. His Excellency General Washington, Generals Lincoln and Knox, with their aides, having dismounted, were standing in an exposed situation waiting the result.

Colonel Cobb, one of General Washington's aides, solicitous for his safety, said to His Excellency, "Sir, you are too much exposed here. Had you not step a little back?"

"Colonel Cobb," replied His Excellency, "if you are afraid, you have the liberty to step back."[81]

These are rhetorical gestures in the face of death, but not in the shallow sense of gesture as empty mimicry. It is uplifting theater, strengthening the primary actor and inspiring the onlooker. The actions of artillery captain Mercer at Waterloo illustrate something of this chutzpah, and also the price one of his men had to pay for it:

It was not without a little difficulty that I succeeded in restraining the people [his gunners] from firing, for they grew impatient. . . . Seeing some exertion beyond words necessary for this purpose, I leaped my horse up the little bank, and began a promenade (by no means agreeable) up and down our front, without even drawing my sword, though these fellows [the French] were within speaking distance of me. This quieted my men; but the tall blue gentlemen, seeing me thus dare them, immediately made a target of me, and commenced a very deliberate practice, to show us what very bad shots they were, and verify the old artillery proverb, "The nearer the target, the safer you are." One fellow certainly made me flinch, but it was a miss; so I shook my finger at him. . . . The rogue grinned as he reloaded, and again took aim. I certainly felt rather foolish at that moment, but was ashamed after such bravado to let him see it, and therefore continued my promenade. As if to prolong my torment, he was a terrible time about it. . . . Whenever I turned, the muzzle of his infernal carbine still followed me. At length bang it went, and whiz came the ball close to the back of my neck, and at the same instant down dropped the leading driver of one of my guns (Miller), into whose forehead the cursed missile had penetrated.[82]

Death was to be accepted not only with a certain equanimity but also, if possible, with a memorable quip. On trumped-up charges of having broken their parole (the word given by captured officers that if released, they would take no further part in the fighting), two Royalist officers during the English Civil War, Sir Charles Lucas and Sir George Lisle, who had been recaptured at Colchester, were condemned to be shot by their Parliamentarian captors: "Lucas was shot first and Lisle stood over his friend's body as the firing party reloaded. Lisle called to them to come closer, to which one replied, 'I'll warrant you, sir, we'll hit you'; with a smile Lisle said, 'Friends, I have been nearer you when you have missed me!' "[83]

A young British officer, Major John André, was captured while spying during the American War of Independence and, because he had been instrumental in abetting General Benedict Arnold's defection to the British, was condemned to hang. Alexander Hamilton described the scene:

> In going to the place of execution, he bowed familiarly as he went along to all those with whom he had been acquainted in his confinement. A smile of complacency expressed the supreme fortitude of his mind. Arrived at the fatal spot, he asked with some emotion, must "I then die in this manner." [He was to be hanged like a common criminal and not shot as would have befitted his rank and station, and although he had petitioned Washington twice, the decision remained.] He was told it had been unavoidable. "I am reconciled to my fate," said he, "but not to the mode." Soon however recollecting himself, he added, "it will be but a momentary pang," and springing upon the cart performed the last offices to himself with a composure that excited the admiration and melted the hearts of the beholders. Upon being told the final moment was at hand, and asked if he had anything to say, he answered: "nothing, but to request you will witness to the world that I die like a brave man."[84]

It was a composure that has always been the ideal of a noble officer: "He is patient, forebearing, and resigned on philosophical principles; he submits to pain because it is irreparable, and to death, because it is his destiny."[85]

There was even a gaiety, a sharpened appreciation of life, when death was embraced: "It's a lottery," reflects Captain Bréaut des Marlots, "even if you get out of this, you'll have to die someday. Do you prefer to live dishonored or to die with honor?" General Antoine Lasalle, one of the most intrepid of Napoleon's cavalry commanders, told friends, "What's the point of living? To earn a reputation, get ahead, make your fortune? Well, I'm general of division at 33, and last year the Emperor gave me an income of 50,000 francs." To which a friend replied, "Then you must live to enjoy it." "Not at all," Lasalle responded. "To have achieved it, that's satisfaction enough. I love battles, being in the noise, the smoke, the movement; so long as you've made your name, and you know your wife and children won't want for anything, that's all that matters. For myself, I'm ready to die tomorrow." He was killed three months later, shot between the eyes on the second day of Wagram, 1809.[86]

Bad and arrogant officers were infected with a narcissistic sense of honor for which their men paid a terrible price. At Minden in 1759, Lieutenant General Saint Pern, "having seen the bloody losses sustained by his poor grenadiers, nevertheless kept them exposed to fire throughout the battle, instead of ordering them to sit on the ground, or descend a few paces to the rear, where they would have been covered by the crest of the hill on which they were standing."[87]

Several factors increased the officers' chances of being killed. One was that they dressed conspicuously and therefore attracted the attention of snipers. Marshal Soult in the Peninsular War complained that his own officers were especially targeted: "When senior officers go to the front, either to make observations or to encourage their troops, they are almost always hit. We lose so many officers that after two consecutive actions the battalion is almost destitute of them. In our casualty lists the proportion is often one officer to eight men. I have seen units where there were only two or three officers left, though not one sixth of the rank and file were *hors de combat*."[88] Ironically, there is an account (perhaps apocryphal) that Soult himself was spotted reconnoitering the British lines at Alba de Tormes in November 1812 but that Lieutenant Colonel John Cameron of Fassiefern, commanding the Scottish Highlanders of the Ninety-Second ordered his men to withhold fire.[89]

Sniping officers was considered—by the officer class—to be bad form and a breach of military etiquette. The common soldier, however, saw it quite differently, as this incident during an action at Vimeiro, Portugal, in 1808 makes clear. A British officer asked a rifleman to take care of a French sharpshooter who was aiming at him. The soldier ignored the request, preferring to target a French officer:

> "Why do you want to kill the officer," cried I, "you rascal?" with as much vexation as he had manifested. "Pecaus ter pe more plunder [because there will be more plunder]," muttered the wretch, keeping his eyes fixed on the object of his ambition. It now immediately occurred to my mind, that, as we were rapidly driving back the enemy, this worthy had calculated on permitting the Voltigeur to pick me off, while he should return the compliment on the French officer; and thus secure the advantage of plundering me first, trusting to the almost certainty of getting up to the enemy before the French officer's carcase should be stripped by his friends.[90]

Unpopular officers ran the risk of being fragged. At Blenheim in 1704 a detested officer of the Fifteenth Foot "faced about to the regiment and took off his hat to give an hussa; and just got out these words, 'Gentlemen, the day is ours!' when a musket ball hit him in the forehead, and killed him instantly."[91] Given that many line officers were required to stand in front of their troops, the risk of being shot, either accidentally or accidentally on purpose, was considerable, as one officer attested: "I served one campaign as captain of infantry, and I confess that I suffered frequent anxieties on this account."[92]

The strict demands of honor ensured that more officers, in numerical proportion to nonofficers, were killed. At Waterloo, for example, the officers were 5 percent of the total force but were killed at a much higher ratio. Almost 50 percent of the 840 British infantry officers at Waterloo and Quatre Bras were killed or wounded (compared with perhaps 20 percent of other ranks). Of 63 British commanding officers, 32 became casualties; the Royal Scots lost 31 out of 36 officers, and the Seventy-Third Highlanders, 22 of 26.[93] If the numbers for the four Peninsular battles of Barrosa, Fuentes del Oñoro, Albuera, and Vitoria are combined, French officers constituted 3.4 percent of the total French army but represented 4.9 percent of the casualties. In other words, a French officer stood a 44 percent higher chance of becoming a casualty than one of his men.

Ironically, even though an officer stood in greater peril than his men of being killed outright in battle, he had a much better chance of surviving if he were wounded. First, he was better fed and therefore likely to be healthier; second, he could depend on swifter and more personalized medical attention, which might include being sent home to recuperate, a luxury certainly not afforded the ordinary soldier.

★   ★   ★

THE DEATHS OF one's colleagues were also treated with a certain detachment, even though the deceased may have been a close companion. Rifleman Harris, describing the agonizing death of his friend Sergeant Fraser, ends the account with: "Within about half-an-hour after this I left Sergeant Fraser, and, indeed, for the time had as completely forgotten him as if he had died a hundred years back. The sight of so much bloodshed around will not suffer the mind to dwell long on any particular casualty, even though it happens to be one's dearest friend."

A French soldier described the almost jocular way a comrade's death was treated: "The frequency of danger made us regard death as one of the most common occurrences of life. We grieved for our comrades when wounded, but if they were dead, we showed an indifference about them often even ironical. When the soldiers in passing recognized a companion numbered with the slain, they would say, 'He is now above want, he will abuse his horse no more, his drinking days are done,' or words to that purpose; which manifested in them a stoical disregard of existence. It was the only funeral oration spoken over the warriors that had fallen."[94]

But even dead comrades could still offer a macabre companionship. "James Ponton was another crony of mine," declared Harris. But Ponton was a little too rash going forward "and was not to be restrained by anything but a bullet when in action. This time he got one which striking him in the thigh, I suppose cut an artery and he died quickly. The Frenchmen's balls were flying very wickedly at that moment; and I crept up to Ponton and took shelter by lying behind and making a rest for my rifle of his dead body. It strikes me that I revenged his death by the assistance of his carcase."[95]

After the battle of Roliça in Portugal in 1808 Rifleman Harris spotted a dead soldier:

He was lying on his side amongst some burnt-up bushes, and whether the heat of the firing here had set these bushes on fire, or from whatever cause they had been ignited, I cannot take it upon me to say; but certain it is . . . that this man, whom we guessed to have been French, was as completely roasted as if he had been spitted before a good kitchen-fire. . . . He was drawn all up like a dried frog. I called the attention of one or two men near me, and we examined him, turning him about with our rifles with no little curiosity. I remember now, with some surprise, that the miserable fate of this poor fellow called forth from us very little sympathy, but seemed only to be the subject of mirth.[96]

When an officer was killed his effects were sold off to fellow officers, whose reaction could, to our tender sensibilities, be shockingly callous. George Robert Gleig, a subaltern in the Eighty-Fifth Foot during the Peninsular War, explained: "A strange compound of good and bad feeling accompanies the progress of the auction. In every party of men, there will always be some whose thoughts, centring entirely in self, regard everything . . . solely as it increases their enjoyments. . . . Even the sale of the clothes and accoutrements of one who but a few weeks or days before was their living, and perhaps favourite companion, furnishes to such men food for mirth; and I am sorry to say, that during the sale of which I now speak, more laughter was heard than redounded to the credit of those who joined in, or produced it. . . . I fear that few laughed more heartily than I."[97]

Officers benefited in other important ways. First, pocketing the pay of men killed in action was a lucrative perquisite. It was not unknown for British officers in the American War of Independence to make eight hundred pounds a year in this way (the equivalent to the annual remuneration of an infantry colonel).[98] Second, with every death a rung up the ladder of promotion became vacant—and one that did not have to be paid for because the families of the fallen could not sell the dead man's commission. A vacancy created by death was filled by seniority. Lieutenant

William Scott, an American officer captured at Bunker Hill, gave a startlingly honest view on the relationship between death in battle and the reward that might accrue: "I offered to enlist upon having a Lieutenant's Commission; which was granted. I imagined myself now in a way of Promotion: if I was killed in battle, there would be an end of me, but if my Captain was killed, I should rise in Rank, & should have a Chance to rise higher."[99]

Ironically, the killed offered all kinds of bounty to the living—a regular harvest. The common soldiers plundered the corpses on the battlefield for wallets, clothing, and boots (the secondary gleaning, which often involved bumping off the wounded, was usually carried out by civilians and camp followers). Those who went to the hospital were also invariably robbed. Major Richard Davenport of the Tenth Dragoons made this doleful report in 1759: "I am sorry I can give Mrs. Moss no other account of her husband than that he died at Münster. As to his things, whatever he had is lost. When a man goes into hospital, his wallet, with his necessaries are sent with him, but nothing ever returns. Those that recover, seldom bring anything back, but those that die are stripped of all. I have lost nine men and have not heard of anything that belonged to them. It is a common practice of a nurse, when a man is in danger, to put on a clean shirt, that he may die in it, and that it may become her perquisite."[100] And as the death rate in the hospital for the common soldier of the eighteenth century was about 40 percent, there was a good living, so to speak, to be made there.

Actions of particularly high risk, such as "forlorn hope" attacks on the breached walls of besieged towns, were surprisingly popular among the attacking troops because they offered the very real prospect of gain either from plunder or, if you beat the odds, a vaulting boost to one's career. It was a kind of Russian roulette in a world where advancement was hard-won and the gamblers took their chances. Sir Thomas Brotherton, a British officer during the Peninsular War, saw many of these chancers: "The volunteers [young men without the money to buy a commission] we had with the army . . . always recklessly exposed themselves in order to render themselves conspicuous, as their object was to get commissions given to them without purchase. The largest proportion of these volunteers were killed, but those who escaped were well rewarded for their adventurous spirit."[101] Captain Sir John Kincaid at Badajoz during the Peninsular War describes the general appetite for forlorn hopes:

> In proportion as the grand crisis approached, the anxiety of the soldiers increased, not on account of any doubt or dread as to the result, but for fear that the place should be surrendered without standing an assault; for, singular as it may appear, although there was a certainty of about one man out of every three being knocked down, there were, perhaps, not three men in the three divisions who would not rather have braved all the chances than receive it tamely from the enemy. So great was the rage for passports into eternity in our battalion on that occasion, that even the officers' servants insisted on taking their places in the ranks.[102]

Kincaid himself took a more pessimistic view of the prospects of the forlorn hope: "The advantage of being on a storming party is considered as giving the prior claim to be 'put out of pain,' for they receive the first fire, which is generally the best, not to mention that they are also expected to receive the earliest salutations from the beams of timber, hand-grenades, and other missiles which the garrison are generally prepared to transfer from the top of the wall, to the tops of the heads of their foremost visitors."[103]

For the common soldier yet another risk had to be faced: the ever-present threat of the ultimate sanction—execution. Officers had the jurisdiction to kill men on the spot who attempted to leave the field but very rarely exercised it, and some armies maintained enforcing units to prevent men "leaking" out of the battle. Nevertheless, it was a death that might be described as the shadow risk of combat. Not doing something could get you killed. Discipline was ferocious in most armies of the period. "Many soldiers," stated Frederick the Great, "can be governed only with sternness and occasionally severity. If discipline fails to keep them in check they are apt to commit the crudest excesses. Since they greatly outnumber their superiors, they can be held in check only through fear."[104]

Desertion rates in all armies were high, and those who were captured, particularly those who had deserted during action, stood a very good chance of being executed. James Fergus, a Scotch-Irish Pennsylvania militiaman, made the following diary entry on May 12, 1778, during the siege of Savannah, Georgia: "Four men, two white and a mulatto and a Negro, were taken outside the lines and brought in, supposed to be deserting to the enemy. The governor, coming by at the time, was asked what should be done with them. He said, 'Hang them up to the beam of the gate,' by which they were standing. This was immediately done, and there they hung all day."[105]

Comrades-in-arms were enlisted to do the executions. Rifleman Harris was just a lad when he was chosen to make up a firing squad:

A private of the 70th Regiment had deserted from that corps . . . he was brought to trial at Portsmouth, and sentenced by general court-martial to be shot.

. . . As for myself, I felt that I would have given a good round sum (had I possessed it) to have been in any situation rather than the one in which I now found myself; and when I looked into the faces of my companions, I saw, by the pallor and anxiety depicted in each countenance, the reflection of my own feelings. When all was ready, we were moved to the front, and the culprit was brought out. He made a short speech to the parade, acknowledging the justice of his sentence, and that drinking and evil company had brought the punishment upon him.

He behaved himself firmly and well, and did not seem at all to flinch. After being blindfolded, he was desired to kneel down behind a coffin . . . we immediately commenced loading.

This was done in the deepest silence, and the next moment we were primed and ready. There was then a dreadful pause . . . and the drum-major, again looking towards us, gave the signal before agreed upon (a flourish of his cane) and we levelled and fired . . . and the poor fellow, pierced by several balls, fell heavily upon his back; and as he lay, with his arms pinioned to his sides, I observed that his hands waved for a few moments, like the fins of a fish, when in the agonies of death. The drum-major also observed the movement, and, making another signal, four of our party immediately stepped up to the prostrate body, and placing the muzzles of our pieces to the head, fired, and put him out of his misery.[106]

Quite often a very sophisticated but sickeningly cruel piece of theater was played out upon the condemned. After the whole gruesome rigamarole of being marched to the place of execution (sometimes carrying their own coffins), stood by their expectant graves, and made to face their executioners, a last-minute reprieve was issued. And if it was not, it was important for the efficacy of this ultimate deterrent that there be an audience of fellow soldiers to bear witness and draw the salutary conclusion. But sometimes the whole thing backfired. The audience, in disgust, occasionally rebelled, as the American Revolutionary soldier John Plumb Martin described:

While lying at, or near the Peekskill, a man belonging to the Cavalry was executed for desertion to the enemy, and as none of the corps to which he belonged were there, no troops were paraded, as was customary on such occasions, except a small guard. The ground on which the gallows was erected was literally covered with pebble stones. A Brigade-Major attended the execution; his duty on these occasions being the same as a High Sheriff's in civil matters. He had, somewhere, procured a ragamuffin fellow for an executioner, to preserve his own immaculate reputation from defilement. After the culprit had hung the time prescribed by law, or custom, the hangman began stripping the corpse; the clothes being his perquisite. He began by trying to pull off his boots, but for want of a boot-jack he could not readily accomplish his aim; he kept pulling and hauling at them, like a dog at a root, until the spectators, who were very numerous (the guard having gone off), growing disgusted, began to make use of the stones, by tossing several at his pretty carcass. The Brigade-Major interfering in behalf of his aid-de-camp, shared the same usage; they were both quickly obliged to "quit the field"; as they retreated the stones flew merrily. They were obliged to keep at a proper distance until the soldiers took their own time to disperse.[107]

FOUR

ALL GLORY . . . ALL HELL

The American Civil War

There is many a boy here today who looks on war as all glory. But, boys, it is really all hell. You can bear this warning voice to generations yet to come. I look upon war with horror, but if it has to come I am there.

—William T. Sherman

I N PURELY MILITARY terms, the War between the States had one foot in the past and one in the future: part Napoleonic and part World War I. It was a war that for the first three years of its four-year course was rooted in the tactical tradition of the black-powder warfare of the previous 150 years or so. And yet, the sheer scale on which it was fought and the advances in weapons technology it utilized—rifled muskets, conoidal bullets, repeating guns, breech-loading rifles, and rifled artillery—would shape the wars that followed.

The increase in the rifled musket's range and accuracy compared to its predecessor, the smoothbore musket, brought death more surely to more men than ever before. Or so the standard argument goes. In fact, such innovations did not make as much difference to the experience of combat as might at first be thought. The innovation of greater importance was the application of the power and skills of an already powerful (and soon to be preeminent) industrial state to the business of war—with all the prerequisites of business: capital, organization, manpower, and natural resources. It was this that predetermined victory, however hard fought and close run it was to be at times.

On one level the Civil War was acted out on the thrilling stage of heroic and bloody theater; on the other, its outcome was determined by the victory of the industrial over the agrarian. Renewable resources of treasure and men, as well as courage and determination, predisposed the outcome. The North, even though hampered by shoddy military leadership during the earlier part of the war, could afford much higher losses of manpower and matériel—in absolute and proportional terms—than could the South, with its smaller population and underdeveloped manufacturing capacity. Even though in many battles fewer Confederate soldiers were killed in action or died of wounds than Federals, those who did represented a higher proportion of the fighting force. It was an actuarial reality that smashed the heart of the Confederate cause as mercilessly as a bullet or shell fragment. The South was forced into a war of attrition that eventually and inevitably ran it into the ground. And it is this aspect of the Civil War that foreshadowed the strategic architecture of the world wars of the following century. Resources provide the stage on which warriors with courage and fortitude, sacrifice and determination, play out their drama. The South had no shortage of all these martial virtues, but it was bled to death. It would lose about one-third more men killed as a proportion of those engaged than the North.

And this was the bloody arithmetic that Grant understood when he sacrificed his own warriors at Spotsylvania and Cold Harbor during the endgame of the war.

Numbers, recorded quantities of the dead, estimates of expenditure, the ledger book of life expended and advantage gained: These were the mark of the age. But even in an era that had begun to revel in the mechanisms and skills of bureaucracy, record keeping (especially in the Confederacy) could be a little inexact, to put it mildly. In addition, toward the end of the war swathes of records of the South's fighting units were destroyed. Numbers were also manipulated. Robert E. Lee became alarmed at the willingness—the almost masochistic relish, even—with which some of his commanders advertised the high casualties they sustained as though they were badges of honor. Lee was forced to issue a General Order in May 1863 discouraging such displays, for fear they gave heart to the enemy, and after the devastating losses at Gettysburg he "seems to have quite systematically and intentionally undercounted his casualties."[1] The manipulation of "body count" was not something invented in the Vietnam War. Ambrose Bierce, who fought on the Union side and wrote Gothic spooky stories about it, describes the aftermath of a battle in his story "The Coup de Grace": "The names of the victorious dead were known and listed. The enemy's fallen had to be content with counting. But of that they got enough; many of them were counted several times, and the total, as given afterward in the official report of the victorious commander, denoted rather a hope than a result."[2]

In the North, tallying was better, reflecting the organizational strengths of an industrializing society, strengths that would, in their own prosaic but important ways, help win the war. Even so, William F. Fox, a Union officer (who would later compile one of the great statistical books about the war, *Regimental Losses in the American Civil War*, 1888), remembered the waywardness of record keeping on campaign: "After a hard-fought battle the regimental commander would, perhaps, write a letter to his wife detailing the operations of his regiment, and some of his men would send their village paper an account of the fight, but no report would be forwarded officially to head quarters. Many colonels regarded the report as an irksome and unnecessary task."[3] (Ironically, even record keeping could prove fatal. In 1893, twenty-two clerks were crushed to death when the floors of Ford's Theatre in Washington, DC, which was being used to store Civil War records, collapsed.)[4]

Disease, as in all previous wars, was a greater killer of soldiers than combat (it accounted for 66 percent of all fatalities in the Civil War).[5] Of the approximately 2,100,000 men[6] who took up arms for the North, 360,000 died (17 percent of all who served), of whom about 110,000 (5.2 percent) were either killed outright in battle (67,058) or died from wounds (43,012).[7] Although the high rate of death from disease is shocking, it was an improvement on the Mexican War of 1846–48, in which seven men died of disease for every one killed in battle.[8] Of the approximately 880,000 Confederates who served, about 250,000 (28 percent) died from all causes.[9] Of these Fox estimates that 94,000 (10.6 percent) were killed or mortally wounded. Thomas L. Livermore, reviewing the statistical evidence in his classic study, *Numbers & Losses in the Civil War in America*, printed in 1900, concludes that "any summing-up of the casualties from [the Confederate] reports must necessarily be incomplete, and the number . . . arrived at by Colonel Fox can be accepted only as a minimum."[10] The numbers may be merely indicative, but they suggest that the South lost about 11 percent of its soldiers killed outright or died of wounds, compared with just over 7 percent for the North—a 30 percent greater killed rate for Confederate warriors.

It needs also to be borne in mind that the numbers of men killed outright or who died of wounds expressed as a percentage of those "who took up arms" needs to be tempered by the fact that not all who wore butternut or blue were involved in combat. Obviously, the death toll rises considerably when viewed as a percentage of combatants only: a computation of quite daunting complexity.

There is often an ambiguous attitude to the number of men killed in war. On the one hand, we are saddened, horrified even, at the price paid. But on the other, the sacrifice is intimately involved with our national mythology. It makes us intensely proud. They underwrite our sense of national worth with their blood. A great mortality is a badge of honor, as Fox puts it, "amply heroic."

Some historians of the Civil War point to its "unprecedented" mortality. "Numbers seemed the only way to capture what was dramatically new about this war: the very size of the cataclysm and its human cost."[11] Fox states categorically that casualties were "unsurpassed in the annals of war."

Having complained that too many commanders in the Civil War "claimed losses for their regiments which are sadly at variance with the records [of the muster rolls of the regiments]," Fox goes on to say that to "the thoughtful, the truth will be sensational enough: the correct figures are amply heroic." As comparison Fox cites the Franco-Prussian War of 1870–71, in which the "Germans took 797,950 men into France. Of this number, 28,277 were killed, or died of wounds—a loss of 3.1 per cent. In the Crimean War, the allied armies lost 3.2 per cent in killed, or deaths from wounds. In the war of 1866, the Austrian army lost 2.6 per cent from the same causes. There are no figures on record to show that, even in the Napoleonic wars, there was ever a greater percentage loss *in killed*."[12]

At Borodino in 1812 ("the bloodiest battle since the introduction of gunpowder"), Fox reckons that of 133,000 French troops engaged, 28,085 became casualties; of 132,000 Russians, "there is nothing to show that its loss was greater than that of its antagonist. Although the number of killed and wounded at Borodino was greater, numerically, than at Waterloo and Gettysburg, the percentage of loss was very much less."[13] It is as though Fox is determined to raise a homegrown American red badge of courage that will stand up proudly in comparison to the Old World.

The point Fox makes, though, is a valid one. It is battle deaths as a *percentage* of men engaged that defines the intensity of combat and thus the lethal risk to individual soldiers. Looking at the history of warfare generally (and particularly over the period of nation-state rather than dynastic conflict), we see that the sharp end (those who actually experience combat) tends to get smaller as a proportion of the total number of men involved. The administrative, supply-and-support "tail," on the other hand, becomes larger. (This "progress," ironically, increases the risk to the *combat* soldier of becoming a casualty.)

Obviously, averages do not reflect what we might call "localized risk" where certain units took massive casualties. The infantry could expect to take about 14 percent casualties (an average taken over twenty-five major battles), compared with 5–10 percent for artillerymen.[14] But it was not unusual for an infantry unit involved in the front of an attack to take 50–60 percent casualties.

For example, on day two of Gettysburg the First Minnesota was ordered to make a suicidal counterattack against the Confederates after they had broken the Union line around the Peach Orchard area. In some accounts, 262 Minnesotans started off to attack the 1,600 Alabamians under General Cadmus Wilcox, and 225 Federals became casualties (85.8 percent)[15]—"the highest percentage of casualties suffered by any Union regiment in a single engagement in the entire war," according to a historian of the regiment. He adds that the "annals of war contain no parallel to this charge. In its desperate valor, complete execution, successful result [the rupture in the Union line was plugged], and in its sacrifice of men in proportion to the number engaged, authentic history has no record with which it can be compared."[16]

Other Union units also suffered horrifically. The Irish Brigade attacking Marye's Heights at the battle of Fredericksburg had 1,150 men hit out of a total of 1,400 (82 percent).[17] The First Maine Heavy Artillery Regiment, being used as attack infantry against the Petersburg defenses, lost 632 out of 900 (70.2 percent).[18] The Fifth New Hampshire sustained more killed in action than any other Union regiment during the whole war— 295 men—and, says Fox, they "occurred entirely in aggressive, hard, stand-up fighting; none of it happened in routs or through blunders."[19]

On the Confederate side, the First Texas took 82 percent casualties at Antietam (Sharpsburg) and had the highest percentage of *killed* to men engaged (20 percent) of any Confederate regiment in a single battle during the whole war; the Twenty-First Georgia lost 198 out of its 242 effectives at the second battle of Bull Run (Manassas)—just shy of 82 percent—and with 16 percent of its effectives killed in that battle was the second in the mortuarial league table for Confederate regiments in a single battle.

Books have been written about what might be called the addiction of Confederate soldiers to the attack, as though lemminglike, they looked for a tactical cliff over which they could throw themselves in some death-embracing ecstasy, responding, so the argument goes, to a Berserker gene passed down from their ancient Celtic forebears.[20] It is a theory that has been much derided (the North, too, after all, did not shy away from taking extraordinary casualties in frontal assaults, as Marye's Heights, Kennesaw Mountain, Cold Harbor, and many others attest. Nor was there a shortage of men of Celtic origin dressed in blue), but there is an interesting idea at its root: that soldiers may be swept to their deaths by the powerful undercurrents of cultural heritage. The frontal attack becomes not only a tactical option but also one driven by expectations of manly valor and national pride. General D. H. Hill remarked on Confederate tactics in the earlier phases of the war: "We were very lavish of blood in those days, and it was thought to be a great thing to charge a battery of artillery or an earth-work lined with infantry . . . the kind of grandeur the South could not afford."[21]

The addiction to the frontal attack had long antecedents, but for the officer class of the American Civil War its most recent and nurturing wellspring was revolutionary and Napoleonic France. Officers who would become influential in both the Confederacy and the Union had attended West Point, where Francophile sentiment was strong, and many had been influenced by the writings of such military theorists as Henri Jomini (a Swiss who fought in the French army attached to Ney's and Napoleon's staffs) and others like him, who placed great emphasis on the moral virtue (courage, obedience, patriotic self-sacrifice) as well as the tactical benefit (covering the killing zone quickly and ejecting the enemy at the point of the bayonet) of the swift and determined frontal attack. Implicit in this philosophy was a rejection of the fancy footwork of the limited warfare of the earlier eighteenth century and an embrace of concentrated force and confrontation: an embodiment of what Victor Davis Hanson calls "the Western way of war."

It was a philosophy that looked back to the heroic tradition of the ancient Romans, with its emphasis on sacrificial courage in the service of the state. It embraced a way of fighting total war, furiously energetic and uncompromising, in the service of an ideological cause, be that revolutionary or imperial France. Although it drew its inspiration from the past, it would also inspire soldiers of the future, be they Confederate, Union, or, in a much more terrible incarnation, military theorists and generals (particularly the French) of World War I.

It is worth remembering, however, that tactical orthodoxy has to be based, to some extent, on the successes of experience. Not all frontal attacks ended up like the Confederate attack at Malvern

Hill in 1862, or Pickett's charge at Gettysburg, or the Irish Brigade at Marye's Heights. There were also many successes, such as Jackson's bayonet charge at the first battle of Bull Run (Manassas) and the Union assault on Missionary Ridge in 1863, as well as the Confederate attack on the first day of Shiloh.

To a large extent the emphasis on the frontal attack was a reflection, as it always had been, of the inadequacies of weapons to inflict battle-winning casualties at long distance. The battle could only be won, it was firmly believed, by literally driving the enemy off the field. The killing had to be done close up. But conventional wisdom has it that the "unprecedentedly high" casualties of the Civil War were due to innovations in weapons technology, particularly the rifled musket, which increased the range of lethality, bringing death to the advancing attackers at much greater distance than hitherto—Napoleonic tactics smacking up against modern weaponry. And yet there is plenty of evidence that the lethality of the rifled musket was less impressive than its specifications might have us believe.

Both armies had British-produced Enfield or American-produced Springfield rifle-bored muzzle-loading muskets (although it was not until 1863 that the Confederacy could claim to have comprehensively rid itself of old smoothbores and, in fact, at the start of the war even the Union relied heavily on smoothbores as rifled muskets tended to be the preserve of regular soldiers).[22] The South had a preponderance of Enfields (it bought three hundred thousand from Britain) because its relatively weak manufacturing capacity made it more reliant on imports.[23] The caliber was a little smaller than that of the Springfield, and the gun was a little lighter, but to all intents and purposes the weapons were pretty evenly matched.

Compared with the smoothbore, the rifled musket was a great improvement. A trained rifleman, firing a conoidal slug under controlled conditions, had a fifty-fifty chance of hitting a man-sized target at 500 yards.[24] If sighted at 300 yards, the bullet of a rifled musket described an arc, within which were two killing zones. The first was the initial 75 yards in which the bullet was on its upward trajectory and could be expected to hit a man of average height. Between 75 and 250 yards its arc took it above head height. Between 250 and 350 yards it descended into its second killing zone, capable of hitting a soldier's head at 250 yards, his torso at 300, and a lower limb at 350.[25]

Battle conditions alter pretty much everything about shooting. Men under pressure, even if well-trained, cannot achieve the accuracy or rate of fire of the firing range. In the Civil War, "many recruits went into battle without having fired a single practice round. . . . Whether firing a Model 1863 muzzle-loader or a gas-operated M1, the average citizen cannot hit the proverbial bull in the behind with a bass fiddle."[26] A sentimental notion persists, however, as it does among some historians of the War of Independence, that Americans had a natural familiarity with muskets because, unlike their European counterparts, they were raised as hunters and would already have had a great facility with firearms.[27] It is true that the South was largely rural and that the single largest group in the army of the North was of farming background (about 48 percent)[28] and therefore might be expected to be familiar with hunting guns. But even for those with some hunting experience the chaos and psychological pressure of battle makes it difficult to translate those skills into combat effectiveness. "The huntsman who loads carefully and then stalks his inoffensive prey is surely in a very different state of mind from the soldier who has to fire off forty rounds in double-quick time against an enemy regiment which is busy returning the compliment. The assumptions of the close-order firefight . . . are surely located in a quite different universe from the genteel expectations of game shooting."[29]

The physical exertion of repeated firing, the vicious recoil, the relative intricacy of reloading procedures, and lack of training all tended to lower the lethality of the rifled musket. A soldier of the Twenty-Sixth North Carolina Regiment on the first day of Gettysburg described a specific difficulty of fighting with a rifled muzzle loader: "[The] men had difficulty in ramming down their cartridges, so slick was the iron ramrod in hands thoroughly wet with perspiration. All expedients were resorted to, but mainly jabbing the ram-rods against the ground and rocks."[30] During the battle of Shiloh in 1862, the Englishman Henry M. Stanley, fighting as a gentleman volunteer in the Dixie Grays (and in later life to become famous as a journalist and explorer), described the "impossibility" of advancing and firing accurately, "owing to our labouring hearts, and the jarring and excitement." The surgeon of the Second Maryland observed that men in battle "drop their cartridges. They load and forget to cap their pieces and get half a dozen rounds into their muskets thinking they have fired them off. Most of them just load and fire without any consciousness of shooting at anything in particular."[31]

Some military theorists before the war predicted a revolution in infantry tactics because of the theoretical extension of range and accuracy over the old smoothbores. Battles would start sooner and would cover a larger area—a prediction of the "empty" battlefield of the twentieth century—but despite the technical possibility of accuracy up to 1,000 yards and "irresistible" fire at 600, the rifled musket was used, as the smoothbore musket in an earlier era had been, at fairly close range. "What is much less clear is whether or not the average soldier in combat actually obtained very much benefit from these improvements, since many of the same factors which had limited range and accuracy in Napoleonic times continued to apply throughout the Civil War. Fields of fire were often very short, the soldiers unskilled in the use of their weapons, and the officers were anxious not to engage in indecisive long range fire . . . tactical theory still rested upon the idea of massed fire at close range."[32]

Of a sample of 113 actions in which range was mentioned by eyewitnesses, 62 percent were at 100 yards or less, and none took place at more than 500 yards.[33] In short, infantrymen were more likely to be killed by musket fire not because the rifled musket was more accurate at longer range but because they were in a confined killing zone close to their adversary. At New Hope Church on May 27, 1864, for example, Sherman sent in Hazen's brigade against a well-established Confederate defensive line. A firefight ensued across a narrow killing zone that, try as they might, the Federals could not penetrate. They left about a third of their men dead or wounded in that zone not more than 15 feet from the rebel line; no one got closer than 10 feet.[34]

If the enhanced range of a rifled musket was not a deciding factor, what about the rate of fire? Compared to the smoothbore, the rifled musket could not deliver lead as speedily. It took longer to ram the ball down against the groove of the rifling. An experienced soldier armed with a smoothbore could get off about four shots a minute in battle conditions, whereas his counterpart with the rifle might manage three.[35] Breechloaders such as the Sharps could increase that rate by about three times, and repeating rifles even more: twenty rounds per minute for the Spencer and about fifty for the Henry. However, these faster-firing rifles, although enormously significant for the future of warfare, had only a limited impact on the general equation of Civil War combat. The South had few of them (and those were captured rather than manufactured), and the North mainly deployed them in their cavalry arm, where they could be highly effective in dismounted action, as Buford's cavalrymen proved in the opening phase of Gettysburg.

In any event, one of the military establishment's main objections to fast-firing rifles was that they promoted the wasteful expenditure of ammunition, which was, after all, a major problem even with single-shot muzzle loaders. The gun maker Oliver Winchester put up a self-serving but prescient defense of repeating rifles that became a tactical given for all future wars in which America was involved—"the greater the expenditure of ammunition the happier the soldier."

> If, as we think, it is a consciousness of power that makes men brave, and a sense of imminent peril that makes "cowards of us all" . . . it is not unreasonable to suppose that such a weapon would give a soldier the courage and coolness needed to send each of his fifteen shots with more unerring certainty than his trembling opponent could send with his single shot? If *to save ammunition,* it is essential that every soldier should remain for sixty seconds while reloading, a helpless target, to receive his opponent's fire from one to fifteen shots, why not reverse the order of progress and turn the ingenuity of inventors to the production of a gun that will require twice the length of time or more to reload, and thus *double the saving of ammunition?* Saving of life does not appear an element worthy of consideration in this connection. Yet this is West Point opinion.[36]

The task of the field commander was often, ironically, to prevent men from firing, at least until they were at close range. The Confederate attack at Gaines's Mill in 1862 was a classic example. A high-risk, high-casualty attack was ordered and the men were to charge "in double-quick time, with trailed arms [the weapon carried horizontally, i.e., not in firing position] and without firing. Had these orders not been strictly obeyed the assault would have been a failure." The oncoming lines took a beating (one thousand casualties), but no one stopped to return fire, "and not a step faltered . . . the pace became more rapid every moment; when the men were within thirty yards . . . a wild yell answered the roar of the Federal musketry and they rushed for the works."[37] Speed is a cornerstone of assault tactics, whether it is Gaines's Mill or Passchendaele or Iwo Jima or Omaha Beach. The massed frontal attack will result in many men being killed; but if done at speed, there will be fewer killed than if the attackers stopped en route to engage in a firefight. Stopping midway simply increases the time the attacker is in the killing zone, and no matter how seductive a protective shelter might be, it could be fatal, as Henry Stanley discovered during the attack of the Dixie Grays at Shiloh:

> Continuing our advance, we . . . were met by a furious storm of bullets, poured on us from the long line of bluecoats. . . . After being exposed for a few seconds to this fearful downpour, we heard the order to "Lie down, men, and continue your firing!" Before me was a prostrate tree, about fifteen inches in diameter, with a narrow strip of light between it and the ground. Behind this shelter a dozen of us flung ourselves. The security it appeared to offer restored me to my individuality. We could fight, and think, and observe, better than out in the open. But it was a terrible period! How the cannon bellowed, and their shells plunged and bounded, and flew with screeching hisses over us! . . . I marveled, as I heard the unintermitting patter, snip, thud, and hum of the bullets, how anyone could live under this raining death. I could hear the balls beating a merciless tattoo on the outer surface of the log. . . . One here and there, found its way under the log, and buried itself in a comrade's body. One man raised his chest, as if to yawn, and jostled me. I turned to him, and saw that a bullet had gored his whole face, and penetrated into his chest. Another ball struck a man a deadly rap on the head, and he turned on his back and showed his ghastly white face to the sky.

"It is getting too warm boys!" cried a soldier, and he uttered a vehement curse upon keeping soldiers hugging the ground until every ounce of courage was chilled. He lifted his head a little too high, and a bullet skimmed over the top of the log and hit him fairly in the centre of his forehead, and he fell heavily on his face. But his thought had been instantaneously general; and the officers, with one voice, ordered the charge; and cries of "Forward, forward!" raised us . . . and changed the complexion of our feelings. The pulse of action beat feverishly once more; and, though overhead was crowded with peril, we were unable to give it so much attention as when we lay stretched on the ground.[38]

The frontal charge is a desperate thing; and running through so many Civil War battles is a melancholy acceptance of inevitable death: "Every man vieing with his fellowman, in steadiness of step and correct alignment, the officers giving low and cautionary commands, many knowing that it was their last hour on earth, but without hesitating moved forward to their inevitable doom and defeat," comments Lieutenant L. D. Young, Fourth Kentucky, on being sent into a suicidal attack by General Braxton Bragg at Murfreesboro (Stones River), on December 31, 1862. And surely there is no more heartbreaking image of this stoicism than the veterans of the Twentieth Maine at the Wilderness watching the "spurts of dust . . . like the big drops of a coming shower along a dusty road" that were erupting all over the field, and then pulling down their caps over their eyes as though this shielding would in some magical way protect them from the murderous storm into which they were about to advance. Or the Irish Brigade advancing up toward Marye's Heights at Fredericksburg, heads bowed into the fury.

There was also a fatally self-reinforcing element to the linear attack with men moving "elbow-to-elbow"—something that, after all, increased their chances of being hit. Men packed together and highly influenced by their peer group become more controllable and less able to make individual decisions about their own fates: "Not to put too fine a point on it, you could ensure that men stood and fought—and died—if you had them all enclosed in serried ranks."[39] William A. Ketcham of the Thirteenth Indiana describes how the influence of his comrades' opinions channeled him toward the acceptance of death in combat:

> After I had got used to fighting and could appreciate my surroundings free from the tremendous excitement in the blood, of the smell of battle, I knew perfectly well all the time that if a cannon ball struck in the right place it would kill or maim. . . . I knew it was always liable to strike me, but I always went where I was ordered to go and the others went, and when I was ordered to run and the others ran, I ran. I had a greater fear of being supposed to be as afraid as I was than I had of being seriously hurt and that is a great deal of sustaining power in an emergency.[40]

Confederate general John Gordon describes how the enemy was allowed to come "within a few rods (a rod equals 16.5 feet)" and then "my rifle flamed and roared in the Federals' faces . . . the effect was appalling. The entire front line, with few exceptions, went down in the consuming blast."[41] At Antietam, Frank Holsinger recalled how the Sixth Georgia rose up from behind a fence and poured a volley "within thirty feet" that decimated our ranks fully one-half; the regiment was demoralized."[42]

Close-order firing also had a devastating effect on men in column, especially when delivered by an adversary arrayed in line. A young company commander of the Sixty-Third Ohio Volunteers describes an action on the second day of the battle of Corinth, October 4, 1862:

The enemy had to come over a bluffish bank a few yards in front of me and as soon as I saw their heads, still coming slowly, I jumped up and said: "Company H, get up." The column was then in full view and only about thirty yards distant. . . . Just in front of me was a bush three or four feet high with sear leaves on it. Hitting this with my sword, I said: "Boys, give them a volley just over this. Ready! Aim! (and jumping around my company to get from the front of their guns) Fire!" In a few seconds the fire was continued along the whole line.

It seems to me that the fire of my company had cut down the head of the column that struck us as deep back as my company was· long. As the smoke cleared away, there was apparently ten yards square of a mass of struggling bodies and butternut clothes. Their column appeared to reel like a rope shaken at the end.[43]

In fact the tactical orthodoxy, as expressed by the leading West Point theorist of the day, Dennis Hart Mahan, writing in 1836, deplored the use of column because it offered a more concentrated target than attack in line: "In a very deep order, the troops readily become huddled by an inequality of motion; the head alone fights . . . and a fire of artillery on it causes the most frightful ravages."[44] Its other disadvantage, as French columns during the Napoleonic Wars discovered, was that it could only present a small "face" of muskets as most men were unable to present and fire because they were boxed in.

And yet the suicidal bloodletting of frontal attacks in great sweeping sacrificial lines has to be set against the merciful ineptitude of most soldiers. It takes a lot of lead to kill a man. There was a natural temptation among the inexperienced soldiers who made up the majority on both sides to fire off their muskets with profligate disregard for any tangible result. Captain Frank Holsinger of the Nineteenth US Colored Infantry observed:

> How natural it is for a man to suppose that if a gun is discharged, he or someone is sure to be hit. He soon finds, however, that the only damage done, in ninety-nine cases out of a hundred, the only thing killed is the powder! It is not infrequently that a whole line of battle (this among raw troops) will fire upon an advancing line, and no perceptible damage ensue. They wonder how men can stand such treatment, when really they have done no damage save the terrific noise incident to the discharge. To undertake to say how many discharges are necessary to the death of a soldier in a battle would be presumptuous, but I have frequently heard the remark that it took a man's weight in lead to kill him.[45]

Captain W. F. Hinman, a Union officer at Murfreesboro (1862) described an encounter at long distance:

> Within half an hour we stirred up the enemy's cavalry. Firing began at once, and continued throughout the day. The companies on the skirmish line were kept busy, but as scarcely anybody got hurt they thought it was a good sport. . . . The shooting made a great deal of noise, although it was about as harmless as a Fourth of July fusillade. But our skirmishers blazed away incessantly. We marched over the body of one rebel who had been killed. Shots enough were fired that day to destroy half of Bragg's army.[46]

A Confederate officer, I. Herman, observed that most infantrymen went through their allocation of cartridges during an engagement of any length. Five thousand men might easily expend 200,000 rounds in a few hours (an average of 40 rounds per man), and in his experience it took 400 rounds for every enemy killed. General Rosencrans at Murfreesboro estimated 145 shots to inflict one casualty (and not necessarily a fatality).[47] No wonder General James Longstreet could inform his less experienced troops that though "the fiery noise of battle is indeed most terrifying, and seems to threaten universal ruin it is not so destructive as it seems, and few soldiers after all are slain. . . . Let officers and men, even under the most formidable fire, preserve a quiet demeanor and self-possessed temper."[48]

George Neese, a rebel gunner, found it "astonishing and wholly incomprehensible" that so many could come through the storm unscathed—"how men standing in line, firing at each other incessantly for hours like they did today, can escape with so few killed and wounded, for when Jackson's infantry emerged from the sulphurous bank of battle smoke that hung along the line the regiment appeared as complete as they were before the fight."[49]

Looking at casualties through the rose-colored lens of the telescope, we see that at Gettysburg, the bloodiest Civil War battle in terms of the total number of casualties, 81 percent of Union and 76 percent of Confederate soldiers came through the three days unhurt. But through the other more sanguine lens we see that one in five Federals and one in four Confederates engaged in the battle became casualties and one in thirty Federals and one in fifteen Confederates were killed.[50]

Although musketry may have been wayward, it was overwhelmingly the main source of death in a Civil War battle. Union field surgeon Charles Johnson declared, "I think wounds from bullets were five times as frequent as those from all other sources. Shell wounds were next in frequency, and then came those from grape and canister. I never saw a wound from a bayonet thrust and but one made by a sword in the hands of an enemy."[51] *The Medical and Surgical History of the War of the Rebellion,* published in six volumes between 1870 and 1888 under the auspices of the surgeon general of the US Army, covers Union and Confederate experience. Of the 246,712 wounds from weapons that were treated during the war, the vast majority (just over 231,000) were from small arms. Next came artillery-induced wounds (13,518), followed by a very small number (922) of bayonet wounds. Obviously, if the wounds were treated the soldier had not been killed outright, but the proportion is at least an indicator of the most likely causes of death. The sites of the wounds also tell a story. Most of the wounds (over 70 percent) recorded in the *Medical and Surgical History* were to the arms and legs, which is understandable because they would have been the more survivable and therefore recorded in wound statistics, although amputation might well claim a life later. In one group of 54 amputees, 32 (60 percent) subsequently died.[52]

It is not surprising that a smaller percentage of wounds were to the face, head, and neck (10.7 percent) and 18.4 percent to the torso because men hit in these areas tended to be killed outright and therefore not become a wounded statistic. As Charles Johnson observed:

> When a minie ball struck a bone it almost never failed to fracture and shatter the contiguous bony structure, and it was rarely that only a round perforation, the size of the bullet, resulted. When a joint was the part the bullet struck, the results were especially serious. . . . Of course, the same was true of wounds of the abdomen and head, though to a much greater degree. Indeed, recovery from wounds of the abdomen and brain almost never occurred. One of the prime objects of the Civil War surgeon was to remove the missile, and, in doing this, he practically never failed to infect the part with his dirty hands and instrument.
>
> When Captain William M. Colby of my company was

brought from the firing-line to our Division Hospital he was
in a comatose state from a bullet that had penetrated his
brain through the upper portion of the occipital bone [the
base of the skull]. The first thing our surgeon did was to run
his index finger its full length into the wound; and this
without even ordinary washing. Next he introduced a dirty
bullet probe. The patient died a day or two later.[53]

Some, though, lived to disprove the rule. Corporal Edson D.
Bemis of the Twelfth Massachusetts Infantry was shot in the left
elbow at Antietam, gut-shot at the Wilderness, and then, almost
at the war's end, shot through the left temple by the ear so that
when he arrived at the hospital, brain matter was oozing from the
wound. After the ball had been removed, the patient began to
recover and by 1870 could write with splendid equanimity, "I am
still in the land of the living. . . . My memory is affected, and I
cannot hear as well as I could before I was wounded."[54]

A head shot was usually fatal, but a body wound might feel
surprisingly innocuous. US Seventh Michigan cavalryman A. B.
Isham reports that the "first sensation of a gunshot wound is not
one of pain. The feeling is simply one of shock, without discomfort, accompanied by a peculiar tingling, as though a slight electric current was playing about the site of injury. Quickly ensues a
marked sense of numbness, involving a considerable area around
the wounded part." Another soldier remembers "no acute sensation of pain, not even any distinct shock, only an instantaneous
consciousness of having been struck; then my breath came hard
and labored, with a croup-like sound."[55] A truly terrible experience, though, was to see the look on the face of a mortally hit
comrade—"a stare of woeful amazement," recalls one soldier,
while another describes a comrade who had been hit in the head,
"gasping in that peculiar, almost indescribable way that a mortally

wounded man has. I shall never forget the pleading expression, speechless yet imploring."[56]

★   ★   ★

TROOPS AND THEIR field officers were caught, as they have been throughout history, in an awful dilemma: on the one hand, having to obey the iron dictates of grand tactics (particularly frontal assaults against well-prepared defenses) that would, in all likelihood, result in many deaths; and on the other, improvising localized tactics that might save their lives but must not be seen, by their lords and masters, to compromise the mission. The terrible experience of the frontal attack led to compensatory tactics that would be repeated in the First World War. Entrenchment was an obvious one, but there was also a movement away from mass to more fluid, fragmented attacking units, which also became a characteristic of World War I combat as the war progressed. More sustained skirmishing as well as attacking in rushes became more frequent. At Spotsylvania in May 1864 the Twelfth New Hampshire took 338 casualties (of whom a staggering 30 percent were killed) out of a starting complement of 549 men; an observer notes that "the terrible experience of the last hour and a half has taught them a lesson that each one is now practicing; for every man has his tree behind which he is fighting."[57] Charles W. Bardeen, a Union soldier at the battle, illustrated the tactical issue: "[A] heavy artillery brigade that had come into active service for the first time was ordered to recapture a baggage train. The general actually formed his men in solid front and charged through the woods. . . . Every confederate bullet was sure of its man, and the dead lay thick; I helped bury . . . more than a hundred. It even failed with its five thousand men to capture the train, and then our poor little brigade, hardly twelve hundred altogether, was sent in, and advanced rapidly, every man keeping under cover in the thick woods and brought in the train, hardly losing a man."[58]

Confederate tactics, too, cannot be seen only in terms of heroic but suicidal frontal attacks. Left to their own devices, men will adapt if it increases their chances of survival, especially if it happens also to decrease their opponent's chances. Captain John W. DeForest, in a faithful though fictionalized account, described how his rebel opponents "aimed better than our men; they covered themselves (in case of need) more carefully and effectively; they could move in a swarm, without much care for alignment or touch of elbows ["touch of elbows" was the standard tightly formed advance prescribed for bayonet attacks]. In short, they fought more like redskins, or like hunters, than we."[59]

★   ★   ★

THERE WAS A parasitical relationship between Civil War artillery and its primary victim, the infantry. Although there had been many innovations in the science of gunnery, particularly in the form of rifled guns and exploding shells, the main source of death was still, as it had been throughout the black-powder era, solid shot delivered either in multiple doses via canister or in one megadose via cannonball. For the artillery to be effective, the infantry had to play along. The guns feasted on men who, through tactical convention, were all too often presented in tight, massed formations, elbow-to-elbow in frontal assault, and artillery fed heartily at close range. Charles Cheney of the Second Wisconsin Infantry at first Bull Run (Manassas) tried to describe what it was like to be under close artillery fire: "None but those who saw it know anything about it. . . . There were hundreds shot down right in my sight; some had their heads shot off from their shoulders by cannon balls, others were shot in two . . . and others shot through the legs and arms. . . . Cannon balls were flying like hail."[60]

"Death from the bullet is ghastly," writes a soldier of the Fourteenth Indiana, "but to see a man's brains dashed out at your side by a grape shot and another body severed by a screeching cannon ball is truly appalling." The smaller balls of canister shot certainly accounted for many more deaths than solid shot or exploding shell, but they lacked the horrific grandeur of a cannonball: "It is a pitiful sight to see man or beast struck with one of those terrible things."[61] The "shock-and-awe" factor was reinforced by the thunderous boom of solid shot, and demoralization was almost as important as lethality: "Dead men did not run to the rear spreading panic and demoralization."[62]

Most artillery on both sides was old-style smoothbore, the aptly named 12-pound Napoleon, 1857 model, firing a 4.62-inch-diameter ball, being the workhorse. The North had many more rifled pieces, such as the Parrott, which gave it something of an advantage in terms of counterbattery actions because of its superior accuracy. On one occasion, in a spectacular example of artillery sniping, Confederate general Leonidas Polk was practically cut in two by a carefully aimed shell from a Hotchkiss rifled artillery piece at Pine Mountain on June 14, 1864. Like musketry, gunnery lethality had more to do with quantity and proximity than with accuracy. It was the uncomplicated and unfussy smoothbore cannon that was the omnivore of the Civil War battlefield. It could be loaded faster than a rifled piece and be switched from solid shot to canister with deadly fluency.

For attacking infantry there were three distinct artillery killing zones to be traversed.

Zone 1: If their starting point was 1,500 yards out from the enemy cannon (a not uncommon jumping-off point), there would first have been approximately 850 yards to traverse (taking about ten minutes at regular pace), within which they might be hit by both percussion-fused shells that exploded on the ground (or not, depending on the reliability of the fuse and the softness of the ground) and shrapnel-like spherical shot that exploded above the attacking troops and scattered pieces of the shell casing as well as the seventy-plus iron balls it contained. During this time each piece of the opposing artillery might get off fifteen to twenty rounds, and the first casualties would begin to fall, although not yet in significant numbers. The problem for the artillerist was that the fuses for the spherical case were crude and the explosion could not always be accurately predicted, a technical difficulty that was compounded when the target was moving rapidly forward. For maximum lethality, spherical shot needed to explode about 75 yards in front and 15–20 feet above the target, which was a challenge for the technology of the time.

Zone 2: The next 300 yards would be taken at the quick step, and during those approximately three and a half minutes, each of the defending cannon would have time to send seven balls plowing their furrows through the oncoming rank and file. With the attackers now at 350 yards away, the gunners would quickly switch to canister. Over the next 250 yards the attackers, now moving at the double-quick step, would have to endure about nine blasts from each gun (for solid shot and shell, two rounds a minute was considered reasonable, compared with three a minute for canister).[63]

Zone 3: For those attackers who had stayed on their feet, there would be an appalling last 100 yards taken at the full-out charge and lasting about thirty seconds, during which time the cannoneers could get off one round of canister at point-blank range.[64] If the situation had become especially tricky for the defenders, the cannon might be "double-shotted"—two cans fired at the same time.

A Civil War soldier, if killed by artillery, would most likely be hit at close range—cut down by canister. Longer-range gunnery tended to be much less lethal, although the Union shells fired at those Confederate troops massing for the attack on the Union center on the third day of Gettysburg caused a considerable number of casualties. A British observer, Arthur Fremantle, embedded with Lee's army, noted the large number of men who had been hit while in the woods on Seminary Ridge about a mile from the Union guns on Cemetery Ridge. "I rode on through the woods. . . . The further I got, the greater became the number of the wounded. At last I came to a perfect stream of them . . . in numbers as great as a crowd in Oxford Street in the middle of the day."[65] In contrast, the Confederate preattack bombardment on the Union center on the third day of Gettysburg, although delivered by more than 150 guns, was a failure. It had an insignificant impact on the Union infantry, who were sheltered by the wall and topography atop Cemetery Ridge. And partly due to some deft maneuvering of the Union artillery, the bombardment also failed to interdict the Federal cannon, which would reassemble and inflict terrible casualties on the attackers. A Federal artilleryman scorned the Confederate bombardment: "Viewed as a display of fireworks, the rebel practice was entirely successful, but as a military demonstration it was the biggest humbug of the season."[66]

In some ways the progression of the fighting on the third day of Gettysburg was a chilling preview of many a First World War battle: the artillery barrage that was meant, but failed, to soften up the defenders; the massed attackers moving at an ordered pace across the deep killing ground of no-man's-land, where they were vulnerable to shrapnel; and the intense defensive firepower at close quarters that destroyed them. An eyewitness on the Federal side describes how the attackers were pulled into a vortex of destruction: "Our skirmishers open a sputtering fire along the front, and, fighting, retire upon the main line. . . . Then the thunders of our guns, first Arnold's, then Cushing's and Woodruff's and the rest, shake and reverberate again through the air, and their sounding shells smite the enemy. . . . All our valuable guns are now active, and from the fire of shells, as the range grows shorter and shorter, they change to shrapnel, and from shrapnel to canister, without wavering or halt, the hardy lines of the enemy move on."[67] A private of the Eighth Virginia remembered from halfway across the valley between the ridges the terrific intensity of the artillery response: "When half the valley had been traversed by the leading column there came such a storm of grape and canister as seemed to take away the breath, causing whole regiments to stoop like men running in a violent sleet."[68] Captain Andrew Cowan of the First New York Independent Battery describes hitting the Confederates with canister at 20 yards: "My last charge (a double header) literally swept the enemy from my front."[69]

★　★　★

IT IS PERHAPS indicative of the overall picture of officer mortality in the Civil War that the first and last general officers to be killed (Brigadier General Robert S. Garnett, hit by a minié ball at Corrick's Ford, on July 13, 1861, and Brigadier General Robert C. Tyler, killed by a sharpshooter on April 16, 1865, at Fort Tyler, Georgia) were both fighting for the South. Where more ordinary Confederate soldiers were killed in proportion to their Union counterparts, so too were Confederate officers. One explanation is that there were simply more Confederate officers in proportion to the men they led, compared with the North. In forty-eight battles analyzed by Thomas Livermore, the officer percentage of the Confederate troops was between 6.5 and 11 percent; on the Union side it ran between 4 and 7 percent.[70]

Other explanations hark back to cultural differences between

South and North. For the officer class of the South a few cultural streams flowed together. There was the "knightly" ethos of the southern gentleman-officer inspired, for example, by the medieval romances of Sir Walter Scott, which enjoyed a particular popularity.[71] Young blades from the South embraced a cavalier swagger, quick to take offense and unhesitatingly willing to put their lives on the line or to take a life should honor demand it. A traveler in the South noted that the "barbarous baseness and cruelty of public opinion [that] dooms young men, when challenged, to fight. They must fight, kill or be killed, and that for some petty offence beneath the notice of the law."[72]

Northern officers, by contrast, were seen by the South as percentage players, businessmen at war. As a Confederate diarist puts it: "The war is one between the Puritan & Cavalier"—the flamboyant Celt versus the dull Anglo-Saxon.[73] Although most of this is utter tosh, for Southern nostalgists past and present, heady with Dixiephilia, it can be intoxicating tosh. In any event, such arguments are meant to explain the higher mortality among Confederate officers.

The underlying truth was that officers of both North and South shared a common code that held them to a very high level of commitment and risk. In the Union army the ratio of officers to men was 1 to 28, but the ratio of officers to men killed in battle was 1 to 17. At Shiloh, 21.3 percent of Union officers became casualties, compared with 17.9 percent of men, and at Gettysburg the proportion was 27 percent to 21 percent.[74]

None, not even the most senior, exempted themselves from the danger of being killed—and an extraordinarily large number of general officers were killed in battle on both sides. Sixty-seven Union general officers (including 11 major generals) were killed outright or died of wounds. Fifty-five percent (235 out of 425) of Confederate general officers became casualties, and of those

73* were killed, including 3 lieutenant generals, 6 major generals, and 1 Army commander—A. S. Johnston, killed at Shiloh. Fifty-four (70 percent) died leading their men in attacks.[75] In one battle alone—Franklin, Tennessee, in April 1863—5 Confederate general officers were killed on the field and 1 later died of wounds.[76] At Gettysburg, 7 Union general officers (including those brevetted) and 5 Confederates were killed or died from wounds received in the battle.[77]

It does not do justice to the bravery of the officers of the North, however, to suggest that such sacrifice was in some way characteristic only of the Confederate officer corps, as in "The Confederacy's code of loyalty, like that of earlier Celts, required officers to lead their men into battle. . . . Confederate Colonel George Grenfell told a foreigner that 'the only way in which an officer could acquire influence over the Confederate soldier was by his personal conduct under fire. They hold a man in great esteem who in action sets them an example of contempt for danger.' "[78] Exactly the same sentiments were applicable to the North.

An insouciant attitude toward death was highly esteemed among the officer class of both sides, and there are many examples of sangfroid in the face of extreme danger. Indeed some, such as George Custer, relished testing their staff officers in "an almost sadistic imposition of the leader's courage on others," by leading staff parades that exposed them to fire. Any who flinched were subjected to his withering scorn. Union cavalry general Alfred

---

* According to William H. Fox, *Regimental Losses in the American Civil War in America: 1861–65* (Albany, NY: Albany Publishing, 1889), 571. Grady MacWhiney and Perry D. Jamieson put it at 77 (*Attack and Die: Civil War Military Tactics and the Southern Heritage* [Tuscaloosa: University of Alabama Press, 1982]), 14, as does Gerald F. Linderman, *Embattled Courage: The Experience of Combat in the American Civil War* (New York: Free Press, 1987), 22.

Torbert also insisted on dragging his staff on tours of the front line (his chief medical officer was killed on one such outing), and on the Confederate side, D. H. Hill liked to "treat" his staff to enemy attention.[79] Grant (without any of the theatrics of a Custer, Torbert, or Hill) also displayed conspicuous coolness when he and his staff came under fire at Shiloh. Leander Stillwell saw him, "on horseback, of course, accompanied by his staff, and was evidently making a personal examination of his lines. He went by us in a gallop, riding between us and the battery, at the head of his staff. The battery was then broadly engaged, shot and shell were whizzing overhead, and cutting off the limbs of trees, but Grant rode through the storm with perfect indifference, seemingly paying no more attention to the missiles than if they had been paper wads."[80]

Although occasionally tarnished by ego and showing off, these displays also had a practical purpose—to get men to fight, either by encouraging them into willing emulation or shaming them into begrudging imitation. Confederate major general Richard Taylor (president Zachary Taylor's son and a very gifted tactician), commanding raw troops who were being hammered by shot and shell as they cowered within their breastworks during an attempted relief of the siege of Vicksburg, realized that it was "absolutely necessary to give the men some morale; and, mounting the breastwork, I made a cigarette, struck fire with my briquet [cigarette lighter] and walked up and down, smoking. Near the line was a low tree with spreading branches, which a young officer, Bradford by name, proposed to climb, as to have a better view. I gave him my field glass, and this plucky youngster sat in his tree as quietly as in a chimney corner, though the branches were cut away [by bullets]. These examples . . . gave confidence to the men, who began to expose themselves."[81]

But there was often a price to pay. A Union officer, desperately trying to halt the retreat after the defeat at Chickamauga, "would walk deliberately up to the rail pile and stand erect and

exposed till his men rallied to him. For hours he did this," until he
was killed.[82] And with a higher chance of being killed compared
with that which his men faced, an officer had to come to terms
with it—one way or another. Fatalism helped. Hilary A. Herbert,
colonel of the Eighth Alabama (wounded at the Wilderness and
after the war, secretary of the navy), was asked if he dwelled much
on the shortened odds of being killed due to his prominence on
the field:

> Yes, very frequently. But why do you ask?
>
> Well, I thought from [the] fact that you never say any-
> thing about it, and then for the manner in which you expose
> yourself . . . recklessly, that you had an idea that you were in
> no danger of being killed.
>
> O, no . . . I know that the probabilities are that a colonel
> of an infantry regiment . . . who does his duty, will in all
> probability be either killed or seriously wounded. I have . . .
> simply made up my mind that I must take my chances. . . .
> That is all there is to it.[83]

Another motivation was of a very different order: simple
ambition. Throughout the history of warfare the god of battle
has flipped his coin: death on the tail, promotion on the face.
During the terrible fighting for the "Bloody Angle" of the Mule
Shoe salient during the battle of Spotsylvania, Brigadier General
Abner M. Perrin of Jubal Early's corps roundly declared, "I shall
come out of this fight a live major general or a dead brigadier."
He was killed in a hail of bullets.[84] Style was important. There
are many accounts of what might be called a rhetorical flourish
in the face of death, like that of a Louisiana captain: artilleryman Robert Stiles described how the officer, whose left arm was
taken off at the shoulder by a shell, swung his horse around in
order to spare his men the sight of the ghastly wound, and called

out jauntily, "Keep it up boys, I'll be back in a moment." He then, considerately, fell dead from his horse when out of sight.[85]

But for some, neither stoicism nor ambition nor the obligations of rank could overcome the fear of death. At Spotsylvania a Union officer was spotted lurking behind a log. He "took a cartridge out of his vest pocket, tore the paper with his strong white teeth, spilled the powder into his right palm, spat on it, and then, first casting a quick glance around to see if he was observed, he rubbed the moistened powder on his face and hands and then dust-coated the war paint. Instantly he was transformed from a trembling coward who lurked behind a tree into an exhausted brave taking a little well-earned repose."[86]

"Men go to war to kill or to get killed . . . and should expect no tenderness," declared General William Tecumseh Sherman. For senior officers there was another intimacy with death in battle— they were responsible for unleashing it. Some were utterly hardened (at least superficially) to the carnage for which they were responsible. Sherman, for example, could recognize, in a detached way, the horror of battle. After the first battle of Bull Run (Manassas), he said, "For the first time I saw the carnage of battle, men lying in every conceivable shape, and mangled in a horrible way; but this did not make a particular impression on me," for he knew that the "very object of war is to produce results by death and slaughter."[87] During the Atlanta campaign he even affected a jaunty callousness, saying: "I begin to regard the death and mangling of a couple of thousand men as a small affair, a kind of morning dash."[88]

Ulysses Grant was not insensitive to the death he orchestrated but suppressed the pity, perhaps out of self-preservation. After the bloody battle of Champion's Hill (1863) during the Vicksburg campaign, he recorded: "While a battle is raging one can see his enemy mowed down by the thousand, or the ten thousand, with great composure; but after the battle these scenes are distressing, and one is naturally disposed to do as much to allevi-ate the suffering of an enemy as a friend."[89] But he had to harden his heart, recognizing that the side "that never counted its dead" would achieve the ultimate victory. On the Confederate side, Lee could be deeply affected by the death he visited on his men, as shown by his anguished reaction after the failure of the Pickett-Pettigrew-Trimball assault on the third day of Gettysburg. On the other hand, Stonewall Jackson adopted a Cromwellian stern-ness as far as the deaths of his own men were concerned. He was doing God's work, and that absolved him from all responsibil-ity: "He places no value on human life," George Pickett wrote of Jackson, "caring for nothing so much as fighting, unless it be praying."[90] Jackson once looked upon a line of his own dead as unaffected as if he were at a review. "Not a muscle quivered," Confederate artillerist Robert Stiles records. "He was the ideal of concentration—imperturbable, resistless."[91] To an officer who had protested that the attack Jackson had just ordered was suicidal and "my regiment would be exterminated," Jackson snapped back: "Colonel, do your duty. I have made every arrangement to care for the wounded and bury the dead."[92]

Other generals were undone by their tender hearts. George McClellan suffered the tortures of the damned: "I am tired of the sickening sight of the battlefield, with its mangled corpses and poor suffering wounded! Victory has no charms for me while pur-chased at such cost. I shall be only too glad when all is over."[93] And on another occasion: "Every poor fellow that is killed or wounded almost haunts me! . . . I have honestly done my best to save as many lives as possible."[94] His concern for minimizing casualties endeared him to his men, if not to his political masters, who had a war to win and needed sterner stuff with which to do it.

★   ★   ★

AND HOW DID ordinary soldiers view death on the battlefield?
Two concepts fought with each other. On the one hand was the
idea of death as noble, heroic, and redeemed by sacrifice, with
the body itself lying, as though as evidence, in peaceful repose.
On the other hand, there was the irredeemable and meaningless
waste, the bodies mutilated beyond any possibility of sentimental embalming. It was, of course, a religious age, perhaps more
fundamentally in the South (whose army was periodically swept
with fervent bouts of revivalism) than the North. For both sides,
religion provided most, though by no means all, the solace that
acted as an inoculation against the horror. (Many others found
that booze did more to reconcile them to mortality than religion
ever could.)

The first contact with violent death was like a smack across
the face. On the second day's fighting at Shiloh, a Union soldier
recorded the shock:

> The first dead soldier we saw had fallen in the road; our
> artillery had crushed and mangled his limbs, and ground
> him into the mire. He lay a bloody, loathsome mass, the
> scraps of his blue uniform furnishing the only distinguish-
> able evidence that a hero there had died. At this sight I
> saw many a manly fellow gulp down his heart. . . . Near
> him lay a slender rebel boy—his face in the mud, his brown
> hair floating in a muddy pool. Soon a dead Major, then
> a Colonel, then the lamented Wallace [General W. H. L.
> Wallace, who died from his wounds three days later], yet
> alive, were passed in quick and sickening succession. The
> gray gloaming of the misty morning gave a ghostly pal-
> lor to the faces of the dead. The disordered hair, dripping
> from the night's rain, the distorted and passion-marked
> faces, the stony, glaring eyes, the blue lips, the glistening
> teeth. . . . Never, perhaps, did raw men go into battle under

such discouraging auspices as did this division. There was everything to depress, nothing to inspirit, and yet determination was written upon their pale faces.[95]

Death could come with stunning swiftness. Leander Stillwell would never forget "how awfully I felt on seeing for the first time a man killed in battle . . . I stared at his body, perfectly horrified! Only a few seconds ago that man was alive and well, and now he was lying on the ground, done for, forever!"[96] Stillwell was transfixed by how swiftly the human could be transformed into a mere object. The writer William Dean Howells also describes the existential shock of what might be called the "absoluteness" of the battlefield dead. It was a spiritual gutting: "At the sight of these dead men whom other men had killed, something went out of him, the habit of his lifetime, that never came back again: the sense of the sacredness of life and the impossibility of destroying it."[97] Union cavalryman Charles Weller reflected on the battle of Chickamauga with despair: "What at the present time is a man's life worth! Comparatively nothing[;] he falls and is forgotten except by his immediate friends." A soldier of the Sixth Iowa mirrored Weller's sentiment; war forced him to "estimate life at its true value—nothing."[98]

There were two main ways of combating this emptiness. One was to invest death with religious and patriotic significance; it was transformed from something final or meaningless into an act consecrated by patriotic nobility and Christian sacrifice. The dead passed over to a better world, not only released from the tawdriness of temporal existence but blessedly rewarded in the afterlife. Stonewall Jackson's last words are a lyrical evocation of that premise: "Let us cross the river and rest under the shade of the trees."[99] A devout Confederate at Gettysburg was hit during the last gasp of the battle, and one of his comrades describes how "a terrific fire burst, thundering, flashing, crashing [and] there lay our noble comrade . . . limb thrice broken, the body gashed with wounds, the top of the skull blown off and the brain actually fallen out." But no matter how appalling this was, it could be redeemed because a "chariot and horses of fire had caught [him] up into Heaven."[100] A nurse wrote to the mother of a deceased soldier that he "had been conscious of his death and . . . not afraid but willing to die . . . he is better off."[101] The age revered the cult of dying well—the *ars moriendi*. Much popular literature and art was devoted to it, and inevitably a good deal was of the maudlin tie-a-yellow-ribbon variety. Joseph Hopkins Twichell, a Union soldier, was no stay-at-home bleeding heart. He had seen "a hideous nightmare . . . too piteous for speech . . . as if the universe would stop with the horror of it," during the Peninsular campaign of 1862, but turned to the plangent sentimentality of the period to deal with it:

They're left behind!
Our steps are turned away:
We forward march, but these forever stay
Halted, till trumpets wake the final day:—
  Good-bye! Good-bye!

They're left behind!
The young and strong and brave:
The sighing pines mourn sweetly o'er their grave;
Mute, moving grief the summer branches wave,
  Good-bye dear friends!

They're left behind!
Comfort!—our heavy souls!
Their battle shout forever onward rolls
Till God's own freedom gathers in the poles!
  Good-bye! Farewell![102]

The other way to deal with death in battle was to embrace and revel in the nihilism, disarming death by a rebellious refusal to sanctify it. Cynicism born of experience became a way of flipping the bird at the fates. Charles Wainwright, a Union colonel, reported that when a mortally wounded man fell against him, he had "no more feeling for him, than if he had tripped over a stump and fallen; nor do I think it would have been different had he been my brother."[103] A Confederate soldier described how "we cook and eat, talk and laugh with the enemy's dead lying all about us as though they were so many hogs."[104] A Federal soldier echoed the sentiment: "We dont mind the sight of dead men no more than if they was dead Hogs. . . . The rebels was laying over the field bloated up as big as a horse and as black as a negro and the boys run over them and serch their pockets . . . unconcerned. . . . I run acros a big graback as black as the ase of spade it startled me a little at first but I stopt to see what he had but he had been tended too so I past on my way rejoicing."[105] Men's souls became annealed by repeated exposure to death: "By being accustomed to sights which would make other men's hearts sick to behold, our men soon became heart-hardened, and sometimes scarcely gave a pitying thought to those who were unfortunate enough to get hit. Men can get accustomed to everything; and the daily sight of blood and mangled bodies so blunted their finer sensibilities as almost to blot out all love, all sympathy from the heart."[106]

For many "heart-hardened" soldiers, chaplains were despised as thinly disguised agents of army authority whose job it was to sell the men on the nobility of death in battle. Abner Small describes how before the battle of Chancellorsville the Union chaplains "were eloquent in their appeals to patriotism, and pictured in glowing colors the glory that would crown the dead and the blazons of promotion that would decorate the surviving heroes." Suddenly, enemy shells start to explode: "The screams of horses, and the shouted commands of officers were almost drowned out by the yells and laughter of the men as the brave chaplains, hatless and bookless, their coat-tails streaming in the wind, fled madly to the rear over stone walls, and hedges and ditches, followed by gleefully shouted counsel: 'Stand firm; put your trust in the Lord!' "[107] And to those flag wavers back in the safety of the civilian world, battle-hardened soldiers were only too willing to prick their patriotic bubble: "We ain't doing much just now," writes Francis Amasa Walker, a Federal soldier anticipating the next attack, "but hope in a few more days to satisfy the public taste with our usual Fall Spectacle—forty percent of us knocked over."[108]

The ever-present possibility of being killed inevitably un-hinged some men, who in their desperation looked to a different kind of magic for protection by investing some mundane object with totemic powers. Colonel C. Irvine Walker recounts how a Confederate private who had previously shown signs of cowardice and had been reprimanded for it took his place in the battle line, "his rifle on his shoulder, and holding up in front of him a frying pan." He moved forward, from frying pan to fire as it were, and was killed.[109]

But for others it enhanced life, making it sharper, more intense. Fear was replaced with an adrenaline surge of exaltation. Rice C. Bull, a Union infantryman at Chancellorsville, describes just such a transformation when the Confederate attackers finally came within range: "Most of us . . . held our fire until we saw the line of smoke that showed that they were on the ridge; then every gun was fired. It was then load and fire at will as fast as we could. Soon the nervousness and fear we had when we began to fight passed away and a feeling of fearlessness and rage took its place."[110] At Antietam (Sharpsburg), Captain Frank Holsinger felt a similar elation: "We now rush forward. We cheer; we are in ecstasies. While shells and canister are still resonant and minnies [minié balls] sizzling spitefully, yet I think this one of the supreme moments of my existence."[111] Major James A. Connolly described the sheer elation of death defied. Following a successful assault on a Confederate fortification during the battle of Jonesboro, the last such during the 1864 Atlanta campaign: "I could have lain down on that blood stained grass, amid the dying and the dead and wept with excess of joy. I have no language to express the rapture one feels in the moment of victory, but I do know that at such a moment one feels as if the joy were worth risking a hundred lives to attain it. Men at home will read of that battle and be glad of our success, but they can never feel as we felt, standing there quivering with excitement, amid the smoke and blood, and fresh horrors and grand trophies of that battle field."[112]

Taking sensual pleasure—eating, drinking, smoking, sleeping —among the carnage was, however bizarre it may appear, a gesture of affirmation of life. After Antietam (Sharpsburg), Union troops bivouacked among the dead Confederates. "Many were black as Negroes," notes David Hunter Strother, "heads and faces hideously swelled, covered with dust until they looked like clods. Killed during the charge and flight, their attitudes were wild and frightful. . . . Among these loathsome earthsoiled vestiges of humanity . . . in the midst of all this carrion our troops sat cooking, eating, jabbering, and smoking; sleeping among the corpses so that but for the color of the skin it was difficult to distinguish the living from the dead."[113]

For some, killing was another dimension of joy, as though by taking a life the killer replenished his own. Byrd Willis, a Confederate, saw a comrade "jumping about, as if in great agony. I immediately ran up to him to ascertain when he was hurt & if I could do any thing of him—but upon reaching him I found that he was not hurt but was executing a species of Indian War Dance around a Poor Yankee (who lay on his back in the last agonies of death) exclaiming I killed him! I killed him! Evidently carried away with excitement and delight."[114]

Captured black soldiers and their white officers ran a considerable risk of being summarily executed. At the infamous Fort Pillow massacre of April 1864, the Confederate general Nathan Bedford Forrest oversaw a systematic killing of black soldiers and some of their white officers, after their surrender. Texan George Gautier described his regiment's actions after it had defeated black troops at Monroe, Louisiana: "I never saw so many dead negroes in my life. We took no prisoners, except the white officers, fourteen in number; these were lined up and shot after the negroes were finished. Next day they were thrown into a wagon, hauled to the Ouchita river and thrown in. Some were hardly dead—that made no difference—in they went."[115]

The defeated whites of both sides would be extremely unlucky to be put to death summarily. However, Confederates who had been involved in the Fort Pillow incident were killed. Although many white Union soldiers shared the racial prejudice of their Southern counterparts, Fort Pillow was an insult to the cause that would have to be paid for in blood: "At the battle of Resaca in May 1864, the 105th Illinois captured a Confederate battery. From underneath one of the gun carriages a big, red-haired man with no shirt fearfully emerged. He wore a tattoo on one arm that read 'Fort Pillow.' His captors read it. He was bayoneted and shot instantly. Another regiment in Sherman's army was reported to have killed twenty-three rebel prisoners, first asking them if they remembered Fort Pillow. The Wisconsin soldier who recorded this incident claimed flatly, 'When there is no officer with us, we take no prisoners.' "[116]

On the obverse side of the coin, the fellowship of warriors, no matter which side they were on, could save the life of a captured soldier. Rice C. Bull of the 123rd New York was captured at Chancellorsville, and when a civilian threatened him and his fellow captors with harm, a Confederate soldier stepped in to remind the civilian that "these are wounded men. You have no right or business to insult them."[117] The point was that soldiers inhabited the world of soldiers, and only they could arbitrate its rules; no others had the right to intercede. The rules were, more often than not, respectful and compassionate. A Union soldier noted that Confederates captured at Port Hudson in July 1863 were brave fighters and "in the twinkling of an eye we were together. . . . The Rebs are mostly large, fine-looking men. They are about as hard up for clothes as we are. . . . They have treated the prisoners [Union soldiers captured earlier] as well as they could, giving them the same sort of food they ate themselves."[118]

Union soldier William Aspinall of the Forty-Seventh Indiana was wounded at Champion Hill near Vicksburg on May 16, 1863:

In the evening some of my comrades brought me blankets, doing without themselves, and made me a bed in a fence corner outside of the hospital. In a little while a Confederate soldier came along. He had been shot somewhere in the bowels and was in great pain. I said—"here partner, I will share my bed with you"—and he laid down beside me. He told me that he was from Savannah, Georgia, and that he could not get well. He wanted me to write to his wife and children and gave me a card with their address. I was to tell them that I had seen him and what had become of their beloved husband and father. Being weak and exhausted from the loss of blood, I dozed off to sleep and left him talking to me. In a little while I awoke and spoke to him two or three times, but he did not answer. I put my hand over on his face; he was cold in death. My foe and friend had crossed the river.[119]

The problem was the marginals, the pathetic bar-stool warriors, who found themselves for a moment enjoying power beyond their expectations: "Whenever we fell into the hands of veteran soldiers who had fought us bravely on the battle-field, we received all of the kind and considerate attention due a prisoner of war, but whenever we were in charge of militia or that class of persons who, too cowardly to take the field, enlist in the home guard, we were treated in the most outrageous manner."[120]

The distinction between honorable and dishonorable extended to categories of killing. Killing pickets (sentries), for example, was considered a kind of assassination, perhaps because their role was essentially passive and they were too easy a target. There was an understanding on both sides that familiarity with each other's pickets afforded protection, and killing them when no other general action was going on was denounced as "a miserable and useless kind of murder." A Southerner who knew he was within range of the enemy felt safe because "we were now real soldiers on both sides and well knew that mere picket shooting helped neither side and was only murder."[121]

Sniping was also considered "dishonorable" and denounced as "murderous villainy," but it was a villainy indulged in by both sides. As a Union private fulminated:

Sharpshooting at North Anna [in 1864] was exceedingly severe and murderous. We were greatly annoyed by it, as a campaign cannot be decided by killing a few hundred enlisted men—killing them most unfairly and when they were of necessity exposed. . . . Our sharpshooters were as bad as the Confederates. . . . They could sneak around trees or lurk behind stumps, or cower in wells or in cellars, and from the safety of their lairs murder a few men. Put the sharpshooters in battle-line and they were no better, no more effective, than the infantry of the line, and they were not half as decent. There was an unwritten code of honor among the infantry that forbade the shooting of men while attending to the imperative calls of nature, and these sharp-shooting brutes were constantly violating that rule. I hated sharpshooters, both Confederate and Union, in those days, and was always glad to see them killed.[122]

As will be seen in the two world wars, "attending to the imperative calls of nature" could be one of the riskiest things a soldier could do.

★   ★   ★

THE DEAD WERE able to offer very tangible benefits to the living. Joshua Chamberlain, later to become the hero of Little Round Top at Gettysburg, found himself pinned among the corpses of the attack on Marye's Heights on December 13, 1862, at Fredericksburg: "The night chill had now woven a misty veil over the field. . . . At last, outwearied and depressed with the desolate scene, my own strength sunk . . . I moved two dead men a little and lay down between them, making a pillow of the breast of a third. The skirt of his overcoat drawn over my face helped also to shield me from the bleak winds. There was some comfort even in this companionship."[123]

There was, of course, as there always has been, the stripping of corpses—the "peeling," as they called it. And sometimes the dead continued their beneficence long after their demise. A Confederate, R. H. Peck, happened to pass over the ground of a particularly hard-fought engagement of nine months earlier: "He would always remember crossing a field where the Yankees had delivered a determined charge. It was only with difficulty that he could keep from stepping on bones still wrapped in torn bits of blue uniform. . . . While crossing the ghastly little field, Peck noticed a man from his regiment who had been a dentist before the war. Busy examining the skulls to see if they contained any gold fillings, he had already extracted quite a number and had his haversack completely full of teeth."[124]

In other ways, too, the ripple of economic benefit radiated from the killed. They provided a rich feeding ground for energetic entrepreneurs. There were search agencies like the official-sounding U.S. Army Agency (in fact a private company located on Bleecker Street in Manhattan) that for a share of the deceased's back pay or the widow's pension would locate the body of a loved one.[125] Embalmers such as Thomas Holmes (who processed four thousand bodies at one hundred dollars each during the war), and the manufacturers of metallic coffins—"Warranted Air-Tight"—that could "be placed in the Parlour without fear of any odor escaping therefrom" (fifty dollars each), literally and metaphorically cleaned up.[126]

Bodies were utilized in other, less physical ways: as agents of propaganda. Confederate surgeon John Wyeth describes how after Chickamauga, "most of the Confederate dead had been gathered in long trenches and buried; but the Union dead were still lying where they fell. For its effect on the survivors it was the policy of the victor to hide his own losses and let those of the other side be seen."[127] A Union soldier, Daniel Crotty, describes how one could "read" the facial expressions of the dead as justification of the righteousness of the cause: "The dead of both friend and foe lie side by side, but it is remarked by all that the pleasant smile on the patriot's face contrasts strangely with the horrid stare of the rebel dead."[128] However, another Union soldier, Frank Wilkeson, dismissed the whole fanciful and self-serving notion: "I do not believe that the face of a dead soldier, lying on a battle-field, ever truthfully indicates the mental or physical anguish, or peacefulness of mind, which he suffered or enjoyed before his death." Wilkeson concludes bluntly, "It goes for nothing. One death was as painless as the other."[129]

And long after the war, the "glorious dead" served yet another profitable function. The grim reality of their deaths was replaced by something altogether more palatable, more stirring . . . more *suitable* as a motivation for the next generation of warriors. Oliver Wendell Holmes Jr., who after the war ascended to the Supreme Court, dramatically represents this transition. As a young officer he had been grievously wounded and almost died. He had been through the grinder and, in the process, lost his appetite for the rhetoric of patriotism: "He had grown weary of such words as 'cowardice,' 'gallantry,' and 'chivalry.' " Disillusioned, he eventually resigned his commission. But by 1885 a complete transformation had taken place. Like some American samurai, he discovered a fervent belief in the mystical importance of a warrior's unquestioning obedience unto death: "In the midst of doubt, the collapse of creeds, there is one thing I do not doubt . . . and that is that the faith is true and adorable which leads a soldier to throw away his life in obedience to a blindly accepted duty, in a cause which he little understands, in a plan of campaign of which he had no notion, under tactics of which he does not see the use. . . . It is only when time has passed that you see that its message was divine . . . our hearts were touched with fire."[130]

FIVE

AN INVESTMENT OF BLOOD

Killing and Honor in Colonial Warfare

★

*I*F SOLDIERS HAVE to die it should not be in warfare emptied of nobility. If fate so dictated their deaths, they would wish to give their lives on the high ground, rather than have them carelessly discarded in the scrubby wasteland of history. But in much colonial warfare the deaths of the invaders were denied a noble dimension. Writing in 1904 about the wars of the second half of the nineteenth century between the United States and the Plains Indians, Cyrus Townsend Brady described something of this erosion:

> The most thankless task that can be undertaken by a nation is warfare against savage or semi-civilized peoples. In it there is usually little glory; nor is there any reward, save the consciousness of disagreeable duty well performed. The risk to the soldier is greater than in ordinary war, since the savages usually torture the wounded and the captured. Success can only be achieved by an arduous, persistent,

wearing down process, which affords little opportunity for scientific fighting, yet which demands military talents of the highest order.

Almost anybody can understand the strategy or the tactics of a pitched battle where the number engaged is large, the casualties heavy, and the results decisive; but very few non-professional critics appreciate a campaign of relentless pursuit by a small army of a smaller body of mobile hostiles, here and there capturing a little band, now and then killing or disabling a few, until in the final round-up the enemy, reduced to perhaps less than a score, surrenders. There is nothing spectacular about the performance, and everybody wonders why it took so long.[1]

An exasperated US soldier of the Indian Wars put it this way: "I don't care who does the fighting, I don't want any more of it. . . . The boys out here have all come to the conclusion that fighting Indians is not what it is cracked up to be, especially when it is fighting on the open prarie [*sic*] against five to one, we always have to fight at such a disadvantage, we always have to shoot at them running, they wont stand and let a fellow shoot at them like a white man."[2]

Brady identifies tactics as a reflection of moral worth. If indigenous enemies will not fight the white man's way, he suggests, it robs the white warrior of the honor associated with a certain confrontational style of war making. In the early days of the English colonization of North America, the whites deplored the natives' "skulking way of war" as underhanded and unfair. The Indians, on the other hand, marveled at the whites' willingness to sacrifice their lives in slugfest confrontations. In the end, they learned from each other. The settlers began to incorporate more loose-order combat techniques, and the Indians learned that "the traditional restraints which had limited deaths in aboriginal warfare were nothing more than liabilities in any serious conflict with the English colonists."[3]

At the center of colonial confrontation was a disparity in weapons technology. It made conquest possible and winning probable. The arquebus and cannon of the conquistadores were much more effective at greater distance than the atlatl, bow, and spear of the Aztecs; the Martini-Henry rifle could kill a Zulu warrior at more than 800 yards (whereas the thrown assegai might be deadly only up to 25 yards), and Gatling and Maxim guns cut great swaths through indigenous armies.

This is not to say that native weaponry could not be effective against the European invaders. The atlatl, the dart-throwing "stick" of prehistoric origin, was much used by the Aztecs against the conquistadores, and Spanish sources claim that it was accurate up to 50 yards and its darts, tipped with obsidian, flint, copper, or fishbone, could pierce armor. The barbed version was particularly lethal because it had to be cut out of the wound, which greatly increased the risk of death from blood loss and infection.[4] Bernal Diaz del Castillo particularly feared Aztec archery because arrows tipped with glasslike obsidian had an even greater tissue penetration than steel heads. He also feared the Aztec slingers armed with the *tematlatl*—a maguey-fiber sling that could hurl stones 200 yards to deadly effect. Aztec warriors used spears both for throwing and for stabbing, as well as war clubs. But almost unique among indigenous warriors, Aztec soldiers were armed with fearsome swords (*macuahuitl*), either single- or double-handed. The Spanish noted with awe that a blow from an obsidian-edged broadsword could decapitate a horse.

In the end, however, what was essentially Stone Age weaponry could not prevail against steel armor, Toledo blades, gunpowder, and mounted lancers: "Perhaps it is hard for modern deskbound scholars to understand the utter dread that existed in the minds of those who were routinely sliced to pieces by Toledo steel, shredded by grapeshot, trampled by mailed knights, ripped to pieces by mastiffs [large dogs trained for combat], and had their limbs lacerated with impunity by musket balls and cross-bow bolts. . . . Throughout contemporary oral Nahuatl and written Spanish accounts, there are dozens of grisly scenes of the dismemberment and disemboweling of Mesoamericans by Spanish steel and shot, accompanied by descriptions of the sheer terror that such mayhem invoked in indigenous populations."[5]

However, most successful colonial wars (from the viewpoint of the invader, at least) were won through attrition. Native Americans, for example, were finally vanquished at the end of the nineteenth century not in glorious set-piece battles (although there were plenty of bloody clashes) but through the sheer doggedness and strength in depth of a vastly more powerful invader who could make an investment not only in matériel but also in soldiers' deaths that would have bankrupted the much more fragile infrastructure of his enemy. As a defeated and starving Sioux chieftain said to the victorious General Nelson Miles in early 1877: "We are poor compared with you and your force. We cannot make a rifle, a round of ammunition, or a knife. In fact, we are at the mercy of those who are taking possession of our country. Your terms are harsh and cruel, but we are going to accept them, and place ourselves at your mercy."[6]

Even in victory the costs to indigenous peoples could be crippling. When the Zulu king Cetshwayo inflicted a crushing defeat on a sizable British force at Isandlwana, annihilating six companies of the Second Warwickshires, a whole battalion of the Twenty-Fourth Regiment and other British units (about 670 men in all), as well as about 500 native auxiliaries, it was one of the most catastrophic defeats visited upon the British Army, but the cost in Zulu dead (something over 2,000) was so crippling that Cetshwayo described it as though an "assegai has been thrust into the belly of the nation."[7] The British brought yet more forces, and shortly thereafter, at the battle of Ulundi (the first battle in which the British employed Gatling guns),[8] the Zulus lost 1,500 killed (compared with 15 British). A British corporal of the Fifty-Eighth Regiment describes how the Zulu dead fell "as though they had been tipped out of carts."[9] It was the end of the Zulu nation as a military power.

The problem for military cultures based on the heroic model of mano-a-mano confrontation of (more or less) equals in pitched battle (what Victor Davis Hanson characterizes as "the Western way of war") is that fighting an enemy who does not share that tradition robs the enterprise of its noble and glorious aura. And this is no small matter, because the idea of the heroic is not a disembodied Platonism floating beyond the blood and guts of human experience. On the contrary, it has been developed over millennia of human combat for a very specific practical purpose. It provides the narrative that encourages men to fight and allows them to come to terms with their possible, perhaps probable, death in battle. Colonial warfare against savages who did not fight by Western rules put stress on the received definition of the heroic.

Aboriginal cultures tended to devise tactics in order to minimize the loss of warriors (although this is not a universal truth. The Zulus of the nineteenth century were particularly profligate with their warriors' lives both on and off the battlefield). Europeans of the colonial era looked on this "oblique" way of waging war as proof of the moral turpitude of the savage. A strategy based on avoidance of mass confrontation, of subterfuge, ambush, and picking off stragglers, of cutting off small groups to be massacred—the "skulking way of war"—did not conform to a heroic template of forthright confrontation.

For the indigenous peoples, colonial warfare was defined by possibility in the face of inevitability: the possibility of localized victories set against the certainty of eventual defeat. Those local successes, however, could be spectacular, like the massacre of Spanish troops by Aztecs on July 1, 1520—*La Noche Triste*—the Little Big Horn in 1876, the Zulu victory over the British at Isandlwana in 1879, the annihilation of Anglo-Egyptian forces by Dervishes at El Obeid in the Sudan in 1883, the Italian disaster at the hands of Ethiopian tribesmen at Adowa in 1896, or the catastrophic defeat of Spanish troops by Riffian irregulars at Annual, Morocco, in 1921.

And these extraordinary victories were crafted because indigenous forces had advantages denied to the invader. By playing to a superior knowledge of local terrain, they could outwit, surprise, and ambush the enemy. In 1883, Hicks "Pasha" (William Hicks), a British officer and a general in the Egyptian Army (although Hicks was essentially a British appointee), marched ten thousand troops (mainly Egyptian, but with a handful of European officers) out into the Sudanese desert to confront a Dervish army under the Mahdi. Hiding within the folds of wadis and hummocks at El Obeid, the Mahdists let the government troops come on and then fell on the unsuspecting invaders and killed every man jack of them, including the unfortunate Hicks, whose head was presented to the Mahdi (and through the years, now thoroughly mummified, became a powerful totem—a wiser head, one might say). "England was horrified and astonished. Lord Fitzmaurice told the House of Lords that there had not been such a complete destruction of so large an army since 'Pharoah's host perished in the Red Sea.' "[10]

Defeating in detail was another tactical option available to the native, and a successful one. Colonel Richard Dodge of the US Army notes with some exasperation:

> His [the Indian's] tactics are always the same; never to receive
> a charge, but by constantly breaking, to separate the enemy
> into detached fragments; then suddenly concentrating to

overwhelm them in detail. Having no trains or impediments of any kind, he is always able to avoid battle if the ground or opportunity does not suit him. The heavier slowly-moving troops, encumbered with trains of supplies, must attack when they can, and therefore almost always at a disadvantage. . . . I know of no single instance where troops have gained any signal advantage over Indians in open fight, and this for the reason that the moment they gain even a slight advantage, the Indians disappear with a celerity that defies pursuit. On the other hand, if the Indians gain the advantage, they press it with a most masterful vigor, and there results a massacre.[11]

The success of guerrilla bait-and-switch tactics is predicated on the willingness of someone to take the bait. The enemy has to be enticed, invited, drawn to his death. And that willingness is itself based on a convergence of factors, one of which is contempt for the "uncivilized" enemy; another is a thirst for the glory that is being denied by these "cowardly" tactics. And this aggressiveness turns around and gets him killed, as Captain W. J. Fetterman, US Cavalry, discovered.

Fetterman was stationed at Fort Phil Kearny in northeastern Wyoming, and during the latter part of 1866 the post had been involved in a series of frustrating actions with hostile Sioux, usually in the form of ambushes on the fort's woodcutting teams. Fetterman's commanding officer, Colonel Henry B. Carrington, was a prudent and defensive soldier who refused to rise to the bait, much to the irritation of junior officers such as William Fetterman, who, according to anecdotal accounts, "offered with eighty men to ride through the whole Sioux nation!" Fetterman shared a general contempt for natives that was echoed by a contemporary soldier, J. E. Welch, writing of the warfare of 1869: "I have never seen Indians face the music like white men. . . . I think it just as impossible to make a civilized man of the Indian as it would be to make a shepherd dog of a wolf, or a manly man of a dude. They do not in my opinion possess a single trait that elevates a man above a brute."[12]

On December 21, 1866, yet another logging detail from the fort was ambushed and Fetterman begged for command of the relief force. His request was granted, and as irony would have it, eighty-one men—almost the exact number with which he had previously boasted he would subdue the whole Sioux nation—rode out. Instead of going directly to the aid of the wood train, as he had been strictly commanded to do, Fetterman, desperate to make a decisive impact and, perhaps, enraged by the mocking warriors who stood on their horses and mooned him, was lured farther and farther up a valley to be ambushed by a much larger Indian force. Everyone in Fetterman's command, armed mainly with muzzle-loading muskets, was killed with what might be called "extreme prejudice." For this was a powerful way in which the invaded might "dissuade" the invader: by leaving a horrific calling card in the shape of mutilated bodies. Fetterman's men had "eyes torn out and laid on the rocks; noses cut off; ears cut off; chins hewn off; teeth chopped out . . . brains taken out and placed on rocks with other members of the body; hands cut off; feet cut off."[13] One body was reported to have more than one hundred arrows in it (ironically it was that of James Wheatley, one of two civilians who had joined the Fetterman party in order to demonstrate the lethality of their new Henry repeater rifles).

The mutilation of bodies and the torture of prisoners, although obviously not an exclusive characteristic of colonial warfare, played a particularly important role in an imperial context. Among the colonizing nations it provided proof positive that the indigenous enemy inhabited a realm of savagery beyond the pale of the rules of civilized warfare. Native warriors became at once both utterly terrifying and completely contemptible. They were nothing but ravening beasts, and wars of conquest could now be recast as wars of moral necessity—the crusade of light and reason against the bloody and black heart of barbarism.

Where our own barbarities are sanctioned by cultural familiarity, the practices of the "other" are always vile beyond belief. Without stumbling through a maze of moral relativism it is possible to recognize the rank hypocrisy behind this view. The conquistadores, for example, were "men who shared what to us now seems an uneven morality: slaughtering unarmed Indians in battle brought no odium, nor did turning an entire conquered population into gangs of indentured serfs. In contrast, human sacrifice, cannibalism, transvestitism, and sodomy provoked moral indignation and outrage."[14] A conquistador prisoner of war suffered the same ritualized death as did any other captive. Not that it was much consolation. Those Spanish soldiers unlucky enough to be captured during *La Noche Triste* were put to death in a public spectacle that the ancient Romans would have appreciated. Bernal Diaz del Castillo passed on an account he had heard from native witnesses:

> When they got them up to a small square in front of the oratory, where their accursed idols are kept, we saw them place plumes on the heads of many of them and with things like fans in their hands they forced them to dance before Huichilobos, and after they had danced they immediately placed them on their backs on some rather narrow stones which had been prepared as places for sacrifice, and with stone knives they sawed open their chests and drew out their palpitating hearts and offered them to the idols that were there, and they kicked the bodies down the steps, and Indian butchers who were waiting below cut off the arms and feet and flayed the skin off the faces, and prepared it

afterwards like glove leather with the beards on . . . and the flesh they ate in chilmole.[15]

The Spaniards also used the bodies of their slain enemies. They found that the fat from newly killed Indians "worked as an excellent salve and healing cream."[16]

Slain warriors retained a potency, and sometimes had to be killed again, spiritually, through mutilation, which will ensure that they could not enjoy the pleasures of the afterlife and, more important, would be rendered powerless to revenge themselves when their killer eventually took his own journey to the nether-world.[17] Being scalped, for example, condemned a North American Indian warrior to wander the outer shades of the happy hunting ground, and for that reason it was a matter of the highest importance to retrieve a comrade's body before it could be scalped. Whites adopted the scalping habit quite early on. Peter Oliver, writing in the summer of 1778, declared: "This Scalping Business hath been encouraged, in the Colonies, for more than a Century past. Premiums have been given, frequently, by the *Massachusetts* Assemblies, for the Scalps of Indians."[18]

Preventing scalping of Indians by US soldiers was sometimes a troublesome chore for officers. R. J. Smith was a teamster with Colonel Carrington's Powder River expeditionary force of 1866 and was involved in the historic Wagon Box fight. Writing to Cyrus Brady (the author of *Indian Fights and Fighters*) in 1904, he points out: "As to the Indians carrying off all their dead and wounded, here you are again mistaken, as many of our men carried away with them scalps etc., taken from the bodies of the dead Indians. . . . The Indians certainly hauled off all their dead and wounded that they could, but did not expose themselves very much in order to get the dead ones near the corral."[19] Sigmund Schlesinger, a scout with Major George Forsyth at the battle of

Beecher's Island on September 17, 1868, describes a gruesome incident in the aftermath:

> When I got there the Indians were being stripped of their equipment, scalps, etc. One of them was shot in the head and his hair was clotted with blood. I took hold of one of his braids and applied my knife to the skin above the ear to secure the scalp, but my hand coming in contact with the blood, I dropped the hair in disgust.
>
> Old Jim Lane saw my hesitation, and taking up the braid, said to me: "My boy, does it make you sick?" Then inserting the point of the knife under the skin, he cut around, took up the other braid, and jerked the scalp from the head.[20]

The men who died with Custer at the Little Big Horn were thoroughly mutilated after death. Almost all (except George Custer) were scalped; some were decapitated and their heads taken to the Indian encampment (the Indians maintained that no men were tortured) but others were posthumously burned and further mutilated in the ritual celebrations following the battle.[21] The wounded were dispatched either by warriors or by the women and youngsters who combed the battlefield afterward—a commonplace of battle in Europe up until the end of the Napoleonic Wars. Faces and penises, as might be imagined, were often the centers of attention—the faces bashed in, the penises either cut off or otherwise mutilated.

An interpreter Isaiah Dorman was found, according to George Herendeen, a soldier who viewed the aftermath of the battle, with "his breast full of arrows and an iron picket pin thrusted through his testicles into the ground, pinning him down. . . . Dorman's penis was cut off and stuffed in his mouth, which was regarded among the Indians as the deepest insult possible."[22] In the Fetterman massacre, many dead US soldiers were found with their severed genitals stuffed into their mouths, as were drummer boys of the Twenty-Fourth Regiment killed at Isandlwana.[23] All of the British dead had been eviscerated.

To say that the sight of dead colleagues butchered like hogs was dispiriting is an understatement. Saving the last bullet for suicide became part of the imperial mythology. To "go to your Gawd like a soldier" with a self-administered bullet to the head, as Kipling advised, was preferable to falling into the hands of the savage (or, heaven forfend, the savage's concubine). Caught by a surge of Zulus on a narrow pass at Hlobane Mountain, in South Africa, a small group of British cavalrymen had the unenviable choice of facing certain death by assegai and war club or launching themselves over the cliff. George "Chops" Mossop "dismounted and wormed his way forward to the head of the pass, which was strewn with struggling bodies. He nudged the man beside him, asking if he thought they could get down. 'Not a hope!' the man replied, and to Mossop's horror put the muzzle of his carbine in his mouth and pulled the trigger. His brains spattered Chops."[24]

After the Fetterman massacre it was alleged that Fetterman and his second-in-command, Captain Frederick Brown, who, like Fetterman, had been itching and agitating for "one chance at the Indians," committed joint suicide. According to Cyrus Brady: "Brown and Fetterman were found lying side by side, each with a bullet wound in the left temple [they were presumably both right-handed]. Their heads were burned and filled with powder around the wounds. Seeing that all was lost, they had evidently stood face to face, and each had shot the other dead with his revolver. They had both sworn to die rather than be taken alive by the Indians, and in the last extremity they had carried out their vows."[25]

Brady's account serves two related parts of the colonial mythology. First, Brown and Fetterman's resolution not to fall alive into the hands of savages marks them as civilized warriors who chose death over the indignity of probable torture. Their suicide is not cowardly in the sense that they are abandoning their men (Brady infers) because they chose a noble and Roman end rather than accept the disgusting death that would probably have been meted out to them by their barbarian enemy. In creating their own heroic narrative they rob the savages of their victory. Second, it reinforces the powerful idea of the blood brotherhood of the officer class, and it was the officer class that drove the engine of colonial expansion. Positive images of sacrifice were a hugely important part of the colonial story in the nineteenth century. Custer, it appears, either resisted the temptation or was killed before he could have committed suicide (a bullet wound to the temple showed no telltale marks of the powder burns that indicate suicide, and the wound to his side would have been equally as fatal as the head shot). Indian accounts assert that US soldiers did end their own lives on that Montana hillside, but there is little forensic evidence to support it.[26]

The "chosen death"—*suicide* seems too thin and mean a word—also offered at least some last vestige of the heroic to those natives who were about to be swept away on the triumphal imperial tide. By 1889 the Cheyenne had been defeated and the fleeing bands hunted down. Two young warriors, Head Chief and Heart Mule, decided to take the manner of their deaths into their own hands. An eyewitness account, reported in the *Army and Navy Journal* of September 27, 1890, described the scene.

[Dressed in their finery], the warriors rode out from a timbered butte across the valley and gaining the highest point of an adjacent hill circled their ponies and sang their death songs. This over they opened fire on the troopers [US First Cavalry] below. In a few minutes they were flanked and driven from the rocks at the crest of the hill and then, although with plenty of room to escape in other directions, they charged down the steep incline, one mounted and the other—whose horse had been shot—on foot. Across the valley they went, under a hail of bullets from fifty carbines, towards the line of fresh troops which had just occupied the opposite crest. . . . One of them deliberately rode through Lieut. Pitcher's line, shooting three horses as he came, but doing no other damage. He was pierced by seven bullets. . . . The second . . . was driven to a cut in the bed of the valley, where he fought desperately until killed.[27]

★　　★　　★

ALTHOUGH IT IS generally true that weapons' superiority was a major factor in killing huge numbers of indigenous warriors, occasionally there were technical glitches that resulted in catastrophic reversals of fortune. At Isandlwana on January 22, 1879, the Martini-Henry rifles of the British defenders overheated, causing the brass-sleeved bullets to expand and jam (there may also have been some problems with ammunition supply, but this is still a matter of contention). The Martini-Henry was, on the whole, an excellent weapon that had already demonstrated its man-stopping ability against Afghans and Kaffirs, but on that January day the guns were so hot they could hardly be held and rounds cooked off prematurely; the thin-brass case of .45-caliber rounds expanded and jammed in the breeches; and men frantically tried to clear them with knives and bayonet points.

At Little Big Horn, Custer's men may have suffered a similar problem with the ejector mechanism of their breech-loading single-shot Springfield model 1873 carbines. In later years one of the Indian participants, Rain in the Face, admittedly a bit of a blowhard, insisted that "we were better armed than the long swords. Their guns wouldn't shoot but once—the thing wouldn't throw out the empty cartridge shells. When we found they could not shoot we saved our bullets by knocking the long swords over with our war clubs—it was just like killing sheep."[28] Although Cyrus Brady says that Rain in the Face's account was corroborated by General Gibbon's command two days after the battle, when "dozens of guns were picked up on the battle-field . . . with the shells still sticking in them, showing that the ejector wouldn't work,"[29] modern-day archeological investigation of the battlefield indicates a relatively low proportion of recovered shells showing signs of having been forced out of the breech.

When indigenous warriors stuck to "irregular" tactics of dispersal, of ambush and subterfuge, they not only stood a better chance of inflicting damage on the invader but also minimized damage to themselves. Sometimes, though, sheer numbers overwhelmed opposition, particularly when invaders lost the cohesion that could maximize their firepower. At Maiwand on July 27, 1880, during the Second Afghan War, Brigadier General George Burrows made some of the same mistakes as Colonel Durnford at Isandlwana. By failing to concentrate his firepower and allowing his force of about 2,500 British and Indians to be caught on open ground by approximately 25,000 Afghans, Burrows's force was overrun. The Sixty-Sixth Regiment tried desperately to retreat in the face of overwhelming odds but lost cohesion. Whittled down to about 200 men, one element of the regiment, with its mortally wounded colonel, was eventually brought to ground around their unfurled colors. And there they died. Of Burrows's original force, over one-third (962) were killed in the battle and during the retreat.[30]

Although tactically the best option for many indigenous armies was to fight in dispersed order, they too were sometimes drawn, like moths to the flame, to heroic full-on frontal assault. And when, in response, their opponents were able to take up tightly configured defensive positions that maximized the density of their firepower, the death toll among the attackers could be staggering.

The Dervish mass attack against the defensive perimeter of General Kitchener's Anglo-Eyptian army at Omdurman on September 2, 1898, was wildly valiant and catastrophically self-destructive. Arrayed in a semicircle behind a *zariba* (a fence of thornbushes that functioned like rolls of barbed wire), Kitchener commanded 8,200 British and 17,000 Egyptian troops. At his back, gunboats mounting one hundred guns stood ready in the Nile. At dawn, a Dervish army of about 50,000 launched a frontal attack that must have been a terrifying thing to behold, but they were cut down by Kitchener's six Maxim guns, field artillery as well as shells from the flotilla, and riflemen firing in disciplined volleys (dumdum bullets adding to the lethality). Not one attacker reached the perimeter. Somewhere in the region of 10,000 Dervish bodies (some accounts put it as high as 15,000) littered the desert: "not a battle but an execution," as a British war correspondent described it. The 48 Anglo-Egyptian casualties sustained came mainly from the nearly disastrous charge of the Twenty-First Lancers, in which the young Winston Churchill took part—a stirring but misguided heroic flourish so beloved of Victorian Britons.

One of the keys to European dominance was the adoption on a.significant scale of the breech-loading rifle in the 1860s. It was a force multiplier that closed down one of the main tactical opportunities offered to indigenous attackers—waiting for the opportunity to penetrate a defense that the fairly lengthy reloading of a rifled musket afforded (the Fetterman massacre being a good example). Almost exactly seven months after the Fetterman incident, a detachment of twenty-eight men of C Company, Twenty-Seventh Infantry under the command of Captain James Powell left Fort Phil Kearny on the last day of July 1867 to supervise civilian woodcutters on nearby Piney Island. Wagons used for hauling the wood had been partially dismantled (the boxlike containers had been taken off the wheels to allow the woodcutters to haul logs using only the running gear). Indian attacks on woodcutting parties were common, and Powell prudently arranged fourteen of these boxes in a protective corral, filling the spaces between them with sacks of grain, logs, and anything else that might provide protection. Rifle loopholes in the wagon sides enabled the men to lie in the wagon-box beds and fire on attackers. His men were armed not with the muzzle loaders with which the Indians were familiar but with the new second Allin modification of the model 1866 Springfield (a conversion of the 1863 muzzle-loading Springfield to a breechloader firing the 1866 .50-caliber center-fire cartridge—the very latest development in self-contained metal-jacketed ammunition). Powell had enough rifles and plenty of ammunition for his men and the civilian contractors.

Within a few days of Powell's arrival on Piney Island a large body of Indians (some estimates put it as high as three thousand) under the Sioux war chief Red Cloud had gathered in a general uprising; and of these, a substantial number were detailed to wipe out Powell's improvised fort. The first phase was a grand mounted charge of about five hundred warriors. Against muzzle-loading muskets, the Indians had every expectation of absorbing the initial volleys and then overrunning the defenders as they reloaded. But at close range the Springfields opened up a devastating and, to the Indians' amazement, continuous fire.

The charge having been bloodily repulsed, Red Cloud, conducting the attacks from a nearby hill, resorted to a skirmish line that poured in rifle and arrow fire. The bullets mainly hit the wagons rather than the men, and the arrows fell into the thick army blankets that had been draped over the wagon boxes. The third and final phase was a magnificent massed charge of the main Indian force. Again, Powell held fire until the range had shortened; his fusillades were of such intensity that they produced "a slaughter such as no living Indian had experienced or heard of."[31] The battle was finally resolved with the arrival of US reinforcements that drove off the now demoralized Sioux and Cheyenne. Powell had lost 5 men killed out of 32 combatants. Red Cloud, when interviewed after the war, said that he attacked Powell with 3,000 braves and lost over half. When asked if 1,500 had been killed, Red Cloud replied, tersely, "I lost them. They never fought again."[32]

The British war against the Abyssinians in the late 1860s proved to be a highly satisfactory testing ground for breechloaders. At Fahla on April 9, 1868, the Abyssinian host streamed down the heights to attack the baggage train of an invading Anglo-Indian force commanded by General Sir Robert Napier. Using breech-loading Snider-Enfields, the invaders left 700 Abyssinian warriors dead and 1,700 wounded. Two of Napier's men died.* Two days later, on the plain of Arogi, the whole bloody scenario was reenacted. The war correspondent G. A. Henty (who later, as a prolific author of adventure books for young Victorians, did much to romanticize the idea of Empire) described the Abyssinians' charge as as "pretty a sight as has ever been presented in modern warfare. . . . Upwards of 5,000 of Theodore's [the Abyssinian emperor's] bravest soldiers sallied out [from the royal fortress of Magdala]; scarce as many hundreds returned to the fortress. Over five hundred were killed, and our soldiers earnestly expressed the hope that it would be unnecessary to storm the fortress, for fighting with these poorly-armed natives was little short of slaughter."[33] Not one of Napier's soldiers was killed.

In addition to breech-loading rifles, the 1860s saw a spurt of weapons innovation that tipped the balance of colonial warfare even more in favor of the invading colonizers. If breech-loading

---

* Although the technique of breechloading had been known since the seventeenth century, breechloaders made their first appearance in the British Army on a very limited scale during the American War of Independence, in the form of the Ferguson rifle.

rifles firing metal-jacketed rounds significantly increased the rate of fire, then repeating rifles such as the magazine-fed, seven-shot, lever-action Spencer, first introduced into the US Army in 1860,* as well as the introduction of machine guns, took it to a different level. In 1862 the American Richard Gatling received a patent for a crank-operated gun capable of firing two hundred rounds per minute. "It bears the same relation to other firearms," boasted Gatling, "that McCormack's Reaper [the mechanical harvesting machine that had revolutionized American agriculture in the nineteenth century] does to the sickle."[34] Interestingly, Gatling viewed his brutally efficient (if sometimes stuttering) killing machine as in some way making warfare more economical of lives. In 1877 he wrote:

> It may be interesting to you to know how I came to invent the gun that bears my name. . . . In 1861, during the opening events of the [American Civil] war . . . I witnessed almost daily the departure of troops to the front and the return of the wounded, sick and dead. The most of the latter lost their lives, not in battle, but by sickness and sickness incident *to the service*. It occurred to me that if I could invent a machine—a gun—that would by its rapidity of fire enable one man to do as much battle duty as a hundred, that it would to a great extent, supersede the necessity of large armies, and consequently exposure to battle and disease would be greatly diminished.[35]

---

* At Beecher's Island on the Arikaree River, Colorado, in September 1868, 50 US Army scouts under Major George Forsyth were attacked by some hundreds of Cheyenne commanded by Roman Nose. Armed with Spencer repeaters, the scouts killed somewhere in excess of 100 braves (including Roman Nose) for the loss of 2 men.

The efficiencies of automated killing were particularly valued
in colonial warfare, where the cost of maintaining armies far from
the home base was onerous. Ironically, the very success of machine
guns in killing cost-effective quantities of natives tainted them
when it came to European warfare, where it was felt, particularly
among the officer class, that mechanization would reduce combat to a competition between meat grinders. Machine guns were
simply part of that unheroic yet irresistible curve that had started
when the first knight was shot out of his saddle by an arquebus.
The resistance was adamant, and it would take the cataclysm of
the First World War to kill off the ancient idea of heroic combat.
Something of this ambiguity—the machine gun as awesome yet
detestable—is plain in a British *Army and Navy Gazette* account
of the 1884 battle of Tel-el-Kebir during the war in Sudan: "The
naval machine gun battery, consisting of six Gatlings . . . reached
the position assigned to it. . . . Having received orders to advance
they came within easy reach of the Tel-el-Kebir earthworks. . . .
Rounds whisked [from] the Gatlings, r-r-r-r-r-rum, r-r-r-r-r-rum,
r-r-r-r-r-rum! That hellish note the soldier so much detests in
action, not for what it has done, so much, as for what it could do,
rattled out."[36]

In the early 1880s Hiram Maxim, an American inventor and
firearms entrepreneur, developed a machine gun that would rely
for reloading on the automatic action of gas pressure rather than
hand cranking. He had reviewed the weakness of the competition:

The workmanship of the guns [Gatling, Gardner, Nord-
enfelt, and Hotchkiss] is exquisite. Their weak point does
not lie here, but arises from another cause, which would be
very difficult to remedy in them. It is said by some military
men that no machine-gun has ever been brought into action
which has not become "jammed" at some critical moment.

[At Abu Klea, Sudan, for example, a British column under Sir Hubert Stewart was attacked by a much larger force of Mahdists on June 16, 1885. The single Gardner machine gun was placed outside the square and got off seventy rounds before jamming and being overrun with the loss of eight British killed.] Even if that is not strictly true, still the liability to accident from this cause is very great. A certain percentage of all cartridges fail to explode promptly at the instant of being struck: to use the technical expression, they "hang fire." Suppose that, while the handle of the gun is being worked at its highest speed, one of these sluggish cartridges happens to enter the barrel. It is struck and instantly, before it explodes, the breech is opened, and the cartridge begins to be withdrawn again out of the barrel. At this instant the explosion takes place, breaks the shell in two, drives the front half out of the breech and sometimes blows up the magazine. At any rate, it always drives the forward end of the cartridge firmly into the chamber of the barrel; and if the magazine does not explode, the next rotation of the crank drives a loaded cartridge into the chamber; the gun then becomes blocked or jammed, and of no further use.[37]

Maxim's gun was, by comparison, self-regulating: "If a round fails to fire, it stops the action of the gun. . . . The gunner can then manually eject a faulty round . . . and continue firing as before; the misfire does not result in the gun becoming jammed solid and thus useless."[38]

By the 1880s, Maxim's machine gun was "bowling over and dropping like nine pins" (to use the sporting analogy favored by British commentators) large numbers of native warriors who through some ancient heroic compulsion for massed frontal attack fed themselves into the killing machine. An observer at

Omdurman salivated: "The Dervishes seemed to rise up out of the ground, making full use of [the available cover]. For a moment it seemed that they might overwhelm Kitchener's forces [as] in dense array, moved to consume their feast of flesh, but their ranks were torn by murderous machine-gun fire. As soon as the gunners found the range, the enemy fell in heaps, and it was evident that to the Maxims went a large measure of credit in repelling the Dervish onslaught. [The official account credits them with three-quarters of all casualties.]"[39]

The war against the Matabele in 1890 was a joint venture between the British state and a private company, Cecil Rhodes's Chartered British South Africa Company, and the Maxim was a massively persuasive voice in the acquisition of Matabeleland. About four thousand Ndebele (the dominant tribe in Matabeleland) attacked a British force of about seven hundred that, apart from rifles and two small artillery pieces, was armed with five Maxims. The machine guns' interlocking fields of fire left fifteen hundred warriors dead. The *Daily News* of London observed: "Most of the Matabele had probably never seen a machine-gun in their lives. Their trust was in their spears, for they had never known an enemy able to withstand them. Even when they found their mistake, they had the heroism to regard it as only a momentary error in their calculations. They retired in perfect order and re-formed for a second rush. Once more, the Maxims swept them down in the dense masses of their concentration. It seems incredible that they should have mustered for another attack, but this actually happened. They came as men foredoomed to failure."[40]

It was a splendid investment. For the loss of fifty white men's lives and a cost of perhaps fifty thousand pounds, the colonists had won 400,000 acres.

And yet, despite the evident success of machine guns in killing large numbers of black men at a discount cost per head, the military establishment back in England resisted embracing the machine gun. It was precisely the fact that it had been used primarily in colonial warfare against enemies considered backward and in every way inferior that tainted the weapon in the eyes of the military hierarchy. It was not quite right, not, somehow, within the tradition of European warfare.

The wars of the British against the Boers of South Africa (the first in 1880–81; the second, 1899–1902) were unlike other colonial wars in that the Boers were white, armed with relatively modern weapons, and pretty skilled in their use. If the heroic tradition of Western warfare was predicated on frontal attack, the British Army fighting the Boers, particularly during the Second South African War, had a foretaste of how that tradition, as tenacious as it was, could be destroyed by the skillful use of modern rifles and artillery artfully deployed behind sound defensive positions protected by barbed wire.

Although the British had already experienced the killing power of Boer riflemen during the First South African War, with bloody defeats at Laing's Nek (for example, a frontal attack cost the Fifty-Eighth Regiment 160 casualties, including all its officers, out of its initial strength of 480) and Majuba Hill (on which the British lost 93 men killed, including their commander, Sir George Colley, and 133 wounded, for the loss of 1 Boer killed and 5 wounded), they nurtured a contempt for what they considered a bunch of hick farmers. In one week—the "Black Week" of December 10–15, 1899—the British suffered 7,000 casualties in actions that included two catastrophic frontal charges, at Magersfontein and Colenso. Nor could they complain that they had not been given fair warning. In November 1899, Lord Methuen, the British commander-in-chief, had made three frontal attacks: at Belmont, Graspan, and the Modder River. In each case entrenched Boers, armed with the superb German-manufactured, magazine-fed Mauser rifle, coolly shot down the attackers, inflicting well over

1,000 casualties for negligible loss. Nothing if not consistent, Methuen committed the Highland Brigade to a frontal attack at Magersfontein, where they met not only withering rifle fire but also three heavy machine guns, Krupp-manufactured artillery, and barbed wire. The rout that followed was comprehensive and shocking. There were more than 800 British casualties including 120 killed. Four days later another British commander, General Sir Redvers Buller, was defeated at Colenso with 143 killed, 755 wounded, and ten of his artillery pieces captured—an unforgivable humiliation. The Boers lost 6 killed and 21 wounded.[41] The whole war would cost the British 22,000 dead, of whom 5,832 were killed in battle, the rest dying from wounds and disease.[42]

In all this there was something chillingly prescient. The barbed wire, the machine guns, the mass attacks against entrenched and prepared riflemen—"a dress parade," wrote Rudyard Kipling in 1903.

SIX

"THIS HIGH PLACE OF SACRIFICE"

"Going West" in World War I

★

In answer to the German bugles or trumpets came the cheerful sounds of our officers' whistles, and the riflemen . . . sprang to action. The great roar of musketry rent the air, varying slightly in intensity from minute to minute as whole companies ceased fire and opened again. . . .

Our rapid fire was appalling [lethal], even to us, and the worst marksman could not miss, as he had only to fire in the "brown" of the masses of the unfortunate enemy, who on the fronts of two of our companies were continually and uselessly reinforced at the short range of three hundred yards. Such tactics amazed us, and after the first shock of seeing men slowly and helplessly falling down as they were hit, gave us a great sense of power and pleasure. It was all so easy.

—Corporal John Lucy, Royal Irish Rifles, at the battle of Mons, 1914[1]

The [leading wave] was now half-way across no-man's-land. "Get ready!" was passed along our front . . . and heads appeared over each shell crater edge as final positions were taken up for the best view and machine guns mounted firmly in place. A few moments later, when the British line was within a hundred yards, the rattle of machine gun and rifle fire broke out along [our] whole line of shell holes. . . . The advance rapidly crumpled under a hail of shell and bullets. All along the line men could be seen throwing up their arms and collapsing, never to move again. . . . The extended lines, though badly shaken and with many gaps, now came on all the faster. Instead of a leisurely walk they covered the ground in short rushes at the double [and] within a few minutes the leading troops had advanced to within a stone's throw of our front trench. . . . Again and again the extended lines of British infantry broke against the German defence like waves against a cliff, only to be beaten back. It was an amazing spectacle of unexampled gallantry, courage and bull-dog determination on both sides.

—A German eyewitness to the first day of the battle
of the Somme, 1916[2]

C ORPORAL LUCY AT Mons and the German observer at the Somme are describing the central strategic tactical truth of the First World War: Defensive capability would usually trump offensive ambitions, and even relatively successful attacks would have a very significant price tag. The lure of the possibility of the offensive breakthrough, the victory of dash, courage, and discipline, the concentration of numbers, the faith in the preparatory bombardment, all were part of the siren call of attacking warfare. The more securely locked into their defenses the protagonists became, the more frantically did the strategists search for the attacking key. The force that drove the First World War and sent so many to their deaths was, ironically, the belief in the holy grail of mobility. Although the spirit was surprisingly willing, the human body, exposed in the pitiless killing grounds of no-man's-land or the trenches, was all too often no match for the homicidal efficiencies of organized rifle fire, concerted machine gunnery, or artillery ordnance in vast number and variety and targeting capability, all aided and abetted by deep swaths of barbed wire that tenaciously defied attempts by the opposing artillery to destroy it. As one military historian succinctly puts it, attackers were "unable to advance, unwilling to retire, meat for artillery fire."[3]

The mortality statistics of the First World War are almost as opaque and slippery as the mud of the Western Front. Data was not methodically collected; commentators sometimes confuse overall casualty statistics with those who were killed, or they add in deaths from disease and other non-battle-related fatalities. However, a consensus suggests that during the course of the war, in all theaters and across all combatants, approximately 8.6 million men were either killed in action or died from wounds. Of the larger combatants, Germany lost 1.8 million; Russia, 1.7 million; France, 1.3 million; Austria-Hungary, 922,000; Britain, 650,000 (and its empire, another 226,000); and Italy, 460,000.[4] America lost approximately 116,000 men from all causes, of which 53,400 were combat fatalities.[5] To put it another way, in France there were 34 deaths per 1,000 population; in Germany, 30; in Britain, 16.[6] The ratio of killed to wounded for the whole war was 3 wounded for every combat death.[7] But in some battles the ratio was far worse. On the first day of the Somme, July 1, 1916, the attacking British troops suffered 38,230 casualties and 19,240 killed: a ratio of just under 2 to 1. An attacking British infantryman on that day had about a one in five chance of being killed.[8]

If the Somme was a massive hemorrhage for the British and French armies (the July–November battle would rack up "official" British casualty figures of 420,000 and 204,000 for the French), it was also an unmitigated catastrophe for the

Germans, who suffered 650,000–680,000 casualties. If the war of attrition—*Materialschlacht* is the German term—had any justification, then it was here on the Somme. After the war the Reichsarchiv (German Imperial Archive) recognized that the "grave loss of blood affected Germany very much more heavily than the Entente. . . . The *Materialschlacht* gnawed terribly into the entrails of the defenders. . . . The consequence was a frightful death-roll of the finest and most highly trained soldiers, whose replacement became impossible. It was in this that the root of the tragedy of the battle lies. . . . The Somme was the muddy grave of the German field army."[9] When General Erich von Falken-hayn (and later Hindenburg and Ludendorff) applied the Ger-man version of *Materialschlacht*, during the grotesque ten-month slugfest at Verdun in 1916, he discovered the central truth of attritional warfare: To make your enemy bleed, you too have to bleed. According to the *French Official War History*, France suf-fered 377,231 casualties, of which 162,308 were killed or missing. The Germans took approximately 337,000 casualties, of whom about 100,000 were killed or missing.[10]

Officers were twice as likely to be killed as the men they led.[11] An anonymous British junior officer wrote in 1917: "I am cer-tainly not the same as I was a year ago. . . . After all, just imagine my life out here: the chances of surviving the next battle for us platoon commanders is about 4 to 1 against!"[12] In the German army the infantry casualty rate as a whole was 13.9 percent, but for the officer class it was a staggering 75.5 percent.[13] During a disastrous attack by the Argyll and Sutherland Highlanders at La Bassée in 1915, of the 16 officers who led their men, 14 were killed (87.5 percent).[14] Corporal Hodges of the Royal Fusiliers had 5 company commanders between April and November 1918, and of those, 4 were killed. One, he recalled, "was not with us long for me to get to know his name. He was the one who was wounded and then killed with stretcher-bearers."[15]

★   ★   ★

AND HOW WERE soldiers killed? What weaponry, rolling off the
production lines in unprecedentedly prodigious quantities, did
them in? And what strategies and tactics—so intricately enmeshed
in that great web of political goals, civilian expectations, weapons
capabilities, available manpower, topography—led men to their
deaths? Death could come in many ways, as Private Bernard
Livermore remembered: "Death from a sniper's bullet, death from
a rifle grenade, death from a Minnie [sometimes referred to as a
"moaning Minnie," slang for *minenwerfer*, a German mortar used
to throw a 100- to 200-pound shell into opposing trenches] or a
toffee apple [stick grenade]; death from shrapnel (possibly from
our own guns) or from gas, if the wind were in the right direction.
Death also might come from bayonet or nail-studded cosh if the
Bosche raided our lines."[16]

The greatest killer, however, was artillery, hence the shockingly high proportion of men whose bodies were never recovered
and who have no known grave. More than 300,000 British and
British Empire dead of the Western Front—40 percent of the total
killed there—were never found.[17] On the Menin Gate memorial at
Ypres alone, the names of 54,896 British and Empire dead whose
bodies were never recovered are recorded. The great vaulted memorial, designed in 1921, proved too small to carry all the names of
the unrecovered dead, so those killed after August 15, 1917, were
recorded on the Memorial to the Missing at Tyne Cot cemetery.
On the memorial at Thiepval there are 73,367 names of men killed
who have no known grave, and that encompasses losses during the
fighting on the Somme (1915–1918). They were either obliterated
or churned into the earth by remorseless artillery fire.

Captain J. C. Dunn, the much-decorated medical officer of the
Second Battalion, Royal Welch Fusiliers, describes the transition

from death by small arms, which was preponderant in the early phase of the war, to artillery as the primary cause as the war progressed. In October 1914, he records, "Most of the deaths were from rifle-fire, shells caused comparatively few." A year later, however, he observes that "the wounds on this front are mostly multiple and often horrible, being nearly all caused by shell or mortar-bomb or grenade."[18] Artillery was a much more efficient killer than infantry. According to Paddy Griffith's calculations, the British infantry lost one casualty (wounded as well as killed) for every 0.5 it caused, whereas artillery lost one casualty for every 10 it caused.[19]

Taking the war overall, small arms, particularly machine guns, accounted for the next largest segment of deaths. In one representative British division, 58 percent fell to artillery, 37 percent to small arms, and 5 percent to other agents (bombs, gas, and bayonets, for example).[20] Of those killed by bullets, about half fell to machine-gun fire, and of all casualties about 25 percent were inflicted by machine-gun fire.[21] Although it caused fewer deaths than artillery, the machine gun became the exemplar of killing on an industrial scale. By 1914 both Britain and Germany were manufacturing machine guns based on Hiram Maxim's patents. Vickers received its license in 1892; Krupp the following year. Leading up to the war the supply of machine guns to the British Army had been minuscule (only eleven per year from 1904).[22]

The officer class of European armies, drawn largely from the landed gentry, was deeply rooted in the preindustrial era. Mechanized warfare lacked the heroic attributes of the rifle and especially the bayonet, and so the antediluvians "clung to their old beliefs in the centrality of man and the decisiveness of personal courage and individual behaviour."[23] Although it was a tension that played out all through the war, nothing could prevent the massive industrialization of combat killing. In 1914, Germany deployed 4,900 machine guns (of which most, 4,000, were on the Western Front); France had 2,500, and the British Expeditionary

Force (BEF) could muster the grand total of 108. By war's end, however, Vickers had made not only 71,350 Maxim-style machine guns but also 133,000 Lewis guns. (Weighing 30 pounds, including a forty-seven-round drum magazine, they were the first truly effective light machine guns.)[24]

Machine guns were just the job for relatively unskilled "operators." The mass levies of citizen-soldiers who replaced the small cadre of professionals (mostly killed off by early 1915) did not have the handcrafted rifle skills, honed over years of practice, of the old sweats (thirty rounds in one minute, all on target at 300 yards, was not unusual) and so "power . . . passed from the artist to the artisan."[25]

That is not to say that the operators did not take pride in their machines. George Coppard remembered his Vickers almost fondly: "This weapon proved to be most successful, being highly efficient, reliable, compact and reasonably light. The tripod was the heaviest component, weighing about 50 pounds; the gun itself weighed 28 pounds without water [water-cooling extended firing time]. With a gun in good tune the rate of fire was well over 600 rounds per minute. There were normally six men in a gun team. Number One was leader and fired the gun, while Number Two controlled the entry of ammo belts into the feed-block. Number Three maintained a supply of ammo to Number Two, and Numbers Four to Six were reserves and carriers."[26] If those six men had been employed as riflemen, each one would have been able to get off approximately twelve rounds per minute for a total of seventy-two rounds: a very poor exchange compared with their machine-gun function. In 1914, machine guns (in the British army two per battalion, twelve battalions to a division) could deliver the equivalent of 9,120 rifles per division. By the end of the war they could deliver the equivalent of 38,000.[27]

In the beginning of the war the Germans had about the same ratio of machine guns to infantry as did the BEF, but they tended to concentrate their guns in separate companies rather than allocating them to infantry battalions under infantry control as the British did until the formation of the Machine Gun Corps in October 1915. At the hands of the Germans the British learned the very bitter lesson of the effectiveness of machine guns deployed in concentration and manned by troops trained specifically in their use. At the battle of Neuve-Chapelle in March 1915, for instance, the Second Scottish Rifles went into the attack preceded by an intensive artillery barrage intended to knock out any resistance in the German front trench:

> Ferrers was first out from "B" company, his monocle in his eye and his sword in his hand. As the guns stopped firing there was a moment of silence. Then the guns started again, firing behind the German lines. . . . Almost at the same moment came another noise, the whip and crack of the enemy machine guns opening up with deadly effect. From the intensity of their fire, and its accuracy, it was clear that the shelling had not been as effective as expected. . . . As the attack progressed the German positions which did most damage were two machine gun posts in front of the Middlesex [the Second Battalion of the Middlesex Regiment was an extension of the attacking line of which the Second Scottish Rifles was a part]. Not only did they virtually wipe out the 2nd Middlesex [battalion sizes varied, but about 600 would be average] with frontal fire, but they caused many of the losses in the 2nd Scottish Rifles with deadly enfilade, or flanking fire [meaning, instead of firing into the attackers frontally, they were firing into their flanks and therefore able to hit a great many more men].[28]

The bloody effectiveness of even a single machine gun is recorded in Robert Graves's classic *Good-bye to All That* (1929).

The Royal Welch Fusiliers (in which Graves was a courageous officer) also found themselves side by side with the Middlesex in an attack near La Bassée on September 25, 1915:

> It had been agreed to advance by platoon rushes with supporting fire. When his [a Royal Welch officer's] platoon had gone about twenty yards, he signalled them to lie down and open covering fire. The din was tremendous. He saw the platoon on his left flopping down too, so he whistled the advance again. Nobody seemed to hear. He jumped up from the shell-hole, wave and signalled "Forward!"
>
> Nobody stirred.
>
> He shouted: "You bloody cowards, are you leaving me to go on alone?"
>
> His platoon-sergeant, groaning with a broken shoulder, gasped: "Not cowards, Sir. Willing enough. But they're all f—ing dead." The Pope's Nose machine-gun, traversing, had caught them as they rose to the whistle.[29]

★   ★   ★

THE ARTILLERY SPOKE its own language, in which sinuous and seductive whispering was interspersed with a vocabulary of screaming brutality. Frederic Manning, a private on the Somme who went on to write one of the best books about the war, the novel *Her Privates We* (1930), describes how the "shells streamed overhead, sighing, whining, and whimpering for blood; the upper air fluttered with them . . . with its increasing roar another shell leaped towards them, and they cowered under the wrath. There was the enormous grunt of its eruption, the sweeping of harpstrings, and part of the trench wall collapsed inwards, burying some men in the landslide."[30] Captain Dunn remembered how the "big howitzer coughed huskily from time to time, and high overhead its shell sizzled and soughed eerily beneath the stillness in the starry sky, to burst so far [away] that the report was muffled and there was no echo although sounds carried far."[31]

"It's an easier matter to describe these sounds than to endure them," writes Ernst Jünger in his classic memoir, *Storm of Steel* (1920), "because one cannot but associate every single sound of flying steel with the idea of death. . . . Imagine you are securely tied to a post, being menaced by a man swinging a heavy hammer. Now the hammer has been taken back over his head, ready to be swung, now it's cleaving the air towards you, on the point of touching your skull, then it's struck the post, and the splinters are flying—that's what it's like to experience heavy shelling in an exposed position."[32]

It was as well to listen carefully and learn the shells' language. One's life could depend on it. P. J. Campbell, a young gunnery officer on the Western Front, was lucky enough to have been given a primer by a more experienced colleague: "He told me how to distinguish shells by the sound they made, and how to tell whether they were going to burst at a safe distance or not. 'When you hear a slow rather tired noise,' he said, 'you've got no need to worry, that one's not going to hurt you. But if it's a rumbling noise like this,' and he imitated the noise that a child makes, playing at trains by himself, 'then you run to the nearest dug-out. And if you hear a sudden whistling scream getting louder and louder and coming straight at you, then you fall flat on the ground and pray, you've no time for anything else.'"[33]

Soldiers became almost affectionately familiar with the characteristics of different types of ordnance. The lethal had become their area of expertise, and they discussed it in the same way they would the relative merits and demerits of different automobiles. The French soldier and novelist Henri Barbusse recalled just such a conversation among aficionados:

Suddenly he bends down. We do the same.

Bsss, bsss . . .

"The fuse! It's gone over."

The shrapnel fuse goes straight up and comes down vertically while the percussion fuse falls out of the shattered shell after the explosion and usually remains buried at the point of impact; but sometimes it takes off and goes wherever it wants, like a huge incandescent pebble. You have to be careful. It can attack you a long time after the explosion and in incredible ways, passing over the parapet and diving into holes.

"Nothing as nasty as a fuse. Now what happened to me was . . ."

"There's worse than that," Bags, of the 11th, interrupts. "Austrian shells: the 130 and 74. Now, they do put the wind up me. . . ."

"That's like the German 105: you don't have time to lie down and get your chops close to the ground. . . ."

"Let me tell you about marine shells: you don't have time to hear them; you've got to get out of the way first."

"There's also that bastard of a new shell which only blows up after ricocheting on the ground and going up and down once or twice. . . . When I know they've got one of those up ahead I shit myself." . . .

"That's nothing, all that, mates," says the new sergeant. . . . "You should see what they chucked at us in Verdun. . . . Nothing except ginormous stuff: 380s, 420s, the two kinds of 44. When you've had a proper shelling down there then you can truly say, 'I've been shelled!' "[34]

The soldiers' almost jocular familiarity served to disarm, in the only way they could, weapons of such terrifying destruction. And so the soldiers gave the different shells nicknames: "A Lazy

Eliza was a long-range shell, probably destined for a distant battery, that rustled harmlessly overhead. But Pissing Jenny and Whistling Percy were shells from German 9-inch naval guns, and the Wipers Express was a heavy gun notably used at the second battle of Ypres. A whiz-bang or a pip-squeak was the shell from a German 77-mm field gun, often fired at such close range that the whistle of the shell's arrival almost coincided with the sound of its explosion. . . . A Coal Box or a Jack Johnson was a heavy shell which burst with a cloud of black smoke."[35]

There was a careful appreciation of the gradations of lethality: "Of a single whiz-bang they would take no notice, but a dozen at the same time could be frightening. Whiz-bangs were the smallest German shells. . . . Next in size were the four-twos. They were more disagreeable, but unless one burst within twenty or thirty yards it was unlikely to hurt you, and a good shelter was proof even against a direct hit by a four-two. But only the strongest kept out a five-nine falling even a hundred yards away . . . there were bigger ones, eight-inch and eleven-inch. These were terrifying."[36]

Technological development in the latter part of the nineteenth century made artillery massively more lethal than earlier guns. From the 1880s the development of advanced explosives such as melenite and lyddite took artillery into another realm, in terms of both range and explosive impact. In the American Civil War, 2,000 yards was about maximum range for most guns, and a very few breech-loading cannon could reach 4,000 yards.[37] In World War I the workhorse British 18-pounder could throw an 18-pound shell 7,000 yards—4 miles—while its German equivalent, the 77-millimeter, could send its 15-pound shell up to 11,700 yards (6.6 miles).[38] The largest guns, such as the French 520-millimeter (20.8-inch) Schneider howitzer, were capable of hurling massive shells vast distances. The Schneider fired a 3,130-pound projectile 11 miles; the American and British 14-inch cannon could send shells weighing 1,400–1,560 pounds between 20 and 30 miles, while the famous German "Paris" gun sent its 264-pound shell about 80 miles, the longest range of the war, and in such a high trajectory that the unfortunate citizens of the City of Light thought they were being bombed by unseen zeppelins.[39]

Other improvements increased artillery lethality. Hydraulic recoil systems made for faster gun laying after each round and speeded up the rate of fire in the hands of an experiencd crew (the famous French 75 could get off twenty-five to thirty rounds a minute).[40] Increasingly sophisticated target location through map reference, aerial photography, and sound ranging with the Tucker microphone, which could pinpoint enemy batteries by listening to the frequencies of incoming shells, made it possible for gunners to locate targets that were far out of sight with much more accuracy. Percussion fuses such as the British 106 and its German equivalent ensured that high-explosive shells detonated immediately on impact to send devastating shock waves horizontally rather than, as before, vertically and less harmfully, when shells often buried themselves in the ground before exploding.

Added to these innovations was the breathtaking amount of ordnance expended. Prior to the Allied attack at Messines (May 26–June 6, 1917), for example, the British fired more than 3.5 *million* shells,[41] and to "read the detailed barrage arrangements at Arras, Messines and Third Ypres (Passchendaele) is to stand in awe and trembling before the sheer scale and power of the aggression."[42] The Germans estimated that in the first year of the war the ratio of casualties caused by artillery compared with infantry was two to one in artillery's favor, but by the last year of the war that ratio had increased to 14 to 1.[43]

Artillery may have been the single-largest killer in the war, but as in earlier and later wars, the amount of ammunition needed to kill a single enemy was startlingly high. Captain J. C. Dunn remarked on November 17, 1915 (admittedly before many of the innovations noted earlier came into effect): "An immense amount of metal can, in fact, be flung about trenches without doing much harm. In the front of a lively sector our casualties . . . have been 1 killed by rifle-bullet and 2 wounded by shell-splinters."[44] Estimates vary from thirty to fourteen hundred shells[45] (an astonishing profligacy exceeded only in the Vietnam War) for one kill, mainly because so much ordnance was used for other purposes, like cutting or, more often than not, failing to cut barbed-wire defenses.[46]

Such statistics, to the dispassionate observer, may seem rather comforting, but to those at the sharp end they had the same actuarial reassurance as Russian roulette. To endure a heavy bombardment was to live in a cacophonous, stinking, screaming madness punctuated by arbitrary obliteration. It was an experience unlike anything in combat before this war. For some, death would have been a blessed relief: "There were times," Corporal Clifford Lane remembered, "after being shelled for hours on end during the latter part of the Somme battle, that all I wanted was to be blown to bits."[47]

To be in this maelstrom was to be suffocated in a violence so profound that time itself was transformed: "Suddenly in front of us and along the whole breadth of the hill, dark flames burst out," remembers Henri Barbusse, "striking the air with appalling explosions. Across the line, from left to right, timed shells fall from the sky and explosives rise from the earth. They form a terrifying curtain that separates us from the world, separates us from the past and the future."[48]

British gunner P. J. Cambell described being caught in a heavy bombardment:

> Then I stopped noticing the crying voices. I was conscious only of my own misery. I lost all count of the shells and all count of time. There was no past to remember or future to think about. Only the present. The present agony of waiting,

waiting for the shell that was coming to destroy us, waiting to die. . . . None of us spoke. I had shut my eyes, I saw nothing. But I could not shut my ears, I heard everything, the screaming of the shells, the screams of pain, the terrifying explosions, the vicious fragments of iron rushing downwards, biting deeply into the earth all round us.

I could not move, I had lost all power over my limbs. My heart throbbed, my face was burning, my throat was parched.[49]

A twenty-year-old junior corporal of the German Ninety-Ninth Reserve Infantry Regiment suffered through the British barrage near Thiepval during the softening-up prior to the battle of the Somme in 1916: "One's head is like a madman's. The tongue sticks to the mouth in terror. Continual bombardment and nothing to eat or drink and little sleep for five days and nights. How much longer can this go on?" For him it ended the next day, when he was killed.[50]

High explosives killed and wounded with terrible violence, but a violence not always manifested by a destroyed body. Captain Dunn records that his battalion was "lightly shelled" at Polygon Wood but "one 4.2 that burst among 3 men sitting in a shell-hole killed them with no more visible mark than some singeing of their clothing."[51] Blast waves had destroyed their vital organs while leaving their outer bodies unnervingly intact. Ernst Jünger described the remarkable effect of a big shell that exploded in the middle of his men: "My one, feeble, consolation was that it might have been even worse. Fusilier Rust, for instance, was standing so close to the bomb blast that the straps on his munitions box caught fire. NCO Pregau, who, admittedly, went on to lose his life the next day, was not even scratched as he stood between two comrades who were torn to ribbons."[52]

But this was freakishly unusual. More often than not, high

explosive ripped men apart. Henri Barbusse re-creates the debate between two French soldiers about whether gas or high explosive was more or less disgusting:

> "That looks like mustard gas. Get your face sacks ready."
> "Pigs!"
> "That's a really unfair move," says Farfadet.
> "What is?" says Barque, jeering.
> "Yes, not decent, I mean, gas . . ."
> "Don't make me laugh," says Barque, "you and your fair and unfair weapons. When you've seen men cut open, chopped in half or split from top to bottom, spread around in pieces by ordinary shells, their bellies gaping and the contents dug out, skulls driven right into the lungs as if from a blow with a mallet or a little neck in place of the head with a blackcurrant jam of brains dripping all round it, on the chest and back . . . when you've seen that then come and tell me about clean, decent weapons of war!"[53]

Their argument is at the core of combat experience in the First World War. The ways in which men were killed all too often robbed them of even a vestige of heroic dignity. They were destroyed within the colorless, featureless anonymity of great numbers, and by weapons of such range and power that they could not so much be engaged on any individual level. Their deaths were due not so much to human acts but to mechanized processes. A reflection of this atomization was the great dread soldiers had not so much about being killed but about being blown to bits. A medical officer in the Royal Fusiliers, Charles Wilson (later to become Lord Moran, Winston Churchill's private physician), observed:

> There were men in France who were ready to go out but who could not meet death in that shape. They were prepared

for it if it came swiftly and cleanly. But that shattering, crude bloody end by a big shell was too much for them. It was something more than death, all their plans for meeting it with decency and credit were suddenly battered down; it was not so much that their lives were in danger as that their self-respect had gone out of their hands. They were at the crisis of their lives dishevelled, plastered with mud and earth and blood; their actions at the mercy of others, they were no longer certain what they might do. That dread experience was the last stone of the house of fear.[54]

Those killed by high explosive could be transmogrified into something bizarrely awesome, even gruesomely aesthetic. Captain Dunn saw the effect of a shell burst: "On the way, two men suddenly rose into the air vertically, 15 feet perhaps, amid a spout of soil. . . . They rose and fell with the easy, graceful poise of acrobats. A rifle, revolving slowly, rose high above them before, still revolving, it fell. The sight recalled, even in these surroundings, a memory of boyhood: a turn that thrilled me in a travelling circus at St. Andrews."[55] And Henri Barbusse describes a comrade hit by high explosive: "I saw his body rising, upright, black, his two arms fully outstretched and a flame in place of his head!"[56]

Shells turned the places of protection—trenches and dugouts—into graves, killing and burying the victim in one instant and convenient act: "Men just disappeared and no one saw them go. A weary Tommy would scratch a hole in the side of the trench's bottom to get out of the way of trampling feet. A minnie would explode, and the earth above him would quietly subside on him. Even if the exact spot was known, what was the good of digging him out? In one stroke he was dead and buried."[57]

It was not always as gentle: "He got it the next morning . . . in the dugout that was caved in by a shell. He was lying down and his chest was crushed. Did they tell you about Franco, who was next to Mondain? The roof falling in broke his spine. He talked after they dug him out and sat him down on the ground. He put his head on one side and said: 'I'm dying.' Then he died. Vigile was with them, too. His body was untouched, but his head was completely flattened, like a pancake, and huge, as wide as this. Seeing him lying on the ground, black and changed in shape, you could have taken him for his shadow."[58]

Shrapnel shells ("woolly bears") exploded above the troops (20 feet was optimum) and pelted them with balls (about 270 per shell) and pieces of shell casing: "A young gunner Subaltern was on his way up to observe a machine-gun position. Just as he got outside my door a shrapnell [*sic*] shell burst full in front of him. The poor fellow was brought in to me absolutely riddled. He lay in my arms until he died, shrieking in his agony and said he hoped I would excuse him for making such a noise as he really could not help it. Pitiful as nothing could be done for him except an injection of morphia."[59]

On occasion, however, death by shrapnel could be quite particular and disconcertingly discriminating: "Lieutenant Julian Tyndale-Briscoe, regarding a 60-foot burst as little more than punctuation to his conversation, found that it mortally wounded an officer and the battery clerk: 'They both died within a minute—very sad—they had only one [shrapnel] bullet each.' " Gerald Burgoyne recalled an incident where the medical officer of a Wiltshire battalion was bending down dressing a wound in a crowded aid post: "A piece [of shrapnel] entering the room killed the doctor at once. The room was crowded at the time, but he was the only person hit."[60]

Artillery had a ravenous and capricious appetite that devoured men in body and spirit. Lord Moran describes the death of the soul of a man almost hit by a Jack Johnson (named after the great American boxer, presumably because it packed a wicked punch):

"It's Sergeant Turner, sir. . . . You see, sir, it burst almost on top of him. . . . It's a miracle, I says, as he's here at all."

I found the Sergeant standing in the trench. He looked at me as if he had something to say but he said nothing. His lip trembled and he was trying to keep his limbs still. He appeared dazed by what he had been through and by this end to everything . . . it was plain to me the game was up and he was done. When this sort of thing happens to a good fellow it is final.[61]

What the guns did not kill by commission they frequently did by omission. The constant complaint of the infantry was the failure of friendly artillery to destroy enemy barbed wire in preparation for an attack. George Coppard surveyed the failed attack around La Boiselle during the first day of the Somme battle:

Hundreds of dead, many of the 37th Brigade, were strung out like wreckage washed up to a high-water mark. Quite as many died on the enemy wire as on the ground, like fish caught in a net. They hung there in grotesque postures. Some looked as though they were praying: they had died on their knees and the wire had prevented their fall. From the way the bodies were equally spread out, whether lying on the wire or lying in front of it, it was clear that there were no gaps in the wire at the time of the attack. Concentrated machine-gun fire from sufficient guns to command every inch of the wire had done its terrible work. . . . Any Tommy could have told them that shell-fire lifts wire up and drops it down, often in a worse tangle than before.[62]

Back in 1915 at the battle of Loos, Sergeant Charles Lippett of the Queen's Royal West Surreys had experienced much the same: "As we approached this wire I could see the bodies of men hanging on it, obviously dead or badly wounded, and there were no gaps in it at all. Our artillery had not cut the wire, even firing 18-pounder shells at it. The shell could land in a certain spot and instead of cutting a neat swathe through the wire to allow the troops through, it just lifted great lumps of it up and made the confusion worse. . . . I couldn't even see where the enemy trench was, the barbed wire was so thick and so deep."[63]

P. J. Campbell knew very well what the problems were: "But most of all it was the wire in front of the trenches that was disconcerting, there was so much and wire was so hard to destroy. It was our job to destroy it, the field gunners'. We had to cut it up using shells that burst on percussion without making much of a hole, heavier guns could have destroyed the wire more effectively, but if they made big craters in the ground, then it was difficult for the infantry to advance."[64] The introduction of the 106 percussion fuse in 1917 went some way to rectifying the situation. Its horizontal blast not only cut wire but also reduced cratering, which in itself could be fatal to those too badly wounded to prevent themselves from drowning in the rain-filled shell holes.

Lieutenant Edwin Campion Vaughan of the Royal Warwicks heard them at Passchendaele in 1917: "From the darkness on all sides came the groans and wails of wounded men; faint, long, sobbing moans of agony, and despairing shrieks. It was too horribly obvious to me that dozens of men with serious wounds must have crawled for safety into shell holes, and now the water was rising above them and, powerless to move, they were slowly drowning."[65]

Henri Barbusse saw them in the Artois:

> Their heads and arms are underwater, but you can see their backs with the leather of their equipment emerging on the surface of the pasty liquid, while their blue cloth trousers are blown up with the feet attached crosswise to these balloon

legs, like the rounded black feet stuck on the shapeless legs of clowns or puppets. From one sunken head the hair is standing upright like waterweed. Here there is a face almost emerging, its head stranded on the edge while the body vanishes into the murky depths. It is looking upwards, its eyes two white holes, its mouth one black one. The puffy yellow skin of this mask looks soft and wrinkled, like cold pastry.[66]

And if enemy shell fire was not sufficiently lethal, there was always the grotesquely misnamed "friendly fire." The French general Alexandre Percin estimated that 75,000 French soldiers were killed by their own artillery.[67] Badly made shells, often with loose driving bands (the soft metal strap around the belly of the shell that bit into the rifling and ensured proper propulsion), were common in the earlier years of the war. On February 27, 1915, the Royal Welch's medical officer recorded, with understandable sarcasm, that "our covering battery fired four rounds somewhat as follows: into Nomansland, into our parapet, behind our line, on to a Company H.Q.; and then telephoned 'Is that enough?' "[68]

On August 10, 1916, Lord Moran recorded a typical incident:

I met Burdett who had taken over "B" Company. . . . "It's our God-damned guns. I can't make out what the hell they are up to," he exclaimed angrily. I pushed on down the trench and suddenly came upon the scene. . . . Shells were bursting all round and in the black smoke men were digging. Muffled appeals for help, very faint and distant came out of the earth and maddened the men who dug harder than ever, and some throwing their spades away burrowed feverishly with their hands like terriers. . . . We were afraid too of injuring those buried heads with the shovels and always through our minds went the thought that it might be too late. Then there was a terrific noise, everything vanished for a moment, and when I could see again Dyson and the two men working beside him had disappeared. They were buried. And then as if they had achieved their purpose in blotting this boy suddenly the guns stopped.[69]

★   ★   ★

THOSE WHO SAW the first release of poison gas on the Western Front—by the Germans on April 22, 1915,* on the northern sector of the Ypres Salient—could have been forgiven for imagining it no more than a distraction: "Two curious greenish-yellow clouds [chlorine] on the ground on either side of Langemarck in front of the German line. These clouds spread laterally, joining up, and moving before a light wind, became a bluish-white mist, such as is seen over water meadows on a frosty night."[70] Its effect, however, was far from attractive, and although it caused relatively few fatalities in comparison to those from other weapons (about 6,000 British, 9,000 German, and 8,000 French; the Russians would lose 56,000, mainly due to a lack of gas masks),[71] it was regarded with horror and contempt as a dirty, underhanded way to conduct warfare.

There were four broad categories of gas: the lachrymators, or "tear gas," which caused intense eye irritation but were not in themselves lethal; the sternutators, "sneeze gas," which caused extreme nasal irritation but again were not in themselves fatal; suffocants, which attacked and corrupted the lungs and were highly dangerous—the most notorious being chlorine and phosgene; and vesicants, primarily "mustard gas," which blistered the skin and, if inhaled, the respiratory tract.

---

* The first use was by Germany against the Russians at Bolimov, west of Warsaw, in January 1915. See Philip Haythornthwaite, *The World War One Source Book* (London: Arms and Armour Press, 1992), 90.

In the early phase of the war, gas was released from tubes mounted in the front trench and, because its delivery depended on wind conditions, could be disconcertingly unpredictable. The German chlorine-gas attack on completely unprepared French colonial troops in April 1915 was immediately successful but not exploited. The first British gas attack, at Loos on September 25, 1915, could have been a disaster, with the gas blowing back into the British trenches, but providentially caused only seven "friendly" deaths.[72]

As the war progressed more sophisticated delivery systems were introduced, such as the mortar-type Livens projector (1917), which lobbed a whole drum of gas (its inventor, Captain W. H. Livens, "expressed the ambition of reducing the cost of killing Germans to a paltry sixteen shillings apiece"),[73] and gas-filled shells fired by regular artillery. In response, gas masks were developed, ranging from the earliest crude pads soaked in urine to rubberized face masks attached to air filters, but they were often cumbersome and suffocatingly uncomfortable. In addition, irritant gases were often delivered in combinations that made wearing a mask extremely uncomfortable if they were inhaled, and lethal if the soldier removed his mask to get some relief.

Phosgene and mustard gas were particularly deadly because once they entered the lungs, they penetrated the cells rapidly and hydrolyzed into hydrochloric acid. The victims essentially drowned in an excess of their own body fluid or, in the case of mustard gas, could die from secondary complications caused by extensive burning. The postmortem examination of a victim of mustard-gas poisoning described the shocking damage:

CASE 9.—C. H. W., 101135, Pvt., R. A. F., 3 Kite Balloon Section. Died, October 23, 1918, at 7.05 a.m., at Base Hospital No. 2. Autopsy, two hours after death, by Capt. B. F. Weems, M.C.

Anatomical diagnosis.-Extensive first and second degree burns of skin; acute conjunctivitis; membrano-ulcerative pharyngitis and tracheitis; laryngitis; membranous bronchitis; lobular pneumonia; congestion and edema [accumulation of fluid] of lungs; interstitial emphysema of lungs; acute fibrinous pleurisy, chronic fibrous pleurisy over right upper lobe; congestion of abdominal viscera; gas-shell wounds of both thighs.

External appearance.-Extensive burns over the trunk and extremities and large, pale yellow blebs [liquid-filled blisters also called *bullae*] upon the anterior surface of both thighs, about the left knee, upon both forearms, and upon the neck and face. Besides these clear bullae, there are large areas of a peculiar dusky, pinkish-purple colour, in most cases adjacent to the bullae and having approximately the same distribution. The face is swollen and covered over the bearded portions by scabby exudate [body fluid]; the skin about both eyes is swollen and discoloured; there is purulent conjunctivitis. A mucopurulent exudate [fluid bubbling up from the lungs] issues from the nostrils. There is extensive gingivitis. Skin over scrotum and penis edematous and in part blistered.[74]

It is no wonder that gas victims sometimes pleaded for a merciful end. Pioneer Georg Zobel witnessed the effects of a British gas attack: "Here and there were men from other units who had been surprised by the gas. They sat or lay and vomited pieces of their corroded lungs. Horrible, this death! And, much as they implored us, nobody dared to give them the *coup de grâce*."[75]

Gas was loathed by combatants not only for the appalling suffering it could cause but because it robbed soldiers of the chance to fight back. Sergeant Major Ernest Shephard was at Hill 60 outside

Ypres on May 1, 1915: "The scene that followed was heartbreaking. Men were caught by fumes and in dreadful agony, coughing and vomiting, rolling on the ground in agony . . . I ran round at intervals and tied up a lot of men's mouths, placed them in sitting positions, and organized parties to assist them. . . . When we found our men were dying from fumes we wanted to charge, but were not allowed to do so. . . . Had we lost as heavily while actually fighting we would have not cared as much, but our dear boys died like rats in a trap, instead of heroes as they all were."[76]

Even the gas mask imposed its own suffocating dehumanization, and this is why, with its bugged-out eyepieces and external trachea, it became such a potent symbol for artists of the war. It seemed to represent men entrapped in a rubberized skull, screaming to get out: "The gas mask makes you feel only half a man," wrote Alan Hanbury-Sparrow of the First Battalion, Royal Berkshire Regiment. "You can't think; the air you breathe has been filtered of all save a few chemical substances. A man doesn't live on what passes through the filter, he merely exists."[77]

★   ★   ★

THE LOCKDOWN OF the Western Front in 1915 ushered in not only trench warfare but also its close relative, subterranean warfare. Mining had been used ever since there were walls to undermine, and in the pregunpowder era the attackers relied on physically weakening walls by creating voids beneath them that would lead to collapse. The advent of gunpowder added the more active ingredient of explosive demolition, the most significant prior to World War I being that blown under the Confederate earthworks defending Petersburg, Virginia, on July 30, 1864, when 8,000 pounds of gunpowder blew a crater 170 feet long and 30 feet deep, killing about three hundred Confederate soldiers in the process.

The development of high-powered explosives such as ammonal offered the possibility of even greater potential damage, and the British in particular invested heavily in mining on the Western Front. The work, though, was not for the faint of heart:

> First of all you go down three or four ladders . . . It's a terrible long way down, and of course you go alone . . . I didn't go far up the gallery where they were working because you can't easily pass along, but the RE [Royal Engineers responsible for British mining operations] officer took me along a gallery that is not being worked, and there, all alone, at the end of it was a man sitting. He was simply sitting, listening. Then I listened through his stethoscope thing* . . . and I could hear the Boche working as plainly as anything. . . . as we went away and left him he looked round at us with staring eyes just like a hunted animal. . . . Of course, while you hear them working, it's all right, they won't blow. But if you don't hear them! God, I wouldn't like to be an RE. It's an awful game.[78]

It was a particularly vicious form of combat. Miners and counterminers would break into each others' tunnels and galleries and fight hand-to-hand with coshes, sharpened spades, pistols, or

---

* French poet-adventurer-soldier Blaise Cendrars was in a stretch of the line riddled with German mines. He found that his pet hedgehog, who, despite lapping up the soldiers' wine, had such acute hearing that he could unerringly locate German miners, "showed every sign of terror and ran off in the opposite direction if he thought there was still time, or rolled himself into a ball at the foot of the trench wall if the enemy was very close. And we instantly took precautions, counter-mines or rapid flight, knowing there was no possibility of error." (Blaise Cendrars, *Lice* (London: Peter Owen, 1973), 145. First published as *La main coupée*, 1946.)

rifles with sawn-off barrels and shortened butts. Counterminers would constantly seek to blow up their counterparts with small mines—camouflets—which even if they did not kill by blast inflicted an even more terrible death by entombment.

The point of it all, though, was to accumulate sufficient explosive beneath the enemy trenches to blow them to kingdom come. The Germans blew ten mines under the Indian Corps at Givenchy on December 20, 1914, causing many deaths.[79] On April 17, 1915, the British blew the top off Hill 60 in the Ypres Salient, beating competing German miners to the punch. But the first truly mighty blast came on the first day of the battle of the Somme, July 1, 1916, at 7:20 a.m., when the British Hawthorn Ridge mine containing about 40,000 pounds of ammonal went off. The explosion could be heard in London. The official history of the German 119th Reserve Regiment records: "During the bombardment there was a terrible explosion which for the moment completely drowned the thunder of the artillery. . . . More than three sections of No. 9 Company were blown into the air, and the neighboring dugouts were broken in or blocked . . . and a gigantic crater . . . gaped like an open wound on the side of the hill."[80]

An even bigger blow, however, came at Messines a year later, on June 7, 1917. Twenty-three mines containing a combined 1 million pounds of explosive spread across a 10-mile front were detonated simultaneously. Major Walter Kranz was watching from a little way behind the German front line on Messines Ridge and saw "nineteen gigantic roses with carmine petals, or as enormous mushrooms, which rose up slowly and majestically out of the ground and then split into pieces with a mighty roar, sending up multi-colored columns of flame mixed with a mass of earth and splinters high into the sky."[81] From the British trenches there "appeared a great green meadow, slowly, taking its time, not hurrying, a smooth curved dome of grass, heaving up, up, up like a rising cake; then, like a cake, it cracked, cracked visibly with bursting brown seams; still the dome rose, towering ten, twenty feet up . . . and then with a roar the black smoke hurtled into the air, followed by masses of pink flame."[82] Ten thousand or so Germans were killed, and "many of the men never came to earth again, except as a rain of blood."[83]

The huge craters themselves became a unique part of the topography of combat—battlegrounds within the battleground. And as it had been with the crater at Petersburg in the American Civil War, the struggle for their control was bitterly and bloodily contested because they could provide vantage points, particularly for snipers, as well as refuges for stranded infantrymen. George Coppard witnessed the blowing of the mine beneath the German Hohenzollern Redoubt in the final stages of the battle of Loos at the end of September 1915. Once the debris had fallen ("a risk to friend and foe alike"),

> the storming party rushed forward to capture the hot and smoking crater. The German flanks bristled with machine guns, and it was a safe bet that they would take a toll of some of our boys before they reached the crater. Those who made it literally dug in their toes to prevent themselves sliding backwards down the steep slope behind them. They lined the rim nearest the enemy, desperately prepared to die in defence of their meager gain. . . . A fierce bombing exchange would break out. Many of the bombs over-shot the rim of the crater and, landing on the bottom, blasted fragments up the slope. . . . Both sides employed snipers at vantage points on the flanks and their deadly work added to the terror. . . . The casualty rate rose rapidly for the first hour after the capture of a crater as alarm spread to neighbouring craters and trenches. Inspired by mutual hate and desperation, the volume of fire from short-range weapons

increased, creating an almost impossible demand for stretcher-bearers. Crater fighters were considered to have a pretty mean chance of survival, twelve hours being reckoned as the limit.[84]

★ ★ ★

WITH THE STRANGULATION of fluid battle and the onset of the rigor mortis of trench warfare, inventive minds turned to what might be called a miniaturized imitation of open warfare: trench raiding. The object was usually to capture enemy troops for interrogation, or simply to inflict demoralizing casualties. It was also employed, in the absence of full-throated battle, to "blood" inexperienced units and have them prove their fighting mettle, and to keep experienced but inactive troops on their toes. To many men, however, it was simply another example of the brass finding ways to get them killed.

Corporal Sidney Amatt of the Essex Regiment described the general idea:

> They never asked for volunteers, they'd say, "You, you, you, and you," and you suddenly found yourself in a raiding party. They went over at night, in silence, and the parties always arranged in the same way. Number one was the rifleman, who carried a rifle, a bayonet, and fifty rounds of ammunition and nothing else. The next man was a grenade thrower and he carried a haversack full of Mills hand bombs. The next man was also a bomb-thrower, he helped the first man replace his stock when it was exhausted. And the last man was a rifle and bayonet man. . . .
>
> The idea was to crawl underneath the German wire and jump into their front-line trench. Then you'd dispose of whoever was holding it, by bayonet if possible, without

making any noise, or by clubbing over the head with the butt. Once you'd established yourself in the trench you'd wend your way round each bay. A rifleman would go first, and he'd stop at the next bay. . . . The bomb-thrower would then throw a grenade towards the next bay, and when that exploded the rifleman who was leading would dash into the trench and dispose of any occupants. . . .

. . . But the raiding parties were rarely successful because by the time we got halfway across no man's land and come up against the Jerry wire, the Germans had usually realised something was going on and opened up their machine-guns on that area. So we'd have to scuttle back to our own lines before we all got killed.[85]

Captain Dunn records the risks of a raid at Cuinchy on April 25, 1916, undertaken by two companies of the Royal Welch:

Another raid has been planned by the C.O. . . . . Fifty-five of B and C Companies are to go for the re-entrants of a small salient on the left of the road. . . . Things went wrong from the start. "Uncle" [one of the officers] sent his contingent up tail first, and so late that they barely got out in time. Then most of them followed Sergeant Joe Williams, who made off half-right, shouting, "Lead on, B Company: lead on, B Company." They ran into uncut wire, were enfiladed by a machine-gun and Joe was killed. That gun was to have been kept quiet by the two new trench-mortars, the Stokes, detailed to protect the right flank, but both broke down when they began to fire. The few of B who followed their officers got into the enemy's trench but found it empty. C Company's 2 officers and 25 men also got in, but all they could bring away was an anti-gas apparatus. Both parties were heavily strafed from behind . . . a second sergeant was left behind dead. Another of the dead was Earnshaw. . . . All four officers were wounded. . . . It was agreed afterwards that the previous day's and the morning's wire-cutting had made him [the Germans] wise, and he was ready—in his second line.[86]

In his play *Journey's End*, R. C. Sheriff, who had served as an officer in the East Surreys and had been wounded at Passchendaele in 1917, has the action pivot on the disastrous outcome of a raid insisted on by headquarters even though it was known that the enemy had been forewarned. The company's commanding officer, Stanhope, tries to dissuade his colonel:

STANHOPE: Meanwhile the Boche are sitting over there with a dozen machine-guns trained on that hole [in their wire]—waiting for our fellows to come.

COLONEL: Well, I can't disobey orders.

STANHOPE: Why didn't the trench-mortars blow a dozen holes in different places—so the Boche wouldn't know which we were going to use?

COLONEL: It took three hours to blow that one. How could they blow a dozen in the time? It's no good worrying about it now. It's too late.[87]

If going out was risky, so was coming back, when nervous sentries could be as lethal as the enemy. Captain H. Blair describes the reception of his returning patrol:

Nearing our wire, I changed places with the corporal, he was leading and I was in rear, for I wanted to warn the listening-post, who might not be expecting us after nearly six hours absence. Not a minute after our change of places two shots were fired from the post. The corporal was hit in the chest and stomach; he died, poor fellow, soon after being got back to the trench. The sentry told me he had been warned that only two had gone on patrol; spotting a third man, he inferred that we were being stalked, and fired. It was a tragic mischance that two snap-shots at 40 yards, by moonlight, at a crawling figure took effect.[88]

The British poet-soldier Siegfried Sassoon, feeling "intensely alive," led a trench raid that ended for him when he foolishly decided "to take a peep at the surrounding country. This was a mistake which ought to have put an end to my terrestrial adventures, for no sooner had I popped my silly head out of the sap than I felt a stupendous blow in the back between my shoulders . . . to my surprise I discovered I wasn't dead."[89]

Sassoon's fellow Royal Welch officer friend and fellow poet Robert Graves felt that night operations, whether trench raiding or patrolling in no-man's-land, at least meant that friendly fire was more or less unaimed, and if one was wounded, the chances of survival were increased because field hospitals would not be overwhelmed with the casualties from a full-scale battle. On the other hand, notes Graves: "Patrolling had its peculiar risks. If a German patrol found a wounded man, they were as likely as not to cut his throat. The bowie-knife was a favourite German patrol weapon because of its silence. (We inclined more to the 'cosh,' a loaded stick.) The most important information that a patrol could bring back was to what regiment and division the troops opposite belonged. So if it were impossible to get a wounded enemy back without danger to oneself, he had to be stripped of his badges. To do that quickly and silently, it might be necessary first to cut his throat or beat in his skull."[90]

★   ★   ★

THE STASIS OF trench warfare encouraged a special breed of
killers. As in the trenches around Petersburg in the American
Civil War, snipers took advantage of their victims' vulnerability
through the carelessness brought on by boredom or inexperience.
In one two-week period in December 1915, for example, British
troops sustained 3,285 casualties, of which about 25 percent were
in all probability head and neck sniper wounds.[91]

George Coppard writes of his mate's death:

> Lulled by the quietness, someone would be foolish and
> carelessly linger with his head above the top of the parapet.
> Then, like a puppet whose strings have suddenly snapped,
> he crashes to the bottom of the trench. There is no gradual
> falling over, but instant collapse. A Jerry sniper with a tele-
> scopic sighted rifle, nicely positioned behind the aperture
> of an armoured plate, has lain patiently, for hours perhaps,
> watching our parapet for the slightest movement. His shot
> is successful and a Tommy is breathing his last, not quite
> lifeless, but dying. The back of the cranium is gone, and the
> grey brain flecked with red is splashed out. A pal of mine
> named Bill Bailey . . . died in this way.[92]

Even in the front line there was something shocking about
the way reassuring domesticity could be instantly and bloodily
smashed. Coppard continues, "There were four of us in a short
section of trench, Bailey, Marshall, myself and another. It was
early morning and stand-to was over. The fire was going nicely
and the bacon was sizzling. I was sitting on the fire-step and just
as I was about to tuck in Bill crashed to the ground. I'll never forget the sound of that shot as it found its billet." After taking Bill

to the first-aid post (where he shortly died), Coppard and his pals returned to the trench "ravenous with hunger." They were hoping to reassemble the shards of normalcy, but the "bacon and bread was on the fire-step, but covered with dirt and pieces of Bill's brain."

Ernst Jünger would have recognized Coppard's unnerving experience of unreality. As he describes:

> A sentry collapses, streaming blood. Shot in the head. His comrades rip the bandage roll out of his tunic and get him bandaged up. "There's no point, Bill." "Come on, he's still breathing, isn't he?" Then the stretcher-bearers come along, to carry him to the dressing-station. The stretcher poles collide with the corners of the fire-bays. No sooner has the man disappeared than everything is back to the way it was before. Someone spreads a few shovelfuls of earth over the red puddle, and everyone goes back to whatever he was doing before. Only a new recruit maybe leans against the revetement, looking a little green about the gills. He is endeavouring to put it all together. Such an incredibly brutal assault, so sudden, with no warning given. It can't be possible, can't be real. Poor fellow, if only you knew what was in store for you.[93]

Sniping takes place in its own ambiguous world. On the one hand it is an act of individual skill, but on the other its anonymity robs it of the kudos usually attached to individual combat. It is valued but reviled, admired but detested:

> The German snipers observed and fired from under the eaves of houses, so it was most difficult to locate them. When a parapet was blown in by a shell, or when a trench caved in with the rain where the men had undercut it for shelter, the sniper looked out for the repair or rescue party. The want of communication trenches, which there had not been time to

get on with, and the places where the sections had not yet dug far out enough to join up, were the causes of many casualties. Snipers covered their working parties; worse still they covered attacks, preventing our men lining the parapet until the attackers were close up. Only in the dark could food and ammunition be brought up and the wounded and dead be taken down.[94]

Although the Allies decried German sniping as "underhanded," they recognized that it was superior to their own, not only in equipment such as superb telescopic sights but also in training, particularly concealment:

The Germans had special regimental snipers, trained in camouflaging themselves. I saw one killed once at Cuinchy, who had been firing all day [a fatal error] from a shell-hole between the lines. He wore a sort of cape made of imitation grass, his face was painted green and brown, and his rifle was also green-fringed. A number of empty cartridges lay beside him [another fatal giveaway of position], and his cap bore the special oak-leaf badge. Few of our battalions attempted to get control of the sniping situation. The Germans had the advantage of having many times more telescopic sights than we did, and bullet-proof steel loop-holes. Also a system by which snipers were kept for months in the same sector until they knew all the loop-holes and shallow places in our trenches, and the tracks that our ration parties used above-ground by night, and where our traverses occurred, and so on, better than most of us did ourselves. British snipers changed their trenches, with their battalions, every week or two, and never had time to study the German trench-geography. But at least we counted on getting rid of the unprofessional sniper. Later we secured an elephant-gun that could send a bullet through enemy loop-holes; and if we failed to locate the loop-hole of a persistent sniper, we tried to dislodge him with a volley of rifle-grenades, or even by ringing up the artillery.[95]

Some snipers would draw a moral line (or at least recognize it). A Canadian marksman confided in the military historian Philip Haythornthwaite that after he had shot a German who was relieving himself in the latrine he felt he was no better than an assassin.[96] And Robert Graves, indulging in some amateur sniping near Cuinchy, was disarmed by a sudden revulsion: "While sniping from a knoll in the support line, where we had a concealed loop-hole, I saw a German, perhaps seven hundred yards away, through my telescopic sights. He was taking a bath in the German third line. I disliked the idea of shooting a naked man, so I handed the rifle to the sergeant with me. 'Here, take this. You're a much better shot than I am.' He got him; but I had not stayed to watch."[97]

★   ★   ★

WHAT WAS LEFT of the warrior code, with its emphasis on individual combat, on a death in some way chosen? There were, of course, many acts of great valor and ennobling self-sacrifice, and there was a kind of individual combat during trench raiding. But the general tenor of warfare had become long-distance, mechanical, anonymous, processed. Nevertheless, within this process there was a need to reassert the power of the individual warrior—and as in all previous wars since the introduction of the gun and cannon, it was the blade that represented the last vestige of the heroic duel. And in World War I that heroic blade was embodied in the bayonet.

The bayonet was the figurative and literal point of the frontal attack. It was by the physical ejection of the enemy from his frontline trenches that defenses could be breached, which reserves could exploit, and victory would be won. The attack with the bayonet also represented the moral fiber of the soldier, and cold steel embodied the aggressive élan that would force the great unlocking of the stalemate.

On the eve of the war, Field Marshal Foch, for example, declared that "the French Army, returning to its traditions, no longer knows any other law than the offensive. . . . All attacks are to be pushed to the extreme with the firm resolution to charge the enemy with the bayonet, in order to destroy him. . . . This result can only be obtained at the price of bloody sacrifices. Any other conception ought to be rejected as contrary to the very nature of war."[98] It was an emphatic reaffirmation of the offensive doctrine of France's revolutionary and Napoleonic armies and would echo Danton's famous invocation of the supremacy of the *attaque a l'outrance: "Il nous faut de l'audace, encore de l'audace, toujours de l'audace et la France est sauvée."*[99] The Germans adhered to the same flamboyant heroic credo: "When the decision to assault originates from the commanders in the rear, notice thereof is given by sounding the signal 'fix bayonets.' . . . As soon as the leading line is to form for the assault, all the trumpeters sound the signal 'forward, double time,' all the drummers beat the drums, and all parts of the force throw themselves with the greatest determination upon the enemy. . . . When immediately in front of the enemy, the men should charge with bayonet and, with a cheer, penetrate the position."[100] (*German Infantry Regulations*, 1899)

The problem proved to be getting to the trenches in the first place, and the frontal attack became the focal point for what many saw as the murderous failure of general staffs in their relentless pursuit of breakthrough. Ironically, in a war that had become literally and metaphorically deadlocked, the strategic obsession, shared by all the general staffs, was with movement and fluidity. Siegfried Sassoon recalls the clash between the tactical realities that inhibited fluid warfare and the official line that insisted upon it: "The Fourth Army School was at Flixécourt. . . . Between Flixécourt and the War . . . there were more than thirty English miles. Mentally, the distance became immeasurable. . . . For instance, although I was closely acquainted with the mine-craters on the Fricourt sector, I would have welcomed a few practical hints on how to patrol those God-forsaken cavities. But the Army School instructors were all in favour of Open Warfare, which was sure to come soon, they said. They had learnt all about it in peacetime; it was essential that we should be taught to 'think in terms of mobility.' "[101]

In the event, disastrous losses for all sides destroyed the possibility of the heroic in the old sense. The impressive extended-order frontal attacks that had characterized the earlier part of the war had to be modified in the face of unacceptable casualties. All the combatant armies on the Western Front developed versions of smaller-scale assault units, less impressive visually but much more pragmatic. Stand-off killing, particularly by artillery and machine guns, reduced the possibility of hand-to-hand fighting, and as a reflection, the incidence of bayonet-inflicted casualties was minuscule: .32 percent, for example, of one sample of 200,000 British casualties.[102] Lord Moran notes: "Hand to hand fighting is vanishing out of war, and even veterans have never met cold steel, which was the way death came to the ancients. Once when I had a bayonet a few inches from my belly I was more frightened than by any shell, but it left nothing behind it. It went out of my mind, it would never happen again."[103]

Nevertheless, there were strenuous attempts throughout the war to keep alive the "spirit" of bayonet fighting. The British *Manual of Bayonet Training* reminds soldiers that "the bayonet is essentially an offensive weapon. In a bayonet assault all ranks go forward to kill or be killed, and only those who have developed skill and strength by constant training will be able to kill. The spirit of the bayonet must be inculcated into all ranks, so that they go forward with that aggressive determination and confidence born of continual practice."[104]

Robert Graves describes the frenzied exhortations of the bayonet instructors at Amiens: "In bayonet-practice, the men had to make horrible grimaces and utter blood-curdling yells as they charged. The instructors' faces were set in a permanently ghastly grin. 'Hurt him, now! In at the belly! Tear his guts out!' they would scream, as the men charged the dummies. 'Now that upper swing at his privates with the butt. Ruin his chances for life! No more little Fritzes! . . . Naaoh! Anyone would think you loved the bloody swine, patting and stroking 'em like that! *Bite him, I say! Stick your teeth in him and worry him! Eat his heart out!*' "[105]

Most instructors themselves were, to use British Army parlance, "all mouth and trousers." When pressed, the officer in charge of British bayonet training admitted that very few had actually been involved in real bayonet fighting. "But we don't insist on their telling the strict truth when asked that question."[106]

Bayonet fighting may have been rare, but it could be ruthlessly effective.* Gunner officer P. J. Campbell recalled entering a

---

* Although there is much evidence to support the idea that bayonet combat was rare, it is interesting to read a contrary opinion, by someone who was at the sharp end. John Laffin was an Australian infantryman in World War II, and in his history of battlefield medicine, *Combat Surgeons* (London: J. M. Dent, 1970), 152, observes: "I think surgeons may be mistaken in their assumption that few wounds are made with the bayonet. Such an assumption ignores the frequent and early fatality of bayonet wounds: a man with a bayonet wound in the throat, stomach or chest does not live long enough to reach the surgeon. Again, a bayonet wound is often a secondary one. That is, soldiers attacking forward after firing at an enemy often kill with the bayonet disabled troops who are nevertheless still firing their rifles or machine guns. I can only say from experience . . . that bayonet fighting occurs more frequently than surgeons believe, although few soldiers would engage in it if they still had a bullet in their firearms."

German trench that had just been captured: "The field in front of me looked utterly peaceful, but only fifty yards away there was that trench, full of dead Germans . . . the grey faces, the poor twisted bodies. They had been bayoneted by the Canadians in the morning, you can't take prisoners in a front-line trench in an attack."[107] Private Stephen Graham remembered that such ruthlessness had been insisted on when clearing an enemy trench: "The second bayonet man kills the wounded. . . . You cannot afford to be encumbered by wounded enemies lying at your feet."[108]

Like most hand-to-hand combat, it was more often than not messy rather than parade-ground clean: "I saw one man single me out and come at me with his bayonet. He made a lunge at my chest, and, as I guarded, his bayonet glanced aside and wounded me in the hip; but I managed to jab him in the left arm and get him on the ground, and when he was there I hammered him on the head with the butt-end of my rifle."[109]

Even with a relatively clean kill there was an appalling intimacy to deal with. Sergeant Stefan Westmann describes bayoneting a Frenchman:

> I was confronted by a French corporal with his bayonet to the ready, just as I had mine. I felt the fear of death in that fraction of a second when I realised that he was after my life, exactly as I was after his. But I was quicker than he was, I pushed his rifle away and ran my bayonet through his chest. He fell, putting his hand on the place where I had hit him, and then I thrust again. Blood came out of his mouth and he died.
>
> I nearly vomited. . . .
>
> I had the dead French soldier in front of me, and how I would have liked him to have raised his hand! I would have shaken it and we would have been the best of friends because he was nothing but a poor boy—like me.[110]

More often than not, however, bayonet confrontations followed the pattern described by Lance Corporal F. Heardman of
the Manchester Pals: "I came face to face with a great big German who had come up unexpectedly out of a shell hole. He had
his rifle and bayonet 'at the ready.' So had I, but mine suddenly felt
only the size of a small boy's play gun and my steel helmet shrank
to the size of a small tin lid. Then, almost before I had time to
realize what was happening, the German threw down his rifle,
put up his arms and shouted 'Kamerad.' I could hardly believe my
eyes."[111]

★　★　★

JUST AS, IN combat, killing and dying are two sides of the same
coin, so are celebration and grief in the act of killing. Sergeant
Westmann may have been devastated by bayoneting to death his
French counterpart, but his comrades seemed to have been utterly
unperturbed by their death dealing:

> My knees were shaking and they asked me, "What's the
> matter with you?" I remembered then that we had been
> told that a good soldier kills without thinking of his adver-
> sary as a human being—the very moment he sees him as
> a fellow man, he's no longer a good soldier. My comrades
> were absolutely undisturbed by what had happened. One of
> them boasted that he had killed a *poilu* with the butt of his
> rifle. Another one had strangled a French captain. A third
> had hit somebody over the head with his spade. They were
> ordinary men like me. One was a tram conductor, another
> a commercial traveller, two were students, the rest farm
> workers—ordinary people who never would have thought
> to harm anybody.[112]

Killing could be a joy unclouded by guilt—a simple relishing of one's skill; as artillery forward observer H. M. Stanford wrote to a pal: "Next day I had the time of my life. I got on to Bosche bombing parties at short range and fairly blew hell out of them with shrapnel whenever they showed. . . . I believe I made a bag of about 20 Huns with one round. . . . One time I saw a Bosche bombing-party appear over the parapet and I hit one man plumb with a percussion [high-explosive shell], disintegrating him and his pal alongside. Another time I got into the middle of six or seven firing over the parapet and the whole lot dropped. . . . Anyhow I had a real hectic day."[113]

Stanford's hunting reference ("I made a bag of about 20 Huns") is both a celebratory flourish and a way to neutralize the guilt of killing by turning it into sport. Artillery observer Julian Tyndale-Biscoe described how German infantry "zig-zagged like rabbits. . . . [I] picked up a rifle and had some pot-shots . . . I saw several bowled over."[114]

As in all wars, killing prisoners was sometimes done with an almost larky flippancy. A British officer who had just witnessed what was tantamount to the murder of a surrendering German officer tries to explain his uneasiness to a colleague: "We took a lot of prisoners in those trenches yesterday morning. Just as we got into their line, an officer came out of a dug-out. He'd got one hand over his head, and a pair of field-glasses in the other. He held out the glasses to S—, and said, 'Here you are sergeant, I surrender.' S— said, 'Thank you, Sir,' and took the glasses in his left hand. At the same moment, he tucked the butt of his rifle under his arm and shot the officer straight through the head. What the hell ought I to do?"[115]

Captain J. C. Dunn records the casual murder of four prisoners: "The next dug-out also contained four men. They came out with their hands up—'Kamerad.' . . . Soon after, a man of ours came along with a wound of the left arm. He was given a revolver, and told to take the four prisoners back to the Company's trench and hand them over to the C.Q.M.S. [company quartermaster sergeant], who was waiting in a deep dug-out to receive prisoners. . . . Those four never got to him. The escort wrote from hospital to a pal in the Company that he thought they were going to slip him, so he shot them, but he was 'sorry at losing the Sergeant-Major's revolver.' "[116]

Jauntiness is possible if the killing is sanitized by distance. It is much more difficult when the results are too close for comfort. Ernst Jünger shot a British soldier as he was emerging from a dugout and after a while went back to the dugout to examine the body: "Outside it lay my British soldier, little more than a boy, who had been hit in the temple. He lay there, looking quite relaxed. I forced myself to look closely at him. It wasn't a case of 'you or me' any more. I often thought back on him; and more with the passing of the years. The state, which relieves us of our responsibility, cannot take away our remorse; and we must exercise it. Sorrow, regret, pursued me deep into my dreams."[117]

★　　★　　★

IN ALL HIS considerable time in combat zones as a medical officer, Lord Moran saw only one man die in terror:

> The men of his company would do anything for him, which is another way of saying that he was no coward. Hit early one morning he was taken to a broken-down farm not far distant, and I was with him until he died many hours later. Though gravely hurt and in great pain he kept cheerful and patient without complaint. He was so certain he was going to get well—he said as much—but a few hours later, when he was worse . . . he took my hand in terror and whispered,

"Am I going to die?" I got up and put a heavy box of dressings against the door.

We who practise physic are compelled to witness things which no man should be asked to face. The wounds we dress are nothing, it is when something has gone in the make-up of a man that this bloody business comes home.[118]

Moran felt that very often "dying men rarely experience pain or apprehension, or terror or remorse; their lives peter to an end, 'like their birth, their death is a sleep and forgetting.' When death is not far off, when a wounded soldier lies very still on his stretcher . . . nature with a kindly gesture dulls the senses, and death like a narcotic comes to steal men almost in their sleep."[119] Ernst Jünger experienced a similar benignity: "The man with the wound in the belly, a very young lad, lay in amongst us, stretched out like a cat in the warm rays of the setting sun. He slipped into death with an almost childlike smile on his face. It was a sight that didn't oppress me, but left me with a fraternal feeling for the dying man."[120]

Violent death may, occasionally, have had its reassuring smile and the gentle shading off into oblivion, but it also had the rictus of terror; the scream of outrage as well as the sigh of acceptance. On the battlefield mortally wounded men called out for their mothers, as though impending death and pain had made children of them again. Robert Graves records how an officer of the Middlesex caught in no-man's-land during a failed attack "had his platoon sergeant beside, screaming with a stomach wound, begging for morphia; he was done for, so Hill gave him five pellets [enough to euthanize the wounded man]."[121]

Lieutenant Edwin Campion Vaughan and his colleague Corporal Breeze were hit by a shell: "As I was blown backwards I saw him thrown into the air to land at my feet, a crumpled heap of torn flesh. . . . I saw the stump of his arm move an inch or two. . . . He was terribly mutilated, both his feet had gone and one arm, his legs and trunk were torn to ribbons and his face was dreadful. But he was conscious and as I bent over him I saw in his remaining eye a gleam of mixed recognition and terror. His feeble hand clutched my equipment, and then the light faded from his eyes."[122]

In contrast, Ernst Jünger was hit seriously twice and on each occasion experienced something death-transcending. The first time: "I felt a sharp jolt on the left side of my breast. Night descended on me! I was finished . . . I supposed I'd been hit in the heart, but the prospect of death neither hurt nor frightened me. As I fell, I saw the smooth, white pebbles in the muddy road; their arrangement made sense, it was as necessary as that of the stars, and certainly great wisdom was hidden in it." The second hit was as revelatory:

In mid-jump . . . I felt a piercing jolt in the chest—as though I had been hit like a game bird. With a sharp cry that cost me all the air I had, I spun on my axis and crashed to the ground.

It had got me at last. At the same time as feeling I had been hit, I felt the bullet taking away my life. I had felt Death's hand once before . . . but this time his grip was firmer and more determined. As I came down heavily on the bottom of the trench, I was convinced it was all over. Strangely, that moment is one of the very few in my life of which I am able to say they were utterly happy. I understood, as in a flash of lightning, the true inner purpose and form of my life. I felt surprise and disbelief that it was to end there and then, but this surprise had something untroubled and almost merry about it. Then I heard the firing grow less, as if I were a stone sinking under the surface of some turbulent water. Where I was going, there was neither war nor enmity.[123]

Escaping the fear of death meant, as Lord Moran said, grasping the nettle. Sergeant Major Richard Tobin describes how this transmutation took place as he was waiting to go into action:

> We stood there in dead silence, you couldn't make noise, and the fellow next to you felt like your best friend, you loved him, although you probably didn't know him a day before. They were both the longest and the shortest hours of my life. An infantryman in the front line feels the coldest, deepest fear.
>
> Then, it was just five minutes to go—then zero—and all hell let loose. There was our barrage, then the German barrage, and over the top we went. As soon as we got over the top the fear and the terror left us. You don't look, you see; you don't listen, you hear; your nose is filled with fumes and death and you taste the top of your mouth. You are one with your weapon, the veneer of civilisation has dropped away.[124]

For some, the possibility of being killed acted as a life-enhancing stimulant. For Siegfried Sassoon, "the idea of death made everything seem vivid and valuable." And for him this was no idle notion hatched in relative security. The day before a major attack he was involved in the highly hazardous job of cutting enemy wire in daylight, but instead of being petrified he found that "it seemed like an escapade, and the excitement was by no means disagreeable. It was rather like going out to weed a neglected garden after being warned that there might be a tiger among the gooseberry bushes. . . . I was cutting the wire by daylight because commonsense warned me that the lives of several hundred soldiers might depend on doing it properly. I was excited and pleased with myself while I was doing it." Trench bombing raids made him feel "intensely alive."[125]

Captain Charles Carrington of the Warwickshire Regiment went into action on that fateful July 1, 1916, and one might have presumed that he would be filled with apprehension. The opposite was the case: "I got up at dawn. I was acting-adjutant of my battalion. . . . I went up to take my command post in the trenches, from where we could see over the country between Gommecourt and Serre. . . . I can only say that I have never been so excited in my life. This was like a boy going to play for the first time in his life. That's how I felt. The noise rose to a crescendo such as I'd never heard before. A noise which made all bombardments that we'd heard in the previous day seem like nothing at all. And the effect of the bombardment created a sort of hysterical feeling."[126]

Bourne, the central character of Frederic Manning's novel, *Her Privates We*, based on his own experiences, describes the exultant spike of adrenaline that could turn the possibility of death into something he felt was glorious:

> For a moment they might have broken and run themselves, and for a moment they might have fought men of their own blood [British troops retreating through Bourne's unit], but they struggled on as Sergeant Tozer yelled at them to leave that bloody tripe alone and get on with it. Bourne, floundering in the viscous mud, was at once the most abject and the most exalted of God's creatures. The effort and rage in him, the sense that others had left them to it, made him pant and sob, but there was some strange intoxication of joy in it, and again all his mind seemed focused into one hard bright point of action. The extremities of pain and pleasure had met and coincided too.[127]

When the angel of death passed men over, choosing others in their stead, the joy of survival might strike us as being shockingly naked:

"... Barbier was killed.

...He had the top of his back taken off by a shell ... as if it had been cut with a razor. Besse had a piece of shrapnel through his belly and his stomach. Barthélemy and Baubex were hit in the head and neck.... You remember little Godefroy? The middle of his body was blown right away. He was emptied of blood on the spot, in an instant, like turning over a pail.... Gougnard had his legs blown off...."

... "So many fine friends less, my dear old Marchal."

... "Yes," says Marchal.

...But he is swept away by a horde of his comrades, shouting at him and ragging him ... they all laugh and jostle one another.

...I look from one face to the next. They are merry and, through the weary lines and stains of earth, they seem triumphant....

...I pick out one of the survivors who is humming a tune and marching along.

... "Well, Vanderborn, you look pretty pleased with yourself!"

... Vanderborn, usually a quiet fellow, shouts to me:

... "It wasn't me this time, see? Here I am!"

And with a sweeping gesture like a madman he claps me on the shoulder.

... Now I understand.

... These men are happy, despite everything, as they emerge from hell—for the very reason that they are emerging. They are coming back, they are saved. Once again, death was there, but spared them....

... This is why, though they are crushed by weariness and still spattered with the recent slaughter, and their brothers have been snatched away ... in spite of everything ...

they rejoice at having survived and enjoy the infinite glory of being on their feet.[128]

The staggering good fortune of not being killed needed to be celebrated with life-affirming sensuality:

"Where's Dixon?"

"Gone west. Blown to fuckin' bits as soon as we got out of the trench, poor bugger. Young Williams 'it same time, 'ad most of his arm blown off. . . ."

They spoke with anxious, low voices, still unsteady and inclined to break; but control was gradually returning; and all that pity carried with it a sense of relief that the speaker, somehow, but quite incredibly, had himself managed to survive.

When breakfast came they at first seemed to have no appetite, but once they had started, they ate like famished wolves, mopping up the last smear of bacon fat and charred fragments from the bottom of the pan with their bread.[129]

To survive a great battle was to be elected to an elite. There had been no shirking or avoidance; but by some wonderful stroke of good luck death had spared them. It was possible to walk out of the terrible fire with a renewed sense of life:

All around me are faces which sleep might not have visited for a week. . . .

. . . The Somme was over, our little bit had been well done and before us there was rest. . . . It is these moments that make war possible. . . .

. . . Certainly it was worth going through a show to come out of it. There was a battle on up there, but we were at peace with all the world.[130]

★   ★   ★

THE DEAD WERE both shocking and yet familiar; gruesome and occasionally gruesomely funny. Battle after battle laid down a sediment of corpses to form archeological strata that men would have to excavate as though through the loam of a compost pile: "The churned-up field was gruesome. In among the living defenders lay the dead. When we dug foxholes, we realized that they were stacked in layers. One company after another, pressed together in the drumfire, had been mown down, then the bodies had been buried under showers of earth sent up by shells, and then the relief company had taken their predecessors' place. And now it was our turn."[131]

Digging and the constant churning of exploding shells created macabre reappearances, as though the dead were, in some unnerving way, reanimated:

> The ground is so full of bodies that landslides uncover the places bristling with feet, half-clothed skeletons and ossuaries of skulls, one beside the other in the sheer wall, like china jars.
>
> In the earth here there are several layers of dead bodies and in places the pounding of the shells has brought up the oldest and placed them or scattered them across the newer ones.[132]

Mud became an oversaturated solution of the killed. Lieutenant John Glubb recalled that in early 1916, "during the battle last month the troops suffered heavily and were too tired to bury their dead. Many of them were merely trampled into the floor of the trench, where they were soon lost in mud and water. We have been digging out a lot of these trenches again, and are constantly coming upon corpses. They are pretty well decomposed, but a pickaxe brings up chips of bone and rags of clothing. The rest is putrid grey matter."[133]

A German soldier even in the early days of trench warfare in 1914 complained:

> Neither the dead nor the wounded can be removed. If you put up as much as a finger above the edge of the trench, the bullets came whizzing round immediately. The dead bodies must therefore be allowed to remain in the trench; that is to say, the dead man is got rid of by digging a grave for him in the floor of the trench. A few days ago . . . a soldier was so badly hit by a shell that he was cut in two [and] could not be removed without risk to the survivors and was therefore allowed to remain. But presently he gave rise to a horrible stench and whatever they did the men could not get away from the mutilated blackened features. . . . One gets hardened in time.[134]

"One gets hardened in time," and the commonplace could render the dead flat-out, music-hall hilarious. Corporal Clifford Lane described a German trench near Thiepval in the summer of 1916:

> It was very hot . . . this trench was full of dead Germans and they'd been there some time. Some were sitting on the steps of these deep dugouts . . . others were lying on the trench floor. We'd seen plenty of dead people before, but we'd never seen anything like this. They were all different colours, from pallid grey to green and black. And they were bloated—that's how a corpse goes in time, they get blown up with gases. We thought it was funny, really, which shows how your mind can get inured to such situations. We started making up the trench and had to tread on one of these

blokes, who was partly buried. Every time we trod on him his tongue would come out, which caused great amusement amongst our people.[135]

Robert Graves encountered a corpse "lying on the fire-step waiting to be taken down to the grave-yard tonight: a sanitary-man, killed in the open while burying lavatory stuff between our support lines. His arm was stretched out stiff when they carried him in and laid him on the fire-step; it stretched right across the trench. His comrades joke as they push it out of the way to get by. 'Out of the light, you old bastard! Do you own this bloody trench?' Or else they shake hands with him familiarly. 'Put it there, Billy Boy.' "[136]

The dead had a useful afterlife in all sorts of ways. Captain Dunn recalls that on October 23, 1914, "the front was under fire, more or less all night . . . we had, I think, 19 men to bury. A large grave had been dug, and the first few poor chaps put into it when the usual nightly attacks started. There was no cover where we were except the grave, so in we went—the quick and the dead together."[137]

During the battle of Passchendaele in 1917 gunner Aubrey Wade crossed a stream, the Steenbeek, by "a bridge composed of a compact mass of human bodies over which I stepped gingerly. I was not at all squeamish, the sight of dead men having long lost its terror for me, but making use of corpses, even enemy corpses, for bridge-building purposes seemed about the limit of callousness. The major said nothing, but stopped to light his pipe on the farther bank."[138]

The dead could also be quite profitable. Gunner Leonard Ounsworth explains how the killed provided increased rations for the survivors: "When you lost men, it was a day or two before you could stop their rations coming up. The Army Service Corps would still be sending up the rations of so many men while you might have lost half of them. And what happened to all that grub? You'd live like fighting cocks on what was left for a day or two."[139] "The bread ration varied," explains Corporal Frederic Hodges, "four or five men to a loaf when we had recently received a new draft to replace casualties, or three to a loaf when we had recently suffered casualties but still received their rations. As the ration party came in sight, the first question we asked was 'How many to a bun?' "[140]

Even after the war ex-soldiers employed to exhume bodies could hit the jackpot. One such at Ypres in 1920 reported: "It's jolly hard work. But it 'as its better side. Some fellers the other day came on a dug-out with three officers in it, and they picked up five thousand francs between 'em."[141]

In a convoluted bit of irony, propaganda points could be scored from the (completely fictitious) profit squeezed from British bodies by the fiendish Hun. George Coppard remembers:

[There was] a piece of psychological propaganda, put about by some War Office person, which brought poor comfort to Tommies. The story swept the world and, being gullible, we in the trenches were taken in by it for a while. With slight variations it indicated that the German war industry was in a bad way, and it was short of fats for making glycerine. To overcome the shortage a vast secret factory had been erected in the Black Forest, to which the bodies of dead British soldiers were dispatched. The bodies, wired together in bundles, were pitchforked on to conveyor belts and moved into the factory for conversion into fats. . . . If the object of the story was to work the British troops into a state of fighting frenzy, then it was a complete and utter wash-out.[142]

If the long-dead proclaimed their own putrid narrative of past battles, the bodies of the freshly slain created a heartbreaking topography—if one had the eye to read it as the poet John Masefield did:

> The field of Gommecourt [the Somme, 1916] is heaped with the bodies of Londoners: the London Scottish lie at the Sixteen Poplars; the Yorkshire are outside Serre; the Warwickshires lie in Serre itself; all the great hill of the Hawthorn Ridge is littered with Middlesex; the Irish are at Hamel, the Kents on the Schwaben, and the Wilts and Dorset on the Leipzig. Men of all the towns and counties of England, Wales, and Scotland lie scattered among the slopes from Ovillers to Maricourt. English dead pave the road to La Boisselle, the Welsh and Scotch are in Mametz. In gullies and sheltered places, where wounded could be brought during the fighting, there are little towns of dead in all these places.[143]

Another poet, Siegfried Sassoon, viewed the same battlefield and also saw a kind of confraternity: "After going a very short distance we made the first of many halts, and I saw, arranged by the roadside, about fifty of the British dead. Many of them were Gordon Highlanders. There were Devons and South Staffordshires among them, but they were beyond regimental rivalry now—their fingers mingled in blood-stained bunches as though acknowledging the companionship of death."[144]

The forced intimacy of "the quick and the dead" could be profound. Ernst Jünger saw it as a kind of resurrection: "The day's sentries were already in position while the trenches had yet to be cleared. Here and there, the sentry posts were covered with dead, and, in among them, as it were, arisen from their bodies, stood the new relief with his rifle. There was an odd rigidity about these composites—it was as though the distinction between alive and dead had momentarily been taken away."[145]

And for the Italian poet-soldier Giuseppe Ungaretti the proximity was transfiguring:

WATCH

CIMA QUATTRO, 23 DECEMBER 1915

A whole night through
thrown down beside
a butchered comrade
with his clenched teeth
turned to the full moon
and the clutching
of his hands
thrust
into my silence
I have written
letters full of love

Never have I
clung
so fast to life[146]

The dead spoke, but the problem was to understand what they said. For Sassoon there was a ferocious repudiation of any uplifting message:

Wherever we looked the mangled effigies of the dead were our *memento mori*. Shell-twisted and dismembered, the Germans maintained the violent attitudes in which they had died. The British had mostly been killed by bullets and bombs, or they looked more resigned. But I can remember a pair of hands (nationality unknown) which protruded from the soaked ashen soil like the roots of a tree turned upside down; one hand seemed to be pointing at the sky with an accusing gesture. Each time I passed the place the protest of those fingers became more expressive of an appeal to God in defiance of those who made the War. Who made the War? I laughed hysterically as the thought passed through my mud-stained mind. But I only laughed mentally, for my box of Stokes gun ammunition left me no breath to spare for an angry guffaw. And the dead were the dead; this was no time to be pitying them or asking silly questions about their outraged lives.[147]

To Henri Barbusse, however, they spoke a quite different language: "No, you can't imagine. All these deaths at once crush the soul. There are not enough of us left. But we have a vague idea of the grandeur of these dead. They have given everything; they gave it little by little, with all their strength, then finally they gave themselves, altogether, all at once. They outdistanced life, and there is something superhuman and perfect in what they did."[148]

★   ★   ★

MEN USED A spectrum of techniques to deal with their fear. One was to simply laugh in the ogre's face. A German soldier, the twenty-five-year-old Alfred Lichtenstein, wrote his jocular "death poem" in 1914 as he left for war:

Before dying I must write my poem.
Quiet, comrades, don't disturb me.
We are off to war—death is our bond.
Oh, if only my girlfriend would stop howling!
What do I care? I am happy to go.
My mother's crying; one needs to be made of iron.

The sun falls to the horizon;
Soon they'll be throwing me into a nice mass-grave.
In the sky the good old sun is glowing red;
In thirteen days I shall probably be dead.[149]

He was killed that year.

Black humor was a protective shield:

But when we were confronted by death, with what light hands we touched the common friend. To a man off his feed Price had offered the mocking counsel: "You had better eat it up, it's as likely as not your last." And to another, down over the death of a pal, "Cheer up, Cockie, it's your turn next." I remember, when bringing in the wounded at Hooge, I heard a man say "Down you go there, you won't trouble any more to-night," and with that the fellow heaved a dead man into a big crater. . . . We simply could not afford to allow death to hover in the offing as the final mystery; it must be brought to earth and robbed of its disturbing influence, by rough gibes and the touch of ridicule. If it was firmly grasped like a nettle soon there was no sting left in it.[150]

Grasping the nettle of the fear of one's own death was one thing, but the sickening foreboding at the possible loss of a friend was an agony that humor of whatever color could not relieve. Lord Moran confides in his wartime diary:

I have ceased to bother much about the odds, the chance of stopping something, but I have another infirmity now. I am for ever worrying about the people I really like. The Boche gunners have certain spots taped, but it is after dark that I begin to get uneasy. Every evening Barty Price starts off for the trenches walking up the Menin Road with an orderly and I cannot settle until I hear him return. I feel certain he will pick up a spare [*hit by a random shell*] and come back on a stretcher done, and I often try to get him to go by day when it is—in spite of the attention of their gunners—much safer.

But he only laughs. I lie reading by candle light and every time I hear a machine gun in the distance he comes into my head and I expect at any moment to see him carried in. The noise of the footsteps in the street above brings my heart into my mouth and I say irritably "Why the devil does he play the fool like this?"[151]

With comradeship came risk: "When you learn or see the death of one of those who had been fighting alongside you and living the very same life it gives you a direct shock which hits you before you understand. It really is almost like suddenly learning of one's annihilation."[152]

Homicidal fury was one way of dealing with grief. In Frederic Manning's *Her Privates We*, Martlow, the young friend of his older mentor, Bourne, is killed:

Martlow was perhaps a couple of yards in front of Bourne, when he swayed a little, his knees collapsed under him, and he pitched forward on to his face, his feet kicking and his whole body convulsive for a moment. Bourne flung himself down beside him, and, putting his arms around his body, lifted him, calling him.

"Kid! You're all right, Kid? He cried eagerly. . . . As Bourne lifted the limp body, the boy's hat came off, showing half the back of his skull shattered where the bullet had come through it; and a little blood welled out on to Bourne's sleeve and the knee of his trousers. . . . Bourne let him settle to earth again . . . the ache in him became a consuming hate that filled him with exultant cruelty. . . ." Kill the buggers! Kill the bloody fucking swine! Kill them!"

All the filth and ordure he had ever heard came from between his clenched teeth . . . a Hun went for Minton, and Bourne got him with the bayonet, under the ribs near the liver, and then, unable to wrench the bayonet out again, pulled the trigger, and it came away easily enough.

"Kill the buggers!" he muttered thickly.[153]

A British soldier was escorting six German prisoners to the rear:

"Look here, Dick, about an hour ago I lost the best pal I ever had, and he was worth all these six Jerries put together. I'm not going to take them far." . . .

Some little time later I saw him coming back. . . . As he passed me again he said, "I done them in as I said, about two hundred yards back. Two bombs did the trick."[154]

At the other end of the emotional gauge the loss of a friend could be met with a stoicism of unnerving rigor: "We took over trenches from Delville Wood to Waterlot Farm . . . we had scarcely moved in when we lost a Company Commander. I went to tell Toby: Pat and he were inseparable. I found him making out a return [of casualties] for the brigade. When I had done he did not look up but sat without a word making holes in a piece of blotting paper with his pen. Then he said, 'Thanks, old thing,' and went on writing."[155]

Booze was the great and universal anesthetic. But perhaps the commonest psychological defense against being killed was resignation—"a universal torpor," Moran calls it, "a wall . . . set up by nature to meet the violence of the hour." A padre, Oswin Creighton, writes of his fears before his division was to make an assault at Gallipoli, where "slaughter seems to be inevitable," but adds that the men "are quite prepared for it."[156] This is how Lance Corporal Marshall of the Accrington Pals experienced it during the carnage of the first day of the Somme: "I saw many men fall back into the trench as they attempted to climb out. Those of us who managed had to walk two yards apart, very slowly, then stop, then walk again. . . . We all had to keep in a line. Machine-gun bullets were sweeping backwards and forwards . . . shells were bursting everywhere. I had no special feeling of fear and I knew that we must all go forward until wounded or killed."[157]

But in this stoicism there was the possibility of something that transcended the "torpor" of animals being led to slaughter—the almost unimaginable victory of glorious defiance: "And I saw it then, as I see it now—a dreadful place, a place of horror and desolation which no imagination could have invented. Also it was a place where a man of strong spirit might know himself utterly powerless against death and destruction, and yet stand up and defy gross darkness and stupefying shell-fire, discovering in himself the invincible resistance of an animal or an insect, and an endurance which he might, in after days, forget or disbelieve."[158]

SEVEN

A CONFRATERNITY OF GHOSTS

How Soldiers Were Killed in World War II

Now in my dial of glass appears
the soldier who is going to die.
He smiles, and moves about in ways
his mother knows, habits of his.
The wires touch his face: I cry
NOW. Death, like a familiar hears

And look, has made a man of dust
of a man of flesh. This sorcery
I do.

—From "How to Kill" by Keith Douglas (killed by
mortar fire in Normandy, June 9, 1944)

*A*S KEITH DOUGLAS squeezed the trigger he experienced the emotional violence of two images, two ideas of humanity, as they elided in the crosshairs: the particular, the individual, and the precious versus the anonymous, generalized, and expendable. He knows the Man but does not know the man.

In a century dedicated to computation, to measurement, to exactitude, there are multitudes who remain uncounted and unaccounted for. In the ocean of the slain so many souls were easily lost in the great rise and fall of the swell. They simply drifted away into the deep blue of history. We have no accurate reckoning. About 16 million (give or take a million) fighting men and women died—roughly double the number of the First World War.[1] "It is testimony to the scale of wartime carnage that the estimates of military losses should vary by margins of millions."[2]

The great killing ground was Russia. It was here that Germany was bled to death. And in the bleeding, the Soviet Union sacrificed fighting men and women on a scale that would have been completely insupportable for their Western Allies. Although the numbers of Soviets and Germans killed on the eastern front are approximate, they are, even in a rough comparison with Western Allied deaths, astonishing. In combat deaths alone the Soviets lost about 6.5 million.[3] In addition, more than 5.7 million Red Army soldiers were captured, of whom probably more than half were killed, primarily by being starved, worked to death, or, in the case of perhaps 600,000 of them, peremptorily shot either on capture or in captivity.[4] During the first six months of the war alone, the Red Army lost two-thirds of its starting strength of just over 3 million men.[5]

David M. Glantz, an authority on the eastern front, calculates German casualties in all theaters over the course of the war at 13.5 million and of these 10.8 million became casualties or were captured on the eastern front.[6] Even after the opening of the second front with D-Day, 65 percent of all German losses took place in the east. By January 1945 the Allies had inflicted about 620,000 "irreplaceable losses" (killed or so badly wounded that they could not return to duty) in the European Theater of Operations, while in the east more than 1.2 million Germans fell during the same period.[7] Germany would suffer about 3.5 million combat-related deaths in all theaters throughout the war.[8]

To put the scale of the Soviet and German losses in some perspective, a US Congressional Research Service report states that American ground forces (Army and Marines) had 291,557 killed or died of wounds in all theaters over the course of the war.[9] Great Britain had about 260,000 servicemen and women killed, with perhaps another 100,000 from the British Empire (for example, Australia and India had each about 24,000 killed; New Zealand, 10,000; South Africa, approximately 7,000).[10] In other words, the Soviets probably lost ten times as many killed as all the other Allies *combined*. In the Soviet view the Great Patriotic War—their war—*was* the war. The Western Allies were helpful, particularly in the supply of matériel, but when it came to the business of dying and killing, it was the Soviet Union that carried by far the bloodiest burden.

★   ★   ★

THE WAR AGAINST Japan offers interesting contrasts as well as parallels to the eastern front. In contrast, compared with the massive human expenditure the Russians needed to defeat their enemy, the Americans (as the major partner in the Allied fight against Japan) were extraordinarily efficient. Taking into account only land forces, the Japanese had about 685,000 men killed fighting the Americans in the Pacific. The US Army and Marines sustained around 55,000 killed. So, roughly twelve times as many Japanese foot soldiers died as did Americans.[11] In individual battles, though, that ratio could rise to more than fifteen Japanese killed for every American.

The Japanese were well established in a string of island

redoubts—Guadalcanal, Saipan, Tinian, Peleliu, Iwo Jima, Tarawa, Okinawa, to name a few—where one might have expected the old formula to work. In the past, assaulting fixed defenses was costly, and defenders enjoyed something like a three-to-one advantage over the attacker; that is, three attackers could expect to become casualties for every defender. However, attackers could usually be reinforced, while the bottled-up defenders were gradually eliminated through attrition. It did not always work that way (disease as well as casualties, for example, might erode attackers more quickly than defenders), but on the whole, if the attacker was willing to pay it, the price would secure the property. In the Pacific that formula was turned on its head.

The discrepancy between the relatively low American death toll in relation to the massive Japanese losses reflected a new way of doing this kind of warfare. A few representative examples make the point. At Guadalcanal (August 7, 1942–February 7, 1943), American dead totaled 1,600 while the Japanese defenders took 14,000 killed (plus 9,000 dead from disease).[12] On Guam (July 21–August 10, 1944) the Japanese were wiped out (18,000–20,000 killed) for the loss of 1,023–1,400 US Army and Marine dead.[13] On Peleliu (September 15–November 28, 1944), 13,600 Japanese were killed at a cost of 1,460 Americans. On the island of Tinian, 328 Marines died, but all of the 9,000 Japanese defenders were killed. And in the last great battle—Okinawa (April 1–June 22, 1945)—7,374 US soldiers and Marines died in the process of killing at least 107,500 Japanese (many others were entombed in the cave systems they had fortified).[14] For a variety of reasons—strategic and logistic, tactical and cultural—the Japanese were annihilated in each of the island fortresses they chose to defend—a "fatality rate . . . rarely seen in the history of warfare."[15]

One of the major factors that connected the eastern and Pacific fronts was the role racism played in driving up the numbers of killed. The Germans in Russia and the Americans (including their allies) and the Japanese in the Pacific saw their enemies in racial terms that enabled and endorsed killing an opponent who had been stripped of any claim to humanity or nobility. Germans viewed the Russians as "Asiatic" *Untermenschen*: a reincarnation of those barbaric hordes that had swept out of the steppes to fall on medieval Christian Europe. On November 25, 1941, Colonel General Hermann Hoth, commander of the Seventeenth Army, told his troops:

> It has become increasingly clear to us . . . that here in the East spiritually unbridgeable conceptions are fighting each other: German sense of honor and race, and a soldierly tradition of many centuries, against an Asiatic mode of thinking and primitive instincts, whipped up by a small number of mostly Jewish intellectuals: fear of the knout [a type of whip], disregard of moral values, levelling down, throwing away one's worthless life.
>
> More than ever we are filled with the thought of a new era, in which the strength of the German people's racial superiority and achievements entrusts it with the leadership of Europe. We clearly recognize our mission to save European culture from the advancing Asiatic barbarism.[16]

The Allied fighting man usually viewed his Japanese counterpart with an equally ferocious contempt. Admiral William "Bull" Halsey, at the conclusion of the conquest of Peleliu in October 1944, sent his congratulations to the infantry: "The sincere admiration of the entire Third Fleet for the hill-blasting, cave smashing extermination of 11,000 slant-eyed gophers." He added gleefully that "we are drowning and burning [them] all over the Pacific, and it is just as much pleasure to burn them as to drown them."[17] Ernie Pyle, the war correspondent most closely in touch with the ordinary fighting Joe, put it this way: "In Europe we felt our enemies, horrible and deadly as they were, were still people. But out here I gathered that the Japanese were looked upon as something subhuman and repulsive: the way some people feel about cockroaches or mice." On seeing captured Japanese, Pyle confessed that they "gave me the creeps, and I wanted to take a mental bath after looking at them."[18]

E. B. Sledge, a Marine and the author of the classic memoir *With the Old Breed at Peleliu and Okinawa* (1981), notes:

> The attitudes held toward the Japanese by noncombatants or even sailors or airmen often did not reflect the deep personal resentment felt by Marine infantrymen. Official histories and memoirs of Marine infantrymen written after the war rarely reflect that hatred. But at the time of battle, Marines felt it deeply, bitterly, and as certainly as danger itself. To deny this hatred or make light of it would be as much a lie as to deny or make light of the esprit de corps or the intense patriotism felt by the Marines with whom I served in the Pacific.
>
> My experiences on Peleliu and Okinawa made me believe that the Japanese held mutual feelings for us. They were a fanatical enemy; that is to say, they believed in their cause with an intensity little understood by many postwar Americans—and possibly many Japanese, as well.
>
> This collective attitude, Marine and Japanese, resulted in savage, ferocious fighting with no holds barred. This was not the dispassionate killing seen on other fronts or in other wars. This was a brutish, primitive hatred.[19]

George MacDonald Fraser, a noncommissioned officer in the British Army in Burma (who would go on to fame and fortune with his *Flashman* novels), admitted to the racist basis of his war with a bluff, unapologetic vigor that probably reflected the views of the vast majority of his comrades and civilian countrymen:

> There is much talk today of guilt as an aftermath of war—guilt over killing the enemy. . . . Much depends on the circumstances, but I doubt if many of [the] Fourteenth Army lose much sleep over dead Japanese. For one thing, they were a no-surrender enemy and if we hadn't killed them they would surely have killed us. But there was more to it than that. It may appal a generation who have been dragooned into considering racism the ultimate crime, but I believe there was a feeling (there was in me) that the Jap was farther down the human scale than the European. . . .
>
> . . . There is no question that he was viewed in an entirely different light from our European enemies. . . . The only good Jap was a dead one. And we were right, then.[20]

A research study during the Pacific war found that an average of 43 percent of American soldiers expressed an enthusiastic desire to kill Japanese. In contrast, only 10 percent of American GIs surveyed in Europe "really wanted to kill German soldiers."[21]

Racism was also an important element of Japanese nationalism. It too created images of the "other" ("barbaric" Americans or "backward" Chinese) that made killing easier. The Japanese, like the Germans, had crafted out of their ancient past a mythological theater that was intoxicatingly inspirational—a collective fabrication rooted in heroic, chivalric militarism. This was a world in which war banners bravely streamed and the sun glinted on gorgeous armor. Its purpose was to energize and inspire a burgeoning nationalism or to revitalize the nation during periods of defeat and humiliation. Japan and Germany were both in thrall to a deep nostalgia and profound sentimentality, an overproof concoction distilled from a mixture of legend and cynically manipulated quasi history that provided the high-octane ideological fuel for a very deadly style of warfare.

The racial element was almost entirely absent when the Allies and Axis fought in North Africa, Italy, and western Europe. Neil McCallum, a British infantry officer in North Africa, reflected on the place of hatred in combat:

> One of us recently received a letter saying, "How you must hate those bastards." We don't . . . there is anger, but not at anyone in particular. The whole thing is too vast for so personal an emotion as hatred. In a sense, the more deeply you become involved in war, the more impersonally you regard it. That may be a sort of native caution: an excess of emotion such as hatred is very unbalancing. In any case, there are plenty of other things to hate—the flies, the heat, the cold, the grub, or not having enough sleep, and all that. But not the enemy, or very rarely.
>
> Hatred belongs at home with the civilians. . . . The feelings of soldiers in action must be fairly standardized, unless they have been whipped up by such obscenities as concentration camps, or deliberate sadistic practices. . . . Such things exert no immediate influence on us, and there is little positive hatred to be drawn from the theoretical. . . . You cannot hate the bastard who is trying to kill you and who you are trying to kill. When war was brief and hand-to-hand hatred might have been possible. . . . We shoot at the enemy on the basic grounds of fear and self-preservation. If you don't shoot first he will shoot you.[22]

When the fierce heat of combat burned off the ideological vapor, soldiers fell back on the sureties that have sustained soldiers throughout the whole history of warfare: the interdependence of survival and comradeship. "After you have spent time at the front," writes Günther Koschorrek, a Wehrmacht machine gunner in Russia, "you no longer fight for *Führer, Volk und Vaterland*. These ideals have long gone. . . . We fight . . . to stay alive and help our front-line comrades to do the same."[23]

Sometimes soldiers did their killing fired up by lofty ideology, but more often they did it because they had to. "To get home," writes historian Paul Fussell, then a young US Army officer in Europe, "you had to end the war. To end the war was the reason you fought it."[24] The political, civilian-sanctioned reasons for fighting were evaporated by the heat of combat, and the war became an internal world ruled and judged by its own laws, so immeasurably distant from the values of "home." War becomes the point and purpose of war, and those at the sharp end watched the "other" world fade into the distant horizon. "If we killed," says Jim Alcock, an American survivor of Anzio, "we could go on living. Whatever we were fighting for seemed irrelevant."[25] Alex Bowlby, a British rifleman in Italy, knew whom he was fighting for: "Mixed up in our counter-clowning was an intense pride. I had never felt so conscious of my regiment as I was then. This was the way to risk one's life. There was no King or Country about it—it was the regiment. And I wouldn't have changed places with anyone."[26]

William Manchester, a Marine during the war in the Pacific and later a very successful writer of popular histories, describes the intensity of this bond: "Those men on the line were my family . . . closer than any friends had been or ever would be. . . . Men, I now knew, do not fight for flag or country, for the Marine Corps or glory or any other abstraction. They fight for one another."[27] John Hogan, a US Seventh Division soldier, was offered a comparatively safe billet away from the rifle company in which he served. He wrote to his parents explaining why he was going to stick with his unit: "There is something about the spirit of the men in this platoon that I have grown to love and I want to help guard it." He describes their shared danger as a "sacrament." Hogan was killed at the Gaja Ridge on Okinawa and was awarded a posthumous Silver Star.[28]

For Allied combat soldiers of all backgrounds personal survival was the ultimate motivation (and in it one sees a humanity utterly absent in the more fanatical elements of the German and Japanese forces for whom the idea of death seems to have had a narcotic attraction). A rifleman of the US Thirty-Second Infantry Division fighting the Japanese was quite clear about the priorities: "Put into the situation that we and thousands of others were, survival for one's self was the first priority by far. The second priority was survival for the man next to you and the man next to him. So, right and wrong, love of country and pride in the unit . . . was a good bit behind."[29]

The constancy of death in combat created this remarkable world with its compelling centripetal force. To be separated from the hub of confraternity could be a torment even as it offered comparative safety. Harry Arnold, of the Ninety-Ninth Division in Europe, described the sense of loss when he and his buddies got a pass to the rear:

> Walking the sidewalks and crossing the streets were the garrison soldiers, resplendent of uniform, upright certain strides, heroic of countenance. They scarcely noticed our passing. Some regarded us stonily and . . . shook with revulsion. . . . It takes some time for the infantryman to realize that he is a breed apart and that, as such, he may have more with the enemy infantry across the way than with the army to his rear. . . . A feeling of unease pervaded our sense of belonging. We somehow felt denied, shunted aside as if an embarrassment to this rear area army. Though we dreaded facing Spandaus, 88s, mortars, and panzers, our gut feeling

told us that we belonged up there somehow . . . going to hell on worn out feet.[30]

It was as if the dead had paid the ultimate price to join an exclusive club—a club to which the living had an open invitation. The experience of death conferred membership and legitimacy on the survivors, as a Thirty-Sixth Infantry Division soldier remembers: "An individual who hasn't experienced the trauma of witnessing sudden death, fatal wounds, extreme heat/cold or smelled gas gangrene is never initiated into that select group of warriors."[31] A Red Army officer wrote to his family in February 1944: "Many of my friends have died. The truth is that we fight together, and the death of each is our own. Sometimes there are moments of such strain that the living envy the dead. Death is not as terrible as we used to think."[32]

★   ★   ★

HOW SOLDIERS DIED was often a reflection of where they fought. Death could take on the countenance of a particularly ghoulish real estate agent, mournfully intoning, "location, location, location." More than 109,000 US infantrymen would die in northwest Europe; 30,000 perished in Italy and almost 55,000 in the Pacific. For an American it was safer to be an infantryman in the Pacific theater, where he had a 2.5 percent chance of being killed (7.3 percent of being wounded), compared with the European theater, where GIs had a 3.5 percent chance of being killed (11.3 percent wounded).[33] As a wounded soldier, though, the chances of survival were much greater in Europe than in the Pacific, where it was more difficult to evacuate men to adequate medical facilities. For Americans in all theaters, 1 in 29 wounded men died (20,810 of 599,724), which was a very significant improvement on World War I, where 1 in 12 wounded men died.[34]

The issues involved in, say, the conquest of the Pacific islands compared with the type of warfare seen on the Russian steppes, or in North Africa, or western Europe, were obviously vastly different. Geography dictated strategic and logistical possibility, which in turn would determine the circumstances in which soldiers were killed.

Weaponry reflected these strategic and tactical differences. Soldiers in the Pacific were much more likely to die by small-arms fire, and Japanese soldiers could expect to die by flamethrower far more frequently than any soldier fighting in other theaters. The flamethrower was a weapon particularly well suited to killing men in the spider holes, caves, and tunnels favored by the Japanese defenders. For soldiers in the open lands of western Europe, North Africa, and Russia, tanks played a major role that was unknown on any remotely comparable scale in the Pacific, where the topography—rugged and often covered in thick jungle—was unsuited to massed tank warfare.

Allied soldiers in the Pacific were less likely to be killed by artillery than were infantry in western Europe and North Africa because the Japanese were relatively deficient in that armament. Within certain tactical situations, Japanese artillery fire was not capable of terrible lethality (during amphibious assaults, however, preregistered artillery could take a fearful toll of assaulting troops) but in the tactical picture as a whole the Japanese were incapable of laying down the massed bombardments available to the Americans, as in the battle for Okinawa, when between March 24 and June 22, 1945, the Japanese were hit by 2.4 million artillery rounds delivered by a combination of ground and naval pieces.[35]

The greater risk of American infantrymen being killed or wounded in the European theater compared with their counterparts in the Pacific was largely due to the superiority of German artillery, which inflicted about 60 percent of all battlefield casualties.[36] Artillery was overall the greatest killer of infantrymen in

World War II, but the chances of being killed if hit by a shell or grenade fragment in the European theater was 25 percent, compared with 16 percent in the Pacific.

This is explained in part by a combination of poor-quality munitions and the limitations placed on Japanese gunners by the need for concealment in order to limit exposure to the devastating counterbattery potential of American land, sea, and air forces. The usual pattern for Japanese artillerymen was to run guns up to the mouth of the cave in which they were concealed, fire a few rounds, and then pull back before they were found by GR-6 sound locators, spotter planes, or visual detection. Conservation of limited ammunition supplies was also an issue. Lack of communication between frontline infantry and the supporting gunners also reduced Japanese artillery lethality. With few radios, instructions were sent either across telephone wire, which was constantly being severed by American bombardment, or by runners, who, desperately exposed, were often cut down.

If geography facilitated the clash of massed forces in the combat in the Soviet Union, Europe, and North Africa, it dictated an altogether more fragmented, small-unit confrontation in the Pacific theater. Ironically, the battlefields of massed confrontation are usually described as "empty" because modern artillery, tanks, mortars, and machine guns killed at relatively long range. It is a type of warfare far distant from the personal confrontation of classic "heroic" combat. One would have thought the in-your-face, cut-and-thrust of jungle warfare conformed much more closely to some ancient heroic model of mano-a-mano fighting. But the opposite was the case. The fighting in the Pacific war reminds us that combat is a bloody gutter-slop: nasty, brutish, and short—an abattoir that is only later cleaned up, perfumed, and decorated with the laurel crown of history.

★   ★   ★

WORLD WAR II brought three broad innovations in land combat: amphibious, tank, and airborne warfare. Amphibious and tank warfare were innovative not so much in concept as in scale; amphibious assault had ancient precedents, and tank warfare had been introduced with great drama in the First World War. Airborne warfare was in a slightly different category. The principle of parachuting was well established by 1914, and although generally unavailable to aircrew of the First World War, parachutes were used by the almost proverbial sitting ducks of the Western Front—observers aloft in tethered balloons—even though, as one historian so delicately and aptly put it, "parachutes fell some way short of perfection in design."[37]

Of the three, an argument can be made that amphibious assault was the major strategic and tactical element of World War II—it kicked in the door. For the Allies—who had to respond to an enemy, whether Japanese or German, who had taken the initiative and controlled their interior lines of supply and communication—attacking their enemies first entailed reaching them: The shell had to be cracked before one could get at the meat. Seaborne assault offered the most effective method that could be supported with the logistical heft to carry the war to the enemy.

Airborne warfare also carried the war to the enemy, but it was practically impossible to sustain logistically. The German drop on Crete in May 1941, although ultimately successful, teetered so close to disaster that it put Hitler off the whole concept of airborne warfare, an aversion Stalin shared following the Soviet debacle at Velikii Bukrin, near Kiev, in September 1943, when two Soviet brigades landed almost literally on top of the Nineteenth Panzer Division, with predictably gruesome results for the jumpers.[38] Allied para-assaults on D-Day and at Arnhem in 1944, no matter how valiant, also exhibited a terrible fragility.

For the soldiers involved in amphibious attack, the risks, paradoxically, harked back to a much older mode of fighting: siege warfare: the terrible assault of the citadel. And although it was certainly innovative in its scale and in the specialized equipment developed for its execution, what might be called the ethos of amphibious assault was rooted in the frontal attack against heavily defended strongholds that had been a major characteristic of combat during the First World War. There was always something of the "forlorn hope" about it: terribly risky, exposed, naked. It took a certain desperate, grim élan and an acceptance of potentially high casualties in order to win the bridgehead.

Another parallel with the infantry assaults of the First World War was the role of preparatory bombardment and, as in that war, the often unrealistic predictions of its ability to suppress the opposition before the assault. The preliminary bombing of the D-Day beaches by the US Eighth and Ninth Army Air Forces was ineffectual, due partly to adverse weather conditions that limited visibility and partly to a nervousness about causing friendly casualties. As Harry Reynolds, an Eighth Army Air Force bombardier/navigator, recalls: "The area was covered with an overcast to about 13,000 feet. We did not want to drop the bombs because we were afraid of hitting our own troops who had advanced in from the beachhead."[39] German batteries at Omaha Beach in particular—which would prove to be the most deadly of all the landing points on D-Day—were left almost untouched by the bombers. Forced to bomb by instruments through the overcast, the 329 B-24s scattered their thirteen thousand bombs as far as 3 miles inland.[40]

For the attacking infantry the result was a disaster. Richard J. Ford of the Twenty-Ninth Infantry Division remembers: "The Air Force was to have bombed the beach creating craters for us to use. They missed the beach by three miles. Their explanation being they were afraid they might hit the landing craft, as the water was full of ships. However, this bomb preparation was to take place long before we got on the beach. As a result, that beach was as smooth and flat as a road and looked about two miles deep. As a result the Germans were in a 'shooting gallery' and we were the 'ducks.' "[41] There were about 10,000 casualties in all sectors on D-Day, of which, at a conservative estimate, about 2,000 were incurred on Omaha. Although it is surprisingly difficult to pinpoint accurate figures, around 4,400 of the 10,000 were killed.[42]

Naval bombardment was more accurate than aerial bombing, but even when delivered in massive concentration it could provide no guarantee that hostile fire would be adequately suppressed. In the Pacific, many amphibious assaults proved to be particularly bloody for the attackers because preliminary bombardment had failed to neutralize Japanese defenses. At Tarawa such a "stunning" tonnage of naval shells fell on the atoll that a Marine wondered why "the whole goddam island doesn't fall apart and sink." Yet somehow, the Japanese survived to pour in artillery fire when the incoming landing craft were 3,000 yards out, heavy machine-gun fire at 2,000 yards, and "everything the enemy had, including sniper fire and heavy mortars," at close range.[43] On Saipan the Japanese, in their interconnected limestone caves, just as the Germans had taken to their deep dugouts in World War I, largely survived the preliminary bombardment to emerge and sweep the reef with such a ferocity of fire that observers on US ships presumed it had been mined, when in fact the explosions were caused solely by artillery and mortar shells. At Iwo Jima, US warships poured in 22,000 shells and B-24s pounded the island for six weeks, none of which seriously interdicted the Japanese capability to hammer the Marines during their approach and on the beach.

The lethal dangers for amphibious assault troops started well before they even came close to the killing ground. Just getting into the Higgins boats (the specialized landing craft developed by Higgins Industries in New Orleans and in general use by mid-1943) could be deadly.[44] Men, encumbered with heavy gear, had to clamber over the sides of the mother ship and make their perilous, swaying way down scramble netting before making an anxious jump into the landing craft. Robert Leckie, a Marine at Guadalcanal, describes the heart-in-mouth experience: "The *George F. Elliott* was rolling in a gentle swell. The nets swayed out and in against her steel sides, bumping us. . . .

Three feet above the rolling Higgins Boats the cargo nets came to an end. One had to jump, weighted with fifty or more pounds of equipment. No time for indecision, for others on the nets above were all but treading [on] your fingers. So there it was—jump—hoping that the Higgins Boat would not roll away and leave only the blue sea to land in."[45]

William Manchester, another Guadalcanal veteran, remembers:

Descent was tricky. . . . A Marine in an amphibious assault was a beast of burden. He shouldered, on the average, 84.3 pounds, which made him the most heavily laden foot soldier in the history of warfare. Some men carried much more: 20-pound BARs, 45-pound 81-millimeter-mortar base plates, 47-pound mortar bipods, 36-pound light machine guns . . . and heavy machine-gun tripods, over 53 pounds. A man thus encumbered was expected to swing down the ropes like Tarzan. It was a dangerous business; anyone who lost his grip and fell clanking between the ship and the landing craft went straight to the bottom of Sealark Channel, and this happened to some. More frequent were misjudgments in jumping from the cargo net to the boat. The great thing was to time your leap so that you landed at the height of the boat's bob. If you miscalculated, the most skillful coxswain couldn't help you. You were walloped, possibly knocked out, possibly crippled, when you hit his deck.[46]

Raymond Gantter, a GI on his way to France in October 1944, recalls: "We had our first casualty as we transferred gingerly from the ship in which we had crossed the Channel to the LST that would deliver us. One of our officers, a grinning and likeable guy, was crushed to death between the LST and the Channel steamer. Climbing down the landing net hung over the side of the larger vessel, he hesitated a moment too long before leaping for the LST. A bad omen."[47]

Once on board the landing craft, the dangers of the approach were exacerbated by the acutest miseries that made men even more vulnerable when they hit the beach. Sergeant John R. Slaughter of the US 116th Infantry heading for Omaha Beach described the scene:

> There was a foot of water in the bottom of the boat and we had to take to the bilge pumps but they couldn't evacuate the water fast enough so we had to use our helmets to bail the water. Everybody was seasick. I'd never been sick before and some of my buddies had filled their puke bags already so I gave my puke bag and my Dramamine tablet away. Then I got sick. What caused me to get sick was the cold. It was probably in the 40s, the wind was blowing and we were soaking wet. I was just shivering. I went into my assault jacket and found a gas cape that we had in case of mustard gas and got under it to shield myself from the wind and the water. Of course lack of oxygen under the cape caused me to get really sick and I came out from under the thing. I started vomiting and I just pulled my helmet and vomited in my helmet, threw it out and washed the helmet out, vomited some more and that's the way we went in.[48]

Amphibious assault shared with all frontal assaults against prepared defenses (whether it was Pickett's charge, or Cold

Harbor, or Passchendaele) the terrifying negotiation of the killing ground that constitutes no-man's-land. The journey to the beach was a period of more or less enforced passivity for the attackers and gave the defenders their best chance of inflicting great pain.

Mortimer Wheeler (who would later become a renowned archeologist) recounts the approach to the Salerno landings in Italy on September 9, 1943: "Meanwhile, another German battery, four 88-millimeters, had got the range of our craft over open sights as we moved slowly in, awaiting our turn at the beach. The captain of the next landing-ship beside us was killed by a direct hit on the bridge. . . . Our turn was next. The rounds came over in sharp salvoes and bracketed us with perfect precision, sending showers of spray over us as we changed course cumbrously to vary range."[49]

In addition to the dangers of incoming artillery and machine-gun fire, heavily laden soldiers simply drowned when they were forced to evacuate their stricken landing craft. Private Bill Bidmead, a British commando at D-Day, "saw men drowning in the shallow water. Wounded, their 90-lb rucksacks weighed them down."[50] During the Allied landings on North Africa (Operation Torch) the men carried 132 pounds, which was "110 pounds too much for a combat soldier to carry and enough to make anyone utterly useless," nor could it be supported by the life jackets they had been issued, according to the quartermaster for the US II Corps.[51]

William Manchester makes the assertion that at Tarawa a coxswain, completely unnerved by the heavy artillery and machine-gun fire hitting the landing craft as they tried to get over the reef, "lost his mind [and] . . . screamed, 'This is as far as I go!' He dropped his ramp and twenty Marines bowed by weapons and ammunition drowned in fifteen feet of water."[52]

Getting through the surf was agony in slow motion. Private Jim Wilkins, a Canadian at Juno Beach on D-Day, remembers:

We were only 500 yards from the beach and were ordered to get down. Minutes later the boat stops and begins to toss in the waves. The ramp goes down and without hesitation my section leader, Corporal John Gibson, jumps out well over his waist in water. He only makes a few yards and is killed. We have landed dead on into a pillbox with a machine gun blazing away at us. We didn't hesitate and jumped into the water. . . . Where was everybody? My section are only half there—some were just floating on their Mae Wests. . . . Kenny keeps yelling "Come on. Come on."

"I'm coming, I'm coming," I yell to him. We are now up to our knees in water and you can hear a kind of buzzing sound all around as well as the sound of the machine gun itself. All of a sudden something slapped the side of my right leg and then a round caught me dead centre up high on my right leg causing a compound fracture. By this time I was flat on my face in the water—I've lost my rifle, my helmet is gone . . . [I] flop over onto my back and start to float to shore where I meet five other riflemen all in very bad shape. The man beside me is dead within minutes.[53]

Getting across the reef and through the surf at Tarawa presented the Japanese gunners with ample slow-moving targets. Many of the Marines in the Higgins boats on the reef had to get out far from the shoreline. Robert Sherrod, reporting for *Time* magazine, watched them jump out into chest-deep water: "It was painfully slow, wading in such deep water. And we had seven hundred yards to walk slowly into this machine-gun fire, looming into larger targets as we rose onto high ground."[54] Harry Smith of the Second Marine Division writes to his girl-friend: "I was one of the first ten men out, and as these first ten scrambled out many of them were hit. A fellow directly in front of me got shot in the head, the force tore his helmet off and as he fell forward into the water I could see that the top of his head had been blown off and his brains dropped into the water. To this day I don't know how I got to shore in such a shower of machine gun and small arms fire. Men were getting shot all around me."[55]

When men have endured that kind of murderous exposure, their first thought, on reaching what they imagined to be the relative safety of the beach, is to go to ground and take whatever kind of cover they could, but when defenders' guns have been preregistered to rake the beachhead, the attackers need to act counterintuitively. Moving into and through fire takes an extraordinary degree of training and courage, for men will most certainly die.

Douglas Grant, a British officer at Sword Beach on D-Day, saw how "men floundered in the loose sand under their top-heavy loads . . . and I ran up and down the line yelling them on with every curse I remembered. . . . Other troops, with the stupidity of sheep, were digging in along the length of the wire; they had not sense enough to realise that the enemy would blast it as conscientiously as a drill routine." Somehow he got his men up and "we ran on . . . our hearts straining to match our wills."[56]

Sublieutenant George Green, a British naval officer taking the ill-fated A Company of the US 116th Infantry Regiment (a Pennsylvania National Guard outfit, "pleasant friendly country lads but not assault troops," as Green described them) under the command of Captain Taylor Fellers, to Omaha Beach notes: "It took some time for the troops to disembark as the craft was bouncing up and down in the heavy surf and the soldiers were hampered by the amount of kit they carried. . . . When they reached the beach the troops lay down and made no attempt to advance towards the obstacles 50 yards away or the menacing cliffs 250 yards further on where the hidden Germans were popping off mortars at us. . . . I heard that Taylor Fellers and all the men in LCA 910 had been killed. Practically everyone else in that first wave we landed at 6:30 was wiped out shortly after landing."[57]

The 116th at Omaha Beach took the heaviest casualties of any of the Allied invaders ("They just murdered them," said an observer). The US War Department's official history describes what happened to the first battalion as it assaulted Dog Green sector:

> All boats came under criss-cross machine-gun fire. . . . As the first men jumped they crumpled and flopped into the water. Then order was lost. It seemed to the men that the only way to get ashore was to dive head first in and swim clear of the fire that was striking the boats. But, as they hit the water, their heavy equipment dragged them down and soon they were struggling to stay afloat. Some were hit in the water and wounded. Some drowned then and there. . . . But some moved safely through the bullet-fire to the sand and then, finding they could not hold there, went back into the water and used it as cover, only their heads sticking out. Those who survived kept moving forward with the tide. . . . Within ten minutes of the ramps being lowered, A Company had become inert, leaderless and almost incapable of action. Every officer and sergeant had been killed or wounded. . . . The men in the water pushed wounded men ashore ahead of them. And those who had reached the sands crawled back into the water pulling others to land to save them from drowning, in many cases only to see the rescued wounded again or to be hit themselves. Within twenty minutes of striking the beach A Company had ceased to be an assault company and had become a forlorn little rescue party bent upon survival and the saving of lives.[58]

In some circumstances digging-in was a fatal breach of a cardinal rule to keep moving through the killing zone. On Iwo Jima the soft black volcanic ash was about as much use as talcum powder in providing shelter. Fire poured into the beachhead, and the "steep-pitched beach sucked hundreds of men seaward in its backwash. Mines blew up Sherman tanks. . . . The invaders were taking heavy mortar and artillery fire. Steel sleeted down on them like the lash of a desert storm. . . . The deaths on Iwo were extraordinarily violent. There seemed to be no clean wounds; just fragments of corpses. It reminded one battalion medical officer of a Bellevue [a New York City hospital] dissecting room. . . . You tripped over strings of viscera fifteen feet long, over bodies which had been cut in half at the waist. Legs and arms, and heads bearing only necks, lay fifty feet from the closest torsos."[59]

Seaborne attack became almost the signature tactic of the Pacific war, again dictated by the particular geography of the island-strewn battle zone. Although the US Army undertook more amphibious assaults than the US Marine Corps (of the forty-three total the Marines spearheaded fourteen),[60] those involving the Marines tended to be more memorably bloody. Guadalcanal, Tarawa, Saipan, Peleliu, Iwo Jima, and Okinawa are the battles that have stamped themselves on the popular imagination, something not hindered by the Corps' skill on the PR front (to an extent that deeply irked the always vigorously self-promoting General Patton, who saw his own exploits with the Third Army in Europe being eclipsed in the press by the headline-grabbing casualty rates incurred by the Marines in the Pacific. It was as though the Marines had inspired some large part of the public's idea of the heroic, while the Army was left to trudge, underappreciated, as the Corps strutted out).

The US Marine Corps cherished and actively promoted an acceptance of casualties in its role as the kicker-in-of-doors in the Pacific. Where the Army might have looked at the door and diligently searched for the key, the Marines preferred the smashing boot. And nothing suited this ethos better than the amphibious assault.[61] The Corps conceded that there might be many bodies left on the beach, but, it fervently believed, the pain in the short term was outweighed by the gain overall. Marines were frankly contemptuous of the conservatism of the US Army, with its emphasis on slower evaluation and exploitation of the tactical situation. Richard C. Kennard, a Marine on Peleliu, puts it bluntly in a letter home: "My only answer to why the Marines get the toughest jobs is because the average leatherneck is a much better fighter. He has far more guts, courage, and better officers. . . . I'm not saying that the Army men are cowards. They are older men as a rule however and not nearly as tough and brave as any single average Marine. These boys out here have a pride in the Marine Corps and will fight to the end no matter what the cost."[62]

What Kennard implies is that the Marines were volunteers for death and glory; the Army, merely conscripts.

Where landings were opposed, Marines had to take a beating in order to establish their footholds. Tarawa (November 20, 1943) was one of the earliest, and assault elements of the Second Marine Division took about 20 percent casualties. Of the 800 men of the Sixth Marines who set off as reinforcements, only 450 made it to the beach.[63] A total of 990 Marines were killed outright or died of wounds—a sacrifice that shocked the American public and forced the Corps to review its amphibious doctrine.[64]

Not all assaults were contested at the waterline, either by accident or intention. At Anzio (September 22, 1944) on the Italian west coast, the Allies enjoyed the benefit of complete surprise, only to squander it by a pusillanimous failure of command to grab the initiative and break out in order to exploit their initial good fortune—a nervous stumble for which the Germans would later exact a very bloody price. When the Marines and Army landed at Okinawa on April 1, 1945, they were only very lightly opposed, the Japanese choosing to draw the Americans inland to do bloody battle from carefully prepared defenses.

At Guadalcanal on August 7, 1942, Robert Leckie remembers his terror as his landing craft approached Red Beach: "I could think of nothing but the shoreline where we were to land. There were other boatloads of marines ahead of us. I fancied firing from behind their prostrate bodies, building a protecting wall of torn and reddened flesh. I could envision a holocaust among the coconuts." But the "Japanese had run" and for "ten minutes we had something like bliss, a flood of well-being following upon our unspeakable relief."[65]

★   ★   ★

THERE WAS NO question about the dying. Donald R. Burgett, a 101st Airborne recruit, remembers that an "instructor . . . told us that we weren't volunteering for any picnic; that most of us would die in combat. 'In fact,' he said, 'if any man lives through three missions, the government will fly that man home and discharge him. You know as well as I do that Uncle Sam isn't going to discharge anyone during wartime, so now you know what your chances are of living through this war. You haven't got a chance!' "[66]

Jumping into thin air a mile, perhaps several, above the all-too-solid earth, while enemy infantry and antiaircraft guns shot at your ever-so-slowly descending and unutterably vulnerable nether regions, was, to put it mildly, fraught. A British paratrooper during the invasion of Sicily in July 1943 felt the understandably acute anxiety common to all airborne infantrymen: "Suddenly we heard the guns ahead—the furious crackle from the quick-firing pom-poms [he didn't know it, but they were being shot at by their own ships] and the deeper intermittent crack of the heavier barrage. At once terror gripped me as

I braced myself to meet the red-hot inverted rain. I had had no experience of flak, and those fountains of red and orange tracer looked quite appalling. There is something specially disturbing about being shot at from below—one's body seems to be much more vital when attacked from that direction."[67]

The whole business from beginning to end was crazily risky. First there were the considerable dangers of training, made especially acute because the practice of airborne warfare was itself a very recent development and there was much learning on the job, which is fine if you are an accountant but less so if you are a parachutist.

Parachute descents had been undertaken in the eighteenth century, and Napoleon had toyed with the idea of sending assault troops by balloon on his aborted invasion of Britain. That extraordinary military visionary Billy Mitchell had pushed strongly for an American parachute force to be dropped behind the German lines in 1918, but nothing came of it, and the serious development of the use of parachutes in combat (as against their use as a means of escape from stricken planes or observation balloons) had to wait until the 1930s, with much of the pioneering work done in Russia, Italy, and Germany.

Although the United States and Britain lagged behind in the development of an airborne arm (they had to be spurred by the arrival of World War II), it was a Briton, Everard Calthrop, and an American, Leslie Leroy Irvin, who greatly progressed the development of the parachute itself. Calthrop's chute—aptly called the "Guardian Angel"—was designed to make escape from an airplane possible and was attached to the aircraft; the chute being deployed from its container by the weight of the falling pilot. Irvin's parachute, on the other hand, was a true free-fall design, the canopy activated by the parachutist pulling a rip cord—the great advantage being that the crewman did not have to be in a fixed position in the plane in order to use the chute. On April 19,

1919, Irvin himself, with a heroic belief in his own design, made the first rip-cord parachute jump. It was a historic success (apart from a broken ankle on landing awkwardly).[68]

Inevitably, equipment failure (including the dreaded "Roman candle," to describe a chute that failed to inflate) and the mistakes of rookie parachutists took their toll during training and in battle. The young Donald Burgett watched

a plane swing along the Chattahoochee River and come in over the drop zone at about 1000 feet. The tiny figures tumbled out in rapid succession and all seemed well until two of the chutes bumped together in midair, and the men became entangled in suspension lines. One chute collapsed but the other one held, and for a moment it looked as if they would still make it O.K. . . . But the man hanging lower than the other pulled his reserve chute. This is something we were specifically instructed not to do. The only time a reserve chute is any good is when the main doesn't open at all or has a serious malfunction. When two men are entangled, the reserve can billow up and collapse the main chutes. . . . Now, as we watched, the smaller chute unfurled into the main canopy of the top man, collapsing it. The chutes looked like bedsheets fluttering behind the figures as they plummeted earthward. Neither one of the men yelled or made a sound; they must have been too busy trying to untangle the snarled lines and fighting for their lives to know how close they were. The whole mess took place in a matter of seconds. . . . They bounced a couple of feet in the air. . . . One of the sergeants leaped from a jeep and worked over the bodies a few minutes, then got back in and drove up to us. Climbing out of the jeep he held two pairs of bloodied jump boots from the two men out there. "Now does anyone want to quit?" . . . No one stepped out of line.[69]

When bodies hit the ground, they sounded "like large ripe pumpkins being thrown down to burst against the ground," or a "large mattress going 'floomp.' "

Inferior design as well as the sheer weight of the equipment could be extremely hazardous to jumpers. The parachute used by the German *Fallschirmjäger*, the RZ-1, pitched the man face-forward so that he had to do a nifty forward roll on landing— something that demanded a very high degree of athletic ability and often resulted in injuries to knees, hands, and face. The design also severely limited the weaponry that could be carried to a pistol and perhaps a submachine gun. The tightness of the harness, the violence of the canopy opening, and the forward-facing gait all meant that any solid objects on him would likely injure him, so his weaponry had to be sent down in separate metal containers. Retrieving these on the battlefield put the *Fallschirmjäger* at a potentially lethal disadvantage: "A German platoon needed fourteen containers for their weapons and ammunition, which meant there was a lot of running about on the drop zone. . . . In Crete [May 1941] the British and Commonwealth troops were already familiar with the need for the parachutists to rally round their containers before they became an effective fighting force, and they merely watched for the colored canopies of the containers and laid their machine-guns on them after they had landed."[70]

In their most famous action, the battle for Crete, German paratroopers took horrific casualties. Of the 22,000 parachutists committed, 5,000 were killed, "most of them coming from the junior leaders—the corporals, sergeants, and young officers. In addition, 2,500 were wounded."[71] After Crete the German airborne arm undertook no more large-scale assaults and mutated into elite light infantry.

The Allied jumpers had the opposite problem. They were loaded "like a military Christmas tree." Their parachutes held them upright so that they would hit the ground (theoretically) feet-first, and "there was scarcely a part of the body which was not covered by some equipment or weapon." One of the US 101st Airborne listed the things he carried:

> Jump suit . . . helmet, boots, gloves, main chute, reserve chute, Mae West, rifle, .45 automatic pistol, trench knife, jump knife, hunting knife, machete, one cartridge belt, two bandoliers, two cans of machine gun ammo, 66 rounds of .45 ammo, one Hawkins mine capable of blowing the track off of a tank, four blocks of TNT, one entrenching tool with two blasting caps taped on the outside of the steel part, three first-aid kits, two morphine needles, one gas mask, a canteen of water, three days' supply of K rations, two days' supply of D rations . . . six fragmentation grenades, one Gammon grenade, one orange smoke and one red smoke grenade, one orange panel, one blanket, one raincoat, one change of socks and underwear, two cartons of cigarettes and a few other odds and ends.[72]

In addition, they often had a musette bag weighing as much as 80 pounds attached by a cord to a leg. So heavily laden were they that getting up to board an aircraft often required a helping hand. They were the modern equivalent of the medieval knight in more ways than one. The sheer amount of gear worn and carried by a knight and a paratrooper signified potency. In another way, though, it was an indicator of their vulnerability. The knight could be attacked from so many angles with such a variety of weapons that he had to be his own mobile fortress. The paratrooper, whose great tactical vulnerability was that, by necessity, he had been projected far from the main army with all the logistical support it offered, needed to replicate in miniature that support. He too was a one-man fortress. Knights died when they were separated from their archers and infantry support, and the significant defeats of airborne warriors came at those times when they too were separated for too long from artillery and reinforcements. One thinks of the British First Airborne at Arnhem and the British First Parachute Brigade at Primosole in Sicily, both of which were eventually outgunned and overrun.

Another parallel, of course, is that both knights and paratroopers reveled in their role as primary assault troops; they celebrated the heroic nature of their elite combat status. It is interesting that in the equipment of the 101st Airborne trooper listed above there are four edged weapons. In the indoctrination of airborne warriors, much emphasis was placed on the fearsome psychological impact of the blade. This is not combat in the empty technological battlefield but something ancient, fierce, and personal. And like the knight or the samurai, the airborne warrior demanded that this special valor be advertised. As an example, the Mohawk hairstyle of the American paratrooper at D-Day announced the very considerable harm—with an association to a much older, much more personal style of killing—that was about to be visited on his enemy.

Just as the unhorsed knight could be betrayed by the very thing that was meant to protect him—his armor—so too was the airborne warrior. As with overburdened amphibious soldiers, should the paratrooper land in water (and it didn't need to be very deep), he stood an excellent chance of being dragged under and drowned, something that happened with sickening frequency. On D-Day, men of the Eighty-Second Airborne landed in an area around the rivers Douve and Merderet that had been deliberately flooded by the Germans, and they drowned, partly because their harnesses were difficult to release.[73]

The chute that was designed to safeguard the paratrooper could also be the instrument of his death. Its very ability to keep him in suspension increased his exposure to enemy ground fire. It was for all an agony of anticipation and for some a bloodily premature extinction. General Sir John Hackett, dropping with the First Airborne at Arnhem, saw "an inert mass . . . swinging down in a parachute harness beside me, a man from whose body the entrails hung, swaying in a reciprocal rhythm."[74] The chute could snag the jumper up on a tree or pole as a helplessly dangling target for enemy infantry, and on the ground it might drag him into God knows what peril.

Private Ken Russell of the US 505th recalls about D-Day: "I don't remember all the stick [the unit] in our plane but I know Private H.T. Bryant, Private Ladislaw 'Laddie' Tlapa and Lieutenant Cadish were most unfortunate. They were the fellows who were shot on the power poles. My close friend Private 1st Class Charles Blankenship was shot still in his chute hanging in a tree." In addition, he remembers that when

we jumped there was a huge fire in a building in town. I didn't know that the heat would suck a parachute towards the fire . . . one trooper landed in the fire . . . I landed on the right side of the roof. This other trooper came down and really got entangled on the steeple. . . . Almost immediately a Nazi soldier came running up from the back side of the church shooting at everything. Sergeant John Ray had landed in the churchyard almost immediately below. . . . This Nazi shot him in the stomach while he was still in his chute. While Ray was dying he somehow got his .45 out and shot the Nazi in the back of the head, killing him. He saved my life . . . it was one of the bravest things I have ever witnessed."[75]

The fate of the airborne warrior was also greatly dependent on the mode of delivery—aircraft or glider—and the crews who flew them. Both had their own unique risks, but both shared the difficulties of navigation, weather, and hostile fire, often in an unholy confluence. The Allied airborne assault on Sicily in 1943—a mixture of glider and airplane delivery—was probably one of the best examples of that deadly nexus.

The British First Air-Landing Brigade went in first on July 10, 1943. The idea was to fly in gliders with the stealth the Germans had used against the Belgian fort of Eben-Emael in May 1940. The operation fell apart. Gale-force winds blew up great sandstorms that obliterated landing sites; there was insufficient fighter cover and inadequate training. Sixty percent of the tugs (the aircraft towing the gliders) detached their gliders prematurely, and once a military glider (unlike lightweight recreational versions) was let loose, it dropped fast. Many gliders crashed into the sea, and 252 troopers were drowned. Of the 52 gliders that had left the North African coast, only 12 landed anywhere near their targets. Of the 2,000 men of the First Air-Landing, 490 were lost, and of the 145 glider pilots, 88 were lost.[76]

Shortly after the British attack, the aircraft-borne US 505th Parachute Infantry Brigade, led by the legendary Colonel James Gavin, a pioneer of airborne warfare, battered by high winds and disoriented by the lack of adequate navigational aids, was dropped up to 60 miles off target with men landing "on stone ridges, olive groves, barbed wire, beaches—and a few in the sea."[77] Their sister regiment, the 504th, was sent in as reinforcement, and before it could even get at the enemy it was hammered by friendly fire that spread like a "contagion" from the beachhead and the anchored Allied fleet. It was, to use a descriptive phrase from the Vietnam War, a "cluster fuck." Due to the congestion of communication, the fleet had not been properly forewarned of the 504th's flyover:

"I looked back," reported a captain in one of the lead planes, "and saw the whole coastline burst into flames." Pilots dove to the deck or swerved back to sea, flinging paratroopers to the floor and tangling their static lines. Men fingered their rosary beads or vomited into their helmets. Bullets ripped through wings and fuselages, and the bay floors grew slick with blood. . . .

Formations disintegrated. Some pilots flipped off their belly lights and tried to thread a path along the shore between fire from the ships and fire from the beach. Others fled for Africa, chased by tracers for thirty miles. Half a dozen planes were hit as paratroopers struggled to get out the door. "Planes tumbled out of the air like burning crosses. . . . Others stopped like a bird shot in flight." . . . Men died in their planes, men died descending in their parachutes, and at least four were shot dead on the ground by comrades convinced they were Germans.[78]

Putting the parachutist on target was, for the pilot of the aircraft or glider, a hugely complex business. Speed and altitude were obviously critical, and navigation was, to put it mildly, a challenge (especially at night and in fog and low cloud as prevailed on D-Day). Because the planes were forced to come in on relatively low trajectories they were highly vulnerable to flak. An observer on the USS *Quincy* on D-Day records the horror when "a yellow ball would start glowing out in the middle of a field of red tracers. This yellow ball would slowly start to fall, forming a tail. Eventually, it would smash into the black loom of land, causing a great sheet of light to flare against the low clouds. Sometimes the yellow ball would explode in mid-air, sending out streamers of burning gasoline. This tableau always brought the same reactions from us sky control observers: a sharp sucking-in of the breath and a muttered 'Poor goddamn bastards.' "[79]

There was much accusation that pilots had cravenly sacrificed paratroopers in order to save their own skins. Donald Burgett of the 101st fumed:

I saw vague, shadowy figures of troopers plunging downward. Their chutes were pulling out of their pack trays and
just starting to unfurl when they hit the ground. Seventeen
men hit the ground before their chutes had time to open.
They made a sound like ripe pumpkins being thrown down
to burst against the ground.

"That dirty son of a bitch of a pilot," I swore to myself,
"he's hedgehopping and killing a bunch of troopers just to
save his own ass. I hope he gets shot down in the Channel
and drowns real slow."

There wasn't any sense in going to those men. . . . If by
some miracle one of them were still alive, he would be better
off to be left alone to die as quickly as possible.[80]

Many historians echoed this notion, accusing Troop Carrier Command pilots of not only releasing men too low but also
increasing airspeed in order to avoid flak, and thereby pitching
the troopers out to suffer terrific prop blast and ferocious shock
when their canopies opened. The truth, however, was that the
planes themselves were grossly overloaded, which forced the drop
speed to be increased in order to prevent stalling. Low cloud cover
and wind gusts of up to 30 knots (a safe limit over a drop zone is
about 13 knots) also contributed to increased casualties.[81]

Glider-borne delivery was equally, if differently, hazardous.
The very notion of taking a fragile plane (British gliders were hardly
more than flying wardrobes; in fact they were made of wood and
fabricated in furniture-making factories) and intentionally crashing it is so counterintuitive as to appear positively deranged—a
point not missed on the would-be glider-borne troops, who failed
to volunteer in droves. In fact, so unattractive was the prospect of
intentional self-destruction that they had to be conscripted, the
inducement of a monthly bonus notwithstanding.[82]

Even before landing, there was a very real danger that if

the glider failed to fly either higher than or lower than the tug ("High-Tow" or "Low-Tow"), it could be shaken to destruction by the turbulence of the tug's slipstream.[83] Landing was a nerve-wracking crapshoot conducted in such congestion, and with such little means to maneuver, that a main cause of death to crew and soldiers was collision with other gliders. Clinton Riddle of the Eighty-Second Airborne saw the remains of a crashed glider in Normandy and remembered: "You could almost step on the bodies from one to the other."[84]

★   ★   ★

THERE WERE SO many ways a soldier could get killed. GI Raymond Gantter pondered the possible fate of his foxhole buddy, Chesty, who disappeared without a trace: "I wonder what did become of him. It's possible that he wandered up to the front that night and was killed, perhaps so mangled that he was unrecognizable and his dog tags lost. Or a German sniper or straggler may have killed him and concealed his body in Hurtgen Forest . . . or he may have stumbled on a mine or booby trap . . . or perhaps he's spent the night in a dugout that collapsed on him burying him alive."[85]

Despite the emphasis on mechanized warfare with the thrilling promise of blitzkriegian speed and finality, much of the fighting followed the much more prosaic tradition of "infantry performing its role with rifles, hand grenades, machine guns, and mortars and using tactics unchanged since the First World War and even the Civil War."[86] Combat in Europe was often drawn out and dogged. The Normandy front was static for two months following D-Day, Monte Cassino lasted six months, the siege of Leningrad lasted two and a half years, and El Alamein has been described as a classic First World War battle, with huge preliminary bombardment, creeping barrages, and infantry break-ins designed to crumble the enemy's fortified line.[87] And in the Pacific much of the fighting was a classic infantry slugfest against entrenched defenders: "Contrary to the common impression that Second World War battles were easy, fast-moving and decisive affairs we find that they were in reality protracted, gruelling, nerve-racking and costly. There were more dangers to counter than there had been in the battles of a quarter century before; and it took a higher level of training and morale to overcome them. The tight-rope on which front-line soldiers walked had become thinner and less stable, reflected in higher levels of accidents, 'psychiatric casualties' and the general destruction of lives and property. War had become inexorably nastier."[88]

For the infantryman, the war was fought amid an unremitting exposure to danger. General Omar Bradley described its extraordinary brutality: "The rifleman fights without promise of either reward or relief. Behind every river there's another hill—and behind that hill, another river. After weeks or months in the line only a wound can offer him the comfort of safety, shelter and a bed. Those who are left to fight, fight on, evading death but knowing that with each day of evasion they have exhausted one more chance for survival. Sooner or later, unless victory comes this chase must end on the litter or in the grave."[89] As a veteran American infantryman put it: "Nobody gets out of a rifle company. It's a door that only opens one way, in. You leave when they carry you out, if you're unlucky, dead, or if you're lucky, wounded. But nobody just walks away. That was the unwritten law."[90]

Without the prospect of rotation out of the combat zone, the grave became a likely destination. For Americans, the last fourteen months of the war saw the heaviest casualties. In October 1942, only 1 in 1,000 US Army members became a casualty. In November, it rose to 4 per 1,000, reflecting the fighting in North Africa, Guadalcanal, and New Guinea. By June 1944, it had soared to 50 per 1,000, hitting its peak in January 1945 with about 56 per 1,000.[91]

As a snapshot the statistics are interesting but hide a much grimmer picture. The rate per thousand is a percentage of the whole army. Unlike World War I, where a much larger proportion of the total armed services was exposed to combat, in World War II the logistical tail was fat and long and comparatively safe. The combat soldiers formed the small arrowhead that carried combat to the enemy, and their chances of being killed or wounded were, of course, considerably greater. Of the roughly 10 million men in the US Army by the war's end, only about 2 million, or 1 in 5, were in the 90 combat divisions (of which 68 were infantry divisions), and of these, about 700,000 were in the infantry: 1 in 14 for the whole Army but absorbing 70 percent of the casualties.[92] Frank Nisi, an infantryman with the Third Infantry Division, described that exclusive club in a letter to his father:

> I would venture to say that only a very small percentage really know what war is all about. By that I mean that of the millions . . . only the Infantry and certain attachments, such as tanks and TDs [tank destroyers], were ever close enough to hear a shot fired in anger. Then that could be broken down still further to exclude the Reg't. Hq. Service Company etc. It gets down to the man with the rifle who has to live in the ground . . . or any place he possibly can, then go without sleep for several days and get up and fight, hike, run, creep, or crawl 25 miles or so. During this time the echelons in rear of him move up in vehicles, get their night's sleep and wait for him to advance again.[93]

In the last six months of 1944, the battle losses far exceeded the US planners' expectations, with 12,000–18,000 GIs killed in each of those months and 40,000–60,000 wounded. The upshot was that young men who had initially been allocated to the logistical tail to take up relatively safe duties of an administrative nature, thanks to their higher intelligence-test scores, now found themselves on the front line. Death in combat had suddenly become a whole lot more democratic.

★   ★   ★

WHAT INSTRUMENTS KILLED soldiers in World War II? Although there had been improvements in all branches of weaponry since the First World War, nothing fundamentally new had emerged. There were sophistications and, crucially, there was more of it, but the underlying architecture of weaponry was not too far removed from that of World War I. Artillery and other kinds of infantry-delivered bombs such as mortars, grenades, and mines (as against aircraft- or ship-delivered munitions) took the heaviest toll. In the US Army, about fifty thousand died by explosive devices of one kind or another, compared with just more than thirty thousand killed by small arms and machine guns.[94] Although this overall picture is accurate, sometimes the individual cause of death could be elusive.

In one of the very few studies of the causes of death for men killed outright in action (one thousand US bodies were examined between April and November 1944 at the US military cemetery at Monte Beni, Italy), a medical team reported:

A man killed in battle will be seen to fall only by his comrades who cannot know with certainty what type of missile caused a man's death. They may know that a man was hit by machinegun or rifle fire or that he encountered a mine, but they cannot state with accuracy the caliber of a high explosive shell which has been fired at them. In any event, even if accurate information regarding missiles is known to a man's comrades, it does not often find its way to the EMT's [emergency medical tags] which are filled in by company aidmen or other medical personnel who arrive on the scene after the action has occurred. Those who actually see the death occur are seldom present when the body is tagged. Ballistic data on EMT's cannot therefore be depended upon since it is not known which ones are accurate. The best method of obtaining accurate information of this type is to perform an autopsy [but] . . . it became evident that the performance of an autopsy in every case was impracticable because of the time required for such a procedure. The first body autopsied in this project was thoroughly dissected in search of the missile. After a period of 3 hours, the missile had still not been found, and the search for it was abandoned.[95]

Nevertheless, the majority of men (87.1 percent) in this sample were found to have been killed by "fragment-producing weapons" (artillery and mortar fire), while 10.9 percent were hit by small arms. Only a tiny fraction were killed by hand grenades (0.1 percent) or land mines (1.9 percent).[96]

No wonder, then, that artillery gripped soldiers with the most intense dread. The poet Louis Simpson, a trooper in the 101st Airborne, explains: "Being shelled is the real work of an infantry soldier, which no one talks about. Everyone has his own way of going about it. In general, it means lying face down and contracting your body into as small a space as possible. In novels you read about soldiers, at such moments, fouling themselves. The opposite is true. As all your parts are contracting, you are more likely to be constipated."[97]

Writing to his family from northwest Europe, Raymond Gantter described artillery's monumental malevolence:

You ask which is more frightening . . . rifle and machine guns versus artillery? If I *have* to make a choice, I'll take small-arms fire. Rifles and machine guns are bad medicine, but they carry this small sugar-coating: a hole in the ground, a hollow, even a tiny hummock of earth, offers reasonable protection against their bullets. Chances are you won't get hurt so long as you lie there. That is, not by small-arms fire. Shrapnel cannot be denied by a hole in the ground, a hollow, or a little mound of dirt. You hear the shell screaming through the air, you estimate where it will fall and tense yourself. Then it hits, the earth bounds under you, trying to push you up, and the air is filled with the buzzing of maddened bumblebees. The hell with Ry-crisp or lettuce-and-lemon diets—for ladies who would be swanlike I recommend a few hours under an artillery barrage.[98]

David Kenyon Webster remembered how shells sought him out:

Three more shells came in, low and angry, and burst in the orchard.

"They're walking 'em toward us," I whispered.

I felt as if a giant with exploding iron fingers were looking for me, tearing up the ground as he came. I wanted to strike at him, to kill him, to stop him before he ripped into me, but I could do nothing. Sit and take it, sit and take it. The giant raked the orchard and tore up the roads and stumbled toward us in a terrible blind wrath as we sat in our hole with our heads between our legs and curses on our lips.[99]

For a British soldier, shells seemed somehow willfully directed by some divine malevolence:

We hit the earth with one thud where we had stood. I could feel the exact spot in the small of my defenceless back (I wish to God we had packs on, I thought . . . not because they're any *use* but it feels better) where the pointed nose of the shell would pierce skin and gristle and bone and explode the charge that would make me feel as if I had a splitting headache all over for a fiftieth of a second before I was spread minutely over the earth and hung up in trees. I held my breath and tried to press deeper into the earth and tensed every muscle as though by sheer will power I could abate the force of that disintegrating shock, cheat death, defy God (O God have mercy on me, please, please, *please* dear God, don't let me die).[100]

To stay or to run? Either decision could bring death or salvation:

"Anti-tank guns!" yells Dorka, thunderstruck, and crosses himself.

At the same moment a second shell hits the mound. . . . Dorka yells and clutches his throat. He looks dumbstruck at his bloody hand and presses it against his wound. Panic-stricken, he jumps out of the hole and runs up the field towards the village. Right behind him another round explodes and rips off both his legs. His backside is thrown into the air and falls, covered in blood, on to the ground. Only seconds have passed, and as I again look towards the front another flash comes from a gun barrel. The shells hit in the mound in front of my position at full force and covers half my hole with dirt. I pull my legs out of the dirt and press myself tightly down on to it. Then the next round explodes immediately in front of me and sends a glowing splinter towards me. I feel a heavy impact on my upper right arm and some light splinters hitting my chest. Blood immediately starts running warm down my arm and dripping out of my sleeve. For a moment I am numb; then I feel a burning sensation, and pain.

You will bleed to death here in this hole! I think, and then I am gripped with a terrible fear. Just get away from here! The fright drives me out of my hole. I press my left hand over my wound and dash away. Instinctively, I do not go the obvious way—up to the houses—but, propelled by terror, I run to the right. . . . I know that the direct-fire gunners [like Webster, he is being shelled by an antitank gun deployed against infantry] must first physically shift their aim in order to pick up a new one—in this case me. The shells start to land around me only after I have been running for a bit. They are firing at me as they would at a rabbit—so I behave like one, by constantly zigzagging. I carry on like this, to force the gunners to adjust their sights all the time.

But I am running out of steam. My lungs are heaving like a pair of bellows and I sense a light dizzy feeling. I can't stop the bleeding with my hand. . . . Wheezing, I keep on running in zigzag fashion, running for dear life, afraid of being blown to bits by the next shell. . . . Well out of breath, I run further into the woodland then fall to the ground.

I am safe.[101]

The gods could be almost playfully malicious:

Strung out in a long, scattered single file, our battalion made its way up the hills, moving at a steady pace. Captain Kessler knelt with his subordinate leaders and studied his maps for a moment, waving the rest of the company on.

"Keep moving," he said in his gravelly voice. "Keep moving."

He was about twenty feet ahead of me to the left of the narrow path we were following. Suddenly he grunted and rolled over on his left side. . . . One of the men he had been kneeling with looked at his eyes. He was dead. A tiny piece of shrapnel from one of the enemy shells exploding in the valley below had struck him in the right side of his head, just under the rim of his helmet. . . . It was a one-in-a-million chance that a piece of shrapnel would travel that distance but it had, and a good company commander was dead as a result of it.[102]

Death could also come with terrifying logic: "The first shell landed a safe distance away, but the second came in only 150 yards from where two engineers, the platoon sergeant, another noncom, and myself were working. We hit the ground—and we feared the shells would fall in a 'ladder' pattern: an artillery design in which the successive shells 'search out' the target as though moving up the rungs of a ladder."[103]

Shrapnel had a way of shredding whatever sangfroid the infantryman might attempt to hide behind:

At first I tried being casual about artillery fire. Shells would hit in the distance then move in, and it seemed humiliating to rush for cover, so I took my time getting out of the way, waiting almost for the warmth of the blast before jumping into my slit trench. It didn't take long to find out what shrapnel could do and then I hit the ground sooner than later, not worried about looking foolish.

A shell fragment could act as bullet, knife, cleaver, bludgeon. It could punch, shear, slice, crush. It could be surgical in its precision or make sadistic excess seem unimaginative.[104]

Tree or airbursts were particularly feared ("the worst," according to William Manchester), producing blast and shrapnel against which foxholes and slit trenches offered little protection. Paul Fussell describes the effect of an airburst on a group of Germans:

> I came upon a perfectly preserved dead waxwork German squad. . . . that caused my mouth to open in wonder. . . . [It] consisted of five German soldiers spread out prone in a semicircular skirmish line. They were still staring forward, alert for signs of the Amis. Behind them, in the center of the semicircle, was an equally rigid German medic with his Red Cross armband who had been crawling forward to do his work. In his left hand, a roll of two-inch bandage; in his right, a pair of surgical scissors. I could infer a plausible narrative. One or more men in the group had been wounded, and as the medic crawled forward to do his duty, his intention was rudely frustrated by an unspeakably loud sharp crack overhead, and instantly the lights went out for all of them. The episode was doubtless a tribute to our proximity artillery fuse, an invaluable invention which arrived on the line that winter, enabling a shell to explode not when it struck something but when it came near to striking something. Here, it must have gone off five or ten yards above its victims. Or perhaps the damage had been done by the kind of artillery stunt called time-on-target—a showy mathematical technique of firing many guns from various places so that regardless of their varying distances from the target, the shells arrive all at the same time. The surprise is devastating, and the destruction immediate and unimaginable. . . .
>
>   . . . It was so cold that the bodies didn't smell, and they'd not begun visibly to decompose, but their open eyes were clouded, and snow had lodged in their ears and the openings in their clothes and the slits in their caps. Their flesh was whitish green. Although they were prone, their knees and

elbows were bent, as if they were athletes terribly surprised while sprinting.[105]

The effects of high explosive were not nearly so aesthetic. Donald Burgett "came upon a sloping hole in the ground used by a French farmer for watering his cattle. We walked down into it and found two dead Germans sitting upright against the wall. An artillery shell had landed in the center and the heat from the explosion had torn away their features. Their lips and ears were missing and the empty eye sockets looked black in the charred and wrinkled skin. The concussion had snapped their hands and feet off at the wrists and ankles."[106]

★   ★   ★

ABOUT A QUARTER of all casualties were caused by small-arms fire (compared with 30–40 percent in World War I and 90 percent in the American Civil War).[107] And although artillery took more lives than small arms did, a soldier hit by a machine-gun round, for example, stood a 50 percent chance of dying, compared with 20 percent if hit by artillery. Of those hit by bullets, almost a quarter were killed, whereas slightly fewer than one-fifth of soldiers struck by artillery died, and only one in ten from mortars.[108] The reason was quite simple. There was a great deal of artillery fire, and although it tended to be scattershot, there was enough of it to take the majority of lives lost in combat. There was less volume of small-arms fire, but what there was tended to be more lethal because it was, more or less, aimed. Surveys of infantrymen's attitudes affirmed that artillery was most feared; machine guns ranked fourth (mortars third, dive bombers second). Yet studies during the war showed that the machine gun was the most deadly weapon—50 percent of the men hit would be killed.[109]

The heavy machine gun, as in the previous world war, was

lethal anywhere it could be installed defensively. The Germans were adept at hilltop defenses, particularly in the North African, Italian, and Normandy campaigns. At the end of the day it was the foot soldier who had to take the hill or cross the river, and the surest and most economical way to stop men climbing hills or crossing rivers was to spray them from a long distance with machine-gun fire. Crossing the Rapido River in Italy in 1944 was a catastrophe for the assaulting Americans. Sergeant Kirby of the Thirty-Sixth (Texas) Infantry Division describes the fearsome effect of heavy machine-gun fire: "We were under constant fire. I saw boats being hit all round me, and guys falling out and swimming. . . . When we got to the other side it was the only scene that I'd seen in the war that lived up to what you see in the movies. I've never seen so many bodies—our own guys. I remember this kid being hit by a machine gun; the bullets hitting him pushed his body along like a tin-can. . . . Just about everybody was hit. I didn't have a single good friend in the company who wasn't killed or wounded."[110]

A Canadian infantry officer, Lieutenant D. Pearce, recounted an attack on Bienen, Germany, in March 1945: "My platoon assaulted in a single extended wave. Ten tumbled down, nailed on the instant by fire from two or maybe three machine guns. . . . The Bren gunners put their weapons to their shoulders but never got a shot away. (I saw them after the battle, both dead, one still holding the aiming position). . . . A rifleman on my left took aim at a German weapon pit, and with a spasm collapsed on my arm. His face turned almost instantly a faint green, and bore a simple smile."[111]

In his novel, *Vessel of Sadness* (1969), based on his World War II combat experience, William Woodruff describes what happens when a machine gun catches a group of British soldiers near Anzio out in the open:

It was then that it happened. In broad daylight they overshot the turning to the right . . . and went smack into a

machine-gun nest. . . . The . . . jeep shuddered to a halt as
if struck by a hundred steel bars. Only then did they realize that the noise they had heard was a machine gun firing
almost in their faces. Sarge called out, "Jump for it!" Those
still able to jump for it did so. But their luck was out. . . . Of
course they should have hit back: "The best defence is always
rapid and well-directed fire." Instead, they fled for their lives
and were at the mercy of their instincts. They never saw the
enemy or his gun. . . . The vegetation jumped and twitched
before their eyes. The bullets hissed and splashed as they
struck the little pools of water close to their faces. They were
sick with fear. It was as if a madman had suddenly got loose
and was running up and down the ditch lashing out with
chains. When the unseen chain hit a man he just crumpled
up or got to his knees and moaned. Sarge shouted, but every
man was for himself. They were terrified of dying.[112]

For infantrymen hit by small-arms and machine-gun fire,
head shots were the most lethal. The soldier's head, despite the
protective helmet, is often the most exposed part of his anatomy:
The head above a foxhole rim; lying prone, head toward the
enemy; advancing in the infantryman's characteristic head-down
stooping run—all tended to make the most vulnerable part of the
body also the most exposed.

American infantrymen armed with the M-1 Garand took a
high proportion of head wounds because their weapons, unlike
those of the Japanese or Germans, were not smokeless and so
attracted counterfire aimed at the muzzle flash, which, if the rifleman was holding the stock to the shoulder as he sighted down the
barrel, greatly increased the chance of being shot in the head.[113]
As airborne trooper Donald Burgett puts it, "They [the Ger-
mans] used a smokeless powder and were hard to locate, whereas
our weapons spewed out billows of smoke that gave our positions

away and kept us moving to keep from getting our brains blown out."[114] But as the only semiautomatic rifle of World War II the Garand did give GIs a jump on the bolt-action rifles of the Germans and Japanese. It was rugged, and the eight-shot capability could save your life. Sidney Richess of the US Fortieth Infantry Division remembers: "During an encounter with an enemy force in a busy gully, an enemy rifleman fired at me at close range but missed. Knowing he was working his bolt . . . my runner . . . fired and wasted the guy."[115]

In a survey of American infantrymen, of those weapons they found most frightening and most lethal, the mortar ranked third after artillery (as represented by the much feared German 88-millimeter) and the dive-bomber.[116] The noise a weapon generates has, throughout history, had an important impact on soldiers' morale—depressing or boosting, depending on which side of the receiving line one happened to be—and the mortar was probably more effective as a wounding rather than a killing weapon. Beyond a 15-yard radius the lethality of the exploding shell fell away sharply. Which was small comfort to the soldier hunkered down in his foxhole convinced that one of those tail-finned beauties was whistling merrily down to send him to Valhalla. But it wounded plenty. In fact, it has been estimated that mortars were responsible for about half the casualties suffered by Allied soldiers in the Pacific and northwest Europe.[117]

Modern mortars are bargain-basement artillery—highly mobile, cheap to manufacture, and not particularly complicated to operate; all of which affords tactical flexibility and makes them a ubiquitous threat to the long-suffering infantryman. The Japanese, unable to make the relatively large investment demanded by full-scale artillery, churned out huge numbers of mortars, and one of the most famous was the nastily effective little "knee mortar" (actually more like a handheld grenade launcher braced against the ground), weighing only 11 pounds, firing a round of about

1½ pounds, and needing only one man to operate it.* Paul Sponaugle was the unappreciative focus of a knee-mortar attack on New Georgia in 1943:

> When I was gone my buddy was killed when a mortar shell hit his hole. My first sergeant called me over to his hole to tell me about my friend. I just got in the hole, took off my helmet, and two knee mortar shells struck that hole. No doubt the Japs saw me jump in. This hole was better than most and had logs and dirt on top. There were three of us in there and I was on top. The explosions were awful. They were right on top of us. The Japs used a knee mortar: a bigger one would have killed us. The first one caused the splinters and made a hole, the second one showered us with shrapnel. I knew I was hit right away. I was pelted with splinters from the logs on the back and had a leg full of shrapnel. At least I was smart enough to stay where I was. The other two were stupid and ran for another hole. That's really asking for it during a mortar barrage. The chances are pretty slim of getting another direct hit. They were both hit in the open.[118]

Light mortars like the US 60-millimeter, weighing in at just over 40 pounds and firing a 10- or 11-pound missile over 1,800 yards, needed two men, while heavies like the US 81-millimeter or the British 3-inch, which could fire a 10-pound shell over 2,500 yards, required three. The big mortars could pack a mighty

---

*It was called a knee mortar because "at first it was thought that the concave base plate meant it was fired while resting on the soldier's thigh, an impression furthered by pictures of Japanese troops posed in this fashion. This was found to be untrue after a few Allied soldiers broke their legs while trying it. The Japanese pictures had been made because the troops looked tough that way." James F. Dunnigan and Albert A. Nofi, *The Pacific War Encyclopedia* (New York: Facts on File, 1998), 265.

wallop. John Masters, a British officer in Burma (later to find fame as a novelist and memoirist), sardonically recalls that if a shell (weighing 60 pounds) from a Japanese heavy mortar "landed on a weapon pit it saved the need for burying parties."[119]

William Manchester was unlucky enough to be on the naughty end of a Japanese "screaming meemie" (a.k.a. "flying sea-bag" or "boxcar Charlie")—a huge 8-inch mortar shell:

> Early the next morning several of us were standing in a tomb courtyard when we heard the familiar shriek. We were on a reverse slope from the enemy; the chances of a shell clearing the top of the hill and landing on us were, we calculated, a thousand to one, and the Nips, as we now knew, had no way of controlling the flight of these missiles. I crept into the doorway of the tomb. I wasn't actually safe there, but I had more protection than Izzy Levy and Rip Thorpe, who were cooking breakfast over hot boxes. The eight-incher beat the thousand to one odds. It landed in the exact center of the courtyard. Rip's body absorbed most of the shock. It disintegrated, and his flesh, blood, brains, and intestines encompassed me. Izzy was blind. So was I—temporarily, though I didn't know that until much later. There was a tremendous roaring inside my head, which was strange, because I was also deaf, both eardrums having been ruptured. My back and left side were pierced by chunks of shrapnel and fragments of Rip's bones.[120]

Mines, like mortars, are also cheap to manufacture, but they enjoy the added advantage of doing their stuff entirely on their own. They simply sit, tirelessly patient, calmly waiting for the victim to be his own executioner. They are a weapon of sublime economy, which is why they have been used with such obscene profusion. Perhaps it was just this passivity that prompted

World War II soldiers to rank mines only seventh on the list of most-feared weapons. And yet they were a great killer of Allied foot soldiers, particularly in North Africa, Italy, and northwest Europe, where the Germans showed a certain genius for mine laying (and its close cousin, booby-trapping). Two were particularly notorious: the "Schu-mine," a wooden box (cheap to make and difficult for mine detectors to locate) containing roughly a quarter-pound block of TNT, enough to blow off a soldier's legs; and the much loathed and feared S-mine, or "Bouncing Betty." S-mines could be set off either by treading on the activating prongs (about 15 pounds of pressure was enough) or by trip wire, whereupon a small charge lifted the bomb to 2 or 3 feet above the ground (roughly genital height) before detonating the main explosive to send hundreds of projectiles horizontally. It was a killer within 20 yards, and still dangerous at 200.

Moving across ground suspected of being mined was done, remembered one soldier, with the wary step of someone gingerly navigating a field of cowpats. But even then, such caution could not guarantee a safe arrival. An American naval officer on Omaha Beach recalled: "Three of my officers were walking down the beaches, which were strewn with mines. They were walking in the wheel ruts of a truck. Twenty paces behind a soldier came by, stepping in the footprints made by the last naval officer. He set off the mine and was blown to pieces."[121] Roscoe C. Blunt Jr. remembered traversing a mined field on the border between Holland and Germany, on November 19, 1944:

I saw a BAKER Company rifleman lying face down on the ground. As I ran toward him, I yelled, "C'mon. Let's keep moving." Then I saw one of his legs had been blown off below the knee and the bloody foot stump was on the ground several feet away. He was still alive. Shuddering at the sight, I yelled, "I'll get you a medic," and kept running.

My heart jumped into my throat when it finally occurred to me I was running full tilt in a field infested with hundreds of wooden Schu mines. "Mines! Mines!" I screamed at the other GIs around me, but for the legless GI I had just passed, it was too late. I skidded to a stop and stared at the ground. Some were buried shallow, the rest just planted on the surface in no particular pattern.

The fear I had not felt back in Palenburg almost paralyzed me now. I stood frozen, afraid even to put my foot down. Slowly, I inched my way forward, putting as little weight as possible on each step. At that moment, I realized for the first time the insidious psychological effect mines have on a soldier. It struck home. I would take my chances with small arms fire or even artillery rather than these silent, deadly devices.

I was pushing my feet along the ground, not wanting to lift them, when an explosion about 100 feet to my left signaled another victim. . . . This man didn't have to worry about being an amputee—both his legs and groin area had been blown away and he was dead before he hit the ground. I was instantly sickened when I shot a glance in his direction and saw his body still twitching on the ground, even in death. The sight of this second shattered body unnerved me. This was a rotten war, a stinking way to die.[122]

As if the mines themselves were not bad enough, they might also bring down yet another world of harm. An officer of the US Twenty-Ninth Division in the Ruhr Valley described how "at the first sound of exploding mines, the Germans would lay down final protective fires with machine gun, mortars and artillery. If the men fell to earth to escape this fire, they might detonate more mines. Some elected to remain erect rather than risk falling on a mine."[123]

★   ★   ★

FROM THEIR INTRODUCTION by the British on the Western Front in 1915, tanks have been held in terror by infantrymen. During the initial encounters with German armor in the early phase of the invasion of the Soviet Union, the Russians found it almost impossible to stop men from panicking. Apart from the obvious danger of being shot by a tank's machine guns or blasted by the main gun, tankers killed soldiers by running them down or crushing or burying them alive by wheeling and churning over their foxholes and slit trenches—"ironing," it was called, with that black humor the infantry of all armies affect. The Russians attempted to inoculate their infantry against this viral fear by training them to dig deep and narrow slit trenches that would not collapse when ironed. To prove the point, Russian commanders then had their own tanks run over the trenches. A Soviet junior officer was able to write to his family in late 1942: "The most important thing is that there is no more 'tank fright' that we saw so much of at the beginning of the war. Every soldier . . . knowingly digs deeper into the earth."[124]

Training or no training, enduring an ironing was a terrifying experience, and panic almost always got the soldier killed. Günter Koschorrek, a German machine gunner on the Russian front, went through it:

The T-34 [the principal Russian battle tank of World War II] turns its turret towards our position and comes at us, its engine roaring. I pull my machine gun into the trench and throw myself down. Grommel and Weichert dash into the bunker. Swina is already lying behind me in the trench.

A harsh metallic shot, and a tank shell explodes exactly where my machine gun once stood. . . . And there it is again—the rattle and the roaring as steel tank tracks grind squealing on their rollers. A deathly noise! I press myself like a worm on to the ground. In the trench everything goes dark: the steel monster is parked directly on top of me, blocking out the daylight.

Now the sharp steel tracks are tearing up the edge of the trench. Frozen blocks of dirt fall on to my back and half cover me. Will the monster bury me alive? I remember soldiers telling me that tanks have turned on top of foxholes until the men below could no longer move and suffocated in the dirt. A hell of a way to die! . . .

The T-34 is now shooting at will in the connecting trenches. He rolls over them and turns round, churning up the frozen ground and filling them. Two soldiers, frightened and desperate, jump up and try to flee the trench, but seconds later they are cut down by the tank's machine gun. Another soldier bravely throws a hand grenade against the tank's turret. It smashes against it like a snowball on a wall. . . .

. . . Another soldier whose nerves cannot stand the pressure of being in the trench gets up and out, and the tank turns around and runs him down, tearing him in half.[125]

Koschorrek's tormentor was eventually destroyed by an antitank gun.

The armored front slope of a tank is called a "glacis." It is a term that harks back to the great age of fortress building in the seventeenth century, when it referred to the earth slope that fell away from the outer walls, the first line of protection to be overcome before the citadel could be breached. And this curious terminological connection between ancient and modern offers a broader understanding of how tankers died in battle.

Part fortress, part knight (tanks came out of and still invoke a cavalry heritage), the tank shares with both not only some of their functions, but their intrinsic vulnerabilities. Just as the fortress could be destroyed by direct fire from specialized heavy-duty armament such as siege cannon, bombards, *perriers,* and mortars, tanks were killed by a variety of munitions delivered by artillery (the most likely way), other tanks, and mobile antitank guns, as well as "tank-busting" aircraft and handheld weapons such as the bazookas, *Panzerfausten,* and PIATs (projector, infantry, anti-tank), wielded by intrepid infantrymen.[126]

The earliest such munition (developed even before the advent of the tank as a means to penetrate the steel shields that protected snipers during World War I) was the solid, hardened-steel, armor-piercing round, the German "K bullet" of World War I. Tank crews were often killed by "bullet splash": "When a lead-cored bullet hit the outside of the armor, it flattened and squeezed out its lead core in a 'splash' which radiated in a circular pattern. Under the force of the impact, the lead became nearly liquid and spread out with an almost explosive velocity. At the range of a foot, bullet splash is very nearly lethal, and the fast-moving liquid lead will force its way through any crack that presents itself."[127]

High-explosive antitank shells (HEAT) were "shaped" or "hollow" charges that, on impact, squirted a molten jet of metal through a relatively small hole in the tank's armor into the interior, igniting ammunition and fuel and causing hideous injury to the crew. It was a classic case of the thing that made the tank strong—its armor—being turned against it. When the armor plating was breached, fragments of the interior skin were transformed into lethal missiles whose impact was intensified within the tank's interior. Keith Douglas, a tank commander (destined to be killed later in the war), looked inside an Italian tank knocked out in North Africa:

> Gradually the objects in the turret became visible: the crew of
> the tank—for, I believe, these tanks did not hold more than
> two—were, so to speak, distributed around the turret. At

first it was difficult to work out how the limbs were arranged. They lay in clumsy embrace, their white faces whiter, as those of dead men in the desert always were, for the light powdering of dust on them. One with a six-inch hole in his head, the whole skull smashed in behind the remains of an ear—the other covered with his own and his friend's blood, held up by the blue steel mechanism of a machine gun, his legs twisting among the dully gleaming gear levers. About them clung that impenetrable silence I have mentioned before, by which I think the dead compel our reverence.[128]

After the battle of El Alamein in 1942, James Ambrose Brown, a South African officer, inspected the inside of a tank that had lost its track to a mine and then been pounded by the fearsome German 88:

To know the truth about tanks, one must see them after the battle, pitted with holes where shells have penetrated the armour, covered with scores where shells gouged out the steel as a spoon gouges out cheese. . . . The interiors of the tanks were for the most part masses of twisted steel, shattered and blackened by fire. But others, unburned, were filled with flies, scraps of bloody clothing, spilled oil and pieces of flesh. Dark blood splashes marred the cool white painted interiors. Telephones, bullets, half eaten food, pathetic rubbish. I read a fragment of a letter I picked up. It was from a girl to the now meaningless thing which lay in the wreckage. A pitiful document it was, full of love and hope. I used to glory in war: now I am beginning to understand.[129]

David Ling, a young troop leader of A Squadron, Forty-Fourth Royal Tank Regiment, had his tank hit. It was like falling down the well in *Alice in Wonderland,* he remembered:

I wondered if there was a bottom and whether I would be brought up with a jolt but this did not happen. Probably I would be gently slowed up. After all, to be stopped instantaneously after such a fall must kill one and that was ludicrous because one cannot be killed twice and I was already dead. Of that there was no doubt in my mind and it was the only lucid truth I knew. . . . I was dead and I didn't seem to mind. . . .

I lay still, as clarity, sanity and reality came back. I was comfortable and in no pain. I knew that I was huddled on the floor of my tank, that we were not moving, that the engine had stopped and that my last clear memory was an urgent call on the radio that some big gun was trying to hit me. Obviously it had. It was black inside and the turret and the air was full of black smoke. With difficulty I peered across the two feet of space separating me from the face of Corporal Hill. . . . "Are you all right, Hill?" "I'm all right, Sir—are you all right?" "Yes, I'm all right." I didn't ask the same of Trooper Bucket, my expert and lovable gunner. . . . Now slumped across his little adjustable seat he sprawled backwards and downwards. His head, split in twain, was poised over my chest while his hot blood poured over and through me, a black glistening stream from the back of his crushed skull. His suntanned face turned half sideways was closed and white with death, shining clearly in that black murk. I remember I struggled to get up and Hill struggled also. We were entangled and I had to move Bucket. I remember I stretched up my arm to push him forward and away— and that two of my fingers went through the hole in his skull, into the warm softness within. I wiped my hand on my blood-drenched clothes.[130]

Rootedness was the essential vulnerability of both fortress and knight. Obviously, the fortress could not avoid the devastating effects of overwhelming firepower and the mounted knight, carrying on his back the simulacrum of the fortress, could suffer the same fate if brought to a halt. The success of German armor in the early years of the war was predicated on its speed. Movement was the tank's hope of salvation. To stop was to court disaster, as Field Marshal Erich von Manstein, the architect of German armored strategy, emphasized: "The safety of a tank formation operating in the enemy's rear largely depends on its ability to keep moving. Once it comes to a halt it will immediately be assailed from all sides by the enemy's reserves."[131] Jock Watt, a British tank commander at the battle for the airfield at Sidi Rezegh, Libya, in November 1941, learned the lesson the hard way:

> Down on the airfield, as the view became clearer it revealed a scene even more chaotic and depressing. My god, what a mess we had got ourselves into! Bodies lay everywhere and obstruction by debris slowed our progress to a crawl, just at a time when speed was vital to get to our target. But where the hell *was* our target? Vehicles were milling about all over the area, with troops of tanks suddenly appearing out of the smoke and dust. It was an impossible situation, open fire on one of these vague, fleeting targets and you could be blasting your own CO to hell.
>
> We stopped to assess the situation but that was a mistake; fire descended upon us from all directions and the noise of screaming shells, explosions, the chatter of machine guns, and the whistle of fragments flying through the air was unbearable. I kept my body as low as possible in the turret and the urgent need to think and act suppressed the fear rising within me. . . .
>
> A violent explosion rocked the tank and a large crater appeared alongside, big enough to hide the tank in. What in the hell was that? Another missile was screaming through

the air and landed just in front of us. Added to the usual artillery, anti-tank and machine gun fire, we were now being targeted by 210mm shells. Someone decided that that was enough and gave the order to "get the hell out of here!" . . . Guiding my driver in this almost blind environment required all my concentration and consequently I failed to detect the smell of burning until the operator screamed, "We are on fire!"[132]

Other points of vulnerability of the mounted knight mirrored in the tank were the chinks in the armor: the joints where armor plates needed to move, or the slits necessary for observation, gun ports, or tracks. Sergeant Edgar Gurney of the British Seventh Parachute Brigade witnessed infantry killing a panzer in Normandy with extraordinary coolness and skill:

Private McGee, who was near the main road, picked up his Bren gun [roughly the equivalent to the US Browning Automatic Rifle], then started to walk up the middle of the road towards the tanks, firing the Bren gun from his hip. As one magazine became empty, he replaced it with a new one. . . . We could hear the bullets ricocheting off the armour steel plating of the leading tank that immediately closed down his visor, thus making him blind to things in front! Corporal Tommy Kileen realized what was happening and ran up the side of the road, taking two Gammon bombs [heavy-duty grenades that exploded on impact] from his pouches. He threw the first bomb which hit the leading tank where the turret and body meets which nearly blew the turret off. He threw the second bomb against the tank's track, which was promptly blown off. The tank now tried to escape but only having one good track it went round in circles, so the crew baled out and tried to escape. They were shot by McGee.[133]

Where the knight was extremely vulnerable as he leaned forward on his horse in order to engage an enemy to his front, thus exposing his unarmored nether regions, so too was the tank at its rear. Its armament tended to point forward, and its heaviest armor plate was deployed on front and sides. This was why tanks, like knights, needed to work with foot soldiers as protection. Without that screen of friendly defenders, enemy infantry had several options to kill them. They could strike with bazooka-type arms, going for the swivel joint of the turret, the fuel tanks, or the tracks, or they could swarm it, as did medieval foot soldiers the stationary knight. The latter was a highly risky option for the infantryman and one mainly employed by the Soviets (in the early stages of the war) and Japanese, who, through lack of antitank guns, were spurred on by the courage of the desperate and inspired by the invention of the determined. Robert C. Dick, a tanker on Leyte, was at the receiving end of one such charge:

One event stands out in my memory, and thinking of it, even now, makes me wonder at the foolishness, and yes, bravery, we all saw during our days of combat. Our platoon was on a narrow road, and by a miracle it wasn't too muddy. We came to a clearing, and as we drove through it I noticed that very deep ditches had been dug on each side. So deep and wide, in fact, a tank could not cross them. There were four tanks in our platoon that day, and we were number three in the column.

As the first tank got to the far edge of the clearing, the Japanese rushed us. They came out of the jungle on all sides, carrying mines attached to long bamboo poles. Before any

of us could react, the tracks had been blown off the lead
tank and also off the last tank. We were stuck right here,
and while I couldn't speak for anyone else, I was stunned.
I just couldn't believe that real Japanese soldiers, guys who
were intent on killing us right now, were in plain view and
swarming all over our tanks. As a driver there was nothing I
could do except watch this unbelievable attack. . . .

There seemed to be an endless number of them, but we
later estimated their strength at around twenty or so. We all
started shooting them off each other's tanks by using our
.30-caliber coax [machine] guns. . . . Right in the middle of
things, a Japanese officer jumped up onto the back of Couch's
tank, and as the turret began to traverse in our direction (in
order to shoot the Japs off our tank), the officer began hacking away at the machine gun barrel with his two-handed
sword! After about three or four whacks he got it turned a
bit sideways, but the blade snapped off about a foot below
the hilt. That's when my gunner, Anderson, shot him off
Couch's tank.[134]

Where the knight's face visor was a potential weakness,
because the slits through which he needed to see were also inviting for a dagger thrust, so too was the tank turret hatch. US
infantryman Roscoe C. Blunt Jr. describes how a tank could be
killed through its "visor":

The tank turned its attention to the infantry squad with
us who were laying down heavy rifle and machine gun fire
in their direction. But .30-caliber bullets against a steel-
enforced Tiger tank were almost as troublesome as fleas
to an elephant. We were in exposed positions and unable
to move forward or backward. The lieutenant motioned
for me to follow him in a flanking attempt around one of

the buildings shielding the Kraut tank, while our driver crawled forward to the riflemen and told them we needed diversionary fire. . . .

Communicating by hand signals and eye language, we quietly swung ourselves on top of the tank. When the lieutenant pulled the tank's hatch cover [in the distraction of combat inadvertently left unlocked] partly open, we heard yelling inside and saw a pair of hands grab at the cover in a tug of war with the lieutenant. I pulled the pin on a fragmentation grenade and shoved it under the heavy, round hatch cover just as the lieutenant released his grip. I saw the grenade was wedged between the hatch cover and the hatch rim, keeping the cover from being slammed shut.

With only four seconds before detonation, I gave the grenade a hard sideways kick and it fell inside as the lieutenant and I dove head-first off the tank and rolled behind one of the buildings. With the muffled explosion and the screams from inside, the hatch cover flew open and white smoke billowed out. We clambered back onto the tank and emptied our pistols down the turret hatch to finish the job.[135]

Just as the belly of a knight's horse was horribly vulnerable to any soldier intrepid enough to get underneath and slash it, so too was the underside of the tank. Top surfaces were often treated to thwart magnetic mines, but the belly of the beast was a different matter. Getting to it, though, required extraordinary courage and skill that might often need to be supplemented by a heaping helping of luck. A *Landser* (German foot soldier) in Russia took on a main Soviet battle tank, the mighty T-34:

Crouching low I started towards the monster pulling the detonation cord, and prepared to fix the [magnetic] charge. I had now five seconds before the grenade exploded and then I noticed, to my horror, that the outside of the tank was covered in concrete. My bomb would not stick on such a surface. . . . The tank suddenly spun on its right track, turned so that it pointed straight at me and moved forward as if to run over me.

I flung myself backwards and fell straight into a partly dug trench and so shallow that I was just below the surface of the ground. Luckily I had fallen face upwards and was still holding tight in my hand the sizzling hand grenade. As the tank rolled over me there was a sudden and total blackness. . . . The shallow earth walls of the trench began to collapse. As the belly of the monster passed over me I reached up instinctively as if to push it away . . . [and] stuck the charge on the smooth, unpasted metal. Barely had the tank passed over me than there was a loud explosion . . . I was alive and the Russians were dead.[136]

No tankers took a more fearful beating than the Soviets, both in the desperate defense of the initial German invasion and in the all-out attack of its repulse. More than 77 percent of Soviet tankers (310,000 out of 403,000) were killed.[137] " 'Have you burned yet?' was a question Russian tank men often asked each other when they met for the first time."[138] Burning to death was the greatest fear and the common fate of many tankers of whichever army. Cyril Joly, a British tank commander in North Africa in 1940, witnessed the fate of an Italian tank:

Ryan was the first to get a kill. He hit an enemy tank which was turning on the slope before him fairly and squarely in the engine, shattering the petrol tanks and starting a fire which spread rapidly. Mixed with the flame, clouds of billowing black smoke rolled across the desert, blocking my view of the enemy entirely. With a dull roar the ammunition then exploded, throwing a mass of debris into the air. A moment later we were horrified to see a figure with face blackened and clothes alight stumbling through the smoke. He staggered for some yards, then fell and in a frenzy of agony rolled frantically in the hard sand in a desperate effort to put out the flames. But to no avail. Gradually his flailing arms and legs moved more slowly, until at last, with a convulsive heave of his body, he lay still.[139]

Churchills and Shermans, both gasoline-fueled, would invariably "brew up" when hit (the Germans called Churchills "Tommy cookers"; Americans called their Shermans "Ronson burners" after the cigarette lighter whose advertising claimed it always lit the first time). Nat Frankel, an American tanker, explained what happened when a Sherman was hit:

A tank, you see, had four gas inlets, and each one was filled with high octane. If any of those four were hit, the whole machine would go up. . . . When that gas got hit, your options were, to say the least, limited. Oh, we had a fire extinguisher, but that was for overheated motors; it was useless for an exploded tank. Now, there were two ways to get out. One was via the turret; the other was through a trapdoor on the opposite side of the driver from the bow gun. Often the turret would be inaccessible to anyone inside the tank; if the machine was hit badly, particularly if it was knocked on its side, the trapdoor would jam as well. At best you would have ninety seconds to get out that door; if it jammed, you would need fifty of those seconds to push it open. That would leave forty seconds for three men to squeeze out. Tick, tick, tick, boom! And what would happen if both the turret and the trapdoor were inoperative? What would happen is, you'd die! It takes twenty minutes for a medium tank to incinerate; and the flames burn slowly, so figure it takes ten minutes for a hearty man within to perish. You wouldn't even be able to struggle, for chances are both exits would be sheeted with flame and smoke. You would sit, read *Good Housekeeping* and die like a dog.[140]

Grayson La Mar of the US 712th Tank Battalion found out all about the hatch problem when his tank was hit in the rear and burst into flame: "It took three tries to get the hatch open. See, the hatch would hit the gun barrel. The gunner was killed and nobody could operate the gun to get the barrel out of the way. Finally, on the third try, I slipped by. If the gun was over a quarter-inch more I'd never had got out."[141]

Many, of course, never did get out, as Gromov, a Russian antitank rifleman, explains: "I fired at [the tank] again. And I saw at once that I'd hit it. It took my breath away. A blue flame ran over the armour, quick like a spark. And I understood at once that my anti-tank shell had got inside and gave off this blue flame. And a little smoke rose. The Germans inside began to scream. I'd never heard people scream this way before, and then immediately there was a crackling inside. It crackled and crackled. The shells had started to explode. And then flames shot out, right into the sky. The tank was done for."[142]

But perhaps the most terrible sound of a tanker's death was a simple click (as the radio connection was severed by a hit):

A squadron of British tanks was coming up in support. The commander calmly directed the battle using cricket parlance: "Harry, I'd like you to go a little further out in the field in the hope of a long catch. . . . Charlie, would you move over to silly mid-off." . . . and so it went on.

We might have been at Lord's in London watching Test

cricket on a warm sunny afternoon and wondering whether the tea break was far away. Suddenly, across the squadron leader's voice came a sharp ominous click. We'd heard it before. We couldn't see the tank but we knew what the click meant. Charlie took over the radio network. The others obeyed his orders calmly, resolutely, as if it were the most natural thing in the world for their comrade to depart suddenly like that—with a click as adieu.[143]

★   ★   ★

AN INFANTRYMAN AT the sharp end lives in a world where risk comes in two sizes: large and larger. There are many tactical "obligations" he is expected to carry out. In fact, almost everything he does in the combat zone (including, as the decorous phrase has it, "answering the call of nature"—in fact, *especially* while answering that urgent summons) puts him in harm's way. But one task in particular represents the jumbo package of risk: the frontal attack across open ground against a prepared enemy—"the basic theme of combat in World War II." It was an old way of dying in a modern war, "as old as warfare itself."

Here are three soldiers, in three very different theaters of the war, recalling three attacks:

Russia, 19 December 1943:

Towards noon, we, the Panzergrenadiere, go into action. We have to cross open country without any cover. The enemy has been waiting for this, and he greets us with a furious bombardment using all his heavy weapons. All hell breaks loose around us, and a tumultuous inferno of violence and unceasing destruction comes pouring down. A score of combat aircraft come screaming over our heads, raining bombs on us and our tanks. The tanks rapidly make smoke to avoid being seen. In the meantime, we are lying flat on the ground without any cover, wishing that we were moles so that we could crawl to safety.

The ground beneath us shakes with the impacts and explosions. All around us we hear painful cries from the wounded calling out for the medics. We run forward through the thundering hell, with only one thought in mind—to somehow find some sort of cover there in front of us. Even though we make it through the artillery crossfire, death waits for us a thousand times over. The Russian machine-gunners hammer away at us with all barrels and the enemy anti-tank weapons and divisional artillery fire at our every movement.

Bursts of hot bullets swish by me and tear up the thin snow cover around . . . I am reminded how many times over the last few weeks I have sped through the enemy's rain of fire. Up till now I have been lucky and have, with God's help, always come through. Will I manage it this time?

I do now what I have always done: I run, bent double, driven on by fear that I'll be hit any moment. My body seems as if it's electrically charged, and I feel hot waves running down my back. . . . Every now and then I throw myself flat on the ground and stick my head in between my shoulders like a tortoise. Thinking that a hit low down in my body could cost me my life, I prefer to cover the distance to the hedge crawling flat on my stomach, feet first. . . .

On the churned-up field behind us the wounded are whimpering, for they can no longer run. They lie among the many dead bodies and roll over in pools of blood, often in their death throes. Less than ten paces behind me I can see Willi Krauze lying in a pool of blood. Willi is dead.[144]

Pelelieu, 16 September 1944:

The mortars had stopped. The first F Company [Fifth Marines] wave was advancing across the airstrip, running low with ranks scattered, breasting a withering machine gun fire that had begun to rake the runway. They were falling. It seemed unreal, it seemed a tableau, phantasmagorical, like a scene from a motion picture. It required an effort of mind to recall that these were flesh-and-blood marines, men whom I knew. . . . Still more was required in facing up to the fact that my turn was next. And here is the point in battle where one needs the rallying cry. Here where the banner must be unfurled or the song sung or the name of the cause flung at the enemy like a challenge. Here is mounted the charge, the thing as old as warfare itself, that either overwhelms the defense and wins the battle, or is broken and brings on defeat. How much less forbidding might have been that avenue of death that I was about to cross had there been some wholly irrational shout—like "Vive l'Empereur," or "The Marine Corps Forever!"—rather than that educated voice which said in a sangfroid that was all at odds with the event, "Well, it's our turn, now." . . .

I began to run. . . . The heat rose in stifling waves. . . . The bullets whispered at times, at other times they were not audible. . . . I ran with my head low, my helmet bumping crazily to obscure my view . . . I was alone and running. . . . There were men to my left, still falling. . . . I ran and threw myself down, caught my breath, rose, and ran again. . . . Suddenly I ran into a shell crater full of men and I stopped running.[145]

Normandy, 13 June 1944:

We had crawled on hands and knees to the edge of the hedgerow that the enemy was entrenched behind. We fixed bayonets and then, on command, charged headlong over the hedgerow into heavy enemy fire to do hand-to-hand battle with the Germans. We pushed forward into fierce enemy fire across grazed-over pastureland toward the next hedgerow—where the bulk of the enemy had withdrawn, leaving their dead behind. They cut us to ribbons as we ran over the open ground, charging after them. At least six enemy machine guns had us in a cross fire, and a mix of 81mm mortar, flat-trajectory 88mm cannon, and high-angle 75mm howitzer fire exploded in our midst, filling the air with searing shards of shrapnel. . . .

I made it over about seven hedgerows and fields, seeing a large number of my comrades wounded, maimed, and killed around me. Still we charged forward into the small-arms and artillery fire. I was slightly ahead of my squad when a German suddenly appeared out of a hedge a few feet away on my left front. He flipped a long-handled potato-masher grenade at me in a nonchalant manner before I could bring my rifle to bear, and then he disappeared back into the hedge.

The explosion knocked me out. My comrades left me where I lay, thinking I was dead. . . . You should never stop an attack to look out for the wounded or the dead—if you do, you most likely will become one of them.[146]

After the initial assault, it would have been nice if the enemy could have been kept at arm's length in a mutually beneficial standoff. But war is not like that. There is a deeply irritating and unremitting pressure to go on and visit yet more violence on one's adversary, thereby inviting him to reciprocate. Patrolling was the infilling between pitched battles that kept men dutifully, if begrudgingly, employed in the business of killing and being killed. Raymond Gantter, recalling his experience in Germany in the winter of 1944–45, recounted the very dubious appeal patrolling had for the foot soldier:

> I think I have never been so cold, so wretched, so frightened. I decided that a patrol was the worst of all war assignments, particularly in winter. (Nothing I experienced in later months changed my mind—patrolling remained the job I hated and dreaded beyond any other.)
>
> It is the slow piling up of fear that is so intolerable. Fear moves swiftly in battle, strikes hard with each shell, each new danger, and as long as there's action, you don't have time to be frightened. But this is a slow fear, heavy and stomach-filling. Slow, slow . . . all your movements are careful and slow, and pain is slow and fear is slow and the beat of your heart is the only rapid rhythm of the night . . . a muttering drum easily punctured and stilled.[147]

Within the world of patrolling there were larger and lesser risks. An American soldier made this distinction: Patrols "were of two types. The combat patrol was sent out to kill Germans and return with prisoners for interrogation. This type of patrol was dangerous. We did not volunteer to go on these patrols because they were deadly; we had to be ordered to go. The other type was the reconnaissance patrol. . . . This type was less dangerous."[148]

In the Pacific theater the chances of being killed on patrol were greater than the risk of holding a defensive perimeter. Bill Crooks, an Australian fighting on New Guinea, remembers: "We did most of our fighting and suffered most of our casualties patrolling. Our fighting in the Pacific was a squad or platoon war, most of it on patrol. People would go out, there would be short, vicious firefights, grenades thrown, and people screaming like mad. It was over fast. And then the men would get going again or stay there dead."[149]

Jungle patrolling, with its limited visibility, was an agony of suspense. "A patrol moves very slowly in the jungle," recalled Robert Leckie:

> Fear of ambush produces the most extreme caution, which reduces speed to a crawl. It is this literally. Each foot is firmly planted before the other is raised, utmost care is taken to avoid twigs, and a sort of crablike rhythm is produced as the eyes and torso travel in the alternating directions of the feet. Left foot, lean, look, listen, pause; right foot, lean, look, listen, pause.
>
> At such speed, it would take a day to move a mile and return. Should the trail be hilly, or especially twisting, it might take longer. On this patrol it had taken twenty minutes to go round one bend, precisely because that curve lay at the foot of a rise and because such a terrain feature is admirably suited for ambush . . . the enemy can deliver a plunging fire into your ranks at the very moment when your own visibility is at zero. He might even allow you to gain the hill, permit you to pass him—and then fire from behind you—a most demoralizing trick.[150]

There was little that was heroic about patrolling, and soldiers knew that it did not rate highly as a military spectacle that would excite the civilian appetite for glorious deeds of martial splendor.

One infantryman in Italy complained: "Since the time . . . the Press was first able to announce, reluctantly and with an undercurrent of disapproval, that 'all is quiet on the Italian Front. Military operations are limited to patrol activity,' patrol warfare has been waged with a pitiless ruthlessness that perhaps would satisfy the recumbent fireside sadists . . . rather than the most gory of large-scale attacks. Swift and noiseless thrusts in the dark; unpremeditated death by an unknown hand from a quarter uncertain; silent attack and counter-attack without ceasing—these are the pigments one must use to paint the picture of patrol warfare."[151]

Certain soldierly occupations carried more than their fair share of risk. Scouts and point men were particularly high up the scale of those most likely to be hit. One scout, Henri Atkins of the US Ninety-Ninth Infantry Division fighting in the Ardennes, did not beat about the bush:

> A point man needs a willingness to die. He is nothing more . . . than a decoy. When he is shot, the enemy position is revealed. Don't confuse this willingness with "bravery." A point man is just doing his job, what he has trained to do. Usually a scout is way out ahead of the attacking forces, ready to signal back enemy contact. He has a chance of survival, but not much of one. The tough question is, why did I volunteer as company first scout . . . when I knew how dangerous the position could be? I didn't get paid more. It was the most dangerous position in a rifle company. I was important to my company. They needed me. I could do the job. I could be counted on. Is that an answer? I don't know, but it's as good an answer as any.[152]

The jungle held perhaps even greater peril for front men. Richard Loucks was with the US Forty-Third Division on New Georgia:

The principal characteristic of the jungle is its density. There are no landmarks. There are trails, and in many places we could move only on them because of the impassibility of vines, underbrush, tree roots. Mangrove swamps, for example, were totally impenetrable. We were, therefore, in great danger because the Japanese knew where we had to go and prepared for us. . . . The scouts out front were particularly vulnerable because they had no instantaneous support from the troops behind them. Often the scouts were on top of the enemy before either side realized what was happening. Since they were moving they were at terrible risk and took many casualties.[153]

So dangerous was the scout/point position that experienced patrol leaders could be shockingly pragmatic: "It was *sacrosanct*," declares one, "that point scouts carried a rifle, as they often were knocked off and we did not want to lose a submachine gun."

Combat medics/aidmen/corpsmen were meant to be protected by the Geneva Convention, and their helmets and armbands, emblazoned with the insignia of the Red Cross, were supposed to provide them with protection from enemy fire. Often it worked . . . often it did not: "The risks our medics took shocked me because their immunity was so scantily guaranteed. There was little in their dress to indicate their calling. Lacking only weapons, they wore the usual GI uniform, and their sole distinctive markings were red crosses on a white ground, painted on the four sides of their helmets, and white armbands, also marked with a red cross. A helmet and an armband, that was all. But helmets got dirty, scratched, chipped; armbands became grimy rags, twisted, narrow bands that were indistinguishable on dark sleeves. I'm surprised that more medics weren't killed."[154] If a medic was in the European theater he did all he could to emphasize his markings; quite the opposite if he were facing the Japanese, who assiduously targeted medics.[155]

Even without the overtly malicious intent of an enemy, medics went where the danger was greatest, and they paid a terrible price. John Worthman, a medic with the US Fourth Infantry Division, estimates that "our regiment had 80 percent of its aidmen lost in Normandy—wounded, killed in action, or captured." But like point man Henri Atkins, Worthman knew that the need far outweighed the risk: "If you have never felt you were really wanted, be an aidman. Forty men are relying on you."[156]

Leo Litwak, a combat medic in northwest Europe, illustrates the extraordinary heroism of most medics (although, as he points out, extreme risk could deter even normally brave men):

> We were probing the high ground near some Belgian village, and a Third Platoon scout was hit by a sniper. He lay in the road up ahead, facedown, on his belly. The company took cover in the woods off the road. Aid man Grace crept to where he could see the scout lying in the road. "He's not moving. You can see he's dead. There's a sniper waiting to knock off anyone who goes out there."
>
> Grace wouldn't go to him.
>
> They called on Cooper, aid man with the Second Platoon. Cooper said the Third Platoon was Grace's responsibility, not his, and he wouldn't go to the scout either.
>
> Sergeant Lucca came to me. "The Third Platoon has a man down out there, and Grace and Cooper won't go."
>
> I took off down the road, full speed, came up over the rise, saw the scout lying in the road, hit the ground next to him, turned him over, saw a nickel-sized wound on his forehead. I couldn't feel a pulse. I put my cheek to his mouth and there was no breath. I expected to be hit the same way, above the eyes, in the middle of the forehead. Either the sniper respected my red cross markings or he'd taken off.[157]

Some were not so lucky. J. D. Jones of the Third Infantry Division saw his medic go to a wounded man even though a previous aidman had just been killed in the attempt: "Sammy turned . . . his helmet to get that big old white blob with the red cross on it, and he was just leaning over the man . . . and they [the Germans] shot him right between the shoulder blades, killed him instantly."[158]

The provisions of the Geneva Convention that sought to protect medics were emphatic that they must be strictly noncombatant, carrying no weapon. And a breach of this protocol could have deadly results. Trooper David Kenyon Webster of the 101st Airborne, fighting in northwest Europe, witnessed just such a retribution: "While I watched the smoke, a German jeep popped out of it and whirled boldly through the village. It was flying a big Red Cross flag and carried two wounded Germans on stretchers in back, and it was such a startling phenomenon, with a big, husky German paratrooper at the wheel, that nobody made a move to stop it. It drove boldly down the middle of the road until it was finally stopped by an officer with more presence of mind than the rest of us. The jeep was commandeered; the driver, a medic, was shot for carrying a pistol; and the two wounded men were left by the side of the road to die."[159]

Those soldiers with specialized jobs that involved carrying large amounts of potentially deadly substances stood a much higher risk of a very speedy trip to the Hereafter. Flamethrowers, for example, had to be operated by men of a sanguine disposition, not to say philosophical resignation. "Snipers really looked for them," recalls a First Division Marine, and understandably there was a certain reluctance to take on the job:

> The lieutenant said, "Sergeant, put someone on that flame-thrower." I sensed we were all trying to shrink up in our uniforms, as none of us wanted that job. Then he said,

"Laughlin, you do it." I had to endure a number of ribald comments, some pity, and some cynical requests for my girl-friend's address. I was very disgruntled at being selected— why me I'll never know—and I considered refusing to do it and then decided against that. [Afterward] I gave loud notice that I wasn't going to have another turn and I was not called on again.[160]

Laughlin's reluctance is entirely understandable. Particularly in battles like Okinawa, where flamethrowers were widely used to kill the Japanese in their cave redoubts, too many men would have witnessed scenes like this:

Horst von der Goltz, Maine '43, who would have become a professor of political science, was leading a flamethrower team . . . when a Nip sniper picked off the operator of the flamethrower. Horst had pinpointed the sniper's cave. He had never been checked out on flamethrowers, but he insisted on strapping this one to his back and creeping toward the cave. Twenty yards from its maw he stood and did what he had seen others do: gripped the valve in his right hand and the trigger in his left. Then he pulled the trigger vigorously, igniting the charge. He didn't know that he was supposed to lean forward, countering the flame's kick. He fell backward, saturated with fuel, and was cremated within seconds.[161]

Carrying explosives such as mines, Bangalore torpedoes,* or satchel charges could be highly prejudicial to one's health. Paul

---

*An ungainly but quite effective device invented in 1912 by an engineer officer in the British Army in India (hence its name) made up of con-necting sections of tube that gave the operator some distance from the TNT charge at the end. It was primarily used to blow gaps in barbed wire and other obstacles.

Fussell recalls that Lieutenant Matt Rose had been decapitated not, as first thought, by a German shell, for "the large black stain on the snow told the truth. Matt Rose had accidentally blown himself up with his own antitank mine, as his assistant, ordered prudently to kneel many yards away, confirmed. It was typical of the boy Matt Rose, and admirable, that he chose to do the hazardous work himself. As the winter [of 1944] went on, we gradually learned that the fuse in the American antitank mine, or its explosive, grew extremely unstable in subfreezing weather."[162]

Harley Reynolds of the US First Infantry Division witnessed the heroic sacrifice of a Bangalore torpedo man, betrayed by his weapon, on Omaha Beach: "He pulled the string to the fuse-lighter and pushed himself backward. The first didn't light. After a few seconds the man calmly crawled forward, exposing himself again. He removed the bad lighter, replaced it with another, and started to repeat his first moves. He turned his head in my direction . . . when he flinched . . . and closed his eyes looking into mine. Death was so fast for him. His eyes seemed to have a question or pleading look in them."[163]

In a sad category of extreme risk were the replacements; men shoved into combat units without adequate training. Toward the end of the war, losses were so great for both the winners and losers that men who were woefully unprepared were flung into the furnace. After the battle of Kursk in the summer of 1943 the Germans were forced to commit new recruits and, in so doing, to take ever greater casualties, which in turn fueled the lethal spiral. With Operation Bagration (the massive Soviet counteroffensive of 1944) chewing up huge numbers of men, the German army had, in a dramatic turning of the tables, begun to resemble that of the Soviets in the early years of the war.

American replacements, for example, could expect only a scant sixty days training and during the bloody endgame of the war, six weeks.[164] Life expectancy for a replacement could be, understandably, pretty brief; the first three days were critical—as for all fledglings and the newly hatched. An officer of the US Thirtieth Division in Normandy reckoned that "there must have been at least 75 or 80 percent turnover in the [rifle] platoons. . . . In order to fill the ranks, the replacements were sent up to their squads without any satisfactory pre-battle orientation." And taking a sample of four American divisions in Italy, by April 1945 only 34 percent of the men had been there since landing in September 1943. Of the 66 percent replacements, more than half had been thrown into combat only two days after joining their units, and a further 20 percent within a week.[165]

The old sweats could be protective (Raymond Gantter remembers that "the old men have been patient with our ignorance, kindly in their tutelage"), but they could also be callous bastards. An American sergeant at Anzio recalls: "One day . . . we got eight new replacements in my platoon. We were supposed to make a little feeling attack that same day. Well, by next day, all eight of them replacements were dead, buddy. But none of us old guys were. We weren't going to send our own guys out on point in a damnfool situation like that. . . . We sent the replacements out ahead."[166] Paratrooper David Kenyon Webster felt sorry for the replacements in his unit who were denied any kind of acclimation and had simply been chucked into the front line. Nevertheless, he admits, when holed up in a house threatened by German artillery, "we immediately cleared out the southeast room, which was most in line with the 88 . . . and put the replacements in it, keeping the warmer, safer . . . room for ourselves."[167]

"Them replacements were dead, buddy. But none of us old guys were." So what did the old guys learn that kept them from being killed? First, the replacements, scared and naive, tended to stick together during action—"It is natural to want to be close to someone else when death reigns," remembers Donald Burgett—but bunching offers a juicy target. Veterans cited it as the main

mistake made by newcomers, and an officer outlined the problem: "In combat we found that green troops would invariably freeze when first coming under fire. They would stop, seek cover, and then try to find the enemy. They could not see any distinct targets. Therefore they did not fire. Their casualties increased."[168]

Under fire, moving forward rather than clumping in reassuring clusters is counterintuitive. Leo Litwak's captain told his squad, "When you hear the order to attack, stand up and start marching and firing and keep marching and firing and don't run, don't hit the ground, don't take cover, don't lose your intervals, always stay in line with the advance. It doesn't matter that you can't see what you're shooting at." This was called marching fire, and was scary to do. "I had to force myself to rise and start marching," remembers Litwak. "I walked into enemy fire and didn't hit the ground, didn't start digging, didn't wiggle on my belly toward the nearest tree, didn't hug the ground and hide my face. I walked at a steady, modest pace, buddies strung out to the left and right, utterly exposed. It was against all my inclinations. I was as terrified and resentful as if I had been offered as a sacrifice to a god in whom I had no faith."[169]

A British officer in Italy encouraged inexperienced men a little more pungently: " 'Get up!' he shouts, hitting them on the arse with his swagger [stick]. 'Get up! They'll get you in the guts! Blow your arse to bits! If you get up they'll only get you in the legs!' "[170]

Exhortation was one thing, but moving into fire was terrifying: "Bullets cracked as they passed close by, at times nipping clothing, at times thudding into a trooper's body. I always got a sick feeling in the pit of my stomach when I started a running attack into frontal fire, knowing that at any moment an enemy bullet might tear through my body. . . . But once we started there was no turning back. There was only one option as far as I was concerned: run forward and kill. Once the enemy was dead there was time to rest."[171]

David Kenyon Webster wrote a fascinating primer on survival in a letter to his parents:

> It has been said that old soldiers never die. Although an air-burst or a stray shot occasionally kills an old soldier, the casualty rate among the veterans is noticeably lower than among green troops or replacements. There are several reasons for this.
>
> The longer a man is in action the more cautious he becomes. The old soldier leaves very little to chance. At one village in Holland, our convoy was fired upon and two-thirds of our company had to dig in in an orchard and spend thirty-six hours under continuous shell fire. Every time there would be a letup, we would dig our slit trenches deeper. . . . When at last we were able to march north to rejoin the undamaged third of our Company . . . we were appalled to find they hadn't even dug in. We immediately started digging and didn't stop until we were four feet down . . . even though there were no 88s in the vicinity. Old soldiers don't take chances.
>
> Old soldiers, too, have learned by bitter experience to be independent and make their own decisions. Once our lieutenant told my squad leader to take his eight men and knock out some antiaircraft guns . . . nine men with rifles fighting dual-purpose 88s and 40mm! . . . By using his own judgment he saved our lives in a situation where a new man would have rushed in blindly. . . .
>
> These hard-learned lessons are revealed nowhere better, however, than when a man is wounded. The veteran rushes to the aid man as fast as possible and gets off the battlefield

with all the speed left him. He doesn't wait to be told what to do. . . .

Perhaps I have made the veterans sound a little cynical. I have omitted some of the positive facts we have learned as we go along. We have learned not to let the artillery and mortars pin us down so badly that we cannot fire at the attacking enemy. We have learned not to be afraid of the sound of German small-arms fire but to keep our heads up and our rifles ready to pick off their operators. A small-arms fight is fun. Artillery, however, takes the joy out of life! A few of us have acquired a surface calm under fire which is the envy of the replacements. I am not one of those few, but I have learned to look at the noise and confusions a little more objectively.

Thus the old soldier, unshaven, dirty, quiet, cautious, cool, always prompted by the motive of self-preservation . . . keeps alive as long as possible. Old soldiers die, but they die hard.[172]

It took time for the newbies to learn vital things, little signs, tricks, that gave them a better chance of survival. The old guys had esoteric knowledge. Robert "Doc Joe" Franklin, a combat medic in Europe, remembers: "Before the end of the war, I could smell Germans too. Their diet of sardines and sharp cheese gave them away in warm weather if they weren't careful to cover their feces."[173] Allied soldiers in the Pacific claimed that Japanese soldiers smelled of fish, while the Japanese said they could smell the "meaty" body odor of the Allies. Russian soldiers advertised their presence with the pungent aroma of *makhorka* tobacco, the "awful smell of which," according to Wehrmacht officer Siegfried Knappe, "got into their thick uniforms and could be smelled for quite a distance."[174]

Combat technique and battlefield wisdom quite often needed

a supernaturally helping hand, and even (perhaps especially) hard-bitten veterans answered an ancient echo that had sustained warriors down the centuries, for magic also had its place in warding off death. Talismans, charms, amulets, and superstitious tics were another kind of protective armory. John Steinbeck, who was with the US Army in Italy, noted:

A great many soldiers carry with them some small article, some touchstone or lucky piece or symbol which, if they are lucky in battle means simply not being hurt. . . . The magic articles are of all kinds. There will be a smooth stone, an odd-shaped piece of metal, small photographs encased in cellophane. Many soldiers consider pictures of their wives or parents to be almost protectors from danger. One soldier had removed the handles from his Colt .45 and had carved new ones out of Plexiglass from a wrecked airplane. Then he had installed photographs of his children under the Plexiglass. . . .

Sometimes coins are considered lucky and rings and pins. . . . One man carries a locket his dead wife wore as a child and another a string of amber beads his mother once made him wear to ward off colds. . . .

It is interesting now that, as time in action goes on, these magics not only become more valuable and dear but become more secret also. And many men make up small rituals to cause their amulets to become active. A smooth stone may be rubbed when the tracers are cutting lines about a man's head. One sergeant holds an Indian-head penny in the palm of his left hand and against the stock of his rifle when he fires. He is just about convinced that he cannot miss if he does this. . . .

As time goes on and dangers multiply and perhaps there is a narrow escape or so, the amulet not only takes on an increasing importance but actually achieves a kind of personality. It becomes a thing to talk to and rely on. . . . There are times in war when the sharpest emotion is not fear, but loneliness and littleness. And it is during these times that the smooth stone or the Indian-head penny or the wooden pig are not only desirable but essential. Whatever atavism may call them up, they appear and they seem to fill a need. The dark world is not far from us—from any of us.[175]

Even the resolutely agnostic and the proudly cynical needed all the help they could get. Paul Fussell, "entirely a skeptic," carried a New Testament in the left breast pocket of his shirt but with a skeptic's embarrassed caveat: "I conceived that even if it didn't provide magical, supernatural safety, it at least—it was a half-inch thick—might slow down shell and grenade fragments and deflect a bayonet thrust to my chest."[176] "Men in combat acquire curious superstitions," recalls Raymond Gantter, "even those who pride themselves on their incredulity. I was ashamed of my own pet charm, but it was no longer private or secret. From a platoon joke it had become a company gag, and whenever we moved out on a push I'd be sure to hear someone yell, 'Hey, Gantter! Got your battle gum?' "[177]

For different horses, different courses: Russians had "taboos about sex—a wounded, even an unconscious, man would die if he touched his own genitals—about swearing, and about the advisability of wearing clean linen before battle. There were many predictions based on vagaries of the weather. Some men believed it was unlucky to swear while loading a gun, others that a man should never swear before a battle. It was also unlucky to give anything to a comrade before going into combat, and soldiers all had tales of borrowed greatcoats that brought death."[178]

The soldier-poet Louis Simpson felt that somehow an adoption of the attitudes of the dead would be a magic camouflage that just might fool the Furies:

> *The path reeled in*
> *Another corpse. It came to him boot first:*
> *A German soldier on his back, spread-eagle,*
> *A big, fresh-blooded, blond, jack-booted man*
> *In dusty gray. Stepping around the fingers,*
> *Around the bucket helmet, Dodd stared down.*
> *A fly lit on his teeth. He looked away*
> *And to the front, where other attitudes*
> *Of death were waiting. He assumed them all,*
> *One by one, in his imagination,*
> *In order to prevent them.*[179]

The Furies, though, all too often scoffed at these precautions and with the manic determination of water or smoke, no matter how tight the seal, found their way in. Men were killed in all kinds of offbeat, half-baked, heartbreaking ways. British rifleman R. L. Crimp, in North Africa in 1942, recorded in his diary his response to a letter from home urging him to "take care of yourself":

Good lord, as if I ever do anything but! Of course I always take all the cover that's going, and keep my swede [head] down as long as possible. But what's the good? Bill Vole moved heaven and earth to get a job with Rear Echelon but when a stray Jerry strafed his convoy miles back he got his just the same. On the last Jerry push, six weeks ago, there was Johnny Gussett in "A" Company carriers, wireless operator. He'd only just joined us from the base, where . . . he'd been sitting pretty for nearly a year. Yet in that one night's skirmishing a Breda shell [from an Italian light machine gun] went through his carrier, through his set and through him. Even Stingo Carstairs . . . speeding by truck into Cairo on leave, hit a tram, then a tree, and finished up in the military cemetery.

So using your loaf doesn't get you far in keeping it safe. You can only wait—and see. . . . "Do look after yourself." Rather a problem, eh, chum?[180]

It was indeed the damnedest thing how a man could get killed. A "safe" distance behind the lines, a tent had been set up in which to show movies. The men were jolly and relieved to be out of the action for a brief respite. Some enemy planes came over and American antiaircraft batteries opened up. Raymond Gantter remembers:

We were a little blasé about the fun outside—we'd seen all this so many times before, and stuff. . . . I was talking to a neighbor when a man sitting a few feet in front of me grunted or coughed and gently, slowly, toppled forward on his face. There was a puzzled hush for a moment, and then, uncertainly, the laughing and talking in the tent resumed. Then someone bent over the fallen man and shouted, "Get a medic!" and our paralysis was broken. We turned him over. His hand and arm were covered with blood and his face was a red mask. Before we could carry him from the tent he was dead. For a long time we could not guess how he'd been hit until someone discovered a two-inch slit in the canvas roof . . . a piece of falling shrapnel from our own ack-ack had knifed through the canvas and pierced his back as he leaned forward, elbows on knees.[181]

The malevolent Fates often conspire to deny the warrior any vestige of the heroic, and what better way to do that than catch him with his pants around his ankles. As Milton Landry of the US Thirty-Sixth Infantry Division commented after being wounded by a grenade while assuming what he delicately calls "the proper position": "You don't read much about it in books."

But it was often a surefire way of getting killed. Dick Peterson of the Twenty-Fifth Division remembers: "Dysentery was rampant on Guadalcanal. . . . The desire to relieve yourself is just tremendous. At night, what do you do? We had passwords, but the Japs were all over and guys were quick to shoot. So do you stay in the hole or go out for a minute and risk getting shot? Those were the alternatives. Most people stayed in the hole, but I'm afraid many of the men shot after dark had their pants down. It was amazing how many ways you could get hurt in World War II."[182]

Meanwhile, thousands of miles away:

It was a beautiful and grim Christmas Eve. Shorty and I spelled each other on guard throughout the bitter cold night. The cold I could endure, but an additional misery landed on me in the middle of the night. I got the GIs [diarrhea]!* That's always a tragedy, of course—although in normal life, with the luxury of a civilized bathroom at hand, it would seem only an embarrassing annoyance—but this time the tragedy was of major proportions. You see, our dugout is on the crest of a hill, smack in the middle of an open field and with never a bush or tree to provide cover. It's not modesty that bothers us, you understand, it's snipers. We peer anxiously in the direction of the German lines, unbutton our pants in the dugout, hold them up with one hand while we clamber out, and get the business over in a hurry. We wipe on the run—our naked and chilled buttocks quivering in anticipation of a bullet. . . . A half-naked man crouching on a hilltop is a defenseless creature, unnerved by the constant sense of his nakedness framed in the sights of an enemy rifle. I winced and shook each time I dropped my

---

*It would be intriguing to know the derivation of this bit of slang. "Government issue," as in government-issued rations that induced diarrhea?

pants, expecting every moment to be caponized by a German sniper who combined marksmanship with a macabre sense of humor.[183]

A common way for a soldier to be killed "off the books," as it were, was by his own comrades. The chaos of jungle warfare made friendly fire particularly lethal. On Bougainville, 16 percent of American deaths were attributable to friendly fire; and on Guadalcanal, it accounted for 12 percent of all casualties.[184] On New Georgia, "the 169th Regiment thought its bivouac area had been penetrated by the Japanese. There was a great deal of confusion as knives were drawn and grenades wildly thrown into the dark. Many Americans stabbed each other. Grenades bounced off trees and exploded amongst the defenders. Some soldiers fired off round after round to no avail. Come morning there was no trace of Japanese dead or wounded but there were numerous American casualties, 50 percent of them hit by fragments from the grenades."[185] These fracture points of panic ran through all armies.

It was bad enough that patrolling was itself one of the deadliest occupations known to the infantryman, but to cap it all, just trying to reenter one's own lines could be hair-raising and often lethal. Paul Fussell learned not to trust passwords when bringing a patrol back through the perimeter: "We learned many simple survival techniques. One was never to assume a friendly soldier knew who you were at night and in his nervousness would refrain from shooting you. We learned that 'passwords' were seldom efficacious: you had to raise your voice to speak them, risking arousing the enemy a hundred yards away, and it was very likely that the password had been forgotten by one or both of you anyway."[186]

A misheard word could be fatal. Robert Leckie remembered a medic killed by friendly fire on Guadalcanal: "When the sentry had challenged him as he returned from relieving himself, he had boggled over the password 'Lilliputian' and so met death: eternity at the mercy of a liquid consonant."[187] George MacDonald Fraser also lost a comrade to a consonant.

> We stood to until dawn, half an hour later, and when the light grew someone spotted the body lying a few yards in front of the pit to our immediate right. It was the Duke. He had been cut almost in half by the Vickers [British machine gun] fire.
>
> It soon became plain what had happened. Someone had got up to go to the latrine, and in the dark had trod on one of the sleeping Jats [Indian troops fighting with the British Army in Burma] who had cried out—not loudly, but still loud enough to wake a third party, who had asked what was up. A fourth man had said something like: "It's just one of the Jats," and a fifth man, probably half-awake, had misheard the last word of the sentence and exclaimed: "Japs?" In an instant someone else had shouted "Japs!" and there was a mad scramble for the pits, with the Jat gunners starting to blaze away—and at some point the Duke must have come awake, remembered that he was away from his pit and his rifle, and made a bee-line for them. Only it was pitch dark, and he had run the wrong way.[188]

There were also "friendly" fatalities on a grand scale. Operation Cobra was a US bombing mission to help American troops break out of the Saint-Lô beachhead in Normandy. The bombers missed their mark and killed 25 Americans on the first day and 111, including Lieutenant General Lesley McNair, the next, and wounded 400-plus more. A couple of weeks later British bombers inadvertently dumped their loads on Canadian and Polish troops near Caen. The Régiment de la Chaudière, for example, suffered 400 killed and wounded.

But nothing compared to accidentally killing a comrade up close:

"Soon be home, Charlie," somebody would say.

"Oh, no," Charlie would reply—almost taken aback by the suggestion. . . .

Bet he didn't know he was going to cop it like that, though. It's a different feeling killing your pals to killing Jerry. Nobody minds you killing Jerry. That's what you're here for. But you have to have a big excuse if you want to knock off your own. There was no excuse here. You were told to stay in the field away from the house—rain or no rain. But hell, it rained so hard you were afloat. So you got into the farm with Harry and another bloke, and you jammed the door. Nobody was going to surprise you. And you sat on the floor of one of the bedrooms with your backs to the wall, and faced the only window looking up to the black sky . . . you all agreed that it would be too dangerous to sleep and you all swore you would stay awake, and you all slept. . . . And then there was the bark of a gun, and all was commotion and fear, and for one sharp second you thought your heart would burst, and the window was filled with a body and the body was grunting and falling down head over heels upon you. And when you saw it was Charlie coming in search of his fate you thought, "Thank God it's Charlie and not the Jerries, and thank God he got it quick." But Charlie didn't get it quick and he wouldn't die, either, and his lifeblood sprayed over you and refused to be stanched. And Harry, who had shot him, felt himself part of Charlie's fate and it unnerved Harry, and he shook Charlie and told him he hadn't meant to kill Charlie, and he asked Charlie to forgive him, and he wept, and he asked Christ to let Charlie speak to him. But Christ didn't hear; nor did Charlie, and Charlie died with his blood saturating you as he lay on you, and the blood ran down your legs all warm and sticky, not like water.[189]

★   ★   ★

THE RELENTLESS EXPOSURE to combat affected a reverse alchemy: the precious metal of "It can't happen to me" was turned into the lead of "It will happen to me." Paul Fussell charts that transformation: "We came to understand what more have known than spoken of, that normally each man begins with a certain full reservoir, or bank account, of bravery, but that each time it's called upon, some is expended, never to be regained. After several months it has all been expended, and it's time for your breakdown. My reservoir was full, indeed overflowing, at St. Dié and so certain did I feel that no harm could come to me—me—that I blithely pressed forward, quite enjoying the challenges and the pleasures of learning a new mode of life. . . . But at the Moder River line in the snow hole, some courage leaked away, and it was distinctly hard for me to leave the hole at night to go out and check on my men."[190] "Perhaps if you are very brave," observed a British soldier, "it diminishes imperceptibly, but it does diminish as a chord on a piano once struck grows steadily weaker and can never behave otherwise."[191]

The soldiers of the Second World War were, perhaps, less inhibited about expressing their fear than those of earlier wars. Ike Roberts, a combat GI in Europe, admits its prevalence as well as its antidote: "As for the actual feeling, the day I hit the front line and every day thereafter I was the same as all the other GIs and our officers—scared as hell and you get more scared at every attack. But when the word comes, scared or not you climb out and go. You know damned well it has to be done and it's up to you. If a man says he's not scared he's one of two things, he's either a fool or a damned liar."[192]

A British artilleryman also recognized that dogged acceptance in a description of fortitude and quiet courage that is heir to centuries of infantry battle: "I stood watching the infantry. Without any show of emotion they got up, picked up their P.I.A.T. mortars, their rifles and ammunition, and walked slowly up the road towards the enemy, with the same bored indifference of a man who goes to work he does not love . . . No hesitation, no rush on the part of anybody. Men move slowly against death, and although the shaft of every stomach was a vacuum of bile and lead no sign was given and I tried to cover my fear." A chaplain watched Canadian infantry preparing to attack the Hitler Line in May 1944: "My boys move in tonight . . . New boys with fear and nerves and anxiety hidden under quick smiles and quick seriousness. Old campaigners with a faraway look. It is the hardest thing to watch without breaking into tears."[193]

Corporal Ralph Pearse of the 2nd West Yorkshire Regiment remembered that "Both Sid Wright and I were sure by this time that we couldn't go on coming through battle after battle alive. Like Sid, I'd become a fighting man and nothing else; no hope of anything else but more fighting, until in the end we knew we must be killed. We didn't care much. We knew it was inevitable."[194] At the extreme of physical and psychological exhaustion what was once feared above all else now is almost welcomed. To be killed, wounded, or captured would be a release, remembers Henri Atkins: "At the time, any one of those possibilities was OK with me. I had been living in such miserable, bitter cold, I didn't really care what happened." Resignation was a kind of liberation, a calmness in the face of almost certain obliteration. The Soviet war correspondent Vasily Grossman talked to an infantry commander who had come through the appalling battering as the Germans swept up to the gates of Moscow:

At Khasin's tank brigade, Captain Kozlov, the commander of the motorised rifle battalion, was philosophising about life and death while talking to me at night. He is a young man with a small beard. Before the war he was studying music at the Moscow Conservatoire. "I have told myself that I will be killed whatever happens, today or tomorrow. And once I realised this, it became so easy for me to live, so simple, and even somehow so clear and pure. My soul is very calm. I go into battle without any fear, because I have no expectations. I am absolutely convinced that a man commanding a motorised rifle battalion will be killed, that he cannot survive. If I didn't have this belief in the inevitability of death, I would be feeling bad and, probably, I wouldn't be able to be so happy, calm and brave in the fighting.[195]

As a young replacement in the terrible battle of the Hürtgen Forest, Raymond Gantter recalls one of the veterans:

I was struck by how old he seemed. Not in physical appearance—in spite of his heavy beard, his haggard eyes, and all the evidence of great weariness, he was still a young man in his early twenties. Nor, in spite of what's written in war novels, was his age heavily implicit in the tragedy of his eyes. No, it was in the way in which he spoke of life and death and mutilation, in his calm acceptance of transiency and impermanence, his serene willingness to receive whatever would come instead of the Quixotic rebellion against fate that every young man has a right to enjoy. I felt young and naïve before his mature and unbegging resignation.[196]

But fatalism could also be a kind of gloriously noodle-headed "Quixotic rebellion." Robert Leckie saw it at work with one of his buddies on Guadalcanal, Scar-Chin, who took to standing outside during bombing raids,

> stirring not a foot even when the thump of the bombs was dangerously close, or when we in the pit below could hear the tinkle of falling shrapnel or the whizz of bomb fragments. . . .
>
> "C'mon down here, Scar-Chin. C'mon, you crazy bastard, before you get your ass blown off."
>
> Scar-Chin would chortle, "What's the difference? They can knock it off down there, too. Makes no difference where you are. If you're gonna get it, you're gonna get it, and there isn't anything you can do about it. When your number comes up, that's it, brother. So why worry?"
>
> There was no arguing with him, nor with his fellow fatalists. Kismet was all the fashion on Guadalcanal. You could hear them saying, It Is Written, in a hundred different ways: "Why worry, you'll go when your time comes."
>
> There is almost no argument against fatalism. Argue until you are weary, but men like Scar-Chin still lounge among the falling bombs. . . . Suggest that it is they, through their own foolhardiness, who choose the time. Impress upon them that they are their own executioner, that they pull their own name out of the hat. . . .
>
> It is a fine argument, an excellent way to pass the time while the bombs fall and Scar-Chin—that disturbing fatalist Scar-Chin—lounges above without a word of rebuttal, himself alone among the exploding steel.[197]

Men might be philosophical about death, but they shared with soldiers down the centuries a particular horror of being killed in a certain way, a way that denied them some kind of saving grace. When Major John André, a British officer and spy captured during the American War of Independence, was sentenced to be executed, he petitioned George Washington to allow him to be shot, as befitted an officer; Washington insisted on the ignominy of a criminal's execution by hanging. More than 160 years later, Laurens van der Post, a South African–born officer in the British Army (later to become famous as a conservationist, anthropologist, and writer), captured behind enemy lines in Java in 1942, faced what seemed to be his imminent execution at the hands of the Japanese: "And curiously enough, the only thing that worried me was *how* I was to be killed . . . I didn't want to be strangled, I didn't want to be hanged, I didn't want to be buried, I didn't want to be bayoneted—all forms of execution I had seen. I wanted to be shot. And I thought: the great thing is to think of an argument, a way of putting it to them so that they shoot you in the morning. This seemed to me of vital importance."[198]

Donald Burgett, a tough young paratrooper intimately acquainted with death in battle, pondered the possibility of his own with a vividness born of experience. Echoing Lord Moran's observation during World War I, he confesses that it is dismemberment that tightened the sphincter:

The thought of death did not really bother me too much. Death is just the other end of being born. It is natural. We come into the world out of a dark, unknowing void and we return to it. What really bothered me was the thought of having my arms and legs torn from my body. Of lying there with my blood spurting out on a shell-ravaged field. Of seeing the jagged ends of splintered bone protruding from the torn, ragged stumps of flesh where my limbs used to be. Of smelling burnt powder and raw iron mixed with fresh human blood. I had experienced this with others in battle too many times. I didn't want it to happen to me. I would rather be killed.[199]

Another way the combat soldier could protect himself from the fear of death was to detach it from the *me* and invest it in the *you*: "We worried more about our buddies," remembers Marine Frank Chadwick. "You made yourself believe that nothing could happen to you, that you had to worry about your friends." But it was a peculiarly schizophrenic attitude. On the one hand, "you knew people were killed and wounded all the time, but deep down you thought it would happen to some other guy."

Responsibility and care, love even, are freighted with the appalling risk of loss. Kenneth Cole, who had his best buddy killed on Iwo Jima, lamented: "I just can't make myself understand that I won't see Boone anymore. Even though you may have seen men die in the same outfit with you it is impossible to make yourself believe that anybody can get killed that is as close to you as Boone was to me. He taught me practically everything I know about being a Marine. If it hadn't been for Boone I would have been a white cross on Bougainville."[200]

The contract of comradeship had to be honored, although perhaps many years later. Alex Bowlby's closest friend, Corporal Jeffreys, was killed in Italy.

> One morning I saw a rifleman from "D" Company. Had there been any casualties I asked?
>
> "No," he said. "It's been pretty cushy. But Corporal Jeffreys is dead. He stepped on a Teller [a German mine] and it went off. He was on patrol."
>
> I walked away quickly, automatically heading for a wood outside the camp. There I sobbed my heart out. I felt as if part of myself had died.
>
> By the evening the grief had bottled itself up. It stayed that way until one November evening fourteen years later, when I cried my way across half London.[201]

Sometimes the dead stranger reached out: "There he is . . . a fellow Marine. His face is not recognized; perhaps I have never met him. None of this seems to matter now. He is my brother. How many times had my fellow Marine felt the slicing and piercing of the Japanese bayonet? There must be at least 30 bayonet wounds. His penis is cut off and shoved into his mouth in the Japanese way of the ultimate insult. His once handsome features and dark complexion are now obscured by ants. . . . I shed . . . tears for his family whom I will not be able to find. To this day I am bothered by this memory."[202]

Charles Lindsay of the Fourth Marines on Okinawa stumbled on the body of a fellow Marine: "A perfect specimen of youth . . . not a scratch on him except a bullet hole thru his helmet. He must have been killed instantly and there was no blood. I opened his pack to get his poncho to cover him from the flies. Out fell a picture of his mother and a picture of a beautiful girl. I placed the pictures inside his jacket and then knelt down and prayed. And then just plain cried. To me he was the whole war."[203]

As bizarre as it might sound, death could be a relief from the weighty responsibility of loving someone in peril. C. Russ Martin was a sergeant in the US First Infantry Division. His twin brother was killed in North Africa. "Twins, we feel for one another, and the minute he got killed I knew it, a sensation and a kind of relief, you know, from worrying about him. I didn't have to worry about him anymore. A boy walked up to me and said, 'You know your brother got killed?' And I said, 'Yes, I do.' "[204]

Another response was to balance loss with revenge, the death received with the death meted out. Donald Burgett, the tough-guy airborne warrior, going into a desperate attack in northwest Europe in 1944, recalls:

Passing one foxhole I saw an infantry man holding his dead buddy in his arms and crying. This puzzled me, and I stopped for a minute to ask him what the trouble was.

"They've killed my buddy," he sobbed, with tears streaming down his cheeks. "But he can't be dead, we went through basic together; the medics have got to save him."

The man was dead all right, shot through the Adam's apple, and I told the infantry man so. "The only thing that you can do for him now is to leave him alone and help kill some of these Krauts."

Looking back I saw that he was still crying and holding the dead man in his arms. "He must be nuts," I thought. I have had buddies killed even in training and didn't feel like that. Not an hour ago Baranski, René, Robbie and LaRose had been killed and several others badly wounded. I felt bad, but we couldn't sit around and cry about it. We had Germans to kill.[205]

Rejecting tough-guy rhetoric (although himself a battle-hardened warrior), William Manchester expresses the need to move past grief: "It was bad form to weep long for a fallen buddy. We moved on, each of us inching along the brink of his own extinction."[206]

★   ★   ★

A FEW REVELED in it; most were disgusted by it, and yet more were reconciled to the necessary truth that killing is what combat soldiers are meant to do: "We were in the business of killing . . . it was what we were trained for; it was our livelihood, in a very real sense. I am not justifying, but explaining, when I say those were the days when, if a selection board chairman asked (and he did): 'Wouldn't you like to stick a bayonet in a German's guts, eh?,' he was not expecting an answer drawn from the Sermon on the Mount."[207]

As with most soldiers throughout history, combat troops in World War II tended to resolve any moral qualms with an uncomplicated directness: In the words of an armored infantryman, "You learn one basic axiom and that is kill or be killed. You learn to think of 'me.' With someone getting killed you say, 'Better him than me.'" And of a medic: "In the heat of all this bitterness, anger, and fear of being done in, it's either you or them."[208] Survival had a way of trumping most other considerations: "You don't fight a kraut by Marquis of Queensberry rules. You shoot him in the back, you blow him apart with mines, you kill or maim him the quickest and most effective way you can with the least danger to yourself. He does the same to you. He tricks you and cheats you, and if you don't beat him at his own game you don't live to appreciate your own nobleness.[209]

An American infantryman in the Pacific theater would have heartily applauded the sentiment: "Hollywood movies do not actually portray the realities of war, as in many cases the enemy is shot from behind or stabbed from behind or blown up from behind easier than front on. This is not a step-by-step hip-swinging, gun-throwing, honor-bound situation. Actually, you were out to save your own neck in the safest, easiest possible way."[210]

Men under great stress cannot help but feel satisfaction—joy even—in killing an enemy who would kill them given half a chance. Is it evidence of innate and primal evil? Of a bloodlust like a lousy inheritance? Or simply that huge sigh of relief—"He. Not me." George MacDonald Fraser recalls being in an attack against a strong Japanese position at Pyawbwe in Burma that had been long anticipated and much feared by the attackers. Finally, they were in the thick of it, and the killing, surprisingly, brought an almost luxurious sense of satisfaction, deliciously unburdened of guilt:

Nick jumped into the wagon [railroad car], and I was on his heels. It was open on the far side, like a picture window; it might have been designed as a firing point for kneeling marksmen. All around the wagon men were yelling with excitement, throwing themselves down on the rubble and blazing away at those running figures, some of whom must have turned to fire at us, for two or three shots clanged against the wagon. But most of them were running, and all we had to do was pick our targets.

This was something new. In my previous contacts with the enemy, everything had been split-second in crisis, with nothing to do but react at speed, snap-shooting. . . . There had been no time to think; it had been scramble and shoot and hope . . . in a way like a goal-mouth scramble. . . .

But in that railway wagon it was more like the moment when you're clear with the ball. . . . There wasn't much time, but enough: to pick a target, hang for an instant on the aim to make sure, take the first pressure according to the manual—and then the second.

It was exciting; no other word for it, and no explanation needed, for honest folk. We all have kindly impulses, fostered by two thousand years of Christian teaching, gentle Jesus, and love thy neighbour, but we have the killer instinct, too, the murderous impulse of the hunter . . . but one must not say so.[211]

Killing, in Fraser's world, was sanitized by distance and sanctified by an ancient tribal dispensation. However, when it was up close and personal, the killer was no longer protected from the consequences, as Raymond Gantter found:

It is hard to write this part, because this is where I killed a man. The first one. The first one I was sure of. It ought to be told simply, because it's important that you should understand what it's like—how you feel when you have trapped a small, running creature between the cold sights of a deliberate gun and pulled the trigger, and suddenly the creature has stopped running and is lying there, and now it's a man and his body is naked, and soft and crumpled. It ought to be told without hint of boast, and yet so that you would see there's something of the bragging boy in the sense of achievement; it ought to be told without sentiment, and yet so you would see what a big thing it is.

I saw a German soldier rise from behind the protective shoulder of the ridge and start to run to the rear, sprinting across the open field toward the hills. Perhaps he was a runner, a messenger—I cannot remember that he carried a weapon. It occurred to me later that he must have been young and very green, because he ran in a straight line, an easy course to follow with the sights of a rifle. He had unbuttoned his overcoat for greater freedom in running, and the skirts flapped like huge blue wings around his legs. He was a moving dot of blue, a clumsy blue object to be stalked deliberately. . . . Now, impaled within the sights, the blue coat was enormous, presented itself to my squinted eye like a cloud, like a house, like a target painted solid blue on the firing range. . . . I squeezed the trigger and he fell. He did not move again, the skirts of the blue overcoat made a patch of unnatural color in the field where he lay.

For a moment I was triumphant and my eyes lingered on my prize, confirming it. There he was! . . . He was there, still lying there, and it wasn't a game any longer. He hadn't risen to his feet, dusted himself off, and thumbed his nose at me gaily before started to run again. He lay there, quiet now, and he hadn't moved, and I laid my rifle on the floor of the attic—carefully, because of the plaster dust—and put my head in my hands. I wanted to be sick, but there wasn't time to be sick. And I thought, Poor bastard . . . he was hungry and cold, too . . . scared and homesick and missing his people and tired of war. And I was sick and ashamed because I never hated him, never him specifically, and I never wanted to kill him. And it was an ugly and an evil thing. . . . Then I picked up my rifle and went back to my job.[212]

★   ★   ★

TWO SOLDIERS ARE killed. Their deaths, humiliating for one, defiant for the other, stand at the polar opposites of combat. A great arc—the spectrum that connects the heroic and unheroic—is made visible. They are particular in that they happened during World War II, but they are also universal, belonging to all wars.

William Manchester kills his first Japanese:

Utterly terrified, I jolted to a stop on the threshold of the shack. I could feel a twitching in my jaw, coming and going like a winky light signaling some disorder. Various valves were opening and closing in my stomach. My mouth was dry, my legs quaking, and my eyes out of focus. Then my vision cleared. I unlocked the safety of my Colt, kicked the door with my right foot, and leapt inside.

My horror returned. I was in an empty room. There was another door opposite the one I had unhinged, which meant another room, which meant the sniper was in there—and had been warned by the crash of the outer door. But I had committed myself. Flight was impossible now. So I smashed into the other room and saw him as a blur to my right. I wheeled that way, crouched, gripped the pistol butt in both hands, and fired.

Not only was he the first Japanese soldier I had ever shot

at; he was the only one I had seen at close quarters. He was a robin-fat, moon-faced, roly-poly little man with his thick, stubby, trunklike legs sheathed in faded khaki puttees and the rest of him squeezed into a uniform that was much too tight. Unlike me, he was wearing a tin hat, dressed to kill. But I was quite safe from him. His Arisaka rifle was strapped on in a sniper's harness, and though he had heard me, and was trying to turn toward me, the harness sling had him trapped. He couldn't disentangle himself from it. His eyes were rolling in panic. Realizing that he couldn't extricate his arms and defend himself, he was backing toward a corner with a curious, crablike motion.

My first shot had missed him, embedding itself in the straw wall, but the second caught him dead-on in the femoral artery. His left thigh blossomed, swiftly turning to mush. A wave of blood gushed from the wound; then another boiled out, sheeting across his legs, pooling on the earthen floor. Mutely he looked down at it. He dipped a hand in it and listlessly smeared his cheek red. His shoulders gave a little spasmodic jerk, as though somebody had whacked him on the back; then he emitted a tremendous, raspy fart, slumped down, and died. I kept firing, wasting government property.

Already I thought I detected the dark brown effluvium of the freshly slain, a sour, pervasive emanation which is different from anything else you have known. Yet seeing death at that range, like smelling it, requires no previous experience. You instantly recognize the spastic convulsion and the rattle, which in his case was not loud, but deprecating and conciliatory, like the manners of civilian Japanese. He continued to sink until he reached the earthen floor. His eyes glazed over. Almost immediately a fly landed on his left eyeball. It was joined by another. I don't know how long I stood there staring. I knew from previous combat what lay ahead for the corpse. It would swell, then bloat, bursting out of the uniform. Then the face would turn from yellow to red, to purple, to green, to black. . . .

Jerking my head to shake off the stupor, I slipped a new, fully loaded magazine into the butt of my .45. Then I began to tremble, and next to shake, all over. I sobbed, in a voice still grainy with fear: "I'm sorry." Then I threw up all over myself. I recognized the half-digested C-ration beans dribbling down my front. . . . Then Barney burst in on me. . . . He said: "Slim, you stink." I said nothing. . . . I remember wondering dumbly: *Is this what they mean by "conspicuous gallantry"?*[213]

Michael Calvert, a British commando-trained officer fighting deep behind Japanese lines with Orde Wingate's Chindit special forces group in Burma in 1943, meets a noble adversary in a fight to the death:

On the beach, as naked as I was, stood a Jap. A pile of clothes lay near his feet and in my first startled glance I took in the insignia of an officer. . . .

While I was still thinking hard the Jap officer stepped into the river and came towards me. I think his mind must have been working much like mine; he could see I was unarmed but if he used his gun it would bring both patrols running and he did not know our strength. . . . Anyway, he wasn't taking any chances on an open fight which would needlessly risk his men's lives. He preferred to tackle me with his bare hands.

He knew his ju-jitsu and the water on his body made him as slippery as an eel, but I was the bigger and the stronger. We fought in silence except for the occasional grunt, and struggled and slipped and thrashed around until we were at times waist deep in the swirling river. It was an ungainly fight, almost in slow motion, for it is extraordinarily difficult to keep balance or move quickly and surely in two or three feet of water. Our breathing became heavier and the Jap got more vicious as he jabbed his fingers at my face in an attempt to blind me. I think it was not till then that I fully realized this would have to be a fight to the death.

I was a trained soldier, taught how to kill with a gun, or a bomb, or a bayonet or even a knife in the thick of battle. Somehow this seemed different, more personal, as the two of us, naked as we were, fought in the water. Apart from anything else I had come to admire this game little Jap. He had all the guts in the world. He could so easily have called up his men. . . .

Now he was putting up a tremendous show and I was hard put to it to hold him. I pulled myself together. Brave or not I had to kill him. Or he would kill me.

I was thankful for one lesson I had learned: never to take my boots off in the jungle outside camp. Other clothes can be scrambled on in a moment but boots take time, and time can cost lives. Even on this occasion I had stuck to my rule, which was just as well. I managed to grab the Jap's right wrist and force his arm behind his back. And I buried my face in his chest to stop him clawing my eyes out. Then as he lashed out with his left arm and both feet, I forced him gradually under water. My boots gave me a firm grip and I shut my eyes and held him under the surface. His struggles grew weaker and weaker, flared again in frantic despair and then he went limp. I held on for a few seconds longer before releasing my grip. Slowly I opened my eyes and for a moment could see nothing except the eddies of water caused by his final efforts to break free. Then his body emerged on the surface a couple of yards away and floated gently off downstream.[214]

EIGHT

DIAMONDS IN THE MIRE

Death and the Heroic in Modern Combat

I don't want to die in this fucking country.

The last words of Staff Sergeant Stevon Booker, a tank commander
with Alpha Company 1/64 Armor, Third Infantry Division,
Baghdad, Iraq, April 5, 2003 as reported in Michael R. Gordon
and General Bernard E. Trainor, *Cobra II: The Inside Story
of the Invasion and Occupation of Iraq.*

If I have to die, let me die in a stand-up fight.

David Bellavia in his war memoir, *House to House* (2007)

*A*STAND-UP FIGHT IN whatever country—Vietnam,
Somalia, the Falklands, Grenada, Iraq, Afghanistan—
is all the soldier asks. (Or, perhaps more accurately, all the *Western* soldier asks.) To give his life or, more likely, have it taken
for some purpose is the first and last clause in the contract he
has made with his country. The cause may not be grand (think
Grenada) or even comprehensible (think Vietnam) to the men

at the sharp end (the politicians, editorialists, and think-tank pointy-heads will provide the ideological scaffolding), but there has to be some lifeline of meaning by which the soldier can haul himself out of the madness and bloody mire of combat. The actions that lead to his death may not, in the strictest sense, be heroic, but in a more general sense his death should be redeemed by purpose. There should at least be some vestige of significance. To give up one's life as a gratuity is not acceptable, although for many warriors it has been the price demanded, and all the more terrible for it.

Looking back, it seems as though the end of World War II also marked the end of a compelling and luminous version of heroic warfare. There was an overwhelming national commitment. The war was noble, the enemy unambiguously evil. The Allies stood foursquare, untroubled by any niggling doubt as to the righteousness of their cause. There were no mass antiwar rallies. Good believed in itself without being undermined by the sneer of irony.

Back then, the enemy was, by unequivocal definition, bad (Germans), bad but silly (Italians), and sometimes truly evil (the Japanese in totality, the Germans partially, as in the SS), but they were the recognizable enemy. They wore uniforms (and if they did not, they were shot out of hand). They may have been bastards, but they stood up and gave a good honest fight. On the whole they fought within the broad context of the rules of the game (although, reprehensibly, the Japanese did not always sing from the same songbook and were therefore disgusting and bestial). It was, give or take a few "irregularities," a symmetrical confrontation, despite some localized disequilibrium. (The Japanese tended to be on the wrong end of this equation, but they were, by common agreement, fanatics, and therefore thoroughly deserved their bloody fate.)

Partisan warfare muddied the waters, but in the end it was quite clear. If the partisans fought for the Allies, they were good, their guerrilla tactics brilliant and daring, their breaking of the rules thrilling and heroic. If they were killed by the Germans, Italians, or Japanese, it was very wicked and provided yet more evidence that our enemies were brutal thugs. When German soldiers had themselves photographed gawping and grinning contemptuously at partisan bodies swinging from makeshift lamppost gallows or dumped into communal pits, we were revolted by the crassness and the cruelty.

The Germans enjoyed killing Communist partisans because they were, as far as the Nazis were concerned, terrorist scum. For the Germans there was no noble link between "partisan" and "patriot." They were simply the vermin of the battlefield, their courage mere fanaticism, their tactics underhanded and despicable.

After World War II it seemed as though the established notions of how wars would be fought changed drastically. With the Great Powers held in a standoff by the mutually assured destruction that their nuclear arsenals guaranteed, the conflicts of the postwar era fragmented into "small wars" of empire as communistic and capitalistic systems fought to maintain their spheres of influence.

There were some exceptions. The mass frontal charges of Chinese infantrymen during the Korean War (complete with rousing bugle calls) strike us now as the last expression of an ancient style of heroic warfare. The pitched battles between Israeli and Arab tank armies during the sixties and seventies had a heroic dimension that harks back to a type of combat freed of the tactical messiness that accompanies the insurgency warfare that characterized Vietnam, the later stages of the invasion of Iraq, and Afghanistan.

★   ★   ★

THE VIETNAM WAR has the tragic distinction of being America's bloodiest post–World War II conflict (and, even bloodier for

North and South Vietnam). Of the 58,000 American troops who died, 48,000 were killed outright in battle or died from wounds (about 6 percent of the approximately 776,000 who saw combat).[1] The ARVN, the South Vietnamese loyalists—who tended to be contemptuously dismissed as cowards and shirkers—lost 224,000. The North Vietnamese army and the Vietcong paid the heaviest price, with 1.1 million killed.[2] In comparison, almost 32,000 American ground troops died in Korea, while their enemy, the People's Republic of China, lost approximately 132,000 killed; South Korea lost over a quarter of a million men killed.

These huge disparities between American lives lost compared with their enemies became even more pronounced during the Persian Gulf and Iraq wars. In the 1991 Gulf War, for example, the coalition forces lost fewer than 150 combatants (a significant proportion to friendly fire), while the hapless Iraqis had 200,000 killed.[3] In the first phase ("shock and awe") of the Iraq War, starting in 2003, 148 US troops were killed in action, and of those a substantial number were from friendly fire; of the 24 British soldiers killed, 9 deaths were caused by US fire.[4] By comparison the Iraqi army had an estimated 100,000 killed and 300,000 wounded.[5] And yet, despite the emphatic disparities in American and enemy dead and the thumping defeats meted out, the Persian Gulf wars have not shone with the clear and unambiguous heroic light of World War II.

On the political and social level, the wars of America and its allies since World War II drove great divisive wedges through their societies. A battle for what might be called the heroic spirit of these wars was waged between liberals and conservatives, with governments sometimes being forced into a little "creative rewriting" to establish a just cause and a compelling moral context (the Gulf of Tonkin incident in the Vietnam War and the potential "mushroom cloud" of WMDs in Iraq being among the more egregious examples).

These rifts had a profound effect on the soldiers sent to fight. No longer secure in the wholehearted support of the nations that had dispatched them, they did what soldiers always do—created their own inward-looking and self-referencing world. If some kind of moral ambiguity clouded the picture, and if they were denied the heroic status that had been awarded to the warriors of World War II, they would create one for themselves. They would find their own diamond in the mire.

In the face of what they felt was either open hostility or simple neglect and indifference, soldiers often developed a fierce and angry defiance, giving the finger to a society they felt did not support them. Their war would have its own down-and-dirty integrity, as unattractive as that might be to the folks back home. It was, as a Vietnam vet puts it, "using whatever means available to beat somebody else whatever the reason, right or wrong." Or, as another put it, "War is fucking people up." "It was a dirty back-alley street fighting—killing the other guy before he kills you."[6] Staff Sergeant David Bellavia of the US First Infantry Division in Iraq turned the dirtiness of his killing business into a defiant statement of pride: "This is our war: we can't shoot at every target, we can't always tell who *is* a target; but we look out for one another and we don't mind doing the nation's dirty work. . . . War's a bitch, wear a helmet."[7] If they were to be rejected, they would turn that rejection into a badge of honor.

The messiness on the social/political level was mirrored on the strategic and tactical. The manner in which the wars were fought was irregular, the enemy combatants often indistinguishable from civilians, the tactics classic guerrilla, whether it be fighting the VC in Vietnam, the mujahideen in Iraq, or the Taliban in Afghanistan. One of the characteristics of heroic warfare is that the combatants must be clearly distinguished as such, whereas the opposite is true in insurgency warfare. In fact, one of the main ways insurgents can offset the weapons superiority of their enemy is by blurring the distinction between combatant and civilian, much to the fury, disgust, and confusion of "regular" troops. Not being able to read cultural signs—literally not being able to see the enemy—presents a huge disadvantage, as Captain Doug Beattie of the Royal Irish Regiment in Helmand Province, Afghanistan, in 2006, recognized:

> Each day there would be a constant stream of people coming to the compound. . . . With my interpreter Namir I would often watch them file past. More than a few of those who turned up wore distinctive black turbans. Didn't our enemies wear this style of headdress? One day I articulated my curiosity:
>
> "Talib?" I enquired warily.
>
> "Not Talib, Captain Doug," came the reply.
>
> A little while later, "Talib?" I enquired again, nodding towards a new arrival.
>
> "Not Talib." . . .
>
> A bit later Namir tapped my shoulder. . . . "Talib!" he said triumphantly.
>
> I looked at the eight men being escorted. . . . "How do you know?"
>
> "Everyone knows who they are."[8]

Dale Canter was in Cu Chi, Vietnam, in 1966 and described the unnerving ambiguity of the locals: "During the day, there was a lot of military traffic in and out, but at night, it still had a very ominous VC presence. . . . I honestly believe that some of these people really liked us. It was kind of a strange mixture. They were VC, some of their family and friends were VC, but when they got to know us, they had a genuine affection. But they had no qualms about reporting our activities and setting us up for ambushes, which would result in the death of many GIs."[9]

Kids and old ladies can get soldiers killed. As a Marine major in "Indian country" in Vietnam, Charles Cooper sent one of his rifle companies out on patrol. "A day or two later they had a couple more men killed. This time it was done by a small child. This kid had waved to the Marines while they were on patrol and signaled them to come over. As they closed in on him he reached down and pulled up an AK-47 and started shooting. Two guys were killed and a few more wounded and this kid capered off toward the village of Son Thang."

The next night a Marine "killer team" went into Son Thang and executed twenty women and children.[10]

In the Iraq and Afghanistan wars the same kind of combatant/civilian "camouflage" constantly caught the invaders off-guard. The initial blitzkrieg phases had been hugely successful. In Afghanistan surgical strikes by special forces and air had unseated the Taliban. But in Iraq, coalition (the U.S.–led Multi-National Force) planners had focused almost entirely on a recognizable enemy, the Republican Guard, and very quickly combat dissolved into a fight with Baathist irregulars, and coalition troops had to contend with what they considered underhanded tactics. In other words, the Iraqis, like the Vietcong, refused to recognize the rules of "heroic" combat as codified over centuries of Western warfare. "The Iraqis were not going to fight on the Americans' terms. The enemy faced by U.S. forces would be largely amorphous, not in uniform, and rarely part of an organized military force."[11] The Iraqis used civilian vehicles, civilian houses as strongpoints, and civilians as shields. An American soldier records a bewilderment that could have come straight out of the Vietnam War: "There's no tanks, there's no BMPs [armored infantry carriers], there's no uniforms. This is not anything we planned to fight. I mean, they're running around in black pajamas."[12]

The rules of engagement that are meant to determine for regular armies the legitimate use of deadly force are critical if civilian casualties are going to be contained and thus make the country more sympathetic to occupation, but they are a constant source of frustration and danger to the occupiers in the chaotic and confusing combat environment of insurgency warfare. Sergeant First Class Anthony Broadhead was part of the American thrust during the opening phase of the Iraq War. In Samawah he discovered just how bewildering the rules of engagement could become when the insurgents did not recognize those rules: "They were using an ambulance to pull up, drop new soldiers, and pick up the dead guys and leave. . . . So they did this all day long. Sergeant McCollough wanted to kill the ambulance and I'm like no, we can't do that. As long as they're not firing, even if they're transporting new soldiers to the battlefield, they got the Red Crescent on it."[13]

In the chaos of insurgency warfare there are wrenching decisions to be made. Captain Ed Hrivnak, a member of a medevac team in Iraq, recalls that a wounded soldier "confides in me that he witnessed some Iraqi children get run over by a convoy. He was in the convoy and they had strict orders not to stop. If a vehicle stops, it is isolated and an inviting target for a rocket-propelled grenade. He tells me that some women and children have been forced out onto the road to break up the convoys so that the Iraqi irregulars can get a clear shot. But the convoys do not stop. He tells me that dealing with the image is worse than the pain of his injury."[14]

Donovan Campbell, a young Marine officer embroiled in the urban warfare of Ramadi, west of Baghdad, describes how officers at the sharp end took a Damoclean sword to the knot of the rules: "Once the firing started and once the targets had been positively identified, though, the in/out of the fight concept would get tossed out of the window. Instead, we would stop our shooting according to the dictate of the Pine Box Rule: If there's any question about whether it's you or the bad guy who is going home in a pine box, you make damn certain that it's the bad guy. Of course we wanted to avoid as many innocent victims as possible, but if someone had already tried to kill us, there was no way we would risk our own lives simply to meet a vague legal condition of extremely dubious validity."[15]

Soldiers from the West, whether in Vietnam, Iraq, or Afghanistan, found themselves enmeshed in a type of warfare utterly alien to their instincts and training. The rules had been bent, and the techniques of combat were not suited to their more formal approach—a potentially fatal combination.

It is said that we always refight the last war, and armies steeped in a tradition of head-on "transparent" combat were caught off-kilter when it came to fighting insurgents. As US ambassador to South Vietnam, retired US Army general Maxwell Taylor advised President Johnson in February 1965: the "white-faced soldier, armed, equipped, and trained as he is, not a suitable guerrilla fighter for Asian forests and jungles. The French tried to adapt their forces to this mission and failed. I doubt that US forces could do much better."[16] Thomas Giltner, a junior infantry officer, described a training regimen that, if anything, was designed to get soldiers killed:

I completed my training at Fort Benning Officers' Candidate School on 13 May 1965. My training for combat in Vietnam was nonexistent. I fired one magazine of an M16 rifle; I took one helicopter ride on one afternoon counterinsurgency problem. The only thing I remember was being carried from one area to another on a simulated airmobile mission and hauling an M60 machine gun around to secure some obscure objective. Our training was conventional—it was Monte Casino, North Africa, the Battle of the Bulge. Mostly, we prepared for mass tactical deployment of large infantry and armor formations. The training of 1944 and 1964 had little apparent change, and that's how I was prepared for my assignment as a rifle platoon leader. . . . We were more concerned with fighting the Red Chinese or the Soviet Union.[17]

As a young officer, Lawrence Tahler recalls of his time in Vietnam: "Few officer leaders knew what they were doing. The top brass were fighting another war and most of us junior officers were trained to take Normandy, not fight insurgents. The grunts knew what was happening, but few officers listened to them. 'What do they know? They're just enlisted men' was too often the prevailing attitude."[18]

★   ★   ★

IF THE OCCUPYING armies lack tactical preparedness, they invariably have the advantages of the hardware their wealth provides, and so the default response tends to be to play that ace card—weapons superiority, in particular artillery and air-delivered devastation. Given the sheer volume of firepower available to the occupying forces, insurgent soldiers will have a much greater chance of being killed by artillery and air-delivered bombs and rockets than by small arms. Ta Quang Thinh, a medic with the North Vietnamese army, remembers: "Most of the wounds I treated were caused by artillery shells. Bombing also caused many shrapnel wounds and concussions."[19] The United States dropped three times as many bombs during the Vietnam War as it had during the whole of World War II. In 1968–69 alone it delivered one and a half times as many as the total dropped on Germany.[20]

A reliance on overwhelming air and artillery superiority was also the case in Iraq and Afghanistan. Captain Doug Beattie was astounded at the power of air support he could call in during his fight with Taliban insurgents in Garmsir in Helmand Province: Apache helicopter gunships ("the real battle winners"); close ground support A-10 Thunderbolts ("Warthogs") armed with a massive seven-barrel Gatling gun capable of firing up to four thousand 30-millimeter shells per minute; F-18 fighter-bombers firing an M-61 Vulcan Gatling gun as well as delivering air-to-ground missiles and rockets; and the huge B-1 bombers with their massive GPS-guided payloads. Beattie used them all, the B-1's in particular. "The sight was awesome. It reminded me of the old footage I had seen from Vietnam, where the US pilots tried to carpet bomb the Vietcong into submission. This was far short of what happened in the 1960s, but gave some insight into the sheer scale of the destructive firepower available to us in Afghanistan."[21]

Within minutes though, Beattie records, the insurgents had returned to the fight with renewed vigor: "The small-arms fire and RPGs [rocket-propelled grenades] being directed towards us had now been joined by mortar rounds . . . the enemy was attacking us from at least three sides."[22] The beleaguered Beattie was reliving another lesson of Vietnam (and, indeed, of so many attacks in modern warfare, be it World War I or the amphibious assaults in the Pacific during World War II)—humongous amounts of high explosive do not always have the desired suppressive effect. The enemy survives, like some backstreet brat tough enough to take his licks and come back to whack the rich kid. Vietnamese insurgent Tran Thi Gung, the only woman in her unit, believed that "the Americans lost many people because they were applying conventional tactics against our ambushes and tunnels. Their shells and bombs were extremely powerful and sometimes they killed people in the tunnels, but it didn't happen as often as you might think. . . . 'A stork can't shit into a bottle.' "[23] Or as S. L. A. Marshall put it, referring to Vietnam (but applicable also to Iraq and Afghanistan): "Elephant guns are used to bang away at rabbits."[24]

★   ★   ★

CONVENTIONAL TROOPS FIGHTING an insurgency war often die because they cannot adapt quickly enough. "It will never cease to amaze me," wrote GI Tom McCabe as he recovered from wounds in a hospital in Vietnam, "how unorthodox this war seems compared to how I imagined it. There are no set lines of battle & it is usually over as fast as it starts."[25] When the unprepared and unsuspecting soldier is transposed to an alien environment, so many things can trip him into the grave. This was especially true in Vietnam, where the US Army was largely composed of draftees (the Marine Corps, in contrast, would only accept volunteers). In Iraq and Afghanistan, where the challenges, both tactical and cultural, were equally great, the troops were professionals by choice, with, one presumes, their military compass needle pointing north.

The tour of duty for most US Army infantrymen in Vietnam was one year. As the war progressed, draftees accounted for a higher proportion of the soldiery, and not surprisingly, their risk of being killed early in their tours was significant. The Army lost 43 percent of all its killed in actions in the first three months of their service; the Marines lost 33.8 percent. American combat troops were twice as likely to be killed in the first half of their tour as in the second.[26] For FNGs (fucking new guys), like FNGs in every war, the learning curve could be tragically steep.

A vet recalls after the war trying to warn a "kid named Donald who wasn't in-country even three months" that he should keep his head down and eyes open because snipers were active.

> Donald took his time and was laughing. . . . Donald sits up facing away from the outside of the perimeter. As I was telling him to keep his eyes open, all of a sudden there's this pow!
> The bullet went through Donald's upper shoulder [and] came out his chest. . . . When it hit the kid he didn't die

right away. His guts were hanging out his mouth and his nose. He like coughed them up when he was shot. . . . I didn't really have a chance to be working with him, to teach him how to stay alive, because by the time he came, we was on the run constantly. He didn't learn how to do what you told him instantly, when he was told to do it.

He looked at me and all I could see were the tears in his eyes. It was like he was saying, "I'm alive, but what do I do? I'm dying."

I debated whether I should put a bullet in his head and take him out of his misery. For some reason I couldn't do it. I looked at him, he was a young kid. He was seventeen.[27]

Some vets, however, felt anything but protective toward FNGs, as the filmmaker Oliver Stone remembers:

I was totally anonymous, just a guy who didn't talk too much and tried to learn things as fast as I could. They [the vets] didn't know your fucking first name. . . . I tried not to get too noticed. Just did my job and shut up. Don't get picked on. I was pretty good at that because some of the other new guys were really irritating to them and believe me, when you were a new guy they would kill you. They don't really care about you, because you're an FNG. They'd put you up on point all the time. If you don't know what you're doing you're dead. And if they really wanted to fuck with you, they'd put you on an LP [listening post]. which is as spooky as hell because you're only two people outside the perimeter.[28]

There were so many things to learn. In themselves they seemed trivial, but the trivial could get a newbie killed. Karl Marlantes, in his fine Vietnam War novel *Matterhorn* (2010), which is richly informed by his own combat experience, describes the preparations for combat of a newly minted junior officer:

> He carefully bloused his trousers against his boots with the steel springs to keep the leeches out and stuck a plastic bottle of insect repellent into the wide rubber band circling his new green camouflage helmet. . . .
>
> Jancowitz grinned at Mellas. "Sir, I'd, uh . . ." He hesitated and then tapped the side of his soft camouflage bush cover.
>
> Mellas looked at Hamilton. "The insect repellent," Hamilton said. "The white stands out in the bush. Makes a great target."
>
> "Then, what's the rubber band for?" Mellas asked, shoving the bottle into his pocket.
>
> "Beats me, sir," Hamilton answered. "Holds the fucking helmet together, I guess."[29]

Even at the other end of the learning curve, death could still squirm its way in through the cracks and chinks. David Hackworth, one of the most highly decorated field commanders of the Vietnam War, noted the numerous ways complacency got even experienced men killed: "Many combat vets come to think they know it all and start taking shortcuts. They blow off the basics and neglect the little things that keep them alive because they get cocky or think it's better for their men's morale. They build a fire at dusk, smoke at night, walk on trails, don't carry their weapons, wear mosquito repellent on ambush or patrol, don't send out flank security on ops. Shortcuts that get you killed."[30]

Fatigue and the craving for some kind of relief were both seductive and deadly. Larry Fontana found that the quest for creature comforts over safe discomfort was a dangerous game to play. The gooks would booby-trap heavily traveled areas. If an old abandoned hooch was next to a roadway that is patrolled daily, stay away! If it isn't booby-trapped, it should be. . . . Shortly before I left to go home, I was ordered to build a bunker for a team of medics. . . . I have to admit, [we] built a hell of a bunker for these guys. . . . Near the bunker was a small, wood-framed building with a corrugated roof on it. It was used to house supplies. After dark, the gooks fired a recoilless rifle into the firebase. The shell hit the roof of the building and made a mess of the inside. . . . Part of the mess were 2 dead medics who were sleeping on cots in the building. I guess they didn't care to sleep on the dirt floor of a fortified bunker. They died for their quest for comfort in a hostile environment. To this day, I still feel no remorse for these men.[31]

And, if according to the adage that war comprises long stretches of tedium punctuated by moments of sheer terror, those long stretches of boredom could prove fatal. Joel Turnipseed describes how men adjusted to being hit by Scud missiles in Saudi Arabia during the 1991 Persian Gulf War:

Being bombed is boring. It was thrilling, at first, to have the Scuds start falling: when the sky flashed and the desert rumbled: when I and the other frightened Marines scattered like roaches from our tents, wearing nothing but gas masks and dog-tags and underwear. . . . By the second or third night of the war, the thrill of being awakened two or three or four times turned to something more like annoyance. . . . You're tired. You've heard sirens all night long. So do you get up and run? No, you light a cigarette. . . . After a couple of weeks of this I didn't even bother to get out of my cot. . . . When the alarms for that fourth SCUD started whirling, half the Pound ignored it.

The bomb exploded right overhead, and the concussive effect of the explosion knocked the wind out of us. Through some pure adrenaline-charged order from our animal brain, we sped out to the shelter. . . .

Hatch turned on American Forces Radio to hear the news. There was no mention of our attack, just the tragic report from the Khobar barracks, where twenty-eight Army soldiers were killed by an Iraqi Scud and a hundred more wounded. . . . Why didn't they run for their bunkers? Maybe because they didn't have time. Or maybe because war is boring. Bombing is tedious. And during war's long drag, we all exhaust our inner resources.[32]

★ ★ ★

ALL WARS ARE different, but those against insurgents share some critical strategic/tactical characteristics that determine the ways in which soldiers will die. A primary factor is the need of occupying forces to seek refuge in strongholds as some respite from the dangers of Indian country. But insurgencies cannot be suppressed from the comparative safety of compounds. The "bad guys" have to be hunted and destroyed, and the occupiers have to stick their necks out and sometimes their heads get chopped off.

Back during the American Revolution, Lord Cornwallis chafed at the constraints imposed by a reliance on what were, in more modern parlance, "firebases": "One maxim appears to me to be absolutely necessary for the safe and honourable conduct of this war," he wrote to his boss, General Sir Henry Clinton, on May 26, 1781, "which is, that we should have as few posts as possible."[33] It was Cornwallis's determination to strike out from the British firebase posts and hunt down his bad guys that led directly, and ironically, to the last post of all—the Saigon of the Revolutionary War—Yorktown.

It might be doubted that if Captain Doug Beattie in Afghanistan in 2006 had Lord Cornwallis in mind, but he echoes the sentiment: "We had a presence Helmand-wide but our tactical bases were in the centre of towns and villages like Gereshk, Sangin and Now Zad. Movement beyond them was not easy; in fact it was downright dangerous. We had toeholds in these semi-urban centres but little or no influence beyond them. In effect these troops were prisoners in their own fortresses."[34]

In Vietnam, Iraq, and Afghanistan, forays were fraught, deadly, and frustrating. Tobias Wolff's classic Vietnam memoir, *In Pharaoh's Army* (1994), gives a vivid idea of the lethality of that exposure, which apart from some technological changes was eerily reminiscent of what whittled away at Cornwallis in the Carolinas or, for that matter, the US Army in the Indian Wars of the nineteenth century:

> The enemy were local guerrillas organized in tight, village-based cadres. Occasionally they combined for an attack on one of our compounds or to ambush a convoy of trucks or boats, or even a large unit isolated in the field and grown sloppy from long periods without contact, but most of the time they worked in small teams and stayed out of sight. They blew us up with homemade mines fashioned from dud howitzer shells, or real American mines bought from our South Vietnamese allies. They dropped mortars on us at night . . . to kill a man or two, or inflict some wounds. . . . Then they hightailed it home before our fire-direction people could vector in on them, slipped into bed, and, as I imagined, laughed themselves to sleep. They booby-trapped our trucks and jeeps. They booby-trapped the trails they knew we'd take, because we always took the same trails, the ones

that looked easy and kept us dry. They sniped at us. And every so often, when they felt called on to prove they were sincere guerrillas and not just farmers acting tough, they crowded a road with animals or children and shot the sentimentalists who stopped.

We did not die by the hundreds in pitched battles. We died a man at a time, at a pace almost casual. You could sometimes begin to feel safe, and then you caught yourself and looked around, and you saw that of the people you'd known at the beginning of your tour a number were dead . . . And you did some nervous arithmetic.[35]

Once "in-country," the occupying soldier was exposed to a whole range of deadly weaponry, but one of the most lethal, whether it be in Vietnam, Iraq, or Afghanistan, was some version of a mine. In Vietnam about 18,500 soldiers were killed by gunshot, while some 16,000 were killed by multiple-fragment wounds caused by mines, booby traps, and "other explosive devices."[36] In 1966 alone, mines and booby traps killed more than 1,000 American soldiers, representing about 25 percent of all combat deaths that year.[37] In Iraq and Afghanistan, improvised explosive devices (IEDs) were the single-greatest cause of coalition deaths. In Afghanistan, for example, IED fatalities in 2009 accounted for over 61 percent of all coalition KIAs.[38]

The same pattern of fatalities was experienced by the Soviet army during its invasion of Afghanistan (1979–89). In the course of the whole war, the Soviets had 14,450 men die from all causes, plus another 53,700 wounded. In the early years the majority of Soviet KIAs were caused by small arms, but as time went on, shrapnel and blast casualties (mainly from mines) accounted for 2.5 times more than those caused by bullets, peaking in 1981–82 at 800 for that year; these figures dropped thereafter as anti-IED measures such as reinforcing vehicles, wearing flak jackets, and riding on the tops of armored vehicles took effect. By 1984 the Soviets were losing only 100 men a year to IEDs.[39]

Captain Francis J. West Jr. spent the spring and early summer of 1966 with the Ninth Marines in South Vietnam. The patchwork quilt of paddies and hedgerows around Hill 55 (where two battalions of French infantry had been wiped out in the French Indochina war) was particularly deadly. Of the Marines, West records, "The enemy they hated, the enemy they feared the most, the enemy they found hardest to combat, was not the VC; it was mines. One company of the regiment—Delta—lost ten KIA and fifty-eight WIA in five weeks. Two men were hit by small arms fire, one by a grenade. Mines inflicted all the other casualties."[40] The mines were everywhere: "There seemed to be no pattern to their emplacement," West remembers. "They had been scattered at trail junctions, at the intersection of rice dikes, along fences, under gates. Having watched the movements of Marine patrols in this area, the enemy buried their mines where they anticipated the Marines would walk. Often they scouted the direction and path a patrol was taking and planted the mines ahead. If their patrol passed that point safely, the VC would scurry out of his hiding place, dig up his mine, and keep it for another day."[41]

Some weapons are so brilliantly malevolent that they have bounded enthusiastically from one war to the next. The Bouncing Betty mine, a horror of World War II, was also terribly feared in Vietnam. It was sublimely evil. Dr. Ronald J. Glasser remembers a conversation between Robert Kurt and his doctor, Peterson, in a hospital in Japan:

> Kurt gritted his teeth but kept on talking about a trooper who'd frozen on a pull-release bouncing betty.
> "But why didn't you help him?" Peterson interrupted as he put down his probe.

Kurt looked up at him, obviously offended. "How?" he said flatly.

"Get him off it," Peterson said, as he put on a new dressing of the wound.

Kurt shrugged. "If we could have, we would have. Look," he said seriously, testing his leg, stretching it out a bit on the bed, "it was a bouncing betty booby trap. They're all pull-release: you step off it, and then 'boom,' the lifting charge goes off and throws the explosive charge up into the air."

"Couldn't you have put something on it and let him step off it?"

"Who you gonna get to do it? The detonator's no bigger than a tit, and you don't know how much pressure you need to hold on to it to keep it from going off. Some of them are really unstable. You don't have to step off it to set it off; just shifting your weight can do it. Your foot goes first. You just have to leave them. You have to."[42]

As far as mines and booby traps were concerned, there were things that should never be done; things that got you killed:

Bobby had always told me from when I first met him, "Don't go through an open gate, don't do it." I was hopping over the fence just getting ready to say, "Don't go over the open gate Bob." Man, he hit that fucking gate and a shaped charge blew his ass all over the place. He was just lying there screaming, "I'm going home! I'm going home! I'm going home!"

. . . The corpsman says, "You're God damn right you're going home."

He stayed awake like that. . . . Then he died. . . . He was

always telling me, "Don't walk through no open gate." . . .
Yeah, look who's talking now. Poor fucker.[43]

The Vietcong used frugality to fashion the infernal. The vast
majority of the IEDs were made from the hundreds of tons of
unexploded American ordnance available to them every month.
Ninety percent were antipersonnel devices, some quite crude but
nevertheless fiendishly effective, as Jerry Johnson, walking point
along a trail west of Saigon, discovered.

> They would take two flat pieces of wood and put a stick
> on either end of it to hold them apart from each other. Then
> they would wrap gum foil around it on each side and run two
> wires to that from a battery. When you tramped on that it
> would complete the circuit and the booby trap would explode.
> We had a tank commander killed . . . two days before he left
> for R&R. [He] was walking over a piece of corrugated steel
> that grounded out his tank, and his tank ran over the slapstick
> [mine] and he was standing on an eighty-pound charge. . . .
> You couldn't find [anything] from the waist down. Half his
> face was gone. That explosion was so violent that when he
> came back down there was pieces of him all over everything.[44]

Dan Vandenberg of the Twenty-Fifth Division in Vietnam
describes what it was like to trip a grenade booby trap:

> Soon, we moved, and I walked over a dike. I had gone
> about 30 yards when I felt something around my ankle. I
> knew it wasn't a vine, and I quickly figured out it was a wire.
> You've got approximately 2 or 2½ seconds once the pin is
> pulled on a hand grenade before it goes off. It took about
> 1½ seconds to figure out what I had tripped on, which left

about a second. A lot of people ask me, why didn't you run, why didn't you dive? First of all, you don't know which way to run: You might run right into it; it could be anything from 2 to 4 feet away. Also, you're using part of that second of time to let sink into your head exactly what you've done. My first thought was, "Aw shit, I've blown it now." And for anybody out there wondering what it feels like to have a hand grenade go off at your feet, it's comparable to someone winding up with a baseball bat and rapping you in the face. Your whole body goes numb, it hurts like hell for the first 10 seconds, and after that, you can't move.[45]

About 77 percent of deaths sustained while traveling in armored personnel carriers in Vietnam were caused by IEDs, a percentage that has increased in Iraq and Afghanistan.[46] The explosive power of IEDs intensifies within the confines of a vehicle, as Tobias Wolff witnessed.

We passed through a string of hamlets. . . . I drove fast to get an edge on the snipers, but snipers weren't the problem on this road. Mines were the problem. If I ran over a touch-fused 105[mm] shell it wouldn't make any difference how fast I was going. I'd seen a two-and-a-half-ton truck blown right off the road by one of those, just a few vehicles ahead of me in a convoy coming back from Saigon. The truck jumped like a bucking horse and landed on its side in the ditch. The rest of us stopped and hit the dirt, waiting for an ambush that never came. When we finally got up and looked in the truck there was nobody there, nothing you could think of as a person. The two Vietnamese soldiers inside had been turned to chowder by the blast coming up through the floor of the cab.[47]

A Marine sergeant and his radioman tripped an IED in Vietnam; journalist Charles Anderson saw the result:

> The mine accomplished just about what the Russians who made it and the North Vietnamese who planted it had in mind. The only things left inviolate on those two human bodies and their clothing was the propriety of boots on feet, although the feet were ripped from their legs. The mine mixed trousers with calf muscles and tendons with genitals with intestines with bladders with shit with livers and spleen and kidneys and stomachs, and jammed the oozy mass upward into lungs and throats. Then it burned hands and arms and chests and faces to the texture and appearance of dried prunes. Just like it was supposed to do. What happens to human beings in mechanized warfare has absolutely no poetic or theatrical possibilities.[48]

Mines and booby traps inflict not only grievous physical but also profound psychological damage—inducing Tobias Wolff's "nervous arithmetic." David Hackworth could see the same computation in his men:

> Most 4/39th soldiers knew that each time they took a step they risked the ugliest of wounds. A bullet makes a hole, a chunk of shrapnel may take off an arm—but a mine turns a soldier into a splattered, shrapnel-punctured basket case.
>
> Many troopers in the battalion had concluded that waging war consisted of crossing a field, hitting a mine, calling for a medic, patching up the wounded, getting a medevac; then moving out again and hitting another mine. They also did the math and figured out that not many of them would be lucky enough to make it through the 365 days it took to rotate home.

"The very words 'booby trap' bring back the smell of blood whenever I hear them," recalls Jim Robertson. "The damned things were so numerous, so varied, and Charley was so good at making and concealing them, that the feeling was that if you stayed in the field long enough, you were going to fall victim to a booby trap. It was just a matter of time."

In a firefight, the grunts knew they had a chance to fight back. If you got ambushed and you didn't get hit in the first burst, you could get your licks in. "But with a booby trap," Robertson remembers, "it was BANG, game over. . . . That was the worst—the frustration and the helplessness."[49]

It was, remembers Dan Krehbiel of the Twenty-Fifth Division, "a different nature of war, a war of booby traps, mines, watching where you walk, and having nobody to shoot back at when somebody gets hurt or blown up." It was warfare mostly robbed of satisfying confrontation.

> We walked right into a huge, booby-trapped area. There were no enemy soldiers, no shooting. The guy in front of me stepped into a *punji* pit [a camouflaged pit in which sharpened stakes have been embedded—a throwback to a hunting technique of our ancient ancestors]. . . . At the same time, three ARVN soldiers walked into a white phosphorous artillery booby trap, a big 155mm shell, and it went off and threw white phosphorous all over them and they burned—they just cooked. All three of them died. . . . Then somebody set off a hand grenade behind us that wounded someone. . . . I was all set to put my gun on automatic and wait for something to move in the bushes. I figured we were going to get overrun or something, but that was it.[50]

A soldier in the US Fifth Stryker Brigade in Afghanistan echoes the frustration: "A lot of guys felt gypped. All the other units have these great stories about firefights, then here we are, we're not getting anything. We had to sit there and just wait to get blown up."[51]

Just occasionally the vengeful gods of war (the same capricious old bastards who infest *The Iliad*) nodded off, to the amazement of one Vietnam NCO vet:

> We get on the fucking helicopters and we take off and fly for maybe an hour, and we come in, and everybody does *everything right*. Y'know, that was the funny part about it, it went decent. . . . We jumped off the helicopter, everybody ran to where they're supposed to—and the first fucking thing over the radio came, "BE ADVISED YOU'RE IN A FRENCH MINEFIELD."
>
> And I remember the first thing I said was, "I don't fucking believe you motherfuckers!" So . . . I said to [my radio man], "Pass it on: We're in a minefield." And seventy-two fucking guys get up and ran out of the minefield. I mean everything went so *perfect*, y'know, and I'm standing there, "I don't fucking believe this. . . . Where the fuck yous going?" And they just ran out. And I grabbed the fucking radio man by the fucking harness and awa-a-ay we go. Like, I mean. *I* did it too! We just ran out of a fucking minefield—and nothing went off.
>
> So then, y'know, you're sitting down and the sweat's rolling off of you. It ain't because of the heat. And everybody talking bullshit, you know. *Now* you're invincible. You just ran out of a fucking minefield. . . . We got a shining star with us.[52]

Sweeping roads for IEDs was like playing Russian roulette, except it was not a discretionary divertissement. Lee Reynolds was an APC crewman in Vietnam.

We did a lot of road security. We'd go out looking for signs of the enemy and "bus" the road, which is, in effect, a stupid minesweeper technique of driving down the road and seeing if you can run over a mine and blow something up. We got a lot of people hurt and killed unnecessarily doing that. I remember writing my girlfriend and telling her about that, and she wrote me back . . . if you know the roads are mined, why don't you stay off the roads? It was brutal logic but initially too overpowering for our colonel. One day, one of our tracks [armored personnel carriers] was demolished by a huge mine. Eight of our people were blown to bits. Shreds of their tissue hung from the trees, and birds came to feed on it. After that happened, we stayed off the roads.[53]

Marine lieutenant Donovan Campbell describes the hair-raising procedure of the early morning IED sweep of a main thoroughfare in Ramadi, Iraq:

Because Michigan was such an important transportation artery for all coalition forces in the area keeping it free and clear of IEDs became a high priority for our company, so almost every morning started off with a platoon patrol straight down the highway from the Outpost. . . . The mission seems sound and practicable in theory; even the term, "route sweep," sounds professional, efficient, antiseptic. The reality is anything but—a route sweep is a nasty mission that can only be accomplished by ugly, primitive, and fairly risky methods.

The Army had performed its sweeps by driving down the highway in fully armored Humvees at forty miles per hour, minimum, looking for whatever suspicious objects they could spot at such high speeds while holding their breaths, just waiting to get exploded. By contrast, we performed our route sweeps by walking down Michigan wearing body armor. Like the Army, we also held our breaths, waiting to get exploded. Walking at five miles an hour rather than driving at forty, we stood a much better chance of spotting unusual objects among the trash and other clutter littering the road. Wearing only body armor, though, we also stood a much worse chance of surviving a blast. Even at the slow speed, Marines still rarely spotted well-camouflaged IEDs until we were about thirty to fifty feet away, well within the kill zone.[54]

Some of the most lethal IEDs looked deceptively innocent, about as scary as a can of Coke. But these "explosively formed penetrators" (EFPs)—shaped charges that projected molten metal into the target—were deadly. Sean Michael Flynn, a company commander with the Sixty-Ninth Regiment of the US Army National Guard in Iraq, describes what happened when one of their Humvees was hit by an EFP: "The EFP that insurgents detonated against Lwin and Ali's truck sat just a few feet away from the vehicle in a pile of brush along a narrow center median. The penetrator shot from the can and entered the Humvee behind Lwin, who was driving. The molten steel killed the Burmese American [Lwin] instantly. Ali was sitting in the gun turret facing rearward. When the round exited Lwin it blew off Ali's hindquarters, before sending shards of steel into Sergeant Maiella's chest cavity and head."

Ali bled to death en route to hospital; Maiella survived.[55]

Next to mines and booby traps, probably the most potent weapon in the insurgent arsenal was the RPG—the rocket-propelled grenade launcher that is heir to the bazooka. Being highly portable, relatively cheap to manufacture, and not complicated to operate, it fits the insurgents' bill nicely. The only problem, from an insurgent point of view, is that the operator has to be quite close to the target, which, together with the highly visible back blast, makes him extremely vulnerable to counterfire.

RPG tactics usually follow a fairly consistent pattern. First, the enemy is brought to a halt, perhaps with an IED or some kind of road blockage, and then he is hit with an RPG. Jim Ross was a Twenty-Fifth Division soldier on an armored personnel carrier in Vietnam:

> Being mechanized infantry, our firepower was so superior to a straight leg infantry unit that we didn't think the enemy to be much competition as far as toe-to-toe battle. When we did, the enemy almost always had the opportunity of striking the first blow. That's one of the main disadvantages of mechanized forces. You move around a lot, you make a terrific target, you can be seen from quite a distance, and you can be heard from even a farther distance, so they had ample time to interdict us if they chose to do so. And very often, they could get away with that without paying any price at all. All they would do was simply set up a 2- or 3-man RPG ambush, attack the lead APC or maybe the tail APC and either damage or destroy the track.[56]

Drivers of trucks in Vietnam were particularly vulnerable because the vehicles were powered by 90 gallons of gasoline and, as novelist (*Paco's Story*) and Twenty-Fifth Infantry Division vet Larry Heinemann recalls: "A gallon of gasoline is equal to nineteen pounds of TNT and a gallon of gasoline has enough energy to lift one thousand pounds one thousand feet into the air instantly. Don't fuck with gasoline. You got ninety gallons here and if an RPG hits the bull's-eye you go up like the head of a match. . . . If anything happens, the driver always dies."[57]

★   ★   ★

IF WE LISTEN closely to the voices of the modern battlefield, we can hear quite distinctly the echoes of ancient ones. Under the Kevlar we can still smell the funky reek of ancient warriors that no amount of modern sanitation seems able to wash away, often to our embarrassment, sometimes to our shame.

Modern warriors speak in old tongues and answer to the ancient gods. The joy of rolling in the primal mud can be wonderfully liberating. The presence of death becomes an exhilarating narcotic. Lance Corporal Thomas P. Noonan wrote to his sister on October 17, 1968, from Vietnam: "Please disregard any small note of flippancy that might reveal itself in this letter. I try to avoid it, but when one is having such a good time it is hard not to be cheerful. I've thrown off the shackles of silly society. I've cast out my razor, divorced my soap, buried my manners, signed my socks to a two-year contract, and proved that you don't have to come in out of the rain. I scale the mountains, swim the rivers, soar through the skies in magic carpet helicopters. My advent is attended by Death and I've got chewing gum stuck in my mustache."[58]

Noonan was killed four months later.

The chaos, paradoxically, can offer clarity not to be found in "ordinary" life: "Basically I enjoyed Vietnam. It was the most vivid part of my life. I enjoyed the anarchy of it. You know, self-law. No one ever bothered you. You know what it's like to walk down the road with twelve guys armed to the teeth and anybody who shoots at you is in trouble? You're living every minute, you're with the guys who really look after you. . . . I missed that a lot when I got back to the States. You really appreciate that now when you're getting fucked over all the time dealing with society."[59]

One can hear the great crazed shout of the atavistic gods of war in the voice of a soldier in Iraq:

> At one point, an insurgent spotter appears . . . I see him point us out to his buddies.

Fuck him.

I stand up on a chair, point back, and roar, "I am become Death, the destroyer of worlds" . . . you fuckers![60]

Or this helicopter gunner in Vietnam:

It turned into a turkey shoot. They were defenseless. . . . I was in there with the best of them. Blowing people off the boats, out of the paddies, down from the trees for Chrissake. Blood lust. I can't think of a better way to describe it. Caught up in the moment. I remember thinking this insane thought, that I'm God and retribution is here, now, in the form of my machine gun and the Miniguns that I take care of and the rockets that we are firing. . . . You begin at that point to understand how genocide takes place.[61]

The power of killing in combat—a sanctioned release for our murderousness—is as though some ancient and psychotic genie that we normally keep stoppered in its civilized bottle has been let loose. We can hear the voice from this soldier in Vietnam:

I would take C-ration cans and booby-trap them with pressure release devices. Very small. You put the explosive inside the C-ration can, turn it upside down so it doesn't look like it's been opened. Then you put it on top of a pressure-release device. When somebody picks it up—*whoosh*—it's all over. We used to love to do that.

I have to admit I enjoyed killing. It gave me a great thrill while I was there. . . . There was a certain joy you had in killing, an exhilaration that is hard to explain. After a fight, guys would be really wired. "Wow, man, did you see that guy get it. Holy shit."[62]

It is so easy and thrilling to let the genie out. Just a twitch of the trigger finger. Staff Sergeant David Bellavia exults in a kill in Al Fallujah, Iraq:

> He doesn't notice me. . . . His back is to me. He casually continues to smoke, with his AK strapped over his right shoulder. At first I think I'm hallucinating. Does this jackoff think there are unionized smoke breaks in battle?
>
> My weapon comes up automatically. I don't even think. In the second it takes to set the rifle on burst-fire, my surprise gives way to cold fury. The muzzle makes contact with the back of his head.
>
> *Fuck a zero. I can't miss now.*
>
> My finger twitches twice. Six rounds tear through his skull. His knees collapse together as if I'd just broken both his legs. As he sinks down he makes a snorting, piggish sound. I lower my barrel and trigger another three-round burst into his chest, just to be sure. . . .
>
> His head bobbles back and forth. He snorts again. . . . His face looks like a bloody Halloween mask and I stomp it with my boot until he finally dies.[63]

Bellavia is reenacting one of the oldest forms of combat in which the real killing is done not face-to-face in heroic confrontation but stealthily, in ambush, from behind. Like murder or assassination, which minimizes the risk to the killer, it is stripped of any pretense of nobility. It is an act of execution, bone simple.

Although intimate killing is a relative rarity in modern warfare, Bellavia also found himself engaged in a type of combat at the other extreme of ambushing: the classic mano-a-mano duel that is at the heart of the heroic tradition. But in the filth and chaos of Al Fallujah, the confrontation is stripped down to the horrific tearing and bludgeoning of a lethal brawl. When the heroic mask slips it reveals the snarling, blood-and-sweat-and-snot-smeared face of true combat. And it was always thus:

The wounded Boogeyman stirs. He's flat on his back, but he still holds his AK [47] in one hand.

I step forward and slam the barrel of my rifle down on his head. He grunts and suddenly swings his AK up. Its barrel slams into my jaw and I feel a tooth break. I reel from the blow, but before I can do anything he backhands me with the AK. This time, the wooden handgrip glances off the bridge of my nose. I taste blood.

I back off and wield my M16 like a baseball bat. Then I step back toward him and swing with everything I've got. The front sight post catches him on the side of the head. I wind up to hit him again . . . his leg flies up from the floor and slams into my crotch.

I stagger backward, pain radiating from my groin. . . .

I leap at my enemy. Before he can respond I land right on top of his chest. A rush of air bursts from his mouth. . . .

I beat him with the inside of my armor plate. I smash it against his face again and again and again until blood flows all over the inside of my shirt. He kicks and flails and screams. . . . He kicks and howls, yet he refuses to submit. . . .

"Shut the fuck up!" I bash his face again. Blood flows over my left hand and I lose my grip on his hair. His head snaps back against the floor. In an instant, his fists are pummeling me. I rock from his counterblows. He lands one on my uninjured jaw and the pain nearly blinds me. He connects with my nose, and blood and snot pour down my throat. I spit blood between my teeth and scream with him. The two of us sound like caged dogs locked in a death match. . . .

He opens his mouth under my hand. For a second I think

this is over. He's going to surrender. Then a ripping pain sears through my arm. He clamped his teeth on the side of my thumb near the knuckle, and now he tears at it, trying to pull meat from bone. . . .

My belt. I have a knife on my belt.

. . . I reach for my belt just as he comes up after me. His face rams my crotch. I feel his teeth clamp onto me. . . .

Finally, suddenly, I become a madman.

My arm comes up over my head, then chops down with every bit of power I have left. . . .

I pounce on him. My body splays over his and I drive the knife right under his collarbone. My first thrust hits solid meat. The blade stops, and my hand slips off the handle and slides down the blade, slicing my pinkie finger. I grab the handle again and squeeze it hard. The blade sinks into him, and he wails with terror and pain. . . .

The knife finally nicks an artery. We both hear a soft liquidy spurting sound. . . .

I'm bathed in warmth from neck to chest. . . . His eyes lose their luster. The hate evaporates. His right hand grabs a tuft of my hair. . . . He is feeble. . . .

His eyes show nothing but fear now. He knows he's going to die. His face is inches from mine, and I see him regard me for a split second. At the end, he says, "Please."

"Surrender!" I cry. I'm almost in tears.

"No . . ." he manages weakly.

His face goes slack. His right hand slips from my hair. It hangs in the air for a moment, then with one last spasm of strength, he brings it to my cheek. It lingers there, and as I look into his dying eyes, he caresses the side of my face.[64]

★   ★   ★

THE MUTILATION AND denigration of the enemy dead—something usually associated with ancient and tribal cultures—is another atavistic need from which modern warfare is not exempt: "The Hardcore troopers wore their black metal Recondo arrowhead pins with pride, but as I found out recently the VC sometimes had the misfortune to wear the Recondo pin too. . . . 'We used the Recondo pins to let Charley know we took them out,' a Hardcore platoon sergeant says. 'We hammered them into VC dead bare chests and sometimes their foreheads.' "[65]

When a GI in Vietnam is taught to desecrate enemy bodies, one is reminded of the way hunting animals have their young play-kill on already-dead prey in order to become acquainted and comfortable with killing. There is purpose to the macabre:

> The first patrol we went to where some Marines had ambushed a bunch of Viet Cong. They had me moving dead bodies. VC and NVA. Push this body here . . . Flip a body over. See people's guts and heads half blown off. I was throwing up all over the place.
>
> "Keep doing it. Drag this body over there. . . . You're going to get used to death before you get in a fire fight and get us all killed." . . .
>
> Next, I had to kick one dead body in the side of the head until part of his brain started coming out the other side. . . . "Kick it," they said. "You are starting to feel what it is like to kill. That man is dead, but in your mind you're killing him again. Man, it ain't no big thing. Look-a-here." And they threw some bodies off the cliff and shit.[66]

But it is not only the echo of ancient curses and murderous screams that the modern warrior hears. Occasionally, out of the primeval sludge of combat, someone finds a diamond, perhaps a poor justification for the whole sorry bloody mess but something precious nevertheless.

In the Twelfth Evac of the Twenty-Fifth Division in Vietnam: "We saw men who came in who displayed feelings of love, gentleness, affection, closeness, and behavior we had never seen between two men before. Not in a homosexual way but in a brotherhood way—closer than brotherhood. Men coming in messed up telling us to work on their friends first. Guys concerned about each other. 'See Smitty down there, how's Smitty doing?' Smitty might be fine compared to the guy who's asking, who might be dying. . . . To see two men love each other made me wonder why we can't be like that in the civilized world. Why does that only exist in the war zone?"[67]

Or this, north of Dak To in the Central Highlands of Vietnam, June 8, 1966:

I had a lot of holes in me and was sort of groggy, but I knew damn well that I wasn't going to die. And there were people on the ground that were just a hell of a lot worse off than I was. There was an army sergeant there named Pellum Bryant who really saved us that day. If it hadn't been for him, the whole thing would have been gone in fifteen minutes. By all reckoning we should have been wiped out—the whole platoon should have been killed. But watching him maneuver, I swear to Christ, it was almost like watching a ballet dancer move back and forth. All of us are strung out on this trail, some at the high end, some at the low end, and I'm in the middle with the command post. Bryant is moving back and forth, left and right, firing as he goes. And not firing blindly—firing with purpose.

It was somebody with superb confidence in himself and what he was doing. Just as a great musician must understand the importance of what he is playing, Pellum Bryant must have had an understanding in the back of his mind that his actions were going to save a lot of people. And all the time he was doing this kind of dance, back and forth, he did not speak a single word.

All of this stands totally separate from whether you like the Vietnam War or don't like it. This is not a word I toss around lightly, but it was *inspiring* to see him in the middle of this stupid damn war. Not to get too elaborate, but it approached the vicinity of the spiritual. . . . A few weeks later he was blown up by a mine.[68]

And in a letter left at the Vietnam Veterans Memorial in Washington, DC:

18 November 1989

Dear Sir,

For twenty two years I have carried your picture in my wallet. I was only eighteen years old that day we faced each other on that trail in Chu Lai, Vietnam. Why you did not take my life I'll never know. You stared at me for so long with your AK-47 and yet you did not fire. Forgive me for taking your life, I was reacting just the way I was trained, to kill V.C. or gooks, hell you weren't even considered human, just gook/target, one in the same.

Since that day in 1967 I have grown a great deal and have a great deal of respect for life and other peoples of the world.

So many times over the years I have stared at your picture and your daughter, I suspect. Each time my heart and guts would burn with the pain of guilt. I have two daughters myself now. One is twenty. The other is twenty two, and has blessed me with two granddaughters, ages one and four.

Today I visit the Vietnam Veterans Memorial in D.C. I have wanted to come here for several years now to say goodbye to many of my former comrades.

Somehow I hope and believe they will know I am here, I truly loved many of them as I'm sure you loved many of your former comrades.

As of today we are no longer enemies. I perceive you as a brave soldier defending his homeland. Above all else, I can respect that importance that that life held for you. I suppose that is why I am here today.

As I leave here today I leave your picture and this letter. It is time for me to continue the life process and release my pain and guilt. Forgive me Sir, I shall try to live my life to the fullest, an opportunity that you and many others were denied.

I'll sign off now Sir, so until we chance to meet again in another time and place, rest in peace.

Respectfully,
101st Airborne Div. Richard A. Luttrell[69]

APPENDIX

FOR PITY'S SAKE

A Brief History of Battlefield Medicine

If you have two wounded soldiers, one with a gunshot wound of the lung, and the other with an arm or a leg blown off, you save the sonofabitch with the lung wound and let the goddamn sonofabitch with an amputated arm or leg go to hell. He is no goddam use to us anymore.

—A medic remembering advice given by General George S. Patton Jr.[1]

Were it not so tragic there would be something comical in the way man invents machines to kill and injure, then uses his ingenuity to provide methods of repairing damages caused by his own destructive genius.

—Mabel Boardman, Red Cross historian, 1915[2]

*I*T IS A peculiar thing, this juggling between our relentlessly destructive inventiveness and our redemptive determination to fight against the dark side. Our technological and logistical genius, so brilliant at the harming, can also put back together what we have undone. We kill and we save, reveling in both.

In the ancient world any kind of serious wound would almost inevitably lead to the soldier's death. There was no way to control this inexorable mortality. Little was known of the mechanisms and chemistry of the body—how the torn could be repaired, or the insidious workings of infection. Only the kindness of comrades, the limited effectiveness of herbal medicines, and above all, the fervent appeals to the gods, put up a fragile barrier between the doomed and the saved. Most were doomed.

This doleful state of affairs persisted pretty much until the Enlightenment of the eighteenth century began the process of putting less emphasis on appeals to the deities and more on scientific inquiry and medical organization. During the American War of Independence, for example, about a quarter of all patriot soldiers admitted to hospital died.[3] In the Civil War it dropped to around 14 percent,[4] but by the First World War the American soldier's chances of surviving hospitalization for wounds had increased dramatically: Slightly over 6 percent were lost; in World War II, 4.5 percent; in Korea, 2.5 percent, and in Vietnam, 1.8 percent.[5] What accounts for such a dramatic improvement? Several factors had to come together, each making a massive individual contribution but not a decisive one, until they acted in concert. They were the organization of medical services, the control of infection, blood transfusion, surgical procedures, and anesthetics.

Medical services, no matter how crude or sophisticated, have first to be delivered to the wounded soldier. For this to happen, there must be some kind of organization. Whether it is the provision of first responders working at the front line of combat, a system of more permanent hospitals with specialist medical staff, or simply the fundamental—and massively important—issue of transportation, there has to be the will and the wherewithal to create a medical organization.

In the ancient Greek world, care of the wounded was primarily the responsibility of comrades-in-arms, who in most instances were obligated by the tribal and familial bonds on which the army was built. Nothing much could be done other than the most basic remedial care of wounds: washing and binding, some anesthetizing with wine, and perhaps the use of natural soporifics and analgesics. The outcome was in the hands of the gods.

Imperial Rome brought its bureaucratic genius to the salvage work of the battlefield. Taxes were levied to finance the army. Permanent military medical personnel worked in the thick of combat. Specialist wound surgeons (*medici vulnerarii*) and a sophisticated system of hospitals (each military camp had its *valetudenarium*) tended to the wounded with a surprising awareness of the need for cleanliness to inhibit infection. Organizationally, the Roman soldier was afforded a level of care that would not be emulated until the nineteenth century.

A casualty of the dissolution of the Roman Empire's brilliant bureaucracy was organized care for wounded and sick soldiers. (Pestilence was the greater killer for most of history. Not until the Franco-Prussian War of 1870–71 did battle deaths outnumber those dying from disease.) In the medieval West there was hardly any provision for the care of ordinary combat troops. Nobles were attended by their retinue, which might include a physician, but even so, their life expectancy from any kind of serious wound would have been on the short side. A historian of medieval epics has reconstructed the ministrations given to a badly wounded knight:

> We see the wounded knight laid upon the ground, his wounds examined, washed and bandaged, often with a wimple from a woman's forehead; the various practices of giving a stimulating wound-drink to relieve faintness, of pouring oil or wine into wounds, of stanching hemorrhage

or relieving pain by sundry herbs, of wound-sucking to prevent internal hemorrhage; the mumbling of charms over wounds; the many balsams, salves and plasters used in wound-dressing; the feeling of the pulse in the cephalic, median and hepatic veins to ascertain the patient's chances of recovery; the danger of suffocation or heat-stroke from the heavy visored helmet and coat of mail; the eventual transportation of the patient by hand, on shield or litters, on horseback or on litters attached to horses; the sumptuous chambers and couches reserved for the high-born, and the calling in of physicians, usually from the famous schools of Palermo or Montpellier in grave cases.[6]

For the ordinary soldier there is little evidence that the armies of the Middle Ages had any effective organization to deal with casualties.

It was not until the mid-eighteenth century that Western nations established institutionalized medical care for their armies or, indeed, for their civilian populations. The first permanent civilian hospital in America, for example, was established in Philadelphia in 1751 and the second in New York twenty years later. Military hospitals, including the fairly general provision of mobile field hospitals to accompany the army on campaign, did not guarantee effective treatment for a number of reasons: inadequate facilities, low-grade staff (in the British Army, for example, there was no army medical school until 1858),[7] lack of ambulances, and a general ignorance (by no means limited to military hospitals) of the principles of hygiene. Although two great military "hospitals" (Les Invalides in Paris, founded in 1676, and the Royal Hospital Chelsea, London, 1682) were established, they were not hospitals in the sense of treating the full range of combat wounded, but more like rest homes for a select number of wounded or aged ex-soldiers. The problem was the inadequacy and scarcity (often nonexistence) of hospitals proximate to the fighting.

All too often, those field hospitals that did follow the army on campaign were as much a threat to the soldier's life as the enemy. The American doctor James Tilton, a pioneer of rational hospital design, viewed the field hospitals servicing the patriot army during the American War of Independence as lethal, where more men "were lost by death and otherwise wasted, at general hospitals, than by all other contingencies that have hitherto affected the army, not excepting the weapons of the enemy."[8] It is probably true that before the twentieth century, fragile medical facilities for soldiers on campaign were overwhelmed by any serious battle. A famous example, in relatively modern history, was the Crimean War (1854–56)—catastrophic even by the laissez-faire standards of the time. George Munro, an officer with the Ninety-Third Sutherland Highlanders, remembered:

> We had a large number of regimental medical officers, but no regimental hospitals, and there were no field hospitals, with proper staff of attendants. We had no ambulance with trained bearers to remove the wounded from the battle-field, and no supplies of nourishment for sick or wounded.
>
> On landing in the Crimea, the regimental hospital was represented by one bell tent, and the medical and surgical equipment by a pair of panniers containing a few medicines, a small supply of dressings, a tin or two of beef-tea, and a little brandy. . . .
>
> The instruments were the private property of the surgeon, paid for out of his own pocket, as one of the conditions attached to promotion. The only means of carrying sick or wounded men consisted of hand-stretchers, entrusted to the [members of the regimental] band.[9]

At the beginning of the American Civil War, care for the wounded was entirely inadequate. At the outset the Union Medical Department consisted of a grand total of 98 officers. The early battles were a disaster on the medical front. At the first battle of Bull Run (Manassas, July 21, 1861) the Union wounded were abandoned, and just over a year later at second Bull Run, many of the wounded were left on the field for three days. The provision of field hospitals during the Peninsular campaign was lamentable. After the battle of Fair Oaks (Seven Pines, May 31, 1862) the Union field hospital had 5 surgeons and no nurses to treat 4,500 casualties.[10] By the end of the war, however, the Union had the most sophisticated mobile military hospital and ambulance system in the world—and one that served pretty much as the organizational model for US battlefield medical care until the Vietnam War. This was due in large measure to the organizational genius of Dr. Jonathan Letterman, medical director of the Army of the Potomac, and William A. Hammond, who was appointed surgeon general in 1862. An illustration of the effectiveness of the Union medical system was that during Grant's bloody campaign through Virginia in the later phase of the war, of the 52,156 gunshot casualties from March 1864 through April 1865, only 2,011 died from their wounds, a 3.2 percent mortality rate compared with the 10–25 percent rate for the period from July 1861 to March 1864.[11]

An organizational element of fundamental importance—transporting the wounded—was, until the late eighteenth century, either nonexistent or so cruelly jarring that it did more to kill men than save them. Improvements in either ambulance services that got the wounded soldier to a medical facility or, conversely, delivered medical services to the soldier in the field have been massively important in increasing casualty survival. All too often the wounded were simply left on the field, helped off by their comrades, or thrown into carts—or they crawled off as best they could.

Although the Austrians had some "flying ambulances" in the 1750s, it was not until the Napoleonic Wars that Napoleon's surgeon general of the Imperial Guard, Dominique-Jean Larrey, emphasized the overwhelming importance of treating traumatically wounded men as soon after their wounding as possible, rather than waiting until the battle was over. The light field ambulances (*ambulances volontes*) he devised did two things: They not only got soldiers off the field and to a surgeon as quickly as possible, but they also delivered medical teams to men while the combat still raged—a model of battlefield medicine on which all modern practice is predicated. Nor did Larrey merely preach the doctrine of fast response. His own actions on the battlefield were inspirationally courageous. At Eylau (1807) he had become so involved in the combat zone that he had to be rescued by a cavalry detachment of the Imperial Guard, and at Waterloo he worked so close to the front line that Wellington recognized him and ordered his gunners to direct their fire elsewhere.[12] In addition, Larrey refused to prioritize treatment on the basis of rank and social distinction, as had been the norm for centuries. The most grievously hurt were dealt with first, which has become the moral basis of triage in all modern military medicine.

Apart from the establishment of a system of divisional field hospitals, ambulance services gave the Union supremacy in battlefield medicine in the later half of the Civil War. In the beginning, though, it was dire. At the first and second battles of Bull Run (Manassas), civilian teamsters hired to drive wagons simply skedaddled (at first Bull Run not one Union casualty reached a hospital by ambulance). On the peninsula an army corps of thirty thousand had ambulance transportation for precisely one hundred men. At Shiloh (April 1862) and Perryville (October 1862) the ambulance service was shambolic. Letterman's reforms of 1862 created a retrieval system that proved itself at Fredericksburg in 1862 and at Gettysburg in 1863, where there were one thousand ambulances and three thousand ambulance drivers and stretcher men.[13]

In the First World War the average time it took to get a wounded US soldier from first responder to definitive care was ten to eighteen hours. In World War II it dropped to six to twelve hours; in Korea, four to six hours; and in Vietnam, one to two hours (although it could be as short as forty minutes).[14] As comforting as these ever speedier responses might seem (and in general they do reflect recovery systems of dramatically increasing effectiveness), it depended very much on where the wounded soldier was fighting. For example, within the tight perimeter of, say, Guadalcanal, a wounded US Marine could be extracted and delivered to a hospital ship in two hours. On the other hand, on Papua New Guinea the wounded had to be hand-carried down the Kokoda Trail for many hours, even days. In North Africa in 1942–43 "a wounded man could spend a day in a motor ambulance or a day and a night on a train reaching treatment."[15] Yet it was in those areas where evacuation was most difficult that air transportation of casualties was pioneered (the first helicopter evacuation, for example, was on April 23, 1944, in Burma).[16] By the end of the war, 212,000 US wounded had been evacuated by air.[17]

★   ★   ★

BEFORE A CASUALTY can be mended by medical intervention, he must not be killed by medical intervention. It was not until the middle of the nineteenth century that such pioneers as Joseph Lister and William Detmold made the scientific link between uncleanliness, bacteria, and infection. Although there had been some understanding that uncleanliness and infection were linked (essentially that the wounded soldier should be treated in "clean" surroundings if possible), there were two problems. First, wartime circumstances often meant that soldiers were operated on under horrifically unhygienic conditions. Second, there was little understanding of how infection was transmitted. So doctors explored wounds with filthy hands and probes, swabbed wounds with sea sponges rinsed out in already contaminated water, irrigated wounds with unsterilized water, licked the silk sutures before threading them through unsterilized needles, wiped bloody instruments on dirty rags, and so on. General Carl Schurz described the scene after Gettysburg: "There stood the surgeons, their sleeves rolled up to the elbows, their bare arms as well as their linen aprons smeared with blood, their knives not seldom held between their teeth, while they were helping a patient on or off the table, or had their hands otherwise occupied; around them pools of blood and amputated arms or legs in heaps, sometimes more than man-high. Antiseptic methods were still unknown at the time. As a wounded man was lifted on the table . . . the surgeon snatched his knife from between his teeth, . . . wiped it rapidly once or twice across his blood-stained apron, and the cutting began."[18]

Gangrene, pyemia, tetanus, erysipelas, osteomyelitis, all blossomed. A Civil War surgeon describes losing a patient to pyemia after surgery:

Many a time have I had the following experience: A poor fellow whose leg or arm I had amputated a few days before would be getting on as well as we then expected—that is to say, he had pain, high fever, was thirsty and restless, but was gradually improving, for he had what we looked on as a favorable symptom—an abundant discharge of pus from his wound. Suddenly, overnight, I would find that his fever had become markedly greater; his tongue dry, his pain and restlessness increased; sleep had deserted his eyelids, his cheeks were flushed; and on removing the dressings I would find the secretions from the wound dried up, and what there were were watery, thin, and foul smelling, and what union of the flaps had taken place had melted away. Pyemia was the verdict, and death the usual result within a few days.[19]

Pyemia had a 98 percent mortality rate. In 1863 William Detmold made a connection between pyemia and puerperal fever—the great killer of women immediately following child-birth—and the connection was the doctor's unclean hands and instruments. Like Lister he recommended thorough hygiene (Lister prescribed washing with carbolic acid), but "there is no evidence that Detmold's precepts were followed."[20] Tetanus, with a death rate of 89 percent, thrived in the manure-rich battlefields of the Civil War and World War I. Stables were often the location of field hospitals in the Civil War and were nurturing environments for *Clostridium tetani*. Erysipelas, a streptococcal infection, was also introduced into wounds by dirty instruments, dressings, and hands. Infected soldiers had a 41 percent chance of dying.[21]

Gangrene killed about 46 percent of its victims. [22] This example happens to be from the notorious Andersonville POW camp in Georgia during the American Civil War but was probably representative of many military hospitals of the period: "Our patients have been crowded together on the same ground with other patients suffering from the various diseases incident to the prisoners, and in very many instances in the same tent, or even on the same bed. Again, we have only one wash pan to the tent, . . . and owing to the great scarcity of bandages we are compelled to use the same bandages several times, and in washing they not unfrequently [*sic*] get changed, and thus the disease may be transmitted from one patient to the other by actual contact."[23] This was the remorseless timetable for one Union soldier:

J. Mailer, aged twenty-four years, admitted August 5, with large sphacelus [dead tissue] covering the whole arm up to within two and a half inches of the shoulder joint. The arm was very much tumefied [swollen], and presented around the border of the large sphacelus a kind of erysipelatous inflammation. This inflamed surface was covered with green and yellow spots; these in turn opened and discharged filthy and very offensive sanies [ulcers]. The pulse beat 120 to the minute, was weak, and had a peculiar vibratory thrill. Tongue dry and glazed, very red at the tip and edges. Bowels a little loose, but not amounting to diarrhea. Appetite weak. Urine scant and highly colored; complained of considerable pain in the affected arm and shoulder; had copious night-sweats; complained of chilliness of mornings and fever in the afternoon. . . . Apply pure nitric acid to the sphacelus, envelope the whole arm in pulverized lini poultices [made from crushed flaxseed].

[August] 6th: Patient no better; is very anxious to have the arm amputated; gangrene extending. Pulse 125 in the morning, 137 in the evening. . . . continued prescription.

[August] 7th: Gangrene still extending above the elbow; presents a pea-green appearance, and emits an intolerable odor. . . . Bowels painful; has mucous discharges. Appetite weak. . . .

[August] 8th: This morning the gangrene has extended into the shoulder joint and half way to the hand. Pulse 140 . . . Has dysentery. Prescription continued about turpentine emulsion. In this condition the patient remained up to the 10th, at which time he began to sink, and as we could do nothing more we continued with the same treatment up to the 14th, at which time the patient died, with the whole arm in a state of sphacelus.[24]

Occasionally, and paradoxically, foul conditions saved men with gangrene. Confederate surgeons who were POWs at the Union stockade at Chattanooga were denied medical supplies, and many men's wounds were left exposed to flies, which inevitably resulted in the wounds becoming infested with maggots. The received wisdom was, not unnaturally, that everything should be done to clean the wound (often with injections of chloroform), but in the case of the maggot-ridden Confederates, their doctors were amazed to discover that because maggots eat only necrotic tissue, they performed a vital scavenging role, and that the recovery rate was better than for those soldiers with conventionally cleaned wounds. It was a lesson relearned during World War I and led to the breeding of maggots specifically for treating osteomyelitis.[25] The discovery of sulfonamide antibiotics in the 1930s and penicillin, first used for battle casualties in 1943, temporarily halted their use but more recently they have made something of a comeback and wound debridement with maggots is now an accepted treatment.

Before the age of asepsis, antibiotics, anesthesia, and blood transfusion, military surgeons were caught between the devil and the deep blue sea. In order to prevent severe injuries to limbs from becoming gangrenous, amputation was widely considered prudent. However, the nonsterile conditions of the operation introduced its own risks: of infection, of fatal hemorrhage (often days after, when the wound had "sloughed," that is, become infected), and the shock to the patient, all of which made amputation extremely hazardous. After the battle of Waterloo, 70 percent of amputees died, and during the Crimean War, 63 percent.[26] Even though the German and French armies had embraced Lister's antiseptic prescriptions with much more enthusiasm than did either the British or American military medical establishments, the losses to amputation during the Franco-Prussian War of 1870–71 were shocking. Georg Friedrich Louis Stromeyer, the most important surgeon in the

Prussian army, lost all of the 36 soldiers whose legs he had amputated. Of the 13,173 amputations (ranging from relatively minor operations to fingers up to major ones to limbs) undertaken by the French, 10,006 (76 percent) died of subsequent infection.[27] During the American Civil War, Union surgeons performed about 30,000 amputations. Of soldiers who had leg amputations, 40 percent died, compared with 12 percent of those who lost arms.[28] For soldiers who had fingers amputated, the death rate was 3 percent; for those who had legs taken off at the hip, it was over 83 percent.[29]

Speed was of the essence if the patient was to stand a chance of surviving amputation. In his *Memoir on Amputations*, Larrey reported that prior to his insistence on dealing with the severely wounded as quickly as possible, there was a 90 percent mortality rate. After his reforms (and his own skill—after Borodino he personally performed two hundred amputations), Larrey could boast that "more than three-fourths have recovered after our amputations, some of whom even lost two limbs."[30]

★   ★   ★

ALTHOUGH ANESTHETICS SUCH as opium, henbane, Indian hemp, mandragora (mandrake), and, of course, alcohol have been used for millennia, it was not until the first half of the nineteenth century that synthetic anesthesia was more or less generally available to the severely wounded soldier (and even then, many had to withstand terrible ordeals, such as amputation, without its benefit). Ether was first used in 1842 in dental surgery and for an amputation in 1846. Chloroform (preferred over ether because it is not as combustible anywhere near a naked flame) became popular and trusted when it was administered to Queen Victoria during her eighth and her ninth (and final) childbirths.

Although chloroform also had attendant dangers—a deep inhalation might overdose and paralyze the heart muscle—most soldiers facing the excruciating rigors of amputation would have accepted the risk in the blink of an eye. At the battle of Missionary Ridge on November 25, 1863, a young Confederate soldier, Albert Jernigan, was badly wounded in his right arm and after some days of tormented wandering ended up in a military hospital. He desperately wanted to save his arm, but

> when the Board of Surgeons consisting of six members met in consultation over my arm, their decision was soon rendered, which was my arm must come off. I had begun to entertain a hope that it might possibly be saved by the performance of what is termed a "resection," that is to split the arm open, take out the fractured bone. . . . This I stated to the Board. But they objected, said it would not do. . . . I told them that if they were ready, they might proceed with the amputation.
>
> They took what is called a bonnet, but shaped more like a funnel, lined inside with raw cotton which was saturated with chloroform, placed it over my nose and mouth, as I lay upon my back, while one of the surgeons stood by holding my hand and feeling my pulse. I soon lost all consciousness of pain. I was perfectly happy. A feeling of indescribable bliss, ecstasy, felicity, or I know not how to describe it, came over me, then all consciousness of being or existence passed from me. I was totally oblivious. I awoke without knowing where or what I was. I opened my eyes. One of the surgeons spoke to me. A thrill as if an electrical shock ran through my frame. I was myself again. My arm was gone.[31]

Alcohol was used liberally as an anesthetic, but some soldiers displayed a breathtaking sangfroid without it. Joseph Townsend, an American Quaker, observed surgeons working on the British wounded after the battle of Brandywine during the American

War of Independence: "I was disposed to see an operation performed by one of the surgeons, who was preparing to amputate a limb by having a brass clamp or screw [Petit's tourniquet, invented in 1718, revolutionized amputations by controlling arterial bleeding] fitted thereon a little above the knee joint. He had his knife in his hand . . . when he recollected that it might be necessary for the wounded man to take something to support him during the operation. He mentioned to some of his attendants to give him a little wine or brandy . . . to which [the patient] replied, 'No, doctor, it is not necessary, my spirits are up enough without it.' "[32]

The invention of the hypodermic syringe in 1853 by Charles Gabriel Pravaz meant that morphine could now be injected as a fast-acting solution, and the discovery of barbiturates in Germany in 1903 led to intravenously delivered anesthetics.

★   ★   ★

EXSANGUINATION MAY SOUND like an arcane rite of the Catholic Church, but it remains the leading killer of soldiers. Loss of blood leads to shock and shock to terminal collapse of the circulatory system. It comes as no surprise that most soldiers who died from their wounds in the pretransfusion era (that is, before World War II) bled to death. But it gives something of a jolt to learn that, according to the US Army Medical Department, hemorrhage is the leading cause of death on the battlefield in modern warfare (over 50 percent) and that "although some soldiers killed on the battlefield are clearly unsalvageable [an interesting if industrial choice of word] and become KIA within minutes of impact . . . it appears that approximately one-third of KIA would be salvageable with the development and fielding of new methods for early intervention."[33] Once a severely bleeding soldier gets to a modern field hospital, his chances of survival are very good indeed, but this was not so for a soldier of, say, the American Civil War, where over 60 percent died. To save lives, transfusion has to be swift, and the efforts of modern battlefield medicine are focused on getting to the wounded soldier as soon after impact as possible.

Unless blood loss can be replaced, the soldier will die of shock. A British medical officer, Captain Gordon R. Ward, discovered at the end of World War I that replacement with the fluid part of blood, plasma (blood minus the red cells), could restore blood pressure and maintain the basic function of the circulatory system. The wounded would need full blood eventually (either by natural regeneration or transfusion) because it is red blood cells that deliver oxygen to tissue, but as an interim intervention, plasma transfusion revolutionized battlefield medicine. The technique of drying plasma was developed between the world wars, which meant that it could be stored for up to five years and was also easily delivered to the combat zone, where it was mixed with distilled water prior to intravenous injection. By 1943 plasma transfusion was widely available. On Tarawa (November 1943), for example, there were 1,000 plasma transfusions each day, with the average patient receiving 1,200 cubic centimeters. Of the 2,519 American wounded, only 2.7 percent died.

Plasma was important as a stopgap, but exsanguinated soldiers who had plasma transfusions could not withstand the rigors of transportation to rear areas for further medical attention because, starved of oxygen delivered by red blood cells, they were far too fragile. They needed whole-blood transfusion, and as close to the fighting as it could be delivered: "Plasma and albumin work wonders on wounded," a combat medic writes, "but whole blood is life itself."[34] From 1943 on there were important advances not only in the collection of blood by Red Cross blood banks but also in preserving it by refrigeration. By war's end about 388,000 pints of blood had been shipped overseas from America alone.[35]

Larrey's principles of speedy rescue of wounded soldiers as well as immediate battle-line ministration remain as applicable today as they did two hundred years ago. The modern army has developed highly mobile medical units that can deploy sophisticated facilities close to combat. These forward surgical teams (FSTs), complete with operating tables, ultrasound machines, computerized diagnostics for blood electrolyte count, X-ray machines, and the whole paraphernalia of an intensive care unit, can be operational close to the front line in sixty minutes. In addition, there is a range of devices that might prevent a wounded soldier from bleeding to death: one-handed tourniquets that a wounded soldier can self-administer as well as hemostatic dressings containing the clotting agents fibrogen and thrombin. However, deep intracavity and noncompressible wounds have always been, and are still, intransigent killers of soldiers. Hemostatic foams injected into the cavity to stop bleeding (think fire extinguisher) as well as drugs that would seal the bleeds may one day be successful on the battlefield. But there are problems. The coagulant foams do not distribute themselves within the cavity and reach the centers of bleeding. They also have to fight against the flow of blood that washes them away.

Blood is hard to stanch.

ACKNOWLEDGMENTS

All of us have stood on others' shoulders in order to see just a little farther. (Through no fault of theirs, although we may see farther we do not necessarily understand what we're seeing.) To recognize these debts in no way implies that those who are acknowledged would agree with this book in whole or in detail. Nor is it, by some suggestion of affinity, a sneaky co-opting of their genius. Although there are so many to whom a great obligation is owed, the journey of this book could not have happened without certain powerful beacon lights to guide by. Like most people working in this field, I owe a great debt to Sir John Keegan for his brilliant brand of deductive history, illuminating the big picture by the light of the particular. Richard Holmes (who died far too young) has been an inspiration; an enthusiast and scholar whose erudition was always irrigated by a wonderful sympathy and a generous heart. Paul Fussell is a historian and memoirist from a liberal tradition that has been on the defensive since the end of the Vietnam War. He confronts and confounds the flag-wavers and war-boosters with a deeply humane skepticism about the heroics of combat. He learned the truth about the appalling messiness of battle the hard way, as a young infantry officer in Europe in World War II. I would guess that Victor Davis Hanson is not of the same political persuasion as Paul Fussell but he also powerfully evokes the gut-torn truth of combat, particularly ancient combat, and writes with an intellectual muscularity and audacious sweep that makes one think twice about getting in the same ring. Paddy Griffith is also a military historian, like John Keegan, who focuses on the specifics of combat and tenaciously follows those leads in order to understand what really happens in battle. Always challenging, his work attacks the clogging sediment of received wisdom.

And then there are the memoirists without whom none of this material would have voice, or form, or flesh. It's a peculiar irony, isn't it, that the writing about death has to be *alive*. And just to highlight the two world wars, writers such as Graves, Sassoon, Blunden, Coppard, Dunn, Barbusse, Jünger, and Cendrars in the first; Manchester, Sajer, Gantter, Leckie, Bowlby, Fussell, Sledge, Fraser, Verney, Mowat, Litwak, and Douglas in the second, have become companions for whom I feel a deep affection and admiration.

★   ★   ★

Although I alone am responsible for any errors in this book, it could not have been written or published without:

Alex Hoyt for finding a publishing home for *The Last Full Measure* and helping me get started as a writer of military history, and Michael Carlisle for his generosity and support. Julian Pavia, my editor at Crown, shepherded the book through the publishing process with impressive intelligence and tact. On more than one occasion his steady head prevented me from losing mine. Margaret Wimberger copyedited the manuscript with great diligence, Chuck Thompson and Chris Fortunato brought a much-appreciated knowledge of military history to reading the proofs. They saved me from the kinds of bloopers that if not caught and corrected will wake you with a sickening jolt in the middle of the night. (And any that may remain are entirely my responsibility.) The designers Song Hee Kim (interior) and Chris Brand (jacket) have my thanks for making a handsome book. I was fortunate in benefitting from the services of two researchers—Phil White in the US and Chad Henshaw in the UK—who took to death and destruction with quite remarkable enthusiasm. I was very lucky indeed to have a historian at West Point, Lieutenant-Colonel Gregory A. Daddis, critique the book in manuscript. His comments were perceptive and extremely helpful. My friends Joan Goodman and Keith Goldsmith gave me books that otherwise I would have missed, and my friend John Peterson, a Vietnam vet and a historian of dazzling, not to say daunting, depth and breadth, let me pick his brain on many an occasion. My brother Paul allowed himself to be dragged around more battlefields, military cemeteries, and monuments than I think he would have wished. But he did it all with good grace, for which I'm always grateful. My wife, Kathryn Court, showed more patience during my all-too-frequent periods of gloomy misgiving and other deeply irritating bouts of bad behavior than I had any right to deserve.

Finally, I want to acknowledge two gallant men, father and son, who share a windswept family graveyard atop a hill overlooking beautiful Parnham House just outside Beaminster, Dorset, England, which once was their home. The father, William Bernard Rhodes-Moorhouse VC, a pilot in the Royal Flying Corps, was killed on May 22, 1915, in an action that won him a Victoria Cross (the first ever to be awarded to an airman). The son, "Willie" H. Rhodes-Moorhouse DFC, was only one year old when his father died. Shortly after winning the Distinguished Flying Cross, he too would be killed in action (September 6, 1940) as a Hurricane pilot during the Battle of Britain. His ashes were scattered over his father's grave. When I first discovered that high and austere place many years ago the need to write this book was born.

NOTES

PREFACE

1. Quoted in Victor Davis Hanson, *Carnage and Culture: Landmark Battles in the Rise of Western Power* (New York: Doubleday, 2001).

CHAPTER ONE

1. Ibid., 60.
2. Lawrence H. Keeley, "Giving War a Chance," in *Deadly Landscapes: Case Studies in Prehistoric Southwestern Warfare,* eds. Glen E. Rice and Steven A. Leblanc (Salt Lake City: University of Utah Press, 2001), 332.
3. John Keegan, *A History of Warfare* (London: Hutchinson, 1993), 387.
4. Robert L. O'Connell, *Of Arms and Men: A History of War, Weapons, and Aggression* (New York: Oxford University Press, 1989), 25.
5. Lawrence H. Keeley, *War Before Civilization: The Myth of the Peaceful Savage* (Oxford: Oxford University Press, 1996), 94.
6. Ibid., 91.
7. Keith F. Otterbein, *How War Began* (College Station: Texas A&M University Press, 2004), 3, 62.
8. Ibid., 40.
9. Jean Guilane and Jean Zammit, *The Origins of War: Violence in Prehistory* (London: Blackwell, 2005), 25, 73.
10. Otterbein, *How War Began,* 50.
11. Ibid., 56.
12. Ibid., 64.
13. Ibid.
14. Keeley, *War Before Civilization,* 49.
15. Ibid.
16. Ibid., 53.
17. Barbara Ehrenreich, *Blood Rites: Origins and History of the Passions of War* (New York: Henry Holt, 1997), 67.

18. Keeley, *War Before Civilization*, 105.

19. Ibid.

20. Otterbein, *How War Began*, 195.

21. Keeley, *War Before Civilization*, 84. Of the approximately 230 tribal groups that Keeley studied throughout the world he found only 8 "that sometimes spared male adult captives for any reason" (213).

22. Guilane and Zammit, *Origins of War*, 88.

23. Keeley, *War Before Civilization*, 99.

24. Ibid., 101.

25. Otterbein, *How War Began*, 161.

26. Quoted in Keeley, *War Before Civilization*, 100.

27. Ibid., 143.

28. Stephen Turnbull, *The Samurai: A Military History* (Oxford: George Philip [Osprey], 1977), 10.

29. O'Connell, *Of Arms and Men*, 33.

30. J. E. Lendon, *Soldiers & Ghosts: A History of Battle in Classical Antiquity* (New Haven, CT: Yale University Press, 2005), 29.

31. Guilane and Zammit, *Origins of War*, 215.

32. Lendon, *Soldiers & Ghosts*, 56.

33. Ibid., 44.

34. Ibid., 83.

35. J. F. C. Fuller, *Armament & History: The Influence of Armament on History from the Dawn of Classical Warfare to the End of the Second World War* (New York: Charles Scribner's Sons, 1945), 24.

36. Lendon, *Soldiers & Ghosts*, 29.

37. Bernard Mishkin, *Rank & Warfare Among the Plains Indians* (Omaha: University of Nebraska Press, 1992), 31.

38. Robert Fagles, trans. *The Iliad* (New York: Viking Penguin, 1990), 551.

39. Ibid., 423–24.

40. Ibid., 425–26.

41. Ibid., 554.

42. Lendon, *Soldiers & Ghosts*, 46.

43. Ibid., 52.

44. H. Frölich, *Die Militärmedicin Homer's* (Stuttgart: Enke, 1879).

45. K. B. Saunders, "Frölich's Table of Homeric Wounds," *Classical Quarterly* 54, no. 1 (2004): 1–17.

46. R. Drews, *The End of the Bronze Age: Changes in Warfare and the Catastrophe, c. 1200 BC* (Princeton, NJ: Princeton University Press, 1993).

47. Fagles, ed., *Iliad*, 426.

48. Ibid., 195.

49. Victor Davis Hanson, *The Western Way of War: Infantry Battle in Classical Greece* (New York, Alred A. Knopf, 1989), 213.

50. Fagles, *Iliad*, 423.

51. Ibid.

52. Ibid.

53. Lendon, *Soldiers & Ghosts*, 41.
54. Hanson, *Western Way of War*, 224.
55. Estimating the weight of ancient armor is just that—estimating. What bronze armor has been excavated is so badly corroded as to make calculations of weight extremely difficult. Jack Coggins in his *Soldiers and Warriors: The Fighting Man; An Illustrated History of the World's Greatest Fighting Forces* (Doubleday, 1966), 19, goes into this in thoughtful detail, and I have tended to use his calculations. Some historians, for example, O'Connell in *Of Arms and Men* and Hanson in *Western Way of War*, favor much heavier weights. O'Connell puts the cuirass alone at 30 pounds (13.6 kg), while Hanson ups it to between 30 and 40 pounds (13.6–18 kg).
56. O'Connell, *Of Arms and Men*, 36, puts the hoplite helmet at 20 pounds (9 kg), which seems excessive, but G. B. Grundy, cited in Hanson, *Western Way of War*, 49, actually wore an excavated helmet of this period and says: "I have tried on a Greek helmet at Delphi, and I have also tried on various helmets of genuine armour dating from various periods in the Middle Ages. The iron of the Greek helmet was extraordinary thick, and its weight was, I should say, nearly double that of the heaviest helmet of the medieval period." Hanson finally plumps for five pounds (2.3 kg), 72.
57. Hanson, *Western Way of War*, 78.
58. Ibid., 79.
59. Ibid.
60. Coggins, *Soldiers and Warriors*, 20.
61. Hanson disagrees. He states that the panoply was disablingly heavy (*Western Way of War*, 78).
62. Ibid., 45.
63. Quoted in Lendon, *Soldiers & Ghosts*, 50.
64. Ibid., 140.
65. Fuller, *Armament & History*, 26.
66. Quoted in ibid., 153.
67. Quoted in ibid., 154.
68. Quoted in Hanson, *Western Way of War*, 91.
69. Cited in ibid., 87.
70. Coggins, *Soldiers and Warriors*, 20.
71. Lendon, *Soldiers & Ghosts*, 186.
72. Quoted in Fuller, *Armament and History*, 25.
73. Hanson, *Western Way of War*, 209.
74. Ibid., 203.
75. Ibid., 201.
76. Quoted in ibid., 124.
77. Quoted in ibid., 203.
78. Lendon, *Soldiers & Ghosts*, 108.
79. Ibid., 152.
80. Hanson, *Carnage and Culture*, 74.
81. Ibid., 77.

82. Ibid., 35.
83. Lendon, *Soldiers & Ghosts*, 136.
84. Hanson, *Carnage and Culture*, 88.
85. Lendon, *Soldiers & Ghosts*, 118.
86. Hanson, *Carnage and Culture*, 88.
87. Ibid., 83, Hanson goes for the higher figure and states that Alexander "killed more Hellenes in a single day than the entire number that had fallen to the Medes at the battles of Marathon, Thermopylae, Salamis, and Plataea combined!"
88. Ibid. For example, Dr. Albert Devine puts the figure for Persian losses at 15,000, including wounded and captured. General Sir John Hackett, ed., *Warfare in the Ancient World* (London: Sidgwick & Jackson, 1989), 116.
89. Quoted in Coggins, *Soldiers and Warriors*, 50. The physics of the *pilum* seems a little contradictory. On the one hand the weapon must have enough straight-on kinetic force and structural integrity to pierce a shield, yet the long iron shank had to be pliable enough to bend when embedded. The penetration could only be achieved if all the force was directly behind the spearhead (and perhaps this was the function of the iron knob at the base of the shank on some *pila*). Any deviation in flight and the shank would have bent prematurely on impact and dispersed the kinetic energy uselessly.
90. Quoted in O'Connell, *Of Arms and Men*, 68.
91. Quoted in Coggins, *Soldiers and Warriors*, 71.
92. Adrian Goldsworthy, *Roman Warfare* (London: Cassell, 2000), 52.
93. Ibid., 54.
94. For example, Hanson estimates 50,000 (*Carnage and Culture*, 104); Polybius puts it at 70,000; Livy at 45,500.
95. Hanson, *Carnage and Culture*, 103.
96. Ibid., 110.
97. John Warry, *Warfare in the Classical World* (Norman: University of Oklahoma Press, 1995), 156.

CHAPTER TWO

1. Bryan Perrett, *The Battle Book* (London: Arms and Armour Press, 1992), 101.
2. Stephen Turnbull, *The Samurai Sourcebook* (London: Arms and Armour, 1998), 150.
3. Quoted in Stephen Turnbull, *The Samurai: A Military History* (Oxford: George Philip [Osprey], 1977), 34.
4. Quoted in Morris Bishop, *The Penguin Book of the Middle Ages* (London: Penguin, 1971).
5. David Nicolle, *Medieval Warfare Source Book*, vol. 2, *Christian Europe and Its Neighbours* (London: Arms and Armour, 1996), 158.
6. Ibid.

7. Matthew Bennett et al., *Fighting Techniques of the Medieval World, AD 500–AD 1500: Equipment, Combat Skills, and Tactics* (New York: St. Martin's, 2005), 33.

8. Hanson, *Carnage and Culture,* 157.

9. Bennett et al., *Fighting Techniques,* 35.

10. Quoted in Robert Hardy, *Longbow: A Social and Military History* (Somerset, UK: Patrick Stephens, 1976), 51.

11. "Battle of Duplin Moor," Battlefield Trust, http://www .battlefieldtrust.com/resource-centre/medieval/battleview. Hardy puts English knights and men-at-arms at 33 killed.

12. Quoted in John Keegan, ed., *The Book of War* (New York: Viking Penguin, 1999), 49.

13. Quoted in ibid., 59.

14. Bert S. Hall, *Weapons and Warfare in Renaissance Europe* (Baltimore: Johns Hopkins University Press, 1997), 15.

15. David Nicolle, *Medieval Warfare Source Book,* vol. 1, *Warfare in Western Christendom* (London: Arms and Armour, 1995), 246.

16. Turnbull, *Samurai,* 45.

17. Jack Coggins, *Soldiers and Warriors: The Fighting Man: An Illustrated History of the World's Greatest Fighting Forces* (New York: Doubleday, 1966), 90.

18. Quoted in ibid., 89.

19. Maurice Keen, *The Pelican History of Medieval Europe* (London: Penguin, 1968), 121.

20. Nicolle, *Medieval Warfare Source Book,* vol. 2, 109; and Eduard Wagner et al., *Medieval Costume, Armour and Weapons* (Mineola, NY: Dover, 2000), plates 26–35.

21. A. V. B. Norman and Don Pottinger, *A History of War and Weapons* (New York: Crowell, 1966), 126.

22. Ewart Oakeshott, *A Knight and His Weapons* (Chester Springs, PA: Dufour, 1964), 49.

23. Quoted in Turnbull, *Samurai Sourcebook,* 205.

24. Norman and Pottinger, *War and Weapons,* 160.

25. Quoted in Philip Haythornthwaite, *The English Civil War, 1642–1651: An Illustrated Military History* (London: Brockhampton, 1998), 48.

26. Ibid., 49.

27. Oska Ratti and Adele Westbrook, *Secrets of the Samurai: The Martial Arts in Feudal Japan* (Boston: Charles E. Tuttle, 1973), 189.

28. Turnbull, *Samurai Sourcebook,* 178.

29. "Arms & Armour," Regia Anglorum, http://www.regia.org/warfare/ sword.htm.

30. Oakeshott, *Knight and His Weapons,* 61.

31. Hardy, *Longbow,* 72.

32. Bennett et al., *Fighting Techniques,* 28.

33. Ewart Oakeshott, *A Knight in Battle* (Chester Springs, PA: Dufour, 1971), 36.

34. Nicolle, *Medieval Warfare Source Book,* vol. 2, 244.

35. R. C. Smail, *Crusading Warfare, 1097–1193* (Cambridge University Press, 1956), 127.

36. Nicolle, *Medieval Warfare Source Book,* vol. 2, 295.

37. Hall, *Weapons and Warfare,* 41, 44.

CHAPTER THREE

1. At the beginning of its war of liberation, America struggled to acquire significant quantities of saltpeter from the British-controlled West Indies. Figuring out how to manufacture enough domestically was a priority that John Adams, for one, felt acutely. To James Warren in October 1775, he writes: "We must bend our attention to salt petre. We must make it. While Britain is Mistress of the Sea and has so much influence with foreign courts we cannot depend upon a supply from abroad. It is certain it can be made here. . . . A gentleman in Maryland made some last June from tobacco house earth . . . the process is so simple a child can make it." Quoted in Henry Steele Commager and Richard B. Morris, eds., *The Spirit of 'Seventy-Six: The Story of the Revolution as Told by Participants* (Harper, 1958), 776. When George Washington discovered, at the war's outset, how little powder was in store, Brigadier General John Sullivan recorded that "he did not utter a word for half an hour." Erna Risch, *Supplying Washington's Army* (Washington, DC: US Army Center of Military History, 1981), 341.

2. Bert S. Hall, *Weapons and Warfare in Renaissance Europe* (Baltimore: Johns Hopkins University Press, 1977), 76.

3. Ibid., 75–76.

4. Quoted in ibid., 67.

5. Ibid.

6. Ibid., 101.

7. Victor Davis Hanson, *Carnage and Culture: Landmark Battles in the Rise of Western Power* (New York: Anchor, 2002).

8. Stephen Turnbull, *The Samurai Sourcebook* (London: Arms and Armour, 1998), 227.

9. Quoted in Hall, *Weapons and Warfare,* 183.

10. Quoted in ibid., 199.

11. Quoted in Christopher Duffy, *The Military Experience in the Age of Reason* (London: Routledge and Kegan Paul, 1987), 222.

12. Quoted in W. H. Fitchett, *Wellington's Men* (London: Smith, Elder, 1900), 363.

13. Quoted in Duffy, *Military Experience,* 116.

14. John Keegan, *The Face of Battle* (London: Jonathan Cape, 1976), 123.

15. Quoted in Fitchett, *Wellington's Men,* 134.

16. Quoted in Duffy, *Military Experience,* 257.

17. Donald R. Morris, *The Washing of the Spears: The Rise and Fall of the Zulu Nation* (New York: Simon & Schuster, 1965), 571.
18. Duffy, *Military Experience,* 224.
19. Quoted in Fitchett, *Wellington's Men,* 380.
20. Quoted in Rory Muir, *Tactics and the Experience of Battle in the Age of Napoleon* (New Haven, CT: Yale University Press, 1998), 124.
21. Quoted in ibid., 125.
22. Quoted in Duffy, *Military Experience,* 226.
23. Quoted in Commager and Morris, *The Spirit of Seventy-Six,* 1111–12.
24. Quoted in John Keegan, *The Face of Battle,* 124.
25. Philip Haythornthwaite, *The English Civil War* (London: Brockhampton, 1998), 30.
26. Arcadi Gluckman, *United States Muskets, Rifles, and Carbines* (Harrisburg, PA: Stackpole, 1959), 33.
27. Richard Holmes, *Redcoat: The British Soldier in the Age of Horse and Musket* (New York: Norton, 2001), 195.
28. Hall, *Weapons and Warfare,* 135.
29. Charles Knowles Bolton, *The Private Soldier Under Washington* (New York: Charles Scribner's Sons, 1902), 115.
30. Gunther E. Rothenberg, *The Art of Warfare in the Age of Napoleon* (London: Batsford, 1977), 64.
31. Quoted in David Hackett Fischer, *Washington's Crossing* (Oxford: Oxford University Press, 2004), 305.
32. Quoted in ibid., 65.
33. Hall, *Weapons and Warfare,* 140.
34. Gluckman, *United States Muskets,* 37.
35. Rothenberg, *Art of Warfare,* 65.
36. Hall, *Weapons and Warfare,* 139.
37. Rothenberg, *Art of Warfare,* 65. Paddy Griffith, in *Forward into Battle: Fighting Tactics from Waterloo to the Near Future* (Novato, CA: Presidio, 1997), 38, claims 800 rounds per casualty.
38. Quoted in David Chandler, *The Art of Warfare in the Age of Marlborough* (London: Batsford, 1976), 131.
39. Griffith, *Forward into Battle,* 28.
40. Major General B. P. Hughes, *Firepower: Weapons Effectiveness on the Battlefield, 1630–1850* (London: Arms and Armour, 1974), 165.
41. John J. Gallagher, *The Battle of Brooklyn, 1776* (Cambridge, Mass.: De Capo, 1995), 130.
42. Muir, *Tactics,* 102.
43. Ibid., 165.
44. Captain Mercer, quoted in Fitchett, *Wellington's Men,* 370.
45. Muir, *Tactics,* 135.
46. Quoted in Jay Luvaas, ed. and trans., *Frederick the Great on the Art of War* (New York: Free Press, 1966), 78.
47. Quoted in Duffy, *Military Experience,* 246.
48. Hall, *Weapons and Warfare,* 136.

49. Duffy, *Military Experience,* 247.
50. Quoted in Fitchett, *Wellington's Men,* 158.
51. Quoted in Holmes, *Redcoat,* 254.
52. Quoted in Hall, *Weapons and Warfare,* 207.
53. Quoted in Griffith, *Forward into Battle,* 25.
54. Quoted in Duffy, *Military Experience,* 205.
55. Howard H. Peckham, *The Toll of Independence: Engagements & Battle Casualties of the American Revolution* (Chicago: University of Chicago Press, 1974), 41, 62.
56. Quoted in Duffy, *Military Experience,* 86.
57. Lt. Col. Dave Grossman, *On Killing: The Psychological Cost of Learning to Kill in War and Society* (Boston: Back Bay, 1995), 123.
58. Quoted in Earl J. Hess, *The Union Soldier in Battle: Enduring the Ordeal of Combat* (Lawrence: University Press of Kansas, 1997), 51.
59. Quoted in Gallagher, *Battle of Brooklyn,* 119.
60. John Rhodehamel, ed., *The American Revolution: Writings from the War of Independence* (New York: Library of America, 2001), 269.
61. Quoted in Duffy, *Military Experience,* 234.
62. Quoted in ibid., 217.
63. Quoted in Fitchett, *Wellington's Men,* 386.
64. James Thatcher, *Military Journal of the American Revolution, 1775–1783* (Corner House Historical, 1998), 284.
65. Hall, *Weapons and Warfare,* 152.
66. Anonymous, *Memoirs of a Sergeant: The 43rd Light Infantry During the Peninsular War* (Stroud, UK: Nonsuch, 2005), 60.
67. Joseph Plumb Martin, *A Narrative of a Revolutionary Soldier* (New York: Signet, 2001), 206.
68. George F. Scheer and Hugh F. Rankin, *Rebels & Redcoats: The American Revolution Through the Eyes of Those Who Fought and Lived It* (Cleveland, OH: World, 1957), 56.
69. Quoted in Fitchett, *Wellington's Men,* 95.
70. Quoted in Commager and Morris, *The Spirit of Seventy-Six,* 1105.
71. Quoted in ibid., 387.
72. Haythornthwaite, *English Civil War,* 53.
73. Quoted in Muir, *Tactics,* 47.
74. Duffy, *Military Experience,* 245; and Muir, *Tactics,* 46.
75. Muir, *Tactics,* 46–47.
76. Philip Haythornthwaite, *Weapons & Equipment of the Napoleonic Wars* (London: Arms and Armour, 1979), 67.
77. Quoted in Griffith, *Forward into Battle,* 31.
78. Quoted in Duffy, *Military Experience,* 76.
79. Quoted in Robert L. O'Connell, *Of Arms and Men: A History of War, Weapons, and Aggression* (Oxford: Oxford University Press, 1996), 118–19.
80. Quoted in Muir, *Tactics,* 262.
81. Quoted in Commager and Morris, *The Spirit of Seventy-Six,* 1233.
82. Quoted in Fitchett, *Wellington's Men,* 388–89.

83. Haythornthwaite, *English Civil War*, 121.
84. Quoted in Rhodehamel, *American Revolution*, 607.
85. Cardinal John Henry Newman in *The Idea of a University* (1852), quoted in Gary Mead, *The Good Soldier: The Biography of Douglas Haig* (London: Atlantic, 2007), 41.
86. Quoted in Muir, *Tactics*, 219.
87. Quoted in Duffy, *Military Experience*, 219.
88. Quoted in Muir, *Tactics*, 191.
89. Philip Haythornthwaite, *The Armies of Wellington* (London: Arms and Armour, 1994), picture caption between 224 and 225.
90. Quoted in Muir, *Tactics*, 66.
91. Quoted in ibid., 178.
92. Quoted in Duffy, *Military Experience*, 220.
93. Richard Holmes, *Acts of War: The Behavior of Men in Battle* (New York: Free Press, 1985), 348.
94. Quoted in Muir, *Tactics*, 221.
95. Quoted in ibid., and Fitchett, *Wellington's Men*, 159.
96. Quoted in Fitchett, *Wellington's Men*, 163.
97. George Robert Gleig, *The Subaltern: A Chronicle of the Peninsular War* (1825; repr., Leo Cooper/Pen and Sword, 2001), 114.
98. Sylvia R. Frey, *The British Soldier in America: A Social History of Military Life in the Revolutionary Period* (Austin: University of Texas Press, 1981), 135.
99. Quoted in John W. Shy, "Hearts and Minds: The Case of 'Long Bill Scott,'" in *Major Problems in the Era of the American Revolution, 1760–1791*, ed. Richard D. Brown (Lexington, MA: D. C. Heath, 1992), 209.
100. Quoted in Duffy, *Military Experience*, 171.
101. Quoted in Holmes, *Redcoat*, 164.
102. Quoted in Fitchett, *Wellington's Men*, 98.
103. Quoted in ibid., 91.
104. Luvaas, *Frederick the Great*, 77.
105. John C. Dann, ed., *The Revolution Remembered: Eyewitness Accounts of the War of Independence* (Chicago: University of Chicago Press, 1980), 183.
106. Quoted in Fitchett, *Wellington's Men*, 146.
107. Martin, *Narrative*, 143.

CHAPTER FOUR

1. Drew Gilpin Faust, *This Republic of Suffering: Death and the American Civil War* (New York: Knopf, 2008), 253.
2. Ambrose Bierce, "The Coup de Grâce," in *Tales of Soldiers and Civilians and Other Stories* (New York: Penguin, 2000), 57.
3. Faust, *Republic of Suffering*, 252.
4. Ibid., 256.

5. George Worthington Adams, *Doctors in Blue: The Medical History of the Union Army in the Civil War* (Baton Rouge: Louisiana State University Press, 1996), 194.

6. Faust, *Republic of Suffering*, 3.

7. William F. Fox, *Regimental Losses in the American Civil War, 1861–1865* (Albany, 1889) Reprint, Gulf Breeze, FL: eBooksonDisk.com, 2002, 24. See also Faust, *Republic of Suffering*, 255, and Gerald F. Linderman, *Embattled Courage: The Experience of Combat in the American Civil War* (New York: Free Press, 1987), 115.

8. Adams, *Doctors in Blue*, 3.

9. Faust, *Republic of Suffering*, 3, 147.

10. Thomas L. Livermore, *Numbers & Losses in the Civil War in America, 1861–65* (Bloomington: Indiana University Press, 1957), 6.

11. Faust, *Republic of Suffering*, 260.

12. Fox, *Regimental Losses*, 46.

13. Faust, *Republic of Suffering*, 47.

14. Paddy Griffith, *Battle Tactics of the Civil War* (New Haven, CT: Yale University Press, 1989), 174.

15. Fox, *Regimental Losses*, 27.

16. Richard Moe, *The Last Full Measure: The Life and Death of the First Minnesota Volunteers* (St. Paul: Minnesota Historical Society Press, 1993), 275.

17. Linderman, *Embattled Courage*, 62.

18. Griffith, *Battle Tactics*, 174.

19. Fox, *Regimental Losses*, 27.

20. Grady McWhiney and Perry D. Jamieson, *Attack and Die: Civil War Military Tactics and the Southern Heritage* (Tuscaloosa: University of Alabama Press, 1982).

21. Quoted in ibid., 108.

22. Brent Nosworthy, *The Bloody Crucible of Courage: Fighting Methods and Combat Experience of the Civil War* (New York: Carroll and Graf, 2003), 186. Also see Brent Nosworthy, *Roll Call to Destiny: The Soldier's Eye View of Civil War Battles* (New York: Basic Books, 2008), 25.

23. Griffith, *Battle Tactics*, 80.

24. Jack Coggins, *Arms and Equipment of the Civil War* (Garden City, NY: Doubleday, 1962), 38.

25. Ibid., 38–39.

26. Ibid., 39.

27. For example, see Nosworthy, *Bloody Crucible*, 588.

28. Fox, *Regimental Losses*, 62.

29. Griffith, *Battle Tactics*, 87.

30. Quoted in Rod Gragg, *Covered with Glory: The 26th North Carolina Infantry at the Battle of Gettysburg* (New York: HarperCollins, 2000), 120.

31. Quoted in Earl J. Hess, *The Union Soldier in Battle: Enduring the Ordeal of Combat* (Lawrence: University Press of Kansas, 1997), 80.
32. Ibid., 74.
33. Paddy Griffith, *Forward into Battle: Fighting Tactics from Waterloo to the Near Future* (Novato, CA: Presidio, 1981), 78.
34. Hess, *Union Soldier*, 84.
35. Coggins, *Arms and Equipment*, 32.
36. Quoted in Nosworthy, *Bloody Crucible*, 616–17.
37. Quoted in Griffith, *Battle Tactics*, 142.
38. Henry Steele Commager, ed., *The Blue and the Gray: The Story of the Civil War as Told by Participants* (Indianapolis: Bobbs-Merrill, 1950), 355–56.
39. Griffith, *Battle Tactics*, 110.
40. Quoted in Hess, *Union Soldier*, 94.
41. Quoted in Coggins, *Arms and Equipment*, 29.
42. Quoted in Commager, *Blue and the Gray*, 306.
43. Quoted in ibid., 367.
44. Quoted in McWhiney and Jamieson, *Attack and Die*, 45.
45. Quoted in Commager, *Blue and the Gray*, 306.
46. Don Congdon, ed., *Combat: The Civil War* (New York: Mallard Press, 1967), 239.
47. Cited in Nosworthy, *Bloody Crucible*, 583.
48. Quoted in ibid., 579.
49. Quoted in ibid., 578.
50. John W. Busey and David C. Martin, *Regimental Strengths and Losses of Gettysburg* (Hightstown, NJ: Longstreet House, 1986), 238, 280.
51. "The Regimental Hospital," Shotgun's Home of the American Civil War, http://www.civilwarhome.com/regimentalhospital.htm.
52. David J. Eicher, *The Longest Night: A Military History of the Civil War* (New York: Simon & Schuster, 2001), 791.
53. "Regimental Hospital."
54. Cited in Eicher, *Longest Night*, 790.
55. Quoted in Hess, *Union Soldier*, 29.
56. Quoted in ibid., 28.
57. Quoted in Linderman, *Embattled Courage*, 138.
58. Quoted in ibid., 139.
59. Griffith, *Battle Tactics*, 155.
60. Quoted in Eicher, *Longest Night*, 100.
61. Both quoted in Hess, *Union Soldier*, 26.
62. Griffith, *Battle Tactics*, 171.
63. Nosworthy, *Bloody Crucible*, 435.
64. Coggins, *Arms and Equipment*, 76–77.
65. Quoted in Commager, *Blue and the Gray*, 636.
66. Quoted in Gragg, *Covered with Glory*, 174.
67. Quoted in ibid., 632.
68. Quoted in Eicher, *Longest Night*, 146.

69. Quoted in McWhiney and Jamieson, *Attack and Die,* 115.
70. Livermore, *Numbers & Losses,* 69–70.
71. Linderman, *Embattled Courage,* 15.
72. Quoted in McWhiney and Jamieson, *Attack and Die,* 171.
73. Quoted in ibid., 172.
74. Fox, *Regimental Losses,* 38.
75. McWhiney and Jamieson, *Attack and Die,* 14.
76. Eicher, *Longest Night,* 774–75.
77. Ibid., 571.
78. McWhiney and Jamieson, *Attack and Die,* 189.
79. Linderman, *Embattled Courage,* 142.
80. Quoted in Commager, *Blue and the Gray,* 363.
81. Quoted in ibid., 46.
82. Cited in Linderman, *Embattled Courage,* 46.
83. Quoted in ibid., 24–25.
84. Quoted in Eicher, *Longest Night,* 678.
85. Quoted in Linderman, *Embattled Courage,* 27.
86. Bell Irvin Wiley, *The Life of Billy Yank: The Common Soldier of the Union* (Baton Rouge: Louisiana State University Press, 1952), 81.
87. Quoted in Linderman, *Embattled Courage,* 206.
88. Quoted in ibid., 207.
89. Ulysses S. Grant, *Personal Memoirs* (1885; repr., New York: Penguin, 1999), 285.
90. Quoted in Linderman, *Embattled Courage,* 178.
91. Quoted in ibid., 178.
92. Quoted in ibid.
93. Quoted in ibid., 203.
94. Quoted in ibid.
95. Quoted in Hess, *Union Soldier,* 8.
96. Quoted in Linderman, *Embattled Courage,* 124.
97. Quoted in ibid., 128.
98. Quoted in Hess, *Union Soldier,* 140.
99. Quoted in Eicher, *Longest Night,* 488.
100. Quoted in Linderman, *Embattled Courage,* 65.
101. Quoted in Faust, *Republic of Suffering,* 20.
102. Quoted in Linderman, *Embattled Courage,* 101.
103. Quoted in Faust, *Republic of Suffering,* 59.
104. Quoted in Reid Mitchell, *Civil War Soldiers: Their Expectations and Their Experiences* (New York: Viking, 1988), 64.
105. Quoted in Wiley, *Billy Yank,* 79.
106. Quoted in Linderman, *Embattled Courage,* 244.
107. Quoted in ibid., 254.
108. Quoted in ibid., 217.
109. Bell Irvin Wiley, *The Life of Johnny Reb: The Common Soldier of the Confederacy* (Baton Rouge: Louisiana State University Press, 1970), 88.
110. Quoted in Hess, *Union Soldier,* 24.
111. Quoted in Commager, *Blue and the Gray,* 307.

112. Quoted in Hess, *Union Soldier,* 93.
113. Quoted in ibid., 149.
114. Quoted in Faust, *Republic of Suffering,* 36–37.
115. Cited in ibid., 45.
116. Mitchell, *Civil War Soldiers,* 193.
117. Quoted in Linderman, *Embattled Courage,* 237.
118. Quoted in Wiley, *Billy Yank,* 352.
119. Scott Walker, *Hell's Broke Loose in Georgia: Survival in a Civil War Regiment* (Athens, GA: University of Georgia Press, 2005), 84.
120. Quoted in Linderman, *Embattled Courage,* 238.
121. Quoted in ibid., 72.
122. Quoted in ibid., 148.
123. Quoted in Commager, *Blue and the Gray,* 248.
124. Nosworthy, *Bloody Crucible,* 229–30.
125. Faust, *Republic of Suffering,* 117.
126. Ibid., 92.
127. Quoted in ibid., 71.
128. Quoted in Linderman, *Embattled Courage,* 127.
129. Quoted in ibid., 127, 159.
130. Ibid., 282.

CHAPTER FIVE

1. Cyrus Townsend Brady, *Indian Fights and Fighters* (1904; repr., Lincoln: University of Nebraska Press, 1971), 339–40.
2. Quoted in Thomas Goodrich, *Scalp Dance: Indian Warfare on the High Plains, 1865–1879* (Harrisburg, PA: Stackpole, 1997), 8.
3. Patrick M. Malone, *The Skulking Way of War: Technology and Tactics Among the New England Indians* (Lanham, MD: Madison, 1991), 80.
4. Ross Hassig, *Aztec Warfare: Imperial Expansion and Political Control* (Norman: University of Oklahoma Press, 1988), 79.
5. Victor Davis Hanson, *Carnage and Culture: Landmark Battles in the Rise of Western Power* (New York: Anchor Books, 2001), 211.
6. Quoted in Brady, *Indian Fights,* 334.
7. Quoted in Donald R. Morris, *The Washing of the Spears: The Rise and Fall of the Zulu Nation* (New York: Simon & Schuster, 1965), 350.
8. Roger Ford, *The Grim Reaper: Machine-Guns and Machine-Gunners in Action* (London: Sidgwick and Jackson, 1996), 17. Byron Farwell asserts that Gatlings were first used at the battle of Charasia in Afghanistan on October 6, 1879. See Byron Farwell, *Queen Victoria's Little Wars* (New York: Harper and Row, 1972), 209.
9. Quoted in Michael Barthorp, *The Zulu War: A Pictorial History* (Blandford, 1980), 56.
10. Farwell, *Little Wars,* 272.
11. Quoted in Goodrich, *Scalp Dance,* 172.
12. Quoted in Brady, *Indian Fights,* 178.

13. Goodrich, *Scalp Dance,* 30.
14. Hanson, *Carnage and Culture,* 204.
15. Quoted in ibid., 191.
16. Ibid., 215.
17. John D. McDermott, *A Guide to the Indian Wars of the West* (Lincoln: University of Nebraska Press, 1998), 75.
18. Quoted in John Rhodehamel, ed., *The American Revolution: Writings from the War of Independence* (New York: Library of America, 2001), 487–88.
19. Quoted in Brady, *Indian Fights,* 69.
20. Quoted in ibid., 118.
21. Douglas D. Scott, P. Willey, and Melissa A. Connor, *They Died with Custer: Soldiers' Bones from the Battle of the Little Big Horn* (Norman: University of Oklahoma Press, 1998), 312.
22. Quoted in Goodrich, *Scalp Dance,* 260.
23. Hanson, *Carnage and Culture,* 282.
24. Morris, *Washing of the Spears,* 486.
25. Brady, *Indian Fights,* 32.
26. Scott, Willey, and Connor, *They Died with Custer,* 308.
27. McDermott, *Indian Wars,* 165–66.
28. Quoted in ibid., 285.
29. Ibid.
30. Farwell, *Little Wars,* 213.
31. Brady, *Indian Fights,* 55.
32. Ibid., 58.
33. Quoted in Donald Featherstone, *Victorian Colonial Warfare: Africa* (London: Blandford 1992), 23.
34. Quoted in John Ellis, *The Social History of the Machine Gun* (London: Croom Helm, 1975), 13.
35. Quoted in ibid., 26–27.
36. Quoted in ibid., 84.
37. Quoted in Ford, *Grim Reaper,* 31–32.
38. Ibid., 32.
39. Quoted in ibid., 53.
40. Quoted in ibid., 47–48.
41. Bryan Perrett, *The Battle Book* (London: Arms and Armour, 1992), 79, 188.
42. Douglas Porch, *Wars of Empire* (London: Cassell, 2000), 164.

CHAPTER SIX

1. Quoted in Richard Holmes, *Tommy: The British Soldier on the Western Front, 1914–1918* (New York: HarperCollins, 2004), 31.
2. Quoted in Ian Passingham, *All the Kaiser's Men: The Life and Death of the German Army on the Western Front, 1914–1918* (Stroud, UK: Sutton, 2003), 112.

3. Roger Ford, *The Grim Reaper: Machine-Guns and Machine-Gunners in Action* (London: Sidgwick and Jackson, 1996), 92.
4. Philip J. Haythornthwaite, *The World War One Source Book* (London: Arms and Armour, 1992), 54.
5. http://www1.va.gov/opa/fact/amwars.asp.
6. Gary Mead, *The Good Soldier: The Biography of Douglas Haig* (London: Atlantic, 2007), 344.
7. Haythornthwaite, *Source Book*, 55. Some historians put the ratio at four to one. See, for example, Ford, *Grim Reaper*, 107.
8. Passingham, *Kaiser's Men*, 107.
9. Quoted in ibid., 124–26.
10. Alistair Horne, *The Price of Glory: Verdun, 1916* (New York: St. Martin's, 1963), 327.
11. Haythornthwaite, *Source Book*, 54; and J. M. Winter, *The Great War and the British People* (London: Macmillan, 1986), 99. Revisionist historians such as Paddy Griffith tend to take issue with what they see as a hysterical focus on high casualties. There were "many instances" of units having had a pretty cushy time (the implication is that this was more representative than the hellishly lethal experience portrayed in so many other accounts): "A 'quiet' sector of the front could be very quiet indeed, almost entirely devoid of the irony conveyed by the title of E. M. Remarque's book *All Quiet on the Western Front*, and this happy condition might apply to over two-thirds of the line on any given day. . . . One battalion . . . 'fought' pretty continuously in the trenches for a whole year, yet suffered a total officer casualty list of just a single individual. So much for the misleading popular idea that the infantry subaltern's life expectancy in the BEF was no more than a fortnight!" Paddy Griffith, *Battle Tactics of the Western Front: The British Army's Art of Attack* (New Haven, CT: Yale University Press, 1994), 15.
12. Quoted in Holmes, *Tommy*, 61.
13. Richard Holmes, *Acts of War: The Behavior of Men in Battle* (New York: Free Press, 1986), 346.
14. Robert Graves, *Good-bye to All That* (1929; repr., London: Penguin, 1960), 134.
15. Quoted in Holmes, *Tommy*, 582.
16. Quoted in ibid., 297.
17. Ibid., 14.
18. Captain J. C. Dunn, *The War the Infantry Knew, 1914–1919* (1938; repr., London: Cardinal, 1989), 80, 148.
19. Griffith, *Battle Tactics*, 43.
20. Ibid., 228. The division was the Ninth (Scottish).
21. Ford, *Grim Reaper*, 133.
22. John Ellis, *The Social History of the Machine Gun* (London: Croom Helm, 1975), 35.
23. Ibid., 16.
24. Ibid., 39. See also Ford, *Grim Reaper*, 95, 114.

25. Ibid., 99.
26. George Coppard, *With a Machine Gun to Cambrai* (London: Her Majesty's Stationery Office, 1969), 37.
27. Haythornthwaite, *Source Book*, 71.
28. Quoted in Ellis, *Social History*, 131.
29. Graves, *Good-bye*, 131.
30. Frederic Manning, *Her Privates We* (first published as *The Middle Parts of Fortune*, 1929) (London: Hogarth, 1986), 212.
31. Dunn, *War the Infantry Knew*, 279.
32. Ernst Jünger, *Storm of Steel*, trans. Allen Lane (1920; repr., London: Penguin, 2003), 80.
33. P. J. Campbell, *In the Cannon's Mouth* (London: Hamish Hamilton, 1977), 34.
34. Henri Barbusse, *Under Fire* (first published in French as *Le feu* [1916]), trans. Robin Buss (London: Penguin, 2003), 197–98.
35. Holmes, *Tommy*, 497–98.
36. Campell, *Cannon's Mouth*, 42.
37. Philip Katcher, *The Civil War Source Book*, 66–67.
38. Haythornthwaite, *Source Book*, 83.
39. Ibid., 86.
40. Joseph Jobé, ed., *Guns: An Illustrated History of Artillery* (New York: Cresent, 1971), 164.
41. Ibid., 89.
42. Griffith, *Battle Tactics*, 85.
43. Haythornthwaite, *Source Book*, 74.
44. Dunn, *War the Infantry Knew*, 167.
45. Holmes, *Acts of War*, 170. Holmes cites J. T. MacCurdy's *The Structure of Morale* (1943), with the caveat that "although he marshals no evidence in support of this assertion, it may not be altogether wide of the mark."
46. Haythornthwaite, *Source Book*, 87.
47. Max Arthur, *Forgotten Voices of the Great War: A History of World War I in the Words of the Men and Women Who Were There* (London: Ebury, 2002), 190.
48. Barbusse, *Under Fire*, 226.
49. Campbell, *Cannon's Mouth*, 80.
50. Passingham, *Kaiser's Men*, 107.
51. Dunn, *War the Infantry Knew*, 401.
52. Jünger, *Storm of Steel*, 227.
53. Barbusse, *Under Fire*, 196.
54. Lord Moran, *Anatomy of Courage* (1945; repr., New York: Avery, 1987), 63.
55. Dunn, *War the Infantry Knew*, 398.
56. Barbusse, *Under Fire*, 154.
57. Coppard, *With a Machine Gun*, 38.
58. Barbusse, *Under Fire*, 46.
59. Quoted in Holmes, *Tommy*, 400.

60. Ibid., 401.
61. Moran, *Anatomy*, 19.
62. Coppard, *With a Machine Gun*, 83.
63. Arthur, *Forgotten Voices*, 103.
64. Campbell, *Cannon's Mouth*, 261.
65. Holmes, *Acts of War*, 186.
66. Barbusse, *Under Fire*, 297–98.
67. Holmes, *Acts of War*, 189.
68. Dunn, *War the Infantry Knew*, 116.
69. Moran, *Anatomy*, 121.
70. Passingham, *Kaiser's Men*, 66.
71. UK National Archives, http://www.learningcurve.gov.uk.
72. Holmes, *Tommy*, 420.
73. Griffith, *Battle Tactics*, 118.
74. "Fatal Exposure to Mustard Gas, WWI," The Medical Front WWI, WWW Virtual Library, http://www.vlib.us/medical/gaswar/mustrdpm.htm.
75. Holmes, *Acts of War*, 188.
76. Quoted in Holmes, *Tommy*, 418.
77. Quoted in ibid., 425.
78. Quoted in ibid., 461.
79. Passingham, *Kaiser's Men*, 43.
80. Quoted in ibid., 109.
81. Quoted in ibid., 162.
82. Quoted in Holmes, *Tommy*, 462.
83. Blaise Cendrars, *Lice*, translated by Nina Rootes (London: Peter Owen, 1973). First published as *La main coupée*, 1946.
84. Coppard, *With a Machine Gun*, 34–36.
85. Quoted in Arthur, *Forgotten Voices*, 176.
86. Dunn, *War the Infantry Knew*, 195–96.
87. R. C. Sherriff, *Journey's End* (1929; repr., Oxford: Heinemann, 1993).
88. Dunn, *War the Infantry Knew*, 150.
89. Siegfried Sassoon, *Memoirs of an Infantry Officer* (1930; repr., London: Faber, 1944), 166–69.
90. Graves, *Good-bye*, 111–12.
91. Passingham, *Kaiser's Men*, 77.
92. Coppard, *With a Machine Gun*, 25.
93. Jünger, *Storm of Steel*, 47.
94. Dunn, *War the Infantry Knew*, 83.
95. Graves, *Good-bye*, 113–14.
96. Haythornthwaite, *Source Book*, 81.
97. Graves, *Good-bye*, 112.
98. Quoted in Ellis, *Social History*, 53–54.
99. David A. Bell, *The First Total War: Napoleon's Europe and the Birth of Modern Warfare* (London: Bloomsbury, 2007), 188.
100. Quoted in ibid., 54.

101. Sassoon, *Memoirs*, 8.
102. Holmes, *Tommy*, 382.
103. Moran, *Anatomy*, 69.
104. Quoted in Sassoon, *Memoirs*, 11.
105. Graves, *Good-bye*, 195–96.
106. Holmes, *Tommy*, 345.
107. Campbell, *Cannon's Mouth*, 251.
108. Holmes, *Tommy*, 548.
109. Quoted in Haythornthwaite, *Source Book*, 66.
110. Quoted in Arthur, *Forgotten Voices*, 70–71.
111. Quoted in Holmes, *Tommy*, 383.
112. Quoted in Arthur, *Forgotten Voices*, 70–71.
113. Quoted in Holmes, *Tommy*, 413.
114. Quoted in ibid., 415.
115. Quoted in ibid., 548.
116. Dunn, *War the Infantry Knew*, 220.
117. Jünger, *Storm of Steel*, 241.
118. Moran, *Anatomy*, 147.
119. Ibid., 16.
120. Jünger, *Storm of Steel*, 248.
121. Graves, *Good-bye*, 134.
122. Quoted in Holmes, *Tommy*, 578.
123. Jünger, *Storm of Steel*, 281–82.
124. Quoted in Arthur, *Forgotten Voices*, 186–87.
125. Sassoon, *Memoirs*, 51, 165.
126. Quoted in Arthur, *Forgotten Voices*, 156.
127. Manning, *Her Privates We*, 215.
128. Barbusse, *Under Fire*, 46–47.
129. Manning, *Her Privates We*, 13.
130. Moran, *Anatomy*, 127.
131. Jünger, *Storm of Steel*, 98.
132. Barbusse, *Under Fire*, 28.
133. Quoted in Holmes, *Tommy*, 452.
134. Quoted in Passingham, *Kaiser's Men*, 42.
135. Quoted in Arthur, *Forgotten Voices*, 162.
136. Graves, *Good-bye*, 97.
137. Dunn, *War the Infantry Knew*, 80.
138. Quoted in Holmes, *Tommy*, 63.
139. Quoted in Arthur, *Forgotten Voices*, 165.
140. Quoted in Holmes, *Tommy*, 322.
141. Quoted in Peter E. Hodgkinson, "Clearing the Dead," *Journal of the Centre for First World War Studies* 3, no. 1 (September 2007): 49.
142. Coppard, *With a Machine Gun*, 114–15.
143. Quoted in Holmes, *Tommy*, 46.
144. Sassoon, *Memoirs*, 58.
145. Jünger, *Storm of Steel*, 85.

146. Patrick Creagh, trans., *Giuseppe Ungaretti: Selected Poems* (London: Penguin, 1971), 28.
147. Sassoon, *Memoirs*, 157.
148. Barbusse, *Under Fire*, 246.
149. Quoted in Passingham, *Kaiser's Men*, 11.
150. Moran, *Anatomy*, 148–49.
151. Ibid., 116.
152. Barbusse, *Under Fire*, 245.
153. Manning, *Her Privates We*, 116.
154. Quoted in Holmes, *Tommy*, 551.
155. Moran, *Anatomy*, 121.
156. Haythornthwaite, *Source Book*, 135.
157. Quoted in Holmes, *Tommy*, 84.
158. Sassoon, *Memoirs*, 153.

CHAPTER SEVEN

1. "Source List and Detailed Death Tolls for Man-made Multicides Throughout History," from Matthew White's invaluable Atlas of Twentieth Century History website: http://necrometrics.com/warstats.htm. His numbers are derived from a review of more than 50 sources.
2. Catherine Merridale, *Ivan's War: Life and Death in the Red Army, 1939–1945* (New York: Metropolitan Books/Henry Holt, 2006), 337.
3. Colonel General G. F. Krivosheev, ed., *Soviet Casualties and Combat Losses in the Twentieth Century* (London: Greenhill, 1997), 85, 96. David M. Glantz and Jonathan House, *When Titans Clashed: How the Red Army Stopped Hitler* (Lawrence: University of Kansas Press, 1995), adopt Krivosheev's numbers (from the original 1993 Russian-language edition). Richard Ellis, *World War II: The Encyclopedia of Facts and Figures* (Madison, WI: Facts on File, 1995), 254, gives Soviet "killed and missing" at 11 million.
4. Omer Bartov, *Hitler's Army: Soldiers, Nazis, and War in the Third Reich* (Oxford: Oxford University Press, 1992), 83.
5. Glantz and House, *When Titans Clashed*, 123.
6. Ibid., 284.
7. Ibid. Ellis, *World War II*, 253, gives a much lower figure for German losses: 7.9 million casualties in all theaters, of whom 3.3 million were killed.
8. http://necrometrics.com/warstats.htm.
9. Congressional Research Service Report for Congress, "American War and Military Operations Casualties: Lists and Statistics," *Congressional Record* S3 (2007), CRS3.
10. http://necrometrics.com/warstats.htm.
11. Ellis, *World War II*, 256.

12. James F. Dunnigan and Albert A. Nofi, *The Pacific War Encyclopedia* (Madison, WI: Facts on File, 1998), 690.
13. Perrett, *Battle Book*, 127; and Dunnigan and Nofi, *Pacific War*, 255.
14. Perrett, *Battle Book*, 224.
15. Michael Bess, *Choices Under Fire: Moral Dimensions of World War II* (New York: Knopf, 2006), 212.
16. Quoted in Bartov, *Hitler's Army*, 130.
17. Paul Fussell, *Wartime: Understanding and Behavior in the Second World War* (New York: Oxford University Press, 1989), 116.
18. Quoted in Craig M. Cameron, *American Samurai: Myth, Imagination and the Conduct of Battle in the First Marine Division, 1941–1951* (Cambridge University Press, 1994), 1.
19. E. B. Sledge, *With the Old Breed at Peleliu and Okinawa* (1981; repr., New York: Ballantine, 2007), 400.
20. George MacDonald Fraser, *Quartered Safe Out Here: A Harrowing Tale of World War II* (New York: Skyhorse, 2007), 125.
21. John C. McManus, *The Deadly Brotherhood: The American Combat Soldier in World War II* (Novato, CA: Presidio, 1998), 172.
22. Quoted in Richard J. Aldrich, *Witness to War: Diaries of the Second World War in Europe and the Middle East* (Garden City, NY: Doubleday, 2004), 541–42.
23. Günter K. Koschorrek, *Blood Red Snow: The Memoirs of a German Soldier on the Eastern Front* (Minneapolis: Zenith, 2005), 255.
24. Fussell, *Wartime*, 140.
25. Quoted in ibid.
26. Alex Bowlby, *The Recollections of Rifleman Bowlby: Italy 1944* (London: Leo Cooper, 1969), 114.
27. William Manchester, *Goodbye, Darkness: A Memoir of the Pacific War* (Boston: Little, Brown, 1979), 391.
28. Lee Kennett, *G.I.: The American Soldier in World War II* (New York: Scribner's, 1987), 140.
29. McManus, *Deadly Brotherhood*, 237.
30. Quoted in ibid., 240.
31. Quoted in ibid., 283.
32. Quoted in Merridale, *Ivan's War*, 233.
33. Ellis, *World War II*, 161.
34. Frank A. Reister, *Medical Statistics in World War II* (Washington, DC: Office of the Surgeon General, Department of the Army, 1975), 16.
35. Thomas M. Huber, "Japanese Counterartillery Methods on Okinawa, April–June 1945," Combined Studies Institute Report 13, *Tactical Responses to Concentrated Artillery*, US Army Combined Arms Center.
36. Kennett, *G.I.*, 152.
37. John Lucas, *The Silken Canopy: A History of the Parachute* (Shrewsbury, UK: Airlife, 1997), 67.

38. Glantz and House, *When Titans Clashed*, 172.

39. Quoted in Gerald Astor, *The Mighty Eighth: The Air War in Europe as Told by the Men Who Fought It* (New York: Dell, 1997), 308.

40. War Chronicle, http://warchronicle.com/16th-infantry.com.

41. 29th Infantry Division Historical Society, http://www .29infantrydivision.org/WWII-stories/Ford_Richard_J_2.html.

42. D-Day Museum and Overlord Embroidery, http://www. ddaymuseum.co.uk.

43. Manchester, *Goodbye*, 224.

44. Gordon L. Rottman, *U.S. World War II Amphibious Tactics: Army & Marine Corps, Pacific Theater* (London: Osprey, 2004), 31. Ironically, Andrew Higgins's inspiration came from a photograph the Marines had shown him in 1941 of a Japanese drop-ramp landing craft—the *Daisatsu*—developed in the late 1920s.

45. Robert Leckie, *Helmet for My Pillow* (New York: iBooks, 2001), 57.

46. Manchester, *Goodbye*, 162.

47. Raymond Gantter, *Roll Me Over: An Infantryman's World War II* (New York: Ballantine, 1997), 4.

48. Quoted in Martin Bowman, *Remembering D-Day: Personal Histories of Everyday Heroes* (New York: HarperCollins, 2005), 118.

49. Quoted in Ronald Lewin, ed., *Voices from the War on Land, 1939–1945* (New York: Vintage, 2007), 205.

50. Ibid.

51. John Ellis, *On the Front Lines: The Experience of War Through the Eyes of Allied Soldiers in World War II* (New York: Wiley, 1991), 61.

52. Manchester, *Goodbye*, 228. This anecdote is reminiscent of a similar accusation made by Stephen Ambrose in *D-Day, June 6, 1944: The Climactic Battle of World War II* (New York: Touchstone, 1994), 337, 343, that a British coxswain ferrying men of the U.S. assault force at Omaha Beach lost his nerve and would not press on to the beach until threatened by an officer with a Colt .45. Ambrose had based his story on an account by another fabulist, S. L. A. Marshall (who would himself be discredited for fabricating evidence to support his thesis that most soldiers were too intimidated to fire their weapons). An American survivor of that boat, Bob Sales, knew the story to be a complete fabrication and confronted Ambrose with his scurrilous fiction. Sales recounts that Ambrose "just laughed it off and said, 'I can't do everything,'" For a full account see http://www .warchronicle.com/correcting-the-record/ambrose-coxswains.

53. Bowman, *Remembering D-Day*, 268.

54. Quoted in Manchester, *Goodbye*, 224.

55. McManus, *Deadly Brotherhood*, 128.

56. Quoted in Lewin, *War on Land*, 252.

57. Bowman, *Remembering D-Day*, 123.

58. Ibid., 117.

59. Manchester, *Goodbye*, 340.

60. Rottman, *Amphibious Tactics*, 9.

61. Cameron, *American Samurai*, 135.

62. Quoted in ibid., 155.

63. Manchester, *Goodbye*, 238.

64. Cameron, *American Samurai*, 142.

65. Leckie, *Helmet*, 58.

66. Donald R. Burgett, *Currahee! A Screaming Eagle at Normandy* (New York: Dell, 2000), 8.

67. Quoted in Lewin, *Voices*, 191.

68. John Lucas, *The Silken Canopy: A History of the Parachute* (Shrewsbury, UK: Airlife, 1997), 87.

69. Burgett, *Currahee!*, 32–33.

70. John Weeks, *The Airborne Soldier* (Poole, UK: Blandford, 1982), 45, 53.

71. John Weeks, *Assault from the Sky: The History of Airborne Warfare* (Newton Abbot, UK: David and Charles, 1978), 66.

72. Burgett, *Currahee!*, 66.

73. Antony Beevor, *D-Day: The Battle for Normandy* (New York: Viking, 2009), 64.

74. Quoted in Fussell, *Wartime*, 271.

75. Bowman, *Remembering D-Day*, 63.

76. Weeks, *Assault*, 57.

77. Ibid., 58.

78. Rick Atkinson, *The Day of Battle: The War in Sicily and Italy, 1943–1944* (New York: Holt, 2007), 108–9.

79. Quoted in Beevor, *D-Day*, 62.

80. Burgett, *Currahee!*, 76.

81. Randy Hils, "An Open Letter to the Airborne Community on the History of OPERATION NEPTUNE, June 6, 1944," http://www.warchronicle.com/correcting–the–record/NEPTUNE–airborne.htm. Hils is particularly scathing about the uncritical acceptance of S. L. A. Marshall's assertions of pilot failure (in his book *Night Drop*) adopted by many subsequent military historians, the most influential being Stephen E. Ambrose in *D-Day, June 6, 1944*.

82. Ellis, *On the Front Lines*, 64.

83. Weeks, *Airborne Soldier*, 102.

84. Quoted in McManus, *Deadly Brotherhood*, 154.

85. Gantter, *Roll Me Over*, 32.

86. Paul Fussell, *The Boys' Crusade: The American Infantry in Northwest Europe, 1944–1945* (New York: Modern Library, 2003), xiii.

87. Paddy Griffith, *Forward into Battle: Fighting Tactics from Waterloo to the Near Future* (Novato, CA: Presidio, 1997), 111. See also Ellis, *On the Front Lines*, 74.

88. Griffith, *Forward into Battle*, 118.

89. Quoted in Ellis, *On the Front Lines*, 52.

90. Quoted in Fussell, *Boys' Crusade*, 96.

91. US Army Medical Department, *Medical Statistics in World War II*,

Office of the Surgeon General, Department of the Army (1975), frontispiece chart.

92. Fussell, *Boys' Crusade,* 10.

93. McManus, *Deadly Brotherhood,* 4.

94. US Army, *Medical Statistics,* 350.

95. William W. Tribby, "Examination of 1,000 American Casualties Killed in Italy," US Army Medical Department Office of Medical History, http://history.amedd.army.mil/booksdocs/wwii/woundblstcs/chapter6.htm, 441.

96. Ibid., 446.

97. Quoted in Ellis, *On the Front Lines,* 70.

98. Gantter, *Roll Me Over,* 304.

99. David Kenyon Webster, *Parachute Infantry: An American Paratrooper's Memoir of D-Day and the Fall of the Third Reich* (New York: Delta/Dell, 2002), 100.

100. Quoted in Ellis, *On the Front Lines,* 70.

101. Koschorrek, *Blood Red Snow,* 284–85.

102. Burgett, *Seven Roads,* 250.

103. Gantter, *Roll Me Over,* 95.

104. Leo Litwak, *Medic: Life and Death in the Last Days of World War II* (Chapel Hill, NC: Algonquin, 2001), 81.

105. Paul Fussell, *Doing Battle: The Making of a Skeptic* (Boston: Back Bay/Little, Brown, 1996), 133–34.

106. Burgett, *Currahee!,* 138.

107. Morris Fishbein, ed., *Doctors at War* (New York: Dutton, 1945), 177.

108. Ibid.

109. Ellis, *On the Front Lines,* 89.

110. Quoted in ibid., 330.

111. Quoted in ibid., 88.

112. William Woodruff, *Vessel of Sadness* (Boston: Abacus, 2004), 54.

113. Bergerud, *Touched with Fire: The Land War in the South Pacific* (New York: Viking, 1996), 287.

114. Burgett, *Currahee!,* 92.

115. Quoted in McManus, *Deadly Brotherhood,* 46.

116. Ellis, *On the Front Lines,* 90.

117. Bergerud, *Touched with Fire,* 319; and Griffith, *Forward into Battle,* 117.

118. Quoted in Bergerud, *Touched with Fire,* 321.

119. Quoted in Lewin, *Voices from the War,* 239.

120. Manchester, *Goodbye,* 384.

121. Quoted in Bowman, *Remembering D-Day,* 107.

122. Roscoe C. Blunt Jr., *Foot Soldier: A Combat Infantryman's War in Europe* (Cambridge, MA: Da Capo, 2002), 69.

123. Quoted in Ellis, *On the Front Lines,* 86.

124. Merridale, *Ivan's War,* 181.

125. Koschorrek, *Blood Red Snow,* 92–94.

126. Trevor Dupuy, *Attrition: Forecasting Battle Casualties and Equipment*

Losses in Modern War (Falls Church, VA: Nova, 1995), 80; and Gordon L. Rothman, *World War II Infantry Anti-Tank Tactics* (London: Osprey, 2005), 15.

127. John Weeks, *Men Against Tanks: A History of Anti-Tank Warfare* (New York: Mason/Charter, 1975), 23.

128. Quoted in Samuel Hynes, *The Soldiers' Tale: Bearing Witness to a Modern War* (New York: Allen Lane/Penguin Press, 1997), 141–42.

129. Quoted in Aldrich, *Witness to War*, 491.

130. Quoted in George Forty, *Tank Warfare in the Second World War: An Oral History* (London: Constable and Robinson, 1998), 76–77.

131. Quoted in Kenneth Macksey, *Tank Warfare: A History of Tanks in Battle* (New York: Stein and Day, 1972), 153.

132. Jock Watt, *A Tankie's Travels* (Bognor Regis: Woodfield, 2006), 73.

133. Bowman, *Remembering D-Day*, 76–77.

134. Robert C. Dick, *Cutthroats: The Adventures of a Sherman Tank Driver in the Pacific* (New York: Ballantine/Presidio, 2006), 93–94.

135. Blunt, *Foot Soldier*, 134.

136. Quoted in Stephen G. Fritz, *Frontsoldaten: The German Soldier in World War II* (Lexington: University Press of Kentucky, 1995), 41.

137. Merridale, *Ivan's War*, 215.

138. Ibid., 216.

139. Quoted in Lewin, *War on Land*, 61.

140. Quoted in Ellis, *On the Front Lines*, 154.

141. Quoted in Forty, *Tank Warfare*, 197.

142. Quoted in Vasily Grossman, *A Writer at War: A Soviet Journalist with the Red Army, 1941–1945*, trans. and eds. Antony Beevor and Luba Vinogradova (New York: Pantheon, 2005), 140.

143. Woodruff, *Vessel*, 95.

144. Koschorrek, *Blood Red Snow*, 172–73.

145. Leckie, *Helmet*, 307–8.

146. Burgett, *Seven Roads*, 14–15.

147. Gantter, *Roll Me Over*, 106.

148. Quoted in McManus, *Deadly Brotherhood*, 118.

149. Quoted in Bergerud, *Touched with Fire*, 362.

150. Leckie, *Helmet*, 232–33.

151. Quoted in Ellis, *On the Front Lines*, 56.

152. Quoted in McManus, *Deadly Brotherhood*, 105.

153. Quoted in Bergerud, *Touched with Fire*, 361.

154. Gantter, *Roll Me Over*, 176.

155. Albert E. Cowdrey, *Fighting for Life: American Military Medicine in World War II* (New York: Free Press, 1994), 252.

156. Quoted in McManus, *Deadly Brotherhood*, 136.

157. Litwak, *Medic*, 36.

158. Quoted in McManus, *Deadly Brotherhood*, 135.

159. Webster, *Parachute Infantry*, 56.

160. Quoted in McManus, *Deadly Brotherhood*, 41.
161. Manchester, *Goodbye*, 376–77.
162. Fussell, *Doing Battle*, 126.
163. Quoted in McManus, *Deadly Brotherhood*, 120.
164. Ellis, *On the Front Lines*, 13.
165. Ibid., 305.
166. Quoted in ibid., 304.
167. Webster, *Parachute Infantry*, 210.
168. Quoted in Kennett, *G.I.*, 134.
169. Litwak, *Medic*, 74.
170. Bowlby, *Recollections*, 64.
171. Burgett, *Seven Roads*, 240.
172. Webster, *Parachute Infantry*, 364–66.
173. Robert "Doc Joe" Franklin, *Medic!: How I Fought World War II with Morphine, Sulfa, and Iodine Swabs* (Lincoln: University of Nebraska Press, 2006), 24.
174. Siegfried Knappe with Ted Brusaw, *Soldat: Reflections of a German Soldier, 1936–1949* (New York: Dell, 1992), 225.
175. Quoted in Aldrich, *Witness to War*, 626–29.
176. Fussell, *Doing Battle*, 136.
177. Gantter, *Roll Me Over*, 322.
178. Merridale, *Ivan's War*, 193.
179. Louis Simpson, "The Runner," from *A Dream of Governors* (1959), in *Selected Poems* (London: Oxford University Press, 1966), 60.
180. Quoted in Aldrich, *Witness*, 474.
181. Gantter, *Roll Me Over*, 158.
182. Quoted in Bergerud, *Touched with Fire*, 380.
183. Gantter, *Roll Me Over*, 97–98.
184. Kennett, *G.I.*, 176; and Cowdrey, *Fighting for Life*, 83.
185. Ellis, *On the Front Lines*, 96.
186. Fussell, *Doing Battle*, 137.
187. Leckie, *Helmet*, 63.
188. Fraser, *Quartered Safe*, 151–52.
189. Woodruff, *Vessel*, 104–6.
190. Fussell, *Doing Battle*, 138.
191. Quoted in Ellis, *On the Front Lines*, 221.
192. Quoted in McManus, *Deadly Brotherhood*, 249.
193. Both quotes in Ellis, *On the Front Lines*, 98.
194. Quoted in ibid., 208.
195. Quoted in Grossman, *Writer at War*, 96.
196. Gantter, *Roll Me Over*, 38.
197. Leckie, *Helmet*, 104–5.
198. Quoted in Lewin, *Voices from the War*, 320–21.
199. Burgett, *Seven Roads*, 19.
200. Quoted in McManus, *Deadly Brotherhood*, 282–83.
201. Bowlby, *Recollections*, 196.

202. Quoted in McManus, *Deadly Brotherhood*, 152.
203. Quoted in ibid., 154.
204. Quoted in ibid., 282.
205. Burgett, *Currahee!*, 149.
206. Manchester, *Goodbye*, 246.
207. Fraser, *Quartered Safe*, 192.
208. Quoted in McManus, *Deadly Brotherhood*, 237.
209. Quoted in ibid., 109.
210. Quoted in ibid.
211. Fraser, *Quartered Safe*, 118.
212. Gantter, *Roll Me Over*, 172–73.
213. Manchester, *Goodbye*, 5–7.
214. Quoted in Lewin, *War on Land*, 116–17.

CHAPTER EIGHT

1. Jonathan Shay, *Achilles in Vietnam: Combat Trauma and the Undoing of Character* (New York: Scribner, 1994), 138.
2. Christian G. Appy, *Vietnam: The Definitive Oral History Told from All Sides* (London: Ebury, 2003), 163.
3. Andrew Wiest and M. K. Barbier, *Infantry Warfare: The Theory and Practice of Infantry Combat in the 20th Century* (Minneapolis: MBI, 2002), 154.
4. US Department of Defense figures. Interestingly, no number is posted for Iraqi casualties. Given the enormous disparity of casualties, the DoD merely states, perhaps a little coyly, that "42 divisions were made combat ineffective."
5. According to Norwich University Master of Arts in Military History website, http://www.u-s-history.com.
6. Quoted in James R. Ebert, *A Life in a Year: The American Infantryman in Vietnam* (New York: Ballantine, 1993), 363.
7. David Bellavia, *House to House* (New York: Pocket Star, 2007), 20.
8. Doug Beattie, *An Ordinary Soldier* (New York: Simon & Schuster, 2008), 77.
9. Quoted in Eric M. Bergerud, *Red Thunder, Tropic Lightning: The World of a Combat Division in Vietnam* (New York: Penguin, 1993), 30.
10. Appy, *Vietnam*, 446–48. Two marines were sentenced to five years (later reduced); one of them later committed suicide.
11. Michael R. Gordon and General Bernard E. Trainor, *Cobra II: The Inside Story of the Invasion and Occupation of Iraq* (New York: Pantheon, 2006), 259.
12. Quoted in ibid., 222.
13. Quoted in ibid., 223.
14. Quoted in *The New Yorker*, June 12, 2006, 124.

15. Donovan Campbell, *Joker One: A Marine Platoon's Story of Courage, Leadership, and Brotherhood* (New York: Random House, 2009), 70.

16. Quoted in Edward F. Murphy, *Semper Fi Vietnam: From Da Nang to the DMZ: Marine Corps Campaigns, 1965–1975* (New York: Presidio, 1997), 6.

17. Quoted in Bergerud, *Red Thunder*, 95.

18. Quoted in Col. David H. Hackworth, *Steel My Soldiers' Hearts* (New York: Simon & Schuster, 2002), 61.

19. Ibid., 20.

20. Ebert, *Life in a Year*, 324.

21. Beattie, *Ordinary Soldier*, 150.

22. Ibid., 152.

23. Quoted in Appy, *Vietnam*, 17.

24. S. L. A. Marshall, *Vietnam: Three Battles* (Cambridge, MA: Da Capo, 1982), 3. First published as *Fields of Bamboo: Three Battles Just Beyond the China Seas* (New York: Dial, 1971). Captain Beattie in his account of his service in Helmand Province, Afghanistan, recounts how he called in a B-1 strike to kill one insurgent: "I thought about what I was about to do. Use 500 lbs of high explosive to destroy a small hut and in doing so finish off one man. What had happened to my compassion? . . . Was I any better than the Luftwaffe pilot who strafes the helpless British aviator floating to the ground by parachute after being shot down?" In Beattie, *Ordinary Soldier*, 188.

25. Quoted in Andrew Carroll, ed., *War Letters: Extraordinary Correspondence from American Wars* (New York: Scribner, 2001), 432.

26. Ebert, *Life in a Year*, 156.

27. Quoted in Mark Baker, ed., *Nam: The Vietnam War in the Words of the Soldiers Who Fought There* (New York: Berkley, 1983), 214.

28. Appy, *Vietnam*, 254.

29. Karl Marlantes, *Matterhorn* (New York: El León Literary Arts/ Atlantic Monthly Press, 2010), 46.

30. Hackworth, *Steel My Soldiers' Hearts*, 60.

31. Quoted in Bergerud, *Red Thunder*, 143–44.

32. Joel Turnipseed, *Baghdad Express: A Gulf War Memoir* (New York: Penguin, 2003), 144–46.

33. Quoted in Henry Steele Commager and Richard B. Morris, *The Spirit of 'Seventy-Six: The Story of the American Revolution as Told by Its Participants* (New York: Harper and Row, 1958), 1225.

34. Beattie, *Ordinary Soldier*, 194.

35. Tobias Wolff, *In Pharaoh's Army: Memoirs of the Lost War* (New York: Vintage, 1994), 7.

36. US National Archives & Records Administration, http://www .archives.gov/research/vietnam-war/casualty-statistics.

37. Ebert, *Life in a Year*, 235.

38. Operation Enduring Freedom, http://icasualties.org/oef/.

39. Lester W. Gran, William A. Jorgenson, and Robert R. Love, "Guerrilla Warfare and Land Mine Casualties Remain Inseparable," *U.S. Army Medical Department Journal,* October–December 1998: 10–16.

40. Captain Francis J. West Jr., *Small Unit Action in Vietnam: Summer 1966* (New York: Arno, 1967), 1.

41. Ibid., 3.

42. Ronald J. Glasser, *365 Days* (New York: Braziller, 1971), 19–20.

43. Baker, *Nam,* 96–98.

44. Quoted in Ebert, *Life in a Year,* 242.

45. Quoted in Bergerud, *Red Thunder,* 198–99.

46. Ibid., 241.

47. Wolff, *Pharaoh's Army,* 4.

48. Quoted in Ebert, *Life in a Year,* 246–47.

49. Hackworth, *Steel My Soldiers' Hearts,* 17.

50. Quoted in Ebert, *Life in a Year,* 177.

51. Quoted in Luke Mogelson, "A Beast in the Heart," *New York Times Magazine,* May 1, 2011, 37.

52. Quoted in Shay, *Achilles in Vietnam,* 138–39.

53. Quoted in Bergerud, *Red Thunder,* 118–19.

54. Campbell, *Joker,* 107.

55. Sean Michael Flynn, *The Fighting 69th: One Remarkable National Guard Unit's Journey from Ground Zero to Baghdad* (New York: Viking, 2007), 232.

56. Quoted in Bergerud, *Red Thunder,* 125.

57. Quoted in Appy, *Vietnam,* 245.

58. Quoted in Carroll, *Letters,* 388.

59. Quoted in Baker, *Nam,* 279.

60. Bellavia, *House to House,* 153.

61. Quoted in Baker, *Nam,* 135.

62. Quoted in ibid., 184.

63. Bellavia, *House to House,* 17–18.

64. Ibid., 262–68.

65. Hackworth, *Steel My Soldiers' Hearts,* 132.

66. Quoted in Baker, *Nam,* 59.

67. Quoted in Bergerud, *Red Thunder,* 211.

68. Quoted in Appy, *Vietnam,* 136.

69. Quoted in Carroll, *Letters,* 441–42.

APPENDIX

1. Quoted in Albert E. Cowdrey, *Fighting for Life: American Military Medicine in World War II* (New York: Free Press, 1994), 118.

2. Quoted in Naythons, Sherwin B. Nuland, and Stanley Burns, *The Face of Mercy: A Photographic History of Medicine at War* (New York: Random House, 1993), 99.

3. Harold L. Peterson, *The Book of the Continental Soldier* (Harrisburg, PA: Stackpole, 1968), 172.

4. Maurice Fishbein, MD, ed., *Doctors at War* (New York: Dutton, 1945), 174.

5. Naythons, Nuland, and Burns, *Face of Mercy*, 232.

6. Quoted in ibid., 20.

7. Sylvia R. Frey, *The British Soldier in America* (Austin: University of Texas Press, 1981), 48.

8. Quoted in Erna Risch, *Supplying Washington's Army* (Washington DC: Center of Millitary History, US Army, 1981), 374.

9. Quoted in Julian Spilsbury, *The Thin Red Line: An Eyewitness History of the Crimean War* (London: Weidenfeld and Nicolson, 2005), 101.

10. George Washington Adams, *Doctors in Blue: The Medical History of the Union Army in the Civil War* (Baton Rouge: Louisiana State University Press, 1952), 72.

11. John T. Greenwood and F. Clifton Berry Jr., *Medics at War: Military Medicine from Colonial Times to the 21st Century* (Annapolis, MD: Naval Institute Press, 2005), 26.

12. Naythons, Nuland, and Burns, *Face of Mercy*, 34.

13. Adams, *Doctors in Blue*, 91.

14. Naythons, Nuland, and Burns, *Face of Mercy*, 237.

15. Cowdrey, *Fighting for Life*, 119.

16. Greenwood, *Medics at War*, 104.

17. Cowdrey, *Fighting for Life*, 119.

18. "The Ghastly Work of the Field Surgeons," Shotgun's Home of the American Civil War, http://www.civilwarhome.com/fieldsurgeons.htm.

19. Adams, *Doctors in Blue*, 139.

20. Ibid., 140.

21. Ibid., 143.

22. Greenwood, *Medics at War*, 30.

23. "Report on Gangrene by A. Thornburgh, Assistant Surgeon, Provisional Army, C.S., C.S. Military Prison Hospital, Andersonville, Ga.," Shotgun's Home of the American Civil War, http://www.civilwarhome.com/andersonvillegangrene.htm.

24. Ibid.

25. Adams, *Doctors in Blue*, 129.

26. Richard Holmes, *Redcoat: The British Soldier in the Age of Horse and Musket*, (New York: W. W. Norton, 2001), 249.

27. Naythorns, Nuland, and Burns, *Face of Mercy*, 84.

28. Greenwood, *Medics at War*, 30.

29. Margaret E. Wagner, ed., *The Library of Congress Civil War Desk Reference* (New York: Simon and Schuster, 2002), 634.

30. Naythorns, Nuland, and Burns, *Face of Mercy*, 34.

31. Quoted in ibid., 64.

32. Quoted in George F. Scheer and Hugh F. Rankin, *Rebels &*

Redcoats: The American Revolution Through the Eyes of Those Who Fought and Lived It (New York: World, 1957), 239.

33. Kathy L. Ryan et al., "Overview of the Homeostasis Research Program: Advances and Future Directions," *Army Medical Department Journal*, July–September 2003: 1.

34. Cowdrey, *Fighting for Life*, 171.

35. Ibid., 172.

BIBLIOGRAPHY

Adams, George Washington. *Doctors in Blue: The Medical History of the Union Army in the Civil War.* Baton Rouge: Louisiana State University Press, 1996.

Aldrich, Richard J. *Witness to War: Diaries of the Second World War in Europe and the Middle East.* Garden City, NY: Doubleday, 2004.

Ambrose, Stephen E. *D-Day, June 6, 1944: The Climactic Battle of World War II.* New York: Touchstone, 1994.

Anderson, M. S. *War and Society in Europe of the Old Regime, 1618–1789.* London: Fontana, 1988.

Anonymous. *Memoirs of a Sergeant: The 43rd Light Infantry During the Peninsular War.* Stroud, UK: Nonsuch, 2005.

Appy, Christian G. *Vietnam: The Definitive Oral History Told from All Sides.* London: Ebury, 2003.

Arthur, Max. *Forgotten Voices of the Great War: A History of World War I in the Words of the Men and Women Who Were There.* London: Ebury, 2002.

Astor, Gerald. *A Blood-Dimmed Tide: The Battle of the Bulge and the Men Who Fought It.* New York: Dell, 1994.

———. *Crisis in the Pacific: The Battles for the Philippine Islands by the Men Who Fought Them.* New York: Dell, 1996.

———. *The Mighty Eighth: The Air War in Europe as Told by the Men Who Fought It.* New York: Dell, 1997.

Atkinson, Rick. *The Day of Battle: The War in Sicily and Italy, 1943–1944.* New York: Holt, 2007.

Baker, Alan. *The Knight.* Hoboken, NJ: Wiley, 2003.

Baker, Mark, ed. *Nam: The Vietnam War in the Words of the Soldiers Who Fought There.* New York: Berkley, 1983.

Bancroft-Hunt, Norman. *Warriors: Warfare and the Native American Indian.* London: Salamander, 1995.

Barbusse, Henri. *Under Fire,* trans. Robin Buss (first published as *Le feu,* 1916). London: Penguin, 2003.

Barthorp, Michael. *The Zulu War: A Pictorial History.* London: Blandford, 1980.

Bartov, Omer. *Hitler's Army: Soldiers, Nazis, and War in the Third Reich.* Oxford: Oxford University Press, 1992.

Beattie, Doug. *An Ordinary Soldier.* New York: Simon & Schuster, 2008.

Beevor, Antony. *D-Day: The Battle for Normandy.* New York: Viking, 2009.

———. *Stalingrad: The Fateful Siege, 1942–1943.* New York: Penguin, 1998.

Bell, David A. *The First Total War: Napoleon's Europe and the Birth of Modern Warfare.* London: Bloomsbury, 2007.

Bellavia, David, with John R. Bruning. *House to House.* New York: Pocket Star, 2007.

Bennett, Matthew, et al. *Fighting Techniques of the Medieval World, AD 500–AD 1500: Equipment, Combat Skills, and Tactics.* New York: St. Martin's, 2005.

Bergerud, Eric. *Red Thunder, Tropic Lightning: The World of the Combat Soldier in Vietnam.* New York: Penguin, 1993.

———. *Touched with Fire: The Land War in the South Pacific.* New York: Viking, 1996.

Bess, Michael. *Choices Under Fire: Moral Dimensions of World War II.* New York: Knopf, 2006.

Bierce, Ambrose. *Tales of Soldiers and Civilians and Other Stories.* New York: Penguin, 2000.

Bilby, Joseph G. *A Revolution in Arms: A History of the First Repeating Rifles.* Yardley, PA: Westholme, 2006.

Bishop, Maurice. *The Penguin Book of the Middle Ages.* London: Penguin, 1971.

Blunden, Edmund. *Undertones of War.* 1928. Reprint, London: Penguin, 1982.

Blunt, Roscoe C. *Foot Soldier: A Combat Infantryman's War in Europe.* Cambridge, MA: Da Capo, 2002.

Bolger, Daniel P. *Death Ground: Today's American Infantry in Battle.* New York: Ballantine, 1999.

Bolton, Charles Knowles. *The Private Soldier Under Washington.* New York: Charles Scribner's Sons, 1902.

Bowlby, Alex. *The Recollections of Rifleman Bowlby: Italy 1944.* London: Leo Cooper, 1969.

Bowman, Martin. *Remembering D-Day: Personal Histories of Everyday Heroes.* New York: HarperCollins, 2005.

Bradley, James. *Flags of Our Fathers.* New York: Bantam, 2000.

Brady, Cyrus Townsend. *Indian Fights and Fighters.* 1904. Reprint, Lincoln: University of Nebraska Press, 1971.

Brown, Richard D., ed. *Major Problems in the Era of the American Revolution, 1760–1791.* Lexington, MA.: D. C. Heath, 1992.

Brumwell, Stephen. *Redcoats: The British Soldier and War in the Americas, 1755–1763.* Cambridge: Cambridge University Press, 2002.

Bryant, Anthony J. *Sekigahara, 1600: The Final Struggle for Power.* Oxford: Osprey, 1995.

Bull, Dr. Stephen. *World War II Infantry Tactics: Squad and Platoon.* Oxford: Osprey, 2004.

———. *World War II Infantry Tactics: Company and Battalion.* Oxford: Osprey, 2005.

Burgett, Donald R. *Currahee! A Screaming Eagle at Normandy.* New York: Dell, 2000.

———. *Seven Roads to Hell: A Screaming Eagle at Bastogne.* New York: Dell, 2000.

Busey, John W., and David C. Martin. *Regimental Strengths and Losses at Gettysburg.* Hightstown, NJ: Longstreet House, 1986.

Cameron, Craig M. *American Samurai: Myth, Imagination and the Conduct of Battle in the First Marine Division, 1941–1951.* Cambridge University Press, 1994.

Campbell, Donovan. *Joker One: A Marine Platoon's Story of Courage, Leadership, and Brotherhood.* New York: Random House, 2009.

Campbell, P. J. *In the Cannon's Mouth.* London: Hamish Hamilton, 1977.

Carroll, Andrew, ed. *War Letters: Extraordinary Correspondence from American Wars.* New York: Scribner, 2001.

Cawthorne, Nigel. *Steel Fist: Tank Warfare, 1939–45.* London: Arcturus, 2003.

Cendrars, Blaise. *Lice.* Translated by Nina Rootes. London: Peter Owen, 1973. First published as *La main coupée,* 1946.

Chandler, David. *The Art of Warfare in the Age of Marlborough.* London: Batsford, 1976.

Cleary, Thomas, trans. *Code of the Samurai: A Modern Translation of the Bushido Shoshinsu of Taira Shigesuke.* Boston: Tuttle, 1999.

———. *The Japanese Art of War: Understanding the Culture of Strategy.* Boston: Shambhala, 2005.

Coggins, Jack. *Arms and Equipment of the Civil War.* Garden City, NY: Doubleday, 1962.

———. *Soldiers and Warriors: An Illustrated History.* New York: Doubleday, 2006.

Commager, Henry Steele. *The Blue and the Gray: The Story of the Civil War as Told by Participants.* Indianapolis: Bobbs-Merrill, 1950.

Commager, Henry Steele, and Richard B. Morris, eds. *The Spirit of Seventy-Six: The Story of the Revolution as Told by Its Participants.* New York: Harper, 1958.

Congdon, Don, ed. *Combat: The Civil War.* New York: Mallard Press, 1967.

Coppard, George. *With a Machine Gun to Cambrai.* London: Her Majesty's Stationery Office, 1969.

Cotterell, Arthur. *Chariot: The Astounding Rise and Fall of the World's First War Machine.* London: Pimlico, 2004.

Cowdrey, Albert E. *Fighting for Life: American Military Medicine in World War II.* New York: Free Press, 1994.

Creagh, Patrick, trans. *Giuseppe Ungaretti: Selected Poems.* London: Penguin, 1971.

Dann, John C., ed. *The Revolution Remembered: Eyewitness Accounts of the War of Independence.* Chicago: University of Chicago Press, 1980.

Diagram Group. *Weapons: An International Encyclopedia from 5000 B.C. to 2000 A.D.* New York: St. Martin's, 1980.

Dick, Robert C. *Cutthroats: The Adventures of a Sherman Tank Driver in the Pacific.* New York: Ballantine/Presidio, 2006

Drews, R. *The End of the Bronze Age: Changes in Warfare and the Catastrophe, c. 1200 BC.* Princeton, NJ: Princeton University Press, 1993.

Duffy, Christopher. *The Military Experience in the Age of Reason.* London: Routledge and Kegan Paul, 1987.

Dunn, Captain J. C. *The War the Infantry Knew, 1914–1919.* 1938. Reprint, London: Cardinal, 1989.

Dunnigan, James F., and Albert A. Nofi. *The Pacific War Encyclopedia.* Madison, WI: Facts on File, 1998.

Dupuy, Col. Trevor N. *Attrition: Forecasting Battle Casualties and Equipment Losses in Modern War.* Falls Church, VA: Nova, 1995.

———. *Numbers, Predictions & War: Using History to Evaluate Combat Factors and Predict the Outcome of Battles.* Indianapolis: Bobbs-Merrill, 1979.

———. *War: History and Theory of Combat.* New York: Paragon House, 1987.

Ebert, James R. *A Life in a Year: The American Infantryman in Vietnam.* New York: Ballantine, 1993.

Ehrenreich, Barbara. *Blood Rites: Origins and History of the Passions of War.* New York: Holt, 1997.

Eicher, David J. *The Longest Night: A Military History of the Civil War.* New York: Simon & Schuster, 2001.

Ellis, John. *On the Front Line: The Experience of War Through the Eyes of the Allied Soldiers of World War II.* New York: Wiley, 1990.

———. *The Social History of the Machine Gun.* London: Croom Helm, 1975.

———. *World War II: The Encyclopedia of Facts and Figures.* Madison, WI: Facts on File, 1995.

Elton, Hugh. *Warfare in Roman Europe, A.D. 350–425.* Oxford: Clarendon, 1996.

Fagles, Robert, trans. *The Iliad.* New York: Viking Penguin, 1990.

Farwell, Byron. *Queen Victoria's Little Wars.* New York: Harper and Row, 1972.

Faust, Drew Gilpin. *This Republic of Suffering: Death and the American Civil War.* New York: Knopf, 2008.

Featherstone, Donald. *Victorian Colonial Warfare: Africa.* London: Blandford, 1992.

Fischer, David Hackett. *Washington's Crossing.* Oxford: Oxford University Press, 2004.

Fishbein, Morris, ed. *Doctors at War.* New York: Dutton, 1945.

Fisher, Tyler. *A Medic's War: One Man's True Odyssey of Hardship, Friendship, and Survival in the Second World War.* San Diego: Aventine, 2005.

Fitchett, W.H. *Wellington's Men.* London: Smith, Elder, 1900.

Flynn, Sean Michael. *The Fighting 69th: One Remarkable National Guard Unit's Journey from Ground Zero to Baghdad.* New York: Viking, 2007.

Ford, Roger. *The Grim Reaper: Machine-Guns and Machine-Gunners in Action.* London: Sidgwick and Jackson, 1996.

Forty, George. *Tank Warfare in the Second World War: An Oral History.* London: Constable, 1998.

Fox, William F. *Regimental Losses in the American Civil War, 1861–1865.* 1880. Reprint, Gulf Breeze, FL: eBooksonDisk.com, 2002.

Franklin, Robert "Doc Joe." *Medic!: How I Fought World War II with Morphine, Sulfa, and Iodine Swabs.* Lincoln: University of Nebraska Press, 2006.

Fraser, George MacDonald. *Quartered Safe Out Here: A Harrowing Tale of World War II.* New York: Skyhorse, 2007.

Frey, Sylvia R. *The British Soldier in America: A Social History of Military Life in the Revolutionary Period.* Austin: University of Texas Press, 1981.

Fritz, Stephen G. *Frontsoldaten: The German Soldier in World War II.* Lexington: University Press of Kentucky, 1995.

Frölich, H. *Die Militärmedicin Homer's.* Stuttgart: Ende, 1879.

Fuller, J. F. C. *Armament & History: The Influence of Armament on History from the Dawn of Classical Warfare to the End of the Second World War.* New York: Scribner's, 1945.

Fussell, Paul. *The Boys' Crusade: The American Infantry in Northwest Europe, 1944–1945.* New York: Modern Library, 2003.

———. *Doing Battle: The Making of a Skeptic.* Boston: Back Bay/Little, Brown, 1996.

———. *The Great War and Modern Memory.* New York: Oxford University Press, 1977.

———. *Wartime: Understanding and Behavior in the Second World War.* New York: Oxford University Press, 1989.

Fussell, Paul, ed. *The Norton Book of Modern War.* New York: Norton, 1991.

Gallagher, John J. *The Battle of Brooklyn, 1776.* Cambridge, MA: Da Capo, 1995.

Gantter, Raymond. *Roll Me Over: An Infantryman's World War II.* New York: Ballantine, 1997.

Glantz, David M., and Jonathan House. *When Titans Clashed: How the Red Army Stopped Hitler.* Lawrence: University of Kansas Press, 1995.

Glasser, Ronald J. *365 Days.* New York: Braziller, 1971.

Gleig, George Robert. *The Subaltern: A Chronicle of the Peninsular War.* 1825. Reprint, London: Leo Cooper/Pen and Sword, 2001.

Gluckman, Arcadi. *United States Muskets, Rifles, and Carbines.* Harrisburg, PA: Stackpole, 1959.

Goldsworthy, Adrian. *Roman Warfare.* London: Cassell, 2000.

Goodrich, Thomas. *Scalp Dance: Indian Warfare on the High Plains, 1865–1879.* Harrisburg, PA: Stackpole, 1997.

Gordon, Michael R., and Gen. Bernard E. Trainor. *Cobra II: The Inside Story of the Invasion and Occupation of Iraq.* New York: Pantheon, 2006.

Gragg, Rod. *Covered with Glory: The 26th North Carolina Infantry at the Battle of Gettysburg.* New York: HarperCollins, 2000.

Gran, Lester W., et al. "Guerrilla Warfare and Land Mine Casualties

Remain Inseparable." *U.S. Army Medical Department Journal,* October–December 1998: 10–16.

Grant, Ulysses S. *Personal Memoirs.* 1885. Reprint, New York: Penguin, 1995.

Graves, Robert. *Good-bye to All That.* 1929. Reprint, London: Penguin, 1960.

Greenwood, John T., and Clifton F. Berry. *Medics at War: Military Medicine from Colonial Times to the 21st Century.* Annapolis: Naval Institute Press, 2005.

Griffith, Paddy. *Battle Tactics of the Civil War.* New Haven: Yale University Press, 1989.

———. *Battle Tactics of the Western Front: The British Army's Art of Attack.* New Haven: Yale University Press, 1994.

———. *Forward into Battle: Fighting Tactics from Waterloo to the Near Future.* Novato, CA: Presidio, 1997.

Grossman, Lt. Col. Dave. *On Killing: The Psychological Cost of Learning to Kill in War and Society.* Boston: Back Bay, 1995.

Grossman, Vasily. *A Writer at War: A Soviet Journalist with the Red Army, 1941–1945.* Trans. and eds. Antony Beevor and Luba Vinogradova, New York: Pantheon, 2005.

Guilane, Jean, and Jean Zammit. *The Origins of War: Violence in Prehistory.* London: Blackwell, 2005.

Hackett, Gen. Sir John, ed. *Warfare in the Ancient World.* London: Sidgwick & Jackson, 1989.

Hackworth, Col. David H. *Steel My Soldiers' Hearts.* New York: Simon & Schuster, 2002.

———. and Julie Sherman. *About Face: The Odyssey of an American Warrior.* New York: Simon & Schuster, 1989.

Hall, Bert S. *Weapons and Warfare in Renaissance Europe.* Baltimore: Johns Hopkins University Press, 1997.

Hanson, Victor Davis. *Carnage and Culture: Landmark Battles in the Rise of Western Power.* New York: Anchor, 2002.

———. *The Western Way of War: Infantry Battle in Classical Greece.* Berkeley: University of California Press, 1994.

Hardy, Robert. *Longbow: A Social and Military History.* Somerset, UK: Sparkford, 1976.

Hart, Peter. *The Somme: The Darkest Hour on the Western Front.* New York: Pegasus, 2008.

Harwell, Richard B., ed. *The Civil War Reader.* New York: Konecky and Konecky, 1957.

Hassig, Ross. *Aztec Warfare: Imperial Expansion and Political Control.* Norman: University of Oklahoma Press, 1988.

Hastings, Max. *Warriors: Portraits from the Battlefield.* New York: Vintage, 2007.

Haythornthwaite, Philip. *The Armies of Wellington.* London: Arms and Armour, 1994.

———. *The English Civil War, 1642–1651: An Illustrated Military History.* London: Brockhampton, 1998.

———. *Weapons & Equipment of the Napoleonic Wars*. London: Arms and Armour, 1979.

———. *The World War One Source Book*. London: Arms and Armour, 1992.

Hess, Earl J. *The Union Soldier in Battle: Enduring the Ordeal of Combat*. Lawrence: University Press of Kansas, 1997.

Hodgkinson, Peter E. "Clearing the Dead." *Journal of the Centre for First World War Studies* 3, no. 1 (September 2007).

Hogg, Ian. *Tank Killing: Anti-Tank Warfare by Men and Machines*. New York: Sarpedon, 1996.

Holmes, Richard. *Acts of War: The Behavior of Men in Battle*. New York: Free Press, 1985.

———. *Redcoat: The British Soldier in the Age of Horse and Musket*. New York: W. W. Norton, 2001.

———. *Tommy: The British Soldier on the Western Front, 1914–1918*. New York: HarperCollins, 2004.

Horne, Alastair. *The Price of Glory: Verdun, 1916*. New York: St. Martin's, 1963.

Huber, Thomas M. "Japanese Counterartillery Methods on Okinawa, April–June 1945." Combined Studies Institute Report 13, *Tactical Responses to Concentrated Artillery*. US Army Combined Arms Center.

Hughes, Maj. Gen. B. P. *Firepower: Weapons Effectiveness on the Battlefield, 1630–1850*. London: Arms and Armour, 1974.

Hynes, Samuel. *The Soldiers' Tale: Bearing Witness to Modern War*. New York: Allen Lane/Penguin Press, 1997.

Jobé, Joseph, ed. *Guns: An Illustrated History of Artillery*. New York: Crescent, 1971.

Johnson, J. H. *Stalemate: Great Trench Warfare Battles*. London: Cassell, 1995.

Jünger, Ernst. *Storm of Steel*. Translated by Michael Hoffmann. 1920. Reprint, London: Penguin, 2003.

Junger, Sebastian. *War*. New York: Twelve, 2010.

Karnow, Stanley. *Vietnam: A History*. New York: Penguin, 1983.

Keegan, John. *A History of Warfare*. London: Hutchinson, 1993.

Keegan, John, and Richard Holmes. *Soldiers: A History of Men in Battle*. New York: Viking, 1986.

Keegan, John, *The Face of Battle*. London: Jonathan Cape, 1976.

———. *Six Armies in Normandy: From D-Day to the Liberation of Paris*. London: Jonathan Cape, 1982.

———. *A History of Warfare*. London: Hutchinson, 1993.

———. *The Book of War*. New York: Viking Penguin, 1999.

Keeley, Lawrence H. *War Before Civilization: The Myth of the Peaceful Savage*. Oxford: Oxford University Press, 1996.

———. "Giving War a Chance," in *Deadly Landscapes: Case Studies in Prehistoric Southwestern Warfare*. Glen E. Rice and Steven A. Leblanc, eds. Salt Lake City: University of Utah Press, 2001.

Kelly, Jack. *Gunpowder: A History of the Explosive That Changed the World*. London: Atlantic, 2004.

Kennett, Lee. *G.I.: The American Soldier in World War II.* New York: Scribner's, 1987.

Knappe, Siegfried, with Ted Brusaw. *Soldat: Reflections of a German Soldier, 1936–1949.* New York: Dell, 1992.

Koschorrek, Günter K. *Blood Red Snow: The Memoirs of a German Soldier on the Eastern Front.* Minneapolis: Zenith, 2005.

Krivosheev, G. F., ed. *Soviet Casualties and Combat Losses in the Twentieth Century.* London: Greenhill, 1997.

Laffin, John. *Combat Surgeons.* Stroud, UK: Sutton, 1999.

Leckie, Robert. *Helmet for My Pillow.* New York: iBooks, 2001.

———. *Okinawa: The Last Battle of World War II.* New York: Penguin, 1995.

Lendon, J. E. *Soldiers & Ghosts: A History of Battle in Classical Antiquity.* New Haven: Yale University Press, 2005.

Lewin, Ronald, ed. *Voices from the War on Land, 1939–1945.* New York: Vintage, 2007.

Linderman, Gerald F. *Embattled Courage: The Experience of Combat in the American Civil War.* New York: Free Press, 1987.

Livermore, Thomas L. *Numbers & Losses in the Civil War in America, 1861–65.* 1900. Reprint, Bloomington: Indiana University Press, 1957.

Livesey, Anthony. *The Historical Atlas of World War I.* New York: Holt, 1994.

Lucas, John. *The Silken Canopy: A History of the Parachute.* Shrewsbury, UK: Airlife, 1997.

Luvaas, Jay, ed. and trans. *Frederick the Great on the Art of War.* New York: Free Press, 1966.

Macdonald, John. *Great Battles of the Civil War.* Edison, NJ: Chartwell, 1988.

Macdonald, Lyn. *Somme.* New York: Dorset, 1983.

Macksey, Kenneth. *Tank Warfare: A History of Tanks in Battle.* New York: Stein and Day, 1972.

Malone, Patrick M. *The Skulking Way of War: Technology and Tactics Among the New England Indians.* Lanham, MD: Madison, 1991.

Manchester, William. *Goodbye, Darkness: A Memoir of the Pacific War.* Boston: Little, Brown, 1979.

Manning, Frederic. *Her Privates We* (published as *The Middle Parts of Fortune*, 1929). London: Hogarth, 1986.

Marlantes, Karl. *Matterhorn.* New York: El León Literary Arts/Atlantic Monthly, 2010.

Marshall, S. L. A. *Vietnam: Three Battles.* Cambridge, MA: Da Capo, 1982.

Martin, Joseph Plumb. *A Narrative of a Revolutionary Soldier.* New York: Signet, 2001.

McDermott, John D. *A Guide to the Indian Wars of the West.* Lincoln: University of Nebraska Press, 1998.

McManus, John C. *The Deadly Brotherhood: The American Combat Soldier in World War II.* Novato, CA: Presidio, 1998.

McNeal, Edgar Holmes, trans. and ed. *Robert of Clari: The Conquest of Constantinople.* New York: Norton, 1969.

McPherson, James M. *Battle Cry of Freedom: The Civil War Era.* New York: Ballantine, 1989.

McWhiney, Grady, and Perry D. Jamieson. *Attack and Die: Civil War Military Tactics and the Southern Heritage.* Tuscaloosa: University of Alabama Press, 1982.

Mead, Gary. *The Good Soldier: The Biography of Douglas Haig.* London: Atlantic, 2007.

Merridale, Catherine. *Ivan's War: Life and Death in the Red Army, 1939–1945.* New York: Metropolitan Books/Henry Holt, 2006.

Messenger, Charles. *Trench Fighting, 1914–18.* New York: Ballantine, 1972.

Mills, Dan. *Sniper One: The Blistering True Story of a British Battle Group Under Siege.* London: Penguin, 2007.

Mitchell, Reid. *Civil War Soldiers: Their Expectations and Their Experiences.* New York: Viking, 1988.

Mishkin, Bernard. *Rank & Warfare Among the Plains Indians.* Omaha: University of Nebraska Press, 1992.

Moe, Richard. *The Last Full Measure: The Life and Death of the First Minnesota Volunteers.* St. Paul: Minnesota Historical Society Press, 1993.

Moore, Lt. Gen. (Ret.) Harold G., and Joseph L. Galloway. *We Were Soldiers Once . . . and Young.* New York: Harper Torch, 1992.

Moran, Lord. *Anatomy of Courage.* 1945. Reprint, New York: Avery, 1987.

Morris, Donald. *The Washing of the Spears: The Rise and Fall of the Zulu Nation.* New York: Simon & Schuster, 1965.

Muir, Rory. *Tactics and Experience of Battle in the Age of Napoleon.* New Haven: Yale University Press, 1998.

Murphy, Edward F. *Semper Fi Vietnam: From Da Nang to the DMZ: Marine Corps Campaigns, 1965–1975.* New York: Presidio, 1997.

Nichols, David, ed. *Ernie's War: The Best of Ernie Pyle's World War II Dispatches.* New York: Random House, 1986.

Nicolle, David. *Medieval War Source Book.* Vol. 1, *Warfare in Western Christendom.* London: Arms and Armour, 1995.

———. *Medieval War Source Book.* Vol. 2, *Christian Europe and Its Neighbours.* London: Arms and Armour, 1996.

Norman, A. V. B., and Don Pottinger. *A History of War and Weapons.* New York: Crowell, 1966.

Nosworthy, Brent. *The Bloody Crucible of Courage: Fighting Methods and Combat Experience of the Civil War.* New York: Carroll and Graf, 2003.

———. *Roll Call to Destiny: The Soldier's Eye View of Civil War Battles.* New York: Basic Books, 2008.

Nuland, Sherwin B., et al. *The Face of Mercy: A Photographic History of Medicine at War.* New York: Random House, 1993.

Oakshott, Ewart. *A Knight and His Weapons.* Chester Spring, PA: Dufour, 1964.

———. *A Knight in Battle.* Chester Spring, PA: Dufour, 1971.

O'Connell, Robert L. *Of Arms and Men: A History of War, Weapons, and Aggression.* New York: Oxford University Press, 1989.

Oman, C. W. C. *The Art of War in the Middle Ages*. Ithaca: Cornell University Press, 1953.

Otterbein, Keith F. *How War Began*. College Station, TX: Texas A&M University Press, 2004.

Overy, Richard. *Why the Allies Won*. New York: Norton, 1995.

Passingham, Ian. *All the Kaiser's Men: The Life and Death of the German Army on the Western Front, 1914–1918*. Stroud, UK: Sutton, 2003.

Peckham, Howard H. *The Toll of Independence: Engagements & Battle Casualties of the American Revolution*. Chicago: University of Chicago Press, 1974.

Perrett, Bryan. *The Battle Book: Crucial Conflicts in History from 1469 BC to the Present*. London: Arms and Armour Press, 1992.

Peterson, Harold I. *The Book of the Continental Soldier*. Harrisburg, PA: Stackpole, 1968.

Pimlott, John. *The Historical Atlas of World War II*. New York: Holt, 1995.

Pohl, John D. *Aztec, Mixtec and Zapotec Armies*. Oxford: Osprey, 1991.

Pohl, John, and Charles M. Robinson. *Aztec and Conquistadores: The Spanish Invasion & the Collapse of the Aztec Empire*. Oxford: Osprey, 2005.

Porch, Douglas. *Wars of Empire*. London: Cassell, 2000.

Ratti, Oscar, and Adele Westbrook. *Secrets of the Samurai: A Survey of the Martial Arts of Feudal Japan*. Edison, NJ: Castle, 1999.

Reiss, Oscar. *Medicine and the American Revolution*. Jefferson, NJ: McFarland, 1998.

Reister, Frank A. *Medical Statistics in World War II*. Washington, DC: Office of the Surgeon General, Department of the Army, 1975.

Rhodehamel, John, ed. *The American Revolution: Writings from the War of Independence*. New York: Library of America, 2001.

Risch, Erna. *Supplying Washington's Army*. Washington, DC: U.S. Army Center of Military History, 1981.

Rothenberg, Gunther. *The Art of Warfare in the Age of Napoleon*. London: Batsford, 1977.

Rothers, Christopher. *The Armies of Agincourt*. Oxford: Osprey, 1981.

Rottman, Gordon L. *U.S. World War II Amphibious Tactics: Army and Marine Corps, Pacific Theater*. Oxford: Osprey, 2004.

———. *World War II Airborne Warfare Tactics*. Oxford: Osprey, 2006.

———. *World War II Infantry Anti-Tank Tactics*. Oxford: Osprey, 2005.

Russ, Martin. *Breakout: The Chosin River Campaign: Korea, 1950*. New York: Penguin, 2000.

Ryan, Kathy L., et al. "Overview of the Homeostasis Research Program: Advances and Future Directions." *Army Medical Department Journal*, July–September 2003: 1.

Sajer, Guy. *Forgotten Soldier* (first published as *Le Soldat Oublié*, Paris: Laffront, 1967). Reprint Dulles, VA: Potomac Books, 2000.

Sassoon, Siegfried. *Memoirs of an Infantry Officer*. 1930. Reprint, London: Faber, 1944.

Saunders, K. B. "Frölich's Table of Homeric Wounds." *Classical Quarterly* 54, no. 1 (May 2004).

Scheer, George F., and Hugh H. Rankin. *Rebels & Redcoats: The American Revolution Through the Eyes of Those Who Fought and Lived It.* Cleveland: World, 1957.

Scott, Douglas D., et al. *They Died with Custer: Soldiers' Bones from the Battle of the Little Big Horn.* Norman: University of Oklahoma Press, 1998.

Shay, Jonathan. *Achilles in Vietnam: Combat Trauma and the Undoing of Character.* New York: Scribner, 1994.

Sherriff, R. C. *Journey's End.* 1929. Reprint, Oxford: Heinemann, 1993.

Simpson, Louis. *Selected Poems.* London: Oxford University Press, 1996.

Sinclaire, Clive. *Samurai: The Weapons and Spirit of the Japanese Warrior.* Guilford, CT: Lyons, 2001.

Sledge, E. B. *With the Old Breed at Peleliu and Okinawa* (first published 1981). Reprint New York: Ballantine, 2007.

Small, R. C. *Crusading Warfare, 1097–1193.* Cambridge: Cambridge University Press, 1956.

Smith, Gary R. *Demo Men: Harrowing True Stories from the Military's Elite Bomb Squads.* New York: Pocket, 1997.

Spalinger, Anthony J. *War in Ancient Egypt.* Oxford: Blackwell, 2005.

Spilsbury, Julian. *The Thin Red Line: An Eyewitness History of the Crimean War.* London: Weidenfeld and Nicolson, 2009.

Steinman, Ron. *The Soldiers' Story: Vietnam in Their Own Words.* New York: Barnes & Noble, 2002.

Symonds, Craig L. *A Battlefield Atlas of the Civil War.* Charleston, SC: Nautical and Aviation, 1983.

Taylor, Colin F. *Native American Hunting and Fighting Skills.* New York: Lyons, 2003.

Thatcher, Dr. James. *Military Journal of the American Revolution, 1775–1783.* New York: Corner House Historical, 1998.

Turnbull, Stephen. *The Knight Triumphant: The High Middle Ages, 1314–1485.* London: Cassell, 2001.

———. *Osaka, 1600: The Last Battle of the Samurai.* Oxford: Osprey, 2006.

———. *The Samurai: A Military History.* Oxford: George Philip [Osprey], 1977.

———. *The Samurai Sourcebook.* London: Arms and Armour, 1998.

Turnipseed, Joel. *Baghdad Express: A Gulf War Memoir.* New York: Penguin, 2003.

U.S. Army Medical Department. *Medical Statistics in World War II.* Washington, DC: Office of the Surgeon General, Department of the Army, 1975.

U.S. Department of Defense. *Emergency War Surgery.* Washington, DC: US Government Printing Office, 1958.

Van Creveld, Martin. *Technology and War: From 2000 B.C. to the Present.* New York: Touchstone, 1991.

Verney, John. *Going to the Wars.* London: Collins, 1955.

Wagner, Eduard, et al. *Medieval Costume, Armour and Weapons.* Mineola, NY: Dover, 2000.

Walker, Scott. *Hell's Broke Loose in Georgia: Survival in a Civil War Regiment.* Athens: University of Georgia Press, 2005.

Warry, John. *Warfare in the Classical World.* Norman: University of Oklahoma Press, 1995.

Watt, Jock. *A Tankie's Travels: World War II Experiences of a Former Member of the Royal Tank Regiment.* Bognor Regis, UK: Woodfield, 2006.

Webster, David Kenyon. *Parachute Infantry: An American Paratrooper's Memoir of D-Day and the Fall of the Third Reich.* New York: Delta/Dell, 2002.

Webster, Graham. *The Roman Imperial Army of the First and Second Centuries A.D.* Norman: University of Oklahoma Press, 1998.

Weeks, John. *The Airborne Soldier.* Poole, UK: Blandford, 1982.

———. *Assault from the Sky: The History of Airborne Warfare.* Newton Abbot, UK: David and Charles, 1978.

Weeks, John. *Men Against Tanks: A History of Anti-Tank Warfare.* New York: Mason/Charter, 1975.

Weller, Jac. *Weapons and Tactics: Hastings to Berlin.* New York: St. Matin's, 1966.

West, Bing. *No True Glory: A Frontline Account of the Battle for Fallujah.* New York: Bantam, 2005.

West, Capt. Francis J., Jr. *Small Unit Action in Vietnam: Summer 1966.* New York: Arno, 1967.

Wiest, Andrew, and M. K. Barbier. *Infantry Warfare: The Theory and Practice of Infantry Combat in the 20th Century.* Minneapolis: MBI, 2002.

Wilcox, Fred A. *Waiting for an Army to Die: The Tragedy of Agent Orange.* Santa Ana, CA: Seven Locks Press, 1989.

Wiley, Bell Irvin. *The Life of Billy Yank: The Common Soldier of the Union.* Baton Rouge: Louisiana State University Press, 1952.

———. *The Life of Johnny Reb: The Common Soldier of the Confederacy.* Baton Rouge: Louisiana State University Press, 1970.

Williams, David. *A People's History of the Civil War: Struggles for the Meaning of Freedom.* New York: New Press, 2005.

Williamson, Henry. *The Patriot's Progress: Being the Vicissitudes of Pte. John Bullock.* 1930. Reprint, London: Sutton, 1999.

Wilson, David M. *The Vikings and Their Origins: Scandinavia in the First Millennium.* London: Thames and Hudson, 1970.

Winter, Denis. *Death's Men: Soldiers of the Great War.* London: Penguin, 1978.

———. *Haig's Command: A Reassessment.* New York: Viking, 1991.

Wolff, Tobias. *In Pharaoh's Army: Memoirs of the Lost War.* New York: Vintage, 1994.

Woodruff, William. *Vessel of Sadness.* Boston: Abacus, 2004.

Wrangham, Richard, and Dale Peterson. *Demonic Males: Apes and the Origins of Human Violence.* Boston: Houghton Mifflin, 1996.

Wright, Patrick. *Tank: The Progress of a Monstrous War Machine.* New York: Viking, 2002.

Index

Abyssinia, 183

Afghanistan, 5, 48; Garmsir, 363–64; coalition forces, 360, 365, 370; coalition forces and weapons superiority, 363–64; combatants and civilians as indistinguishable, 359, 360; IEDs, 371, 375; insurgency warfare and, 356, 358, 359, 364, 377–78; insurgency weapons, 364; Second Afghan War, 180; Soviet casualties, 371–72; Taliban, 360, 363

Africa: Meru, 13; war against Matabele, 187; Zulu and colonial warfare, 11, 81–82, 168, 169–70, 171, 177

Alcock, Jim, 258

Alexander the Great, 27, 40–42, 46

Amatt, Sidney, 218–19

American Civil War: accuracy of fire and battle conditions, 130–32; ammunition use, 133, 138–39; Andersonville POW camp, 400–401; battlefield medicine, 139–40, 392, 396, 397, 399–402, 403, 404, 405–6; bayonets and, 98–99, 129, 139; black soldiers and US Colored Infantry, 138, 160; cannon fire, 143–47; captives, treatment of, 160–62; casualties, artillery and the infantry, 105, 143–47; casualties, North vs. South, 122–27, 147; casualties, tetanus and, 400; casualties, weapons and types of wounds, 139–42, 143–44, 145, 294; casualties and Confederate cultural heritage, 127–28, 147–48; casualties and

confined killing zones, 132, 133–37, 142–43; casualties and disease, 124; casualties and frontal attack, 127–29, 134, 135, 137, 142–43; casualties and localized risk, 126; casualties and tactics, 136–37; casualties compared to other conflicts, 125; cavalry, 132; chaplains in, 157–58; common soldiers' view of death, 154–63; comradeship of soldiers, 160–61; dead soldiers and corpses, treatment of, 163–65; death and ineptitude, 137–38; death and solace of religion, 155–56; embalming, 164; fatalism and, 135–36, 151; fear of death, 152; fields of fire and killing zones, 129–32; Gettysburg Address, xi; the heroic and, 122, 128; honorable and dishonorable killing, 162–63; infantry, 94, 126, 131, 132, 135–37, 143–47; infantry, three killing zones and, 144–45; killing and joy, 159; manipulation of body counts, 123; nihilism, 157; officers and ambition, 151; officers and code of honor, 148–49; officers and death in combat, 41, 128, 147–53, 149n; officers and reaction to soldiers' deaths, 152–53; officers and style, 151–52; officer's sangfroid and death, 149–51; range of guns and artillery, 201; rifles, types of, 129–30, 132; subterranean warfare (mining), 214, 217, 222; as transitional, 121; Union ambulance corps, 397;

SHLOMO BARAK

SPACE

IS ALL THERE IS

A THEORY OF EVERYTHING - TOE
THE PHYSICAL REALITY AS
SPACE DEFORMATIONS AND WAVES

Producer & International Distributor
eBookPro Publishing
www.ebook-pro.com

Space Is All There Is
Shlomo Barak

Editor: Roger M. Kaye

Contact: shlomobarak@yahoo.com
ISBN 978-965-90727-5-0

SPACE

IS ALL THERE IS

A THEORY OF EVERYTHING - TOE
THE PHYSICAL REALITY AS
SPACE DEFORMATIONS AND WAVES

DR. SHLOMO BARAK

EDITED BY ROGER M. KAYE

CONTENTS

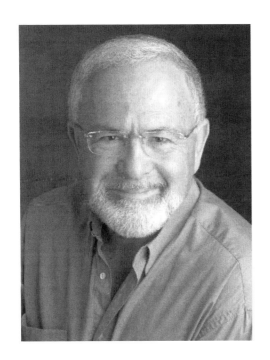

Dear readers,

This book is for you scientists, engineers, mathematicians, teachers and for you who are seeking knowledge. Here I present, in a simple way, my theory that explains light particles, the particles that make up atoms, and subjects relating to the entire universe. Physicists name this kind of a total theory of the physical reality A Theory of Everything – TOE. My TOE is based on 22 of my scientific papers, published recently, and a book, listed in Chapter W.

In my theory, Space is all there is and nothing is alien to it. "All there is" are space deformations and waves: some are straight-moving wavepackets, like the particles of light, and others are circulating wavepackets like electrons. This theory yields both theoretical results and calculations that so far, no other theory has been able to provide. More than that, it is a realization of Einstein's vision, expressed by him in many of his articles and books.

This book is important for physicists, since it presents a paradigm shift, and resolves many of the cardinal issues that have been left open. Mathematicians will find in my book my new geometry of deformed spaces that complements the Riemannian geometry of bent manifolds. The beginning of this book is simple but becomes more complicated from each chapter to the next.

ENJOY

PROLOGUE (Recommended for physicists)

The Current Paradigm

The current paradigm in physics, despite the successes of the excellent theories that construct it, is facing many obstacles. Many principles remain unproven, attributes of elementary particles cannot be derived and calculated, and mysteries are un-resolved. This situation results from the lack of a deeper theoretical layer.

The GDM – My Theory of Everything (TOE)

The missing theoretical layer is my **GeometroDynamic Model (GDM)** of reality, in which **Space Is All There Is**. The GDM provides answers as to what are: **charge, elementary particles, inertia (mass), gravitation**, and relates to additional fundamental subjects. The GDM does not, at large, contradict the paradigm; it simply serves as a realistic and tangible deeper theoretical layer – **simplicity and beauty at its peak.**

GDM RESULTS (The first of their kind in physics)

Some results, the **masses and radii of the elementary particles**, out of the many published in the Barak papers, are presented below. The Standard Model of elementary particles and String Theory, **wrongly** consider elementary particles to be alien to space, point-like or string-like, and structureless. This is why both theories **fail** to derive and calculate these masses and radii.

Electron/Positron Mass

$$M_e = \frac{s^2 \sqrt{2}}{\pi(1+\pi\,\alpha)} \cdot \sqrt{G^{-1}\alpha\hbar c^{-3}}$$

$s = 1 \quad [s] = LT^{-1}$

For the electron/positron charge, which is a white/black hole, s is light velocity at the event horizon, as the far-away observer measures.

M_e (calculated) $= 0.91036 \cdot 10^{-27} gr$

M_e (measured) $= 0.910938356(11) \cdot 10^{-27} gr$

M_e (measured) / M_e (calculated) $= 1.0006$ **!!!**

Muon/Anti-Muon Mass

M_μ (calculated) = 112.5 ·Mev/c^2

M_μ (measured) = 105.8·Mev/c^2

Quarks/Anti-Quarks Masses

M_d (calculated) = $9M_e$ = 4.5 MeV/c^2

M_d (measured) = 4.8 $\pm$ 0.5 MeV/c^2

$M_{\tilde{u}}$ (calculated) = $4.5M_e$ = 2.25 MeV/c^2

$M_{\tilde{u}}$ (measured) = 2.3 $\pm$ 0.8 MeV/c^2

The Elementary Charge Radius

$r_p = \sqrt{2}/(2s^2) \cdot \sqrt{G\alpha\hbar c}$

r_p(calculated) = 0.8774 ·10^{-13}cm

r_p(measured) = 0.8768(69) ·10^{-13}cm

r_p(calculated)/r_p(measured) = 1.0007   **!!!**

11

The Extended (unified) General Relativity (GR) Equation

By defining charge as nothing but curved space and using the Lorentz Transformation we derive the entire Maxwellian Electromagnetic theory, without any phenomenology. This result enables us to extend Einstein's equation of General Relativity (GR) to become an equation that incorporates not only the energy/momentum tensor ($T_m^{\mu\nu}$), but also the charge/current tensor ($T_q^{\mu\nu}$).

This equation becomes a macroscopic/microscopic equation of the entire physical reality. Charge and angular momentum are quantized and thus we predict that the curvature of spacetime is also quantized.

$$\mathbf{R^{\mu\nu} - 1/2 R g^{\mu\nu} = 8\pi G/c^4 \cdot T_m{}^{\mu\nu} + 4\pi G^{1/2}/s^2 \cdot T_q{}^{\mu\nu}}$$

where $S = 1$ and $[S] = LT^{-1}$. In the GDM $[L] = $ cm and $[T] = $ sec.

In the past, efforts were made to incorporate the energy/momentum tensor of the electromagnetic field in the GR equation. The common denominator of all these efforts to unify gravitation and electromagnetism was the idea that only energy/momentum curves spacetime. In contrast, we show that the right-hand-side of the GR equation expresses curving by angular momentum and charge. Curving by angular momentum is related to frame dragging, by the elementary spins, whereas charge is simply curved space. Charge and angular momentum are quantized and thus we predict that curvature of spacetime is also quantized. Thus, the creation or annihilation of pairs is supposed to result in a double quantum change in curvature

The GDM Idea

The elastic and vibrating three-dimensional Space Lattice **is all there is**.

Elementary particles are Transversal or Longitudinal wavepackets of this vibrating space.

The GDM Method of Unification

The GDM approach to the issue of unification is as follows: **Instead** of adding spatial dimensions, which we consider a formal, even artificial, way of unification, we have explored the possibility that **all phenomena** have a common denominator. This common denominator is the **Geometrodynamics of spacetime**, since in the

GDM **space is all there is**. Thus, Riemannian geometry, applied to deformed spaces rather than to bent manifolds becomes our mathematical tool to explore the reality.

The GDM Goals

The GDM is a model of the physical reality, in which **space is all there is.**

This expresses the drive to reductionism.

The GDM explains known, but currently unexplained, phenomena.

This expresses the drive to understand.

The GDM predicts new phenomena that can be confirmed experimentally.

This is the requirement for specificity and falsifiability.

The GDM logically infers laws of physics.

No phenomenology and hence no need to ask where the laws come from.

The Constants of Nature

$c_T = c$ Velocity of transversal Space vibrations (EM waves) $[c_T]=LT^{-1}$

[c_L Velocity of longitudinal Space vibrations ($c_L > c_T$)] $[c_L]=LT^{-1}$

$\hbar$ Planck Constant $[\hbar]=L^5T^{-1}$

G Gravitational Constant $[G]=T^{-2}$

α Fine Structure Constant $[\alpha]=1$

Since $c_L/c = \pi/2 \cdot (1 \mid \pi\, \alpha)$ we exclude c_L from the list and choose the known α instead. Longitudinal electromagnetic waves have recently been detected. In the GDM the elastic space vibrates transversely and/or longitudinally.

Note that in the current paradigm the number of constants is 20.

A Constant of Nature is a physical quantity that, measured locally by observers anywhere in space, and with any relative velocity with respect to each other and to space, results in the same value (invariance).

Note that a Constant of Nature is not necessarily regarded as a constant by an observer that observes other regions of space rather than his own. Our discussions on light velocity, both in SR and GR, will clarify this statement.

Motion and "Rest"

In the GDM **there is no rest** - only motion at the waves' velocities.

Elementary particles at **"rest"** are circularly rotating wavepackets. Their virtual geometric centers are at rest. When they move the wavepackets describe spirals.

The Units of the GDM

In the GDM all units are expressed by the unit of length L (**cm**) and the unit of time T (**sec**) only. A conversion from the **GDM system** of units to the **cgs system** enables calculations of known phenomena and of new, GDM-predicted, phenomena.

Einstein's vision

A. Einstein (1924)

In the present situation we are de facto forced to make a distinction between matter and fields, while we hope that later generations will be able to overcome this dualistic concept, and replace it with a unitary one, such as the field theory of today has sought in vain.

A. Einstein (1936)

$$R_{ik} - \frac{1}{2} g_{ik} R = \frac{8\pi G}{c^4} T_{ik}$$

..... is similar to a building, one wing of which is made of fine marble (left part of the equation), but the other wing of which is built of low-grade wood (right side of equation). The phenomenological representation of matter is, in fact, only a crude substitute for a representation which would do justice to all known properties of matter.

A. Einstein (1933)

…. the axiomatic basis of theoretical physics cannot be extracted from experience but must be freely invented…

The GDM realizes Einstein's vision.

A.   This Book

We all have curiosity, but each to a different extent. We all want to understand reality, but everyone is interested in a different aspect of it. My curiosity, from childhood, was largely focused on the physical reality. I wanted to know why, for example, water flows in one pipe, while an electric current requires two "tubes" – a pair of metal wires. I expected to receive the answer from my father, who worked for the Electric Company, but he was not a technical man and could not give me the answer. I, a five-year-old boy, was amazed, a little annoyed, I asked him: you work for the Electric Company and you're not curious to know what is electricity?

In my youth (1950s), I built myself a laboratory for electrical experiments. I built radio receivers and audio amplifiers, and I also helped build the school's natural science laboratory.

Electricity "electrified" me, but what is electricity?

What is an electrical charge?

Why are there only two types of charge (+) and (-)?

What is attraction and repulsion between charges?

Why does charge appear in equal portions?

What gives charge its stability?

What is the field of a charge?

What is the radius of a charge?

I used to subscribe to journals like "Technology and Science for Youth", "The Young Technician" (I have them to this day). I sought advice from teachers and electrical engineers but did not get the answers I wanted. After graduating in mathematics and physics, I went on to gain a PhD in physics, but answers came there none! And today, in the year 2020, there are still no answers. But, with all due caution and modesty, I finally have them, and I want to share them with you.

While in high school, I was troubled by the question of infinity. Intuitively, there is only one infinity. Thus, there can be no large infinity and no small infinity.

While wandering through the bookstores in Ramat Gan (there were several) I came across a book by **Frankel**, at the time my teacher, on the **theory of Sets** (I still have the book), which was developed by **Cantor**. I was in shock that took some weeks to pass.

I learnt how to compare infinite Sets and to scc that there are both large and small. In life, intuition can be helpful, but in science it might be a pitfall.

When I was an adult, and even before studying at the university, I learned that there are both true and false statements but there are also those which cannot be determined.

The language of physics is mathematics and geometry. Allegedly "on solid ground" but it is not, as was shown by **Kurt Gödel** in his **incompleteness theorems** (I have kept the book). We bring just a simple example of the mess that he created, **Goldbach**'s conjecture. Consider the following statement:

Any even number greater than 2 is the sum of two prime numbers. This statement claims that it is possible that it is correct - **true** - and may not be correct – **false**, but it is also possible that **in principle** it cannot be determined if it is true or false.

It was another lesson in modesty.

And now in my third age I have decided to dedicate my time to the study of the physical reality. I was aware of the numerous unsolved problems in the study of the particles as in the study of the universe and the endeavors to build a theory titled:

Theory Of Everything - TOE of the physical reality.

All this seems to me a wonderful challenge for the Third Age, and especially now that nothing can, on the face of it, destroy my tranquility or harm my concentration.

We pause here to learn something about the history of science and the aspiration to build a **TOE**. We can only then see the size and scope of the mission I have taken on myself, see Chapter **D**.

B. A Brief History of Physical Thought

First and foremost, to give you an idea of the difficulty of breaking a paradigm, which is what I am trying to do.

On the Ancients

Anaxagoras (500 – 428 BCE) was a Greek philosopher and astronomer. He believed that there is no absolute total formation and destruction **and no empty space**. Only later will we see that he was right.

Aristotle (322 – 384 BCE) developed many theories about nature and the way in which it works. Aristotle gave these theories the name, **physics**, although today many of these explanations would be included in the science of biology. Aristotle believed that nature is purposeful, meaning that a good explanation for an activity or event is one in terms of the purpose for which it was made.

Physics also describes activities and events by the means of the purpose for which they occur. But physics **mainly** explores the reasons for events. Aristotle adopted the theory of "the four elements", which also enables it to explain material changes in a purposeful manner.

The main principles of the Aristotelian physics are (there is no need to delve into them):

1. **Natural places**. Each element "aspires" to be in a different location relative to the center of the Earth, which is also the center of the Universe.

2. **Attraction/float**. An object moves in the direction of the location it aspires to reach.

3. **Straight line movement**. Movement in response to this force is in a straight line and at a fixed speed.

4. **Speed/density ratio**. Speed of movement is in inverse proportion to the density of the medium.

5. **Void is not possible**. Because, according to the previous rule, the speed of an object in emptiness is infinite.

6. **The Aether spreads in everything**. All points in space are filled with material.

7. **Infinite universe**. Space cannot have borders.

8. **Continuity theory**. Between atoms is emptiness, so material cannot be atomic.

9. **The fifth Essence or Aether**. Objects outside of the Earth are not made of earthly matter.

10. **The Eternal and Incorruptible Cosmos**. The sun and the planets are perfect spheres and do not change.

11. **Circular motion**. Planets move in a perfect circular motion.

These principles **are incorrect** and rely solely on observations and **logical thinking**. Aristotle **did not experiment**. Aristotle, for example, inadvertently stated that a heavy body falls to the ground faster than a light body. It was Galileo who conducted an experiment and proved that the **free fall** was identical for the two bodies. But Aristotle's physics became the dominant **paradigm** for about 1800 years, until Galileo's time.

What caused all those who dealt with science to be submissive to Aristotle's ideas for 1800 years? - God!

Today, too, physics has been under the influence of a paradigm for more than 100 years. This paradigm, which has promoted science in an astonishing way, is no longer able to answer my weighty questions.

I seek to change the paradigm and this transformation, as you will see, does indeed answer my questions.

Archimedes (287 – 212 BCE) was a Greek mathematician, **physicist**, and philosopher. His book **"The Sand Reckoner"**, concludes that the planets surround the sun. This was about 1750 years before **Copernicus** (1473-1543) (so where were they all?). Archimedes model was forgotten Fig. (B1).

Three hundred years later **Ptolemies** (Talmi) model appeared, Fig. (B2), that ruled till Copernicus.

It is important to emphasize: Neither the Sun revolving around the Earth – the **Geocentric** concept, nor the Earth revolving around the Sun – the **Heliocentric** concept, is correct.

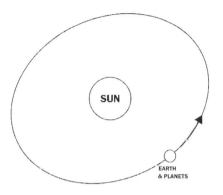

Fig. (B1) The Heliocentric System today and also according to

Archimedes and Copernicus

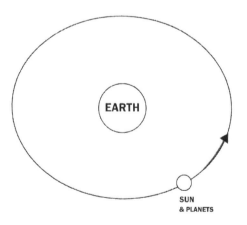

Fig. (B2) Ptolemies Geocentric System

As every physicist knows, two bodies moving around each other are actually moving around the common center of mass of both bodies, see Fig.(B3). The same applies to the Earth and the Sun. Because the Sun's mass is almost a million times larger than that of the Earth, the common center of mass is in the Sun. Thus, the heliocentric convention applies, although it is only an approximation.

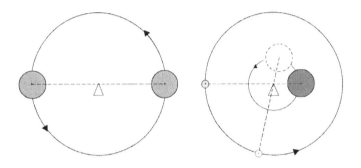

Fig. (B3) Common Center of Mass

Lucretius (55 – 99 BCE). His great work **on the nature of the universe** summarizes the main principle of the Epicurean school. The work is divided into six books: The second book, for example, discusses atomic theory and even raises the idea of worlds other than our own. This book is only a literary attempt to present an entire **Theory of Everything - TOE.**

The Three Philosophers

The Rambam, **Ibn Rushd**, **Thomas Aquinas** - In the twelfth and thirteenth centuries, these three philosophers emphasized the fact that there are two approaches to the physical truth: The serious approach to reality is the most complex and therefore difficult, if not impossible, to understand. The simplistic approach – accessible to most people, makes for easy understanding. The story of the world's creation in the Book of Genesis is an example of this (Rambam - Maimonides).

The Rambam, in his book, a Guide for the Perplexed instructs his disciple, an astronomer who is pretending to understand the composition of the heavens. Be satisfied, says the Rambam, with a model of the celestial movements and prove to us that this model is compatible with your observations.

New Physics

Galileo Galilei (1564 –1642**)** was not only the father of the new physics, and overthrower of the Aristotelian paradigm, which had been dominate for 1800 years, but he also initiated the first start-up company.

Galileo's father was a guitar player, part of a group that created the opera. Seeing his son reading Aristotle's book, he noted that Aristotle's theory of harmonies is wrong. As a proof of his claim, he demonstrated with his guitar. Galileo, noting Aristotle's argument that, in free fall, a heavy body falls faster than a light body wondered if Aristotle was also wrong on this.

Galileo decided that the real test for Aristotle's idea was an experiment. Dropping heavy and light bodies from the top of the tower in Pisa, he soon found than Aristotle was indeed wrong

This experiment demonstrated the importance of experimental physics. It established that the only test for the validity of a claim is an experiment or observation.

Galileo investigated movement and is known as the Father of Kinematics (the Theory of Motion). The Venetian Navy was interested in improving performance. Galileo's knowledge of kinematics gave birth to ballistics, the science of the flight behavior of projectiles. The funding of this research was a matter of some importance for Galileo.

In addition, the Navy contracted with Galileo for polishing lenses and building telescopes. This enabled the navy to discover approaching enemy ships, and Galileo to explore the heavens. The Venetian navy had made an investment in a scientist's venture.

Newton (1643 – 1727) Wrote the **Mathematical Principles of Natural Philosophy**, including his physical research in kinetics and the three laws of motion – **Dynamics**, and the force of **gravity** – **Gravitation**. He thus laid the foundations of classical mechanics. The mathematical model for the motion of celestial bodies was based on **Kepler laws** and other observations. Newton proved the laws of Kepler based on the gravitational central force. Assisted by the same principles he explained the cycles of Comets, the circulation of Tides, and other phenomena. His prediction that the shape of Earth was ellipsoidal was validated. Newton's determination that the universe is subject to mathematical principles has been a major influence on the Philosophy of Science.

In optics Newton invented and built the first reflecting telescope and developed a new theory of color. He worked on an atomic theory of light, whereby it consists of a flow of particles, now known as **photons**. He formulated the empirical law of cooling, and studied the first mathematical theory of sound.

Newton also developed calculus, thereby providing physics with a **language - mathematics**.

Boskovich

- Croatian (1787 – 1711) in his book, **A Theory of Natural Philosophy,** presented for the first time a complete, unified, theory of the physical reality – a TOE. It was, of course, wrong.

Einstein (1879 – 1955) was known primarily for the **Theory of Special Relativity** and the **Theory of General Relativity**. This book takes a close look at these theories, and therefore, at this juncture, we concentrate on a limited number of fundamental matters relating to the teachings of this great man.

At the beginning of his scientific career, there was nothing known about the essence of space and Einstein considered it as a reference frame only. He thus kept with the view of Newton and others that speed is only relative and that there is no Special Reference System. This is of decisive importance in the development of the Theory of Special Relativity.

From this theory we see that the perception of space and time are **subjective**. Two observers, Reuven and Shimon, move in carriages relative to each other, at a fixed speed and on a straight line.

Each of our two observers carries an identical yardstick and clock and they look at each other.

Reuven will find that both Shimon's yardstick and his carriage are shorter than his, and Shimon's clock is slower than his.

Shimon, on the other hand, will see the exact same situation for Reuven.

This is a situation that can only be observed at speeds close to the speed of light.

Of necessarily, there is no real change — This is a completely symmetrical situation. The only change is the observers' perception of space and time which is completely subjective.

Today, this result is accepted by nearly all physicists. It is a major component of the current paradigm of physics.

However, since 1905, when the theory was presented, and Einstein's death in 1955, we have learned several new things about space.

With this new knowledge, me and others conclude that **space** is a **special reference system** and that there is a special meaning for **speed relative to space.**

My understanding is that all bodies, including yardsticks and carriages, in their motion relative to space, undergo a real contraction that increases with their speed.

Clocks in motion undergo a real retardation that increases with their speed.

Adopting this approach removes the subjectivism from the perception of space and time.

No, there is no need to throw out the Theory of Special Relativity. But it should be updated in the spirit of Einstein's teacher**, Lorenz**, who also explained that the **Aether** is a special reference system.

Today the role of the **Aether** is taken by **space**.

The General Theory of Relativity, accepted by all physicists, is the heart of our theory. However, in order to understand it, it is necessary to adopt my geometry of **Deformed Space** that I have created and which we will further discuss in Chapter **G**.

Wheeler (1911 – 2008), a disciple of Einstein, formulated the view that space is the only thing that exists and there is nothing else. Together with his students Misner and Thorne, Wheeler published this essentially intuitive view in a canonical book - Gravitation.

His view, which is actually a TOE, Wheeler called **The Geodynamics** of Space. I have adopted this expression, since my view is similar, and call my model of physical reality:

Spacetime **G**eometro**D**ynamic **M**odel of the physical reality – **GDM.**

Feynman (1918 – 1988) was a disciple of Wheeler. His contribution to science and the teaching of science compares favorably with that of the greatest of his predecessors. He constructed a calculation formalism for fields and, first and foremost, for the electromagnetic field named QUANTUM ELECTRO DYNAMICS - QED. This formalism yielded important results, but Feynman himself admitted that we don't really understand how it works (I recently published an article that explains both why and how).

Based on the success of this formalism came the perception that an elementary particle is an excitation of the field that is associated with it. That a particle is a sort of wave-packet. But on the other hand, it is point-like and structureless.

This determination, which is only a speculation, is an obstacle, since without finite size and structure, it is impossible to build models for particles nor to calculate their properties.

Einstein, Feynman and the Paradigm

Einstein's Special Theory of Relativity, Feynman's calculation formalism, and the accompanying concepts are the main components of the paradigm.

They were useful in building the paradigm and brought many benefits. Today, however, the paradigm must undergo a shift as it is unable to answer the questions shown in the next chapter, and many others that have remained unanswered for decades.

If we consider the Aether and Space (which is not a vacuum, but has properties) to be the same physical entity, then Einstein could have adopted my theory. Note his comments:

Einstein (1920) Ether and the Theory of Relativity

… the hypothesis of ether in itself is not in conflict with the special theory of relativity.

… According to the general theory of relativity space without ether is unthinkable;

C. Some Open Questions in the Paradigm and Why They Are Unresolved

Gravity

Particles and star masses bend space and other masses move according to the bending.

So, what is this bending?

How can a particle, if it is a point, bend space?

How does a particle, if it is a point, feel the bending and know which way to move?

What is attraction or perhaps repulsion between bodies?

Electromagnetism

What is an electrical charge?

Why are there only two types of charge?

What is the attraction and repulsion between chargers?

Why does charge appear in the same and equal portions?

What gives charge its stability?

What is the field of a charge?

And if charge does have size, what is it?

The Electron

What is its structure, if it has one?

Why does it have inertia, that implies mass?

What is the size of the mass?

Why does its mass increase in motion?

Why does it contract in motion, if this is indeed a real contraction?

The Universe

What is dark energy?

What is dark matter?

Why does the universe expand?

Why is the space Euclidian (flat)?

Where is anti-matter?

We will settle for this and mention that **we have all the answers**.

Physicists, who have been long aware of these questions, begin to understand that a new physics is required – a TOE.

Thus, the timing of the appearance of my articles and book is appropriate.

Why Are There No Answers?

There are three Pillars of Physics:

Einstein's   Special Theory of Relativity

Einstein's   General Theory of Relativity

Feynman's   Quantum Field Theory

These theories are the heart of the current Paradigm. They have yielded excellent results so far but are helpless in face of the above questions. We will explain why.

We also explain what to adopt, what should be changed and what needs to be completed to provide answers.

Special Relativity

Special relativity refers to speed (constant velocity) in a straight line as a relative variable (parameter). Reuven moves relative to Shimon as Shimon moves relative to Reuven. One, as if at rest, sees the other in motion.

Note that the speed in a straight line, with no acceleration, does not allow you to know if you are moving at all. In this theory, only relative motion has any meaning.

Such an approach, as we will explain, does not allow us to answer the questions in the above list that refer to an electron.

According to this theory, an observer in one system concludes that in the system of a second observer moving relative to the first observer, both the carriage and the yardstick inside contract and time is dilated. See Fig. (C1) for (Lorentz) **Length Contraction** and Fig. (C2) for (Larmor) **Time Dilation**, as the observer at "rest" observes.

However, the second observer will come to the same conclusions as the first observer. There is full symmetry here and therefore both the length contraction and the time dilation **are not real**. So, what is wrong?

About 25 years after the death of Einstein, it was discovered that space is filled with the noise of electromagnetic waves, with wavelengths of millimeters, a remnant of The Big Bang.

Fig. (C1) Length Contraction

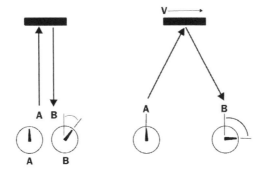

Fig. (C2) Time Dilation

This cosmic background noise is known as the **Cosmic Microwave Background (CMB)** or Thermal Radiation Bath.

The highest amplitude in this radiation has a wavelength of

2 millimeters. When moving relative to the radiation bath, that is, relative to space in which the radiation resides, a shortening of the 2 mm wavelength ensues, looking forward, as a result of the motion.

Looking In the opposite direction, a wavelength increase ensues. The greater the speed, the greater the shift in the wavelength.

From the size of the shift we get the speed relative to space.

This shift in wavelength due to speed is known as the **Doppler Shift.**

The conclusion is that space becomes a **Special Frame** (Universal) and everyone can measure their speed relative to space.

Unfortunately, the community of physicists did not take this fact on board.

With this new knowledge, the speed of the solar system in relation to space was measured. It was found to be about 371 kilometers per second from the cluster of galaxies Aquarius to the cluster of galaxies Leo and Virgo.

This fact that space is a universal framework opens a new approach to the conclusions arising from the Theory of Relativity. In this theory, the shortening of yardsticks and bodies as well as time dilation, which are seen by observers in frames other than their own, is only imaginary. But now, in light of the existence of a Universal system, it is possible to examine the possibility that the shortening of yardsticks and the change in the rhythm of clocks as a result of their speed relative to space is real, Fig. (C3).

This was the opinion of Lorenz, Einstein's mentor. But there was nothing, on which to base his suppositions, and they were rejected.

Today, with the detection of the cosmic background radiation we argue, as we expand below, that we should, in principle, return to Lorenz's approach.

This will open the way to solving the issues that we have raised. The formalism of Einstein's theory will be preserved, but the meaning of the theory, as we have explained, will change beyond all recognition.

Based on the new meaning, we can build a model of the electron and the other particles, and answer the questions that, so far, have had no answers.

Fig. (C3) Real Contraction of Bodies (C the velocity of light 300,000 km/second)

General Relativity

Einstein himself believed, and said, that general relativity will always be at the heart of any future physics (he did not mention special relativity). Einstein did not know just how right he was and why. To understand his theory, we must learn about the process that preceded its creation. Galileo, is the father of **Kinematics** – the Theory of Motion. He knew how to describe the path of moving bodies, like the Venetian Navy's shells, but did not know why they moved the way they moved.

Newton was the first to add the 'Why' to Galileo's understanding of 'How' bodies moved in the way that Galileo described. Newton showed that the motion of bodies is determined by the forces that bodies apply on each other. This branch of physics is called **Dynamics.**

Tycho Brahe (1541-1601) conducted observations of the solar system's planets and created tables loaded with numbers. **Johannes Kepler (1594-1600)** examined these tables and concluded the kinematics of the planetary motion around the Sun in three laws known as **Kepler's laws**.

So now, a room full of tables has been reduced to just three laws. From Kepler's laws, Newton deduced that a central force applied by the Sun on the stars around dictates their paths. This force is known as Gravity. Newton, like all his contemporaries, thought that space, in which all the bodies move, is empty – vacuum – and without end. **Newton** proved, as a derivative of Kepler's laws, that the force between two bodies, such as the Sun and a planet, is proportional to their masses, and inversely proportional to the square of the distance between them.

This is the Law of **Universal Gravitation**. But how it is that two bodies can affect each other when they are in empty space. And how fast does the effect spread. What this force is and what is its origin was not clear then and is only partly clear today.

It was Einstein, in his Theory of General Relativity, who made a very significant step towards the understanding of gravity, thus allowing me to give the full answers. First of all, he realized that it would make sense to suppose that the bodies were in a real, **non-empty medium**, and that it was this medium that transferred the force of Gravity. Moreover, the speed of the spread of force in the medium is the same as the speed of waves in it. This medium, he determined, is **space**. This is a revolutionary determination. Instead of an empty space without any attributes, that serves as a reference frame only, we now have a non-empty space and can study its properties.

In order to learn about the features of space **Einstein** conducted a **thought experiment** (in the human brain rather than in practice) as described in Fig. (C4). This figure shows identical four carriages in which the following things occur:

In A, in a carriage positioned on the Earth's surface, a stone falls from a top shelf with the acceleration of free fall on to the floor of the carriage. At B the carriage accelerates upward with the same acceleration as free fall. A stone also falls from a top shelf, which is at the same height. The fall time must be the same (and it is indeed), since an observer, watching from inside has no way to know whether it is on the ground or someone is pulling it up with a rope. From this thought experiment, Einstein determined that the response of a mass to gravitation was equivalent to its response to acceleration (inertia). From here (historically I am not precise), we derive the **Equivalence Principle**, the **equivalence of gravitational and inertial mass.**

This law has been confirmed to a very high level of accuracy in many experiments. But it has not yet been proven theoretically, in spite of more than a century that has passed since its discovery. However, I have presented an article that proves that not only are gravitational and inertial mass equivalent, but they are **identical.**

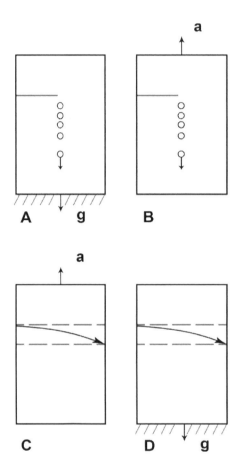

Fig. (C4) A Light Beam in a Gravitational Field

But let us continue.

In C, a light beam is sent from the shelf toward the right wall and parallel to the ceiling. If the carriage is at rest (or in constant motion in a straight line) the beam will hit the wall right in front of it. Both the beam's exit point and contact point are at the same height below the ceiling. If, however, the carriage is accelerated upwards, as the figure shows, the beam will hit the opposite side at a lower point. All this because of the final speed of the beam and the fact that while it is moving to the right the right wall moves upwards. In practice, this experiment is almost impossible because of the enormous speed of light.

From this thought experiment Einstein came in three steps to an amazing conclusion.

Cases A and B show that we cannot know what acceleration we are undergoing, that is, normal acceleration or the acceleration of free fall as the result of gravitation (Einstein, in his day, could not have thought otherwise. See Note at the end of this section). Therefore, of necessity, in case D where the carriage is not accelerated but is positioned on the Earth, it should get the same downward shift.

Eddington exploited a solar eclipse (1919) and demonstrated that a light beam from a distant star was bent as it passed the Sun.

Space is the medium in which a beam of light travels, ostensibly in a straight line. If it bends, it means that the Sun's mass is distorting space - bending it.

As a result of his thought experiment, Einstein concluded that gravity is nothing but bent space. This bending dictates the energy and motion of masses and light beams.

Here is Einstein's equation that expresses this idea:

$$R^{\mu\nu} - 1/2Rg^{\mu\nu} = 8\pi G/C^4 \cdot T_m^{\mu\nu}$$

The right-hand side of the equation represents energy and mass (which today is considered energy and nothing more), while the left-hand side represents bent space.

Einstein asked his friend **Marcel Grossman** to find a way to express the bending of space. His recommendation was the only suitable geometry at the time – **Riemannian geometry.**

Since then, many have tried to turn the equation into a general expression that applies to all the existing fields, not just the Gravitational field – the **Unified Field Formula** – as it is known.

The **first successful attempt**, by me, (note the addition of a new term in the right wing), is shown below:

$$R^{\mu\nu} - 1/2 R g^{\mu\nu} = 8\pi G/C^4 \cdot T_m^{\mu\nu} + 4\pi G^{1/2}/s^2 \cdot T_q^{\mu\nu}$$

Where S = 1 and [S] = LT^{-1}

So how did it come about, after more than a hundred years, that I now have a **Unified Equation** of gravity and electromagnetism?

The Theory of General Relativity relies on Riemannian Geometry which deals with bent (curved) surfaces (manifolds) and not with deformed spaces. The surface of a ball is, for example, a curved surface. A surface like this is two-dimensional, its curving is in the three-dimensional space, and its geometry is not Euclidean. On the other hand, my new geometry – **Barak Geometry** – deals with a deformed three-dimensional space. On the difference between bent manifolds and deformed spaces see Chapter **E** and **G**. In the Geometry Chapter **H** you will find the explanation of why Barak Geometry serves the General Theory of relativity better than Riemannian. It shows that a star does not bend space around it, as is believed today even though it is impossible to imagine it, but rather contracts space around it.

In addition, in Chapter **J**, I show that the electrical charge and its field are deformed space, and therefore electromagnetism and gravitation have a common denominator. From here the road to a Unified Field Formula (of gravitation and electricity) is long but paved.

By adopting the new geometry, whereas the Riemannian "formalism" remains the same as it was, our perception and understanding of general relativity has changed.

Referring to charge and its field as a spatial deformation creates a common denominator that enables the construction of the Unified Field Formula.

In other words, this provides proof that the gravitational and electromagnetic forces are expressions of a single force, the mechanical stretching and contracting (like a spring) of space.

Unification of all forces is the proof that they are nothing but the tension of space

So far, I have considered only the union between gravity and electromagnetism, but there are two more forces, the weak force and strong force. I will look at these forces, which appear to be nothing but electrical in nature, later. I will show that all four forces are expressions the elasticity of space. This reinforces our determination that there is nothing other than space and the only force is its elasticity.

Thus, the above extended equation becomes the equation of all forces, an equation of the macroscopic and microscopic worlds.

Time

Now we consider time as understood by Einstein:

Masses curve space and its curvature dictates the rate of clocks that are at different points in space (that is, dictates "the Flow of Time").

This is explained later on in Chapter **S**, but it is important to emphasize that the field formula refers to both space and time, or space-time. This is not simply a phrase.

Note (relates to previous Reservations) that Motion relative to a source of radiation can be determined, and the speed calculated, using the Doppler Effect. This is the effect in which motion towards a source encounters radiation with a shorter wavelength than at rest relative to the source. Moving from a source, radiation with a longer wavelength is encountered. Today, we know that the Universe is filled with microwave radiation, a relic of the Big Bang. This is called the **Cosmic Microwave Background, CMB,** and we will return to discuss it. The observer of a carriage can open a window and measure their motion relative to space and know that if there is no motion, gravity is working on it and if it is in motion it is accelerated.

For this matter to be fully understood, we suppose that space is filled not with microwave radiation (with a wavelength of millimeters), but with a uniform green radiation (with a wavelength of half a thousandth of a millimeter). If we move quickly relative to space, we will discover that space looks blue (shorter wavelength than green), behind us red (longer wavelength than green) and to the side (perpendicular to our motion) green. Further reservation, and this Einstein should have known, there is no parallel gravitational field to the parallel vertical walls of the carriage since a gravitational field is necessarily radial.

Quantum Field Theory (QFT)

This theory deals with all the elementary particles, but not only them. The first to be studied, were the electron and the photon, this study created **Quantum Electrodynamics - QED**. Today, this theory is part of **Quantum Field Theory- QFT**, and we concentrate on this. This theory was developed, following the contributions of many others, by **Feynman**.

The main idea of this theory is that the force between particles is a result of the exchange of certain force-carrying particles. This means that the force-carrying particle is alternately absorbed and emitted by the other particles.

As an example: between an electron, which carries a negative electrical charge, and a nearby electron, a photon moves back and forth which causes repulsion between them. We know from experience that two charges with the same sign (+) or (-) repel each other, and here we supposedly have an explanation.

To explain attraction between particles with opposite charges such as an electron and a positron (identical to an electron, except for its positive charge) we return to the photon. Of course, it is not reasonable to assume that the exchange can cause both attraction and repulsion, but not to worry, the mathematical formalism of the theory sets things straight.

Thanks to Feynman, this idea gave rise to a mathematical formalism that produced, with the help of Feynman Diagrams, see an example Fig. (C5), excellent results in various fields. In the title of this fig. Feynman expresses his wonder how come that the experimental number that expresses the amplitude of the interaction of a photon with an electron is the square root of the known **fine structure constant** α (**I have the answer).**

Feynman's formalism enabled the introduction of the known **Standard Model of Elementary Particles.**

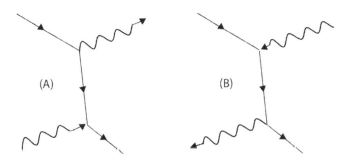

$$-\sqrt{\alpha} \sim -0.08542455\ldots$$

It's one of the greatest damn mysteries of physics: a magic number that comes to us with no understanding by man. you might say the "hand of god" wrote that number, and "we don't know how he pushed his pencil."

Fig. (C5) The Great Riddle

The Standard Model of Elementary Particles

This model has continued to produce results for decades, but some issues remain open. One example, out of many, is the question of the source of inertia of particles (the Higgs particle was supposed to explain inertia, but this explanation is problematic) and the ability to calculate their masses. Knowing how to calculate the masses of elementary particles is the **ultimate test** in physics. So here you are - My calculation, **the only one ever**, of the electron mass:

Electron/Positron Mass M$_e$

$$M_e = \frac{s^2\sqrt{2}}{\pi(1+\pi\,\alpha)} \cdot \sqrt{G^{-1}\alpha\hbar c^{-3}} \qquad s=1 \; ([s^2] = L^2T^{-2})$$

α, represents the **Fine Structure Constant.** G, h and c are the known constants. A dimensionality check: $[G^{-1}] = ML^{-3}T^2$ $[\alpha] = 1$

$[\hbar] = ML^2T^{-1}$ $[C^{-3}] = L^{-3}t^3$ Thus: $M = [s^2\sqrt{G^{-1}\alpha\hbar c^{-3}}] =$

$L^2T^{-2}(ML^{-3}t^2 \cdot ML^2T^{-1} \cdot L^{-3}t^3)^{1/2} = l^2t^2(M^2L^{4t}T^4)^{-1/2} = l^2t^2ML^{-2t}T^2 = M$

M$_e$ (**calculated**) = 0.91036 · 10^{-27}gr

M$_e$ (**measured**) = 0.910938356 (11) · 10^{-27}gr

We have here 0.06% accuracy!

So why did the Standard Model stop from bringing results? The reason is simple: This model is based on **QFT**. In this model fields are imbedded in space one for each type of particle. In a given field, like that of the electron and the other particles, every excitation is a particle. Therefore, we have particles that are point-like and structureless. This is exactly **the drawback of the model.**

After all, how does a photon dancing create attraction or repulsion? How does an electron swallow or emit a dancing photon? How can you understand and calculate traits of a particle if it is a point? and more ….

And yet: The mathematical formalism of Feynman is excellent, and if you just ignore his perception of the reality and embrace my own, there are answers to the questions.

Examples of this are given below.

In summary, we have seen that Einstein and Feynman contributed much to the advancement of Physics, but they also raised obstacles. However, with my model - the GDM, their theories continue to be beneficial.

D. The Mission I Took on Myself –

To Build a TOE

In the middle of November 1993, at Palmahim Beach, I dove to "my" cave at 15 meters depth. This time not to go fishing, but to think. A nice fish that looked especially smart, approached me. I asked him what is your view of the world, what is your TOE? He said, "all is water". And what is your worldview? He asked, what is your TOE? "All is space." I replied.

This answer did not happen by chance.

In my second year at the university, I learned the theory of electricity – Maxwell's electromagnetism. I came back and thought about the essence of the elementary charge unit, carried by various particles like the electron. The units of charge are of two types, marked arbitrarily (+) and (−) and with no meaning, other than to distinguish between them. These charges have the property that those with the same symbols repel each other, while those with different symbols attract each other.

I asked myself: this bivalency, the (+) and (−), and this attraction and repulsion, how can we explain it? The following idea occurred to me:

If space is all that there is, then a concentrated contraction can, for example, be a positive charge while an expansion (dilution) be the negative charge. This is how you get the bivalency. As for the repulsion and attraction: A pair of charges with the same sign, whether they are two contractions or two expansions, create (the couple) tension in space that can only be weakened if they distance themselves from each other. And a pair of charges with different signs create tension in space that can only be reduced as they get closer together.

This explanation requires an extension, and our analogy in which space is a spring mattress can help. Let's say the mattress is soft, so the tensions are very low or zero. Note that a spring can be stretched or contracted, and in both cases, tension is created and this also occurs in space. A positive elementary charge is a microscopic contracted area that also contracts its surroundings, a contraction that decreases with distance, and this is the electric field of the charge.

When in space two positive charges are close to each other, the contraction is the sum of the contractions contributed by each charge. For the contraction, and hence the energy, to be reduced the charges must move away from each other – repulsion.

When in space two negative charges are close to each other, they include an expansion that is the sum of the expansions of each charge. For the expansion, and hence the energy, to be reduced the charges must move away from each other – repulsion.

When in space a positive and negative charge are close to each other space contraction by one is canceled by space expansion by the other. For the tensions and the energy of tensions to decline, the charges must come close to each other – hence attraction.

So far, this is a nice explanation by the way of analogy and nothing more. But imagine that I can summarize this story just by one mathematical definition of the **density of electrical charge.**

Moreover, from this definition alone I have derived and proved all of Maxwell's theory of electromagnetism.

Maxwell's theory is a phenomenological theory that rests entirely on experience, while I have constructed the entire theory on logical inferences, based on the above one definition only. This matter has been subject to peer scrutiny, published and is stimulating much interest.

So, I had an idea that space is everything, and I wanted to see if indeed it is. I was motivated and I had both time and means.

Therefore, I decided to devote 25 years (that's what it took), which was supposed to end on my Eightieth birthday, to build the Theory of Everything, the TOE. I declared my intentions to my spouse, sons and friends.

It was a crazy decision, because, after all, what could be my chance of success?

So why did I think I might be a person (a person and not the person) suitable for the task? I derived the confidence that I am the right person by looking back at my life. I completed a doctorate at the

Hebrew University of Jerusalem with a research thesis in Physics (on the essence of light). To the dismay of my tutor and mentor Prof. Yatsiv, I did not continue in academia. I had, from early childhood, already found a much more important task that concerned the security of the State of Israel. I was able to successfully complete this task.

From this success, I have derived the courage, technological knowledge, experience in leading people, and thinking out of the box, that is necessary to establish a start-up company.

And indeed, based on one of my inventions, I founded one of the first hi-tech companies in Israel. I turned it into a multinational company, that was eventually sold for billions of dollars. I went on to establish other companies.

So, what does all this have to do with physics? You may be surprised to learn that even scientific communities are influenced by the spirit of time – the **Zeitgeist**, and they have characteristic elements in sociology and the psychology of communities.

The variety of my life experiences has enabled me to understand these elements in the community of physicists, and to understand how they have shaped the paradigms of both the past and the present. And, in particular, to understand where the mines are laid.

An example is the dispute between Lorenz and his disciple Einstein that was resolved in favor of the latter. Was this dispute affected by the spirit of Logical Positivism, also called Logical Empiricism, that arose in Vienna at that time – I wonder.

There are, of course, more examples, but I will hold back.

The majority of scientists make use of the basic principles they have learned and read. These elements are considered to be almost impossible to appeal. But despite their training and talents, they are sometimes faced with a wall, problems that refuse to be resolved. Only a few scientists are able to breach this wall.

As an example, consider the orbit of the hot planet, Mercury, revolving around the Sun. Calculating its path using Newton's Law of Gravitation gives a result that deviates slightly from observations.

Only after many years, Einstein adopted an alternative theory to that of Newton, General Relativity, to show that calculation correlates to observation. Newton's theory, however, does not have to be discarded, it is an approximation, which follows General Relativity for the case of weak gravitation.

And another reason why I thought I might be suitable for the task.

I have never been an academic, anxious for his position, and afraid of exceeding the paradigm and hence being known as a crackpot.

While I am not an academic, over the years I have kept myself fit, not only physically but also professionally. Step by step, towards the 23rd year, since I started my project, I was able to calculate the masses of the elementary particles and found them to fit the experimental results.

In physics, this is the determining factor: Do you know how to calculate things, that so far no one has succeeded. Therefore, I believed that my project was proceeding successfully, and it was time to publish my work in a series of scientific articles. I have published

22 complex, professional scientific articles, which have received considerable attention.

This is nice, it proves there is interest, **but no more than that**. Real recognition is a long and painful matter when it comes to overcoming common perceptions.

Aristotle's Paradigm ruled for 1800 years before Galileo disproved it with the fall of bodies from the tower in Pisa.

Archimedes, in his book the Sand Reckoner, presented a model of the solar system, where the planets revolve around the Sun and not around the Earth.

This model was forgotten and only about 1800 years later the scientific world started to take an interest in the heliocentric model of Copernicus. In these matters, it seems, a lot of patience is required - something I have in abundance.

The day that marked 25 years since I began the project, was, as I had planned my 80th birthday. On the same day I published my eBook which is a collection of my articles that I had published till then, under the title:

A Spacetime GeometroDynamic Model (GDM) of the Physical Reality

In Hebrew, the name of my book begins with the word **Model**, so what is a model?

We have already used this word but in a more intuitive way.

A model is a collection of mathematical equations and geometric descriptions that refer to variables (parameters) and constants. Models are applicable in all sciences. In physics, variables and constants are physical quantities.

In our model we express all the physical quantities using just the density of space. We use only two units: a unit of length – for example a centimeter, and a unit of time – for example a second.

Some examples of a model

A model of the number of daily infections of the corona virus in a given city.

Constants: The city's area, the number of residents, their ages and background diseases, the number of apartments, their distribution by area and the number of rooms.

Variables: The distance between people.

Equations: Infection by the virus as a function of the distance between people. Infection by the virus as a function of age etc.

A model of the Solar system should predict the planetary trajectories.

Constants: The masses of the Sun and the planets and their locations in relation to the Sun.

Variables: Distances

Equations: Newton's Law of Universal Gravitation

The Objective of a model:

To create a concise language to describe the phenomena –

reductionism.

Describe causal relationships – **Understanding.**

Predict phenomena that have not yet been observed - **specificity and test of validity.**

On Causality and Reductionism

From the dawn of humanity, we have sought to know the cause of the events that surround us, are with us and are inside us.

At the heart of this desire is the understanding that every result has a reason -**the principle of causality**.

In the event of an occurrence that consists of a complex of sub-occurrences, we seek to know if there is a primary reason.

This is the desire to reduce a multitude of things to a minimum-**reductionism**. We also want to know what objects around us, and we ourselves, are made of.

We recognize that these objects may consist of individual objects, which are themselves not complex. These objects are referred to as **elementary objects**.

This is the recognition that a complex object can be presented as a number of fundamental objects, once again - reductionism. It is the striving to reduce a multitude of things to the simplest possible object.

The ancient Greeks, for example, thought that there are four elementary things: Earth, air, water, and fire. The Greek **Democritus** later raised the explanation that materials are composed of basic particles, which are indivisible – **atoms.** Today, physicists believe that various atoms (more than a hundred) are built from a limited number of elementary particles. The number of elementary particles in atoms and others is 15 and with the anti-particles 29. We will see that some of them are not elementary at all.

The ancients also believed that the cause of reason was the will of the gods. But the aspiration to reductionism gave rise to faith in one God - **monotheism**. It was the **Akhenaten** the Egyptian, Judaism, Christianity, and Islam that preached this belief. Believers in monotheism are divided on many subjects, but we are interested in the dispute as to whether God (if there is one) is outside of the universe and dominates it – **transcendental**, or is the universe itself, as was the opinion of the philosopher Spinoza and others. This view is called **pantheism**.

In this book we present, simply and briefly, the possibility of extreme reductionism in recognition of physical reality. This option is also in favor for pantheism.

Science

Science is the subject of research that builds **models** that are meant to be compatible with reality. Psychology, sociology, chemistry, medicine, and of course, physics are examples of this.

Mathematics, on the other hand, is an art, the result of thoughts that can be completely detached from reality.

Truth

Physics does not deal with **truth**, which is the absolute determination that this is the way things are and there is no room for further investigation.

So, because for every reason there is a previous reason, the chain be infinite. Either way, all that physics does is the construction of models with temporary validity (**tentative**) that match reality in a one to one correspondence (**isomorphism**).

When a new phenomenon is discovered that does not support the model its validity expires.

Geometrodynamics is the second word in the name of my model and it refers to my main idea that there is nothing other than space. We expand on this issue in the next chapter.

E. Geometrodynamics and the Character and Purpose of this Book

When your research leans on the common and well-known Paradigm you do analytic work. When you want to explore the **unknown and outside the paradigm**, you must activate your imagination and make speculations that are not accepted so that you can build a new model of reality. A model whose validity is tested by applying it to reality. And the test of its benefits is its ability to predict new phenomena and to provide original insights.

In my model of reality, **there is nothing other than space**.

Meaning that every object in the universe whether a table, electron, we ourselves, the stars or the galaxies, are made from the elastic, cellular space which is made of cells that can resize themselves — See Fig. (E1) and Fig. (E2).

That's why I want to say that any material particle, for example, is a type of deformation, such as the contracting or the expanding of space – see Fig. (E3) and Fig. (E4). This disturbance is of a finite size in its expansion or contraction and **passes through space.** Meaning that what passes is the just shape of this particle, its geometry, and nothing else. Hence the expression Geometrodynamics.

Fig. (E1) Cellular Space

Fig. (E2) Kelvin's Cellular Space made of Octahedrons

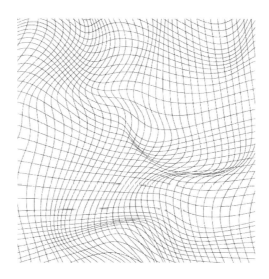

Fig. (E3) A Deformed Cellular Space

There is theoretical evidence that space is cellular and it has to do with space energy density calculations. The idea that space is elastic is a conclusion of General Relativity, and more so with my geometry.

Space as a Lattice

By attributing a cellular structure to space, we can explain its expansion, its elasticity and can introduce a cut-off in the wavelength of the vacuum state spectrum of its vibrations. Without this limitation on the wavelength, infinite energy densities arise. The need for a cut-off is addressed by **Sakharov**, **Misner** et al, and by **Zeldovich**. In addition, the **Bekenstein Bound** sets a limit to the information available about the other side of the horizon of a black hole. **Smolin** argues that:

There is no way to reconcile this with the view that space is continuous for that implies that each finite volume can contain an infinite amount of information.

I relate to space as a 3D elastic, deformable lattice, rather than a bent manifold. I have created a new geometry applicable for these 3D elastic, deformable lattices.

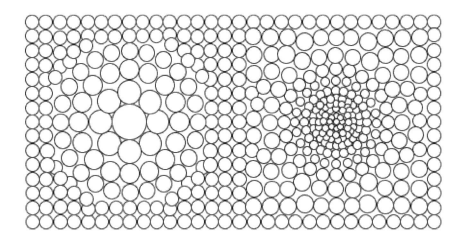

Fig. (E4) Electrical Charge: Left Negative - Right Positive

Fig. (E4) shows a two-dimensional representation of an elementary electrical charge that in reality is three-dimensional.

It is also possible to see the figure as the cross-section of the charge.

Let a sphere with a radius of several cells from the center represents the charge. The cells outside this circle are then considered the electric field of the charge. No sharp boundary between the charge and its field

A movement of the charge and its field to the right means that the cells remain in place and only the deformation moves to the right. This is Geometrodynamics.

This is undoubtedly not simple to take in – the idea that we ourselves are not matter but rather a moving geometry.

This model is the maximum possible reductionism.

This possibility, on the face of it, and especially for those who are not physicists, may be seen as deluded and unacceptable. Only physicists have the tools to examine the validity of the model. The general public can only be impressed by the fact that this is the maximum simplicity - **the Ultimate Beauty**.

From this determination that there is nothing foreign to space and there is nothing but space we want to create a new, concise and comprehensive description of the physical reality for the general public. This work is based on 25 years of research and has recently been published in 22 scientific articles and a book mainly in the journal HAL, see Chapter **W**. These publications can also be found on my web site,

https://cv.archives-ouvertes.fr/shlomo-barak.

The nature of the above kind of study is accepted by the community of theoretical physicists. I first asked myself, what is the most reductionist model of reality possible. I came to the conclusion that space is everything. Then I asked whether it was possible to invent the existing physics and beyond, while testing its compatibility with reality.

The invention of a model, using one's imagination, was **Einstein's** recommendation for the theoretical physicist.

In this matter, physics differs from other sciences. In medicine, the medical researcher recognizes the relevant biology. In biological research, the relevant chemistry, and in chemistry, the relevant physics.

But in physics where will you go? It's endless. You're in the underworld. You already know (I think that I know) an elementary electric charge is a contraction or a dilation moving in space. You know that the space is cellular and elastic, but from what is it made, and what happens in a black hole. Can space rupture, what happened in the Big Bang? There are endless questions still open, still awaiting answers. That's what makes physics different, and that's what makes me so happy. It takes imagination and courage to fight for your opinion against the accepted one.

F. On Physical Reality

In this chapter, which you might find exhausting, we discuss the key concepts that will be required below.

The Essence of Space

In the past, space was considered a reference frame only — a frame for the objects in it. Take out the objects and space become meaningless. Today, most physicists are convinced that space is a kind of material entity, a cellular structure which has features similar to an elastic medium.

We know that our universe is expanding. We know that it is deformed (General Relativity). And this is, of course, tangible evidence of its being elastic. We know theoretically that it is cellular. We know a few more things, but nothing about its essence, from what is space made. And yet this limited knowledge is sufficient to justify our model of reality.

Dimensions of Space

There are just three dimensions of space. We have no need of multiple dimensions, as String Theory suggests.

Space Waves

An elastic space, of necessity, vibrates - that is it creates waves. Such waves are transverse waves and longitudinal waves, see below. All physicists agree, however, that gravitational waves, which have recently been discovered, are indeed transverse waves.

We claim that the electromagnetic waves – waves of Light, Radar, X-rays, Radio, etc. are also transvers waves of space. The transverse and longitudinal waves have different motion speeds.

Waves in General and the Transverse and Longitudinal Waves in Particular

Waves occur in a media. The media does not move. Waves are a disturbance in the media, which can be a local change in density or a local change, back and forth, of the media's components. It is this disturbance that is in motion.

In a pool of calm water, the surface of the water is flat. Dropping a stone in the center of the pool causes the water at the point of impact to move up and down relative to the calm waters. This is the disturbance that moves out towards the pool's banks.

The height and depth that the water rises above and below the level of the calm water is the **amplitude**, and the distance between two peaks of the wave is the **wavelength**. The time that elapses between one peak and the next is the **period time,** and the number of cycles that occur in a unit of time is the **frequency**. In this example, we use the dimensions of length, measured in inches or meters. In the case of an electric wave we use the dimensions of voltage, measured in Volts.

On a Transverse Wave

The example above is approximately that of a transvers wave.

In the case of a transverse space wave the up and down motion is due to the contraction and dilation of the space cells perpendicularly to the direction of propagation of the wave. The amplitude in this case is given in units of length.

On a Longitudinal Wave

A longitudinal wave is a contraction and expansion of the medium (a change of its density) along the direction of propagation and alternately this disturbance moves at a speed that exceeds that of a transverse wave moving in the same medium.

In this case, amplitude expresses the size of the change in density. A sound wave is a longitudinal wave in the air.

A spatial wave is the movement of local contractions and expansions of the medium's cells.

Wave Packages

Waves of different frequencies can form, in one small area, contractions or expansions of space, or swing between the two states. This disturbance in space necessarily moves at the speed of the waves. Such disturbance is called a **Wave Packet.**

Distorted Space and its Geometry (With a Hint of General Relativity)

Cellular space means a space consisting of cells. And elastic space means a distorted space that in part is expanding and in part is contracting. Expanding – the space cells are growing, contracting – the space cells are shrinking.

In such a space there is no use for the geometry of Euclid, which relates only to a uniform (**homogenous**) space, which is also the same in any direction (**isotropic**), see Fig. (F1). We need, therefore, a new geometry. In the new geometry, for example, the sum of the triangle's angles needs not necessarily be 180 degrees. The ratio between the circumference of the circle and the diameter need not necessarily be π =3.14

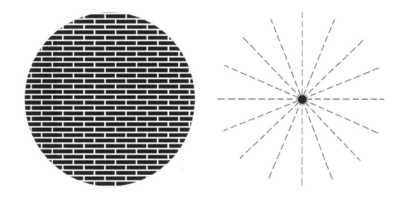

FIG. (F1) Left - Homogeneity   Right - Isotropy

Space Cells

Space cells are extremely small. They have never been seen and their lengths have not been measured. Theoretical estimates put their length – Plank's length – at trillions and trillions of times smaller than the length of the hydrogen atom.

Space Density

Space density is the number of space cells in a volume unit (e.g. cubic centimeters). The density of space is represented by the Greek letter:

ρ

The Elementary Particles

The material elementary particles, on which we expand later, incorporate an elementary charge, which is a longitudinal wave packet.

Longitudinal wave packets are characterized by being a contraction or expansion of space, or a swinging between the two modes (oscillation). Such particles are not strangers to space –they are wave packets that travel at the speed of a longitudinal wave.

In today's physics, the elementary particles are perceived as point-like and structureless. We, however, prove that they have a finite volume and a defined structure.

Rest and Motion

A material elementary particle, such as the electron, if it is in the state of "rest" relative to space, of necessity, it moves in a circle with the speed of a longitudinal wave. The center of the circle, which is a geometric point only, is at rest in relative to space.

A non-material particle, such as a photon, moves in a "straight" line (a geodesic), that curves with space, and the speed of a transverse wave.

Therefore, there is no rest – only movement relative to space at the speed of the waves. There are only two speeds, that of transverse waves and that of longitudinal waves.

Yardsticks and Distance

The distance between two points is measured using a yardstick.

We could, in theory, use a space cell as a yardstick.

In this case the distance between two points is the number of space cells between them on a straight line (or a geodesic).

If space is homogenous and isotropic – Euclidian as it is customary to call it - then between two points there is only one straight line, and therefore the distance is well defined.

If, however, space is deformed (not Euclidian) then it is possible to bridge the two points in different ways with different lengths. The shortest length, that is the smallest number of cells make up its length, is called the **Geodesic** line.

In a deformed space the size of the cells along the path is not necessarily uniform, but only their number is relevant.

There is also the possibility that a surface is curved, like that of a ball. In this case the cells are equal in size, and the geodesic line is that of the Arc of a Great Circle – the circle that is centered on the center of the ball and passes through the two points.

The Yardstick and the Distance as Seen by Different Observers

A uniform yardstick (standard) is a yardstick that has an equal number of space cells along its length. Observers in various places in space could, in principle, count cells to determine if the yardstick they are holding is standard or not. Note that in various places in space the sizes of space cells might differ, but the length of the yardstick is determined by their number only.

But a cell count is impossible. So how can these observers make measurements, and communicate between themselves, if they are at distant points in a deformed space, where its cells can have different sizes?

It is important to understand that not only space or the yardstick is deformed but so is the observer who is also made of cells.

An observer may not know anything from the study of their immediate surroundings, for example that they are themselves deformed, contracted, or expanded, relative to somewhere else in space. They may be able to know, if they investigate their larger environment that will reveal any deformation in space around them.

As an example, compare the measurements of an observer in a space station with those of an observer on a planet (Earth for example). The observer in the space station was equipped, before going into space, with the same yardstick as the observer on the planet.

We know, and will expand on this later, that a star deforms the space around it (gravitation). This deformation is reduced as the distance from the star increases.

Observing each other from a distance, they will both agree that, on the face of it, the observer in space has a longer yardstick than the observer on the planet as the cells in their expanded space are larger.

Such a view is not necessary today since the Theory of General Relativity enables the calculation of the phenomenon.

Barak's Geometry as Opposed to Riemannian Geometry

General relativity is based on Riemannian geometry, which deals with curved surfaces (manifolds) and not deformed spaces. The surface of a ball is, for example a curved surface. A surface like this is two-dimensional manifold, embedded in a three-dimensional space, and its geometry is not Euclidian.

On the other hand, our new geometry, Barak's Geometry, deals with deformed 3D spaces. Chapter **H** explains why Barak's serves the Theory of General Relativity more successfully than Riemann's. It shows that a star does not bend the space around it, as is believed today — but really cannot be imagined, but rather contracts space around it.

Clocks and Time

We don't know what is time, we only know what is motion, as the Greek philosopher Aristotle also believed. We can construct devices that are called clocks, in which the movement of the dials depict the "passage of time." Each cycle of the clock represents a unit of time. The measurement of the elapsed time between events is a measure of the number of time cycles that have elapsed between the events. We cannot attribute to time any meaning. We can only use the concept of time as a reference to the above.

Clocks and Time as Seen by Different Observers

We know, and there is experimental confirmation, that the rate of a clock is influenced by the spatial deformation. The same clock in a contracted space is slow, while in an expanded space – fast. That is, the same timepiece, in a space station, will be faster than if on the Earth. As a result, measuring time between events by different observers, one in space and the other on the Earth, will yield different results. The GPS system takes it into account; hence, it is so accurate.

Velocity and Acceleration

Distance and time are considered fundamental properties of reality. Therefore, the velocity that is the division of distance by time is considered to be resultant.

Since we hold that only movement has meaning, not time, we choose distance and speed as the fundamental properties of reality.

Acceleration is an increase of speed and deacceleration a reduction.

Velocity is relative. This was clear to Newton, and as such it is also considered by Einstein in his Theory of Special Relativity. I agree, but consider space to be a special reference system and that velocity relative to space affects bodies.

This velocity relative to space can be measured by the Doppler Shift of the Cosmic Microwave Background (CMB) radiation.

Speed of Light

The speed of light is the speed of an electromagnetic wave in space. This is also the speed of its particles – photons. I will further discuss electromagnetism and photons but for now, I only mention that I will show that electromagnetic waves are transverse waves of space.

Yardsticks and Clocks in Motion

I show that bodies, in their motion relative to space, contract as their speed increases and that clocks slow down.

These are real changes. In the Theory of Special Relativity, these are only imaginary changes.

Endless Space and its Universes

I assume that space is endless. In a tiny part of it is our universe, which we know is finite, with a well-known and well-defined radius and a measurable and well-known rate of expansion. Therefore, I assume that it is possible that there are many other universes in space.

Laws of Nature

A law of nature is a mathematical connection between physical quantities, which is always valid – at anytime and anywhere for all those who examine it. An example is the Laws of Electromagnetism.

I demonstrate that, given all we have shown so far, I can logically deduce all the laws of nature. This is contrary to the conventional understanding that these laws are **phenomenological** - deduced from experiment and observation only, and that they are laws whose source is unclear.

Constants of Nature

Constants of Nature are physical quantities, whose values when measured, are the same for anytime and anywhere. And for all who measure them. An example of a constant of nature is the speed of light.

It is customary to believe that there are some twenty constants of nature. We suggest that there are only four.

The Speed of Light as a Constant of Nature

We return to the observers on the space station and on the Earth. In space the yardstick is longer, and the clock is faster than on the Earth, where the yardstick is shorter and the clock slower. Although, originally both yardsticks and clocks were the same.

This is because on Earth space is denser than far away in space. The speed of light can be measured as follows: Let light pass along a yardstick from end to end and we measure its transition time. In space the light transverses a longer distance but the transition time is also longer because the clock is ticking faster. On Earth light transverses a shorter distance with a shorter transition time because the clock is ticking slower. In both cases, dividing the distance by the transit time gives the same result, the speed of light and therefore I refer to it as a constant of nature.

Note that the number of clock cycles, or beats, between two events determines the length of time between them. A fast rate indicates a long time while a slow rate indicates a short time. In the case of a non-deformed space, for two observers moving relative to space, one at a greater speed than the other, we get exactly the same situation and the same result as before. The fast observer is like an observer on Earth, while the slow observer is like an observer in space.

Symmetry in Nature and the Laws of Conservation

Emmy Noether proved the connection between symmetry in Nature and the Laws of Conservation.

We provide some examples:

Symmetry of displacement in time - the same occurrence (phenomenon) exactly repeats itself periodically (and remains fixed in time). In this case, the Law of **Energy Conservation** is held.

We compress a spring and tie it so that it does not open. Then it will remain so for a minute, an hour, a day, a year, and there is a **symmetry of displacement in time**. But the spring remains contracted, and so does the energy of contraction, and it is really the Conservation of Energy.

If a particular phenomenon exactly repeats itself, independent of its position in space, this is a **symmetry of displacement in space**, and in this case the Law of **Conservation of Linear Momentum** is held.

A body (particle) with a mass, is in rapid (uniform) motion on a straight line. In this case, the body has linear momentum which is the product of its mass and its speed.

If, in every place in space (symmetrical displacement), the mass (a scalar) is the same, and speed - its value and direction (a vector) is the same, then their multiplication that gives **the linear momentum** (a vector) is the same everywhere and **conservation of the linear momentum** is held.

If a particular phenomenon is preserved on rotation – **rotational symmetry** –then **circular momentum is conserved.**

It seems so simple - what is there to prove? It's hard for me to explain.

Please note, in the eyes of theoretical physicists, these are just words. Words do not convince them, the language of physics is mathematics, not English or Hebrew.

An additional symmetry that exists in nature relates to the laws of nature. Consider, for example, a particular occurrence, in a given frame, according to a certain Law of Nature. If the same occurrence occurs in a frame moving with fixed speed, in a straight line relative to the first frame, and obeys the same law, then there is a valid symmetry of the same law in both frames and in all of the frames that move relative to one another.

Such symmetry exists for Maxwell's laws of electromagnetism but not for Newton's laws, and therefore Einstein was forced to modify them.

Transition Law – **Transformation** – which determines how an occurrence in a given frame appears in a second frame, is called **Boost.**

An example of a Boost is a law according to which a particle at rest in a co-ordinate frame appears as a moving particle, at some speed along a straight direction, in another frame.

The Universe

Our universe (probably) has spherical symmetry and a known radius that is growing with time. This radius at the time of the big bang, which started the expansion, was almost a point. This universe contains ordinary material, radiation and mysterious Dark Matter, and Dark Energy. The quantitative ratio between them is measured and well known. But what is dark matter remains dark for almost 80 years and dark energy for 40 years.

The endless space, that includes our universe and others and all that happens in it, I call the Cosmos.

G. The New Geometry of the Deformed Space Lattice

Riemannian geometry is the mathematics of the Theory of General Relativity. This geometry deals with curved manifolds (explanation below).

The Theory of General Relativity focuses on our 3-D space and proves to us that it is a curved 3-D manifold in a 4-D hyperspace (this has nothing to do with the dimension of Time) and achieves excellent results. We **cannot imagine** this curving in 4-D, but we can make calculations.

Physicists have become accustomed to this situation. But this is precisely why they cannot solve various problems which we will discuss and solve.

Therefore, we present a **new geometry** with concepts such as those of the Riemannian geometry and with the same calculation formalism, but in contrast can be imagined and, hence, be useful in resolving the open issues.

Fig. (G1) Manifolds: Plane (Euclidian)& Bent (Un Euclidian)

The new geometry assumes that space is cellular, that space consists of cells. There is no reason that space in Riemannian geometry should not be considered cellular as well, but it does not make any difference.

The difference between the two geometries is double:

In the new geometry, the infinite global space is Euclidian, three-dimensional and elastic. But this elasticity is manifested mainly locally.

Being an elastic, deformed space means a change in the size of its cells. Thus, this space is no longer Euclidian (see explanation below). Note that in infinite space a local volume is an electron, the Earth, and even our universe, which is finite.

In Riemannian geometry, the global space is also three dimensional, **but if it is cellular, then the cells retain their size.** Our three-dimensional space is an elastic three-dimensional manifold that can be curved within a four-dimensional hyperspace.

Here we are getting lost, our imagination just can't handle it. But the mathematical formalism is valid and working. There is something here that does not match with common sense: if the manifold is deformed how can the cell size be maintained?

After reading the material below, it is advised to reread this introduction from the beginning of the chapter.

Riemannian Geometry

A curved single-dimensional line in a

two - dimensional plane

Fig. (G2) a Curved Line on a Plane

At a point, where the line is curved, a circle is tightly pressed to the curve – an **Osculatory circle**. The circle's radius at this point is called the **radius of curvature**. The smaller the radius the larger the curvature. The curvature of a line is termed positive if the osculatory circle is below the line and negative if above.

A Curved (2-D) Manifold in (3-D) Space

The two - dimensional manifold in Fig. (G3) is the surface of a ball. This manifold is curved, a positive curvature in a three-dimensional space. The radius of the osculatory circle, which is pushed to the point P is the radius R_0 of the ball

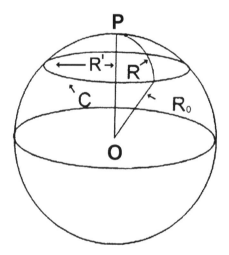

Fig. (G3) A Positively Curved manifold IN 3D SPACE

The smaller this radius, the greater is the curvature. If the manifold is not necessarily the surface of a ball, for example an ellipsoid, then take the largest osculatory radius, **R** and multiply it by smallest osculatory radius R. This product, **RR**, is the square of the average radius, while

K = 1/**RR** is the **Gaussian Curvature** of the manifold at point P. This curvature is considered positive since the two radii are from the same side of the manifold.

This is all valid for us, as observers outside the manifold, but within the 3-dimentional space around. A flat, two-dimensional observer on the surface of the ball, cannot see that this surface is curved. This observer will be able to realize that its manifold is curved only if they perform the following measurements on it:

Measure the distance from the point P to the circle whose circumference, C, is also measured.

The distance to the circle is its measured radius, R. Assuming that the manifold is flat, the radius that is calculated according to Euclidian geometry should be: R' = C/2π

If R = R'   the manifold is flat.

If R > R'   the observer on the manifold knows that the curvature is positive.

The **excess radius** is   δr = R − R' > 0

There is a one-to-one mathematical correspondence between the excess radius and the Gaussian curvature. Therefore, an observer on the manifold and an outside observer will agree on the manifold's geometry.

Fig. (G4) Negative Bent Manifold Around Point P

In Fig. (G4) a negatively curved manifold appears around the point P. At this point, on the saddle appears a section of an osculatory circle (radius **R**), that faces upward and a similar section (radius R) that faces downward.

Since they are on either side of the manifold, the curvature is considered to be negative. The average of the radius squared, as in the previous case, is the product of the radii of these circles, and the Gaussian curvature is also the same as earlier but with a negative sign:

$K = -1/\mathbf{R}R$.

This is our conclusion as external observers. The inner observer, located on the manifold should again make measurements around P. They would see that the calculated R' the result of dividing the circumference of the circle around P by 2π, is greater than the measured R. Thus,

$\delta r = R - R' < 0$

and again, the observer residing on the manifold and exterior observer agree on the nature of the curvature of the manifold.

Everything is fine, but how can you imagine a 3-D curved manifold in a 4-D hyperspace? Well, we remind you, you can't.

The New Barak Geometry

Fig. (G5) shows a deformed plane in the sense that around the point P space cells are growing. Note, that each circle represents a spatial cell or a set of spatial cells.

For the two - dimensional observer on the plane, and even for us outside viewers, to learn about the geometry of this two-dimensional space, we must make measurements. We note that, in contrast to the case of the manifolds, here the two internal and external observers see and measure the same reality.

From the center, we move on a straight line and count the cells, in Fig. (G5) there are 8. This is the measured radius - 8 units of length. From the eighth cell we move along the circumference of the circle and count its cells – 36 longitudinal units.

The measured radius is R = 8 and the measured circumference is C = 36, but the calculated radius R' is:

R' = 36/2 π = 5.86

and therefore, the excess positive radius is:

$\delta R = R - R' > 0$

Thus, Fig. (**G**5) represents a positive deformed space around P.

It is also possible to say that in case of a positive deformation the ratio between the circumference and the measured radius is less than 2π, that is: C/R= 36/8 = 4.5 < 2π

$R_{measured} = 8$

$C_{measured} = 36$

$C/R = 36/8 = 4.5 < 2\pi$

$R_{measured} > R_{calculated}$

The Excess Radius

$\delta = R_{measured} - R_{calculated} > 0$

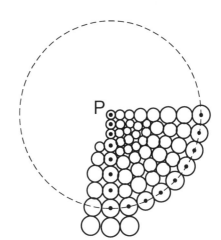

Fig. (G5) A Cellular Plane with Positive Deformation

Fig. (G6) shows a deformed plane in the sense that around the point P space cells are getting smaller. Note, that each circle represents a spatial cell or a set of spatial cells.

Here too we move from the center on a straight line and count the cells; in Fig. (G6) they number 8. This is the radius that we measured - eight units of length. From the eighth cell we move along the circumference of the circle and count the number of cells of which there are 64 - the number of longitudinal units.

$R_{MEAs} = 8$

$C_{meas} = 64$

$C/R = 10.2 > 2\pi$

$R_{MEAs} < R_{Cal}$

The Excess Radius

$\delta = R_{MEAs} - R_{Cal} < 0$

Fig. (G6) A Cellular Plane with Negative Deformation

The measured radius is R = 8 and measured circumference is:

C = 64, but the calculated radius R' is:

R' = 64/2 π = 10.2

and therefore, the excess radius is negative:

δr = R − R' < 0

Thus Fig. (G6) represents a negative deformed space around P.

It is also possible to say that, for a negative deformation the ratio between the circumference and the measured radius is greater than 2π, that is:

C/R = 64/8 = 8 >2π

Recall: in an **undeformed** space, cells are equal and Euclidian geometry is valid.

So far, we have looked at the concepts in the different geometries, and found that there is no need for any change in the Theory of General Relativity. It is, however, essential to understand its meaning, see the next Chapter.

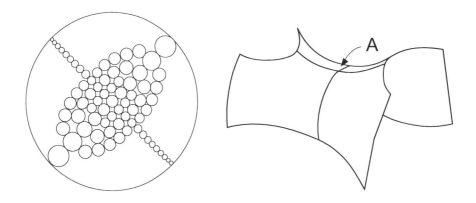

Fig. (G7) A Saddle as a 2D Manifold (Right) and as a 2D Deformed Space (Left)

Geodesic Line

On a warped (curved) manifold, the shortest distance between two points, A and B, is not, as we might think, a straight line. The shortest line is the **Geodesic line**. In the case of the surface of a ball, it is the arc of a great circle, whose center is that of the ball, and goes through points A and B.

For the case of a deformed 2-D space, Fig. (G8) shows, for an observer in this space, the shortest distance between A and B is not the dashed line, whose length is 7-cells plus two half cells, but rather the solid line whose length is 5-cells plus two half cells.

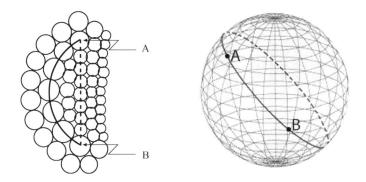

Fig. (G8) A Geodesic on a Spherical Surface (Right) and on a Deformed 2D Space (Left)

Parallel Transport of Vectors on A Curved Manifold and in A Deformed Space

Parallel Transport on a Manifold

This sub-Section is only for experts in geometry (taken from one of my books)

Fig. (7-5) shows the parallel transport of a vector on the surface of a sphere, where parallel transport means that both the tip and the back of the vector are equally displaced along the geodesic. We now transport a vector from O to P, and back through P'. The vector turns through an angle $\delta\vartheta$ so that $\mathbf{v}' = \mathbf{v} + \delta\mathbf{v}$. The curvature, k,

of the surface is defined in terms of δv as the vector, v, is moved

around an infinitesimal closed path with an infinitesimal area, σ.

(7-47) $\delta V = KV$

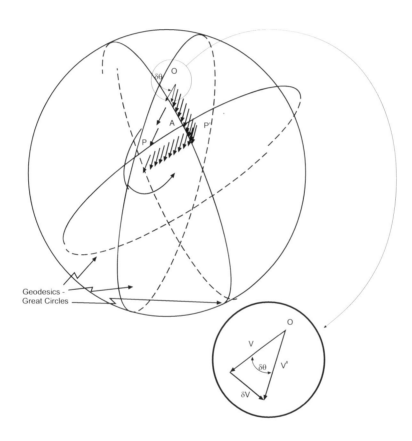

Fig. (7-5) Parallel Transport on a manifold

For a spherical surface with radius r, the curvature is $k = 1/r^2$.

Note that when a vector, v, is parallel transported along a geodesic, the angle subtended by the vector and the geodesic (i.e., the tangent of the geodesic) is unchanged.

Parallel Transport in an Elastic Space

Fig. (7-6) shows a deformed two-dimensional space or a two-dimensional cross-section of a higher dimension elastic space. The transport from O to P directly, or via P', yields an angle $\delta\vartheta$, and

$$\delta V = K v \sigma \qquad \text{the same as (7-47)}$$

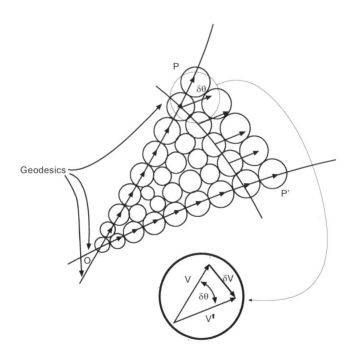

Fig. (7-6) Parallel Transport in a deformed space

On Another Difference Between the Two Geometries

On a curved manifold, it is possible that in the vicinity of a point there will be additional points with the same curvature.

On the surface of a ball, for example, there will be the same curvature around all the points on it. This characteristic is known as **global curvature.**

In a deformed space, if there is contraction or expansion around a point, then around adjacent points the deformation is, of necessity, different. This is known as a **local deformation.**

Adopting my geometry, with local deformations, enables the solving of a serious problem in cosmology.

The Flat Universe Problem

From observations and measurements cosmologists concluded that space in our universe is a three-dimensional manifold without curvature, **flat** in their language, that is **Euclidian**.

The problem of the cosmologists is that they do not understand how, from all possible curvatures, nature "chose", zero curvature – a flat universe as shown by the option on the right in Fig. (G9).

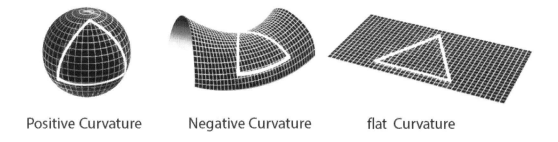

Positive Curvature   Negative Curvature   flat Curvature

Fig. (G9) Curvature of the Universe

My geometry provides a simple explanation. In the universe there is spatial contraction only around each galaxy and star, and this is local contraction. Therefore, space in the universe remains Euclidian. Of course, all the many equations that cosmologists have developed appear to say otherwise, but I will not look further at this.

How Do I Link the Two Geometries?

I have developed a rather simple formula, which gives the geodesic curvature, K, around a point according to (as a function of) the change in the density of space ρ around this point (appears in the article that I published on geometries).

$$K = \frac{4\pi}{45}\left(\frac{\nabla\rho}{\rho}\right)^2$$

In practical terms, there is no need to change the equations of General Relativity that use Riemannian geometry.

A positive deformation means space density increases toward a point. A negative deformation means space density decreases toward a point. Zero deformation means uniform density. All this affects our understanding of, for example, the behavior of light in space

H. The New Geometry and the New Physics

The New Meaning of Gravity in General Relativity

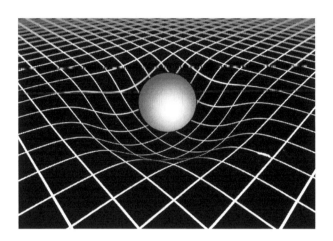

Fig. (H1) The Curving of Space by a Stellar Mass

Fig. (H1) is a typical illustration. This is how curvature by a mass is presented in all books. It is **meaningless** as we cannot imagine a curved three-dimensional space manifold bent in a four-dimensional hyperspace.

Fig. (H2) shows the true deformation of space by a mass, which is merely **space contraction**.

Fig. (H3) shows, again, the true deformation of space by a mass at point P - a deformation which is nothing but a contraction of space around P, the reduction in space cell's sizes - a positive "curvature".

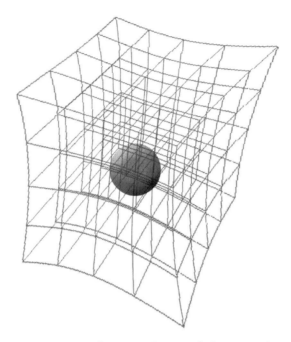

Fig. (H2) The True Deformation of Space by a Mass

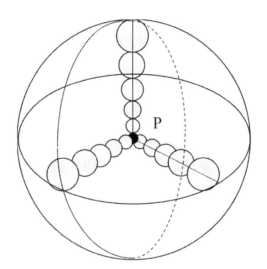

Fig. (H3) The True Deformation of Space by a Mass at

Point P

From the above, I conclude that gravity is a contraction of space!!!

This understanding finally allows us to answer (later in the book) questions in science that have been open for hundreds of years:

- Why does a ray of light curve when passing near a mass?
- How does mass contract space?
- How does another mass feel this contraction and move accordingly?
- How to build a Unified Field Formula (the Physicists' yearning)?

Why does a ray of light curve when passing near a mass?

The usual explanation is this:

Mass curves space. A ray of light should, therefore, move on a geodesic line, which means to curve. Although this is a valid explanation, it does not satisfy me.

My explanation:

A mass contracts space around it. In its vicinity, space is dense but its density, from the mass outwards, falls. Space is analogous to glass, in that its refractive index is large near the mass but decreases with the distance from it.

Space, close to a mass, is also analogous to compressed air, high density near the mass falls with increasing distance from it.

The study of optics tells us that a ray of light passing through a medium with a variable index of refraction is curved, see Fig. (H4).

These examples are a good analogy. The explanation is simpler. Space is the medium whose waves are light waves with their speed dependent on the density of space (as we explain, this does not contradict the fact that the speed of the light is a constant of nature).

When a ray of light passes through a media with a variable density the upper part of the ray (at a relatively large distance from the center of the mass) moves faster than the lower part (at a relatively smaller distance from the center of the mass). Of necessity the wave front is tilted, and the ray is curved.

This explanation is from our virtual point of view as observers out of the universe (**far observers**). For spectators in the media, in space, both their yardstick and their clock vary with the density of space and will, therefore, always give the same value for the speed of light.

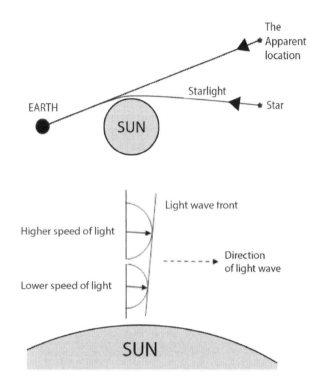

Fig. (H4) Deflection of a Light Beam

—

So, which explanation do you prefer? Tell me.

Black Hole - White Hole (Homage to Kusturica)

The needy, no matter what they receive from us: clothes, food, money, they want more and more. They swallow everything - like a **Black Hole**. In contrast, there are the needy that reject everything we offer them – like a **White Hole**.

But, let's be serious.

The solution to the equations of the Theory of General Relativity, for the case of the mass of a star is the **Schwarzschild Metric** for multi-dimensional, curved space.

This metric is kind of a Pythagorean theorem for a multi-dimensional curved space. More than this, we don't need to know, not now, not later. There are several terms in this metric. In the denominator of one of them, the following expression appears

$$r - \frac{2GM}{c^2}$$

Where

M – mass

G – Newton's Gravitational Constant

r – distance from the center of the mass

c – speed of light

If and when:

$$r = \frac{2GM}{c^2}$$

then, in the denominator of the same metric, a zero appears. It is understandable for it to tend to infinity. In this case the same star is considered a black hole. The radius for which the above equality holds, is called the **Schwarzschild radius** and is marked with a subscript S.

$$r_s = \frac{2GM}{c^2}$$

Now we know that if the ratio between mass M and its radius satisfies:

$$M/r > \frac{c^2}{2G}$$

then **we have a black hole** before us. The above ratio is about 10^{28}, a huge number. A black hole swallows light approaching it from the outside and prevents it exiting from the inside. Now we can know why. We have already learned that mass contracts the space around itself, but here it really compresses it. In such dense space, the speed of light falls sharply.

The space in a black hole, then, can be compared to a glass ball with a high refractive index in relation to the space around it. In this case, a beam of light that penetrates the ball is reflected around its walls and may be swallowed inside. A beam that originates inside will also be reflected and cannot escape.

A **white hole** is the opposite of a black hole. This is a space zone that is highly expanded relative to the space around it - in the same ratio as a black hole is compressed relative to the space surrounding it. In this zone, then, the speed of light is higher relative to its standard speed in space farther away outside. This time any light ray that reaches the white hole will be returned from it, while an inside ray will be held there. This is actually the interaction of a photon with an electron, as imagined by Feynman, because an electron, as we explain, is a white hole. It is clear that a mass cannot create a white hole, because it contracts the space around and inside it. Against this the process where a photon becomes an electron and positron (pair production) allows, as we show, to create a black hole which is the positive elementary charge and a white hole that is the negative elementary charge.

I.   "Ironing" Space and the Ricci Flow

Topology is a branch of mathematics that deals with the study of the properties of space under continuous deformations (such as contraction, tension, and expansion).

Ricci Flow is a branch of topology. It appears here to explain the behavior of space - its dynamics under deformation (contraction, dilation). We have some evidence that space behaves as we describe but not assurance. However, this explanation does have value. It is included in the discussion of the essence of attraction and repulsion between charges that appears in Chapter **J** and completes the model.

By "ironing", we mean the process in which deformed zones of space gradually reduce the deformation, thanks to elasticity, so that the inner tension and the energy of tension decreases to a minimum.

We explain: a loose spring does not have internal tension. If we stretch it with an external force (with our muscles) it creates an internal force that opposes the force we apply. By stretching the spring, we do work. This increases the energy of the spring, the energy of tension. If we remove the force from the spring the internal tension will return the spring to its original relaxed state.

The tension and energy return to their initial values before the stretching. This situation applies to all systems in the universe including space. But physicists love brevity and generality, so they refer only to energy and determine that there is a tendency to minimum energy.

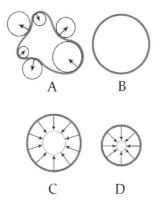

Fig. (I1) Ricci Flow in a Plane

Fig. (I2) Ricci Flow Transforms a Cube to a Sphere

Fig. (I1), shows a two-dimensional, deformed manifold. Its demarcations are curved. The areas of the deformation are drawn with their osculatory circuits that have radii which are the corresponding radii of curvature. As you remember, the curvature K is: K = 1/R.

The Ricci flow equation is:

$$\frac{\partial}{\partial t} g(t) = -2 \operatorname{Ric}(g(t))$$

It tells us that the speed of dissipation of the curving is according to the amount of the curvature and in the direction of its radius.

And so, A goes to C. We get a circle where each of its points has the same osculatory circle, and therefore it continues to contract, to a point, see D. If, in this process it is required, that the area of the manifold should be preserved, then the transition from A is to B.

Fig. (I 2) shows, on the left, a 3D cube, with the biggest deformation at the corners. Therefore, the Ricci flow gradually transforms the cube to a sphere, under the constraint that the volume is preserved.

J.   Electric Charge and its Field as Deformed Space

Charge and the Field

An electrical charge is made up of elementary charges, all of which are exactly the same size, whether they are positive or negative. In my model, a positive elementary charge has spherical symmetry, and is a concentration, around a central point, of small space cells compared to the standard cell size far away in space. Far from this point, they grow to reach the standard cell size. This gradual change is continuous – there is no sharp boundary separating the concentration that is considered charge and the continuation of it, which is considered to be the electric field.

It was **Einstein's vision** that, one day, someone would create such a model. Fig. (J1) illustrates the description I have set out here. It shows the cross section of a three-dimensional spherical charge. At the bottom of the figure is a graph describing the density of space as a function of its position along the cross-section of the charge. ρ is the space density (the number of space cells per volume unit), while ρ_0 is the standard space density.

Since there is no sharp border between the charge and its field, care is required to choose the definition of the charge radius, r_0.

Every cell is analogous to a spring. A standard spatial cell, with no bodies around it, is analogous to a loose spring that has no tension, and therefore the energy of its tension is zero.

A cell that is small compared to a standard cell is analogous to a compressed spring, and hence it stores energy of compression.

A cell that is large compared to a standard cell is analogous to a stretched spring, and therefore it stores the energy of tension.

We choose (define) the radius of a charge as the radius for which the energy in the charge equals the energy in its field. This choice is arbitrary but allows us to calculate the radius and to show that it matches the measured radius.

This definition is related to a difficult issue, which till now remained unanswered. Feynman called this issue a major failure in our understanding of Electrical Theory. This is the issue of **where the energy is located - in the charge or in the field.**

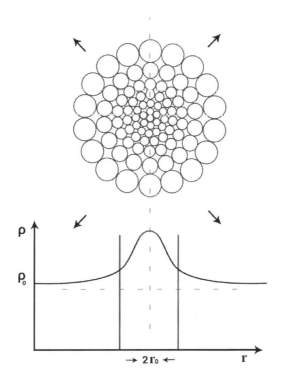

Fig. (J1) Positive Elementary Electric Charge

We explain this: calculating the energy of a charge (electrostatic), and of that the field, supposedly separately, gives the same result.

However, it is clear that there is no duplication of the energy, so the question is - where is it? Our model provides a clear answer: there is no separation between the charge and the field, so the calculated energy is the energy of both charge and field together.

According to the definition of the radius half of this energy is in the "charge" and half in the "field". This is an essential component in the calculation of the radius.

The ongoing discussion and the figures presented here may create a false impression that my theory is purely descriptive. This is not the case. My theory includes all the formalisms necessary for a physical theory.

As an example, I mention that from the definition of electrical charge density q, as a function of the density of space ρ, I derive all Maxwell's Electromagnetic Theory as a logical inference, while Maxwell's theory is phenomenological (based solely on experimental laws). This is an unprecedented achievement in physics based on visual imagination (confirmed by known physicists and published in a peer reviewed journal).

$$q = \frac{1}{4\pi} \frac{\rho - \rho_0}{\rho}$$

Many of the best physicists have proposed the intuitive suggestion that an electrical charge is a kind of **microscopic black hole**, which explains its stability. Since a positive elementary charge, according to my theory, is a positive curving of space, and since General Relativity deals with curved space, **I have shown** (proved rigorously) that it is indeed the case. I have proved that a positive elementary charge is really **a black hole,** and a negative charge is a **white hole** - there is such a thing and we discuss it below.

From all this I managed to calculate the radius of the elementary charge (the same for both types of charge) which is:

$$r_0 = \sqrt{2}/(2S^2) \cdot \sqrt{G\alpha\hbar C} \qquad \text{Where } S = 1, \ [S] = LT^{-1}$$

r_0 (calculated) $= 0.8774 \cdot 10^{13}$cm

Fortunately, **the radius of a positive elementary charge** found in the proton, (a particle that lies in atomic nuclei but can also be isolated outside them) was measured precisely and is:

r_P (measured) $= 0.8768(69) \cdot 10^{13}$ cm

and indeed, if we compare the calculated radius with the measured value we get:

r_0 (calculated) $/ r_p$ (measured) $= 0.8774 \cdot 10^{13} / 0.8768 \cdot 10^{-13} \sim 1.0007$

The accuracy of my calculation validates my model of the elementary charge, which I have discussed here.

I add that both black and white holes are very stable, which answers the question of the stability of the charges.

This is the place to point out that in my model of the electron and positron, the elementary charge revolves in a circle with radius R, and that this rotation gives it spin and as a result its magnetic moment. The calculation of R is much easier than that of r_0.

And, the ratio r_0/R is exactly the Fine Structure Constant α.

The character of the Fine Structure Constant has been, according to Feynman, one of the greatest riddles of Nature. We now have the answer.

Fig. (**J2**) presents a negative elementary electrical charge. This charge is a concentration of cells that are much larger than the standard cell size. This concentration decreases and tends to the standard size. It is, therefore, a negative deformation. The radius of the negative charge, r_0, is the same as that of the positive charge, as I proved.

The bottom of the figure shows a graph describing the density of space as a function of the position along the cross-section of the charge. ρ is the density of space (the number of space cells per unit volume) and ρ_0 the standard space density. In this case, the density of both the charge and its field is lower than the standard density.

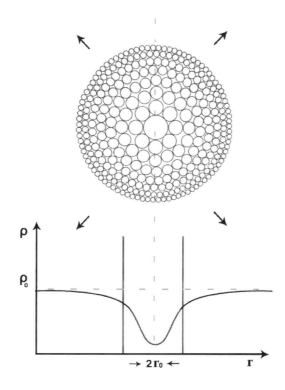

Fig. (J2) A Negative Elementary Electric Charge

We are now able to understand the meaning of attraction and repulsion. I hope you prefer my explanation over that of the "Dancing Photon".

Attraction and Repulsion

Fig. (J3) shows two positive charges and, enlarged, the area of the meeting of their fields. In this area we see the space cells (the drawing shows only the space cells that are on the line connecting the two charges). In this area and in the space between the two charges is the tension of contraction and therefore also the energy of contraction. A reduction in tension and energy is possible if the charges are separate one from the other and move away (just as a compressed spring return to its relaxed state).

Note that the meeting of the fields introduces deformation to space (Barak geometry) that Ricci flow requires to fade away. This deformation has cylindrical symmetry around the line that connects the two charges and therefore, of necessity, the deformation can fade only as the charges distance themselves from each other.

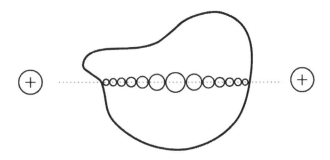

Fig. (J3) Repulsion

Fig. (J4) shows two negative charges and the enlarged area of the encounter between their fields. In this area we see the space cells (in the drawing only the space cells on the line connecting the two charges). In this area and in all the space between the charges there is stretching and therefore also stretching energy. Reducing tension and decreasing energy is possible if the charges move away from each other (as a tense spring returns to its relaxed state). Note that also here (Barak's geometry) Ricci flow explains the repulsion.

Figure (J5) shows two charges, one negative and one positive, and the area where their fields meet. This enlarged area shows the space cells (only the space cells on the line connecting the two charges).

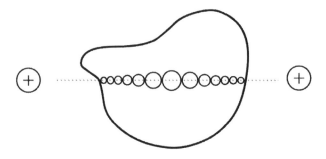

Fig. (J4) Repulsion

In this area, and in the space towards the center between the charges, on the right cells are contracted and on the left are expanded. Space energy can be reduced if the charges get close, so that the contraction and expansion cancel each other.

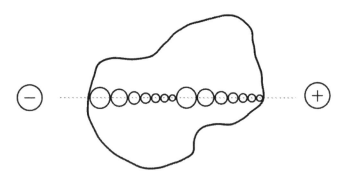

Fig. (J5) Attraction

If the charges come into contact, they annihilate each other and are replaced by two photons.

There is no naked elementary charge in nature, it is always integrated into a particle. An example of such a particle is the electron, built, as it appears, from a negative elementary charge that revolves in a circle that gives it angular momentum, which is referred to as the spin.

The reason for this kind of appearance lies in the source of the particle. Later I will explain that the electron and its companion the positron are created in a process where a photon (if energetic enough) revolves around an atom's nucleus. In tight circulation and with minimum energy, which is the couple's energy. This process is referred to as **pair production**. This is possible, as I explain, because the photon has all the necessary properties to become a couple. The photon, for example, has a single spin that is split between the couple – a single half for each.

Potential and Field (for Physicists)

The density of a charge, a scalar, is proportional to the electric potential. But the density of the charge is proportional to the density of space. It can be said that potential is an expression of spatial density. The electric field, a vector, is simply an expression of the gradient in the density of space.

On the Electric Field

Classical physics does not have an electric field that exists in its own right. If the charge disappears, so does the field. In the current physics, there is no elementary charge that exists in its own right. Elementary charge is a characteristic of charge-carrying particles. There are infinite fields, one for each type of particle, and the particle is nothing but an event in the field – an excitation. These fields are intertwined in space and adopt its topology.

As opposed to this I am satisfied with just one single "field" that is the infinite space. The electric field is nothing but a spatial deformation just like gravitation. The electron's charge, for example, deforms space, some 42 orders of magnitude more than its mass.

On a Magnetic Field

The ancients played with magnets and realized that a magnet has two poles – North and South. Any attempt to separate the poles failed. However, it was clear that there was a positive electrical charge separate from a negative electrical charge. Therefore, it was believed that magnetism and electricity were separate entities.

Maxwell (1862), after accumulating much experimental evidence, built the phenomenological electromagnetic theory. In this theory, magnetism and electricity are different expressions of the same phenomenon. I explain:

There is no magnetic field that stands by itself. The magnetic field has been invented purely for convenience, and do not let the appearance of such equations confuse you. When an electrical charge is in motion, its interaction with other charges is complex and contains the expression:

$$\frac{1}{c}\left(v' \times E\right)$$

where V is the speed of the charge, E its field strength and C the speed of light.

For convenience of using this expression in equations, we denote it by the letter **B** and call it the strength of the **magnetic field.** You are surprised, I know, but this is not my invention.

K. Gravity and General Relativity

How Mass Contracts Space

Einstein proved to us that the presence of mass in space curves space but did not explain how the mass does it. I offer an explanation, the first of its kind, based on my replacement of curving with contraction.

Since each mass is composed of particles, the first question is how does the electron mass, for example, contract space.

The electron, as I explained, is a revolving negative elemental charge that gives it the spin (a chapter is dedicated to the detailed model). The charge deforms space – expands it – But also the spin of the charge, and thus of the mass (for which the charge is responsible because it is just the energy of the deformation) deforms space by causing it to contract. This contraction occurs because the charge, by revolving, "drags" space around it. This is the gravitational deformation, 42 orders of magnitude smaller than that of the charge.

This phenomenon of dragging space by a rotating mass is a prediction of General Relativity. This phenomenon is called **Frame Dragging.**

This phenomenon is confirmed by observational evidence. In a detailed discussion in one of my articles, I show that this is a possible explanation for the source of gravity. Contraction, whose source is spin, has no spherical symmetry and the reader rightly asks how this comply with spherical symmetry in macro, that is in a star. In a star the direction of spins is random and hence the symmetry. There is some questionable evidence that, for a body of material, in which there is a certain alignment of spins, spherical symmetry deviates from perfect. Such an experiment of confirmation or repudiation would be of considerable importance.

Now ask yourself what chance do physicists, dealing with QFT in the standard model of the particles, have to answer the question of how the mass curves space, if they think that a particle is point-like and structureless.

Please note that the current physics describes phenomena but finds it difficult to investigate them.

How a Mass Senses the Distortion of Space and Moves Accordingly – Free Fall

Again I, first and foremost, ask the question about the electron. The answer is complex and requires an understanding of the model of the electron. At this stage, I bring only the main points in my explanation that is given in detail below and also appear in several articles I have published.

Contracted space means that the density of space near a large mass is large and falls with distance from the mass. A density gradient is formed. But density determines the speed of light.

You may be surprised by this statement since you have been taught that the speed of light is a Constant of Nature. But you have forgotten, or may not know, what is a Constant of Nature. Please return to the definition that I have given.

I emphasize that the speed of waves in a medium depends inversely on its density. That is, near the mass, the speed of light is lower but increases as the distance increases. A gradient in the speed of light is formed.

At a distance where gravity is no longer noticeable, the speed of light is the standard speed in space.

An electron has spin that is its angular momentum.

This angular momentum, J, is dependent on the electron's mass, M, its speed of rotation, V, and the spin radius, R.

$J = MVR$

Conservation of Angular Momentum means that if V, in this case the speed of light, is getting smaller, then M and R must become larger.

M is larger only if R is smaller, and R is smaller if the electron is accelerated.

The result is that the electron falls in **free fall,** accelerated toward the mass where the light speed is lower. The electron can sense **the speed of light** only because it has a **finite size** so that its different parts are at different heights above the mass. The electron, having mass, creates also a gradient, and therefore the large mass falls free towards the electron. However, the ratio of the accelerations in this mutual fall is as the ratio of the masses.

This free and mutual fall is mistakenly perceived as an attraction between the masses. Let me remind you that I have explained attraction and repulsion in the chapter concerning charges.

Now comes a surprise: we have already studied that similar space deformations – positive in this case of gravitation – repel each other. Inevitable conclusion is that ...

Masses repel each other. Can this understanding explain the expansion of the universe? - We wonder.

The long-awaited union between electromagnetism and gravitation

From the day of the birth of general relativity, there have been many efforts, mostly by **Einstein** himself, to unite gravitation with electromagnetism. This effort was to yield an expansion of the field equation so that it would include the two types of phenomena. While these efforts failed, I have succeeded because I managed to create a common basis for both theories.

I have proven that charge and its field are nothing but spatial deformation. And I proved that mass also does not curve space but deforms it. This enables me to present the **Consolidated** field formula:

$$R^{\mu\nu} - 1/2 R g^{\mu\nu} = 8\pi G/C^4 \cdot T_m{}^{\mu\nu} + 4\,\pi G^{1/2}/s^2 \cdot T_q{}^{\mu\nu}$$

Where S = 1 and [S] = LT^{-1}

Note the added term on the right-hand side of the equation.

On gravitation and the possibility that it is quantized

General Relativity predicts the existence of gravitational waves. Recently they have been discovered in huge facilities in several places on Earth. So far there has not been found a theoretical way to present these waves as collections of particles - known by the name Gravitons. These hypothetic particles have not been found yet.

I present a model of the graviton that fits the attributes of the gravitational waves.

Note that the loss or addition of mass to a star can be by emission or absorption of small particles like elementary particles. This can weaken or strengthen the gravitational field possibly by emission or absorption of gravitons.

An example: The electrically neutral particle, with smallest mass, that a star can lose or gain is the positronium. This short-lived atom consists of an electron and a positron, which surround each other. Their spins can be oriented parallel or anti-parallel. This orientation is irrelevant to gravitation. Hence, this atom contributes to gravitation two whole units of gravitation, which the mass and its field can lose or gain. All this reminds us the graviton, Chapter O.

L.   The Standard Model of the "elementary" particles

Elementary particles are the particles whose different combinations comprise each and every material in the universe and they themselves are not made from others.

The **Standard Model** is based on **Quantum Field Theory – QFT-** and offers as a summary of experiments and theoretical work the table of particles that appear in Fig. (L1) **The Particle Table (Wikipedia).** In this table on the left column appears the word Quarks that relates to the family of six particles on the right. Under it appears the word Leptons that relates to another family of six particles on the right. Above you see Roman letters that indicate the column of particle's generations: First Second and Third. The first column to the left is the one of the first-generation particles, which are mostly common in nature. On the right-hand side appear the force carrying particles that dance between the material particles. A similar table of twelve Anti Quarks and Anti Leptons not presented here brings the total number of the elementary particles to 29.

Fig. (L1) Elementary Particles of the Standard Model

(Wikipedia)

The existence of Quarks was theorized by **Gell-Mann** and **Zweig** in 1964 and were discovered in SLAC lab. in 1968.

Problems that the standard model does not resolve

There is no understanding of the characteristics of the particles their origin and how to calculate their masses. And so, they relate to the masses as **Nature Constants** – along with the constants of classical physics they amount to 20.

It is unclear why there are three generations of particles (marked in the Table with Roman numerals from above).

Although the **Higgs boson** was presented as responsible for **inertia** but to say the least that is not serious.

It is worth noting that the atmosphere among physicists, these days, working on the standard model is that they should seek **physics beyond it**.

The Four Forces operating among the particles according to the standard Model:

Electromagnetism operates in short and long distances between electrical charges. The strength of the force is taken as a reference with the value 1.

The strong force, operates between quarks and protons and neutrons, is short-range and its strength relative to the electromagnetic force is about 100.

The weak force, operates in radioactive reactions, is short-range and its strength is 4 orders of magnitude smaller than the electromagnetic force.

Gravitation, operates between masses, is both short, and long-range with strength which is 42 orders of magnitude smaller than that of the electromagnetic force.

An order of magnitude is 10 times, whether smaller or larger, than a given quantity.

Two orders of magnitude is (10 times more than)^2=100 and so on.

 Glashow, Salam and Weinberg have shown that the weak force is an electromagnetic force.

The "unification" of forces

There is a wish among physicists to show that all the forces in nature are actually different aspects of a single force termed the **unifying force**.

My alternative model of the particles, is much simpler and in contrast to the Standard Model

In the next Chapter I show that quarks are made of Leptons and hence, they are not elementary.

I calculate the quarks masses. The results are within the error range of the experimental measurements.

I show why there are no single quarks in nature, but pairs and triples of them.

I show the structure of the Mesons and Baryons that are made of quarks.

I show the source of inertia.

I calculate the Leptons masses.

I unify all the four forces.

In Chapter **K** I show that gravitation and electromagnetism are actually the tension force in space. Later in Chapter **N** I show that the strong force is also electromagnetic. To sum it up: all the forces are actually one force, which is the tension in space.

I settle for the photon and add the Graviton from the particles that "carry" force. I show their structure and derive their attributes.

I reduce the number of Constants of Nature in my model from 20 in the standard model to only 4: The velocity of light c, the constant of gravitation G, Planck constant h and the Fine Structure Constant α.

Before I begin in an orderly manner with my model, I examine two of the most important issues that are related to each other, which have remained open for dozens of years. These issues are:

What is the essence of quarks?

Where is anti-matter?

Atoms are made of a nucleus that carry a number of elementary positive charges and the same number of electrons circulating around it. They are named atoms of **Matter**. In the Lab. it was possible to create short-lived atoms of hydrogen with a negative nucleus and circulating positrons. This kind of atoms are named **Anti-Matter**. But such atoms are not found in nature. Cosmologists and astrophysicists do not understand where is the anti-matter in our universe, and whether it was created in the first place.

In Chapter **M I resolve the issue by showing that the amount of matter equals exactly the amount of anti-matter in each and every atom in our universe.**

M. The Essence of Quarks- and the Question Where is the Anti-Matter?

The problems that require a solution

We have two first-generation quarks with their characteristics, that other than the size of the mass, appear also in a pair of second-generation quarks and in a third-generation pair. A total of 6 quarks. These couples carry the two types of electrical charge, and there are three other similar pairs with the opposite types of charge. And in total, 12 quarks.

Quarks are considered elementary, but they are always found in non-segregated threes or couples. This inexplicable trait in the current paradigm, termed **Confinement,** is explained later.

The quarks carry two types of electrical charge: 1/3 or 2/3 of the elementary charge, whether negative or positive. Such fractional charges were never discovered separately from the quarks. This phenomenon is inexplicable in the current paradigm, but it is explained here below.

The various Quarks masses have been measured. Since no one knows what their essence is, it is also not known how to calculate these masses. The calculation of these masses appears here in this Chapter.

In order to continue an introduction to the **Electron** and **Positron** is required, since I am going to show you that the **Quarks** are made of these particles

In 1897, **Thomson** discovered the **electron** that carries a negative electrical charge. It turned out that every negative, small or large electrical charge is made up of a number, of individual elementary charges that carry the same amount of charge. Hence, all the electrons have exactly the same charge unit.

A Positron is a fundamental particle similar to the electron, since its mass and spin are identical to those of the electron. In contrast, its electrical charge is equal to the electron charge but with the opposite type of charge, namely positive. Hence, the positron name.

The positron's existence was predicted by **the Dirac equation**, which was published in 1928 by **Dirac,** although Dirac himself did not come to this conclusion directly. The positron, termed **the anti-particle** of the electron, was first discovered   by **Anderson** in 1932.

The essence of Quarks as I understand Them

In my model, the quarks are nothing but electrons or positrons that move in winding tracks. A similar idea was expressed in the year 1982 by **Sakharov**.

Every sub-track in this model, is nothing but a quark. This idea explains: Why is it impossible to find single isolated quarks, why their electrical charge is supposedly a fraction of the elementary charge and many other things. In such a model we expel at once 12 elementary particles from the long list.

The couple of the first generation are according to the Standard Model:

The quark d (down) with a negative electric charge -1/3 of the elementary charge.

The quark u (up) with positive electric charge of +2/3 of the elementary charge.

And their anti-particles:

The quark $\tilde{d}$ (anti-down) with a positive electric charge +1/3 of the elementary charge.

The quark $\tilde{u}$ (anti-up) with negative electric charge -2/3 of the elementary charge.

Note that the electron has a negative electrical charge (-), while its anti-particle positron is a positive charge (+). Here, the attributing of type of charge, + or -, to a particle or an anti -particle, is different (just a matter of denoting, but not something of fundamental nature).

In addition to the charge, Elementary particles also have angular momentum, **a spin,** given in units of $\hbar$. This spin appears in half integers 0, 1/2, 1, 3/2, 2, etc. of $\hbar$. This half integers are notated by the letter **s**.

The Quark d (down)

Fig. (**M**1) shows a trio of d quarks which are sub-tracks of a twisted electron at "rest". In a translational motion the trio becomes a trio of spirals.

In our model of quarks, we assign charge to each sub-track according to the time the electron (positron) spends on this sub-track. We, of course, assume that the tangential velocity is c.

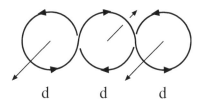

d   d   d

FIG. (M1) The Quark d

The electron spends one third of its full revolution time in each of the sub-tracks. We therefore assign it a charge of $1/3\ Q_0$. The resultant spin of this trio of quarks is $S = \frac{1}{2}$, due to the quarks individual spins, as Fig. (M1) shows. Each sub-track has the same spin as that of the electron. We refer to the sub-track of an electron as the quark, d, and to the sub-track of a positron as the anti-quark, $\tilde{d}$. It is still not fully

clear why the track is twisted.

It is thus clear that the quarks are **not** independent fundamental

particles, and therefore individual quarks do not exist.

Fig. (M2) shows again a trio of d quarks, but in this case with

S = 3/2:

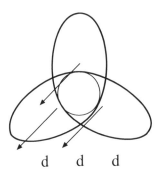

d   d   d

Fig. (M2) The Quark d

The Quark ũ (anti-up)

If one twist in Fig. (M1) opens up; we get the structures shown in

Fig. (M3) and Fig. (M4), which represent **mesons**.

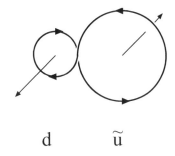

d   ũ

Fig. (M3) Meson S = 0

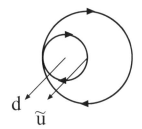

d
ũ

Fig. (M4) Meson S = 1

An electron spends two thirds of its time in the sub-track with the double radius, therefore, we assign it a charge $2/3\ Q_0$ and refer to it as the quark ũ. For a positron, we refer to it as the quark u.

This simple model of quarks enables me to derive and accurately calculate their masses, for the first time in physics.

A Derivation and Calculation of the Quarks Masses

We know the electron mass M_e. From this mass, based on our quark model, we derive the masses $M_{\tilde{u}}$ and M_d of the first-generation quarks, which are also the masses M_u and $M_{\tilde{d}}$ of their anti-particles. The electron angular momentum $L = M_e R_e^2 \omega$ must be conserved. Hence it is the same L for each of the sub-tracks of the d quark, see Fig. (M1). For the $\tilde{u}$ quark it is 2L, since the L of its companion d quark points in the opposite direction, see Fig. (M3). For the quarks, ω is the same, but R and M are different and conversely related. In a twisted track, which is a set of three quarks, ddd, the radius of each sub-track is $R = \dfrac{1}{3} R_e$.

The length of the electron wavepacket is conserved, hence:

$$2\pi R_e = 2\pi \frac{1}{3} R_e \times 3$$

The known relation $L = MR^2\omega$ gives:

$$M_d = \frac{L}{\omega R^2} = \frac{L}{\omega} \frac{1}{\left(\dfrac{1}{3} R_e\right)^2} = 9 \frac{L}{\omega R_e^2} = 9 M_e \qquad (m1)$$

For a twisted track of a pair of quarks, like $d\tilde{u}$, we get for $\tilde{u}$ a sub-track with $R = \dfrac{2}{3} R_e$, spin 2L and a mass:

$$M_{\tilde{u}} = 2 \frac{9}{4} M_e = 4.5\, M_e \qquad\qquad (m2)$$

From (1) and (2) and $M_e = 0.51$ MeV we obtain the following results (3) and (4):

$$M_d = 4.5 \text{ MeV} \qquad\qquad (m3)$$

A recent experimental value is:

$M_d = 4.8 +/- 0.5$ MeV.

$$M_{\tilde{u}} = 2.\,25 \text{ MeV} \qquad\qquad (m4)$$

A recent experimental value is:

$M_{\tilde{u}} = 2.3 +/- 0.8$ MeV.

As you can see my results are within the error range of the measurements.

Let us now see if we can give a simple answer to the question

where is the anti-matter?

In the Universe the Number of Electrons Equals the Number of Positrons

Atoms are built from a nucleus with a number of positive elementary electrical charges, and with the same number of negative electrons revolving around it. But the nucleus is built of quarks only, which according to our model are made of electrons and positrons. A Neutron is made of an equal number of electrons and positions (twisted topologically to become quarks). A Proton is made of electrons and positrons, as is the Neutron, but has one electron (three quarks) less. An atom is made of an equal number of protons and electrons. And hence:

In each and every atom in the entire Universe the Number of Electrons Equals the Number of Positrons.

This conclusion solves the long-standing issue of **where is the anti-matter? It is here all the time.**

So far, there is no evidence for the existence of stars and galaxies made of anti-matter (anti-hydrogen was first created in the laboratory in 1997).

The question: Why, at large, is the universe composed of matter only?

Now becomes: Why we do not see in nature atoms made of anti-protons and positrons?

In our GeometroDynamic Model of the Physical Reality (GDM) there is no **charge conjugation**. A negative charged nucleus curves space around it negatively. This might be the reason for instability in the orbital motion of a positron around it (hence anti-hydrogen created in the laboratory should have a limited lifetime.

The Mesons and Baryons

Fig (M3) and Fig. (M4) show mesons, which are a twisted electron or positron with only one twist. Fig. (M5) shows a meson composed of a twisted electron together with a twisted positron.

Overlapped dashed and solid circles represent the electromagnetic bond, of opposite charges, between the relevant quarks. These quarks that create a bond are **not numbered** as originating quarks of a particle, be it a meson, baryon or any other particle.

Note that in particle diagrams a **solid line** indicates an electron, and a **dashed line** a positron.

It seems that this electromagnetic bond, of opposite charges, between the relevant quarks is the known "strong force".

This subject is also discussed in Chapter **N**.

The π Family with Spin S=0

A single twisted track has a very short lifetime, as can be seen for the π$^+$ and π$^-$ mesons. For the π^0 meson, the lifetime is much shorter due to annihilation.

$$\pi^+ \rightarrow e^+ + \nu_e \quad 2.6 \cdot 10^{-8} \text{ sec}$$
$$\pi^0 \rightarrow 2\gamma \qquad 0.8 \cdot 10^{-16} \text{ sec}$$

A possible decay is:

$$\pi^0 \rightarrow \gamma + e^+ + e^- \quad \text{and even} \quad \pi^0 \rightarrow 2e^+ + 2e^-$$

The ρ Family with Spin S=1

From the reaction $\pi^+ \rightarrow e^+ + \nu_e$ and similar reactions, it seems as if a neutrino is incorporated in the π^+ construction.

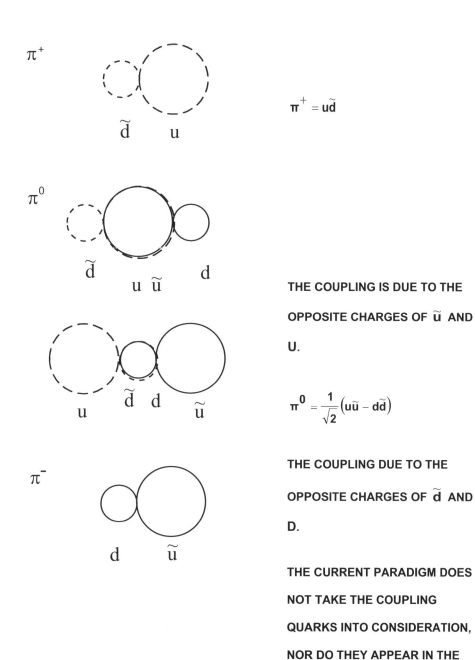

π^+

$\tilde{d}$ u

$\pi^+ = u\tilde{d}$

π^0

$\tilde{d}$ u $\tilde{u}$ d

THE COUPLING IS DUE TO THE OPPOSITE CHARGES OF $\tilde{u}$ AND U.

u $\tilde{d}$ d $\tilde{u}$

$$\pi^0 = \frac{1}{\sqrt{2}}\left(u\tilde{u} - d\tilde{d}\right)$$

π^-

d $\tilde{u}$

THE COUPLING DUE TO THE OPPOSITE CHARGES OF $\tilde{d}$ AND D.

THE CURRENT PARADIGM DOES NOT TAKE THE COUPLING QUARKS INTO CONSIDERATION, NOR DO THEY APPEAR IN THE NOTATION.

$\pi^- = \tilde{u}d$

Fig. (M5) The Π Mesons

$\rho^+ = \tilde{d}u$

$\rho^0 = \dfrac{1}{\sqrt{2}}\left(\tilde{u}u - \tilde{d}d\right)$

$\rho^- = \tilde{u}d$

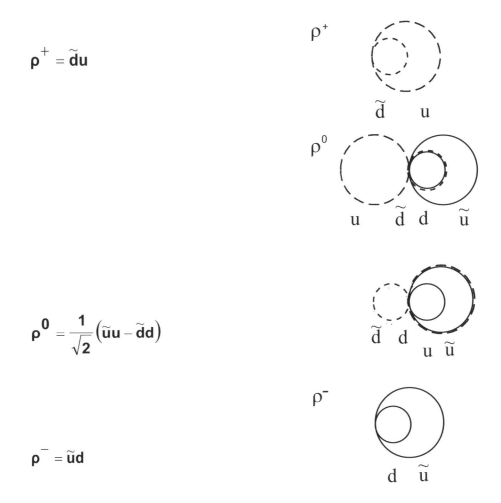

Fig. (M6) The P Mesons

Baryons

The **baryons** are composed of three quarks. As an example,

consider the family, with the members: Δ^{++} Δ^{+} Δ^{0} Δ^{-}, that have the

spin S = 3/2.

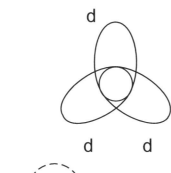

d

d   d

Q = -1

S = 3/2

DDD

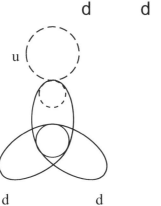

u

d   d

Q = 0

Δ⁰

S = 3/2

UDD

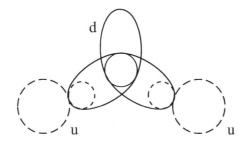

d

u   u

Q = +1

Δ⁺

S = 3/2

UUD

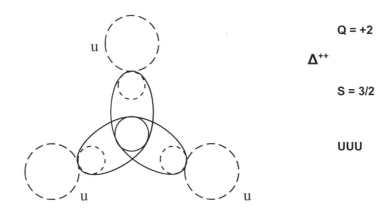

FIG. (M7) The Δ Baryon

N.   On the Neutron & Proton & Strong Force

I model the nucleon (proton or neutron) as kind of a motor with a neutral stator cage, which contains a large number of quarks, and a rotor, which contains only a few quarks termed: **valance quarks**. This rotor determines the charge and spin of the nucleon. My rotor models of the proton and neutron enable me to derive and calculate the **proton charge radius**. My result is well within the error range of the experimental result.

The Stator Model

The stator is composed of a number of twisted positrons and an identical number of twisted electrons. The total number of quarks, in the stator shown in Fig. (N1), is 3x3 + 3x3 = 18

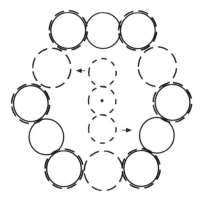

Fig. (N1) The Stator Structure and the Rotor

Note that the total number of quarks that construct a stator can also be much larger. The stator total charge is zero. The net charge of the nucleon (proton or neutron) comes from the rotor.

The spin contribution, of the stator type cage, to the total spin of the nucleon, might be zero, since in this case the magnetic interaction lowers the cage (structure of the stator) energy. The spin of the nucleon is thus, probably, the spin of its "rotor" which is $S = \frac{1}{2}$, as Fig. (N2) and Fig. (N4) show. This issue, of where the spin of the nucleon comes from, is known as the "proton spin crisis".

The Rotor Model

The **neutron** rotor, see the simplistic model in Fig. (N2), is composed of an electron and a positron in the form of three **valence quarks,** which are a pair of d quarks and one u quark. The mass of this rotor is $M_{neutron\ rotor} \sim 2M_d + 1M_u \sim 11.25 Mev.$

Qcharge unit **= 0**

Neutron

S = 1/2

dud

Fig. (N2) The Neutron Rotor

Fig. (N3) shows the spatial charge distribution, known from scattering experiments. This is compatible with Fig. (N2), and with the fact that, despite having no charge, the neutron has a magnetic moment opposite to its spin direction.

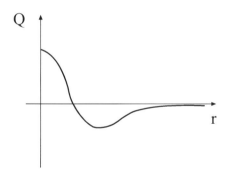

Fig. (N3) Neutron Charge Distribution

The **proton** rotor, see the simplistic model in Fig. (N4), is composed of one electron and two positrons in the form of three valence quarks, u, u, d. The charge distribution, shown in Fig. (N5), is compatible with the proposed model.

The mass of this rotor is:

$M_{proton\ rotor} \sim 1M_d + 2M_u \sim 9\ Mev.$

We, thus, arrive at a heavier neutron than the proton, which complies with experimental data.

$Q_{charge\ unit} = 1$

Proton

$S = 1/2$

udu

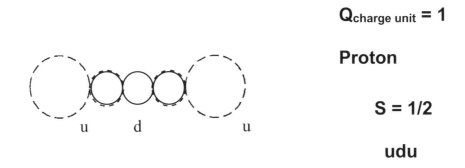

Fig. (N4) The Proton Rotor

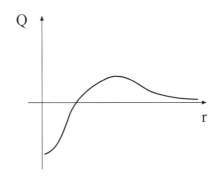

Fig. (N5) Proton Charge Distribution

The disintegration reaction of a free neutron, with a lifetime of ~10 minutes, is:

$$N \rightarrow P + e^- + \tilde{v}_e$$

And now we know **where the electron comes from**.

The mass difference between the Neutron and the Proton

The stators are identical hence, the difference in mass comes from the rotors. The masses of the rotors (in units of energy Mev):

$M_{neutron\ rotor} \sim 2M_d + 1M_u \sim 11.25 Mev$

$M_{proton\ rotor} \sim 1M_d + 2M_u \sim 9\ Mev.$ Hence, the difference is:

$M_{neutron\ rotor} - M_{proton\ rotor} \sim 2.25\ Mev,$

And indeed, the mass of the neutron is larger than that of the proton. But my theoretical result should have matched the experimental measured difference which is:

$M_{neutron} - M_{proton} = 1.29\ Mev.$

I do not have an explanation for this discrepancy.

On the Strong Force

The Force between Quarks

Figures in Chapter **M**, which represent mesons and baryons, show couples of sub-tracks of an electron and a positron, which construct a bond. This indicates that the holding force of these structures, the force between quarks, is probably electromagnetic.

The Force between a Proton and a Neutron, and between Two Protons

On the possibility that the **strong force** is actually an electromagnetic force I learned from **Yukawa and Feynman.**

The **strong force** is short distance and about 100 times stronger than the electromagnetic force. This is **an attractive force only,** and **spin independent** (ignoring weak magnetic interactions).

Yukawa suggested that the source of this force is the exchange of a π^+ meson. And **Feynman** presented a prof that an exchange of a particle can generate an attractive force. He also was very explicit on the possibility that this idea shows that the strong force is electromagnetic.

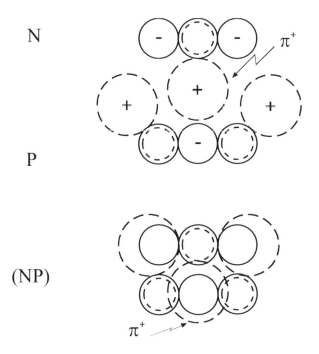

Fig. (N6) The (NP) Strong Force

Fig. (N6) shows how an electric field between three pairs of charges, of the neutron rotor and proton rotor, create an attracting force that binds them.

Note that when the neutron and proton are far apart, the inner distribution of charge is blurred and the effective field decays rapidly, which explains the short range. Note also that according to my GDM the radius of a particle is inversely proportional to its mass.

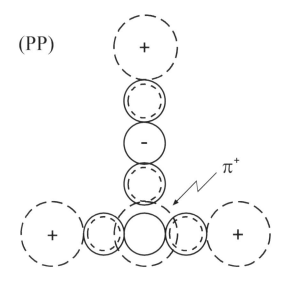

Fig. (N7) The (PP) Strong Force

The mass of a quark is about 10 times larger than that of an electron hence, its radius is 10 times smaller. The electric field is inversely proportional to the square of the radius hence its strength is 100 times larger and so is the force it applies on a nearby charge. We now consider the force between two protons, Fig. (N7). Here, as well, there is an attractive force at short range, but as the distance increases this force becomes repulsive since the particles have the same charge sign.

We consider the binding force, for both the neutron and proton, and proton and proton cases, to be the result of a π^+ meson exchange.

This meson is merely a twisted positron, and its movement back and forth, is the "exchange". This is the Yukawa theory of meson exchange, as the source of the Strong Force.

Feynman explains how an exchange of a particle can generate an attractive force. He describes the force between two protons of the ion H_2^+ as the result of the electron exchange between the protons. The reaction is:

$$(H, P) \underset{\leftarrow}{\overset{\rightarrow}{}} (P, H)$$

*The **attractive force** comes from the reduced energy of the system due to the possibility of the electron jumping from one proton to the other. In such a jump the system changes from the configuration (hydrogen atom, proton) to the configuration (proton, hydrogen atom), or switches back.*

Feynman further shows how the force between a proton and a neutron can be explained by the exchange of a Π^+ meson. Feynman concludes:

*Now we might ask the following question: could it be that forces between other kinds of particles have an analogous origin? What about, for example, **the nuclear force between a neutron and a proton, or between two protons?** In* *an attempt to explain the nature of nuclear forces, Yukawa proposed that the force between two nucleons is due to a similar exchange effect - only, in this case, due to the virtual exchange, not of an electron, but of a new particle, which he called a meson.*

The exchange in this case is:

$$P^+ \underset{\leftarrow}{\overset{\rightarrow}{}} N^0 + \Pi^+$$

The Π^+ meson is emitted from the proton to convert it into a neutron, and by combining with the other neutron to convert it into a proton, and vice versa.

The Standard Model, however, considers meson exchange as a complex effect of color interactions, and not a primary cause.

Based on the above and my GDM I am convinced that the Strong Force is an electromagnetic force. Hence, we have achieved the result that all the forces in nature are merely different manifestations of the same force of tension in space.

Note that this result emerged from my imagined quarks. It was Einstein how said that imagination is more important than knowledge.

O. My Model of Massless Elementary Particles

In this chapter I discuss massless particles (like the photon) and in the next massive particles (like the electron). Hence, we have to understand first and discuss the difference between energy and mass.

On Mass and Energy

In this chapter I discuss energetic particles, which move at the speed of light. They are massless particles. On the other hand, everybody is aware of the known relation:

U (Energy) = **M** (Mass) x **c²** (Square of light velocity),

as if energy is always mass. This notion is wrong. Mass is nothing but energy, but energy is not always mass. Energy is mass, depends on the way it is "packed". A package that attributes to the energy **inertia** (namely you have to apply force in order to accelerate the "package") is having a **mass**.

If no force is applied, a body is at rest or moves on a straight line with a constant velocity. This is Newton's first law. In order to change the velocity, one has to apply a force **F** on the body to accelerate it - an acceleration **a**. The ratio: **F/a = M defines M.**

This is Newton's second law.

The Elementary Particles in the GDM

The massless particles are:

ADAM and **EVE**

They construct the **Photon, Graviton,** and the **Neutrino.**

The massive particles are:

The **Electron** and the **Positron** of the first generation.

The **Muon** and the **Anti-Muon** of the second generation.

The **Tau** and the **Anti-Tau** of the third generation.

All of them are created in the process of pair production from a photon and also in other processes.

The Photoms

In my model there is only one pair of elementary particles – the Photoms.

In my scientific papers I called them photoms, since **they are actually the ground state vibrations of the electromagnetic field** (PHOTON AT THE BOTTOM IS A PHOTOM)

This pair construct all the other particles, as I show here and in the next chapter.

One photom is named **ADAM** (negative photom) and the other- **EVE** (positive photom).

Particles visualized as Springs

Let us assume that ADAM and EVE are two identical springs, see Fig. (O1). ADAM (C) is stretched periodically whereas EVE (B) is contracted periodically. (A) is the state of no tension. Both the amplitude and the frequency of these springs can take any value.

If they have the same frequency their energy of stretch equals that of contraction. If they are coupled, they will have the same frequency. Let the stretching and contracting be perpendicular to their motion through space and rotating. This rotation attributes to them the spin.

Fig. (O1) EVE and ADAM as "Springs"

Let me now present a particle which is composed of these elementary photoms.

A "photon", see Fig. (O2), is composed of two coupled springs – ADAM and EVE. They vibrate at the same frequency and with the same phase; when ADAM is stretched to the maximum EVE is contracted to the minimum. The energy of the photon is the energy of the springs and its frequency is their frequency. Since they rotate, after each half cycle they are in an upside-down position. This rotation is the photon's spin.

EVE   ADAM

Fig. (O2) The Photon as Two "Springs"

Elementary Particles as the Vibrations of the Space Lattice

The lattice is composed of cells and to each of them we can relate as a spring. This spring can serve as an ADAM or an EVE, depending on the circumstances. But these cells are very friendly with their neighbors, they do not keep their vibrations to themselves, they transfer them to the next cell in line. This transfer is the particle's motion which is on a straight line (the geodesic actually), whereas the vibration is perpendicular to the line of motion. The cells themselves do not move; they stay where they are. The particle is not the spring from the previous sub-section it is the vibration that moves on. The velocity of its motion is the velocity of transvers waves in space – the velocity of light (300,000 kilometers per second). This velocity and the velocity of longitudinal waves are the only real velocities that exist.

Note that nothing is alien to space. The particles are merely the vibrations of space taking place in volumes of space that contain many space cells and move on continuously. **There is no rest only motion.** When a particle moves on a circle we can relate to the virtual center of the circle as if it is at **rest.** And of course, there is a possibility that this center moves slowly, much less than the light velocity. In this case the particle (the vibration) moves on a spiral, see Chapter **P**.

In Figs **O**3,4,6,9, and 10 we present in the following order the particles: ADAM, EVE, Photon, Graviton, Neutrino. I show how ADAM and EVE create all the other particles. In all these cases the particle, namely the vibration, enters from left and moves to the right (the vibration is always perpendicular to line of motion) circulating clockwise, as we look from behind and forwards. This circulation attributes to the particle its spin. This circulation is termed a circulation with **right helicity.**

In Figs **O**3,4,6,9, and 10, we see arrows towards the line of propagation or from it. The arrow's direction towards the line indicates the contraction of the space cells, and its direction from the line outwards it indicates the dilation (stretching) of these cells. The maximum contraction or dilation occurs close to the line of motion. These contractions and dilations change with time in a sinusoidal cycle. The arrows appear where the contraction and dilation are at the maximum. If the entrance from the left is at time "zero" then the arrows appear first after a quarter of a cycle and then again after three quarters of a cycle. The reader should try to create a clear picture of these motions in their mind.

Fig. (O3) represents the fundamental particle **EVE**

Fig. (O4) represents the fundamental particle **ADAM**

Recall that contracted space is positive charge whereas dilated space is negative charge.

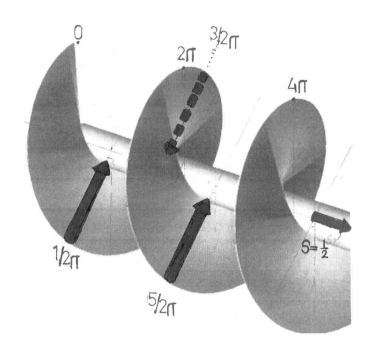

Fig. (O3) The Fundamental Particle EVE

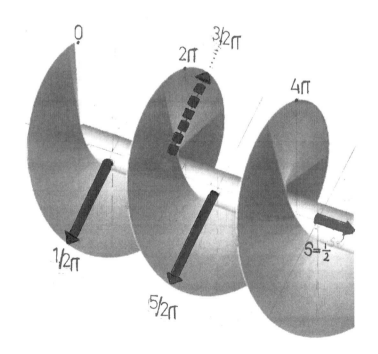

Fig. (O4) The Fundamental Particle ADAM

Photoms - the Ground State Photons

QED attributes to a photon in its ground state one half of the energy, half of the momentum, and half of the spin. To distinguish a photon from a ground state photon, we name it a **Photom** (a photon at the bottom is a photom). In the GDM, however, there are two types of photoms.

EVE The Positive Photom: This photom is an oscillating contraction of space (positive charge), close to the line of propagation. This oscillation is in a plane or in a rotating plane, around the line of propagation.

ADAM The Negative Photom: This photom is an oscillating dilation of space (negative charge) close to the line of propagation. This oscillation is in a plane or in a rotating plane, around the line of propagation.

I consider these photoms more fundamental than the photon – they construct the photon.

I show that EVE carries the oscillating positive elementary charge (that of the positron), whereas ADAM carries the oscillating elementary negative charge (that of the electron) Hence I consider them as the "positron" and "electron" of the **Dirac Sea**, and show that **vacuum polarization** is due to them. This way I dispel the need for a separate ground state (vacuum state) for the electromagnetic field and a separate ground state for the electron and positron field (Dirac sea).

The number of EVE and of ADAM photom particles in a volume unit of space

Here I use a calculation known as the counting of space vibrations in a given unit of volume – the reader should care only about the end result.

The spatial density of an ensemble of photoms of a given λ and a bandwidth $d\lambda$, is:

$n(v) = 8\pi v^2/c^3 \cdot dv$ but $v=c/\lambda$ and $dv=c/\lambda^2 \cdot d\lambda$

Hence: $n(\lambda)=8\pi/\lambda^4 \cdot d\lambda$

For photoms of $\lambda = 500nm$ and a bandwidth $d\lambda = 0.5nm$

the **spatial density** (which should interest the reader) is:

$n(\lambda) \sim 2 \cdot 10^{11}$ **photoms per cubic centimeter.**

This huge number is of utmost importance in the understanding of the nature of light and the understanding of the essence of Quantum Phenomena.

Condensation and Dispersion – the Key to the Understanding of Quantum Phenomena

Fig. (O5), shows a symbolic space lattice, which is like a 3D fisherman's net. Imagine that each vertical plane, in Fig. (O5), going into the page, is a plane in which a photon or a photom is moving. If two adjacent photons or photoms of the same frequency oscillate in anti-phase side by side (**Left**) they stretch the lattice horizontally and move apart to ease the tension. The result is **dispersion** - a reduced spatial density of the photons or photoms. If, however, they oscillate in phase (**Right**), they move together to ease the tension and the result is **condensation** - higher density. A similar situation occurs if they move one below or above the other.

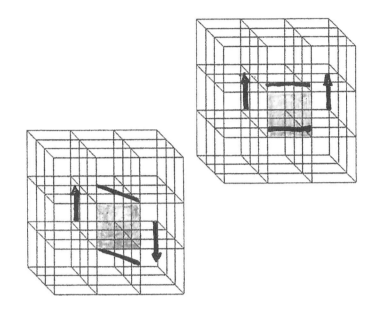

Fig. (O5) Dispersion and Condensation

Interference with Classical Waves – Ensembles of Photoms or Photons (See also Chapter T)

Photons or photoms, of the same wavelength, when they are in phase and closely packed, move as a classical wave. Let a wave front, of such a classical wave, hit the double slit; if the photons or photoms, which are coming from the two slits and hit the screen, are in phase (on the screen) they create maxima zones on the screen, and minima if out of phase. In other words; intensity is reduced in zones of **destructive** interference whereas in zones of **constructive** interference intensity is enhanced. Photons and photoms entering these zones, however, are **neither annihilated nor created** and the total energy is conserved. No annihilation or creation takes place, only **a spatial displacement of the particles,** as I have shown in the previous sub-section, that results in a reduction in their density (intensity) in one zone and an increase in their density (intensity) in the other.

The sun deflects the light of a far star by about a milliradian. The deflection that creates the above dispersion or condensation is much larger. We can only imagine the internal forces in the space lattice.

On Interference with Individual Photons and the quantum enigma, see Chapter T.

ADAM EVE and the Photon

On the photon we know the following:

Light is a stream of photons.

The energy of a photon U depends on its frequency υ times the Planck constant h, named after the physicist Planck:

$$U = h \cdot \upsilon$$

The photon lacks inertia, it does not own mass (despite the fact that energy and mass are equivalent) and it moves at the speed of light – after all this is light.

The photon has intrinsic angular momentum known as its **Spin.**

Spin, in general, comes in units **S**, which are half integers:

1/2, 1, 3/2, 2, 5/2, 3 ...... of $\hbar = h/2\pi$.

The photon's spin is S=1 and its intrinsic angular momentum is $\hbar$.

In quantum field theory - QFT - the photon is considered an excitation of the electromagnetic field. The lowest energy level of this field is embedded with excitations which have half of the photon's energy and half of its spin. We consider them to be our ADAM and EVE. These particles pack space separately with enormous densities. But sometimes ADAMs and EVEs adhere to create pairs and become photons, Fig. (O6), two pairs to become gravitons, and sometimes to become neutrinos.

Note again that EVE carries the oscillating positive elementary charge (that of the positron), whereas ADAM carries the oscillating elementary negative charge (that of the electron) Hence I consider them as the "positron" and "electron" of the **Dirac Sea**, and show that vacuum polarization is due to them.

All this means that the photon caries the two oscillating charges, but its net charge from a distance is zero since the charges cancel out the fields of each other. Physicists will understand that the **photon is an oscillating dipole that confines its oscillating field (**no transmission of energy**).**

We know that an energetic enough photon can get close to the atomic nucleus and be converted in a process known **as pair production** to become a pair of electron and positron. Now it is clear from where the elementary charges of the electron and positron came. And since the elementary charges are of equal size, but of different signs, the charge of the photon is zero. Hence the oscillating charge of ADAM equals that of EVE. This fact strengthens my understanding that fractions of the elementary charges, like those supposedly in quarks do not exist.

Fig. (O6) The Photon

More on the Photon

Photon Energy and the Nature of Planck Constant $\hbar$

The expression for the photon's energy is $U = K\lambda^2/2\pi^2$ where K is an attribute of space similar to the K of a spring. If the "Space Spring Constant K" is **a function of ω only** we guess that it can be:

$$K = M\omega^2 = (U/c^2)\omega^2 = \hbar\omega^3 / c^2$$

where $\hbar$, **not yet identified,** is a constant of proportionality.

Necessarily $U = \hbar\omega$ where $\hbar$ becomes the known quantum constant.

Thus, a classical functionality of $K(\omega) \propto \omega^3$ leads **to the basic quantum mechanical result for the energy and reveals the nature of the Planck constant.**

The Photon's Volume

My model of the photon enables me for the first time in physics to determine the volume of a photon as function of its wavelength λ.

$$V_{Photon} = 6.75 \cdot 10^{-7} \cdot \lambda^3 cm^3$$

The shorter is λ, the more compact is the photon.

For λ = 500nm Green light, we get:

$V_{Photon} = 6.75 \cdot 10^{-7} \cdot \lambda^3 \sim 8 \cdot 10^{-20} cm^3$.

Indeed, a point.

The Photon Spin $\hbar$

My model of the photon enables me to find out theoretically the photon spin L, for a circular polarized photon. Its linear momentum $P = U/c$ times its radius of rotation $R_e = \lambda/2\pi$, gives $L = PR_e = U/c \cdot \lambda/2\pi$ but $U = \hbar\omega$. Hence, the known result:

$L = \hbar$

Space Polarizations - The Polarization of the Vacuum

A scattering experiment, conducted in the TRISTAN accelerator in Japan in 1997, found that the closer electrons get to each other, the field they sense is larger than expected. The explanation, given by **Koltick** (1997), was that in the immediate vicinity of the electron the creation and annihilation of pairs of electrons and positrons screen the charge of the electron by polarization, see Fig. (O7). This is the **Polarization of the Vacuum**. My explanation is somewhat different. Photoms can create space polarization. ADAM particles surround a positive charge and EVE particles adhere to their backs, see Fig. (O7), hence, space acts like a dielectric media and screens the positive charge.

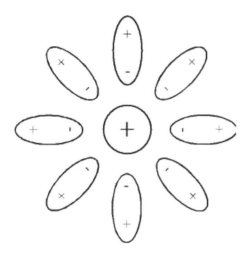

Fig. (O7) The "Net" Charge (Tristan Accelerator Japan 1997)

Thus, from a distance the charge will appear as carrying a smaller charge. If we approach the charge through the screen, the closer, we get the larger the charge will appear.

Based on this understanding we can dispel the need for virtual creation and annihilation of electron-positron pairs.

ADAM and EVE and the Graviton

Gravitational waves have recently been detected. These space waves are predicted by General Relativity. As of today, there is no theoretical proof, or observational evidence, for the existence of quanta of these waves. These quanta are considered by some to be the "force-carrying" mediators between masses - the Gravitons.

Here I suggest a model of the, as yet hypothetical, Graviton. We also relate to the effort to quantize gravitation, and raise arguments in support of the existence of Gravitons.

The Gravitational Wave

Fig. (O8) shows the effect of a linear polarized gravitational wave on a ring of particles, moving towards us perpendicularly to the page and through it, in different times. These times are the quarters of the cycle time T. This wave is a transversal wave of contracted and dilated space, where the contraction and dilation are perpendicular to each other and to the direction of propagation. Hence it moves at the light velocity c.

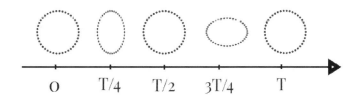

Fig. (O8) The Gravitational Wave

At T = 0 space is the standard normal space. After T/4 space is stretched (dilated) vertically and contracted horizontally. At T/2 space is the standard normal space, and at 3T/4 space is contracted vertically and stretched (dilated) horizontally.

Necessarily the Graviton description should comply with that of the gravitational wave.

The Graviton

The Graviton is composed of a pair of two ADAM particles back to back and a pair of two EVE particles back to back, Fig. (O9).

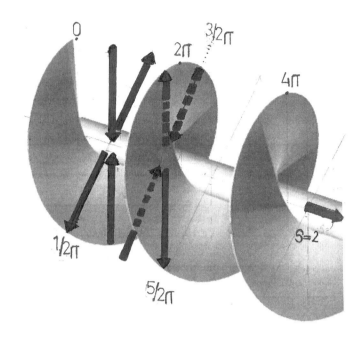

Fig. (O9) The Graviton

When the ADAMs stretch the EVEs contract. Each of the photoms

contributes spin s = 1/2 and together a total spin of

s = 2.

Note how this model complies with the gravitational wave Fig. (O8).

The Spin Energy and Size of the Graviton G

The G Spin

The spin of each photom is 1/2 $\hbar$. Since the graviton is constructed

of 4 photoms its spin must be 2, hence:

L_G = 2 $\hbar$

We could also relate to the fact that in pair annihilation, in order to conserve angular momentum, two photons are created, and hence the above equation.

The Graviton Energy

The Graviton energy is simply the gain of gravitational energy lost in the annihilation of a pair of a particle and its anti-particle. Let a pair with mass M' be located on the surface of a mass M. The gravitational energy of the system M' and M due to the presence of M' is:

E_G = GMM'/R, R being the radius of M. The annihilation of the pair is a loss of energy to the system, since the photons created in the annihilation process leave the system. It is a long-standing issue as to where did the gravitational energy disappear. We contend that this energy is carried by a graviton, which also leaves the system. This understanding enables us to calculate typical graviton energies. Since the graviton is a transversal wavepacket it moves at the velocity c and its energy U is related to its angular frequency ω by: U = $\hbar\omega$

The Graviton Size

The size of a graviton seems to be like that of the photon, where λ is the wavelength of the graviton. Its volume is:

$$V_{Graviton} = 6.75 \cdot 10^{-7} \cdot \lambda^3 \, cm^3$$

The Quantization of Space Curvature and the Graviton

Einstein's Field Equation of General Relativity deals with spacetime curving by Energy/Momentum, which is due to angular momentum, as we have shown. By incorporating in this equation, the additional curving by Charge/Current, we have extended the equation to become relevant not only to the **macroscopic** world, of mainly neutral bodies, but also to the **microscopic** world of elementary particles. This equation expresses the idea that space curvature is quantized, since both angular momentum and charge are quantized.

The Quantized Space Curvature

The quantization of spacetime curvature is due to quantized angular momentum and charge. Thus, the creation of a pair of a particle and its anti-particle contributes twice to the curving by spin (and relevant energy). There is no contribution to curvature by a pair of bivalent elementary charges since the contributions of positive and negative curving cancel out. Note that in our theory - the GDM gravitation is space contraction. Thus, "quantizing gravitation" means that the amount of contraction jumps from one value to another by a quantum of contraction. The annihilation of a pair of a particle and its anti-particle subtracts twice the curving by spin (and relevant energy). This loss in curving (contraction), which is necessarily quantized, is a loss in space torsion and its relevant energy. This is more than a clue as to how the graviton is constructed.

ADAM EVE and the Neutrino

We know that the spin of the neutrino is $s = 1/2$, it moves at the speed of light c, and its mass is about one million times smaller than that of the electron. The neutrino appears mainly in interactions in which the weak force is involved. Hence, we are wondering whether the neutrino is incorporated in the structures of combinations of quarks as responsible for their twisted trucks.

In my model, Fig. (O10), the neutrino is EVE in one half cycle and ADAM in the other half.

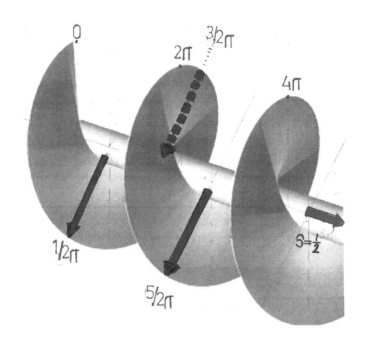

Fig. (O10), The Neutrino

We and the reality in which we live is a huge collection of

vibrations moving at the speed of light, but the centers of their

tracks are moving at slower speeds. Space is the 3D arena in

which these patterns of vibrations move. It is their geometry of

patterns that actually move, hence the name

Geometrodynamics given to my model of the reality - GDM.

P. My Model of Massive Elementary Particles

It is worth noting that my model brings results that no-body, so far, has been able to provide, for example the calculations of the particles' masses. As of today, these masses are considered constants of nature, since nobody knows how to calculate them.

Each and every particle in this category contains an elementary electric charge. Further discussion on the nature of these elementary charges is our starting point.

The Bivalent Elementary Charges as Kind of Black and White Holes

Susskind (2004) wrote:

*One of the deepest lessons we have learned over the past decade is that **there is no fundamental difference between elementary particles and black holes**. As repeatedly emphasized by Gerard 't Hooft (1990), black holes are the natural extension of the* *elementary particle spectrum. This is especially clear in string theory where black holes are simply highly-excited string states. Does that mean that we should count every particle as a black hole?*

Relating just to the elementary charge, our answer to this question is **affirmative**.

This idea was first expressed by Salam and Strathdee (1977), Holzhey and Wilczek (1992), and also Sen (1995).

The intuition of these distinguished physicists is my inspiration.

My attribution of space deformation to an elementary charge, and the fact that charge is quantized, led me to pursue the possibility that positive and negative elementary charges are hitherto unrecognized kind of electrical black and white holes, respectively. This led me to the derivation and calculation, using cgs units, of the radii and masses presented in the following sub-Sections.

My Results for the Radii of the Elementary Charges

My calculated **radius r_p of the elementary positive charge,** based on general relativity, is:

r_p(calculated) = 0.8774 10^{-13} cm,   (p1)

This is also the **radius r_p of the proton's elementary positive**

charge (not the proton radius), which was measured by **Pohl** (2010)

and is:

r_p(measured) = 0.8768(69) 10^{-13} cm.

My calculated result is well within the experimental error range with

an accuracy of 0. 07%

This is also the **anti-proton** charge radius that can be and should

be measured, and the **radii of the elementary negative and**

positive charges of the electron and positron

Based on these radii I derive and calculate the **Mass M_e of the**

Electron/Positron

On Pair Production

Pair production is the creation of an elementary particle and its

antiparticle, by the interaction of an energetic photon with matter.

The electron and positron pair is an example.

In the GDM, and also in **Loudon's** (2000) book, a photon is considered a transverse wavepacket, whereas I consider an elementary charge a longitudinal circulating wavepacket (of contracted or dilated space) A similar concept, suggested by Sakharov (1982) is titled: The Knot-Like Topological Structure of Elementary Charges. Pair production seems to be a **mode conversion** of the transverse wavepacket (the photon) into two longitudinal wavepackets rather than an extraction of an electron from Dirac's sea (the common conception). This conversion takes place during the circulation of an, energetic enough, photon around a positive nucleus. This circulation is possible, since the proton's charge is an electric black hole, which deforms space drastically. The photon spin 1 is divided equally between the particles (conservation of angular momentum) to attribute spin ½ for each particle of the pair.

Derivation and Calculation of the Longitudinal Wavepacket Velocity c_L and Feynman's Self Interactions

In the paradigm longitudinal electromagnetic waves do not exist theoretically and very few have been looking for them. In the GDM they exist theoretically and recently they have also been revealed. Here I present my way to calculate their velocity c_L.

QED uses the concept of virtual photons and Feynman Diagrams, to perform accurate calculations. The idea is that particles exchange virtual photons and can also **self-interact**. This section shows how **a classical approach to self-interaction** can yield a result for c_L. The buildup of a field around a suddenly created charge propagates, from the charge onwards, at velocity C. The sudden destruction of the charge causes the field around it to vanish at the same speed. Imagine, now, a circulating charge that moves with velocity c_L, where $c_L > C$.

In this case, if to move along half a circle takes less time than for the field to vanish along the diameter, **the charge will be affected by its own field** created when it passed the opposite point on the diameter, **as if** the charge, still existed on the other side of the diameter. We refer to this virtual charge as the **image** of the charge. **Self-interaction** is thus the interaction of a charge with its image, as we phrase it. Imagine the electron charge circulating with velocity c_L around a point. Self-interaction occurs if the time to circulate a half circle, $\pi r_e / c_L$, is shorter than, or equal to, the time for its propagating or retreating field to cross the diameter $2 r_e / c$. Thus, self- interaction takes place if at least:

$\pi\, r_e / c_L = 2\, r_e / c.$ The requirement for self-interaction is thus:

$c_L / c \geq \pi/2$ The minimal value of this ratio is:

$c_L / c = \pi/2$ By constructing a more accurate model of the electron I arrive at:

$c_L / c = \pi / 2\,(1 + \pi\,\alpha)$

$c_L / c = 1.6068$ (p2)

Based on the above I arrive at the next Section.

My Derivation and Calculation of the Electron Mass M_e

Here is my result, **the first of its kind in physics,** for the

mass of the electron/positron M_e:

$$M_e = \frac{s^2\sqrt{2}}{\pi(1+\pi\,\alpha)} \cdot \sqrt{G^{-1}\alpha\hbar c^{-3}} \qquad s = 1\ ([s^2] = L^2T^{-2})$$

α is the fine structure constant, c the light velocity, G the

gravitational constant and $\hbar$ Planck constant

Dimensionality test:

$[G^{-1}] = ML^{-3}T^2 \quad [\alpha] = 1 \quad [\hbar] = ML^2T^{-1} \quad [c^{-3}] = L^{-3}T^3$

$M = [s^2\sqrt{G^{-1}\alpha\hbar c^{-3}}] = L^2T^{-2}(ML^{-3}T^2{\cdot}ML^2T^{-1}{\cdot}L^{-3}T^3)^{1/2} =$

$L^2T^{-2}(M^2L^{-4}T^4)^{-1/2} = L^2T^{-2}ML^{-2}T^2 = M$

M_e (calculated) $= 0.91036 \cdot 10^{-27}$gr

M_e (measured) $= 0.910938356(11) \cdot 10^{-27}$gr

The **accuracy** here is 0.06% !

I arrived at this result 23 years after starting my enterprise. I knew that my idea was good but I was not so sure if I could deliver. Only a few years ago I became convinced that I achieved my goal and started to publish my scientific papers.

The Stability of the Self-Circulation and the Anomalous Gyroscopic Moment

The self-circulation is kept stable by the **attractive** Lorentz force

$\mathbf{F} = Q/c\ \mathbf{v}_x\mathbf{B}$, towards the center of the circulation. The magnetic field $\mathbf{B}$, which the charge senses, is created by the circulation of its image. This force balances the **repulsive** force $F = Q \cdot Q/(2r_e)^2$ between the charge and its image. The magnetic field created by the circulating charge is $\mathbf{B} = 1/c\ \mathbf{v}_x\mathbf{E}$.   Hence:

$\mathbf{F}=(Q/c)\mathbf{v}_x\mathbf{B}=(Q/c)\mathbf{v}_x(1/c)\mathbf{v}_x\mathbf{E}$ but $v = c$ and this equation becomes

$\mathbf{F} = Q\mathbf{E}$ or $F = Q \cdot Q/(2r_e)^2$ This centripetal force balances the repulsive force above. Note that this calculation is not dependent on whether we use c or c_L.

The **anomalous gyroscopic moment** is considered a quantum mechanical phenomenon that **cannot** be explained by classical physics.

Note, however, that the circulation of the self-interacting charge with its own "image" is a current of **"two"** charges that double **E** and hence double **B** = 1/c **v**$_x$**E.** These "two" charges are circulating along the larger circle of radius R$_e$ related to the spin. We **wonder** if this is the cause for the factor 2 in the anomalous gyroscopic moment, as Dirac showed.

The Derivation and Calculations of the Muon and Tau Masses

The Muon

A photon that enters the pair-production process, by circulating the proton charge, might be converted into the heavy muon and anti-muon pair. This happens if the energy U$_{photon}$ is high enough to retain the angular momentum of the particle/anti-particle L =$1/2\hbar$, by circulation with radius r$_e$ and velocity c$_L$, around the proton charge alone and with no need for an additional larger circulation with radius

R_e. Hence:

$1/2\ \hbar = (U_\mu /c_L)\ r_e$ or:

$U_\mu = 1/2\ \hbar\ c_L /r_e$

Using (p2) for c_L and (p1) for r_e we get:

U_μ (calculated) $= 180.15\ 10^{-6}$erg $=112.5$ MeV   or:

$M_\mu = 112.5$ MeV/c^2

According to CODATA 2014:

U_μ(experimental) $= 105.6583745(24)$ MeV

M_μ(experimental) $= 105.6583745(24)$ MeV/c^2

The calculated result shows a deviation of ~ 6 % from the

experimental CODATA value.

The Tau
According to the CODATA 2014:

$U_\tau /U_\mu\ = 1776.84/105.66 = 16.82$

$L = P\cdot R = (U_\tau /c')\ r$ and if L is retained then r/c' should be

$(1/16.82)\ r_\mu /c_L$ or:

r/c' = (1/16.82)1.378 10^{-13} / 1.5348 310^{10} = 1.779 10^{-25} sec.   This result occurs if r < r_μ , which means that the elementary charge rotates around an inside point. But for rotation inside a black or white hole c'< c_L. Thus, r might be even smaller than r_μ/16.82.

Note that the elementary charge of both the tau and the muon moves at the longitudinal velocity and there is no circulation that brings the overall average velocity down to that of the transverse velocity, c. In this case, the charge moves faster than the photons it radiates, which explains the short lifetime of these particles. In the case of the electron, the compound circulation of the charge brings down the average velocity to the light velocity, c. Hence, photons cannot be radiated (or radiated but re-absorbed). This explains the stability of the electron.

On the Three Generations of Quarks

It seems that these generations are the twisted circulations of the electron, muon and tau particles.

The Electron in Motion and Lorentz Transformation

"Rest" and Motion in the GDM

Every disturbance in space must move at the velocity of its elastic

waves, c_L or c_T.

A transverse disturbance in space moves at the speed of light

$c = c_T$, whereas a longitudinal disturbance moves at a higher

speed c_L

Note that a longitudinal wavepacket is necessarily a moving dilation,

contraction or an oscillation between the two.

As a consequence, **there is no state of rest**. "Rest" is defined,

therefore, as a situation in which a disturbance, although moving at

velocity c_L or c_T, is on a closed track. This orbital movement,

Dirac's Zitterbewegung, is the spin of elementary particles.

On constant translational velocity v, and accelerated motion, relative to space.

"Rest"

Fig. (P1) is a simple description of the electron (positron) at "Rest" and in Motion. The gray sphere (circle) represents the zone of drastically dilated (contracted) space, which is the electric charge. In this discussion we omit, for simplicity, the inner circulation of the charge, with radius r_e. We also do not show in Fig. (P1) that the circulation plane is **not** perpendicular to the velocity vector **v**.

"Rest" is described on the left of Fig. (P1). The zone of dilated space (charge) of our electron revolves, in the xy plane, around the origin with a radius R_0 (in the previous sections we notated this radius as R_e). In this case: $c = \omega R_o$. From now on, when we relate to the electron we also relate to the positron, unless otherwise is mentioned.

Motion

For simplicity we ignore in the following sections the inner circulation of the electric charge.

Fig. (P1), on the right, describes a translational motion. Motion is the situation in which the circle of revolution of the wavepacket becomes a spiral. On this spiral the **length of a revolution** is retained, since angular momentum is retained (explained below). Hence the spiral radius R is smaller than R_0. This is in analogy to a stretched spring. According to Fig. (P1):

$R = 1/\gamma \; R_0$

Note that R_0 is our R_e in the previous sections.

The resultant electron motion, however, is always at the wave velocity c. Thus, a translational motion at constant velocity, v, does not involve any exertion of force (a proof of Newton's first law). It is also obvious that necessarily $v < c$.

From this alone we derive similar **results** to that of the Theory of Special Relativity (SR), but without SR.

The **length of a revolution** is retained despite the reduction in R since angular momentum is retained. And the angular momentum is retained since the **energy is increasing.**

$$c_1^2 = c^2 - v^2 \quad \text{or:}$$

$$c_1 = c\left(1 - \beta^2\right)^{\frac{1}{2}} = \frac{1}{\gamma}c$$

$$\text{where:} \quad \beta = \frac{v}{c}$$

$$\text{and:} \quad \gamma = \left(1 - \beta^2\right)^{-\frac{1}{2}}$$

Fig. (P1) Rest (left) and Motion (right)

Lorentz Transformation (LT)

Our model of the moving electron yields the LT. In a way, it is similar to the contracted particle in motion, used by **Lorentz** (1904) to derive his LT. Note that both models attribute the LT to the contraction of particles due to their motion. This contraction is also the reason for the slowing down of the rates of clocks. See Chapter **S, On Time.**

Newton's first law, and the **SR conclusion** that no particle or signal can move at a speed that exceeds the light/wave velocity c, are thus a natural result of our model. The helical motion, which is an electric current formally in the direction - z, is related to the magnetic field **B** and the vector potential **A**. The Circular Track is stable since the **centrifugal** force is balanced by an equal but opposite **centripetal** force. The Lorentz force, created by the magnetic field of the circulating charge acting on itself, is the required centripetal force.

The Electron Inertia

At rest, the energy of the electron is U_0, linear tangential momentum is

$P_o = U_0/c$ and the angular momentum is $L_0 = P_o R_o$.

In motion, energy, linear momentum and angular momentum are U,

$P = U/c$ and $L = PR$ respectively.

The conservation of angular momentum $L = L_0$ (which is $1/2\,\hbar$ for the electron) implies that:

$PR = P_o R_o$ hence, $UR = U_0 R_0$ but:

$$R = 1/\gamma\ R_0 \tag{p3}$$

Thus:

$$U = \gamma\,U_0 \tag{p4}$$

Considering the energy as purely electromagnetic, where the elementary charge Q is a sphere of radius r_0 , the relations

$U_0 = Q^2/2r_0$, $U = Q^2/2r$ and (p2) give:

$$r = 1/\gamma \; r_0 \tag{p5}$$

For $v \ll c$ (53) is:

$$r = (1 - v^2/2c^2) \; r_0 \tag{p6}$$

Acceleration is accompanied by an increase of energy U, and a reduction in the radii R and r. The applied force, needed to accelerate the particle, is doing work to curve space more strongly and thus to reduce r. This force is needed to increase stress and cause more strain in order to enlarge the curvature. Thus, we arrive at **Newton's Second Law** and understand **Inertia.**

Note that we have replaced Newton's axiomatic laws by our postulated model of an elementary particle. Some of the merits in this **replacement**, as we show here and elsewhere, are:

- It leads to the proof of the equivalence of gravitational mass and inertial mass. And, more than that, it shows that **gravitational mass is inertial mass**.

- It proves that **mass** is not a fundamental attribute of matter.

- It proves that **inertia** is an intrinsic attribute of matter, with no need for an additional field to induce it (**Higgs Field**).

Note that $L = 1/2\, \hbar$, $R = 1/2\, \hbar c/U$, $U_0 = Q^2/2r_0$ and $r = Q^2/2U$ give:

$\alpha = r/R = Q^2/\hbar c$ **Fine Structure Constant.**   (p7)

This result reveals the meaning of α.

Note also that at "rest" the angular momentum can point in any direction, whereas in motion it can point, in the direction of motion or opposite to it. This attribute is related to **Space Quantization.**

Relativistic Mass

Our "relativistic" relation (p2) gives:

$$U = \gamma U_0 = U_0\left(1 - \frac{v^2}{c^2}\right)^{-\frac{1}{2}} \simeq U_0 + \frac{\frac{1}{2}U_0 v^2}{c^2} \qquad \text{The second term:}$$

$$\frac{\frac{1}{2}U_0 v^2}{c^2} = \frac{1}{2}(U_0/c^2)v^2 \ ,$$

is identified as the **kinetic energy** where:

$$M_0 = U_0 / c^2 \qquad\qquad\qquad\qquad (p8)$$

Thus, **inertial mass** becomes merely a **practical term.** We also get:

$$M = \gamma M_0 \qquad\qquad\qquad\qquad (p9)$$

The literature distinguishes between the **kinetic energy** $\frac{1}{2}M_0 v^2$, which a particle possesses by virtue of its motion, and its **internal energy** $M_0 c^2$. But here, the kinetic energy is also an internal energy of deformation (the reduction in size of r and R) that cannot be distinguished from the rest energy.

Note that our model for the moving electron, presented here, uses the simplified version of the much more detailed model of the electron at "rest" that appears elsewhere.

Q. The Cosmic Microwave Background (CMB)

At large, the CMB is isotropic and homogenous blackbody radiation, with a peak temperature of 2.7°k. The CMB was predicted theoretically by **Gamow** and discovered accidentally by **Penzias and Wilson**. In 1989 the CMB was again measured, this time by the Cosmic Background Explorer (COBE) satellite, see Fig. (Q1).

An observer's motion relative to the background radiation is accompanied by a Doppler shift, see Chapter **C**. This shift enables the measurement of the observer's velocity relative to the radiation bath (i.e., space's vibrations) "attached" to space.

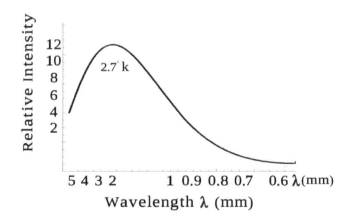

FIG. (Q1) The Cosmic Background

Velocity Relative to the Global Space

A CMB anisotropy was first observed by **Smoot** et al and interpreted as the result of the above Doppler shift.

Fig. (Q2) shows the vector of the velocity, in kilometers per second, of the solar system relative to space. Recently, the velocity of the Earth around the Sun and its rotational velocity have been derived from the Doppler shift.

The solar system velocity relative to space, see Fig. (Q2), is:

$v = 371.0 \pm 0.5$ km sec^{-1}.

This velocity is towards a point whose equatorial coordinates are:

$(\alpha, \delta) = (11.20^h \pm 0.01^h, -7.22^0 \pm 0.08^0)$.

This direction points, approximately, from the cluster of galaxies, Aquarius, towards the cluster Leo-Virgo.

Say the peak of the background radiation is green. An observer, seeing green in all directions, knows they are at rest relative to space. An observer, seeing blue in one direction, red in the opposite direction, and green on the sides, knows they are moving in the direction of the blue.

Similarly, we can also make a distinction regarding acceleration. An observer moving in a circle notices that tangentially to the circle there is no symmetry, the horizon in one direction looks red, and in the other, blue.

FIG. (Q2) Sun Velocity Relative to Space (Scientific American)

Coleman and Glashow, and myself adopted the idea that space is a **special frame**. Experiments to reveal the Earth Velocity Relative to the Global Space by measurements of light velocity in and opposite the Earth velocity vector direction failed. The full isotropy obtained is explained elsewhere.

Space Aether and the Theories of Relativity

In the past space was considered a frame of reference only. Absolute void (emptiness, vacuum) with no meaning without the embedded objects in it. Take out the objects and you have taken from space its meaning.

Later in the past physicists realized that waves accrue in media. Namely waves are the vibrations of a media, like sea waves in the sea or sound waves in the air. But then electromagnetic waves were discovered and the fact that light is an electromagnetic wave.

Immediately rose the question - what is the media of these waves. And since no evidence was found that could identify such a media the idea of the aether was invented. Necessarily it was assumed that this aether occupies the entire space. In this book I explain that the media of electromagnetic waves is space. Hence, we can relate to the terms space and aether as synonyms.

See what Einstein himself wrote about this subject:

Einstein (1920) Ether and the Theory of Relativity

> **… the hypothesis of ether in itself is not in conflict with the special theory of relativity.**

> **… According to the general theory of relativity space without ether is unthinkable**;

R. Updated Special Relativity

Special Relativity (SR) – A Reassessment

In SR, length contraction and time dilation are **not real**. In SR, neither space nor time is objective. Only **spacetime is objective and absolute**, since the interval ΔS^2 is invariant under Lorentz Transformation. In the GDM, physical objects get shorter in the direction of motion relative to space. Hence, the spatial distance between two disconnected objects, moving in the same direction and at the same velocity, is **retained.** SR considers these two objects to reside in **the same** inertial frame. Thus, an observer in another inertial frame concludes that **not only** the objects get shorter, but also the spatial distance between them.

I came across this situation reading Bell's book "Speakable and unspeakable in quantum mechanics".

Case Study

Consider two rockets in a frame **k**, a distance L_0 from each other and at **rest** relative to space. The rockets start to move till they both acquire velocity v, relative to the rest space frame **k**. We assume a

very slow and identical acceleration for both rockets until they reach

this velocity. The two rockets now reside in a new reference frame **k'**

moving at the velocity v relative to **k.**

In Fig. (R1) a beam of light travels from a source S, on the left rocket,

to a mirror M, on the right rocket, and back to a detector D.

According to the GDM, **for an observer at rest** in the space frame

k, $L = L_0$ regardless of the rockets motion, and the time taken for the

light to travel is:

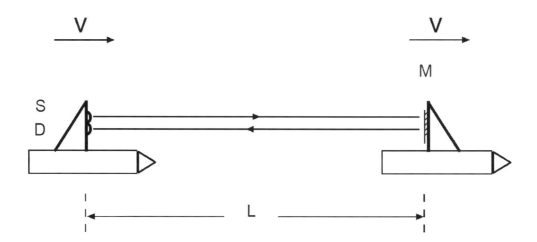

Fig. (R1) Two Rockets

$$\Delta T = \frac{L_0}{c+v} + \frac{L_0}{c-v} = \frac{2L_0}{c} \frac{1}{1-\frac{v^2}{c^2}} = \gamma^2 \Delta T_0 \qquad (r1)$$

where $\Delta T_0 = 2L_0/c$

For the observer on the left rocket

$\Delta T = \gamma \, \Delta T_0$ (r2)

since the unit of time of his clock is dilated.

In SR the two rockets reside in the same reference frame k',

moving relative to k. Hence relative to k the distance $L = \dfrac{L_0}{\gamma}$ is

contracted and the travel time is:

$\Delta T = \gamma \, \Delta T_0$ (r3)

This difference, between (r3) and (r1), is the difference between the

predictions of the GDM and SR, **if** one considers k' a legitimate

frame in SR.

Simultaneity

From the previous Chapter **Q**, it is obvious that observers resting in space can determine whether certain events occurred simultaneously or at different times. The same goes for observers traveling at velocity, v, relative to space. They could also confirm within their system moving at velocity v relative to space whether certain events happened simultaneously or at different times. Events that occurred simultaneously for the observers within the resting system are also simultaneous for observers in motion – and vice versa.

Understandably, in SR, because of Einstein's synchronization procedures, what is simultaneous in one system is not simultaneous in another that is moving relative to the first.

In order to clarify this issue, consider again the moving carriage example Fig. (R2).

Let us suppose that the Earth is at rest relative to space. On earth there is a track that heads off in some direction, with an observer standing by its side. Let us suppose that a carriage travels on this track at velocity v relative to the track (and anyway relative to space) and within the carriage is an internal observer. The carriage has two doors A and B, see Fig. (R2). At the center is a multi-directional pulsating light source. When a pulse reaches detectors D_A, D_B, the doors open. The observer at the side of the track has two cameras, C_A and C_B, able to see a wide-angle view of doors A and B, respectively. These cameras are equipped with equal length cables, at whose ends lay monitors M_A and M_B, which the external observer watches.

If the carriage is at rest relative to the track, and sends a pulse of light, then the doors open simultaneously for both the internal observer and the external observer.

If the carriage is moving relative to the track, and a pulse of light is sent, then it reaches detector D_A after a period of time:

FIG. (R2) Simultaneity

$$\Delta T_A = \frac{L}{2} \frac{1}{c - v}$$
and to D_B after:

$$\Delta T_B = \frac{L}{2} \frac{L}{c + v}$$
The external observer sees door B open

before door A, seeing that:

$$\Delta T_B < \Delta T_A$$

For the internal observer to determine what happened, they must

see the light returning from the doors to the center of the cabin – to

the observer.

The time of return from door A:

$$\Delta T_A' = \frac{L}{2} \frac{1}{c+v}$$

whereas from door B:

$$\Delta T_B' = \frac{L}{2} \frac{1}{c-v}$$

so, the total time it takes to

and from door A:

$$\Delta T_A'' = \Delta T_A + \Delta T_A' = \frac{L}{c} \frac{1}{1 - \frac{v^2}{c^2}}$$

whereas from door B:

$$\Delta T_B'' = \Delta T_B + \Delta T_B' = \frac{L}{c} \frac{1}{1 - \frac{v^2}{c^2}}$$

seeing that:

$$\Delta T_A'' = \Delta T_B''$$

for the internal observer, the doors appear to open simultaneously.

However, since the internal observer knows how to measure v, they can calculate and deduce that the doors did not open simultaneously. Therefore, there is no place for Einstein's SR argument about the relativity of simultaneity. There is no need, anyway, for a new perception of the causality principle.

Note

Einstein's SR gives no meaning to velocity v relative to the "stationary system", because it "can't be" measured.

Since $\Delta T_A'' = \Delta T_B''$ we can arbitrarily make the simplest assumption $\Delta T_A = \Delta T_A' = \Delta T_B = \Delta T_B'$. This is equivalent to stating that the speed of light in the carriage is c in every direction, or in every inertial system. From this Einstein derived the relativity of simultaneity and the relativity of the shortening of length and of the clock slowing down. And from this, the objective meaning is removed from time and space.

A Spherical Light Wave

Spherical wave fronts are emitted from the origin, O, of a co-ordinate system, **k**, starting at time, t_0. System **k** is at rest in space. **k'** is another co-ordinate system that happens to coincide with **k** at t_0 but moves at the speed v along x.

From Einstein's principle of constant light velocity, it is understood that in both **k** and **k'** an observer sees spherical wave fronts and, therefore:

$$x^2 + y^2 + z^2 - c^2t^2 = x'^2 + y'^2 + z'^2 - c^2t'^2$$

From this and the principle of relativity, Einstein 1905 (1923) obtained the **Lorentz Transformation** (LT).

We now consider the spherical wave fronts and try to understand what is really happening.

The observer in system **k**, obviously, sees a spherical wave. The observer in **k'** is, on the face of it, **supposed** to see contracted wave fronts in front of them and dilated wave fronts behind them, as shown in Fig. (R3), i.e., to see distorted wave fronts. But what does "to see" really mean? "To see" means to get back some scattered or reflected light, which is possible only if there are some scattering particles or mirrors in system **k'**. If there are such elements in **k'**, which are physically linked to it, the light that the observer sees has traveled back and forth and, since the lengths in **k'** are contracted, the observer in **k' does in fact see** spherical wave fronts.

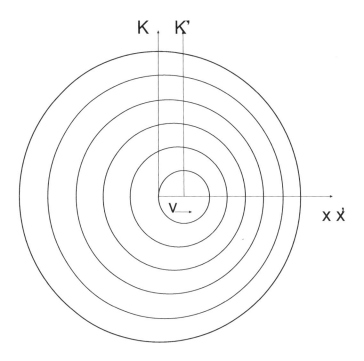

FIG. (R3) Spherical Light Wave

The Contraction of Macroscopic Bodies

Fitzgerald and **Lorentz** (1904) explained the then lack of ability to discover motion relative to the aether (**Michelson** and **Morley** 1887) assuming that the lengths of bodies are contracted in the direction of their motion:

$$L = L_0 \left(1 - \frac{v^2}{c^2}\right)^{\frac{1}{2}} = \frac{1}{\gamma} L_0$$ **Lorentz Length Contraction** (r4)

The translational velocity v is with respect to space, as we see it. An observer moving in space would not notice any contraction, since not only the yardstick but also, they are contracted. However, they can always measure their velocity relative to space and calculate their own contraction. At this stage we can only speculate as to why and how a macroscopic body in motion is contracted.

We consider a possible explanation for macroscopic contraction.

According to Bell, and our exploration elsewhere the electric field of a moving charge is:

$$E' = \frac{HQ}{r'^2} \frac{1 - \beta^2}{\left(1 - \beta^2 \sin^2 \theta'\right)^{3/2}}$$ (r5)

We denote the distance from the charge Q, momentarily at the origin, to the point (x',z') where the field is measured:

$r' = \left(x'^2 + z'^2\right)^{1/2}$. θ' denotes the angle between this radius vector and the velocity of the charge Q, which is moving in the positive x' direction in the frame k'. Then, since z' = r' sin θ', (4) is the magnitude of the field.

For low speeds the field reduces simply to E' ≈ HQ/r'^{2}. But if β^2 is not negligible, at the same distance from the charge, the field is stronger at right angles to the motion than in the direction of the motion. Fig. (R4) shows a simple representation of the field indicating field lines in the x'z' plane. For the field in the x'y' plane we get an identical representation. Fig. (R4) shows that the field perpendicular to the direction of motion gets stronger whereas in the direction of motion - weaker. This phenomenon explains **macroscopic contraction**, since the orbits of electrons in atoms are distorted to become ellipses with their shorter axis in the direction of motion.

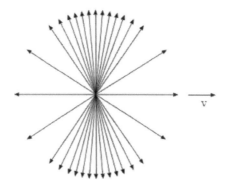

Fig. (R4) The Field of a Uniformly Moving Charge

The Direction of Emission from A Moving Radiator

A Macroscopic Radiator.

Fig. (R5) shows a projector. A point radiator is located at 0, the focal

point of parabolic mirror.

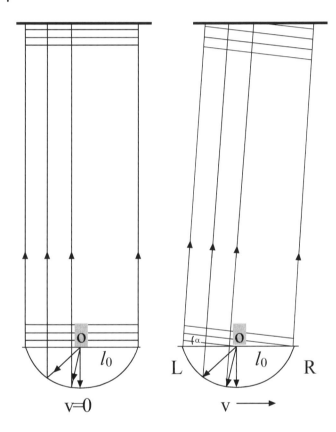

Fig. (R5) A Macroscopic Radiator

When the projector does not move, v = 0, the radiation reaches both

edges of the reflector at the same time, and the outgoing beam from

the reflector moves toward the ceiling with its wave front parallel to the ceiling. When the projector is on the move, v ≠ 0, the radiation from 0 reaches the left side of the parabolic mirror, before it reaches the right side, thus tilting the wave front and, actually, deflecting the beam.

This deflection accrues with any source of light whether macroscopic or microscopic. The conclusion is, thus, that **the motion of an emitter affects the synchrotron radiation.**

A source of light radiates isotropically when at rest relative to space, See Fig. (R6) left. When it moves the intensity in the direction of motion is stronger than behind, See Fig. (R6) right.

This effect, termed **synchrotron radiation,** complies with our understanding.

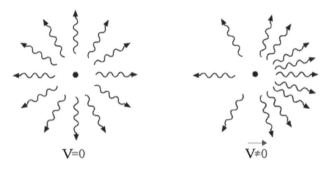

$V=0$ $V \neq 0$

FIG. (R6) Synchrotron Radiation

S. On Time

Real motion is only that of the transvers or longitudinal waves. Space is a special frame and motion relative to space causes real contraction and deflection. These phenomena dispel the need for relating to time as a fundamental attribute of reality. The saying that "Time is Money", albeit with a different connotation, expresses our understanding that Time is indeed like Money.

Larmor Time Dilation

The Cell

Fig. (**S**1) and Fig. (**S**2) show a cell with sides L_0. The cell is equipped with a source S and detector D, on one side, and a mirror on the opposite side. If the cell is at rest relative to space, the time it takes for the light beam to reach the mirror from source S and back to detector D is ΔT_0:

$$\Delta T_0 = \frac{2L_0}{c} \tag{s1}$$

A Moving Cell with a Beam Perpendicular to its Motion

Fig. (S1) shows the source S and detector D on the "floor", and the mirror on the "ceiling". If the cell moves in a direction perpendicular to the direction of the beam of light, the observer resting in space (outside the cell) sees a deflected beam:

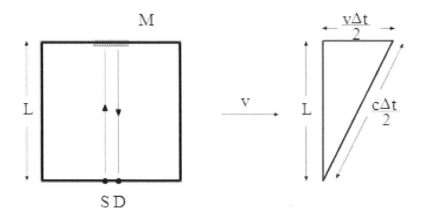

Fig. (S1) A Moving Cell

$$\left(\frac{c\Delta T}{2}\right)^2 = L^2 + \left(\frac{v\Delta T}{2}\right)^2$$

L = L₀ since there is **no contraction** in the direction perpendicular to the direction of motion.

Hence: $4L_0^2 = \left(c^2 - v^2\right)\Delta T^2$ and

$$\Delta T = \frac{2L_0}{c} \frac{1}{\left(1 - \dfrac{v^2}{c^2}\right)^{\frac{1}{2}}} \qquad \gamma = 1 / \left(1 - v^2/c^2\right)^{1/2} \quad \text{or}$$

$\Delta T = \gamma \Delta T_0$ **Larmor Time Dilation**   (s2)

A Moving Cell with a Beam Parallel to its Motion

Fig. (S2) shows the source S and detector D on one side, and the mirror on the other side. When the cell and the light beam move at speed v relative to space:

$$\Delta T = \frac{L}{c+v} + \frac{L}{c-v} = \frac{2L}{c} \frac{1}{1 - \dfrac{v^2}{c^2}} = \frac{2L}{c} \gamma^2 \qquad (s3)$$

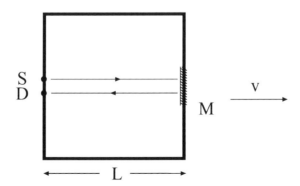

Fig. (S2) A Moving Cell

According to equation (s4):

$$L = \frac{L_0}{\gamma} \qquad \textbf{Lorentz Length Contraction} \qquad \text{(s4)}$$

and again

$$\Delta T = \gamma \Delta T_0 \qquad \textbf{Larmor Time Dilation} \qquad \text{(s5)}$$

Based on (s2) and (s5) **we conclude time to be a scalar**.

On the Lifetime of the Muon

SR Interpretation

The muon particle decays via the weak interaction into an electron and a pair of neutrinos after 2.2 microseconds. In the late 1990s, scientists at Brookhaven National Laboratory, used the Alternative Gradient Synchrotron (AGS) to produce a beam of muons circulating around a 14m-diameter ring at a speed of 0.9994·c. Muons lifetime, at rest, is 2.2 microseconds.

 If this is also the lifetime at this speed, they would manage no more than 15 turns of the ring before they disintegrate. But the muons managed around 433 turns, which means their lifetime was extended by a factor of 28.8 to just over 60 microseconds.

And indeed, for a speed of 0.9994·c the Lorentz factor of time-

dilation is: γ = 28.87.

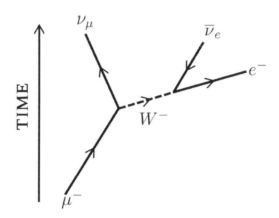

Fig. (S3) Feynman Diagram of the Muon Decay

SR predicts, as observed, that these speedy muons should live 28.87

times longer than at rest.

According to SR, we can also argue that space in the frame of the

muon, which moves with a tangential velocity 0.9994·c relative to the

Lab frame, is contracted, a Lorentz contraction, by the same

γ = 28.87. And as a result, the muon with its lifetime of 2.2

microseconds, moves 433 times around this contracted

circumference. The fact that there are two alternate SR explanations is confusing.

GDM Interpretation

Fig. (S3) shows that the muon disintegrates via its interaction with the vibrating space around it. Hence the smaller it becomes the weaker is the interaction. The interaction dependence on γ is, therefore, reflected in the dependence of the particle's lifetime on γ:

$$T = \gamma T_0$$

Conclusion

We consider both length contraction, and light deflection to be real. Thus, we have dispelled the need to relate to time as a fundamental attribute of reality. Time appears as simply the division of Distance by Velocity. By virtue of motion, or deformed space, objects and light velocity change in a way that keeps light velocity constant, hence the term **constant of nature**, but time by itself has no meaning.

This conclusion has implications as to how we relate to the **first term** in the Schwarzschild metric:

$$ds^2 = -g_{00}c^2 dt^2 + 2g_{0r}dr\,dt + g_{rr}dr^2 + r^2\left(d\theta^2 + \sin^2\theta\,d\varphi^2\right).$$

Some physicists wrongly consider c to be **constant** whereas it is time that changes. We, in contrast, consider c to be a **variable**, but a **constant of nature**.

Note that a mass contracts space around it hence, accordingly light velocity c at the mass, is slower than that in inter-galactic space. Space is contracted, but so is the local observer close to the mass and their yardstick. Thus, the value for c, measured by the local observer, is the same as for the far-away observer. This is the reason for considering c a constant of nature, despite being a variable.

T.   THE PHOTON AND THE QUANTUM ENIGMA

In this chapter we dispel the need to attribute a **dualistic nature** to photons, namely that a photon is both a particle and a wave. The method used in resolving this case is applicable also to other issues of Quantum Mechanics.

Interference with Classical Waves – Ensembles of Photons

Photons or photoms, of the same wavelength, when they are in phase and closely packed, move as a classical wave. Let a wave front, of such a classical wave, hit the double slit, see Fig. (T1); if secondary waves, which are coming from the two slits and hit the screen, are in phase (on the screen) they create maxima zones of intensity on the screen, and minima if out of phase. In other words; intensity is reduced in zones of **destructive** interference whereas in zones of **constructive** interference intensity is enhanced. But these waves are ensembles of photons and photoms, see Fig. (T2) and (T3), entering these zones, and they are neither annihilated nor created and the total energy is conserved. No annihilation or creation takes place, only **a spatial displacement** of the particles that result in a reduction in their density (intensity) in one zone and an increase in their density (intensity) in the other.

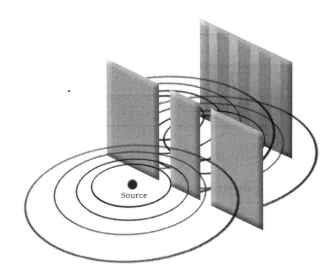

Fig.(T1) Interference with Classical EM Waves

The Table below gives some information about the slits.

WAVELENGTH	0.0005 mm (GREEN)
SLIT WIDTH	0.04 mm
SLIT SPACE	0.250 mm

Fig.(T2) Interference with Photons

This displacement is due to the interaction of the photons with the space lattice, as we have already explained in Chapter **O.** This explanation is the first of its kind, and is applicable to other quantum issues. Hence, we can relate to the ensemble of photons in phase as a wave, see Fig. (T3). **But what about single photons?** What happens when we reduce the intensity of the source of light to the degree in which only single photons are delivered towards the slits. And at a rate that ensures that when one photon is on its way to the screen the next photon is not yet emitted. All this to ensure that no interaction takes place between the photons on their way to the screen.

Fig. (T3) Interference of Waves and Particles

Note that when single photons reach the screen right after the experiment started, we see on the screen "snow" (no pattern), see Fig.(T4) up. Only with time the accumulation of photons reveals the interference pattern, see Fig.(T4) middle and down.

In the current paradigm this phenomenon is explained by attributing a dualistic nature to a single photon: the photon is both a particle and a wave. I beg to differ and suggest the following explanation, based on the understanding of "spontaneous" emission.

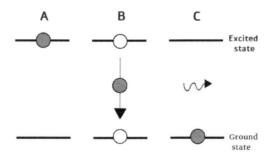

Fig. (T4) The Gradual Development of the Pattern

Stimulated and Spontaneous Emission

Fig. (T5) shows on the left an atom on a high energy level (upper line) above the lower energy level (bottom line-ground state). If a photon, with the same energy as that of the difference in the energy levels of the atom, arrives it can induce the emission of an identical photon by the atom, and its fall to the ground state. This process is termed **Stimulated Emission**.

A   B   C

Excited state

Ground state

Fig. (T5) Stimulated and Spontaneous Emission

However, the atom can also emit a photon without an inducing photon from outside. This kind of emission is termed **Spontaneous Emission.** Some physicists, myself included, are convinced that in this case it is a photom (ground state photon) that induces the emission. Let me remind you that a photom is an ADAM or EVE. Below is evidence in support of my Spontaneous Emission idea. Fig. (T6) shows a beam of exited atoms running through a narrow tube. The rate of emission of photons from these atoms is reduced drastically compared to their rate outside the tube – more than ten times. The explanation is simple: In this tube modes of vibrations, namely photoms, perpendicular to the tube axis and with a wavelength twice the inner diameter of the tube cannot exist. Hence the number of photoms is drastically reduced and so is the spontaneous emission.

Fig. (T6) Damping Spontaneous Emission

In another experiment a mirror is placed close and parallel to a beam of exited atoms. This time the emission rate is doubled, since the mirror reflects incoming photoms back towards the beam, thus doubling their number per unit volume.

Interference with Individual Photons

There is a body of both experimental and theoretical work that shows how the vacuum state of the electromagnetic field (photoms) induces "spontaneous" emission, see the sub-section above. Thus, the basic state is that of a single photon plus a single photom. When one photom, out of the many that construct a wave front of photoms with a frequency that matches a transition in an excited atom (in the source), hits the exited atom it has a probability to induce emission in phase with a photon. The probability of the photon to hit a certain spot on the screen is thus the classical probability of the inducing photom to arrive at this same spot. But the photoms arrive as a classical wave and hence their unseen interference pattern on the screen. This explains the many, one at a time, photons accumulation effect that builds the interference pattern, see Fig. (T4).

This dispels the need to attribute a dualistic nature to photons and solves the collapse issue of the "wavefunction" (although there is no such thing for a photon). Note that the width and the height of the slits, as well as the distance between them, see the table above, comply with our understanding of the photon and photom nature, and the interference experiment.

In the year 2011 it was shown in a "Weak-Experiment" that a single photon, in the Double Slit experiment, goes all the way from the source to the screen through only one slit. The photon follows a trajectory known as the **D. Bohm trajectory**.

Our "mechanism" by which the photon is "guided" is also relevant to other elementary particles, atoms, molecules, and even microscopic bodies. The **statistical nature** of the process of single photons interference is clear, but inferentially it is **deterministic**.

This photoms wave is actually the **De Broglie guiding wave**.

As you can see there is no need for a new formalism in order to support my explanation. All it takes is imagination.

as **Einstein** said:

Imagination is more important than knowledge.

My explanation is even more convincing in the case of the following experiment.

PFLEEGOR & MANDEL's EXPERIMENT (1967)

Interference effects produced by the superposition of the light beams from two independent single-mode lasers have been investigated experimentally. It is found that interference takes place even under conditions in which the light intensities are so low, with high probability, one photon is absorbed before the next one is emitted by one or the other laser. Since the average number of registered photons per trial was only about 10, photon correlation techniques were required to demonstrate the interference. The interpretation of the experiment, and the question whether it demonstrates interference between two photons, are discussed.

The demonstration, a few years ago, that two light beams derived from two independent lasers can give rise to observable interference fringes led to a certain amount of debate. The discussion centered in part on the appropriate description of the state of a laser field, and on the question whether the experiment **disproved** a famous statement of Dirac (1958) that …**each photon interferes only with itself. Interference between different photons never occurs.**

In this experiment, as shown in Fig. (T7) we get an interference pattern of laser beams delivered from two identical lasers. When one of the lasers is off, the pattern disappears (the result of all relevant theories). **However, if we reduce the intensity of the lasers to the extent that statistically the time of flight to the screen is shorter than the time between sequential deliveries of photons, we still get an interference pattern.**

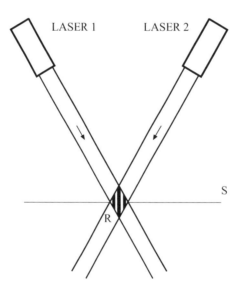

FIG. (T 7) Pfleeger and Mandel's Experiment

Suppose we adopt Dirac's argument that a photon interferes with itself, how do we get an interference pattern in the Pfleeger and Mandel experiment, without using two slits, or some similar device.

The guiding interference pattern, as I see it, is built by the "interference" of identical bunched photoms (waves) coming through the two lasers and the photons simply "ride" on them.

On EM Waves

Waves we encounter in nature are, most of the time, spherical waves rather than plane waves. However, far from a radiator, a spherical wave appears to be approximately a plane wave. Far from the radiator the electrical field of the wave $\mathbf{E}$ decreases as $1/r$ and hence its intensity, which is proportional to $\mathbf{E}^2$ decreases as $1/r^2$. Thus, the classical approach complies with the quantum approach. In this case, the intensity at a far distance r depends on the number of photons that are crossing a unit area and hence the dependence on $1/r^2$.

U.   The Universe

Fig. (U1) gives the distribution of energy/mass in the universe. We know a lot on 4.9 % of this content (white section), which relates, obviously, to the content of this book. We know to some extent on Dark Matter (gray section), but very little on Dark Energy (dark section).

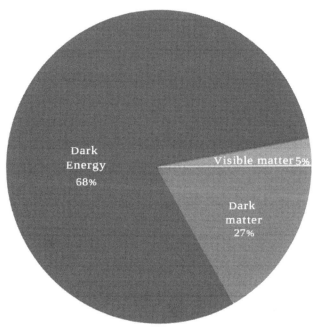

Fig. (U1) The Distribution of Energy/Mass in the

Universe

In this Chapter we discuss four of the cardinal issues in cosmology:

Why is the geometry of our universe Euclidian?

Chapter G covers the subject.

What is Dark Matter? this question has been open already

~ 85 years.

Why is the universe expanding? this question has been open

~ 90 years.

What is Dark Energy? this question has been open ~ 20 years.

Dark Matter

The measurement of the velocity of outlying stars revolving around galaxies is presented by the curve B in Fig. (U2). The expected curve according to the Newtonian theory of gravity was supposed to yield the curve A. This discrepancy is explained in three different ways:

Around galaxies there are halos of invisible mater – **dark   matter**, that interact only gravitationally with visible matter. This   opinion is held by the majority of physicists.

At a large distance from the centers of galaxies Newton's law of gravitation does not hold anymore and should be replaced by a new law. This law was found phenomenologically 30 years ago by Milgrom. No one so far has been able to prove this law theoretically.

My opinion, that differs from the above opinions, but complies with the Milgrom law, is presented below.

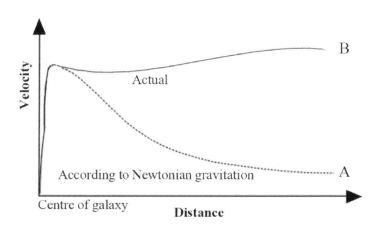

Fig. (U2) Rotation Curves in Galaxies

Dark Matter Resolution

I contend that Dark Matter is a Misinterpretation of Gradients in Space Density Around Galaxies.

General Relativity (GR) and its low field approximation - Newtonian gravitation - are nothing but deformed space. In Chapter G On bent (curved) manifolds and deformed spaces I show that the deformation of space is related to space density. Hence, gravitation is a gradient in space density. Inhomogeneous space expansion (gradients) around galaxies, due to the absence of Hubble space flow inside them, can thus create a central acceleration (gravitational field) that is wrongly interpreted as the result of the presence of Dark Matter.

Rotation Curves

The issue of Rotation Curves in galaxies led, in 1933, to the **Zwicky** hypothesis of Dark Matter (DM). Alternatively, it led, in 1983, to the suggestions by **Milgrom** to modify Newtonian Gravity (**MOND**) and by Bekenstein, in 2004, to modify General Relativity **with Tensor–Vector–Scalar gravity** (TeVeS).

I, however, dispel the need for both DM and a modification of GR. Based on the fact that space expansion in and around galaxies is inhomogeneous, I show that the phenomenological MOND equation indeed represents a new kind of central acceleration.

Again, on Light Velocity

The discussion here will clarify the fact that observers in all zones of space, regardless of their space densities, will claim to get the same result measuring light velocity with their standard yardsticks and clocks. Hence, we relate to Light Velocity as a **constant of nature.**

However, each and every faraway observer finds that according to his measurements and understanding light velocity elsewhere, where local observers reside, might vary according to space density in their locality. This is the result of light velocity dependence on the permittivity and permeability of space. But the permittivity and permeability of space depend on the density of space. Hence, we should not consider light velocity as a constant and should relate to the **coordinate speed of light** of GR as a real speed.

The Metric and Light Velocity

Schwarzschild, in 1916, was the first to find a solution to Einstein's field equation - a general spacetime metric - for the exterior of a spherically-symmetric star of radius R, i.e., for r > R:

$$ds^2 = -g_{00}c^2dt^2 + 2g_{0r}dr\,dt + g_{rr}dr^2 + r^2\left(d\theta^2 + \sin^2\theta\,d\varphi^2\right) \qquad (u1)$$

The metric's elements g_{00}, g_{0r} and g_{rr} are functions of r and t.

According to [13] the line element ds^2 is:

$$ds^2 = -e^{-\frac{2GM}{c^2 r}} c^2 dt^2 + e^{\frac{2GM}{c^2 r}} dr^2 + r^2\left(d\theta^2 + \sin^2\theta\, d\varphi^2\right) \qquad \text{(u2)}$$

We denote a **gravitational scale factor**, a:

$$a = e^{-\frac{GM}{c^2 r}} \qquad \text{(u3)}$$

For the surface of the sun or the edge of our galaxy:

$GM/rc^2 \sim 10^{-6}$ and thus, $GM/rc^2 \ll 1$.

For $GM/rc^2 \ll 1$ equation (u3) is approximated as:

$a = (1 - GM/rc^2)$ $a < 1$ $r \rightarrow \infty$ $a \rightarrow 1$ (u4)

We rewrite equation (u2) to become:

$$ds^2 = -a^2 c^2 dt^2 + a^{-2} dr^2 + r^2\left(d\theta^2 + \sin^2\theta\, d\varphi^2\right) \qquad \text{(u5)}$$

The metric in equation (u5) is derived by a faraway observer OB1 – far away from the center of a mass, M, that serves as the origin of their co-ordinates.

For OB1, a radial distance interval, dl, close to M, contains a smaller number of their yardstick units, dr, than dr_0, the number of the local observer OB2 yardstick units that dl contains. This is the result of the OB2 yardstick contraction (curving), which is the contraction of their local space. Hence:

$$dr_0 = a^{-1}dr \quad a < 1 \tag{u6}$$

From the **synchronization of clocks**, **Rindler** arrives (p. 184) at:

$$dt_0 = adt \quad a < 1 \tag{u7}$$

Thus, for OB1, a time interval, dт, contains a larger number of time units, dt, than the number of time units, dt_0, for OB2.

The 4D **spacetime interval** between two events; the "emission" of a short pulse of light at point A and the "arrival" of this pulse at point B is:

$$ds^2 = 0.$$

Hence, using equation (u5):

$$-a^2c^2dt^2 + a^{-2}dr^2 = 0 \qquad\qquad\qquad (u8)$$

$$acdt = a^{-1}dr \qquad\qquad\qquad (u9)$$

$$dr/dt = a^2c \qquad\qquad\qquad (u10)$$

This, $dr/dt = c'$, for OB1, is the light velocity close to a mass M. Light velocity, for OB1, far away from M, is c (standard light velocity), whereas $dr/dt = c' < c$.

This, $dr/dt = c'$, is a local, real and slower, light velocity since, according to equation (u4), $a < 1$.

In the literature dr/dt in equation (u10) is called the **coordinate speed of light**. This is a misleading name, since dr/dt should be considered a **real speed**.

Substituting dr from equation (u6) and dt from equation (u7) in equation (u8) gives:

$$dr/dt = adr_0/a^{-1}dt_0 = a^2dr_0/dt_0 \qquad\qquad\qquad (u11)$$

Comparing equation (u11) to equation (u10), gives:

$$dr_0/dt_0 = c \qquad (u12)$$

And from (u11) again:

$$c' = a^2c \qquad (u13)$$

The results here and my discussion elsewhere lead me to conclude that OB1 and OB2 measuring light velocity locally in their own zones of space arrive at the same result.

Due to this invariance, light velocity is considered **"a constant of nature"**, despite the fact that in different zones of space it behaves differently.

In conclusion:

$$dr_0 = a^{-1}dr \qquad (u6)$$

$$dt_0 = adt \qquad (u7)$$

$$c' = a^2c \qquad (u13)$$

The Gravitational Field as a Gradient in Light Velocity

Substituting a, equation (u4), in equation (u10), gives for the case $GM/rc^2 \ll 1$:

$dr/dt = a^2c = (1- GM/rc^2)^2c \sim (1- 2GM/rc^2)c = (1+ 2\varphi/c^2)c$ (u14)

From (u14) and $dr/dt = c'$ we get the gravitational potential φ:

$\varphi = \frac{1}{2} c (c'- c)$ (u15)

Note that $c' < c$, which complies with $\varphi < 0$. The field strength (central acceleration g) is thus:

$E_g = g = - d\varphi/dr = - \frac{1}{2} cdc'/dr$ (u16)

$\mathbf{E_g} = \mathbf{g} = - 1/2 c\nabla\mathbf{c'}$ (u17)

Thus, the gravitational field (central acceleration) can be considered a gradient in light velocity.

Note that c' is not a scalar, it is a vector $\mathbf{c'}$, and $\nabla\mathbf{c'}$ is a gradient of a vector. This gradient involves Christoffel symbols which are involved in the GR field equation.

To check our derivation, we take (u14) and $c' = dr/dt$ and get:

$c' = (1- 2GM/rc^2)c$ (u18)

$dc'/dr = 2GM/r^2c$ (u19)

Hence, according to equation (u16) the **central acceleration** is:

$g = \frac{1}{2} cdc'/dr = GM/r^2$ (u20)

$$\mathbf{g} = -(GM/r^3)\,\mathbf{r} \qquad\qquad\qquad\qquad\qquad (u21)$$

Note that M is a **gravitational mass**, since it comes from Einstein's GR field equation.

Note also that equations (u16) and (u17) are **general equations**, not necessarily limited to the Newtonian gravitational field.

This understanding leads to the understanding of free fall and yields the proof of the equivalence of inertial mass and gravitational mass.

The Overlooked Central Acceleration

The **Cosmological Scale Factor** (CSF), a, in the epoch of galaxies formation 500–700 Myr (Mega years)

($z = 8$–11) after the Big-Bang, is notated a_b. Taking $z = 9$ gives:

$a_b = 1/(z+1) = 0.1$, whereas the present CSF in the intergalactic space is $a_0 = 1$.

$$a_b = 0.1 \qquad a_0 = 1 \qquad\qquad\qquad\qquad\qquad (u22)$$

Note that the CSF, a, in this section **is not** the gravitational scale factor, a, although both relate to space density.

Space in the universe expands, but space within galaxies does not.

We, however, assume that at some point in the galaxy or on its

outskirts space starts to expand gradually to reach $a_0 = 1$.

A **toy function** for a variable CSF, in and around galaxies, is:

$$a = a_b + (a_0 - a_b)[1 - \exp(- r/(R/4))] \qquad (u23)$$

R is the Hubble sphere radius. For $r = 0$, $a = a_b$ and for $r \to R$,

$a = 0.98$, which is close to $a_0 = 1$.

Note that the radius of the universe is many times larger than the

Hubble sphere radius R. Taking R/4 is **arbitrary**, but based on the

size of "dark matter halos" it is **reasonable**; **it should**, however, be

supported by observations.

Substituting the values $a_b = 0.1$ and $a_0 = 1$, of equation (u22), in

equation (u23) gives:

$$a = 0.1 + 0.9[1 - \exp(- 4r/R)] \qquad (u24)$$

For $r << R$ equation (u24) becomes:

$$a = 0.1 + 3.6r/R \qquad (u25)$$

According to equations (u13) and (u25) and using the Hubble parameter $H = c/R$ (defined as $H = \dot{a}/a$) gives for $r \ll R$ the following value for dc'/dr:

$$dc'/dr = c\, d/dr\, (a^2) = c\, 2a\, da/dr = 2 \cdot a \cdot 3.6 \cdot c\, /R$$

Taking for a its average value $(a_b + a_0)/2 \sim 0.5$ gives:

$$dc'/dr = 0.36H \qquad\qquad\qquad (u26)$$

The H value as of today - the Hubble constant H_0, is:

$$H_0 = 2.26 \pm 0.25 \times 10^{-18}\ \text{sec}^{-1}.$$

Substituting this value (without the error range, since we are using an artificial toy function) in equation (u26) gives:

$$dc'/dr = 0.36\, H_0 = 0.81 \times 10^{-18}\text{sec}^{-1} \qquad\qquad (u27)$$

The value for the **central acceleration**, due to the inhomogeneous space density, as of today, is calculated using equations (u16) and (u27):

$$g = -\tfrac{1}{2}\, c\, dc'/dr = -1.22 \times 10^{-8}\ \text{cm s}^{-2}. \qquad\qquad (u28)$$

This acceleration, notated g_0, is:

$$g_0 = -1.22 \times 10^{-8}\ \text{cm s}^{-2} \qquad\qquad\qquad (u29)$$

The **geometric average (mean)** of the Newtonian **central acceleration** $g_N = -GM/r^2$, and g_0 gives:

$$g = -\frac{\sqrt{g_0 GM}}{r} \qquad (u30)$$

Equation (u30) **resembles** the **Milgrom MOND phenomenological** equation. According to MOND, for central accelerations smaller than g_0, the Newtonian central acceleration should be modified to become equation (u30). Our g_0, in contrast, is **a real** additional central acceleration. Thus, it is clear that our understanding is not related at all to MOND. We adhere to GR and its weak field Newtonian approximation and dispel the need to modify them.

Note the fit of our value for g_0, in equation (u29), to the observed MOND g_0, which is:

$$g_0 = -1.2 \pm 0.2 \times 10^{-8} \text{ cm s}^{-2}. \qquad (u31)$$

Note, that the MOND theory uses the notation a_0 rather than g_0.

We take the **geometric average (mean)**, since central accelerations are related to radii of space curvatures. This subject, however, is beyond the scope of this paper.

Gravitation is the contraction of space, whereas space expansion is the dilation of space. g_N is the result of gravitational space contraction (curving) whereas g_0 is the result of space dilation (curving). Let r_0 denote the distance from the center of a galaxy at which space contraction was balanced by space dilation, in the epoch of the galaxy's creation. This balance at r_0, with the larger g_0 **of that time**, is expressed by the equality $g_N = g_0$, or:

$$GM/r_0^2 = g_0 \qquad (u32)$$

Thus:

$$r_0 = (GM/g_0)^{1/2} \qquad (u33)$$

Note the following:

With time H becomes smaller and so does the gradient in light velocity, see equation (u26). Thus, the zone of balance, at r_0, see (u33), moves forward, away from the center of the galaxy, as if "Dark Matter Halos" grow with time.

Our central acceleration, equation (u17), is based on a gradient in light velocity; hence we can explain lensing, including the lensing of empty zones of space with inhomogeneous space density.

Summary

The inhomogeneous expansion of space around galaxies creates a universal, so far overlooked, central acceleration, g_0 that explains Rotation Curves. Thus, I dispel the need for Dark Matter or a modification of the laws of physics. We simply have to understand them.

Space Expansion

Three are the options related to space expansion:

Galaxies move through space and drag with them the gravitational deformation, namely the contraction of space.

Galaxies hold space inside them and stretch space as they move apart due to large scale gravitational repulsion.

Galaxies partially move through space and partially drag space.

I have not come across a discussion nor new facts that could help me determine which is the case.

The first option does not comply with the fact that there is no expansion within galaxies.

The second option does not comply with the fact that there are cases in which a fast galaxy is getting detached from its Dark Matter halo.

Dark Energy

Some facts are worth mentioning:

Mass and dark matter density in the universe are getting smaller with space expansion

Radiation density in the universe is getting smaller with space expansion, which means that it is space that expands.

Dark energy density **is not** affected by space expansion.

Dark energy density is not related to space energy due to zero-point fluctuations density, which is many orders of magnitude larger than Dark Energy density.

Dark Energy density is close to twice the energy density of matter (including Dark Matter).

V.   Summary

I have constructed a TOE of the physical reality, in which there is nothing but space. All the laws are derived as logical inferences. The unit of length and the unit of time are the only units needed in my model. All the particles are constructed from the photoms ADAM and EVE. And the only one force is the tension of space.

 If we and the infinite space are one and the same, then there is sense in Spinoza's notion that SPACE is GOD.

Halleluiah

*However, if we do discover a complete theory… then we shall take part in the discussion of the question of **why it is that we and the universe exist**.*

If we find the answer to that, it would be the ultimate triumph of human reason.

S. HAWKING (1987)

W. The Author HAL Web Site and Papers

DOMAINS
› List

AFFILIATIONS

- Taga Innovations

PRODUCTION YEAR

- 2020 2
- 2019 2
- 2018 5
- 2017 9
- 2016 4

Number of documents
22

Dr. Shlomo Barak

Dr. Barak was born and lives in Israel.

He holds a Ph.D. in Physics from the Hebrew University of Jerusalem.

He contributed to the defense of his country.

He contributed to technology and to the economy of his country.

His contribution to science is this collection of papers.

Taga Innovations   16 Beit Hillel St. Tel Aviv 67017 Israel

email: shlomo@tagapro.com

PREPRINTS, WORKING PAPERS, ...22 DOCUMENTS

Shlomo Barak. The Unification of Gravitation and Electromagnetism. 2020. ⟨hal-02616267⟩

Shlomo Barak. The QED Coupling Constant for an Electron to Emit or Absorb a Photon is Shown to be the Square Root of the Fine Structure Constant α. 2020. ⟨hal-02626064⟩

Shlomo Barak. On Bent Manifolds and Deformed Spaces. 2019. ⟨hal-01498435v3⟩

Shlomo Barak. On the Essence of Electric Charge: Part 2 How Charge Curves Space. 2019. ⟨hal-01402667v5⟩

Shlomo Barak. The Constancy of One-Way Light Velocity and the Possibility that Space is a Foamy Fluid. 2018. ⟨hal-01625000v2⟩

Shlomo Barak. The GeometroDynamic Model (GDM) of Reality in 80 THESES: A Realization of Einstein's Vision. 2018. ⟨hal-01524357v2⟩

Shlomo Barak. A GeometroDynamic Model (GDM) of Reality A Realization of Einstein's Vision. 2018. ⟨hal-01435685v4⟩

Shlomo Barak, Arie Zigler, Jenya Papeer. Isotropic One-Way Times of Flight of Laser Pulses and Einstein's "compressible fluid" Space. 2018. ⟨hal-01966893⟩

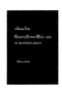

Shlomo Barak. A SPACETIME GEOMETRODYNAMIC MODEL (GDM) OF THE PHYSICAL REALITY. 2018. ⟨hal-01935260⟩

Shlomo Barak. Time is not Fundamental - unlike Distance and Velocity. 2017. ⟨hal-01502214⟩

Shlomo Barak. The GeometroDynamic Model (GDM) Versus String Theory (ST). 2017. ⟨hal-01524356⟩

Shlomo Barak. A Theoretical Derivation of the Milgrom MOND Equation. 2017. ⟨hal-01471151v4⟩

Shlomo Barak. On the Essence of Gravitation and Inertia Part 1: Inertia and Free Fall of an Elementary Particle. 2017. ⟨hal-01404143v7⟩

Shlomo Barak. Equations of Physics and Space Density. 2017. ⟨hal-01625004⟩

Shlomo Barak. The Electron and the Quantum Enigma. 2017. ⟨hal-01631624⟩

Shlomo Barak. Space as a Special Frame and Starlight Aberration. 2017. ⟨hal-01498454⟩

Shlomo Barak. Electromagnetism as the Geometrodynamics of Space. 2017. ⟨hal-01498448⟩

Shlomo Barak. The Graviton. 2017. ⟨hal-01524355⟩

Shlomo Barak. On the Essence of Electric Charge Part 1: Charge as Deformed Space. 2016. ⟨hal-01401332⟩

Shlomo Barak. On the Essence of Gravitation and Inertia Part 2: The Curving of Space by an Elementary Particle. 2016. ⟨hal-01405460⟩

Shlomo Barak. Where is Anti-Matter?. 2016. ⟨hal-01423547⟩

Shlomo Barak. The Photon and the Quantum Enigma.

2016. ⟨hal-0142

Printed in Germany
by Amazon Distribution
GmbH, Leipzig

21139271R00173